Prophets and Conspirators in Prerevolutionary Russia

Prophets and Conspirators in Prerevolutionary Russia

with a new introduction by the author

Adam B. Ulam

Transaction Publishers
New Brunswick (U.S.A.) and London (U.K.)

New material this edition © 1998 by Transaction Publishers, New Brunswick, New Jersey. Originally published in 1977 by The Viking Press.

This book is printed on acid-free paper that meets the American National Standard for Permanence of Paper for Printed Library Materials.

Library of Congress Catalog Number: 98-5462
ISBN: 0-7658-0443-3
Printed in the United States of America

Library of Congress Cataloging-in-Publication Data

Ulam, Adam Bruno, 1922–
Prophets and conspirators in prerevolutionary Russia / Adam B.
Ulam ; with a new introduction by the author.
    p.   cm.
   Originally published: In the name of the people : prophets and
conspirators in prerevolutionary Russia. New York : Viking Press, 1977.
   Includes bibliographical references and index.
   ISBN 0-7658-0443-3 (alk. paper)
   1. Russia—Politics and government—1855–1881. 2. Russia—Intellectual
life—1801–1917. 3. Revolutionaries—Russia—Biography. I. Ulam, Adam
Bruno, 1922–   In the name of the people. II. Title.
DK221.U38   1998
974.08'1'092—dc21   98-5462
   [B]   CIP

CONTENTS

v

Contents

LIST OF ILLUSTRATIONS
(Following page 98)

vii

INTRODUCTION TO THE TRANSACTION EDITION

Russia of the second half of the nineteenth century was truly a country of paradoxes. The empire's government has long been considered the model of unalloyed autocracy, that in a Europe where representative institutions, even if not yet democracy, were becoming the norm. But equally notorious was another feature of the country's political life: nowhere else, especially during the last four decades of the century, did revolutionary conspiratorial activities seem as widespread and diverse as those directed against the absolutist powers of the tsar. The Russian revolutionary exile plotting to bring freedom to his country became a familiar figure to the late Victorian era; his fictional image was found in the pages of writers as diverse as Joseph Conrad, Conan Doyle, and Jules Verne. And indeed the all-powerful government of the world's largest state would be periodically shaken, be it by an insurrection in its Polish provinces or by a terror campaign by Russian conspirators.

It is no wonder that in a Europe ever more peaceful and libertarian that political exoticism of Russian society bred the belief that an orderly political development, not to mention democracy, was somehow inconsistent with the Russian national character. The greatness of Russian culture, certainly in literature, music, and the fine arts, seemed only to accentuate the country's political and social backwardness.

Well, what we have seen in this century makes such judgments much less convincing. We have witnessed the vicious circle of political repression—revolutionary violence and terrorism too often and in too many nations to ascribe those phenomena to some peculiarity in Russian nature. The most repressive rule of the tsars pales in comparison with what had been wrought by Hitler, Stalin, Mao, and their imitators. Conspiratorial terror, which some purported to see as an understandable, and perhaps justifiable reaction against tsarist repression, has in our times often been directed against law-abiding and democratic governments. And so again we must question glib generalizations about individual terror being a specific mark of nineteenth-century Russian society.

ix

At the same time a study of that society is highly instructive in telling us what historical and political conditions favor the genesis and efflorescence of revolutionary violence, and how that violence may prove counteractive by blocking liberal reforms. Some of the attitudes of young rebels at other times and in other countries are reminiscent of those of "the men and women of the 1860s"— the heyday of Russian radicalism. To be sure one hundred years and vastly different political situations in the two countries separate those rebellions against the establishment. And yet in both cases we find some common ingredients: social radicalism, the call for full emancipation of women, the rejection of the traditional sexual mores. The revolutionary wave subsided during the 1880s and 1890s but the rebellious youths influenced the subsequent course of Russian history down to our own days and the crash of the successor of the empire—the Soviet Union.

For one the rebellious decades left as their legacy a chasm between the imperial government, and what in radical parlance was called "society," the educated part of the nation. Not that most of the latter could at any given moment be counted as revolutionaries, or believers in violence. But to many members of the intelligentsia, even those quite moderate in their politics, the state would always be identified with repression, and the revolutionary, even if seen as reprehensible in his methods and misguided in his goals, would still be viewed as a fighter for freedom. The warnings that a revolutionary movement itself could open a path to tyranny would be viewed with incredulity, something which helps explain the relative ease with which the Bolsheviks seized power in 1917. And by the same token those who in the Soviet state would raise their voice against oppression and for freedom would be branded by the Communist rulers as counterrevolutionaries.

The events and figures described in this book would also deeply influence the future course and nature of the radical movements in Russia, and after the coming of Communism, in the rest of the world. A nineteenth-century radical *had* to be a conspirator—no public opposition to the tsarist government was permitted by the law. But then after 1906 Russia became what may be described as a semi-constitutional state, and political parties could operate in the open. And yet the more radical among them persisted in clinging to the conspiratorial pattern as well as participating in elections and other public activities. And indeed even when they achieved the monopoly of power the Communists' method of rule remained largely conspiratorial: the multimillion party and the vast country ruled by a handful of men at the top and/or a single leader, fashioning their policies in the secrecy of the Politburo, no wider body in fact privy to their decision making. It took Gorbachev and *glasnost* to alter that pattern and to enable the Soviet citizen to know why and how decisions controlling his life were being made. And *glasnost* brought Communism down.

Communism has claimed to be the legitimate heir of the Russian revolutionary tradition. Officially Lenin's Bolsheviks began as a faction within the Russian Social Democratic Party, and as such pledged to adhere by the rules of the international socialist movement. Those rules banned terroristic methods and *coup d'etat*, while they stressed democracy as the ultimate goal of the movement. Yet from the beginning Lenin's followers flaunted those rules, the example of their nineteenth-century predecessors suggesting to them other paths to power than those prescribed by Karl Marx and other theorists of socialism.

Lenin himself was very likely spurred into revolutionary activity by the martyrdom of his brother, executed in 1887 for participation in an attempted assassination of the tsar. Another figure in these pages, Peter Tkachev, coined a motto that might well epitomize Lenin's career: "The revolutionary does not *prepare* but *makes* the revolution." And like the Bolsheviks after 1917 Tkachev had no compunctions in advocating mass terror by the revolutionaries once power was theirs.

For all the emotional ties to the preceding generation of revolutionaries Lenin also drew lessons from their failures: they sought their goals by individual heroics rather than securing mass support for their movement. Populism, a catch-all name for those movements, exaggerated the revolutionary potential of the peasantry, and ignored that of the industrial workers. Both in their aims and their internal structure the Populists often veered toward anarchism. For all his emotional bonds to Populism, Lenin remained intellectually a Marxist: a strong centralized state is a necessary stage in the march toward socialism.

The revolutionary decades thus offer a preview of Russia's drama in the twentieth century. As in the post-Stalin Soviet Union we see the government oscillating between attempts to curb the autocracy, and resorting to more stringent forms of repression. The tsarist regime was confronted by the dilemma that would become only too familiar to the architects of *perestroika*: How far can you push reforms in an authoritarian system without bringing down the whole structure? He would sign any constitution placed before him, declared Alexander II, if he was not convinced that the empire would then fall to pieces. But conversely the unfortunate monarch's end was a vivid illustration of the maxim that those who make revolutions by halves dig their own graves. In our own times, though less literally, a similar fate has overtaken that other partway reformer, Mikhail Gorbachev.

Lenin aside, few other main actors in the turbulent events that led to 1917 seem to have absorbed the lessons of our revolutionary drama. But once in power the Bolsheviks certainly drew upon some of those lessons. They had seen how attempts at liberalization shook their tsarist predecessors' empire in the 1860s and 1870s and eventually contributed to its downfall. For all of its autocratic ways the imperial regime was, by the Communists' standards, weak and irresolute. It tolerated some enclaves of autonomy and freedom in society, was often half-hearted in suppressing dissent, and was ineffective in controlling the intelligentsia. And it is among the latter and student youth that the call to revolution finds greatest resonance. And so the Soviet state would not observe such restraints. Occasionally under Lenin and routinely with Stalin mass terror would be employed to secure absolute submissiveness of society. And even under the latter's successors well into the 1980s the state would cling to rigid controls over its subjects' lives.

Yet fearful of each other, and some of them genuinely repentant about what went on under Stalin, his heirs neither wished nor could afford to rule in his manner. And so there was now room for civic courage and dissidence, in a sense the resurgence of the protest against the repressive state initiated by the nineteenth-century revolutionaries.

But the social dissidents drew their own lessons from the past struggles. They did not repeat their predecessors' errors, and saw clearly the immorality and futility of seeking political change through terrorist acts. They challenged the Communist regime by speaking up, and by their writings. Much as nineteenth-century Russian society may have admired the revolutionary's self-sacrifice, its political effect was often offset by the revulsion against violence in his struggle. The modern dissident eschewed the bomb and dagger. And though such "passive" protest against the state, which was much more powerful than its tsarist predecessor, might have appeared futile, who can say that Solzhenitsyn and Sakharov did not chose a better way of educating their society about the iniquities of its rulers?

The nineteenth-century revolutionary fought most often under the banner of a specific ideology. Here again his Soviet equivalent learned an appropriate lesson from the past. Seventy years of Communism have shown only too well how a revolutionary appeal joined with a sectarian dogma may lead to a new form of tyranny. Few of the Soviet dissidents could have been described as political ideologues. They pleaded for freedom and democracy in the most basic sense of those terms.

One must not exaggerate the rule of the dissidents in bringing about the collapse of Communism. They were but a tiny minority within their society. And the initiative in the process that led to the implosion of the Soviet state came from above. But by publicly demonstrating their civic courage, by being ready to suffer imprisonment and exile, that relative handful of brave men and women paved the way to *glasnost* and thus ultimately prevailed where their revolutionary forebears had failed.

But the revolutionary scene deserves our attention not only because of its political significance. The hackneyed "stranger than fiction" fits exactly the lives of its heroes. Where else would you find a ferocious young terrorist who spent his twenty years of solitary confinement acquiring encyclopedic knowledge, while complaining that time flies too fast when one is in jail? When he was released he took up flying, turned liberal, and supported the tsarist government in World War I. Dmitri Morozov concluded his long life as a member of the Soviet Academy of Sciences. Exotic in a different way was the career of Serge Degayev. A revolutionary, he was recruited by the police as an informer only to revert to terrorism. Spirited abroad the erstwhile *agent provocateur* and assassin was eventually transformed into Alexander Pell, a respected professor of mathematics in an American college. And so perhaps there is something peculiarly Russian if not about the politics of our tale then about the personalities of its actors.

Adam B. Ulam
April 1998

FOREWORD

There is much in the saga of the Russian revolutionary movement that will strike the contemporary reader as amazingly modern. But apart from any relevance it might have to our own problems, the story itself is intrinsically of the highest interest. It is little wonder that some of the most memorable works of Russian literature are based on true incidents in the struggle of a handful of men and women against the most powerful autocracy of the nineteenth century.

Anyone writing on this subject must acknowledge his debt to the indefatigable labors of Russian historians of both the pre- and post-Revolution vintage, as well as to such magisterial Western works as Franco Venturi's *Roots of Revolution*. I am also indebted to my colleagues at the Russian Research Center, Professors Abbott Gleason of Brown University and Daniel Field of Barnard College for their advice, to Elisabeth Sifton for her rigorous editorial work, and to my secretary, Mrs. Christine Balm, for her cheerfulness and endurance in coping with my manuscript. Messrs. Ted Everett and Bruce Karr were very helpful as my research assistants.

A.B.U.
Cambridge, Massachusetts
July, 1976

xv

INTRODUCTION

ONE SHOT

It had been the almost daily custom of Alexander II, when in his capital, to stroll in a St. Petersburg public park in the afternoon. Absence from the vast pile and the grounds of the Winter Palace provided for the forty-seven-year-old emperor a brief release from the gruelling dilemmas of his autocratic power, and possibly also privacy to reflect on current concerns of a more intimate nature. From the security standpoint, this regular and well-known habit of the emperor was foolhardy. To be sure, entrances to the Summer Garden were guarded by policemen with instructions not to admit badly dressed or suspicious-acting persons (these two categories still being regarded—though in view of recent Russian history, most ill-advisedly—as almost synonymous). But it would have been easy for an agile would-be assassin to scale the fence, or to attack the tsar when he was leaving or entering the carriage, with its imperial arms, stationed in front of the main entrance, which usually attracted a crowd of respectful onlookers. And often, as on this spring day in 1866, Alexander would take his walk unaccompanied even by an aide-de-camp, just with his Gordon setter Milord.

But it was against the emperor's concept of his office as well as his temperament to observe even minimal precautions. It was the obverse side of the autocratic principle that the Tsar of All Russia, father of his people, should be able to move unguarded among them. Special precautions might be in order for constitutional monarchs, who allowed themselves to be separated from their peoples, or for elected officials who, as the recent fate of Mr. Lincoln indicated, became targets of partisan hatred. It was they who

I

had to be trailed by detectives and police agents. The very rumors about the existence of conspiratorial societies, as well as the recent troubles among his Polish subjects, made it all the more imperative that the tsar not betray the slightest sign of apprehension or depart from his daily routine. He would not be so heedless of danger when in Warsaw, but here in the heart of Russia, where even his late despot father had walked freely in public places, it appeared inconceivable that anybody, be he a revolutionary or a rebellious Pole, would dare to raise his hand against the Tsar Liberator.

And then, Alexander was amply endowed with physical courage and obstinacy when it came to anything that might interfere with his habits and pleasures. It is quite possible that he would still not have changed his routine on this day of April 4, 1866, had he known that on March 14 the chancery of the governor general of St. Petersburg had received a most unusual communication. An anonymous writer disclosed that on the preceding evening a stranger had handed him a sealed envelope with instructions to open it in one week, and to circulate the letter among university students. Of course curiosity immediately prevailed and he now disclosed the contents. It was bloodcurdling: a proclamation addressed "to worker friends," the author of which, after recounting his anguish at the misery of the Russian people, announced his determination "to kill the scoundrel-Tsar"; should he fail and die, let others be inspired to take up the task.[1] The sender never presented himself at the chancery to help identify and apprehend the would-be assassin. The tsar was not warned. Nor is it likely that the horrendous communication even reached the desk of the governor general of St. Petersburg, Prince Alexander Suvorov. His subordinates were well aware that the humane and liberal-minded prince did not put much stock in wild stories circulated by reactionary groups about subversive conspiracies afoot among university youth. The alleged proclamation might well have been forged by such a source, if not indeed by a rival branch of bureaucracy—the Third Department of His Majesty's Chancery, i.e., the political police, by some of whose officials the prince himself was regarded as being close to revolutionary. And so no precautions were taken.

The emperor did not stay in the park for long. He may well have hoped to encounter some charming female subject of his, but instead he ran into his imperial relatives, the Duke of Leuchtenburg and his sister. And so after a brief chat he took his leave of them and returned to his carriage. The two policemen at the gate ran up to offer their services, one to open the door, the other to hold the emperor's greatcoat; no one was paying attention to the gaping onlookers who stood quite close to the carriage. And their eyes

---

[1] M. M. Klevensky and K. G. Kotelnikov, eds., *The Karakozov Attempt: A Stenographic Report of the Trial of D. Karakozov, I. Khudyakov, and N. Ishutin*, Moscow 1928, I, 294.

in turn were bound to be riveted on the manly figure of the master of Russia. With one exception: for Osip Komissarov, a peasant-born hatter's apprentice, this happened to be his nameday,[2] and if, as it seems reasonable to assume, he had already begun to celebrate it in the customary manner, he may well have experienced that restlessness and inability to focus one's eyes which such manner of celebrating occasionally induces. His gaze wandering around, Komissarov spotted a young man who was making his way through the crowd and who, when finally in front of him, pulled out a pistol. Komissarov jostled the man's elbow just before the shot rang out; the bullet passed harmlessly over the emperor's head.

Legend has the crowd seizing the would-be assassin and manhandling him while he allegedly exclaimed, "Fools [or in another version, "brothers"], I have done it for you." In the same vein, Karakozov, to give the stranger his name, is supposed when brought before Alexander to have boldly denounced the tsar for having cheated the peasants. In fact, as the trial transcript shows, the crowd simply "froze" in horror and at first did nothing (Komissarov himself, after his historic deed, temporarily passed out). Karakozov might well have tried to shoot again and succeeded—he still had another bullet in his double-barrelled pistol. Instead he attempted to flee, but the two policemen caught up with him about one hundred feet away, and disarmed him.

Here the emperor displayed that fearlessness which bordered on obtuseness and which within fifteen years would cost him his life. There could have been an accomplice in the crowd; the prisoner was not being held too securely,[3] and he kept reaching into his pocket where he had a vial of acid. But a tsar must not show any of the reactions of an ordinary mortal, who sensibly would have sought shelter or driven off immediately. He walked up to Karakozov and addressed him as if he were some importuning petitioner: "Who are you?"

"A Russian."

"What do you want?"

"Nothing," said Karakozov, "nothing."

Alexander, having inspected the gun, ordered the prisoner to be delivered to Prince Vasili Dolgorukov, chief of the Third Department and the Corps of Gendarmes. The policemen proposed to accomplish this mission by dragging the culprit on foot across half of St. Petersburg, even though by now they were being followed by a crowd, but finally they had the inspiration that an attempt might be made to rescue or to lynch him, and so it was in a hired cab that the would-be assassin reached police headquarters.

So much for the facts of this fateful afternoon. But as we have recently

---

[2] Usually more of an occasion in old Russia than a birthday.

[3] St. Petersburg policemen wore sabres but until 1879 were not armed with revolvers.

and unhappily learned, facts concerning a political assassination or an attempt at one are seldom allowed to pass into history, so to speak, undisturbed. Within an hour, the capital and soon all of Russia was full of the wildest stories and conjectures. That the emperor had been shot at and had escaped injury could not be disputed. But surely, the bulk of the loyal subjects believed, the criminal could not be a real Russian; he had to be a Pole. Only the staunchest reactionaries were willing to grant that he might be one of the "nihilists," those students and young intellectuals who had been creating so much trouble in the last few years; and some even whispered that he would turn out to be connected with the "Constantine party," an imaginary secret court camarilla headed by none other than the emperor's brother, Grand Duke Constantine, and Prince Suvorov. After a few days, the identity of the prisoner was indisputably established by his landlord: he was Dmitri Karakozov, of pure Russian descent from a petty gentry family in the province of Penza.[4] Moreover (the camp of reaction had every reason to feel smug) Karakozov had been expelled for participation in student disorders from the universities of Kazan and Moscow and had recently been connected with a group of young men whose background and activities were of a most suspicious nature.

While all of this could never be subsequently questioned, the role of Komissarov, the man "through whom it has pleased Providence to spare the Precious Life of the Beloved Monarch," as the official communiqué put it, became immediately, and remains today, a matter of violent contention. To loyal subjects, it was peculiarly fitting that it should have been a man of the people who saved the emperor who had freed the serfs. By the same token, for the radicals who considered Alexander's peasant reform a fraud, the official version was suspect: most likely the drunken boor was scratching himself and accidentally nudged Karakozov. To the all-out revolutionaries and to most Soviet historians, the whole story is humbug: Komissarov had nothing to do with Karakozov's unfortunate miss. It was an alert official who, having examined various innocent bystanders, decided that Komissarov was the most suitable person for the role of savior of "His Majesty's Sacred Person" from the hand of a degenerate *intelligent,* thus once more demonstrating how Divine Providence and simple folk watched over the lives of the Russian tsars, just like in the famous seventeenth-century tale dramatized in Glinka's popular opera.[5] Though at this distance it is impossi-

---

[4]During the preliminary investigation Karakozov continued to give a false name and to maintain he was a peasant.

[5]*Life for the Tsar,* renamed in Soviet times *Ivan Susanin,* whose hero is killed by a troop of Polish invaders whom he had intentionally misled concerning the whereabouts of the boy tsar, Michael, the founder of the Romanov dynasty. Every major Russian stage was now performing the opera, though the Polish dances in the score often had to be skipped because the audience booed them so strenuously.

ble to arrive at a certain verdict, one must lean toward the standard version, simply because if a deliberate hoax was intended, no official would have selected a person as imbecilic as Osip Komissarov. Even the most fervent believers of the story of the tsar's providential rescue complained that Providence should have chosen a more attractive and intelligent person as its instrument. Lionized by society, dragged through countless thanksgiving services and meetings, the erstwhile hatter's apprentice could never, despite special tutoring, deliver himself of more than a few ungrammatical expressions of loyalty and gratitude. He was ennobled, given an estate and a generous allowance, and eventually the embarrassing savior had to be shipped out of the capital. In so-called progressive circles there were soon rumors that Komissarov committed suicide in a fit of contrition and/or drunkenness. In fact, though his original proclivities were strengthened by the newly discovered delights of brandy, he was to live and drink for twenty-six more years.

There can be no question that the popular reaction to the events of April 4 was one first of genuine horror and then of thankfulness. Unlike what happened fifteen years later, when the general mood after his assassination expressed revulsion against the deed rather than affection for the victim, in 1866 Alexander still enjoyed the fervent loyalty of the great majority of his subjects. Once it became known that Karakozov was a nobleman, another fantastic rumor made the rounds among the common folk: that the nobles tried to kill the tsar because he had freed the peasants.[6]

But relief and joy were shared by all classes, and of course even those who were indifferent or disappointed at the outcome of the drama of April 4 hastened to proffer their expressions of loyalty and joy. For two weeks, the gates of the Winter Palace remained open to admit deputations of all kinds; crowds would gather continuously on the great square in front of the palace, waiting for the tsar to appear and hailing him with the imperial anthem. All of Russia seemed to be seized with a paroxysm of joy, which a caustic political exile compared to an outbreak of plague: "patriotic syphilis." And indeed parts of the celebration bore a clearly contrived character. As a distinguished Soviet writer was to note, "Cities, nationalities, social classes, seemed to be in competition to express their patriotic feelings." Messages of congratulations and of loyal sentiments arrived at the Winter Palace from "Armenians, . . . cab drivers, Jews, the Old Believers, Moscow Greeks,

---

[6]The absurd story found its way to Washington, D.C., where the Congress of the United States, in voting a solemn address of friendship and congratulations to the emperor on his providential delivery, ascribed the dastardly act to an "enemy of the Emancipation." The resolution was conveyed to St. Petersburg by a special government embassy headed by Assistant Secretary of the Navy Gustavus Fox, who told the tsar that the Americans, still lamenting the assassination of *their* late leader, shared the joy of "our friends and allies the Russian people" in having avoided such a calamity. Tatishchev, *Emperor Alexander II,* St. Petersburg 1903, I, 12–13.

shopkeepers of the Marinski market, the corps de ballet, the Finnish Senate, the Academy of Sciences, the guild of apothecaries, inmates of major jails [!], municipalities of Kiev, Odessa, Warsaw, Yalta. . . ."⁷ What especially rejoiced the hearts of the loyal and chagrined the radicals was the news that patriotic exultation extended to the sphere traditionally considered as the breeding ground of subversive (or, conversely, progressive) ideas: students of Moscow University organized a mass meeting and, after appropriate speeches, marched, singing the national anthem, to a thanksgiving service. Prone to extremes, whatever passions agitated them, the students followed the church services with an act which even to a moderate liberal was a scandalous betrayal of everything the young should stand for: several hundred strong, they marched to the editorial offices of the newspaper edited by the archreactionary Michael Katkov, and raised a cheer for this staunch defender of absolutism, this chief propagandist of a Russian chauvinism so drastic in nature that it brought upon him the displeasure of the government itself. Only a few years before, student manifestations and disorders in St. Petersburg and Moscow had reached such proportions that, the police being unable to deal with them, regular troops had to be called in. And as for the Thanksgiving Mass for the tsar, it brought memories of recent church rites on quite a different occasion: in 1862 many Russian students had participated in memorial services arranged by their Polish colleagues to honor five Warsaw citizens shot down by the tsar's soldiers in the course of a demonstration for Polish national independence.

During those April days, it was difficult if not indeed dangerous to refuse to join in the patriotic frenzy. There was probably little if any calculation behind the action of the Moscow students. But many older citizens who had had even the slightest connection with or reputation for radicalism hastened with public expressions of loyal sentiments. Patriotic hooliganism was quite frequent: men displaying those unmistakable outward signs of radicalism, i.e., wearing their hair long or sporting blue-tinted glasses, were in danger of being set upon and roughed up by wandering bands of loyalists. Some of the latter carried portraits of the tsar or of Komissarov, and any passerby was well advised to doff his hat to them.⁸ Thus, even before the investigation established the broader ramifications of Karakozov's attempt, the urban masses as well as some government officials were certain of the existence of a widespread plot, threads of which would lead eventually to the inspirers of all of Russia's recent troubles: treasonous Poles as well as left-wing Russian intellectuals and writers. These, after all, had been responsible for such calamities as the arson in St. Petersburg in 1862, the Polish insurrection in 1863, and the many attempts to incite mutinies in the army and uprisings

⁷Kornei Chukovsky, *Studies About Nekrasov,* Moscow 1930, 99.
⁸*Ibid.,* 104.

among the peasants. Some of those inciters had been apprehended and were now expiating their crimes in Siberia. But it was obvious that only the tip of an iceberg had been revealed.

And so acute apprehension filled the Russian intellectual and literary establishment. Newspapers and magazines which previously specialized in veiled (because of censorship) diatribes against Russia's political and social system now published stories and editorials extolling the wise policies and generous reforms associated with the reign of Alexander. The explosion of bad poetry appropriate to the occasion was not to be equalled in quality or volume until the mournful dirges inspired by Stalin's death. This time of course the motif was one of joy and gratitude. If "Stalin is always alive in our hearts" was to be the theme of the later occasion, the poems now, whether from the hand of the lowest hack or of Russia's greatest living poet, never failed to include homage to the tsar, "the source of Russia's happiness" and to his savior, "thou simple son of the people" and/or "instrument of Divine Providence."

Apprehension was to change to something approaching outright panic when it became known on April 7 who it was that would conduct the investigations into the circumstances and background of the attempted regicide. Some persons in the emperor's entourage and the reactionary press had for long hinted that officials charged with responsibility for public order were guilty of scandalous negligence, if not indeed something worse. Such views, to give them their due, were not without some substance: Prince Suvorov was by conviction and temperament ideally suited to be a constitutional minister rather than a vigilant servant of an autocracy, and Prince Dolgorukov, chief of the secret police, owed his present crucial position to a quality not uncommon among tsarist bureaucrats with powerful connections: he had shown himself utterly unqualified for his previous high office.[9] A grand seigneur of his type could not be expected to be assiduous in performing his duties—the chief one being attentive perusal of his agents' voluminous reports about what they had learned from paid informers among cabmen, janitors, cooks and other domestic servants of people who were suspected of sheltering a "subversive turn of mind" (this comes closest to the almost untranslatable police expression), or (a lesser charge) "untrustworthy attitudes." Files of the Third Department contained occasional reports going back to 1862 of some student or young artillery officer[10] casually questioning attendants at the Summer Garden as to the emperor's walking habits. And yet nothing had been done.

In the opinion of all right-thinking Russians, there was only one man

---

[9]He had been minister of war during the disastrous Crimean campaign.

[10]The artillery branch of the officer corps was believed, as we shall see later, to be almost as prone to revolutionary infection as the students.

whose illustrious record showed him capable of getting to the bottom of the Karakozov affair and exposing the deeper roots of treason. Yielding to this clamor, Alexander II summoned Count Michael Muraviev to head the inquest and to supersede and command normal police and investigatory agencies. The seventy-year-old general was known to many of his even quite conservative countrymen as "Muraviev the Hangman." In 1863, already enjoying a reputation as a ruthless and bullying bureaucrat, he had been appointed as the military governor of the Lithuanian provinces into which Polish insurrection had spilled over from the Kingdom of Poland.[11] Within a few months, Muraviev had subdued guerrilla warfare there by methods which, though they might seem unexceptional by the standards of Hitler's Germany or Stalin's Russia, were so barbarous by those of the nineteenth century that they were denounced throughout Europe. Captured Poles were treated not as prisoners of war but as criminals, with gallows or hard labor in Siberia a frequent sentence at courts-martial. Muraviev accompanied his victorious feats with the policy of forcible russification: Polish landowners, even when not directly involved in the uprising, had their properties confiscated, Byelorussian peasants of the Catholic rite were forced to convert to the Russian Orthodox Church. Whole towns and villages were ravaged and assessed fines if a few of their inhabitants had fled to the insurgent bands. On returning from Lithuania, Muraviev became the subject of public adulation such as no wielder of mass terror was to enjoy again until the Soviet period. But there was a difference. This time many enlightened Russians, including personages as high as Grand Duke Constantine and Prince Suvarov, refused to join in the chorus of praise for the "Hangman of Vilna" and avoided him socially. He himself felt these snubs deeply and attributed them to a thoroughly un-Russian concern for world public opinion. It may be apocryphal that when asked what elements among the Polish population he considered least dangerous, Muraviev replied, "Those who have been hanged." In any case, and here again is a suggestive analogy with the Stalin era, he is on record as describing a particularly dangerous type of his own countrymen as "a cosmopolite follower of Western ideas." Alexander II, who felt personal revulsion against Muraviev, took the first convenient occasion to ease him into retirement. He was raised to be a count but denied the distinction he most coveted, that of adjutant general, an honorary military aide with the right of personal access to the sovereign.

Now this man was made the great inquisitor, even if not, as the radicals exaggeratedly believed, the dictator of Russia. His task was made easier by Karakozov's carelessness. In the latter's pockets had been found (along with a vial of prussic acid, packages of strychnine, and morphine) a written

---

[11]While the majority of the rural population in the region were of Lithuanian or Byelorussian nationality, most of the gentry and townsmen were Polish.

proclamation identical with that which the anonymous sender had dispatched to Prince Suvorov's office on March 14. In Karakozov's rented room further incriminating evidence was found, leading straight to the Moscow radical circle headed by his first cousin, Nicholas Ishutin. Following this thread, the investigation uncovered the weird background of Karakozov's attempt: a conspiracy within a conspiracy, links (real and alleged) between members of the circle and practically every revolutionary or dissent movement of the last five years: Russian political exiles abroad, Polish insurgents, mysterious organizations which had issued revolutionary manifestoes in 1861 and 1862, the radical press and intellectuals. But even before the facts could be winnowed out from these suspicions and police informers' exaggerations and lies, Muraviev ordered wholesale arrests of any who could be suspected of having a "subversive turn of mind." Among those detained and questioned were some of the leading radical writers and publicists of the day. Those who were fortunate enough to escape the dragnet still lived in fear of a nighttime knock on their door. Expressive of this fear was the event which at the time shook the literary and political world almost as much as Karakozov's shot.

Nicholas Nekrasov was the acknowledged leader of the progressive tendency in Russian literature, as well as one of the outstanding poets of his generation. His poetry, which sang of the sufferings of the Russian people, inspired radical and revolutionary youth almost as much as the prose writings of his friend and collaborator, the martyred Chernyshevsky, now serving at hard labor in Siberia. After the latter's arrest in 1862, Nekrasov managed to continue to publish *The Contemporary,* the magazine in which at one time or another the most famous names in Russian literature had appeared, but which was also the fountainhead of progressivism—or, in the opinion of the right, the main source of seditious ideas infecting society. That he was able to get away with it was due to two reasons. Being, as he himself acknowledged, of a thoroughly unheroic nature, Nekrasov, unlike his friend, confined his radicalism to his passionate poetry. That in itself would not have been a sufficient protection for the writer or his magazine. But in addition the people's poet happened to be a bon vivant and frequenter of aristocratic salons, and he had considerable "pull" in the highest circles. Not infrequently a highly placed gambling partner in that center of St. Petersburg high life, the English Club, would help Nekrasov out of a serious scrape with the authorities. A successful entrepreneur and, when his gambling luck held, a man of means, the poet–publisher occasionally used more direct approaches to mollify censors or other officials.

But, in the months after the attempted assassination, Muraviev was armed against such influences, and unremittingly hostile to *The Contempo-*

rary. And so, in a desperate effort to save his beloved journal and possibly his own skin, Nekrasov did something which would haunt him and fill him with bitter shame until the end of his days. He had already published some painful verses celebrating "the tsar who along an arduous path leads his country to happiness" and the "peasant, nursed at the bosom of Christian Russian folk," who providentially saved him. But this was what was expected at this difficult time. The next step in this poetic self-abasement took place on April 16 at a dinner given at the English Club for the new honorary member, Count Muraviev. Following the coffee, Nekrasov asked the guest of honor for permission to read some verses, and on receiving an approving grunt read a panegyric to the "hangman." It was never printed, but those present, whether amused or shocked by Nekrasov's performance, were united in testifying that his poem contained the lines, "All Russia hails you and implores you not to spare the guilty," which in addition to being repulsive was simply senseless: Muraviev had been called upon to conduct the investigation of the accused, not to sentence them.[12] One of the latter, in jail at the time, was to comment when he learned of the poet's feat that it would have been less vile for Nekrasov to offer to build the gallows for them at his own expense.[13] Some fellow poets now felt inspired to write about Nekrasov: "He called for chastising those . . . whom he himself filled with the nonsense of his vile views and spawned in his journal. What a *liberal*, not to use another word."[14] Or, from a former friend, "Away from the chaste Muse's temple, you meretricious slave!"

In any case, *The Contemporary* was shut down. But Nekrasov soon acquired another journal; liberal and Marxist historians have for the most part forgiven him for his personal weaknesses. Who else sang so passionately about the sufferings of the Russian people, and of those martyred for freedom?

In Soviet writings about the period, the years after 1866 are those of "white terror." This, even if we don't define terror in twentieth-century terms, is a considerable exaggeration. After all, there can be no question, as we shall see, that most of those brought to trial in connection with the Karakozov attempt had in fact been engaged in a conspiracy. Yet some of the lesser actors in the drama got off amazingly lightly; a few among these even ended up as government officials. Still, the single shot of a deranged former student did have fateful consequences and changed the course of Russian history.

[12]The scene described in Chukovsky, 89–92.
[13]Ivan Khudyakov, *Notes of a Karakozovite*, Moscow 1930, 150.
[14]Chukovsky, 84.

The government turned to the right. Prince Dolgorukov on the very day of the assassination attempt offered his resignation as the head of the Third Department and was replaced by Peter Shuvalov, a much more energetic and less scrupulous sniffer-out of subversion. Alexander wanted to retain his old friend Prince Suvorov as governor of the capital, but demanded that he take on as police chief General Fyodor Trepov, who while in the same position in Warsaw had earned a Muraviev-like reputation. Suvorov would not hear of this and, refusing a new high office, retired to his estates. (General Trepov, who first achieved notoriety by being slapped in public by a Polish patriot, was one day to be shot in his office by a young woman because he had ordered a prisoner birched: Vera Zasulich's deed opened a new era of revolutionary terror.) But the greatest loss incurred in the post-1866 days by the government and the country was undoubtedly the dismissal of the minister of education, Alexander Golovnin. In the five years that he had presided over his department this enlightened man had doubled its previously niggardly budget, most of the increase going for new schools, higher salaries for teachers, and scholarships for students. Insofar as it was in his power, Golovnin had promoted university self-government and tried to meet the legitimate aspirations of the youth. And now, of course, the right claimed that the disastrous results of this mollycoddling of intellectuals and immature youth were clear for all to see: young men from the lower classes, instead of receiving a practical education to fit them for occupations proper to their station in life, had been initiated into subversive foreign ideas; witness Karakozov and most of his associates. Golovnin's successor, Dmitri Tolstoy, was well qualified to curtail such "abuses." He retained his old office as Procurator General of the Holy Synod, i.e., minister of Church affairs, and this was a hopeful augury that the religious and moral side of education would again receive due emphasis, to counteract "the fatal attitude of the students infected for most part by atheism and gross materialism in the moral sphere and extreme revolutionary anarchism in the political one."[15] The first steps of the new minister did not betray such hopes. He cancelled his predecessor's orders for the opening of several new *gymnasia*,[16] especially those planned for the Polish areas, and instead diverted the funds to an increased number of two-year schools where plebians would learn all they needed: religion, reading, and writing.

It was not in the emperor's nature to yield entirely to reaction, and he did not undo most of the reforms of the earlier years nor dispense with the services of other liberal councillors. There would be further progressive measures during his reign. But the momentum of Russia's modernization and liberalization had been lost. Even to a radical historian, the period

---

[15]Tatishchev, II, 262.
[16]Eight-year high schools leading to the university.

1856–66 is known as the era of Great Reforms. The reforms represented a great leap in some cases: judicial institutions, for example, were moved from a condition which would have been anachronistic in sixteenth-century Western Europe to the modern age. Peter the Great had modernized the Russian *state* and made it a world power; Alexander II and his bureaucrats had managed, to be sure in a somewhat faltering way, to bring Russian *society* from that servile condition which Talleyrand had characterized in a remark to Alexander I in 1809: "Sire, you are a civilized sovereign of an uncivilized nation," which remark the emperor found quite justified.[17] They achieved the change not only by abolishing serfdom but also by such measures as banning corporal punishment in the armed forces and eliminating the most horrendous punishments (heavy flogging, branding, etc.) for crimes committed by nonnoblemen.[18] To be sure, the sum total of the reforms did not amount to freedom for the individual or a constitutional system of government. But one might expect that, though the tsar himself was a firm believer in autocracy, the very momentum and logic of social change would bring Russia's political system more in line with those of Europe before too long. Now such hopes lay shattered and would revive only briefly and ephemerally near the reign's end, and under much less propitious circumstances.

Most fundamentally, the consequences of the shot revealed the fatal weakness of the three main principles, or forces, contending for the mastery of Russian life: autocracy, liberalism, and revolution. When threatened, autocracy could respond mainly by repression and seek support not among conservatives, for in the true sense of the term this element was almost totally absent in Russian society of the nineteenth century, but only among reactionaries. Liberalism as understood in the West had fervent followers among Russia's bureaucrats, landed aristocrats, and intellectuals. But it lacked both the power of reaction and the passion of radicalism. Paradoxically, a typical liberal, even if himself a high official, was bound to sense his alienation from the government and his embarrassment at being a servant of autocracy. By the same token, and especially if he was an intellectual, he would experience an occasional twinge of guilt when contrasting his role with that of a revolutionary who had fought for liberty not by writing drafts of reforms or petitions to the tsar, but by deeds which might cost him his freedom or his life. The idea of revolution failed to find a response for the rest of the century; it was to have no roots among the object of its solicitude and its alleged justification, the mass of the people. Despairing of, in some

[17]As well as Talleyrand's sly and at the time treasonous description of Napoleon's France, "a civilized nation ruled by a barbarian."

[18]Birching, as we have seen, was retained. We must remember that corporal punishment was practiced in the US Navy until the 1860s and did not disappear from British criminal justice until quite recently.

cases despising, the inert masses, the revolutionary would seek his goal through means at once childish and criminal; this often led him to deceive not only those for whom he worked and fought, but himself as well.

This tragic situation, which contains some of the seeds of twentieth-century totalitarianism, was influenced, but not foreordained, by special characteristics of the Russian character, or of Russian history. Its main cause lies in a peculiar combination of personalities and circumstances which unfolded only a few years before the event of April 4, 1866.

I

MAKERS OF THE REVOLUTIONARY WORLD

THE YEAR 1861 was a time of great
expectations. For most Russians the future was full of promise; the country
had awakened from a long sleep; Russia and, with her, their own lives were
going to be transformed in a way that no one had believed possible five or
six years before. The most out-of-the-way village, with hardly a literate
person among its inhabitants, had already heard the wonderful, if somehow
hardly believable or comprehensible, rumor that the tsar intended to give
the peasants freedom and land. They would no longer be obligated to work
on the nobleman's land, or pay him or the government agent quit rent, no
longer live in constant fear that if they displeased one of those potentates
they could be whipped, jailed, or worst of all, sent into the army for
twenty-five years of soldiering.

The majority of the landowners had for some time acquiesced in the end
of serfdom as inevitable, and were not displeased. It was becoming increasingly embarrassing and occasionally dangerous to exercise such arbitrary
powers over fellow human beings. If the landed nobility kept interposing
objections to the government's draft of the reform, or dragged its feet in
coming up with counterproposals, it was mainly in the hope of securing for
itself the best possible bargain in the financial provisions of the emancipation. And to be sure an enlightened minority was ready to incur material
sacrifices so that the curse and shame of serfdom could be lifted from their
country and Russia might rejoin the civilized world.

For them and for many people in the official and intellectual world, abolition of the demeaning servitude of the majority of their countrymen was the first fundamental step in the overall national reconstruction and rebirth which would bring Russia into the nineteenth century. Government committees were also already at work drafting, to be sure with excruciating slowness, laws that would liquidate or at least moderate such features of Old Russia as the barbarous system of corporal punishments for the lower classes, or the common soldier's lot, which could be described without too much exaggeration as a lifetime sentence at hard labor. It was already assumed that Russia would receive an up-to-date judicial system with such Western trimmings as juries and an independent bar in place of . . . well, no one could find the proper term, but only express horror at what passed for administration of justice, whether civil or criminal. Schemes were afoot for introducing local self-government; these were modest in scope and competence, with representation weighted in favor of the possessing classes, but they planned to include those whom one would, for the first time, be able to call fellow citizens, the peasants. Press censorship had already been relaxed.

In brief, it was a hopeful atmosphere, even for those liberals who would be satisfied with nothing short of a real constitution and a national system of representation, but who realized that the emperor, not to mention his more conservative advisers, would resolutely reject such ideas for the moment. To most political observers, both foreign and domestic, Russia appeared filled with loyalist and monarchist fervor: in addition to the traditional love and reverence which surrounded the Russian tsar (we shall see how much this statement must be qualified), Alexander II aroused admiration and gratitude even among unruly intellectuals and youth, and even Russian political exiles in the West, though carping about the "system," professed personal devotion to the monarch.

Yet a perspicacious observer would have noted an undercurrent of a different kind of excitement in Russia. Those who were infected by it shared in the general enthusiasm which had greeted both the actual and prospective changes, but their expectations were of a drastically different nature from that of most of their fellow countrymen: they expected, prayed for, and were already beginning to work for a revolution. The era of the Great Reform is also the period of the beginning of that revolutionary conspiratorial tradition which, though it had flared up briefly before, in 1825, only now acquired a permanent foothold in Russian life, especially among the educated class. It was to flicker continuously, and occasionally erupt, until the last explosion in 1917–18 swept it away along with other elements of Old Russia.

Revolutionaries fed their hopes on the same developments which gladdened the heart of monarchists and liberals, but they interpreted them differently. Take the proposed abolition of serfdom: can you destroy the peasants' habit of servile obedience without arousing their older, though latent, instinct of anarchism? The new land legislation was bound to be complex and incomprehensible to the common man; its provisions would inevitably fall short of the peasants' wildly exaggerated hopes. How could the end result be anything but widespread dissatisfaction, culminating in one of those vast uprisings which had punctuated the centuries of serfdom and as late as 1773 had shaken the foundations of the empire? As for the rest of the reforms, the cumulative weight of Russia's backwardness, of her oppressive social and political system, was too great to be lifted by a few new laws. They were fine insofar as the government was disarming itself before society. There would be an interval of gratitude, of loyal addresses to the tsar, but then the whole rotten system, its main props undermined, would collapse in a flame of revolution that would consume the monarchy and other features of the establishment (including, the most radical revolutionaries hoped, private property and the family).

The people who indulged in such dreams were a tiny minority among the educated class. But they included men from spheres one does not usually associate with revolutionary dreams and plots: officers of the General Staff of the Imperial Army, fairly high-ranking civilian officials, editors and writers of serious literary journals, rich landowners. And (a typical pattern in a revolutionary situation) a sizable number of their fellows, while rejecting extremist goals and methods, still admired what they believed to be the idealism of such and felt an occasional twinge of embarrassment at their own moderation (or was it faintheartedness?).

What accounts for this ubiquity of revolutionary sentiment, for the sudden fashion for conspiracy in Russia, which for almost four decades had been immune from the revolutionary turbulence that swept the rest of the Continent, and which was now apparently committed to peaceful evolution, modernism, and constitutionalism? The careers of three men provide a major part of the answer to this question. In virtue of what these men did and thought, and in virtue of the forces they represented and set in motion, Nicholas Romanov, Alexander Herzen, and Nicholas Chernyshevsky created the Russian revolutionary tradition.

ONE

NICHOLAS ROMANOV

Nicholas I died on February 18, 1855.[1] In all of Russia's history, only one other man's death was to elicit such feelings of relief and (at the same time) trepidation. As with Stalin, until the actual moment of the announcement no one could have imagined Russia without the man who "Like the dread spirit . . . stood over us"[2] for thirty years. And, also as in Stalin's case, Nicholas' influence on his country did not cease with his physical disappearance: what the emperor did and did not do continued to weigh heavily on Russian history until the end of the imperial system and the deposition of his great-grandson in 1917. But there the analogy ends, for one of the most enduring legacies of Nicholas' time was that uncompromising revolutionary spirit which later entered the vital organs of Russian society and stayed there until exorcised by the Revolution itself. His very success in keeping Russia in his iron grip, isolated not only from Western ideas and progress but seemingly from the forces of history itself, made it almost inevitable that any attempt to undo the evil effects of that isolation would be tardy and unsatisfactory and that the long-suppressed thirst for freedom would, after a brief interval of relief, turn into lust for revolution.

In reading the memoirs of many revolutionaries who grew up in Nicholas' reign, one occasionally detects a kind of perverse nostalgia for the bad

[1]Dates of events in Russia are given in the old style which was used until February 1918, and which in the nineteenth century was twelve days behind the Western calendar.
[2]Alexander Tvardovsky, "Horizon Beyond Horizon," *New World* (1960), No. 5, 9.

old times as contrasted with the turbulent 1860s and 1870s; in the earlier period an enlightened person could hate the regime and feel unreservedly ashamed of being Russian, without even a momentary twinge of doubt that perhaps the government *was* doing something for the country and the people. When it came to action, the same person would probably be doing the only possible thing, i.e., serving the hateful government. One could get into trouble, possibly be sent to Siberia, just by singing a risqué song at a private party, or by publishing a philosophical or literary paper with the slightest hint of unorthodoxy, or (if one were a nobleman) by wearing a beard, which somehow was to Nicholas prima facie evidence of a "subversive turn of mind," perhaps of some dangerous populistic tendency.[3] It would be simply inconceivable to engage in any kind of political, let alone radical, *activity.* The secret dissenter was thus spared the dilemma so real to the men and women of the 1860s: whether to work for revolutionary change through propaganda among schoolchildren, students, or, more riskily, peasants and soldiers, or to join an uncompromisingly revolutionary conspiracy. Nicholas Shelgunov, one of the most typical revolutionaries of the 1860s, recalled the old emperor's times as almost a work of art in despotism: "everybody knew his place." No matter what your abilities or proclivities, whether born to be a poet, revolutionary, or statesman, your destiny was, as the phrase went in Russia, "to serve," i.e., to become a servant of the state. As to which state office, state school, or army regiment you would serve the tsar in—this was again largely preordained by your family's background, means, and connections. For a nobleman or a man from the lower classes who had received what passed for higher education, a completely private existence was virtually unthinkable. No matter how rich, how much drawn by a muse, or how unfit for bureaucratic or military life, one had to begin by serving. One could, after a while, resign,[4] but unless there was a convincing excuse such as illness or need to manage the family estate, one ran the risk of drawing the attention of the authorities to oneself as an eccentric or worse. It might appear that the bucolic existence of a gentleman farmer was one possible escape. But the landowner was considered, and in view of his power over his serfs in fact was, an agent of the government. Russia did not need an extensive police force, said one monarch,[5] because every landowner was, in a way, a police chief. In the same vein, those landed estates were for Shelgunov the basis of the whole social order: "Russia consisted of some 100,000 little autocracies."[6]

---

[3]Peasants and merchants were of course expected to wear beards.
[4]*Compulsory* state service for every nobleman, instituted by Peter I, was abolished by Peter III in 1762.
[5]Variously identified as Catherine the Great, Paul I, and Nicholas himself.
[6]*Memoirs of N. V. Shelgunov and His Circle,* Moscow 1967, I, 73.

Nicholas' masterwork of autocracy reflected not only his temperament but the traumas of his early years. When he was five years old, his father, Emperor Paul, had been murdered, and if not the assassination at least the plot to depose the unbalanced tsar had had the assent of the heir, Nicholas' much older brother, Alexander I. Nicholas' own ascent to the throne was also marked by bloodshed. Profiting by a temporary confusion over the succession, members of secret officers' societies tried on December 14, 1825, to stage a coup.[7] The mutiny was suppressed in the course of one day, but its aftereffects were to dominate his thirty-year reign. Five of the leaders of the Decembrist coup were hanged, about one hundred and twenty others, among whom were members of the noblest families in Russia, were sentenced to punishments ranging from lifelong exile in Siberia (where their wives could join them only if they forsook their rank and the right ever to return home) to being degraded to the rank of private.[8] Not until the vengeful monarch's death were survivors allowed to return to European Russia.

A born autocrat, Nicholas became a reactionary and suspicious tyrant. He was not devoid of intelligence and a certain sense of chivalry, but after December 14 he became convinced that to tamper with any major element of the political and social status quo was to court disaster. Alexander I had played at being a reformer, had looked through his fingers at the spread of liberal and radical ideas among the officer corps—and what was the end result? Nicholas recognized that serfdom was a blight and the main cause of Russia's backwardness in relation to the rest of Europe, but he resolutely rejected the thought of any basic reform on this score. His solicitude for the status quo and for extirpation of subversive novelties extended beyond his empire. When revolutionary tremors shook Europe in 1830–31 and 1848, Nicholas stood ready to protect legitimacy abroad with Russian troops. His designs were frustrated the first time by an untimely rebellion of his Polish subjects, but in 1849 he sent his soldiers into Hungary to save the Habsburgs' rule from a national rebellion.[9]

But while unsuccessful abroad, at home Nicholas managed to freeze Russian social life into something resembling a coma. One could not keep all dangerous foreign innovations and ideas from stealing across the em-

[7]Next in line to the childless Alexander was Grand Duke Constantine Pavlovich who, in view of his morganatic marriage, agreed in a family compact (kept secret until Alexander I's sudden death) to yield to Nicholas. The revolutionary officers exploited their soldiers' ignorance by persuading them that Nicholas was a usurper, and tried to seize the capitol, not for Constantine to be sure, but for their own purposes.

[8]Common soldiers were "merely" flogged and redistributed among loyal regiments.

[9]But unlike a similar Russian intervention in 1956, the Russian aid was not to a submissive satellite. "Austria," said a Viennese statesman at the time, "will astound the world by its ingratitude." And to be sure, in a few years the Habsburg empire adopted an unfriendly attitude toward its savior.

pire's frontiers, but the tsar and his ministers certainly tried. Europe had entered the railway age and seemingly no other government had reasons so pressing to promote communications, even if only from the military considerations so close to the emperor's heart. But as a minister of communication perceptively noted, railways promoted travel, the latter made people acquire new ideas and impressions. . . . At the end of Nicholas' reign vast Russia had about 500 miles of rail-track, a fraction of the mileage in such comparatively small countries as Britain and France.

But Nicholas' primary goal in repression was to bar any ideological coexistence, to use a modern term, with "Europe." It was, after all, the exposure to Europe, especially during the Napoleonic wars, which had infected so many Russian officers serving abroad with ideas that found their fruition in the secret societies and the Decembrists. Permission for travel abroad, especially after the storms of 1848, was quite difficult for Russians to obtain. Still, people read foreign books and then wrote articles and essays into which, in the guise of seemingly innocent philosophical and literary criticism, they smuggled subversive ideas. The emperor himself took a hand at the censor's job, and he was not easy to fool. One police official wrote to a colleague, "His Majesty has deigned to find that everything in this article is but a critique of high policy in spite of the fact that the writer asserts . . . he speaks not of politics but of literature. One has only to apply a certain amount of attention to perceive that the author discussing literature as it were has something quite different in mind: that by the word *enlightenment* he means *liberty,* that the *mind's activity* means for him *revolution,* and the *skillfully contrived middle ground* nothing if not a *constitution.*"[10] One does not have to repeat the well-known story of Nicholas' humiliating treatment of Russia's greatest poet: the slights Pushkin had to suffer as both an individual and an artist contributed to the tragic sequence of events which ended with his death in a duel. It would be likewise superfluous to discourse about the condition of the press in Nicholean times; sufficient to note that even the most servile editor was occasionally jailed for a few days or had his journal suspended because of a quite apolitical criticism of a book or play which had caught the emperor's attention.

In no other European state—and this was to remain true until twentieth-century totalitarianism—was every aspect of life controlled so fully by the bureaucracy. Looking back on the Nicholean era, a man as reactionary as Katkov was constrained to exclaim that there was no real spiritual life then but only officialdom (the head of the ministry of church affairs was usually a general); no science or literature but everywhere officialdom, which not

---

[10]Quoted in Sidney Monas, *Third Section Police and Society in Russia Under Nicholas I,* Cambridge, Mass., 1961, 154.

only regulated these spheres of activity but, in a way unusual even for an authoritarian system, permeated them, and choked off all that strained to be free and spontaneous.

By the same token many people, including some of the architects of this system of repression and obscurantism, sensed occasionally that it was not only sapping the country's vital forces but undermining the foundations of the autocracy itself. Someday, no one could tell when or how, revolution might become the legacy of tyranny. From our perspective it is clear that the Nicholean era produced the belief, which would harden into a veritable dogma in Russian political life, that the "government," no matter how well-meaning, is the natural enemy of "society"[11] and that officialdom, no matter how many enlightened people are found in high places, is the natural enemy both of progress and of the "people."[12] There would be times when the government and officials would be able to repress their enemies seemingly once and for all, as under Nicholas I, or, under vastly different circumstances, under Stalin. There would be periods of détente and even of seeming *rapprochement* between the hostile forces, as during the first years of Alexander II or of Khrushchev, but then the struggle would be renewed.

These comparisons with the Soviet period are, to be sure, misleading because no nineteenth-century police state, not even that of Nicholas, could approach the twentieth century in the art of repression; and when it came to that other essential ingredient of totalitarianism, indoctrination, Russia could not hold a candle even to such a primitive specimen as Mussolini's Italy. Take the secret police organized by Nicholas I in 1826 under the innocent title of the Third Department (sometimes translated as Section). It never had on its staff more than a few dozen harassed and overworked officials, who scoured police and informers' reports as well as some quite nonpolitical appeals to the emperor touching on the petitioners' private troubles, requests for passports to go abroad, etc. The head of the Department was also chief of the many-thousand-strong Corps of Gendarmes, and if he happened also to be a personal friend of the monarch (as was the case of the two incumbents of the office under Nicholas, Count Alexander Benckendorff and Prince Alexis Orlov), he was a very powerful personage indeed. But none of these could have dreamed of the vast and sinister powers of a Beria or Himmler; their undermanned institution could not approach the hideous ubiquity and efficiency of the Gestapo and the KGB.

---

[11]It is a peculiarity of the vocabulary of political debate in nineteenth-century Russia that the word "state" was seldom used. There was on the one hand the "government" ("they" to a radical) and on the other "society," a term which became synonymous with the *intelligentsia,* i.e., the educated, thinking, and usually critical component of society.

[12]Again a peculiarity of Russian political semantics, the term "officialdom" sometimes was and sometimes was not meant to include the tsar (to most peasants it did not); "people," which in Russian is the same word as "nation," usually meant the mass of people, i.e., the peasants.

Such latter-day sophistications of the craft as systematic infiltration of suspected organizations, foreign agents, or the use of torture to extract information, were as yet unheard-of or in their infancy.[13] Well informed as to what was going on in St. Petersburg, the Third Department was much less so when it came to Moscow or Kiev, and it had to depend on the local officials or on amateurs' help when it came to real or potential scandal or subversion in some distant part of the empire.

Such mechanical imperfections of the apparatus of repression made it inevitable that those few seeds of dissent and revolution which were able to survive in the infertile soil of Nicholas' Russia grew more sturdily there than anywhere else. How could literature *not* become a formidable instrument for criticizing the government and society if Turgenev, because of his *Huntsman's Sketches,* a charming and apolitical picture of country life with just an *implied* criticism of serfdom, could be arrested and banished to his estates for several months? How could young Russians fail to bite deeper into and acquire a more lasting taste for the forbidden fruit of socialism, if young Dostoyevsky, for mere attendance at a discussion group devoted to the utopian ideas of Charles Fourier, was condemned to death, arraigned with other culprits for execution, and only at the last moment (as had been prearranged all along) "pardoned" to several years at hard labor? Foreign philosophies and books were eagerly investigated for and usually found to contain startling revolutionary messages. Yet even the most suspicious censor would not ban an esoteric treatise written in German, and to young Alexander Herzen "the philosophy of Hegel is the *algebra* of revolution; it frees man to an extraordinary degree and leaves not a stone upon stone of the whole Christian world, the world of traditions which have outlived themselves."[14] What better antidote for youth's seemingly morbid preoccupation with social problems and injustices than French novels, say those by George Sand? Yet emancipation of women and the loosening of family authority became central themes of the revolutionary movement of the 1860s.

Modern totalitarianism keeps its hold on people's minds not so much through mere repression but also because its vast propaganda and indoctrination resources enable it, as it were, to outshout dissent. But a nineteenth-century autocracy could only preach and punish. The philosophy it preached to all loyal subjects rested on the words of Nicholas' minister of education, on the principles of Orthodoxy, Autocracy, and Nationality. Or, as Count Benckendorff explained, in justifying a punishment to be visited

---

[13]For the period covered by this book, there is no authenticated case of the use of physical torture to extract information.

[14]Quoted in Martin Malia, *Alexander Herzen and the Birth of Russian Socialism,* Cambridge, Mass., 1961, 228.

upon the author of a critical essay about Russian history: "Russia's past has been admirable; her present is more than magnificent; as to her future, it is beyond the power of the boldest imagination to portray. —There, my friend, is the point of view from which Russian history should be conceived and written."[15]

This brings to mind another fatal attribute of Russian reality under Nicholas—one which, quite apart from politics, was from the point of view of any thinking man simply preposterous. In the middle 1850s, a group of writers headed by A. K. Tolstoy, a talented poet and dramatist, invented one of the most enduring satirical figures in Russian literature, Kozma Prutkov, a minor bureaucrat who is at the same time a scribbler of hilariously funny nonsense verse and prose. Among Prutkov's papers is found one entitled "A Project," obviously a draft for a memorandum to be submitted to the higher authorities. The author reflects on the danger signs in society, "Youth, science, immaturity. . . . Nonsense. . . . Lack of respect toward one's elders . . . [insistence on] 'one's own views.' . . . But can there be any independent thinking among people who are not trusted by the authorities? . . . If the writers knew something worthwhile they would be in the employ of the government; he who is not is clearly unworthy, therefore it is a waste of time to listen to him." After more in the same vein, the author comes to the "Conclusion: on the basis of the above, on the one hand taking into consideration the obvious necessity of establishing a uniform point of view in our vast fatherland, and on the other hand seeing the impossibility of reaching this blessed goal without the establishment of an official journal, we find that the latter is the most urgent need of our society and a necessary condition for its flourishing development."[16] The stereotype (not quite fair as we shall see) of the Russian bureaucrat as venal, stupid, and brutal was so firmly established that Nicholas in a rare fit of broadmindedness permitted and laughed at the production of Gogol's *Inspector*.

Nicholas himself, while judging despotism necessary, perceived perhaps more clearly than his subordinates its self-defeating nature. The usual platitude about Russia, "a giant with feet of clay," ought perhaps to be changed for his era to a "giant with a sclerotic brain." The nation's "feet," its human resources, were very much alive. They had enabled, and would continue to enable, the country to survive the results of social oppression and political idiocy. But the governmental system was not only repressive but preposterously unreasonable.

[15]Cited in Monas, 169. Compare what the Party secretary for ideological affairs explained to Solzhenitsyn when the writer sought permission to publish *The Cancer Ward:* "He specified to me what one should not do and what the Party was on its guard against in literature: 1) pessimism; 2) slandering [of Soviet reality]; 3) underhanded attacks." Alexander Solzhenitsyn, *The Calf Kept Butting An Oak,* Paris 1975 (in Russian), 109.

[16]Kozma Prutkov, *Works,* Moscow 1933, 380, 382.

The emperor's despotism was enhanced by his awareness of how vulnerable the whole system was. The principle of legitimacy could have but little meaning to the educated classes, who remembered how the ruling monarch's father had been assassinated, his grandfather deposed by his own wife (and then also murdered); and how throughout the eighteenth century a coterie of officials and officers of the Guards decided who should occupy the throne. The army is the traditional bulwark of authoritarian regimes of questionable legitimacy. Nicholas I was a passionate militarist, and Europe's largest standing army was the main object of his solicitude and of the state's expenditures. But the Decembrists had shown how unreliable the officer corps could be, and their relatives, friends, and erstwhile secret sympathizers still were among the elite of Russian society.[17]

As to the condition of the common soldier, it brings to mind what Dr. Johnson said of the British navy in the pre-Nelson era: that if a man had to choose whether to become a sailor or go to jail, he should unhesitatingly opt for the latter because a naval vessel was the kind of jail which occasionally sank. Infantry was drawn mostly from the serfs: the landlord and/or village assembly often selected the local lout or, conversely, some independent-minded peasant who threatened to become a troublemaker. And, since the term of service was twenty-five years, a married recruit (as a rule, bachelors were preferred) said goodbye to family life. (His wife often became the village prostitute.) Hygienic conditions in every European army of the time were by modern standards abominable, but especially so in Russia; out of a standing force of 700,000–800,000 men, 35,000–40,000 died annually of non-combat-related diseases and ailments.[18] On becoming a soldier one was rather ironically freed from serfdom, but this meant that the infrequent survivor of military duty would be freed only to become a servant or beggar, since he no longer had any claim on the communal land.[19] Discipline in such an army could be maintained only through unrelenting brutality, and punishments included having to run the gauntlet;[20] men fainted under the lash and were then resuscitated so that the sentence, whether 100 or 1000 strokes, could be completed. It becomes understandable that many intelligent and sensitive men who, as officers, had to witness or to preside over such barbarities were drawn to radical and even revolution-

[17]Several members of the famous Muraviev clan had been among the most active Decembrist conspirators, one ending up on the gallows. Even Michael, the future "hangman," was mildly implicated and briefly detained. Hence the saying that the Muraviev family could be divided into "those who hang, and those who get hanged."

[18]V. A. Dyakov, "The Soldiers Movement, 1856–1865," a volume in M. V. Nechkina, ed., *The Revolutionary Situation in Russia, 1859–1861,* Moscow 1970, 73.

[19]To be fair, there were cases of soldiers rising through the ranks and being commissioned: inconceivable in the British army of the same period.

[20]An imprecise expression: the victim was actually dragged slowly so that each of his fellow soldiers would be sure to strike a blow.

ary ideas, and that to some of them, Russia's system and the institution on which it was based—serfdom—was a matter not only of national shame but of national danger as well. An army of this kind could be counted on in a conflict with Turkey, or against numerically inferior Polish or Hungarian insurgents, or against the Caucasian and Central Asian tribesmen with whom Nicholas warred intermittently throughout his reign. But would it measure up to a modern European force?

Yet for the balance of Nicholas' reign, subversion remained latent, and even the thought of dissent or reform was paralyzed by fear. This fear, and the conviction that one must comply with accepted rules and customs no matter how obsolete or unreasonable, permeated all spheres of society and dominated most minds, even those of a naturally rebellious turn. The emperor—whose physical presence matched his reputation; he was very tall, and austerely handsome in his prime—would by a sudden personal appearance panic the most loyal official and render him speechless. A minister, in turn, would bully even high dignitaries of his department and put a distance between himself and them. And so it went down the table of ranks, with immediate superiors objects of dread to be propitiated by servility and, often, by bribes. Since everything—the church, one's school, in some ways even one's family—was mixed up with the state, a small boy being whipped by a teacher somehow felt it was the government which was punishing him. A leading revolutionary of the 1860s wrote about his childhood, "We had grown up in some unconscious fear of the government, and it took me quite a long time to emancipate myself fully from it."[21] Russia during the last years of Nicholas' regime, as every thoughtful person had to conclude, lagged further and further behind "Europe," not only in social and economic development but even in military efficiency. The most loyal and patriotic subject could not help noticing that once you crossed the border from Europe into Russia the atmosphere become heavier, common people more servile and bedraggled, their social betters more preoccupied and watchful, all the amenities of life shabbier. A critic of Russian reality circa 1850 might well have felt about his country's rulers what Solzhenitsyn said about their successors in 1967: "God has afflicted them with stupidity so that they would perish . . . (and all the same they don't perish!)."[22] But unlike the great modern writer, he could not have sought a partial explanation of this apparent paradox in Western blindness and moral weakness, especially among the liberal *intelligentsia*. In European politics, Nicholas' Russia was increasingly isolated, and to a Western liberal she was an object of execration.

And then came the Crimean War. When military defeat threatens the

[21]Shelgunov, I, 35.
[22]Solzhenitsyn, 232.

nation's existence, Russians traditionally rally all their forces behind the government, no matter how cruel and inefficient. So it was in 1812 and so it would be again in 1941–42. But when Russia's survival did not appear to be at stake military humiliation would bring to the surface the undercurrent of revolutionary feeling, as would be the case in 1905 and 1917. Similarly the first calamitous phase of the Crimean War killed Nicholas' system, as in a sense it led to the death of the emperor himself.

The conflict itself appears, in Western historiography and even more so in popular literature, as one of those "small," almost semicomical wars of fortunate Victorian times. If it is remembered by the general reader at all, it is only on account of the heroic inanity of the Charge of the Light Brigade, the career of Florence Nightingale, and perhaps also because a young artillery officer, Leo Tolstoy, first attracted widespread attention with his stories about Sevastapol under siege. But for Nicholas' regime the conflict in the Crimea was not a small war. It destroyed the rationale of his whole despotic system: the conviction that for all her backwardness Russia was the most powerful country on the continent, her army first in the world. The empire mobilized two million men, a prodigious number for those times, but all the factors of economic, social, and hence military weakness made themselves immediately felt. The Russian soldier fought with his traditional tenacity, but his elderly commanders were for the most part incompetent, the supply system was shot through with corruption, and the failure to develop an adequate communications network made it inevitable that no reinforcements could be brought to avoid the main defeat, the fall of the great fortress of Sevastopol after 350 days of fighting which cost the Russian army 18,000 killed and 70,000 wounded. It was only the almost equally incompetent conduct of the war by the other side—the inept command of the French, British, and Turkish forces—which saved the empire from other and more serious disasters. The peace was lenient, and apart from some minor territorial losses involved only a blow to national pride. The long-standing goal of the Russian empire's foreign policy, to end Turkey's rule over the Balkan Slavs and to hoist the Russian flag over Constantinople, now seemed further away than ever.

But even to his most loyal and conservative subjects, Nicholas' system now stood revealed as bankrupt. Conservatives blamed the emperor for having been so solicitous about absolutism and legitimacy that he forgot Russia's national interest; he had saved the Hapsburgs, yet now Austria threatened war unless Russia would bow to Britain's and France's conditions for peace. Seemingly endowed with an iron constitution, the fifty-eight-year-old monarch suddenly developed pneumonia. In his palace, he insisted on a simple camp bed covered by a soldier's greatcoat—circumstances symbolic more of his country's backwardness than, as he had intended, of the military foundation of Russia's greatness. (Few of Russia's rulers, into our own times, die of natural causes without some fantastic rumors subsequently circulating as to the real circumstances of their end. Many years after the event a radical journalist still believed that Nicholas, feeling betrayed and humiliated, took his own life.[23])

Alexander II ascended the throne on February 19, 1855, and suddenly there was a different Russia. Early in the new reign Nicholas Serno-Solovievich, a young official and radical (at the time not an unusual combination), decided that the government was taking too long with the peasant reform. He prepared a memorandum on the subject and armed with it stole into the garden of one of the emperor's residences. Alexander was taking a walk with a little son of his when the madcap young man confronted him and tried to thrust the paper into his hand. He should go through official channels, said the emperor dryly, and continued his walk. "Daddy, this man is still following us," said the little grand duke after a while. Exasperated, Alexander took the paper. In a few days, Serno-Solovievich was commanded to appear at Prince Orlov's. Nicholas' dreaded minister of police had been relegated to another office, and, just as within a few weeks of Stalin's death his erstwhile subordinates all professed themselves believers in "socialist legality," Prince Orlov had moved with the times. Still, Serno-Solovievich, who had now reflected on his venture, went with a feeling that the interview might end in his being sent to Siberia or a lunatic asylum.[24] "My boy," said the old prince, "do you know what the late emperor would have done if you had dared to thrust such a paper upon him? Why, he would have sent you to a place where no one would ever find your bones! But our current sovereign, Alexander Nikolayevich, is so kind that he asked me to kiss you. Here." The aged bureaucrat pressed the astounded youth to his bosom.[25]

Alas, no other action was taken on Serno-Solovievich's radical scheme to free the serfs. Disillusioned, he turned, as we shall see, into a revolutionary and conspirator, ending his short life in a place and under circumstances more or less fitting Prince Orlov's description.

[23]Shelgunov, I, 234.

[24]Another technique of dealing with political dissenters in which Nicholas' police anticipated that of the Soviet Union.

[25]Michael Lemke, *Studies in the Liberation Movement of the Sixties,* St. Petersburg 1908, 43–44.

TWO

ALEXANDER HERZEN

"After all, the writer is a teacher of the people; surely that's what we have always understood . . . and a great writer is, so to speak, a second government."[1] To be precise, Russian society, has conceived of the writer's function in this way only since 1857, when the first copies of a Russian journal, "printed at the Free Russian Press, 5 Thornhill Place, Caledonian Road," in London and "registered at the General Post Office for transmission beyond the United Kingdom," reached the emperor's subjects. But by 1860 for many of the readers of the slim (usually eight or ten pages) bimonthly *Kolokol,* or *Bell,* its editor and main writer, Alexander Herzen, was a moral and political force which challenged and rivaled that of the emperor.

As a political journalist and polemicist, Herzen displayed an artistry and enjoyed an influence which in themselves would secure him a place in history, though he was to meet his match in these respects. He was a great writer, but this was the time of literary giants—why should nineteenth-century Russia, first under despotism and even when still unfree, produce one of the greatest flowerings of literature in world history? Not even the combination of these qualities with Herzen's other achievement, to be sure more debatable, as a social thinker, would fully explain the sway he held over the minds of his contemporaries, nor the enduring charm and influence of his personality. Soviet and Western historians alike point out that his domination of radical and reformist thought in Russia began to decline

---

[1] Alexander Solzhenitsyn, *The First Circle,* Thomas P. Whitney, trans., New York 1968, 358.

31

sharply in 1861 and by 1863 was a thing of the past, and to some extent this verdict is justified. But Herzen's main achievement was to create the vernacular and ethos of revolution and freedom from which every successive generation of Russian radical drew its noblest (and sometimes, alas, most unrealistic) objectives and its rhetoric. Leninism, while annexing Herzen as one of its collateral ancestors (with some disparaging qualifications: he was "representative of the generation of revolutionaries who came from the gentry and never quite overcame their class origin," a "utopian socialist"), seemingly pulverized this whole tradition. But miraculously it has been reborn in our own day: some of the leading Soviet dissenters, notably Alexander Solzhenitsyn, are in many ways spiritual descendants of the great exile.

Herzen was born in 1812, the natural son of a rich nobleman. His illegitimate birth was not allowed to interfere with his education, social standing, or fortune. Did it affect him in a more subtle way? There is perhaps a trace of grand seigneur self-consciousness in Herzen, of the rank that was his by origin and temperament and intellect. As such he found the atmosphere of Nicholas's Russia stifling. Perhaps in a different society he would have become a Whig statesman and man of letters, or a philosopher-historian of pre-Bismarckian Germany. In Russia he was bound to grow up a revolutionary. With a group of friends in a Moscow intellectual circle he imbibed deeply German philosophy and French socialist ideas. A couple of youthful indiscretions, which nowhere else but in Nicholas' empire would have attracted the attention of the authorities, caused this son of a rich and influential man to be sent to an honorable but still irksome exile in the form of governmental clerkships in the provinces. There the young idealist acquired that knowledge and loathing for the ways of bureaucracy which was to become so prominent in Herzen the political journalist.

Passion for revolution had come earlier. The first impulse was provided when he was thirteen, by the drama and martyrdom of the Decembrists. As teen-agers, Herzen and Nicholas Ogarev, with whose life his was to be so tragically intertwined, swore a solemn oath to devote their careers to freeing the Russian people. In 1847, having come into an inheritance, and profiting by a temporary lull in police watchfulness over noblemen with "untrustworthy" attitudes (it is questionable whether a man with his record could have received a passport between 1848 and 1855), Herzen and his family left for Europe.

Herzen left too early in the century to have firsthand knowledge of his country as anything but a vast prison, and too late in his own life ever to find himself at home in the West. Love of Russia combined with hatred for its institutions was to lead him to prescribe rather fanciful remedies for her political and social ills, while passion for Western ideas of freedom and social justice only fed his dislike, which soon turned into loathing, of what he saw as the reality of West European politics. A rebel by nature, he was yet temperamentally adverse to conspiracy and violence. Later he was to write, concerning the young hotheads (brought up on his ideas) who were disseminating terrorist manifestos, that he himself had long before ceased to lust for the enemy's blood, whether in war or in politics: "whenever anybody's blood is spilled tears will flow." But when it came to the crunch it was almost impossible for Herzen to throw his weight on the side of moderation, to condemn a revolutionary conspiracy no matter how reckless or sanguinary its objectives, or even to refuse for long to join one. Personally hating many of the newer type of revolutionaries, in turn treated by them with irritation because of his allegedly "lordly ways" and humanitarian scruples, Herzen in the end helped them with his moral influence, his pen, and his money.

This political tragedy—and certainly that is what it was, from the point of view of what is known as the Russian liberation movement—was partly explained and probably enhanced by the personal tragedy of Herzen's life. A ceaseless wanderer among ideas,[2] he moved restlessly throughout Europe between his self-exile in 1847 and his death in 1870. Even in England, which was his base between 1852 and 1864, he often changed his residence and would dash repeatedly to the Continent. In fact wherever he was he lived in the same milieu—a self-imposed ghetto of Russian political emigrés with a sprinkling of Polish, Italian, or other radicals, revolutionaries, and the like who passed in and out of his circle. Only between 1857 and 1862, when he was "a second government," was his household a meeting place and object of pilgrimage for a wider cross section of Russians who found themselves abroad. The first Russian radical who achieved a European reputation, Herzen still had but limited contacts with the British and French "establishments," whether in politics or letters. Like most Russian exiles from his day to our own, he carried his country and its tragedy wherever he went.

This restlessness and noisy solitude—for Herzen was never really alone, but always had some personal or political drama of his fellow exiles taking place under his roof—reflected the veritable curse which seemed to hang over the Herzen family once it abandoned its homeland. His mother and her deaf-mute son were drowned in an improbable accident. Natalia Herzen's liaison with a contemptible man whom her husband had befriended and supported, which became a public scandal among the international revolutionary set,[3] brought Herzen himself to the verge of a collapse. And

[2]One of the "angry young men" of the sixties wrote of Herzen and not entirely unfairly, "You are a specialist in enthusiasm . . . like a teen-ager in your infatuations . . . your ideals are one day Proudhon, tomorrow Mazzini, then Victor Hugo. . . ." Michael Lemke, *Studies in the Liberation Movement of the Sixties,* St. Petersburg 1908, 272.

[3]It reached the ears and evoked comments from people as dissimilar as Karl Marx and Richard Wagner, the latter still considered, because of a youthful escapade, "a brother democrat." E. H. Carr, *The Romantic Exiles,* London 1949, 138–39.

the Herzens' reconciliation was followed not long afterward by Natalia's death from the aftereffects of bearing a (dead) child.

The next installment of personal tragedy was longer lasting and had an important effect on Herzen's political life. In 1856, his oldest and closest friend, Nicholas Ogarev, joined him in London with his second wife, born Natalia Tuchkova. A staunch nonconformist, a mediocre poet, and already afflicted by alcoholism, Ogarev became Herzen's closest partner in his radical and journalistic ventures. But, unlike his friend, Ogarev had a passion for conspiracy and a penchant for violence. It was not an adolescent but a twenty-seven-year-old man who wrote the following verse: "My heart is filled with love for the masses and with the wrath of a Robespierre. I yearn to set up the guillotine as an instrument of justice."[4]

The second Natalia almost immediately became Herzen's mistress. The relationship was not allowed to interfere with the two men's friendship and close collaboration; all three continued living under the same roof. But the situation could not but strengthen Ogarev's addiction to alcohol and to the company of streetwalkers. And—possibly another escape—his mind in its lucid moments would turn from fantasies about the guillotine more and more toward plans for real-life conspiracies. A sense of personal guilt made Herzen defer to his unfortunate friend's visions of Russia reborn through conspiracy and violent upheaval.

Natalia, much younger than the two friends (b. 1829), was neither to bring Herzen happiness nor find it with him. Of a sensuous and apolitical nature, she longed for normal family life, and grew weary of the procession of revolutionary eccentrics who passed through her unusual household. Her domineering ways made life at home insufferable for Herzen's children by his first marriage, and she begrudged Ogarev the surrogate of domestic happiness he found in a permanent relation with a former London prostitute. The birth of her and Herzen's children, first of Liza in 1858 and then of twins in 1861, alleviated the tension, but then in 1864 another hideous tragedy struck: the twins died. In that year the whole ménage resumed its wandering over the Continent, neither of the lovers being able to endure for long either cohabitation or total separation.

It was against this background that Herzen's last fourteen years unfolded, the first seven of triumph and power, the latter of decline and awareness of political defeat. Even during the last phase he remained indomitable in spirit, still engrossed in Russian and international revolutionary politics, still adding to his autobiography.

My Past and Thoughts is a masterpiece of its kind, one of the most fetching and moving examples of the autobiographical genre in any lan-

---

[4]Quoted in E. L. Rudnitskaya, *N. P. Ogarev in the Russian Revolutionary Movement,* Moscow 1969, 47.

guage. At times deeply personal, as in the story of his love for, estrangement from, and then reconciliation with his wife, it is mainly written in the "witness to my times" fashion but with none of the triteness which later came to be associated with most exercises in this manner. We have a wonderfully sensitive portrayal of the Russia of his youth, of that Russia in exile which he largely created, of the Europe of the revolutionaries. As in any great autobiographical work, the artist reveals more about the subject than he might have wished. (There is an amusing juxtaposition in two neighboring passages: the first is an eloquent critique of the West, and of the materialistic pursuits and mentality of its bourgeoisie; then Herzen turns to his own private affairs. The tsarist government has put a lien on his remaining property in Russia, and Herzen turns for help to the one potentate of whom even Nicholas I must stand in awe, the head of the Paris banking house of Rothschild. The banker intimates to St. Petersburg that the imperial government, chronically broke, might have even greater difficulties in the international money market unless it deferred to his client. Roles are seemingly reversed; Herzen concludes: like a "merchant of the second class" the tsar must humbly obey the emperor of bankers and turn over his patrimony to the political criminal.[5])

Even before his most active political period, Herzen had formulated the first coherent political philosophy of Russian dissent. The Decembrists had had only very hazy notions of what they would put in the place of autocracy. Some had leaned toward a constitutional monarchy with a limited franchise; some, notably Paul Pestel, had been of the Jacobin turn of mind, envisaging nationalization of land and a revolutionary dictatorship. Herzen's populism had as its main ingredients agrarian socialism and an emphatic rejection of the Western model of parliamentarian, centralized political authority. This populism, which in a variety of formulations would remain the dominant revolutionary philosophy of Russia until the end of the nineteenth century, reflected a deep Russian nationalism combined with an unconscious feeling of inferiority and envy vis-à-vis the West. Consciously Herzen came to loathe *meschchanstvo*,[6] which according to him had dominated the Western political system ever since the failure of the revolution of 1848, and, behind the rhetoric of democracy, progress, and equality, subordinated politics and everything vital in society to crass materialism.

And so backward Russia would still one day show the world the way to

---

[5]Which Herzen already was, in view of his refusal to return to Russia upon the expiration of his passport.

[6]*Meschchanstvo* in Russian may have one of three meanings. The first, unimportant from our point of view, was the *legal* term for the *lower* urban middle class. Then, most often it was used as a synonym for the bourgeoisie, the middle class as a whole. To Herzen, *meschchanstvo* was meant to convey the spirit of middle-class philistinism, pettiness, and concern for gain.

a higher and freer civilization than the one created in the West. The peasant, the representative Russian man, was fortunately free of the materialistic craving of the French or English bourgeois or, for that matter, worker. (Perceptively Herzen saw in the industrial proletarian of the day the bourgeois of tomorrow.) The idea of private property, in the corrupt Western sense, was alien to the peasant; he was in fact an instinctive socialist. From time immemorial the Russian peasant had lived in an *obshchina*—a commune. The peasants' land was vested in the commune as a whole. The commune's assembly, or *mir*,[7] would periodically redistribute plots of land among its members, arbitrate the peasants' disputes, and handle similar problems (subject of course to the overall authority of the landlord or, on state lands, the government's steward). Hence once the autocracy and serfdom were abolished Russia would be gradually transformed into a federation of free peasant communes and municipalities. His poor oppressed country would yet show the world how to avoid the evils of industrialism and *meschchanstvo,* how to achieve real grass-roots democracy, and how to build socialism, which, unlike the kind preached by Karl Marx, would dispense with the centralized state and the squalid life of the factory. (Herzen could not stand Marx on either ideological or personal grounds, sentiments that were heartily reciprocated.)

As we can now see, and as some of Herzen's contemporaries were beginning to perceive, his major premise, the concept of the peasant commune and the Russian peasant's mentality, was historically incorrect and psychologically fallacious. And, since he was not a fanatic, as everything we have already seen indicates, he did not reject the possibility of a gradual or somewhat different way of achieving his ideal for Russian society. But to the end he held firmly to the conviction that it had to be a Russian way and not one suggested by London or Paris. In 1851, at the moment of his greatest disenchantment with Western Europe, he wrote, "Our laws begin with the overwhelmingly true formula, 'The emperor has been pleased to order'; your laws begin with a shocking untruth: a derisive invocation of the authority of the French nation, with the words 'liberty, fraternity, and equality.' " Then follows his famous pledge: "Russia will never be Protestant [i.e., moderate and materialistic], she will never be mediocre [i.e., prosaic and middle-class], Russia will never make a revolution just to get rid of Nicholas and to replace him by tsar-representatives, tsar-judges, tsar-policemen."[8] Compare a modern Russian writer speaking of his struggle against the Soviet regime: "One could not hope for any help from the West, and besides, we should never accept help there. If the twentieth

---

[7] The word also means "world" and "peace."

[8] Alexander Herzen, *Works,* Michael Lemke, ed., VI, Petersburg [sic: the official name of the capital had been Petrograd since 1915] 1919, 456–57.

century will leave a lesson for mankind, then we shall have to teach this lesson to the West rather than the West to us; the West's excessive well-being has weakened its will and intellect."[9] Well, the poor "rotten" West! Has it done so much worse than Russia during the century which separates these two great writers?

Great writers are not always at their best when they indulge in majestic proclamations on transcendental themes of philosophy and history. But fortunately for his country and for himself, Herzen laid aside his brooding reflections about the decline of the West and the light which must come from the East, and displayed his superlative talent as a political polemicist and his genius as an advocate of freedom. In 1853 he set up in London the Free Russian Press. At first it was intended to print and then try to smuggle into Russia those works of Russia's literary greats which could not be printed or which had been suppressed by censorship under Nicholas, as well as Herzen's own and others' essays on forbidden topics, e.g., serfdom. Such was the state of mind at the time that Herzen's friends in Russia, even those of the most liberal convictions, begged him to desist from his venture: it would only further incense the despot, enhance repression, and bring easily foreseeable consequences for those found possessing the forbidden literature or caught corresponding with London. And indeed such was the fear that hung over Russian society that during the first two years, except for a few copies smuggled into the empire by some proverbially reckless Poles, only one publication of the Free Press was purchased by some brave Petersburg bookstore owner on his way home.[10]

But then came the wonderful morning in March 1855 when the million-aire exile dispatched his servants to summon his friends urgently and to replenish his stock of champagne! Nicholas I was dead.[11] And immediately Herzen was seized by a new idea: he would now publish a regular magazine, and not just a stray pamphlet or book. On July 25, the anniversary of the hanging of the five Decembrists whose portraits adorned the issue, appeared the *Polar Star:* "a Russian periodical, solely devoted to the task of Russian freedom and to propagating within Russia free ideas. . . ." By 1856 the London bookstore dealing in Russian publications was doing a brisk business in the *Polar Star:* every visitor from Alexander II's realm wanted to bring home that wonder of wonders, that thing unseen and inconceivable during the three-hundred-year history of Russian printing, a journal untouched by the hand of the censor. The Free Russian Press gave the Russian readers poems by Pushkin and Lermontov, which though they had passed

[9]Alexander Solzhenitsyn, *The Calf Kept Butting An Oak,* Paris 1975 (in Russian), 134.

[10]M. Klevensky, "Herzen as Publisher," in *Literary Heritage,* XLI-XLII (Moscow 1941), 573.

[11]Dates of events in the West and hence of the issues of Herzen's journal are of course according to the Western calendar, i.e., twelve days after the Russian.

from hand to hand could never have been published under Nicholas, and made the wider public acquainted with Belinsky's famous letter to Gogol, where, while criticizing the great humorist for the fatuously reactionary views of his latter period, the critic presented a crushing indictment of Russian society. Compare this with the situation not so long before, when the last word in the title *History of the Athenian Republic* had led to the learned treatise's being banned, and when the censor would not authorize an article on potato blight because detailed discussion of the subject might cast doubts on the ever benevolent designs of Providence and hence encourage atheism.

The encouraging news from Russia led Herzen to acquire a habit which was always to embarrass his admirers (especially the radicals among them) and amuse his enemies, and which to tell the truth does occasionally make him look silly. He would now and then issue public letters to the new emperor. To be sure, he was not alone in this activity even among the radicals, especially during the time of great expectations. Yet one winces as one reads in the first of the lot, written on March 10, 1855, the following modest avowal: "And just now the whole English nation has greeted me as the representative of the Russian people."[12] And while this statement must have been due to too much of the celebratory champagne—for the overwhelming majority of the British establishment, not to mention the British people in general, was then, and remained, ignorant of the presence among them of the great Russian—the rest of the letter expressed Herzen's genuine faith in the new monarch and in the possibility of "revolution from above," feelings which he was not to abandon entirely until 1861. How lucky Alexander was not to ascend the throne under the bloody circumstances which signalled the successions of his uncle and father! How fortunate he had been in his education, and in the reputation for kindness which surrounded him as the Heir![13] Herzen recalls how Alexander had been greeted by the common people with love and hope during his travels throughout Russia. And he avows that, though there seems to be an unbridgeable chasm between them—"I am a staunch Socialist, You the Autocrat"—still, "You truly love Russia and You can do so much for the Russian people." And so Herzen, for the sake of their common love, is willing to make a great sacrifice: he will lay aside hostility toward the autocracy, cease his attacks upon it, as long as he sees that the tsar is working for the people. "Sire, give us freedom of speech. . . . We have so much to say to the world and ourselves. . . . Give land to the peasants . . . remove from Russia the fearful blot of serfdom, heal the lash wounds on the backs of our brothers—those hideous stigmata

[12]Quoted in Vladimir Burtsev, *One Hundred Years,* London 1897 (in Russian), 19.
[13]Alexander had tried, and with some success, to persuade his father to soften conditions of exile for the surviving Decembrists.

of inhumanity." Let the emperor not think him presumptuous, but "you will not often hear the real voice of a free Russian."[14]

What in 1855 sounded a bit pretentious shortly became a reality, insofar as the enlightened part of Russian society was concerned. The two Alexanders were soon confronting each other on almost equal terms.

It was Ogarev who, according to his wife, persuaded Herzen that propaganda for freedom in Russia required a more supple instrument than the thick and infrequent issues of the *Polar Star.* "Yes, Ogarev," exclaimed Herzen, "let us publish a journal; we shall call it *The Bell;* we shall strike the Assembly Bell[15] just the two of us . . . but maybe somebody will answer."[16] And the Russian people did answer. *The Bell* at the height of its popularity around 1860 had a circulation of perhaps 3000,[17] but for the readership within Russia we must multiply this at least tenfold. Theoretically *The Bell* remained illegal and its propagation a criminal offense, but during the early years of Alexander's reign the government looked the other way; in fact many officials and, it is said, the emperor himself read it regularly. *The Bell* quickly became a more accurate chronicle of Russian life than any journal published within the country. Anonymous and not so anonymous correspondents in Russia sent information to London in such volume that a special supplement had to be introduced; an alert Petersburg bureaucrat would have to follow the journal in order to find out not only the state of Russian public opinion but sometimes also what was happening in his own ministry. It may come as a surprise to Americans of the Watergate era that it was a nineteenth-century Russian exile who was the father of investigative journalism. But here a gentleman from Saratov informs *The Bell* and all of Russia about the thieving ways of the local governor; there a clerk in the committee drafting the peasant law lays bare the intrigues of reactionary officials who wish to frustrate the emperor's intentions. And in a lighter vein the country learns how a high dignitary uses his influence to spare his daughter the legal consequences of having committed bigamy. Liberals wrote to Herzen asking him to use his enormous influence to quiet the minds of the young: a phrase in the editorial by Iskander—Herzen's usual *nom de plume*—might make the hotheads think that revolution *was* the only way out. Radicals meanwhile implored *The Bell* not to preach moderation and not to advocate patience or faith in the emperor's good intentions. Almost everybody acknowledged Herzen's vast influence: "you

[14]Cited in Burtsev, 21.

[15]In the ancient Russian city-republic of Novgorod, a great bell summoned the people to political meetings. When Ivan III suppressed the freedoms of Novgorod, he removed the Assembly Bell.

[16]Klevensky, 575.

[17]A recent Soviet work gives 1861 circulation as 10,000 (Rudnitskaya, 287), but this runs well over all other estimates.

are a great force, you are a power in the State."[18]

That Herzen acquired such a following was due among other things to his newly revealed skill as a political polemicist. His editorials and commentaries have an elegance, charm, and wit which elevate them far above standard radical pamphleteering with its "people-yes" pomposity and heavy sarcasm about the powers that be. And it was of enormous help to *The Bell* that the educated classes in Russia had been starved for a really free Russian word, for political and social arguments offered in straightforward terms and not in the "Aesopian" language employed by writers at home, who even under the now more lenient censorship had to offer their social critique in the guise of literary criticism or in commentaries about French or Italian politics.

Very soon after Alexander's accession it became easy for Russians to obtain passports to go abroad. And so the Herzen residence came to be a sort of Winter Palace in exile where every Russian traveller of note, whatever his station in life or his political conviction, would seek an audience. Even the material circumstances under which the emperor of dissent and his court lived were described at first with awe, then, as the new generation of radicals grew estranged, with sarcasm, suggesting the opulence of a Rothschild or an English duke. Actually, though by Russian (not to mention exile) standards Herzen was a very rich man, the material amenities of his household were not atypical of those of an upper-middle-class Londoner. He had to support what might be described as his extended family, was generous to his friends and hangers-on, and of course spent freely on the Cause.

In 1859 there appeared in Herzen's circle one Vasili Kelsiev. A twenty-four-year-old employee of the Russian-American Company that ran trade in Alaska, Kelsiev had just had the misfortune to be ordered from the company's home office in Petersburg to its field of operations—Alaska. During a layover in London he discovered that he could no longer work for an agency of the autocracy, and decided he would join the exciting world of revolutionaries. We shall meet Kelsiev again as an important actor in Herzen's misbegotten conspiracies, but here we are focussing on Kelsiev as the author of what must be judged a masterpiece of a uniquely Russian genre of literature: the confessions and recantations of political prisoners. For in 1867, wearied of his revolutionist's existence, Kelsiev turned himself over to the tsarist authorities. While in jail he was asked to write down an account of his activities and his reflections thereon for the benefit of the Third Department and Count Shuvalov. Having discharged this obligation, he was freed, and for the remaining few years of his life tried to earn his

[18]I. Linkov, *The Revolutionary Struggle of A. I. Herzen and N. P. Ogarev and the Secret Society "Land and Freedom" of the Sixties,* Moscow 1964, 101.

living as a *littérateur*. But nothing he wrote then, nor had written as a revolutionary agitator, could approach the vigor and vividness of his famous *Confession*. One would not expect in a work written under such circumstances perceptive philosophic-historical reflections, or touches of humor. Yet both are there in Kelsiev's account of his past and thoughts.

Why had Kelsiev become a revolutionary? Well, already as a boy he had felt, like many others of his generation, that the government was insincere. "Why do they keep truth away from us? . . . Why is everything decided by the government in secret? Isn't this proof of bad conscience, if not indeed of evil intentions? . . . *It was the government that appeared to us as a conspiracy.*" Then take the Russian national propensity to excess in everything: Kelsiev brings up the example—and we must assume he does not do it with tongue in cheek—of the rulers of the old Russian state. All they set out to do, he remarks, was to free the Russian land from the Tartars. But once they started, not only did they chase the Tartars away, they annexed the Tartars' own country, then helped themselves to a large part of Poland and central Asia, and the end is still not in sight: the Turks in Constantinople, the Austrians in Vienna, and the Hungarians all realize that the day is not far off when *they* may fall prey to this unfortunate trait of the Russian national character—not to be able to stop once they start. The chief of police must not be surprised that youthful doubts led him, Kelsiev, to become an ardent revolutionary.[19]

But we must turn away from these gems to Kelsiev's description of Herzen's world. Any ordinary Russian visitor to London, he explains, would immediately go to Trubner's bookstore, where *The Bell*, etc., was sold. The proprietor, a man in Herzen's confidence, would then convey the visitor's written petition for an audience to Herzen, who would decide whether, where, and when he would grant it. Some applicants, e.g., government officials, would prefer not to be seen in Herzen's house and thereby become known to the Russian colony. Some (here Kelsiev must be referring to the time after 1861 when Herzen and Ogarev were connected with revolutionary conspiracies in Russia) would want to have meetings with "the second government" under conditions of special secrecy—the Third Department already had agents among the colony. But also, and in the true imperial manner, once a week on Sunday at five Herzen and Ogarev granted a general audience; every Russian in London not identified as a spy might come and have tea. Many of the visitors were surprised if not shocked at the moderation of Herzen's political views, adds Kelsiev, perhaps out of some remnant of a sense of decency; and in general this would have been true until 1861.

Kelsiev offers an unflattering, if not entirely unrealistic panorama of the

---

[19]"Kelsiev's Confession," in *Literary Heritage*, XLI-XLII (Moscow 1941), 270–71. My italics.

international revolutionary set in London, of which Herzen was one of the main stars (also on account of his largesse):

> Among the French there were two parties, the revolutionaries . . . and the socialists, each blaming the other for the failure of the revolution [of 1848–49].
> . . . Mazzini could not forgive the French for occupying Rome, which ruined the Italian revolution; and the French could not understand why Italy should not remain divided out of the consideration for France, the leading country of Europe, the center of civilization, science, and taste, France which for the sake of mankind should dominate Europe . . . and here you have Mazzini putting Italy above France.
> . . . No one could live in peace with the Hungarians. They were aristocrats, proud of their genealogy and their "historic rights" to rule over Slovaks, Slovenians, Croats, etc. . . . The German could not forgive the Hungarians their rebellion against Vienna, the Italians their insensitivity to the blessings of German culture, and the French their demand to "straighten out" their frontiers by annexing the Rhineland. As for the Poles! They are divided into several groups fighting each other, but they all try to persuade the German exiles that Danzig and Königsberg should be parts of Poland. They are furious at the Italians, for the "Italian question" has diverted the attention of European liberal opinion from the sufferings of Poland. The only people they can get along with are the French—not the emigrés, but the Bonapartists, for they hoped for help from Napoleon III's government.[20]

But Count Shuvalov was not satisfied with such amusing vignettes or with the amplitude of the *Confession* (it comes to two hundred pages of close print). He prodded Kelsiev for details and names. Kelsiev had been too enthusiastic in describing people met in Herzen's salon: "One saw governors, generals, merchants, writers, society ladies, students . . . a veritable cascade of [Russian] society . . . ladies asking for autographs . . . people for advice on their family affairs." Well, asked the police chief, *who* in particular and *what* did they have to say? To his credit, Kelsiev would name only those who by 1867 were already known to the authorities as revolutionaries (some were in jail or dead) or people who were above suspicion, like Count Leo Tolstoy and the renowned reactionary writer Alexis Pisemsky.[21] He did acknowledge that even during his "moderate" phase Herzen hobnobbed with some revolutionary eccentrics such as Vladimir Engelson. Here was another man considerably ahead of his time. He wrote pamphlets in what he assumed to be popular language to stir up the peasants against the government. Herzen printed them with some reluctance, but balked when during the Crimean War Engelson proposed to have them dropped from balloons over Russia to provoke a popular uprising. This pioneer of aerial propaganda met also with a negative response from the French government to which he submitted the proposal. Engelson explained that while

[20] *Ibid.*, 276.
[21] *Ibid.*, 418.

illiterate peasants might not be able to read his seditious literature, the mere sight of books floating down from the air would have a deeply upsetting effect on the superstitious Russian folk; this would hasten the defeat of Nicholas' armies. But Engelson also was beyond Count Shuvalov's long reach—he had died in 1857.

Kelsiev's account gives a valuable insight into the splendors and frustrations, both political and psychological, of Herzen's position in Russian society between 1857 and 1862. Leo Tolstoy met Herzen briefly at the height of his fame, and his initial reaction to him, as to practically all of his contemporary fellow greats, was ambivalent: he admired his writings; he thought him too self-centered. But later the great writer put his finger on the main element of Herzen's tragedy, which was also Russia's: he had to live and work abroad, and hence what we have called here his "second government" was perforce short-lived. After its disappearance, no other person was ever able to mobilize Russian public opinion to the same extent and to make it a countervailing force to the autocracy. Tolstoy was fond of quoting a famous passage of Herzen's, and even he could not know how dreadfully prophetic it was to prove: "If all our progress takes place *only* through the government, we will give the world an unprecedented example of an autocracy armed with all the achievement of freedom; of slavery and oppression supported by all the discoveries of technology and science. This would be Genghis Khan having at his disposal telegraphs, steamships, railways...."[22] And by the same token, Tolstoy believed Herzen's influence could have saved Russian radicalism from its future infatuation with terror. In 1906, in the wake of the first Russian Revolution, the aged Christian anarchist and enemy of violence of all sorts still reverted to this thought: "It was a veritable tragedy for Russia that Herzen did not live here and that his writings did not quite reach Russian society. If he had lived in Russia, his influence would have saved our revolutionary youth from many mistakes."[23]

But during those triumphant years 1857–60 it still appeared of little consequence that Herzen was physically absent from Russia. In fact, since the press in Russia was still not allowed to discuss openly such vital problems as the abolition of serfdom and other reforms, the voice of *The Bell* rang more clearly from London, and Herzen had more influence in putting the heat on the government to hurry up than he could have had as an editor in Moscow or Petersburg. And there seemed—but how brief this was to be —nobody on the horizon who might challenge his influence over the educated class and the young. The passionate voice of the London exile calling for removal of the disgrace and barbarity of serfdom undoubtedly speeded

[22]Herzen, *Works,* IX, Petersburg 1919, 27.
[23]N. Gusev, "Herzen and Tolstoy," in *Literary Heritage,* XLI-XLII (Moscow 1941), 519.

up the Russian government's hitherto torpid progress toward the reform.

Though faced with outright opposition and dilatory tactics on the part of more conservative bureaucrats and gentry, Alexander II in November 1857 for the first time clearly and publicly announced his determination to free the serfs. There ensued a few months of universal (except among out-and-out reactionaries) enthusiasm and seeming national unity, which was not to recur until a similar mirage appeared during a few weeks in February and March 1917. Subsequently Herzen was bitterly criticized for his rapture over the emperor's promise, but at the moment and with some justification he saw that he had had a share in bringing about the historic declaration. "We face not just an heir of Nicholas, but a mighty statesman who has opened a new path for Russia. He is as much the heir of December 14 as of Nicholas. He is working with us for the greatness of our future."[24] The emperor had pardoned the surviving Decembrists. He had promised the peasants freedom. He was no longer an autocrat but the national leader. But, warned Herzen as his peer, the tsar could not dare to stop at half measures. Let him not listen to the reactionary landlords, "those defenders of the lash . . . bespattered with blood . . . those thieves who would take infants from peasant mothers . . . traffickers in women, profiteers in selling soldiers."[25] Let those "wolves" come out of their lairs and state openly their opposition to freeing the serfs. What could they do if united against them were both the government and freedom, the educated class and the people? As for himself, on behalf of free Russia he could no longer oppose the emperor who would liberate peasants. "Thou hast conquered, O Galilean."

Even the greatest admirer of Herzen must admit that the last phrase was an affectation and a ludicrous comparison: Alexander was not Christ, and it would be difficult to find any meaningful parallels between Emperor Julian the Apostate on his deathbed and Herzen alive and unconquered in London. But it is testimony to the nobility of his character that he could be so naively enthusiastic and trusting when the object of his dreams and strivings—freedom for the Russian people—seemed on the point of consummation.

Such enthusiasm by its very nature could not last. Freeing the serfs was the matter closest to Herzen's heart and mind, and he was to watch the slow unfolding of the actual reform with all the anxiety of a father separated from his child, whose guardian appears at times to neglect or even pervert his charge. Will the Galilean turn out to be a false prophet? Will the court camarilla emasculate the emancipation and rob it of any real meaning? The news that a reactionary bureaucrat had replaced a fervent believer in the

---

[24] *The Bell,* No. 9 (February 1858).

[25] Actually, the law prohibited, but not always effectively, the landlords from breaking up their serfs' families, or taking bribes to keep peasants out of the army.

reform as the head of the commission drafting the legislation threw Herzen into despairing wrath and made him bitter about Alexander. On June 1, 1860, *The Bell* castigated the emperor for allowing the whole matter to drag, for letting the sacred task of liberation become mired in the endless red tape of commissions and drafts. Russia (i.e., Herzen) had waited patiently for five years on the strength of a few humane and hopeful phrases; now "our" patience and willingness to collaborate was ended. Should not one toll the bell for all the true believers, to warn them that the time had passed when "one could expect everything from the government," to tell them that they must take the task into their own hands? It was *almost* a call for revolution; Herzen had not yet *entirely* given up hope in the tsar.

But it was not just procrastination over the reform which brought doubts and anxiety to Herzen. (Like most revolutionaries and radicals, he under-estimated the vast economic, administrative, and social complexities in working out the emancipation law, probably the greatest task of social engineering in modern history, until Stalin's and Mao's collectivizations). Suddenly the second ruler of Russia began to perceive that there were people and forces in *his* realm, among Russia's educated class and the young people, who were growing impatient with his reign and who, despite their still universal professions of loyalty and even enthusiasm, were begin-ning to seek new ways, thirst for new leaders. The danger signs appeared first in the social milieu which for lack of a better English word must be described as plebeian (in Russian, *raznochintsy*). These were for the most part young people born in the interstices of the Russian social system, so to speak, sons of priests,[26] petty officials, ruined gentry, etc. In Nicholas' time they would for the most part have followed their fathers' occupations or, at most, sought advancement up the social ladder through state service. A classical example is provided by Ilya Ulyanov, Lenin's father, himself the son of a poor tailor, who advanced through the university and a teaching career to the post of director of primary schools in 1874, which brought with it elevation to the hereditary nobility. But now there was enhanced social mobility; universities were being expanded, and so was scholarship money for needy students. It was no longer almost obligatory or even fashionable to become a civil servant. Every ambitious young man wanted to write. Passion for writing had become for young men (and, not infrequently, women) what a business career was becoming in America after the Civil War, a national vocation. If one did not feel qualified to be a scholar or if one did not have the gift to become another Pushkin or Turgenev, then there was the exciting career of serious journalism. Censorship had been relaxed and many a young "plebeian" now felt that he could give the world

---

[26]Parish priests in the Russian Orthodox Church were practically a hereditary caste, higher ecclesiastical positions being reserved for priests from the monastic clergy.

the benefit of his reflections on philosophy, literature, foreign and (if done circumspectly) domestic politics without the risks and humiliations that attended such endeavors in the late emperor's time. This literary itch not only afflicted those who were underprivileged (this currently fashionable word seems particularly apt for the "plebeians") but extended to the young and middle-aged of all strata: university and even high school students rushed to Petersburg and Moscow to give the journals their thick manuscripts on Turgenev's latest novel, or Goncharov, or Italian politics; army and even police officers blossomed forth as novelists and poets; country gentlemen, if diffident of emulating such fellow members of their class as Pushkin or Tolstoy, sought a more modest niche as authors of treatises and memoranda on the economic and social problems confronting new Russia.

Herzen was both a shining exemplar for and catalyst of this literary explosion. But writing is almost synonymous with criticizing, for the young, and Herzen was old (in his middle forties) and his intellectual background and interests a bit passé for the "new men." He had been brought up on German philosophy, and everybody under thirty knew that instead of those obscure profundities of Hegel and Schelling it was science that was the key to philosophy and the understanding of society. Thorough Russian that he was, Herzen was still cosmopolitan in his outlook and temperament. The younger Russian radical, even if erudite about European socialism and politics, was profoundly "nativist" and could not share the great exile's admiration for Western revolutionary heroes and intellectuals; for him they were mostly windbags and poseurs. If an opportunity arose Russia would produce its own, more effective Mazzinis and Garibaldis. And wasn't Herzen a bit ridiculous in his intermittent enthusiasm for the emperor, and in his insistence that some political enemies, like various proponents of English parliamentarism for Russia, should be argued with politely rather than unmasked as phrase-mongers and poltroons?

The center of the budding cultural revolution was *The Contemporary,* whose publishers were Nekrasov and Ivan Panayev and whose main critics in 1858–59 were the thirty-year-old Nicholas Chernyshevsky and Nicholas Dobrolyubov, barely in his twenties. Though the latter two freely acknowledged Herzen's leadership in progressive thought, and Dobrolyubov indeed was an occasional correspondent for *The Bell,* there were already dissonances between the two centers of what was becoming known as the Russian liberation movement. The younger men were already irreverent about the generation of dissenters who had grown up in the 1830s and 1840s. "Young men have been realizing the impermanence and uselessness of their alliance with those 'mature' sages," wrote Dobrolyubov. To be sure, he (rather condescendingly) excluded Herzen and Ogarev (without naming them because of censorship) from a list of useless sages: "Of course there are in that generation men who are different. . . . They have *until now* preserved freshness and youthful vigor. They have remained men of the future."[27] The man of letters and taste in Herzen could not but be taken aback by the effrontery of the twenty-two-year-old, who in addition considered the glorious past and present of Russian literature as useless because most of it did not deal with the social problem from the "correct" point of view: "We have already explained that we consider literature as reflecting society and not as something separate and completely independent. . . . It is precisely because of that that we have spoken so severely about the recent past of our literature, because we still have hopes for its potential [future]."[28] This already sounds like a Soviet literary bureaucrat laying down the law for those who depart from the path of socialist realism.

Though he shared their basic premises, Herzen could not but be incensed by the contemptuous and opprobrious tone in which Chernyshevsky and Dobrolyubov spoke of the liberals among the Russian gentry whose plans for the peasant reform fell short of their own more radical ideas. To talk thus, Herzen believed, was to strengthen the hand of the most reactionary bureaucrats and landowners, who would block or frustrate the all-important tasks. For another thing, the abuse of these well-meaning if misguided people seemed to him, and quite correctly, to indicate a misdirected class hatred. They were deriding and slandering not the reactionary "wolves" whom he himself had lashed, but a progressive element and tradition within the nobility which had produced the Decembrists, Pushkin, Turgenev (a special target of *The Contemporary* once he had stopped writing for it), and of course Ogarev and Herzen, among others.

Himself intemperate when aroused, Herzen found the key to the young critics' presumption and bad manners in the fact that they retained in their mentality the traits of the "servants' room, the theological seminary,[29] and the barracks." In another rather unfortunate outburst entitled (in English) "Very Dangerous," he wrote that authors of indiscriminate attacks upon liberals might, as reward for their services to reaction, be decorated with the order of St. Stanislaus.[30] (This was a double sarcasm. The order of St. Stanislaus was so widely bestowed by the tsarist government that once, when a general's house was burglarized and the only thing of value left behind were the insignia of St. Stanislaus, a wit suggested that the thief must himself already have been a recipient of the order.)

Herzen's growing estrangement from the circle around *The Contempo-*

---

[27]N. Dobrolyubov, "Some Literary Trifles of the Past Year," in *The Contemporary* (January 1, 1859). My italics.

[28]N. Dobrolyubov, "Some Literary Trifles of the Past Year, Part II," in *The Contemporary* (April 1859).

[29]Where Chernyshevsky and Dobrolyubov, both priests' sons, received their intermediate education.

[30]*The Bell* (June 1, 1859).

rary was also connected with a personal vendetta he carried on against its editors, Nekrasov and Panayev. Here it is necessary to digress briefly into a great scandal which shook the Russian radical literary world of the 1850s and 1860s, not so much for the sake of what might be called historical voyeurism but because of its serious political consequences.

Nekrasov and Panayev shared for some time not only the editorship of this leading Russian magazine but Mme. Panayeva as well. Or rather, Nekrasov replaced his friend both as her real husband and as the magazine's main editor, an arrangement which did not disturb Panayev unduly, as he found consolation with other women and had no head for the business side of publishing. Since all three continued to live in the same quarters, this setup might at first appear to bear a close resemblance to that of the Herzev–Ogarev household in London. In fact, however, both the atmosphere and the personalities involved in the two triangles were startlingly different. Though the Nekrasov ménage had its moments of tragedy— Avdotia Panayeva's miscarriages, and the poet's bout with venereal disease, which aggravated his lifelong hypochondria—it had none of the tension and gloom which hung over the life of the exiles. The three Nekrasov figures were much more mercurial than their corresponding numbers in London. Avdotia Panayeva (b. 1819), a great beauty, was a consummate cook (in the nineteenth-century meaning of the term as the planner and supervisor of great meals) and, with some help from Nekrasov, a novelist. No wonder that her salon and country villa became magnets for the literary world of Petersburg, even for high government officials and visiting foreign celebrities such as Alexander Dumas the elder. Despite her penchant for high life (though it was not so compulsive as Nekrasov's), she succeeded in charming characters of austere republican virtue like Dobrolyubov and Chernyshevsky—though the latter in his old age delivered himself of a cryptic statement about her, saying that after Panayev's death (in 1862) Nekrasov should have married Avdotia, "but then, she was an impossible woman."[31]

Alas, this charming and charitable woman was party to or at least instrumental in a criminal fraud. It involved Ogarev, but even before Ogarev's arrival in London in 1856 Herzen had heard the weird story of how his friend had been swindled by Nekrasov and/or Panayeva.

It is an extraordinary tale. In 1836 Ogarev had married one Maria Lvovna Roslavleva. Like practically everything Ogarev undertook, this marriage turned out to be a disaster. Maria Lvovna was an empty-headed woman and a nymphomaniac to boot. In 1841 Ogarev gave his wife a promissory note

[31]Quoted in L. F. Panteleyev, *Memoirs*, Moscow 1958, 476. In fact, shortly after her husband's death the great romance came to an end. Avdotia at forty-five married a minor writer and became the mother of a daughter. Nekrasov wrote a poem: "All that was precious in our lives; all that we held most dear we placed at the same altar and this flame has not died." Quoted in Kornei Chukovsky's introduction to A. Y. Panayeva, *Memoirs*, Moscow 1972, 10.

on one of his estates.[32] Soon afterward they became estranged, and in 1846 Mme. Ogareva, who was a great friend of Nekrasov and Panayeva, left to live abroad. In 1849 Ogarev asked Maria Lvovna for a divorce, which, egged on by Panayeva, she refused to grant. Instead she instituted a suit against her husband for the money he formally owed her. Ogarev was already in hot water on other counts. He was living openly with Natalia Tuchkova, daughter of a man with "untrustworthy views." (Alexis Tuchkov had had some connection with the Decembrists, and was, the local authorities asserted, "spoiling" his serfs and sporting a beard.) The sum of these transgressions in Nicholas' Russia led to the whole family, including Natalia's brother-in-law, being summoned before the Third Department and Ogarev spending four weeks in jail. Not surprisingly, he lost the civil suit and had to turn over one of his remaining properties to his vengeful wife, who continued to live abroad while leaving the management of her business affairs in Russia to her great friend Avdotia Panayeva. The latter had a rather shady relative of hers manage the property, and finally they sold it for the then considerable sum of 85,000 silver rubles.

In 1853 Maria Lvovna died in virtual poverty in Paris; as it turned out, only a trickle of money, not more than 3,000 rubles, had ever reached her from her friends in Russia. Ogarev and his now wedded Natalia were trying desperately to get passports to go abroad and were in no position to do anything about the swindle, which had become a public secret in the literary world of Petersburg. Rumors ranged from partial exculpation of the theft on grounds that it served a high social purpose (the purloined money was used to help *The Contemporary* out of its financial troubles), through worldly explanations (Nekrasov lost most of the money at cards), to the most opprobrious gossip (Ogarev was prevented from pursuing the matter because Nekrasov threatened to denounce him to the Third Department).[33] But once Ogarev was abroad, Herzen openly branded Nekrasov and Panayeva as thieves. He was not mollified by the poet's protestations, conveyed through Turgenev, that all the fault was Panayeva's and that he, Nekrasov, had gallantly decided for the sake of the woman he loved to endure all the slanders in silence.

It took a civil suit, decided in a Petersburg court in 1859, to make Panayeva disgorge the 85,000 rubles to Maria Ogareva's heirs.[34] Most of the money was in fact paid by Nekrasov. His story, that the fraud was entirely

---

[32]Ogarev, who had inherited lands with four thousand serfs, or "souls," as the phrase went, did everything possible consciously and unconsciously to lose his great wealth. Already in 1842 he had said, "to become a man I must become a proletarian." See Y. S. Cherniak, *Ogarev, Nekrasov, Herzen and Chernyshevsky in the Dispute About Ogarev's Inheritance*, Moscow, 1933, 54.

[33]*Ibid.*, 195.

[34]*Ibid.*, 186.

of Avdotia's doing, was endorsed somewhat unchivalrously and unrealistically by most Russian historians of the period, eager to salvage as much as possible of the reputation of the people's poet. But for Herzen the whole sordid story branded not only Nekrasov (whom as a poet he appreciated) but the whole group around *The Contemporary*. They had repeatedly denounced the Tsarist officialdom for its corruption, and here they were showing themselves completely insensitive to the fact that their intimate friend and collaborator, with the help of his mistress, had swindled an unbalanced woman who had trusted them, and that he had thus compounded the personal tragedy of Ogarev, their fellow radical.[35]

But Herzen still could not face an open split with the radicals in Russia, who if rebellious and wayward were still his spiritual children. In a sense his dilemma forecast the later tragedy of Russian radicalism. From 1903 on the Mensheviks never ceased to attack the tactics and decry the unscrupulousness of Lenin and his followers. Yet not even after the February Revolution did they have the courage to break openly and clearly with the Bolsheviks. The initiative for the break came from the Bolsheviks, and even then many Mensheviks could not bring themselves to oppose the undemocratic aspirations of their erstwhile comrades; to do so would help the common enemy—reaction.

Obviously a summit meeting was needed to avoid a split in what was already referred to as the liberation movement. In June 1859 Chernyshevsky travelled to London for a four-day parley with Herzen. The result was a sort of détente: personal or even ideological differences would not prevent *The Bell* and *The Contemporary* from working for the common goal; their dialogue would become more subdued. Their negative impressions of each other, however, were, if anything, strengthened. "What a sharp mind, what a sharp mind," Chernyshevsky wrote, "but how far behind the times! He seems to act as if he were still dazzling his opponents in Moscow drawing rooms. But things are now moving with extraordinary speed. *One month brings more than what used to take ten years.* Look at him closely, at heart he is still a Moscow gentleman."[36] To paraphrase a future leader of the movement that put Chernyshevsky above Herzen (though it is doubtful that poor Nikita Khrushchev ever read either), the younger man was ready "to bury" Herzen and his camp. But Herzen was not ready to be superseded. Yes, Chernyshevsky was an amazingly erudite man, he remarked. All the more surprising how conceited he was: "He is convinced that *The Contemporary* is the navel of Russia. And us, old sinners, they have already buried.

---

[35]Ogarev's troubles with his first wife and the consequent delay in leaving Russia had undoubtedly aggravated his epilepsy and his tendency to alcoholism.

[36]For a radical of the time Moscow was synonymous if not with conservatism then with genteel liberalism, as against the more progressive atmosphere of St. Petersburg.

But they are a bit premature; we are well, we shall live."[37]

These negative responses were confined to private communications among the writers' friends. Outwardly the political alliance between the two groups continued, though not without strain. Yet even on the eve of embarking on a joint conspiratorial venture, Herzen could not endure what might be called spiritual coexistence with *The Contemporary*'s crew. The more he encountered people of the Chernyshevsky stamp, the more he was repelled by their narrow censorious attitude toward social problems, especially since these self-proclaimed ascetics and enemies of privilege tolerated a Nekrasov in their midst. His feelings exploded in an October 15, 1860 *Bell* piece, "Superfluous Men and Bilious People." Perhaps his own generation displayed some kinship with the "superfluous men" immortalized by Pushkin and Lermontov, as *The Contemporary* would have it; perhaps they all bore traces of their aristocratic upbringing, of the drawing-room levity and fashionable sentimentality of the Romantic Age. But how else, he wrote, could they have survived the Nicholas era, especially after some of those "superfluous men," allegedly unmindful of all but their private lives, had met the fate of the Decembrists? "Superfluous men were then as necessary, as it is necessary now that they should cease to exist." But God forbid that they should be replaced by that other type also formed by the terrible era 1825–55, the "plebeians" (though Herzen does not spell out their class origins) who were distorted by the evil times in a yet different way: "people who for the most part already lost their freshness in their youth . . . became overripe before their time, . . . stricken by old age before reaching legal maturity. These are not superfluous . . . but irascible men, sick in soul and body . . . from humiliations they had to endure; people who will not look you in the eye, who still exude the bile and poison they had to absorb." Perhaps this bilious generation represents an advance over the "superfluous" one, but it is sick and "must heal itself or die."

This remarkable psychological characterization, which as only an obtuse reader could miss focused in ruthless detail on Chernyshevsky and Dobrolyubov, was accompanied by Herzen's imaginary dialogue with a representative of the "bilious people." Why, the latter asks, should he show any sympathy for those "useless, empty aristocrats who live undisturbed and quite comfortably?" They are hardly the victims of political oppression, those "superfluous men"! Perhaps so, replies Herzen, but he will cite the example of a man now active compared to whom those allegedly useless aristocrats were veritable saints. We have had all sorts of people in the Russian literary world, Herzen observes, but for the most part they were honest; "swindlers, cheats, forgers of false promissory notes, and denouncers were usually found among government officials." We have not, until

[37]Quoted in A. A. Kornilov, *The Social Movement Under Alexander II*, Moscow 1909, 103.

now, seen people who "lie and trade on their art just as a prostitute lies with her body and sells her charms"; a "man who perorates against injustice, curses and brands with shame [our] social infamy and backwardness, and at the same time fills his coffers with money openly stolen from his friends."[38]

And yet Herzen was on the point of embarking upon a revolutionary conspiracy with these same "bilious people." That he was to do so was in no small measure due to the presence at his side of Nicholas Ogarev. The traditional view has long been that "poor Nicholas" was, whether in political or personal affairs, but wax in Herzen's hands. But Natalia perceived more correctly the relationship between her lover and her husband, at least insofar as politics was concerned: "Herzen always conceded to Ogarev, even when he knew Ogarev was wrong."[39]

The January 1861 issue of *The Bell* opened with two editorials. A long one by Ogarev condemned in advance the forthcoming peasant reforms, and implied that Russia could not expect to be given freedom—it would have to seize it. Herzen's editorial contained a tribute to a recently deceased political opponent: Constantine Aksakov, a Slavophile, a believer in Russia's own way and destiny distinct from the West, but unlike Herzen also a conservative and traditionalist. Recalling their sharp political quarrels, Herzen wrote, "I do not remember that we ever doubted their warm love for Russia or that they ever questioned ours." But now destiny drove him to march arm in arm with the "bilious men." They would bury if not his reputation then his beloved *Bell;* and to a great majority of his countrymen the erstwhile "second government" would become a traitor to Russia's cause.

[38]Herzen, *Works,* X, 414–22 passim.
[39]N. A. Tuchkova-Ogareva, *Memoirs,* Moscow 1859, 187.

THREE

THE NEW MEN AND CHERNYSHEVSKY

The excitement within Russian society during the late 1850s and early 1860s was generated not only by the talk about and expectation of great reforms, by the radicals' quarrels and the government's apprehensions. The death of Nicholas, and then the humiliation offered by the autocracy when in the Treaty of Paris of 1856 it acknowledged Russia's defeat in the Crimean War, had sent an electric charge throughout Russian society. For a while this most backward and politically most unfree of European countries became the most liberal one, insofar as the manners and morals of its educated class were concerned. Everywhere else in Europe this was the height of the so-called Victorian era, with everything that implies in terms of bourgeois respectability as the ruling creed for the family and society. But in Russia when you follow private lives in the 1860s and observe the outward characteristics of young men and women—not only celebrities but ordinary members of the *intelligentsia*—you find discussions of the generation gap, about whether and how far art and literature should be relevant, and you seem to be not in the empire of the tsars, with its serfs and Siberian exiles, but in our own turbulent 1960s and 1970s. A perceptive writer whom we have already quoted, Nicholas Shelgunov, noted this overnight revolution in manners and morals. Born in 1824, his stereotype of family life included wives as slaves of their husbands, children trembling before their parents and whipped mercilessly for the slightest offense in school. Now, teen-agers assumed that air of slightly contemptuous familiarity with their elders which we know so well. Children had once addressed their parents as "mummy," "daddy," "you"; it now became "mother," "father," and, most shockingly, "thou."[1] Young men of advanced ideas grew their hair long, and of course young ladies of the same persuasion cropped theirs. Physical punishment of minors became so repugnant to the educated classes that even much later, during the period of reaction, an average Russian parent or schoolteacher would not dream of enacting practices used into the twentieth century by British schoolmasters.

But above all, there was a women's and sexual revolution. Its first expression was the popularity of what might be called blank marriages. Young ladies, if denied permission by their parents to live separately or to attend university lectures (a thing until now unheard-of) or to go abroad to receive a formal higher education, would seek out young men who would marry them, on the strict understanding that they would not attempt to enforce their marital rights or hamper their wives' freedom in any other way. It was a marriage of this kind that enabled Sophia Kovalevskaya, born Korvin-Krukovska, to study mathematics in Germany and to become the first distinguished woman in the annals of the science.

Soon the very phrase "marital rights" and the institution of marriage itself acquired unprogressive connotations. What became popular was the so-called civic marriage—not to be confused with a civil marriage, which was impossible under Russian law, and bearing but a superficial resemblance to what in Anglo-Saxon terminology is called a common-law marriage. A civic marriage was not only the union of a man and a woman without any church and state sanction, but it had as prerequisite that each partner be of progressive views and, regardless of whether he or she already had a legal spouse, that they scorn clandestinity and live together (and, if so inclined, procreate) openly.[2]

The new interest in the emancipation of women had, like everything else in the Russian radical movement, been stimulated by books and ideas from the West. It was a French feminist who declared, "All vices and misfortunes, general and particular, are the result of the inferior role of women in the state, society, family, and education."[3] But again, what was elsewhere

---

[1]Which in Russian carries the implication of extreme familiarity and in this context a certain disrespect. See *Memoirs of N.V. Shelgunov and His Circle,* Moscow 1967, I, 140.

[2]Thus Alexander II and his brother, Grand Duke Constantine, entered in their middle years into what to an uninitiated person might appear to be model "civic marriages." But because of the imperial status of the people concerned, most progressive historians refer to these unions as liaisons and to the ladies concerned not as civic wives but as mistresses. Another imperial brother was considered mentally unhinged because, unwilling to indulge in transient affairs appropriate to a prince, or even in a "civic marriage," he sought to divorce his spouse and to marry officially the object of his love. This last lady was so free with her favors that to secure them by matrimony was, a Petersburg wit declared, similar to a man offering to pay for the right to stroll in a public park.

[3]Quoted in Shelgunov, II, 76.

a new and not as yet influential fashion became a veritable cult in Russian radicalism.

If this cult needed a male saint, there is no question but that Nicholas Shelgunov, a colonel in the Forestry Corps,[4] must be a very serious candidate. His wife, Liudmila, kept a salon where she entertained and wooed leading literary figures of the 1850s. (Once she tried to cast her spell over young Leo Tolstoy, and one trembles to think of the consequences to Russian and world literature had she been successful.) Finally, with her husband's full approval, she became the civic wife of Michael Mikhailov, a poet and translator. Not only did Shelgunov become Mikhailov's closest friend, but, as we shall see later on, both men collaborated in important conspiratorial work. Mme. Shelgunova's collaboration with the poet produced a son, Michael, in 1860; her husband's, a series of revolutionary proclamations in 1861, for which Mikhailov was arrested. Under investigation he chivalrously took all the blame on himself to save his friends and was sentenced to hard labor in Siberia. The current gossip laid the blame on Mme. Shelgunova. In any case she now persuaded her husband that they should set out together for Siberia and help their friend escape.

This madcap venture ended as one might have expected. After a brief reunion, Shelgunov was sent back to Petersburg and imprisoned. Mikhailov's confinement was made stricter (he was to die in 1865). Mme. Shelgunova left for Switzerland, where, in Geneva, she ran a boarding house for Russian exiles and struck up a friendship with one whom we shall also meet again, Alexander Serno-Solovievich. With him she had another son, Nicholas, born in 1864. The romance did not run smoothly, and finally Liudmila had her lover confined in a mental asylum, while sending their child to her husband, currently in exile in northern Russia.[5] Throughout, Shelgunov never ceased to write tender letters to "my darling little friend, Liudmila," expressed joy at the happy result of her confinement, and declared his impatience to receive and care for little Nicholas.

There was a sort of happy ending. Liudmila returned to Russia, and though she was unwilling to stay permanently with her husband, who was still barred from living in the main cities, she would visit him occasionally, one such reunion finally producing a child of *both* Shelgunovs! In 1877 the old revolutionary was finally allowed to return to the capital, where he moved close to the new generation of radicals. Again in hot water with the government in the 1880s, he was briefly arrested and exiled again. His

---

[4]For reasons peculiar to Nicholas' Russia, this very unmartial profession was organized along military lines.

[5]In her own memoirs Shelgunova is expansive about Mikhailov but rather matter-of-fact about his successor: "Alexander Serno-Solovievich lived for five years abroad, sometimes at large and sometimes in a madhouse, as he was mentally ill, as his mother had been. He ended his days by suicide." Shelgunov, II, 120.

funeral in 1891 was the occasion of a demonstration by progressive youth, but no one then realized how much Shelgunov himself had been involved in the revolutionary conspiracies of 1860–62, the details of which were to become known only after the 1917 Revolution. What the youth honored in him was his having been a friend of such revolutionaries as Mikhailov and a model for all progressive husbands—a real man of the sixties. Liudmila survived her husband by a few years. Reactionary gossip credited her (quite untruthfully) with converting both Mikhailov and Shelgunov to the radical cause and even with authorship of the revolutionary proclamations of 1861; she did these things, said spiteful tongues, because of her ambition to become the first woman to pass into history as a great revolutionary.[6] If so, she failed. To be sure, Soviet historians give her higher marks than Panayeva or Tuchkova-Ogareva for social consciousness. But in the biographical dictionary of the revolutionary figures of the 1860s published in Moscow in 1928, Nicholas Shelgunov has a long and laudatory entry and there is no mention of Liudmila Michaelis Shelgunova.

Apart from its own inherent interest, the Shelgunov saga is instructive insofar as it throws light on the frequent assertions, made by both his admirers and his enemies, that it was Nicholas Chernyshevsky who molded the minds of men of the sixties. It was, as we have seen, Nicholas I's Russia which made a rebel out of Shelgunov; all his dammed-up impulses to rebellion and nonconformity erupted with revolutionary fervor when the edifice of the autocracy, once so awe-inspiring and invulnerable, showed itself, with the accession of Alexander, brittle and, quite likely, doomed. And Shelgunova's amatory explorations would in all likelihood never have passed the bounds of conventional adultery had not free love become a form of social protest and an imperative for all new men and women. Chernyshevsky's *What Is To Be Done?*, with its portraits and canonization of these new men and women, did not appear until 1863. He was not the *maker* of the new world, but he took what was perhaps a passing fad and made it a religion at whose altar generations of Russian revolutionaries would worship, even those of different ideological persuasions, such as Plekhanov and Lenin.

Before his martyrdom and the fantastic success of his novel made Chernyshevsky a revolutionary saint, this bookish awkward man became a prototype for the Russian revolutionary leader. He was never "a second government," just as he was not a great writer. But somehow, from his ponderous articles in *The Contemporary* and from his own personality, there emanated a revolutionary credo which most radical young people in those feverish years found irresistible: no reform, Chernyshevsky suggested, no benevolence real or feigned on the part of the government can absolve

[6]T. A. Bogdanovich, *Loves of the People of the Sixties*, Leningrad 1929, 380.

honest and thinking men from the duty of working for a violent overthrow of the status quo. Only from such an upheaval, no matter what its cost, can a just and healthy society emerge.

There is no mystery as to why Chernyshevsky should have had so much appeal to the young. Herzen hit on only half the truth when he described Chernyshevsky as a person who was "stricken by old age before his time." Behind the apparent overseriousness Chernyshevsky retained in his nature the kind of adolescent feeling which is an important part of the makeup of the conspiratorial mind. How preoccupied he was with fighting! The word "struggle" appears in his writings almost as often as in the work of his worshipper, Lenin, even in his essays on esthetics: "Looking at human life from the point of view of reason rather than fantasy, we must say 'all important human activity requires incessant struggle with nature or other people.' "[7] Or on the duty of the critic: he has before him, he writes, two poems equally unrealistic in their mawkish sentimental representation of life, one by a minor poet and the other by Goethe; which one is socially more harmful? "Which of these two poems should be *attacked* full blast, if you consider (as every reasonable man should) that mawkish idealization of life is for the Germans a very harmful disease?"[8] Of course Goethe's! Because he is a great poet he may fool more people into believing that life is cakes and ale, rather than a relentless struggle against injustice, oppression, etc. The same line of reasoning leads the youthful Chernyshevsky (he was then twenty-six) to "struggle" against Pushkin. To be sure Pushkin was *for his time* a great poet, he says, but excessive transports over Pushkin, indeed too frequent reading of his poetry, takes one's mind off the important social issues of the day; there is no question that his friend Nekrasov is a much greater poet than Pushkin, for he writes about the people's sufferings.

This kind of comment goes even beyond the requirements of socialist realism as practiced currently in the Soviet Union, for no Soviet critic would dare to put Nekrasov on a level with Pushkin or to assert, as Chernyshevsky did in his old age, and after *War and Peace* and *Anna Karenina,* that Tolstoy was considered a great national writer mainly because he was a count. This is in line with Mao Tse-tung's warning against Chinese classical poetry, reading of which hampers people from doing more important things (such as reading Mao's own writings). But Chernyshevsky's attack upon art for art's sake has another revealing side: he seems to take a childish pleasure in trampling on idols and in delivering, with sophomoric seriousness, definitive judgments such as, "Sublime beauty is found only in life."[9]

Yet one cannot find the entire answer to his popularity in his ability to

[7] N. G. Chernyshevsky, *Works,* Moscow 1949, II, 179.
[8] *Ibid.,* II, 257. My italics.
[9] *Ibid.,* II, 90.

synchronize with youth's eternal need for defiance and its suspicion of authority. Chernyshevsky came from the people and to the end he retained that certain shyness and patient endurance of adversity inherited from a long line of parish-priest ancestors. His education and his first steps as teacher and critic were taken in the last years of Nicholas' reign, when, like many men of his class and aspirations, he had to endure those humiliations of which Herzen was to speak in his comments on the "bilious" people. His repressed rage could then find only such expressions as his warning to the girl he loved that she should think twice about marrying him since, if there ever arose a revolutionary movement in Russia, he would feel bound, though of a meek and even cowardly nature, to join it. Humility, again the product of his early religious upbringing and serious experiences, was to be an abiding trait. In the beginning of *What Is To Be Done?* he wrote sincerely (and, alas, truthfully), "I don't have the shadow of an artistic talent. I even use the language poorly." But this feeling of personal worthlessness was combined with an enormous conceit about the mission with which history (had he remained a believer he would have said Providence) had entrusted him.[10] On the eve of his exile to Siberia he wrote to his wife, "Our life belongs to history; hundreds of years will pass and our names will still be dear to the people." This incongruous mixture of emotion and atavistic religious feeling served him well in creating a new faith for a generation which, like himself, had lost the old one and which, unlike people of Herzen's age and class, did not have spiritual roots in the Western Enlightenment.

Thus Chernyshevsky could "relate" to the "new men" in a way that was quite beyond the power of Herzen and other contemporary political figures. Reading his oft-expressed statements of love for such young people as Dobrolyubov and Vladimir Obruchev and about their own adoration of their guide, an old-school historian might raise his eyebrows, and a devotee of psycho-history triumphantly decide he had made a significant discovery. But they would be wrong. Of few historical figures can it be argued so confidently that once married he had no cravings, conscious or otherwise, except for his lawfully wedded wife. To be sure, his generally Victorian view of the conjugal bond was tinged by a certain masochism and at least verbal concessions to the spirit of the age. To his friends who warned him about his fiancée's character he said, "It is all the same to me if I have someone else's child. I shall tell her, should you prefer to come back to me, my dear, don't be embarrassed." This was certainly not quite à la Shelgunov, who would have found it terribly old-fashioned for his wife even to go away temporarily if she wanted a child by another man. Besides, one suspects in Chernyshevsky's case the declaration was very largely a pose; he felt deeply

---

[10]Even as a radical and atheist, Chernyshevsky still liked to attend church services, and crossed himself when passing a church.

his wife's frivolity and her irritation over his bookish life, which on at least one occasion led her to break into Chernyshevsky's study, drag him away from his writing table, and force him to dance. But Olga Chernyshevskaya's other recollections in her old age—how she had been wooed by grand dukes, and how while her husband was engaged in his sanctum on some weighty treatise she would deceive him in the drawing room with a fellow revolutionary—sound suspiciously like fantasies.[11]

He was awkward, ill-at-ease, and artificial not only with literary celebrities and people of higher social status, but with older people in general; his nervous giggle would drive even his admirers to distraction. This behavior proceeded not only from the reasons we have already mentioned but from awareness of his physical unattractiveness and his parochialism. Like many nearsighted people who start wearing glasses rather late, he always gave the impression of being half blind. And the boy from the lower Volga who had never been in Paris or Rome, or belonged to one of those intellectual circles in Moscow or Petersburg in his youth, could not overcome a feeling of being out of place even when he was renowned as one of Russia's leading intellectuals. This has also probably a lot to do with his need to chastise and unmask Russia's alleged greats, even in areas where he did not claim the slightest competence. (The great mathematician Nicholas Lobachevsky was, according to him, an imposter: who ever heard of such a thing as "curved space"?[12])

By the same token Chernyshevsky was natural, understanding, and tender with young people and knew how to earn their devotion. He had taught but briefly, in Petersburg military schools and a Saratov *gymnasium,* but many of his pupils and associates were to become lifelong followers. Years later a judge examining a political offender would ask if by any chance he had studied under Chernyshevsky. At the height of his fame his dominance over the university students was legendary. Prince Suvorov recalled to Shelgunov how in the 1860s whenever he felt that some trouble was brewing in the capital he would send a message to Chernyshevsky to use his influence to stop it.[13] When the fires of the spring of 1862 broke out in St. Petersburg, Dostoyevsky, convinced like many others that they were the work of the "nihilists," ran to Chernyshevsky, the only man he thought could prevent further conflagrations.

But of course the main source of Chernyshevsky's power which extended

---

[11]Vladimir Nabokov, in his venomous chapter on Chernyshevsky in *The Gift,* New York 1952 (in Russian), 264, takes them at face value. Russian ladies of the era, including the highest born, like Princess Yurievskaya, Alexander II's morganatic wife, were not far behind the current Anglo-American fashion of divulging intimate details of their lives to strangers.

[12]*Ibid.,* 269. Here Lenin was to prove a faithful disciple when he wrote that those who advance the absurd notion that there are more than three dimensions are theologians in a scientific guise.

[13]Shelgunov, I, 157.

beyond his exile and his grave grew out of his political journalism. *The Contemporary* became his tribune through which, it is not too much to say, he changed the course of Russian history. His concentration on journalism was largely fortuitous. Approval of his doctoral thesis, *On the Esthetic Relation of Art To Reality,* written in 1853, was long delayed, first by the faculty then by the ministry of education, and by the time the degree was granted in 1858, Chernyshevsky was launched on a more splendid career than that of a university teacher. In 1855 he became a regular contributor to *The Contemporary.* By 1857 he was virtual co-editor with Nekrasov of the journal.

The Contemporary began as one of those thick literary journals, the tradition of which has carried into our own times and is represented by Soviet literary magazines such as *New World* and *October.* When times would allow, as after Nicholas' death, *The Contemporary* under Nekrasov (or as after Stalin's, *New World* under Tvardovsky) would take on a discreet but distinct political coloring. Nekrasov, whose other characteristics we have already discussed, was an editor of genius with an unerring knack for seeking out the most talented and promising contributors for his journal. Many of his actions become understandable if not forgivable if one keeps in mind that *The Contemporary* was for him an object of fatherly love and pride and by no means just a source of income and influence. In 1856 he scored a major coup: four writers—Turgenev, then acknowledged as Russia's leading man of letters; Leo Tolstoy, the most promising among the young; Alexander Ostrovsky, the country's outstanding dramatist; and Dmitri Grigorovich, a much lesser light but then very popular—agreed to submit all their future writings exclusively to *The Contemporary* in return for a large share of net profits.[14] The magazine seemed, and in fact was, launched on a most glorious as well as profitable career. The rather large fly in the ointment proved to be Chernyshevsky's growing influence, and his determination to turn the journal increasingly in the direction of social and, insofar as censorship would allow, political criticism. And quite apart from questions of editorial policy, the leading literary contributors could not stand Chernyshevsky, both because of what they considered his vulgar views on art and even more on account of his personality. As early as 1855 it became a private joke among some of the noble-born *literati* to say that Chernyshevsky smelled of bedbugs. Closer contact with the man who was already attracting a large following among the young did not endear him to the giants of Russian literature. In 1857 Leo Tolstoy was to write in a letter, "It is a shame to have this man smelling of bedbugs around. One cannot stand his thin unpleasant little voice telling all those silly would-be

[14]William F. Woehrlin, *Chernyshevsky: The Man and the Journalist,* Cambridge, Mass., 1971, 92.

witticisms; and what drives him to babble heatedly in conversation is the fact that he does not know how to talk and his voice sounds obscene."[15] It is impossible not to agree with Soviet critics when they regard such judgments as reflecting class prejudices, but they go too far when they ignore the shattering impression that Chernyshevsky's esthetic views must have had on real artists.

In any case, coexistence in *The Contemporary* between Chernyshevsky and the literary greats could not be lasting. Gradually his opponents terminated their connection with the magazine, the last of them, Turgenev, in 1860. By 1859 the title page of *The Contemporary* bore a subtitle: *Literary and Political Journal*. If the literary man in Nekrasov bewailed the defection of Tolstoy and Turgenev (the former would in any case have found it impossible to stay long in any group or magazine without quarrelling), then the entrepreneur in him must have been pleased: the subscription list grew every year, and by 1861 it was about 7000. Its closest rival, *The Russian Word*, had about 4000. There is no question that this growth reflected the popularity of Chernyshevsky and his protégé, Nicholas Dobrolyubov, who joined the journal in 1857 at the age of twenty-one.[16] Since Dobrolyubov not only shared his friend's views but expressed them in writing more skillfully and passionately, he almost overshadowed Chernyshevsky as the target of abuse by the opposite camp. Chernyshevsky was an ordinary snake, but Dobrolyubov was a viper, said Turgenev. And few failed to notice that not only Dobrolyubov but some other new contributors to *The Contemporary* came from the same sphere as their leader: priests' sons and former students in church seminaries.

Dobrolyubov's influence on his mentor might in some ways be compared to that of Ogarev on Herzen. Not that Dobrolybov drove Chernyshevsky to the left and helped make an active revolutionary out of a radical—Chernyshevsky did not need any pushing in that direction. But the latter was by nature a cautious and patient man, and Dobrolyubov, a passionate youngster convinced, being consumptive and diabetic, that he did not have much time before him, helped to push the older man beyond what he himself would have thought prudent or timely in revolutionary activity.

In January 1858, concurrently with his activity on *The Contemporary*, Chernyshevsky embarked on another editorial job which, though short-lived, was to have very serious consequences. He became a co-editor of *The Military Review*, a new journal sponsored by the war ministry. This appears to have been a strange choice because he was already known as a man of

---

[15]Quoted in Kornei Chukovsky, *Men and Books of the Sixties*, Moscow 1934, 58.

[16]Also such gimmicks of Nekrasov's as free gifts of books to new subscribers. In 1858, e.g., they received the fresh Russian translation of *Uncle Tom's Cabin*, not only a current literary best seller but in view of its subject most timely when the liberation of the "Russian Negroes"—serfs—was on everybody's mind.

unorthodox views, to put it mildly. But this was precisely the point. Dmitri Milyutin, then chief of the planning section of the war ministry and soon (1861) to become its head and one of the great reformers of the era, believed that the Crimean War had shown that the mind of the professional officer needed shaking up and exposure to new social and political ideas. Chernyshevsky, whose erudition, though based exclusively on book learning of the politics and economics of the West, was already legendary, appeared the ideal man to expand the narrow horizons of the average noble officer; he would help to prepare the ground for Milyutin's ambitious goal, a real citizens' army for Russia, rather than one of armed and illiterate slaves disciplined through the lash and officered by a hidebound caste. Strangely enough both Chernyshevsky's personality and ideas proved to have a magnetic effect on quite a few of his military associates and young officers. Perhaps opposites attract; just as many years later West Pointers in the Pentagon were to be awed by academic experts, some of them with thick foreign accents, so the more progressive Russian officer of the 1860s was impressed by this man of the people, not ignorant and servile like the ones they were accustomed to, but learned and defiant. One such was the journal's co-editor, a brilliant young staff officer named Nicholas Obruchev, and we shall hear a great deal about him. But with his contacts established, Chernyshevsky within a year thought it more prudent to resign his editorship of the *Military Review*. By that time he was making enough on *The Contemporary* to satisfy his wife's fancies.

In reading his famous articles, one is at first puzzled as to why they caused such excitement or why they have been credited with such a revolutionary impact. They are long, flatly written treatises, single paragraphs sometimes running for fifty pages of close print, often studded with statistics. Imagine an average article in an American sociological or political-science review but four or five times its length! But this length and form often served to put the most vigilant censor to sleep, while the "perspicacious reader," as Chernyshevsky repeatedly addressed him, enjoyed the delicious game of seeking and usually finding some heretical or outright revolutionary allusion to the Russian reality in the midst of statistical data or an endless discussion of contemporary Italian politics. Take the forty-four pages of the March 1859 review of politics in the West which brought Herzen to the boiling point. There Chernyshevsky launches into a ridicule of those Western liberals who became incensed at the way King Ferdinand II of Naples first flirted with the political reformers in his kingdom and then, once the danger of revolution had in his opinion passed, had them imprisoned and chained.[17] What could those moderate reformers expect? They were fools to trust the tyrant, and he was quite right to lock them up

[17]Chernyshevsky, VI, 150–52.

once he no longer needed to quiet public opinion. To be sure—and here one almost hears Chernyshevsky's chuckle—"in our age liberal superstitions in Western Europe are very strong, and humanity requires that excessive severity not be used when not needed," so those people should have been merely imprisoned, not chained as well. But then, he, Chernyshevsky, is not the judge, and perhaps "the Neapolitan government . . . would not have employed severe measures unless they were really necessary." Who, except the censor who passed it, could miss the clear hint of how silly, how deserving of all that came to them, were those Russian liberals who expected constitutions and other boons from their government!

The expectation of liberals and even radicals à la Herzen was that the progressive bureaucrats in Alexander II's entourage such as the Milyutin brothers[18] would be able to overcome the prejudices of their more conservative colleagues, as well as the class interest of the landowning aristocracy as a whole. Here is Chernyshevsky in July 1859 discussing the reasons why the Austrian army was being beaten by the French: "These reasons, beyond any accident of personality or circumstances, lie in the very structure of the state—in the bureaucratic-aristocratic basis of the whole organization." Even if the Austrians were able to score an accidental victory, the course of the war would not be affected: "The soldiers . . . would still remain the same soldiers, exhausted by needless marches, fatigued by senseless military exercises, hungry, incapable of fighting another battle; their commanders would be the same incompetent people. . . ." The lesson? "Some think that bureaucracy tends to be hostile to aristocracy—perhaps so, in some theoretical scheme. But in fact they get along with each other excellently. They scratch each other's back."[19] No commentary is required.

The revolutionary and the socialist in Chernyshevsky already stand before us by 1859. It is silly, he tells his disciples as clearly as one could in Russia, to get excited about reforms, constitutions, even national emancipation. What do those things mean to the "mass of the people, which is indifferent to all those ideas, whether of reaction, constitutionalism, or political revolution, and which is imbued only by dull dissatisfaction about material conditions of the status quo? These ignorant, almost dumb, *in ordinary times* almost comatose masses do not play any part in current Italian developments, just as they play no part in most of the political affairs of Western Europe." The masses—and how often will this word be used by Lenin and his disciples—are in fact indifferent to politics unless the latter affects the material conditions of their lives, and they do not care to have the right to vote unless there should be an economic revolution, etc. "The

[18]Dmitri's brother Nicholas, deputy minister of the interior, was one of the most active and progressive participants in the drafting of the peasant reform.
[19]Chernyshevsky, VI, 318, 319.

masses think that if there are not to be [new] agrarian laws or a change in the relationship of labor to capital, they would rather be let alone in peace, let things stagnate, as long as they can earn some livelihood." Most reformers, most revolutionaries thus leave the masses indifferent, since they do not have the courage to demand *economic* changes, in fact are unaware that such changes are the only thing the masses are interested in. And thus, since these liberals do no know how to arouse the multitude, they are bound to end up as prey to a triumphant and vengeful reaction. "I am speaking, of course, of Italy."[20]

Was then Chernyshevsky, as Lenin characterized him and as every Soviet writer feels bound to repeat, a "revolutionary democrat?" No. Nothing was further from his way of thinking than that notional device of Marxism: that the emancipation of the working class must be achieved by the working class itself. How could this be, if to him the masses were ordinarily dumb and comatose, interested only in scraping up some means of survival no matter how miserable?

Who *can* rouse the people from their lethargy and turn their wrath against the exploiters? At one time Chernyshevsky was ready to believe it would be the tsar. The publication of Alexander II's rescripts, with their promise of ending serfdom, had thrown Chernyshevsky into a rapture even surpassing that of Herzen, and with his ecclesiastical background he found a more appropriate device for his eulogy of the emperor than the London exile's "Thou hast conquered, O Galilean." His article of February 1858 began with the psalmist's "Thou has beloved truth and hated injustice; and that is why thou hast been anointed by God."

Herzen had qualified his enthusiasm by warning the emperor that the peasant reform was but the first step, but Chernyshevsky's confidence for the moment knew no bounds and evoked a prophecy: "The blessings promised to the peacemakers and to the meek crown Alexander II with a felicity which none of Europe's sovereigns ever achieved—the happiness both to begin and to complete the freeing of his subjects."[21] Soviet and most liberal Russian historians have always been enormously embarrassed by this outburst of their hero. Some have tried rather absurdly to see it as a ruse designed to lull the censor's suspicions about the highly critical discussion of the emancipation proposals which allegedly follows in the same article.[22] Yet no one who has struggled through the rest of the essay could find it easy to endorse such a view: the remainder is devoted to an attack on those Russians who would defend serfdom! Nor can the supplementary explanation from the same sources hold much water: that Chernyshevsky was deceived by the tsar; that he thought the serfs not only would be eman-

---

[20] *Ibid.*, VI, 369 (my italics), 375.

[21] *Ibid.*, V, 70.

[22] N. M. Sikorsky, *The Contemporary and the Peasant Reform of 1861*, Moscow 1957, 14.

cipated, but would receive the land which they cultivated for free, along with their freedom; that as he realized the deception he turned against Alexander II.[23] But in fact Chernyshevsky was ready throughout 1858 to consider various ways in which landlords would be compensated for land going to their erstwhile serfs, and in June wrote, "The peasants can in fact buy out the land exclusively with their own means." He also said, "Should the government wish to assume the whole purchase price, such magnanimity . . . would [eventually] be rewarded by an increase in state income. . . ."[24]

What was, then, the reason for this revolutionary's enthusiasm for the emperor? One must not discount the natural elation of every thinking Russian of the time that the majority of his fellow countrymen would be freed of their demeaning status, no matter what the details. But there was a specific personal reason for Chernyshevsky's prostrating himself before the man whom in three years he would excoriate as the chief landowner, deceiving and lying to his people. What is striking in the eulogy is his repeated reference to Peter the Great: Alexander's reforms "can in their grandeur and beneficence be compared only with the reform achieved by Peter the Great. . . . With the reign of Alexander II there begins a new era for Russia, just as one had begun with Peter's. . . . The glittering achievements of Peter the Great's era and the colossal personality of Peter himself overwhelm our imagination."[25] Why this enthusiasm on the part of a so-called populist and revolutionary democrat for a despot who, while he modernized Russia and made her a world power, did so by methods often surpassing those of his predecessors in barbarism? Of all classes of Russian society, the common folk benefited least, in fact actually suffered from Peter's reforms: he left serfdom more firmly entrenched than it had been before; introduced that military levy on the peasant which, as we have seen, was probably the greatest curse of village life; increased taxes on the Old Believers (religious dissenters); and Peter's whim to build a new capital in a hurry cost the lives of thousands of conscript laborers. Ivan the Terrible killed his son in a fit of rage, but Peter had his own tortured and executed for political reasons of no great urgency. He locked Russia into a bureaucratic-militaristic mold, based on foreign (mostly German) examples, which ever since had been execrated by radical and reformer, whether of the nationalist (Slavophile), liberal (Westernizing), or outright socialist persuasion. Why should such a man arouse Chernyshevsky's admiration and be a model for the new emperor?

Because, with all that, Peter was in a sense a revolutionary. He stripped

---

[23]"The peasants ought to pay nothing for the land they had farmed until then." Franco Venturi thus interprets Chernyshevsky's position in 1858. *Roots of Revolution,* New York 1960, 153.

[24]Chernyshevsky, V, 529, 543.

[25]*Ibid.,* V, 65, 69, 70.

Russia's ancient nobility of its prerogatives, subdued and humiliated the most aristocratic personages in his realm, and executed traitors (at one time lending his own hand to the task) i.e., those who held to the old ways. He made the Orthodox Church, already submissive, a department of the state, raised lowborn people to be his closest advisers, made a servant girl his empress.

Chernyshevsky was not alone among radicals in his admiration for this brutal, if greatly talented tyrant who had kicked Russia into the modern, if not quite the civilized world. Of Shelgunov in his old age an acquaintance recalled that he had enormously admired Peter as a dictator, but not in virtue of his imperial position. And one finds the same sentiments among quite a few other "men of the sixties." For all their blueprints for postrevolutionary Russia—a free federation of regions composed of self-governing peasant communes, etc.—none of them in their heart of hearts really believed that the "dark," illiterate peasant masses were capable of ruling themselves or, without the guidance of a revolutionary elite, even of articulating what they wanted. And unlike the "men of the seventies," these theorizers were not populists in the sense of having any concern with what the peasants wanted or how they lived, or with wanting to help cure their existential ills before the tocsin of the revolution rang. The attitudes in this first generation of revolutionaries ranged from a self-deception, undoubtedly sincere in the case of people like Herzen and Chernyshevsky, which persuaded them that they knew what the peasants ought to want, to a quite cynical view of peasant masses as combustible material for conflagration. Paradoxically, the "men of the sixties" were much closer in their political mentality, with its clear elitist undertones, to Lenin and his Bolsheviks, than were the revolutionaries of the 1870s and early 1880s.

Perhaps Alexander would have continued to earn the admiration of Chernyshevsky and his followers had he tried in Peter's manner to force Russia into modernity, had he cut off the heads of obdurate bureaucrats and aristocrats, tried to force the lethargic peasants to acquire the skills of, say, a Prussian farmer, in brief had he turned out to be a sort of nineteenth-century crowned Stalin. One may consider the enthusiasm with which the Communist Party youth, many of them former admirers of Trotsky, greeted the rapid industrialization and collectivization which occurred in the early 1930s and how they rendered homage to its architect, Stalin. But in 1859–60 it became patently obvious that here was no crowned revolutionary, but a conservative and conventional ruler, pulled to and fro by conflicting advisors, deeply desirous of reforming Russia and making her rejoin the civilized world but at the same time determined to keep his autocratic powers, feeling duty-bound to free the serfs but also to protect the interests of the landowning nobility, which he considered the bulwark of his throne. In brief, not a demiurge, a "colossal personality which would overwhelm our imagination," but the type a revolutionary hates most: a prudent and humane reformer.

Who and what, then, would save and regenerate Russia? Chernyshevsky's answer was clear: those people who, brought up under the hateful conditions of Nicholas' time, had already lost or would soon lose any illusions that change for the better might come from the emperor and his minions, whether well-meaning liberals or old-style bureaucrats. These people—students, young officers, intellectuals—had already discarded the old superstitions about religion, the family, and the sanctity of private property. Yet they were still confused as to what could be done to bring down the whole system, now more hateful than ever because filled with hypocrisy and false promises. A few knew what the new path must be, however. In *What Is To Be Done?* Chernyshevsky, because of modesty (and the censor), did not name the people who would lead the new men into the promised land of revolution, but otherwise he was quite explicit: "We did not see these men six years ago . . . but it matters little what we think of them now; in a few years we shall appeal to them; we shall say, 'Save us,' and whatever they say will be done by all."

To galvanize the new men into action one had first to convince or neutralize the influence of "the second government" in distant London, from which Herzen was still feeding the Russian youth pap about the emperor perhaps seeing the light. And so in the March 1, 1860, issue of *The Bell* an anonymous "Russian from the provinces," never identified but almost certainly Dobrolyubov or Chernyshevsky, threw a challenge down to the old generation of revolutionaries on behalf of the new men:

All that is alive and honest in Russia met with rapture the beginning of your struggle . . . and we have all awaited your unmasking of the main source of our historic misfortune, this unfortunate cringing before the emperor's image, your exposing of the abomination of this servile submissiveness. But instead . . . from the shores of the Thames you send eulogies to Alexander II and his wife.

Herzen bears a heavy responsibility because his every word resounds throughout Russia. But he does not know what is really going on in his country; liberal professors, landowners and bureaucrats fill him with fables about the government's progressive intentions. In fact things were better under Nicholas because then everyone who loved the Russian people was convinced that only force would change things; and Nicholas himself saw that his system was crumbling, and that is why he committed suicide [sic!]. But now things are worse. Poor Alexander, say the liberals, his good intentions are being sabotaged by his bureaucrats. But isn't he an autocrat, and can't he chase out these allegedly disobedient clerks?

A personal animosity to Herzen shines throughout this letter. Isn't it true that Herzen corresponds with the empress? A fine "Galilean," your emperor who persecutes the Old Believers! A fine Tsar Liberator, who schemes how to cheat the peasant out of his land! "Now change your tune, let your *Bell* sound not to a thanksgiving service, but ring the tocsin. *Call upon Russia to raise the axe*—remember that for hundreds of years the belief in the tsars' good intentions has ruined our land. It is not up to you to feed us such illusions."[26]

In his answer Herzen exhibited that fatal weakness of the Russian moderate when confronted with an attack from the left, a weakness which was to persist until October 25, 1917, and beyond. His tone is apologetic: "Have I been completely wrong? Who during the recent past has done something useful for Russia except the sovereign? Let us render unto Caesar that which is Caesar's." But he admits that Russia may have "to lift the axe," and, having admitted the possibility, he cannot help betraying his fascination with the idea of a revolutionary conspiracy: "Having called for the axe, one must have a disciplined movement, one must have an organization, one must have plans, one must be strong and ready for sacrifices, prepared to seize not only the axe's handle but its edge should the axe disintegrate. Are you ready for this?"[27]

The "new men" were confident that they were. But when they tried they would discover that instead of having seized the handle of the axe, they had grasped its sharp cutting edge.

[26]My italics.
[27]*The Bell* (March 1, 1860).

II

A REVOLUTIONARY
MYSTERY STORY

WHEN IN 1904 General Nicholas Obruchev died at the age of seventy-four, newspapers throughout Russia and Europe noted the passing of one of the empire's most distinguished public figures, a faithful servant of his sovereign and state. Obituaries of the general noted that he had been the recipient of the highest honors and imperial favors to which a Russian subject could aspire. First in his class in the Imperial War Academy in 1854, colonel at the age of twenty-eight, major general at thirty-six, he reached the rank of full general and became chief of the General Staff at what was, by the usual standard in European armies, the boyish age of fifty; then adjutant general to His Majesty and member of the State Council.[1] In view of his interest in the arts, Obruchev was elected a member of the Imperial Academy. As Chief of Staff between 1881 and 1897 he helped to draft the Franco-Russian military alliance and contingency plans for campaigns against Germany and Austro-Hungary. He was the recipient of the highest order within the gift of his emperor—the great ribbon of St. Andrew.[2] Everything in his record bespoke loyalty and fidelity to duty, to that army to which—as the address signed on his retirement by all the senior generals asserted—Nicholas Obruchev

[1]The closest thing pre-1906 Russia had to a legislature; its members were of course nominated by the emperor.
[2]If he was never made field marshal it was only because in imperial, unlike Soviet Russia, this rank was bestowed but rarely, usually on commanders-in-chief of victorious campaigns.

"devoted all his forces, intellect, and entire soul."[3]

Yet in 1904 there were quite a few people still alive who knew that the most remarkable thing in Nicholas Obruchev's career was that it had not come to an end some forty years before, by sentence of a court-martial to death before a firing squad for treason, conspiracy, and incitement to mutiny. For this defender of the autocracy, head of the army after Alexander II's assassination, between 1860 and 1863 had been a key figure in a series of conspiracies designed to overthrow the imperial government. He had plotted and co-authored a proclamation to the soldiers to subvert their loyalty to the tsar. He had worked closely with the Polish rebels who were preparing a national uprising to detach their country from the empire. Some of Obruchev's fellow military plotters were indeed apprehended and executed. Some of his civilian co-conspirators (such as his first cousin Vladimir), though compared with him they were but minor cogs in the revolutionary organization, spent long years at hard labor and exile in Siberia. But no trial or even an official investigation interrupted Nicholas Obruchev's brilliant career. Not that he avoided suspicion. There was a file on him in the Third Department which bore witness to his close association with Chernyshevsky, not only in 1858, when they were co-editors of the *Military Review,* but also in 1861–62, when the revolutionary writer was under regular surveillance by the secret police. Obruchev was one of the signatories of the obituary for Dobrolyubov in 1861. In 1863, when the division of which he was chief of staff was ordered into action to fight the Polish rebels, Obruchev pleaded illness and took a year's leave from the army; in fact the conflict between his duties as a soldier and as a revolutionary had brought about a temporary breakdown. And in 1868, as we shall see, a dispute in Russia's highest bureaucratic circles drove the head of the Third Department, Peter Shuvalov, to try to "get the goods" on Obruchev.

All in all it is a fantastic story, and though we shall try to unravel the evidence for the general–revolutionary's remarkable good luck, some mystery must remain clinging to his tale. Not only his: it is quite likely that official parties or court receptions in the 1890s in St. Petersburg included among the guests not only Obruchev but a deputy minister of finance, a privy councillor, and a member of the senate,[4] all of whom had been leading participants in the revolutionary plots of the 1860s. (How fortunate for these gentlemen, and for many many other respectable members of the bureaucracy, the bar, the armed forces, that imperial Russia did not have investigative congressional committees. There were, to be sure, quite a few candidates for the role of Joseph McCarthy, but the autocracy enjoyed some advantages: when the emperor decided that it was a "red herring" to

---

[3]To the Memory of N. N. Obruchev," in *Russian Antiquity,* Vol. 158 (April–June, 1914), 69.
[4]Russia's highest administrative and judicial body.

question a distinguished state servant's past, that was that.)

The tale of the 1860s is, then, in many respects a veritable mystery story, with many aspects of the classical whodunit. Who wrote the various revolutionary proclamations which agitated the government and society? Who was it that protected people like Nicholas Obruchev and kept them from the long reach of the Third Department? Indefatigable archival researches of Soviet historians have helped to clear up some of these mysteries, but far from all. And then there are questions of deeper historical and psychological importance. What persuaded Herzen and Chernyshevsky to pass beyond mere fascination with the idea of conspiracy and thrust themselves into the midst of revolutionary enterprises, in the success of which they, certainly Herzen, never really believed? Were the Great Russian and the Land and Freedom conspiracies seriously planned and purposeful attempts at revolution? Were they even real underground political parties, as some recent Soviet historians would have them? Or were they just madcap enterprises undertaken by a handful of conspirators, who saw thousands of followers and co-conspirators in young people ready only to talk excitedly about revolution and to read with quickened hearts those emotional appeals and prophecies of rebellion which now rained on Russia? Were the Russian peasants really ready to "lift the axe," to rise up in a nationwide revolt? Or were the peasant disorders and occasional uprisings that preceded and followed the Emancipation Edict of 1861 only sporadic and localized expressions of the peasants' bewilderment and disappointed hopes?

FOUR

THE BIRTH OF CONSPIRACY

In the beginning Russia displayed what might be described as a nationwide passion for secret societies and circles. Young people, when confronted by an overwhelming authority, whether the state's, the family's, or the school's, naturally seek a means of expressing their need for privacy and fellowship in some form of communal grouping designed to escape the solicitous eye of elders and superiors. This natural tendency, which under other conditions produces such innocuous organizations as American fraternities and sororities, had been so long thwarted in Nicholas' Russia that the freer air of Alexander's times produced a veritable explosion of student and young-officer circles and societies. Many of them, like the associations of students from a given province or city that arose at the few existing universities, or the groups designed to collect and circulate books not available in the university libraries, were quite open and licensed or at least tolerated by the authorities. But this being Russia, a tinge of conspiracy colored even the most innocent of them. A students' library would almost certainly circulate Herzen's *Bell* and *Polar Star,* an illegal activity, strictly speaking, but until 1862 not accompanied by any danger, just titillating enough to give young men a taste for conspiracy and a sense of superiority vis-à-vis the indulgent authorities. An organization might be devoted to collecting funds to enable an impecunious student to pursue his studies at Moscow or Petersburg University, and this laudable task would lead to discussions about social inequities and various ways of remedying or abolishing them. A professor of mathematics in the higher artillery school wrote poetry and philosophical essays on the side; in contemporary Russia this was not as unusual as it would have been, say, in England, so nobody thought it particularly odd or dangerous when Peter Lavrov invited a number of his pupils to his home, where they would discuss the social and political issues of the day.

The regime's good-natured toleration of such developments induced, as might have been expected, a certain contempt toward the authorities on the part of the more daring and rebellious young men. Already in 1856 among the students of Kharkov University a circle had developed which specialized in composing and circulating parodies of solemn imperial manifestos, such as those written on the conclusion of a peace, or on the birth of a new grand duke, and in rephrasing Herzen's editorials in *The Bell* in a more radical form. It is difficult to follow the Soviet historian in describing such pranks as those of a "secret revolutionary organization."[1] But one can see in the activity of the Kharkov group and similar circles which soon arose in cities like Perm and Kazan the first seeds of an idea essential to the actual revolutionary enterprises of the early 1860s: the idea that the government is so inept and/or weak that one can mount a conspiracy under its very own nose without its realizing it until too late. To be sure, the playful activities of Kharkov and Kiev students were interrupted by a "bust" of their circle in 1860, but the penalty meted out was mild: they were forced to settle down in other cities of European Russia, where some of them embarked on more serious revolutionary propaganda. The most curious punishment was administered to the man whom the authorities believed (with some reason) to be the chief instigator of "untrustworthy attitudes" among the Kiev students, Professor Plato Pavlov: he was forced to exchange his professorship in a provincial university for one in St. Petersburg!

Pavlov was a pioneer of special Sunday schools for adults. On the surface this was a most constructive idea, in the execution of which the government hastened to render every possible assistance. Workers and other lower-class people in the cities were badly in need of education, beginning with the three basic R's. Here were students and young intellectuals offering their services, often freely, for the good of the people and undoubted benefit of society; state agencies, especially the war ministry, made their facilities available for classrooms; highly placed personages gave financial help when the local authorities' resources proved inadequate. The minister of the interior expressed high approval of this patriotic enterprise, uneasy only over the idea of young men teaching women, and hoped that the spiritual needs of the students would not be neglected; perhaps some divinity students might lend help?[2] By the end of 1860 Petersburg had fourteen male and five female

---

[1] J. I. Linkov, *The Revolutionary Struggle of A. I. Herzen and N. P. Ogarev and the Secret Society "Land and Freedom" of the Sixties,* Moscow 1964, 79.

[2] The poor man neglected to observe that church seminaries had produced and were still producing people like Chernyshevsky and Dobrolyubov.

Sunday schools for adults. The idea spread like wildfire. In all of European Russia there were 274 such establishments, among them thirty-one for females. Even the chief of the Third Department gave his approval to the idea of educating the lower classes, though he had the tragic foresight to warn that the whole enterprise should be watched, so that "correct, soberly thought-out guidance should avert any possibility of its turning into harmful channels."[3]

To be sure, two years later when a government commission investigated the eleemosynary project, some of its members must have been shocked to learn what was being taught in some of those schools and who some of the volunteer teachers were. (We shall meet the latter in connection with various conspiracies, including Karakozov's.) The horrified investigators heard of teachers using revolutionary proclamations as texts; an ingenious instructor who made a dictionary handbook for the use of his class, some of the definitions being "political rights—civic rights, e.g., equality," "republic—the form of government where the people rule" (not that its author could be suspected of sympathies for liberals, whom he defined as "gentlemen, landlords who gape around without doing anything, go to the theatre and balls"). Another volunteer teacher, by profession an officer in the Engineer Corps, was more explicit: the manuscript he used as the text for his lectures contained such information as that Christ was an impostor who had deceived millions; that the emperor, if he wanted to represent the nation, must chase out "courtiers, aristocrats, and officials, and choose men with new ideas."[4] (Nor were such pedagogical methods employed by the "new men" only in adult education. Nicholas Ishutin, whom we have already mentioned in connection with Karakozov, taught for a while in an elementary school. He would write on the blackboard 1 and then 70 million, and ask the children how could it be that one man, the emperor, could be greater than 70 million of his subjects? And in the same spirit of making learning relevant, he would explain during a lesson on biology that an eagle, the imperial emblem, was the most rapacious and bloodthirsty of all birds.[5])

What was happening, then, was that social activism, to use a current term, was running in channels hostile to the establishment. Young students and officers were reading Herzen and Chernyshevsky and were growing contemptuous of the government, hostile to Russia's social system, and skeptical of the Emperor's ability to reform it. The "silent majority"—not only the vast mass of peasants and the urban lower class, but even the

[3] *See* Michael Lemke, *Studies in the Liberation Movement of the Sixties,* St. Petersburg 1908, 417, 403.

[4] *Ibid.,* 420, 425. It is interesting to note, and we shall see it again, how even the most radical revolutionaries hesitated to attack the emperor directly when addressing common people.

[5] R. V. Filippov, *The Revolutionary Organization of N. A. Ishutin and I. A. Khudyakov,* Petrozavodsk 1964, 162.

educated—still remained loyal, in the sense that they could not imagine Russia without a tsar and hoped that changes, when they came, would be peaceful. The prestige of the emperor and the power of the state seemed to render any outright challenge to established authority unrealistic. Even if you could galvanize them into action rather than talk, what could those few hundred students and few dozen officers do against the vast power of the Autocrat? For the revolutionary like Ogarev or Dobrolyubov, who by temperament and conviction believed that only a violent upheaval could save Russia from the autocracy or something even worse, the phony constitutionalism of the West, the problem was first of all to turn minority dissent into revolutionary passion and militancy, and then to make the inert masses "lift up the axe." Ogarev in 1857 composed a paper to convince his skeptical friend Herzen that a revolutionary conspiracy in Russia "is desirable, possible, and necessary."[6] Had not the Christians, in the beginning a secret society hated and persecuted by the multitude, eventually conquered the people's mind and thus overthrown the oppressive Roman Empire? This was not a very apt historical analogy, of course: it was a Roman emperor who made Christianity the official cult, and where were the barbarians who delivered the coup de grace? For the moment Herzen remained unconvinced.

Dobrolyubov put his hopes on progressive officers. Quite a few of them, as we have seen, had been connected with the circle around *The Contemporary*. Had his health allowed it he would undoubtedly have promoted the idea of a military conspiracy more vigorously and pushed Chernyshevsky in the same direction. But the gruelling dilemma remained: how were the "new men" to "get a handle" on the masses, make them, as in Chernyshevsky's fantasy, proclaim, "Save us, and whatever you say will be done by all."

In 1861 the revolutionaries thought they had the answer: the imperial government, they believed, faced an almost inevitable catastrophe. Dissatisfaction with the actual form of the serfs' emancipation would bring revolt throughout the country. At the same time everything pointed to another national uprising in the Polish sector of Alexander II's realm, and this in turn was almost certain to bring about an intervention of the Western Powers on behalf of the Poles, and another humiliation of the empire, as in the Crimean War. So there was an imperative need for something more concrete in the way of revolutionary organization than officers' and students' circles, and subversive propaganda in the Sunday schools. One had to organize a clandestine party, both to guide the activity of the aroused masses and to snatch power from the defeated autocracy.

The Emancipation Edict was signed by Alexander II on February 19, 1861, on the anniversary of his accession to the throne. It is a date surpassed in

[6]Linkov, 55.

importance to Russian history only by October 25, 1917. But public announcement of the new law was delayed until March 5. The reason for the delay was simple: the latter day coincided with an Orthodox Church fast, when the faithful in addition to other deprivations were supposed to be abstinent. To announce the emancipation on the day when the law was actually signed would have provoked, prudent ministers believed, the most gigantic mass binge in Russian history.

The government was not quite sure whether this alcoholic explosion would have resulted from joy or from the disappointed hopes of millions of its peasant subjects. But as the momentous date approached it slowly dawned upon the emperor and his advisers that whatever the reaction of the peasants to the provisions of the law, the mere fact that a centuries-old institution was being uprooted, and through legislation so complex that not even the few literates among the serfs could fully understand its meaning, was bound to create trouble.

By the end of the 1850s the serf population of the empire was approximately 43 million "souls" of both sexes, of whom 22 million were the property of individual landowners, some 19 million of the state, and about 2 million of the private estates of the imperial family.[7] The latter two categories were liberated shortly before or after the edict of February 19, and, compared with the problems inherent in emancipating the landlords' serfs, changing their status was relatively simple. The crux lay in the 22 million souls owned by some 30,000 noble families. The juridical-economic-psychological meaning of serfdom and the law for its abrogation are both so complex that the modern reader will be baffled by even the most erudite and competent account of either. But one can at least begin to understand the difficulty of formulating and administering the law, and the initial befuddlement of the average peasant about what exactly was being done to him.

Serfs as persons until 1861 were the personal property of their masters. The masters could order them whipped, confined to correction houses for up to three months, in extreme cases have them exiled to Siberia.[8] In fact, though not in law, he could order them to marry against their will, and decide which peasant lads would go into the army, etc. The serf on his part had no right to sue his master, enter into marriage or any contractual obligation without his sanction, engage in a craft without his permission. He could be transferred from being a land cultivator to a domestic servant of his lord.

Yet in general it could not be said of the average serf that his status was

[7] Lazar Volin, *A Century of Russian Agriculture from Alexander II to Khrushchev,* Cambridge, Mass., 1970, 21.

[8] P. Z. Zayonchkovsky, *The Abolition of Serfdom in Russia,* Moscow 1954, 11.

simply that of a slave. The landlord had an obligation to keep his serfs from destitution. An unusually sadistic master would be warned by the authorities, and there were cases of a notoriously vicious landlord being punished by imprisonment or exile. The average landowner was neither an ogre who worked his serfs to death and kept harems of village girls, nor the other stereotype, the humane master who educated talented peasant boys at his own expense and then emancipated them or, like Ogarev, freed them with very favorable financial provisions. Prudence dictated that a landlord or his steward, living with his family among peasants and with constables or troops miles away, should observe a modicum of humanity and take the counsel of village-commune elders on such matters as marriage, and whom to send away for a twenty-five-year stint in the army.

In any case the degrading institution of personal serfdom was definitely and forever abolished by the Edict, even though in the case of household serfs, their masters retained some disciplinary rights for the transitional period of two years. For the first time in at least three hundred years the Russian peasant was to have personal freedom and, insofar as possible in a class and autocratic society, be called a citizen. This in itself was a reason for rejoicing for every right-thinking Russian.

But thereafter began the difficulty. The economic side of serfdom was a fantastically complicated mosaic of laws and customs. The great majority of serfs were what might be called unfree tenants. For the land which provided them with livelihood they paid their landlords either in money or, especially in the fertile regions of the south, by working some days of the week on the land directly owned by their master, sometimes by a combination of the two. Some serfs worked in cities and towns as craftsmen, industrial workers, or even entrepreneurs, paying a part of their earnings to the landlord from whose village they had come. In Russia proper and in the easternmost Ukraine, peasant land was pooled—one can almost say "owned" collectively—by the commune, which would periodically redistribute it among the peasant families according to size and needs; elsewhere, especially in the western provinces settled by the Ukrainians, Byelorussians, and Lithuanians and in the Kingdom of Poland, individual peasant holdings were the rule.

Not without much prior argument pro and con, the Edict contained two basic decisions on the economic aspect of the emancipation question: the peasants should in principle receive as their property the land they had held as unfree tenants; and the communal system of ownership should be retained wherever it had held before.

To free the peasants without giving them land would have led, the government feared (and correctly so), to chaos if not indeed to a widespread peasant revolution. The serfs firmly believed that the land they cultivated was in a true sense *theirs:* "we are yours but the land is ours" was the stereotypical peasant definition of his relationship to his master. The decision to retain the peasant commune was not so much due to the fact that it was beloved by some conservatives as an ancient Slavic institution (which it was not), or because in the opinion of radicals such as Herzen it expressed the essential egalitarian and socialist mentality of the peasant (which it did not), but simply because it was the most convenient way of assuring that the peasants would meet their financial, military, and other obligations. To tamper with the *obschchina*-commune at a time like this was to increase the chances, already considerable, of complete chaos in the Russian countryside.

But while the government refused to compensate the landlords for the loss of their "baptised property," as serfs had been called in a famous article by Herzen, it felt it could not, without ruining them, refuse to pay the nobility for the arable land which would now become the peasants'. Arrangements for the new economic relationships in the countryside were to be worked out *within two years* by agreements between the peasants (i.e., in most cases their communes) and the landlords, helped by special arbitrators elected from the local gentry, who together were to work out schemes suitable to each locality—how much land to be retained by the landlords, how much to go to the peasants' allotments, etc. Now the landlord did not *have* to sell the latter, but the peasant *had* to buy it if the landlord insisted. If no sale was effected, the ex-serf had to discharge his obligations for the land, of which he was now in effect a perpetual leasor, either by payment or by work on his master's land, in accordance with the amount of payment or quota of work days fixed by the third party—the arbitrator. In fact it was justifiably expected that most landlords would decide upon an outright sale: many of them were in debt, and now that their authority over the peasants' *persons* had lapsed, they knew it was unrealistic to expect their former serfs to break their backs tilling the ex-masters' lands or meeting their rent payments.[9] To finance the peasants' purchase of "their" lands, the state was to pay the landlords in interest-bearing bonds. "Peasants who had purchased the allotments with government aid were placed under the obligation to pay the Treasury annually six per cent of the total sum advanced by the government for a period of forty-nine years."[10]

The great difficulty—especially from the point of view of many peasants and radicals—was that many peasants' allotments were smaller than the ones they had enjoyed as serfs. This was especially true in the south, where the landlords found farming quite profitable and the government appeased

---

[9]The arrangement, let us note, was much more favorable to the peasant than the situation, say, in contemporary Ireland, where the landlord could screw up the rent or terminate the lease at his own terms.

[10]Alexander Gerschenkron in *The Cambridge Economic History of Europe,* VI, Cambridge, Eng., 1965, 737.

them by increasing their shares, at the expense of the lands previously cultivated by their serfs. These "cutoffs" became and would remain an issue in Russian politics for the next fifty years.

All in all it was a stupendous piece of legislation and administration, such as, it is fair to say, no other European government could have effected at the time, even from the purely technical point of view. Most of its authors sincerely believed that they had arrived at a just and practical compromise between the rights of property (which from the point of view of the conservative landlord the government was brutally violating, by compelling him to part with what was his own) and the needs and aspirations of most of the peasants, as well as the spirit of the age. To the modern Soviet historian the Emancipation Edict is a fraud: the government in collusion with the nobility stole part of the lands of the peasants and saddled them with financial burdens which meant that legal serfdom was merely replaced by economic bondage. The verdict of an American economist, while more temperate, is still severe: "The peasantry released from serfdom received insufficient allotment of land for which it had to pay a disproportionately high purchase price."[11]

But our judgments must be set within the context of the times. We have seen that even Chernyshevsky in 1858 had written that the landlords should be compensated for the land the ex-serfs would receive, and thought it fair that the latter should at least share in the burden. Of course it is true that there was an element of class legislation about the whole business; Russia was a class society. But being also an autocracy, the government displayed more solicitude about the peasant than did, say, the British Parliament about the English agricultural worker until about the middle of the century, and about the Irish peasant until the end of the century or, for that matter, than did the American Congress about the economic status of the Negroes following their emancipation.

The immediate consequences of the Edict were viewed by the government with trepidation. This was not so much on account of any specific provisions as because it realized that the mere expression "emancipation" or "freedom" would act like a spark on the powder box of the peasants' long-pent-up frustrations, that the illiterate masses might take it to mean that immediate stoppage of work and payment of dues were authorized. Throughout March the Edict was read from church pulpits, special emissaries and officers were dispatched to distant parts of the Empire, troops were put on the alert. (The emperor had the unfortunate idea to turn over the text of the Edict drafted by Nicholas Milyutin to the Moscow Metropolitan Philaret for editorial reworking. This worthy ecclesiastic, staunch enemy of the emancipation on the grounds that it would lead to widespread license and

[11]Gerschenkron, 741.

anarchy, couched the original businesslike exposition of the proclamation in archaic language which made it all the more difficult for the masses to understand, strengthening their suspicion that the tsar had intended to give the peasants more than the law now actually stipulated. Thus the text included: "And now we hopefully expect that the serfs, having in mind the better future before them, will understand and with gratitude accept this important sacrifice made by the nobility for the improvement of their well-being." This did not square at all with the peasants' notion of the tsar's omnipotence, and probably had the opposite effect to the one intended.)

It is then not surprising that the great edict was often greeted by its beneficiaries with considerable puzzlement, and that in places rumors began to circulate that the tsar had intended to give the serfs freedom and land right away, but that the nobles tried to deceive him and the people; that this was just the "first freedom" and that soon the tsar would issue another edict granting immediate benefits and absolving the peasants from any payment for the land. It was natural that peasant riots would erupt in a number of places. Overnight the authority of the landlords, those "thousands of police chiefs," collapsed or at least was made questionable. The peasants became not so much mutinous as simply rudderless, ready to give credence to the wildest rumors.

The most serious incident took place in Kazan province, in a village appropriately named Bezdna, which in Russian means "bottomless," "abyss." There a local man, Anton Petrov, hitherto considered a cross between the village idiot and the traditional "holy fool," began to tell the peasants that the Edict was phony, and that he was in possession of the real emancipation manifesto, "written in golden letters," entitling peasants to take over their lands immediately. Petrov, an Old Believer, was literate[12] and his preachings attracted crowds of peasants. His message grew more inflammatory: "If the landowner steps off his own land, try to make him go away by words; if he does not obey, bang him on the head. The tsar will reward you."[13] General Apraxin hastened from Kazan with just 200 infantrymen. What then happened is fairly accurately described by an anonymous report from Russia in *The Bell.*[14] At the news that soldiers were approaching, peasants sent their womenfolk away and gathered to protect their prophet. Apraxin demanded that they surrender Petrov. "The people did not obey. They said that they did not know, maybe he was an impostor; that they stood for truth and for their Father-Tsar, who was being deceived

---

[12]The Old Believers, who split from the Orthodox Church in the seventeenth century, contained a higher proportion of literates than did the bulk of the peasants, since they sought the literal meaning of the Scriptures.

[13]Quoted in Zayonchkovsky, 160.

[14]Of June 1, 1861. The events described took place in April.

by landlords and officials. Petrov told the people that nothing would happen to them . . . that they would be free, that he would be invited to Petersburg and would bring back from the Tsar real freedom for them." Apraxin, instead of waiting for reinforcements to awe the crowd, panicked and ordered his soldiers to shoot. Forty-one peasants were killed, seventy wounded. Captured, Petrov was tried by court-martial and, though clearly insane, shot.

The events in Bezdna provided a powerful stimulus for those who thought revolution. To be sure, the peasants there did not "lift up the axe." Theirs was but passive resistance in protecting a man they believed spoke for the emperor. But would the peasants' feelings not turn to *active* rage, and their misguided loyalty to the tsar to a sense of betrayal, when they realized that it was he who had put the additional burdens on them and taken away some of the land they believed was theirs? If not immediately then surely within two years, when the new land and peasant obligations were supposed to be worked out. In April and May 1861 some of our heroes turned from talking about revolution to discussing details of actual conspiracies, and the target date in most of those discussions was the spring of 1863. Always quick on the trigger, Ogarev concluded a fiery editorial in *The Bell* of June 15, 1861, thus: "Old serfdom has been replaced by a new one, in fact, serfdom has not been abolished: *the people have been deceived by the tsar.*"

Conspirators more realistic than he had to face the depressing fact that for all the incidents like the one at Bezdna, most peasants met the Edict with approval. What was worse, from their point of view, the majority of the educated classes greeted it with enthusiasm. The incorrigible Herzen reverted momentarily to shameless eulogies not only of Alexander II but also of the Grand Duke Constantine, whom he credited with a large share in the defeat of the reactionary nobles' last-ditch objections. "Alexander II has done much, very much; his name already stands higher than that of any of his predecessors."[15] And Constantine Nikolayevich "was a strong supporter of his brother in the task of Emancipation and when Alexander embraced him . . . he did it for all of Russia." Longin Panteleyev, at the time a very radical-minded student in Petersburg and soon to get into all sorts of trouble and conspiracies, summarized the response of his contemporaries to the Edict: their main interest in the reform was that it should free the serfs, even without land, he said; "the general opinion was that this would still have been a blessing, though incomplete."[16] To be sure, the educated classes expected new boons from the emperor. As Herzen reminded his readers, he had written in the beginning of the reign that Russia expected from Alexander the abolition of corporal punishment, public judicial proceedings, and

[15] *The Bell* (April 1, 1861).
[16] L. F. Panteleyev, *Memoirs,* Moscow 1958, 160.

a free press, in addition to the emancipation of peasants with land. Nothing about a constitution! And that from a confirmed socialist and, in principle, a republican.

This general attitude was a bitter pill for people such as Ogarev, Dobrolyubov (then in the last stages of his illness), and those young officers like Nicholas Obruchev who were influenced by Chernyshevsky; they craved political action and viewed with dread, even if unconscious, the vista of peaceful reforms that would leave the main source of evil in Russian society—the autocracy—unaffected. The countryside was not nearly so disturbed as even the government had expected. Petersburg workers and artisans, some twenty thousand strong, marched on the Winter Palace, but only to deliver an address of thanks to the emperor (many of them were serfs). The educated class in the wake of February 19 seemed to lose its half distrustful–half contemptuous attitude. Some, to be sure, hoped that the eventual fruit of the reforms would be Russia's peaceful transformation into a constitutional monarchy à la England. But to a true revolutionary this prospect was even more depressing than the continuation of the autocracy.

As against this generally unpromising picture there were some portents of revolutionary hope. The emperor, though he embarked resolutely on the road to reform, was as determined as were his worst enemies that it should not lead to a constitution. He appeared determined to heed the advice given by his dying father, "Hold onto everything." Following the Edict, he hoped to stifle constitutional hopes by dismissing some of his more progressive officials and replacing them with conservative bureaucrats.

Bezdna and some similar though smaller-scale incidents pierced the educated classes' smugness over the ending of serfdom. Students at Kazan arranged a memorial mass for the Bezdna dead, and Athanasius Shchapov, a professor at the university, delivered a fiery sermon hailing Petrov and his fellow victims as martyrs. Shchapov and the priests who celebrated the mass were arrested. They were then ordered by the Holy Synod (Shchapov being in holy orders) to be confined in the Solovetsk monastery, on the island of the same name in the White Sea (where one of the first Soviet forced-labor camps would one day be situated). But by this time the government was fighting nationwide student unrest, and it was thought politic to pardon the popular professor and assign him to a clerkship in the ministry of the interior.

Perhaps the most hopeful thing from the would-be conspirator's point of view was that the Polish pot began to boil again. As with Britain vis-à-vis Ireland, so Russia's troubles had always been Poland's opportunity. On his accession Alexander II had decided to modify his father's ruthless attitude toward that nation.[17] He had wanted to give the Poles a larger share in the

---

[17]In 1835 Nicholas, contemplating the possibility of assassination on a forthcoming trip to his Polish domain, wrote the following instruction to his then teen-age son: "Never give freedom

running of their own country, but as he had said to the Polish nobles who greeted him in Warsaw in 1856, "no vain dreams, gentlemen"—those vain dreams being the restoration of the legislative autonomy which the Kingdom of Poland had enjoyed before the insurrection of 1830, not to mention its national independence. But the indecisive policies of the first years of his reign brought those "vain dreams" to the pitch of delirium. On his next visit to the Polish capital, in 1860, Alexander met with a virtual social boycott by all classes of Polish society. (He had the bad taste to schedule a meeting there with the Prince Regent of Prussia and the Emperor of Austria, the other "proprietors" of the partitioned nation. This was, Herzen observed, like talking about the gallows in the family home of a man who has been hanged.) On February 15, 1861, one of the nationalist demonstrations which were becoming endemic in Warsaw was terminated by Russian soldiers shooting into the crowd; five men were killed. Turbulence in Poland was in turn the Russian revolutionary's opportunity.

In the spring of 1860 two officers of the Russian general staff were sent on long missions abroad. One was Colonel Nicholas Obruchev, head of what was known as the statistical department (whose functions included what we would call intelligence), and another was Captain Sigismund Sierakowski. They were to study foreign military establishments—this was a kind of gentlemanly spying which was an accepted practice in the European armies of the period and as such tolerated, up to a point, by the host countries. But unknown to their superiors both officers had other purposes in the West. Obruchev was the central figure in a clandestine circle of officers connected with *The Contemporary* or at least with Chernyshevsky and Dobrolyubov. Sierakowski, a Pole, played a similar role in a similar group of about thirty Polish-born officers in Petersburg.[18] (The Russian army contained quite a high proportion of Polish officers. That Nicholas I, who had sent thousands of Poles to Siberia, should tolerate Poles in high military and civil employments shows the distance which separates even the most brutal nineteenth-century despot from a Hitler.) In addition to their official duties they were going to contact Russian and Polish revolutionary groups abroad. It is difficult to determine whether their missions were synchronized, but Sierakowski had been Obruchev's student in the General Staff Academy, and in addition he was a close acquaintance of Chernyshevsky.[19] The latter now became a central point of attraction. around which whirled various revolutionary circles and enterprises, but, so far as

to the Poles, try to continue the difficult task of russification of that country." Quoted in *The Red Archive*, III, Moscow 1923, 293.

[18]This group was made up mostly of graduates of the academies of the general staff, artillery, and engineering. Joseph Kowalski, *Russian Revolutionary Democracy and the January* [1863] *Uprising*, Warsaw 1949, 90.

[19]V. A. Dyakov and I. S. Miller, *The Revolutionary Movement in the Russian Army and the* [*Polish*] *Uprising of 1863*, Moscow 1964, 123.

we know, he himself was still too cautious to engage in active conspiratorial work in 1860.

On his "official" trips Sierakowski not only met Polish political emigrés in Paris, where ever since the suppression of the insurrection of 1830–31 there existed a sort of unofficial Polish government in exile, but of course hastened to Herzen in London.[20] Always a strong Polonophile, Herzen was also, as we have seen, one of the senior statesmen in that informal International of revolutionaries which had existed in Europe since the hectic days of the 1840s, its members always ready to render assistance by personal participation or, as in Herzen's case, with their pen, in any new outbreak whether in France, Italy, or Poland. The mere word "revolution," for whatever cause, whether the liberation of Poland or Hungary, the national unification of Italy, etc., had not lost the magic it had exerted on progressive European minds since 1789. The vocation of revolutionary struggled for mastery of Herzen against his temperament, basically opposed to plots and violence, and his practical sense.[21] And so he could not help encouraging Polish revolutionary emissaries like Sierakowski, despite his firm conviction that at the time a Polish national uprising against Russia would end in a defeat more catastrophic than 1831.

In May 1861 a more important visitor appeared in London and spent at least two months in the Herzen–Ogarev circle. Tuchkova-Ogareva in her memoirs (their first edition appeared in tsarist times) identifies him merely as a colonel with a fierce moustache, but we know it was Nicholas Obruchev.[22] He evidently developed a close personal relationship with Ogarev. Together (their relative contributions in the authorship have never been determined) they wrote two revolutionary proclamations, "What the People Need," and "What the Army Should Do," which, when published in *The Bell* on July 1 and November 8, respectively, drastically changed the orientation of the journal and sounded the tocsin for a Russian revolution.[23]

What made Herzen open his journal to violent revolutionary propaganda? There is an oft-told story of how on April 10, 1861, he arranged a banquet to celebrate the Emancipation and to eulogize once more the Tsar Liberator. But by the time the guests sat down the news reached them of new shootings in Warsaw. On March 27[24] another crowd had got out of hand; again soldiers had fired. This time casualties were more numerous—

[20]V. M. Misko, *The Polish Insurrection of 1863*, Moscow 1962, 45.

[21]The latter led him occasionally to take rather questionable steps for a man of his convictions. On the outbreak of the American Civil War he sold his US bonds at a loss, being convinced that the slave-owning states would prevail.

[22]N. A. Tuchkova-Ogareva, *Memoirs*, Moscow 1895, 336.

[23]Obruchev's collaboration in the second article must have been at least partly by mail, since it refers to events of September and by that time he was out of England.

[24]Which in the West would have been April 9.

the official list said ten but some spoke of as many as one hundred. In an emotional outburst Herzen addressed the tsar in *The Bell:* "You, Alexander Nikolayevich, why did you rob us of our joyful occasion? Do we have so many occasions for it? Have we since we were born celebrated much else besides funerals?" Instead of the toast to the emperor Herzen drank "for the full unconditional independence of Poland."

Sincere though he undoubtedly was, one suspects that Herzen's breach with Alexander had other and perhaps more important reasons. He must have been under almost unbearable pressure from Ogarev and some correspondents from Russia to stop his eulogies of the monarch and to surge once more to the forefront of the liberation movement. He had not reacted so violently to the Warsaw shootings a month earlier. And the emperor was no more directly responsible for the March massacre in Warsaw than for the April one in Bezdna. But it gave Herzen an opportunity to get out from what his emotions rather than his reason told him was a false position.

And so in the spring of 1861 the acquiescence in, if not indeed euphoria over, the Emancipation began to give way to revolutionary excitement, but as yet only among the radicals. Suddenly in several circles and independently of each other the idea arose of issuing and circulating revolutionary proclamations. Some were issued on behalf of real or alleged conspiracies or parties; some—like of course the anonymous editorials by Ogarev and Obruchev in *The Bell*—professed to speak to and on behalf of Russian society as a whole; some were addressed to the young, others to soldiers, ex-serfs, etc. But let us note certain characteristics that the proclamation literature had in common. Secretly conceived and published—to the point where the authorship and the printing place of many remain matters of dispute today—they all were aimed at the widest possible publicity and were intended to become known to the enemy, i.e., the government. Their youthful, almost adolescent bravado in effect said to the tsar and his advisers: You have been issuing all sorts of pompous and lying manifestos and edicts; we, a clandestine minority, challenge you to a duel which the Russian people will decide. They all raised social and economic as well as political issues, and the general orientation was to a populistic kind of socialism. The emotional flavor of the proclamations was strongly antimonarchical, yet few of them reached the point of demanding abolition of the monarchy. Even the most unrealistic and fanatical revolutionary knew how deeply the peasants believed in the tsar. Another striking element in all of them was that they were couched in violent and provocative language; consciously or unconsciously the authors phrased their argument as if to convince the government that the path of reform was fruitless since it only stimulated ever more radical demands, thus practically forcing it into more repression, outraging public opinion, and dissipating public illusions about the emperor's liberal intentions.

The story and content of one proclamation whose authorship is well established throw vivid light on the mentality of the early revolutionaries. At the end of 1860 young Vsevolod Kostomarov (b. 1837) approached some people in Chernyshevsky's circle, most particularly the poet Mikhailov, whom we have already met, for help in the literary career he intended. Kostomarov's credentials seemed more impressive as a radical than as a poet. He resigned from the army as sublieutenant and showed Mikhailov some of his revolutionary poems which he had printed on his own hand press. In the spring of 1861 Kostomarov was given, evidently by Mikhailov and without the identification of its authors, some revolutionary writings, which he promised to print. They included a revolutionary appeal to the peasants, written most likely by Chernyshevsky himself, and one to the soldiers, undoubtedly the work of Mikhailov's great friend Shelgunov.[25] But for some reason, probably because his wife wanted to go abroad, Nicholas Shelgunov decided that he would have his main revolutionary composition, *To The Young Generation,* printed in a more professional manner on Herzen's press in London. It was composed with Mikhailov's help in the middle of April, and in the summer the Shelgunov–Mikhailov triangle set out for Europe. Mikhailov left his beloved Liudmila with her husband in Paris[26] and rushed with the text of the proclamation to London. Herzen tried very hard to dissuade him from having it printed and distributed, finding it foolishly inflammatory. But could he and the Russian Free Press refuse to print a revolutionary appeal? In the middle of July Mikhailov was back in Russia with six hundred copies of the manifesto, distributing them through the mails as well as to friends, among them Kostomarov.

Reading *To the Young Generation* one is surprised, even if one accepts the premises of Russian radicalism, that Herzen did agree to have it printed on his press. Quite apart from anything else, it is difficult to see how Shelgunov, then thirty-seven and a man not without some journalistic ability, could have written a composition so puerile in spots and so inept as propaganda.[27] Thus the Emancipation Edict was criticized on two principal grounds: "In the first place the sovereign deceived the people and did not give them real freedom, the kind of which the people dream and which they need;" and secondly, of equal importance, "he stole from the people an occasion for joyful celebration by announcing the law not on February 19 but during the great fast"! Similar inconsistencies crowd other pages. The author is quite positive "that we do not need a tsar . . . God's anointed, an

---

[25] *Memoirs of N. V. Shelgunov and His Circle,* Moscow 1967, I, 12.

[26] Possibly because on a previous visit the trio had made to Herzen in 1859 Tuchkova-Ogareva had given a very cold reception to Mme. Shelgunova, whom she found materialistic and unsympathetic.

[27] The text of the proclamation is in Michael Lemke, *Political Trials in Russia of the Sixties,* Moscow 1923, 62–80.

ermine mantle covering hereditary incompetence. We want as the head [of state] a simple mortal, a man of the people, who will be elected by them"; but then, after this slashing attack on hereditary monarchy the author goes on lamely to say, "we demand that the expenses of the imperial family be cut down." And there is a strange hankering after violence: "If to accomplish our aspirations, to divide land among the people, it is necessary to cut the throats of one hundred thousand landowners, we should not flinch at that."

On the ideological side the proclamation is a hodgepodge of various Western socialist doctrines as well as more specifically Russian versions as expounded by Herzen and Chernyshevsky. Thus Shelgunov paraphrases Saint-Simon's famous statement of elitist socialism: what would happen if the emperor, his ministers, the court, the whole nobility would suddenly disappear? he asks. The country would be better off without all those parasites. But how calamitous would be the disappearance of the aristocracy of mind, among which Shelgunov (ignoring Marxism) includes not only scientists, writers, and artists but also manufacturers. But then, a bow to Herzen, the proclamation urges communal ownership of land and a ban on individual ownership.

The broadside takes a cue from both Herzen and Chernyshevsky in rejecting the vaunted foreign models of liberalism and parliamentarism, but its dismissal of the "rotten West" sounds almost comical taking into account Shelgunov's gloomy assessment of Russia, past and present: "We are a backward nation and therein lies our salvation. We ought to bless destiny that we haven't lived the life of Europe. . . . We have plenty of opportunity to avoid the disastrous situation in which Europe finds itself today." And then, forgetful of this eulogy of the completely independent character of Russian life, Shelgunov asserts that his countrymen have for long aped the French and the Germans and now some of them would like to imitate Britain and her institutions.

Who is to put into effect the rather confused political philosophy advocated by the proclamation? The "new men," of course. "We turn principally to you because only in you do we see people ready to sacrifice their individual interests for the benefit of the whole country." They are to agitate among the people and soldiers, they are the real leaders of the nation. Let them reject the harmful teachings of foreign economists and political theorists and strive first of all for freedom. "By rejecting material calculations and striving for freedom, for a restoration of our rights, we shall conquer felicity, and with it, of course, prosperity. That is what we want so badly —money."[28] Hard to believe, but this is a literal translation. Probably it was Shelgunov's attempt to paraphrase Chernyshevsky's theory of "wise selfish-

[28] *Ibid.*, 66.

ness," derived from the English Utilitarians, which held that man is indeed led by self-interest, but that the highest expression of this self-interest is, for a wise man, service to society.

It is easy to see why the Third Department let itself be convinced that the main author of this extraordinary piece was the poet Mikhailov or perhaps even Mme. Shelgunova, rather than her husband, a government official and publicist of experience and sound reputation. Mikhailov was not the first victim of the political fever of the 1860s, but his was the first arrest which shook the political and literary group in Petersburg which centered around *The Contemporary.* He was denounced to the Third Department by Vsevolod Kostomarov, who thus began his brief but infamous role as helper to the secret police.

It is difficult to decide whether Vsevolod was a scoundrel or simply a weak character, but no such doubt need exist in relation to his brother Nicholas. This promising nineteen-year-old notified the Third Department on August 14–18 that his brother kept and printed subversive literature in their apartment in Moscow. Vsevolod was arrested on August 25 and not only "sang" but wrote a letter implicating Mikhailov, which supposedly he had been unable to destroy prior to his seizure by the police. The poet was arrested on September 14 and to protect Shelgunov took full blame for the essay on himself, denying only his authorship of the more inflammatory passages, such as those about murdering a hundred thousand landlords. We already know his subsequent fate.

By the time *To The Young Generation* hit the streets there had been other leaflets circulating, mainly in Petersburg and Moscow. There began a fantastic tragicomedy which many contemporaries were to describe. You would be sitting home, Shelgunov was subsequently to recall, half nostalgically, half in the spirit of "how foolish we were!", and the bell would ring. A friend would enter, hand you a proclamation, and then without word leave. One thinks of the retired major in Dostoyevsky's famous scene: "In his youth through his hands passed whole packages of *The Bell* and of the proclamations, and though he would have been scared even to open them, he would have considered it utterly base to refuse to circulate them."[29] Subversive literature was found in theatre seats, plastered on the walls, everywhere.

The most important documents in terms of the actual revolutionary movement were several issues, appearing between July and September, of what some historians rather pretentiously call a revolutionary journal, *The Great Russian (Velikorus).* Unlike *To The Young Generation,* which was the work of only two men, *The Great Russian* had behind it a revolutionary organization, though how large it was we still don't know. But it is fairly

[29] *The Possessed,* Paris 1960 (in Russian), 416.

well established that the nucleus of the secret committee behind the publication was composed of several officers, the chief one being Nicholas Obruchev, his main co-adjutors artillery captain Vladimir Luginin and Prince
Nicholas Trubetskoy, a former aide-de-camp to a member of the imperial
house.[30]

Since we are already acquainted with some of the fantastic incongruities
of the 1860s, we will not be unduly surprised to hear that it is widely held
that this subversive, indeed in the eyes of the government treasonous,
publication was produced on the printing press of the General Staff,[31] nor
that its very name strongly suggests that some of the participants in the
conspiratorial organization were Polish-born officers of the imperial army
such as Sierakowski and another future hero of the Polish insurrection,
Jaroslav Dombrowski. A very distinctive feature of *The Great Russian*—
i.e., an organ allegedly speaking on behalf of what we would call today
Russians (Ukrainians at the time were generally referred to as Little Russians, and official doctrine denied the existence of a separate Ukrainian or
Little Russian nation, its language being considered by the government a
peasant dialect)—was precisely its insistence on the right of non-Russian
areas to secede from the empire. "Russians who believe in justice ought to
demand the unconditional liberation of Poland. . . . Our rule over her is
maintained only by armed force. . . . Our national pride and love for our
own people . . . demand this."[32] Russian rule in Poland was illegal, it went
on, since the Congress of Vienna provided only for a personal union of the
Polish Kingdom with the empire. And it cost the Russians money to
maintain a huge army there. Going beyond what some of the most radical
revolutionaries were ready to plead at the time, members of the Great
Russian committee then urged self-determination for what we call today the
Ukraine. "The same need to dispense with military rule demands that the
population of southern Russia be given full freedom to dispose of its destiny
by its own will. . . . It is well known that this nation is opposed to being
dominated by us. . . . We Great Russians are strong enough to live by
ourselves."[33] No civilized nation should be held in bondage by another one;
in fact—and this passage strengthens the suspicion of Polish co-authorship
of the declaration—some Ukrainians may prefer to join an independent
Poland, "because in all those places the people, if not Polish in nationality,

[30]Luginin subsequently went abroad to study, returned home in 1867, and pursued a distinguished scientific career as a chemist. About Trubetskoy's postconspiratorial life the biographical dictionary of the revolutionaries of the 1860s has the following melancholy final entry:
"arrested in 1872 in Orel as a loitering beggar." A. A. Shilov and M. G. Karnoukhova, *Activists
of the Revolutionary Movement in Russia,* Moscow 1928, I, 410.
[31]N. N. Novikova, *The Revolutionaries of 1861,* Moscow 1968, 44.
[32]Quoted in Lemke, *Studies in the Liberation Movement of the Sixties,* 361.
[33]Quoted in *ibid.,* 362.

are so in spirit." This far even Herzen was not ready to go; of course Kiev was a Russian city, he used to say.

Politically the program of *The Great Russian* was both more moderate and more serious than that of *To The Young Generation.* To be sure, there were inflammatory flourishes: the "educated classes" to which it appealed were stronger than the "dumb and cowardly" government, etc. And the committee admits that it is not united on social and political questions. Some want all of the land to go to the peasants free of charge, even that held directly by the landlords; more moderate members would have the nobility keep a proper share. Some want to retain the hereditary monarchy provided Alexander would agree to becoming a constitutional sovereign with a parliament, a responsible government, and full civic freedoms; others believe the monarchy should be overthrown, "an easy task in view of the frustrations of the peasants, dissatisfaction among the landlords, the frustration of the educated class, and the financial bankruptcy [of the state]."[34] All in all the committee agrees to give the emperor a chance and to conduct nationwide agitation to press the tsar for a constitution.

The main clue to the precise membership of this conspiracy (this time the word is appropriate), and who the actual authors of its declarations were, was held by and probably died with Vladimir Obruchev. First cousin of Nicholas, he had finished the higher military school in 1858 at the age of twenty-two with distinction, and had counted on a career as brilliant as that of his cousin. But he was assigned to the Quartermaster Corps instead of the General Staff, and writing his recollections as an old man Vladimir was quite frank in avowing that this undeserved slight helped turn him into a revolutionary. He soon resigned his commission and became part of the little world which worshipped Chernyshevsky and Dobrolyubov. He did some work for *The Contemporary,* and his relationship with its guiding spirit became very close. In his Siberian exile Chernyshevsky later wrote a novel whose hero was his youthful disciple and worshipper, whom he portrays with great warmth.

And indeed the story of Vladimir Obruchev might tempt a modern novelist. He tells us[35] that in the summer of 1861 "someone" asked him to help circulate *The Great Russian.* (Though writing as a graybeard, Vladimir still communicates to us the feelings of a young man asked to participate in an exciting venture.) Of course the logical thing would have been to send the dangerous literature by mail and to disguise his handwriting when addressing it. But the young fool did not think this sporting enough, so he delivered it in person and compounded his recklessness by hiring for the purpose one of those elite Petersburg cabmen with especially fast horses. He

[34]Quoted in *ibid.,* 364.
[35]In the *European Messenger,* V (St. Petersburg 1907), 122–55.

had always wanted to ride in such a cab (the equivalent of a Rolls Royce) but had never been able to afford it on his own! With a fast horse awaiting him, and with his ability (for which he had been famous in school) to run upstairs and downstairs faster than anybody else, he was sure, this incredible conspirator tells us, that he could escape any police trap. Of course his "chauffeur" denounced this unusual customer to the authorities. On October 4, 1861, Vladimir was in the custody of the Third Department.

The secret police were at first lenient with the boy: he was a general's son and he expressed contrition. All might go well with him, said the investigators, if he would only give them the name of the man who told him to circulate the subversive petition. But Obruchev wouldn't then, nor would he do so even forty-five years later, when he wrote his recollections. The emperor's cousin, Prince Peter of Oldenburg, known for his ability to "relate" to the young, as we would say today, was sent to soften him up. But Obruchev told the prince he would rather suffer the fate of a criminal than betray the man who had trusted him and thus lose his honor.

Historians are thus left to speculate as to the identity of the man who sent Obruchev on his foolhardy adventure: was it Chernyshevsky himself, or Nicholas Serno-Solovievich, both of whom were soon to be arrested and charged with other crimes? Though he declined to give names, in his brief recollections Vladimir does throw out some perhaps unwitting hints about the identity of the mystery man. In the course of one of the examinations, he tells us, Count Shuvalov, then second in command of the secret police, asked him suddenly if he did not have a brother or cousin who had worked with Chernyshevsky. Years later, when Vladimir was serving his exile in Irkutsk in Siberia, Shuvalov, by now head of the Third Department, again asked local authorities to try to pry the name of the stranger from Obruchev, holding out as bait that he would then be able to rejoin his mother in European Russia. But by now it was 1868, *The Great Russian* was ancient history, Chernyshevsky was himself in exile, Serno-Solovievich was dead. What prompted Count Shuvalov's renewed query and Obruchev's continued obstinacy?

In that same year of 1868 Shuvalov was engaged in a sharp intrabureaucracy power struggle with the minister of war, D. M. Milyutin,[36] and it would have helped if he could confirm an original suspicion and prove that Milyutin's right-hand man, Major General Nicholas Obruchev, had been the key man in the conspiracy which in 1861–63 proposed to dismember the empire. To be sure, Nicholas Obruchev could not have actually handed the fateful leaflets to Vladimir, who began his dangerous mission in September, since as we have seen the former was still abroad. But very likely the name of the

[36]*See* the introduction to the *Diary of D. M. Milyutin,* P. Z. Zayonchkovsky, ed., Moscow 1947, I, 32.

man who did would have enabled Shuvalov to establish Colonel Obruchev's complicity.

Vladimir paid heavily for his chivalry. He was sentenced to five years of hard labor and, following that, lifetime exile in Siberia. In May 1862 the foolish and heroic young man underwent the horror of "civic execution." He was conveyed to a public square and stood in front of the gallows while the sentence was read and the executioner broke the sword signifying Obruchev's degradation from the nobility. Then a convict's cloak was thrown over him. The mood of the crowd was ugly; to the Petersburg artisans and workers, here was a noble who had schemed against the tsar who liberated them. There were shouts that he should be decapitated or at least publicly flogged. He was then returned to prison to be chained for his long trip. Here he was visited by the kindly Prince Suvorov, and the account of their conversation lends support to our thesis. Drawing him apart from the guards and speaking in French, the governor general of St. Petersburg asked Obruchev whom he would like to see before his departure. His sister and his cousin, said the convict. "Your cousin?" asked Suvorov in a warning tone of voice. Vladimir caught the slip and corrected himself. He meant, he said, his brother-in-law.[37] Suvorov obviously knew something the Third Department did not.

Vladimir Obruchev's later career turned out better than might have been expected. Authorities in Siberia were often indulgent to political prisoners with good connections, and hard labor was interpreted as work in a carpentry shop or service as a clerk. In 1872 he was allowed to return to European Russia. In 1877, upon the outbreak of the Russo-Turkish War, Obruchev volunteered for front duty. He was then allowed to re-enter government service and he retired as major general at the age of seventy. Not bad for an erstwhile state criminal, but quite different from the career of the man he saved, his cousin Nicholas, about whom Vladimir allows himself in his memoirs just a hint of sarcasm.

There is no question that Vladimir retained to the last (he died in 1912) many of his youthful revolutionary beliefs. In fact when he reminisced about tsarist officials of those distant times, such as Prince Orlov or his tormentor Count Peter Shuvalov, his language grows almost (in 1907 it could not be exactly) as scabrous as that of the proclamations he had helped to circulate. His wife, who survived into the Soviet era, was granted a pension as the widow of a revolutionary.

[37]Obruchev, in the *European Herald,* V, 152.

FIVE

LAND AND FREEDOM

Historians must often resist the temptation to pull the subject of their discourse by the sleeve, so to speak, and implore it to do this or that. But in that hectic summer of 1861 the temptation is almost overwhelming: one wants to say, the government should *not* allow the proclamations to get its goat, and it should *not* embark upon a course, not so much of repression as of chicanery, against that most volatile element in the population, the students. And Herzen should *not* let himself dissipate his enormous moral authority by first endorsing and then joining in a conspiracy he did not believe in.

If it could have, Tsar Nicholas' government would have abolished universities altogether, such was its horror at the student disorders abroad, especially in Germany, and its disapproval of the universities' role in the revolutions of 1848. As it was, the number of university students in Russia was strictly limited, and the teaching of philosophy and anything bearing on current politics was forbidden. Alexander's era began with the abolition of these restrictions. The number of students in St. Petersburg University increased threefold between 1855 and 1861. They were no longer required to wear uniforms. Poorer students were exempted from paying tuition, and this helped to bring an influx of youths from the lower classes. Jews were now admitted to institutions of higher education, and in 1860 the first women appeared at the universities, to be sure as yet only as auditors.[1]

---

[1] The presence of ladies served to improve the general tone of university life, wrote L. F. Panteleyev, *Memoirs*, Moscow 1958, 215. Previously young men led rowdy lives at local bars

It is not surprising that this abrupt transition from a status which might be likened to that of the inmates of reform schools to acceptance as mature men had an intoxicating effect on many students. In the Continental manner, Russian students were not confined to colleges and dormitories, and their exuberant energies were not partially absorbed by sports and games. As the "hope of the nation," they were treated by the authorities with indulgence, and as Nicholas I or any of his ministers might have predicted, this was bound to lead to trouble. Quite apart from any political issues, the young men began to feel that they were of course the best judges of what sort of education they should be getting, and of the credentials of the men who taught them. Not infrequently a professor thought dull or otherwise objectionable would have his lectures boycotted or interrupted, or even in some cases would be "invited" by the students to leave the profession. Student expertise on the pedagogical qualifications of their teachers is, though some even today maintain the opposite, not infallible, and the student manner of showing disapproval not infrequently heartless. A foreign scholar might be laughed out of his composure or even his job because his listeners disliked his Germanic accent or pedantry. Russian history was taught at Petersburg University by Serge Soloviev, one of the greatest scholars and teachers of the subject, whose monumental history of the Russian state is considered a masterpiece of its kind even by his Soviet successors. But most students at the time considered Soloviev a bore and a reactionary: he talked about the *state* rather than the *people,* as his rival, Nicholas Kostomarov, did, who in addition enjoyed the aura of being a radical in trouble with the government on account of his Ukrainophile views.

Where the local curator (the government-appointed head of the university, usually chosen from outside it) was liberal, the students enjoyed freedoms unattainable to their fellow citizens. Thus between 1855 and 1861 the indulgent curator of Petersburg University, Prince Gregory Schcherbatov, allowed his students considerable latitude in organizing their own libraries, associations, and special funds for the underprivileged among their comrades; in fact it was a virtual student self-government. And as we have seen, such activities began unawares to take on a political coloration.

By 1860 many professors, and not only conservatives but some quite liberal-minded ones, felt that things had gone far enough and that university regulations had to be strengthened. But instead of acting gradually and tactfully, the government moved from the one extreme of its previous leniency to the other—a series of drastic restrictions which seemed to augur

---

and brothels (where they were charged reduced fees) rather than attending lectures. With women present they became not only more decorous in speech and habits but more engrossed in the great social issues of the day, women's emancipation being one of the principal ones.

a return to pre-1855 conditions. A rescript of May 31, 1861, banned unauthorized student assemblies; the student self-help societies and libraries were to be controlled henceforth by university councils (i.e., professors); and a severe limitation was put on the number of those freed from tuition—a heavy blow which would help to turn many students into revolutionaries (the fees were hardly excessive, fifty rubles per year, but to an impecunious youth like Ivan Khudyakov, a future accomplice in the Karakozov plot, it was convincing proof that the government meant to limit higher education to those who were well-to-do).[2]

Disorders erupted in the beginning of the fall semester of 1861. Students in Petersburg marched on the residence of the curator (no longer Schcherbatov but a retired general); Moscow students, not to be outdone by those of the younger capital, massed before the house of the governor general. In both cities the students' demands touched on the restoration of previous rights: freedom from university fees for the poor, students' control of their own organizations. But there were also inflammatory political speeches and pamphlets. A professor who tried to convince one of his demonstrating pupils that they were doing harm to their school and their learning received this classic reply: "What does learning have to do with this, Alexander Vasilievich? We are deciding important contemporary social issues."[3]

The government officials responsible for dealing with the disorders were, everyone subsequently agreed, completely incompetent. In any case they were convinced that they faced a real insurrection. The minister of education, Efim Putiatin, a naval officer by profession, dealt with students as if they were mutinous men from the lower deck. He and Petersburg's governor sanctioned the arrest of the leaders and, when this predictably led to bigger demonstrations in October, brought out troops and had some 300 students clamped down in the fortress of Petropavlovsk. A similar "bust" and mass arrests took place about the same time in Moscow. In both capitals the students were followed by jeering crowds of the city proletariat as they marched to their place of internment, and in some cases they were seized from the police and beaten up.

On October 18 Alexander II, who had been absent during the imbroglio, returned to Petersburg. He was genuinely appalled at the brutal measures his subordinates had taken and proceeded to fire those primarily responsible. The new governor of St. Petersburg became Prince Suvorov, whose reputation for liberalism and humanity would be amply justified. The bumbling Admiral Putiatin was replaced in the ministry of education by a close collaborator of the liberal Grand Duke Constantine, Alexander Golovnin.

---

[2] Tatishchev, *Emperor Alexander II,* St. Petersburg 1903, I, 395.

[3] L. Gessen, "St. Petersburg University in the Fall of 1861," in B. V. Gorev and B. N. Kozmin, eds., *The Revolutionary Movement of the Sixties,* Moscow 1932, 12.

For the next few years Golovnin, despite all the difficulties put in his path by both the revolutionary and the reactionary camps, was to strive to expand and improve education at all levels.

The arrested students were soon released. Only a few of them were exiled to the provinces. Petersburg University remained closed for the year, but to enable the poorer among the students to transfer to other institutions the emperor allocated funds to be distributed by a committee elected by students released from imprisonment.[4] In brief, granted the brutality and stupidity of the government's initial action, it is difficult to see in its subsequent moves that pattern of brutality and insensitivity to the young which most historians (not only Soviet ones) discern. But mild martyrdom is precisely the most potent revolutionary intoxicant, expecially for the young. The brief time that some of them spent in the dreaded fortresses like that of Petropavlovsk, and even then under the most lenient of conditions, gave them a sense of community with such martyrs for freedom as the Decembrists, and a touch of superiority toward their comrades who had missed this bracing experience and had meekly signed the pledge of good behavior promising obedience to university rules. The mood of the urban mobs must have given the more thoughtful of the young heroes pause, but they consoled themselves with the story (untrue) that the proletariat's hostility toward men who would liberate them (i.e., the students) was due to rumors spread by the police that the students wanted to restore serfdom!

Herzen's emotional response to the news about the student disorders betrays how far by the fall of 1861 he had thrown in his lot with Ogarev and Chernyshevsky, and dreamed of a violent overthrow of the existing system. The government, he wrote in *The Bell* of November 1, has shown itself to be "a gang of scoundrels, robbers, and whores." Events in Russia as well as in Poland now made him see the approach of a revolution. (Police and troops on October 15 had surrounded one of the Warsaw churches, and the Catholic clergy, declaring it a sacrilege, closed down all places of worship.)

In Russia they have closed down universities; in Poland churches, profaned by the police, shut down themselves. . . . From all parts of our enormous country—from the Don and the Ural, from the Volga to the Dnieper—one hears groans, one hears the growing murmur. This is just the beginning of the roar of a tidal wave, which after that terribly oppressive period of calm boils up, pregnant with storms. *To the people, to the people*—there is your place, you exiles from seats of learning. Demonstrate . . . that you will become warriors on behalf of the Russian people. Glory to you, you have begun a new era. You have understood that the time of whispers, discreet criticisms and [reading] forbidden books has passed. Glory to you, our young brothers, and our blessing! Oh, if you only knew how our hearts beat excitedly! How we were close to tears when we read about the *student day* in Petersburg!

[4]Panteleyev, 259.

A contemporary drawing of the Karakozov Attempt
(M.A. Antonovich, *Shestidesyatiye Gody*, Moscow, 1928)

Tsar Nicholas I (Bettmann Archive)

Tsar Alexander II (Bettmann Archive)

Nicholas Ogarev (Sovfoto)

Alexander Herzen (Sovfoto)

Natalia Tuchkova-Ogareva, Nicholas Ogarev and Alexander Herzen
(*Literaturnoye Nasledstvo*, Nos. 39-40, Moscow, 1940)

Nicholas Chernyshevsky
(New York Public Library)

Nicholas Nekrasov (M.A. Antonovich,
Shestidesyatiye Gody, Moscow, 1928)

Nicholas Dobrolyubov
(New York Public Library)

Nicholas Obruchev
(*Literaturnoye Nasledstvo*,
No. 62, Moscow, 1950)

Some of the Petersburg students arrested in the riots of 1861
(*Literaturnoye Nasledstvo*, No. 62, Moscow, 1950)

Nicholas Serno-Solovievich
(*Literaturnoye Nasledstvo*,
No. 62, Moscow, 1950)

Serge Nechayev
(*Katorga Issylka*,
No. 14, Moscow, 1925)

Michael Bakunin (New York Public Library)

Dmitri Karakozov
(A.A. Shilov, Karakozov,
Petrograd, 1919)

Some members of the Female Commune: Sophia Perovskaya in front,
Sophia Leshern von Hertzfeldt in the rear (*Byloe*, No. 8, 1906, St. Petersburg)

Vera Figner (New York Public Library)

Vera Zasulich (Culver Pictures)

Fyodor Trepov (Culver Pictures)

George Plekhanov (Sovfoto)

Alexander Mikhailov (A.P. Priblyeva-Korva and
V. Figner, *A.D. Mikhailov*, Leningrad, 1925)

Peter Kropotkin (Sovfoto)

Andrew Zhelyabov
(*Byloe*, No. 7, 1906, St. Petersburg)

Lev Tikhomirov
(S.S. Volk, *Narodnaya Volya*, Moscow, 1966)

Nicholas Morozov
(Morozov, *Povesti Moei Zhizni*, Vol. 1, Moscow, 1961)

Stephen Khalturin
(Sovfoto)

Olga Liubatovich
(*Byloe*, No. 6, 1906, St. Petersburg)

Alexander II with Princess Yurievskaya and their illegitimate children
(Feoktistov, *Vospominaniya*, Leningrad, 1929)

Now in his most reckless phase, Herzen unwittingly betrayed the blue-print for a national uprising as it was seen by revolutionaries in London and at home. The government had now irreversibly alienated the young generation, the new men, went the argument. These would now spread out through Russia enlightening the masses as to the true character of the government and unmasking the tsar as their oppressor. Already in the August 15 *Bell* Herzen had written:

Oh, if my words could reach you, tiller and sufferer of Russian soil; you whom *that* Russia, the one of lackeys, despises. . . . If my voice could reach you, I would teach you to despise your priests, put over you by the Petersburg Synod and the *German* tsar. You do not know them, you are fooled by their vestments, by their evangelical words—you hate your landlord and your parish priest . . . and you are right. But you still believe in the tsar and the bishops. . . . Don't! The Tsar is with them [the landlords] and they are his kind of people. He through a false emancipation sought to fool the people . . . [ordered] shootings and flogging.[5]

Quite a transition in Herzen: in four months Alexander II, no longer the Tsar Liberator, had become the hated "German Tsar." (In the same August issue Herzen had some practical advice for the revolutionaries in Russia: they should set up secret printing presses, he said, and continue to unmask the government and its alleged reforms.)

We can now begin tracing the clues to the great mystery of the revolutionary movement of the 1860s: the organization of Land and Freedom. The two key dates are undoubtedly July 1861, when, with illegal proclamations already circulating in Russia (in *The Great Russian*), Ogarev published "What the People Need" in *The Bell;* and December 1861, when some of the students released from prison, quite likely under the influence of such inflammatory appeals as Herzen's in the November 1 *Bell,* decided "to go to the people." How would they begin? Some of the young men had of course already been in contact with the radical circle around *The Contemporary,* particularly with Chernyshevsky. And in July the two organs for Russian radical thought, *The Bell* and *The Contemporary,* had already established a liaison with a view to mounting a political conspiracy.

The key man in establishing the liaison appears almost certainly to have been Nicholas Obruchev. He had already been involved in the secret committee of *The Great Russian* and was a friend of Chernyshevsky, and in May to June 1861, having become an intimate of Herzen's and Ogarev's in London, he lent his hand to the latter's composition "What the People Need."

That editorial bears some resemblance to the contents of *The Great Russian* insofar as it combined an inflammatory tone with rather cautious political conclusions. Thus "greed makes tsars, landowners, and officials

[5]My italics.

trade in people's land, their blood, and cheat the nation." But then, instead of taking an outright republican stand, the authors propose to "save the tsar from the officials" with a nationwide representative system based in the lowest instance on the peasant commune. Peasants were to get their land in full and free, but, rather surprisingly, the proclamation proposed that the landlords be compensated by "the imperial treasury," paying them sixty million rubles annually for thirty-seven years! Ogarev fancied himself an economist and argued that such compensation could easily be afforded without raising taxes if the state were to cut down expenses on the army and on the tsar's "stables and kennels." Who was to put this program into effect? Like a true propaganda broadside it promised something to everybody. Until recently the people had believed that the tsar was their friend, but now "our tsar orders soldiers to shoot into the people. . . . They say that he is kind, but what worse things could he have done if he were evil?" Then who? There are people's friends among officers, "who will teach soldiers that it is a mortal sin to shoot peasants," and also among landlords and merchants. And then there is another kind of people's friend: "a man who has neither peasants nor money, but who throughout his whole life has thought, learned, written, and published with one purpose in mind, to give people land and freedom." This was an unmistakable reference to Chernyshevsky and his ilk.

And the thing that reveals "What the People Need" as an obvious prospectus for a conspiracy and eventual revolution is its final advice that the masses should not dissipate their strength in isolated riots; they should "quietly collect forces, seek out dependable men who will help with advice and leadership, with word and deed, . . . ready to sacrifice their fortune and life. This way we shall be able . . . firmly and calmly . . . against the tsar and the nobles, to stand up for communal land, national freedom, and human truth."

The underground political party for which this July editorial was a virtual prospectus was supposed to gather under its umbrella radicals of quite diverse views—from those who would abolish monarchy and institute agrarian socialism to those who would retain the tsar and compensate nobles for liberating their serfs. Now one major obstacle in the way of such a union was the continuing discord between Herzen and his circle in London, and *The Contemporary* crowd in Petersburg. (In 1861 Chernyshevsky had conveyed a message to Herzen that he should not, from his safety in London, stir up the young in Russia.[6] He probably did this to cover his own tracks, since he himself was doing pretty much the same thing at home.)

But there was one man who could bring the squabbling giants together

---

[6]J. I. Linkov, *The Revolutionary Struggle of A. I. Herzen and N. P. Ogarev and the Secret Society "Land and Freedom" of the Sixties,* Moscow 1964, 192.

and make them join at least in blessing a conspiratorial enterprise—and that was Nicholas Obruchev. In July he delegated an acquaintance, Alexander Sleptsov, who had visited Herzen in 1860 and again in the spring of 1861, to contact Chernyshevsky and feel him out on the subject of a conspiratorial venture. Sleptsov (b. 1835) was at the time an official of the Imperial Chancery, and Chernyshevsky, who was seeing him for the first time, would not have talked with him as he did had the young official not carried a letter of introduction from Obruchev.[7] Sleptsov, as he recalls in his memoirs,[8] did not beat around the bush: he had seen Mazzini and Herzen, he reported, and they believed the moment was approaching for a revolutionary situation in Russia. "And here, Nicholas Gavrilovich, I wanted to talk with you and hear what you have to say." Chernyshevsky, who upon opening Obruchev's letter had taken his visitor to his study without introducing him to the guests who had as usual gathered at his house that evening, did not waste words: "What do you plan to do, organize a secret society?" Well, replied Sleptsov, they should evaluate the situation before doing anything. The talk then turned to the recently circulated *Great Russian;* was Sleptsov satisfied with its program? For the beginning, yes, said Sleptsov. Here Chernyshevsky dropped his reserve: "One should first study the situation and decide on what basis one could unite various circles. But they say there will *be a peasant uprising in 1863;* do you believe that?"[9] Now it was Sleptsov who grew wary. Had Chernyshevsky, he asked, put his own hand to a revolutionary proclamation? No, replied Chernyshevsky, he had not and it would be impossible for him to do so. For all his trust in Obruchev, he was not putting all his cards on the table before a man he was seeing for the first time.

Other meetings followed between Sleptsov and the sage of *The Contemporary,* and thus was the groundwork laid for that alliance between the London and St. Petersburg radicals, out of which was to grow Land and Freedom (in Russian, *Zemlya i Volya*), the closest thing to an underground revolutionary party Russia had ever known.

As we have seen, by the time he met Sleptsov Chernyshevsky *had* written a revolutionary proclamation; but *Greetings to the Landlords' Peasants from Their Well-Wishers,* which was entrusted to Vsevolod Kostomarov, was confiscated among his papers by the Third Department (which never learned who its author was) and was never circulated.[10] Its tone made clear the Chernyshevsky-Dobrolyubov convic-

[7]M. V. Nechkina, "The Formation of the First Land and Freedom," in a volume of M. V. Nechkina, ed., *The Revolutionary Situation in Russia, 1859–1861,* Moscow 1960, 292–93.

[8]Sleptsov's recollections were first relayed to Herzen's editor, the historian Michael Lemke. This passage from Alexander Herzen, *Works,* Michael Lemke, ed., Petersburg 1919, 427.

[9]My italics.

[10]Its text in N. G. Chernyshevsky, *Works,* XVI, Moscow 1953, 947–52.

tion that the flawed peasant reform would fail to satisfy the serfs and that by 1863 rural Russia might be seized by a vast revolt. It listed all the by now traditional criticisms of the Edict: that it was not to take effect for two years and even then the *mujik*[11] would be tied to the land for seven years; that the landlord could arbitrarily chase the peasant off his allotted land (this was quite untrue and demogogic); that the tsar had lied to the *mujiks* (and why not, "he himself is a landlord"). Chernyshevsky, who was far from being an admirer of Western institutions, then painted an alluring picture of life in the West for his prospective peasant readers. The language here strained at folksiness. In France there was perfect equality of all classes; in England there was no compulsory military service. Above all equal justice prevails; no one in the West has heard of judges taking bribes and (an even more questionable assertion) all power is vested in people's communes. Even their "tsar" is just like a Russian village elder. If the English or French "tsar" misbehaves, then the people say to him, "You Tsar, stop being our tsar, you do not please us, we are replacing you, go in peace where you will but far away, otherwise we shall put you in jail and put you on trial for disobedience." Such wonderful things could happen in Russia too, if the *mujiks* united and listened to their well-wishers.

Thus by July 1861 Chernyshevsky, while still cautious in his public writings, was ready to launch upon revolutionary agitation among the peasants. The tone of his composition was more demagogic, in places outright deceptive, in comparison to the Ogarev-Obruchev editorial of July 1, but then Chernyshevsky's pamphlet was addressed specifically to the "dark" peasant masses. The theme common to both (as well as to Shelgunov's manifesto, *Greetings to the Russian Soldiers From Their Well-Wishers,* also intercepted and never circulated) was the absence of any appeal for an immediate uprising. On the contrary, in all three proclamations (of which of course only *What the People Need* was circulated in Russia) everyone was urged to stay quiet and save their strength until such time as their "friends" and "well-wishers" called upon them to rise.

The problem before the "well-wishers" was therefore to create a viable underground organization. And on this count the situation until late fall of 1861 looked unpromising. To be sure young people and the *intelligentsia* read and in some cases helped circulate *To the Young Generation* and *The Great Russian,* but this was done more in the spirit of titillation than as a revolutionary endeavor. This depressing conclusion is supported by an anonymous article in *The Bell* of September 15, entitled "An Answer to the

---

[11]Another synonym for peasant, literally "little man." For some reason the term, perhaps because of its exotic sound, became a favorite of foreign writers when referring to the peasants in Russia.

Great Russian," whose author[12] asserted that the majority of "society" was indifferent to political issues. To be sure, a militant minority among the educated classes "holds with the people but does not have any ties with it. . . ." The good intentions of this minority are useless "because it is powerless, and the people [peasants] lack any initiative." Still, the author's conclusion is that a revolutionary organization must be set up. It would not be so difficult to organize a political underground in Russia, he suggests. The size of the country and the population makes strict police supervision very difficult, and underground activity should be easier than elsewhere in Europe. Also, "spying is contrary to our national character. Even the most submissive officials engage in it unwillingly and not with great diligence." Perhaps so in 1861, but how quickly were things to change thereafter! Serno-Solovievich was fortunate to be spared the foreknowledge of how this alleged Russian characteristic was to be affected by decades of conspiracy, by the Revolution, and by Stalinism.

In the October 1 *Bell* Ogarev gave his enthusiastic approval to the idea of a nationwide political underground. He now expanded his action program of July 1 to include, possibly under the influence of the *Great Russian,* national self-determination as both part of the program and an organizational principle of the secret society. The Poles would help but only in conjunction with an all-Russian uprising: "Therefore we beg the Poles not to start things prematurely with their own forces, which would prove insufficient. Such a harmful step would deprive Russia of the help she expects from Poland and would long postpone their common liberation. . . . The Polish [secret] society and [similar] Lithuanian, Ukrainian, and Russian societies should be parts of a common front and should act together." How would these secret societies operate? They should have cells everywhere—in schools, factories, government offices, and especially within the army. "Without the army it would be impossible to do anything."

The scenarios for a Russian revolution as written by Ogarev (and N. Obruchev?) in London and by Chernyshevsky and his group in Petersburg had much in common, but their points of emphasis were somewhat different. Ogarev relied principally on the military conspiracy and the outbreak of nationalist secessionist movement in various parts of the empire, followed by widespread peasant disorders. For Chernyshevsky the starting point was the expected peasant revolution in 1863. Both groups, though against the conviction of their leaders, were half ready to accept a constitutional monarchy, but only as a transitional stage toward a republican and socialist Russia and only because they believed that any constitutional concession made by the emperor would make the present government so impotent that a "real" revolution would be much easier.

[12]Most likely Nicholas Serno-Solovievich.

But both groups as they moved to coalesce realized the formidable obstacles in the way of a successful conspiracy, not to mention a full-fledged revolution. In the first place the "new men" were a minority within the minority of the educated classes. In the second place there was the peasants' infuriating trust in the tsar. And then the government, which had seemed so helpless and tolerant (in the revolutionaries' eyes the latter was of course synonymous with the former) in coping with radical propaganda, whose officials and officers hobnobbed almost openly with Herzen and Chernyshevsky, suddenly in 1861, showed its teeth with the arrests of Mikhailov, Vladimir Obruchev, and some others. It is possible that the projected consolidation of all radical groups into a united revolutionary conspiracy would have remained on paper only or fizzled out altogether, had it not been for the mass arrest of the students in September-October 1861. By the time they were released in December, most of them were ready for exhilarating political action and many of them knew where to go to find it. Unwittingly, by its badly thought-out actions, the tsar's government had helped to create what we would now call a revolutionary subculture in Russian society, had prepared the soil for the subsequent revolutionary crop of the 1860s, almost all the work of alumni of the Petropavlovsk and Kronstadt fortresses.

In describing the first steps of Land and Freedom in October 1861, Sleptsov stresses that its initial recruiting efforts were among "those students who after the university riots in both capitals . . . intended to go abroad to continue their studies."[13] Of course in December recruitment was intensified and newcomers were militant, and since the universities remained closed and many of the released students went home, circumstances offered an ideal way of spreading the conspiratorial gospel to the provinces.

Who were the first organizers? Sleptsov mentions in addition to himself the brothers Nicholas and Alexander Serno-Solovievich, Nicholas Obruchev, and the poet-satirist Vasili Kurochkin (b. 1831). Kurochkin was the editor of a humor magazine, *The Spark.* His brother Nicholas, a doctor by profession and like practically everybody we encounter in these pages a writer on the side, was also to play an important part in Land and Freedom and subsequent revolutionary movements. There was a determined effort to draw in journalists, especially ones who were popular with students and officers. This was not difficult, since many journalists had already gravitated toward the radical course. Gregory Blagosvetlov had typical credentials for a revolutionary of the 1860s: the son of a priest, he had been a teacher in a military school, from which he had been dismissed as early as 1856 "for a subversive turn of mind," and then, after an almost obligatory visit to Herzen (in 1860), he became the editor of *The Russian Word,* a magazine which among the "new men" enjoyed a popularity second only to *The*

[13]See Herzen, XVI, 74.

Contemporary. A particularly valuable acquisition was Alexander Pogoski. Of Polish descent, he had been involved as a schoolboy in some activity connected with the insurrection of 1830–31 and to escape its consequences had enlisted at sixteen as a common soldier. In 1853, already a major, he resigned from the army and took civil employment,[14] and then in 1858 became editor of and chief contributor to *Soldiers' Talk.* Again one can discern the influence of Nicholas Obruchev in the fact that this journal, designed to instruct and broaden the horizons of literate soldiers, was entrusted to a Pole known to be of advanced social views. To have a magazine with such an audience in the hands of a fellow conspirator who knew at first hand the mentality of the rank and file was of course very valuable. Since the official watchdog censor of *Soldiers' Talk* was himself a man of radical ideas, Pogoski could occasionally slip in a story or poem which might induce a thoughtful soldier-reader to develop "untrustworthy attitudes."[15] Another journalistic recruit to the cause was Gregory Yeliseyev, a contributor to *The Contemporary,* who, it was rumored, conceived in 1861 a fantastic plot to kidnap the tsesarevich[16] and hold him until the tsar granted Russia a constitution.[17]

As for the Master himself, stories vary. Some sources are emphatic that Chernyshevsky joined the conspiracy at the beginning. Others quote him as saying that though in general sympathy with the enterprise, he felt that especially in view of Dobrolyubov's approaching end (d. November 17, 1861) he had to save his energies for *The Contemporary.* And he probably suspected that ever since Mikhailov's and Vladimir Obruchev's arrests the Third Department had him under surveillance.

Thus by the late fall of 1861 the secret organization which in August 1862 adopted formally the name of Land and Freedom was in existence. The name itself came naturally enough from the first words of the Ogarev-Obruchev manifesto of July 1: "What the people need is land and freedom." Sleptsov's statement (as related to him by Ogarev) that the name was suggested by Herzen—"it is to be sure a bit pretentious, but honest and clear"[18]—is credible enough, as some other recollections of Sleptsov's are not. It is in line with Herzen's appeal to the young of November 1 to go to

---

[14]J. E. Barenbaum, "Popular Journalism of A. F. Pogoski during the Revolutionary Situation," in Nechkina, ed., 197–99.

[15]The censor in question, V. N. Beketov, was the same one who passed Chernyshevsky's *What Is To Be Done?* and was subsequently fired. *Ibid.,* 202.

[16]This was the official title of the heir apparent to the throne. "Tsarevich," despite the almost universal Western misuse of the term, was a colloquialism for any of the emperor's sons.

[17]Panteleyev, 246. The story, which would have been credible in 1865–66, sounds a bit improbable for 1861, but it is characteristic of Yeliseyev's reputation. He was, said Chernyshevsky, "for all his gray hair, the youngest in spirit of the whole *Contemporary* crowd."

[18]*See* Herzen, XVI, 73.

the people, and his assertion that the time for mere whispering and the reading of forbidden literature behind closed doors had passed.

The July 1 manifesto thus became so to speak the political platform of Land and Freedom. It was broad enough in its postulates to appeal to all shades of radicals, from those who favored a constitutional monarchy to outright revolutionaries. And indeed in January 1862 Chernyshevsky, in an article which had not been passed by the censor and was addressed in fact to the government, urged a constitution and political freedom for Russia as the only way to deflect the coming storm, i.e., a peasant rebellion in 1863.[19] But it is likely that this moderation, rather than reflecting his real beliefs of the moment, was a tactical move to deflect the government's attention both from himself and from the conspiracy of which he was if not a formal member, then the main inspirer. In fact some of his fellow revolutionaries chafed under their self-proclaimed resolve to defer the bid for power until the spring of 1863.

On November 8, 1861, *The Bell* printed the most violent appeal yet for revolution or, more precisely, for a soldiers' mutiny against the tsar: "What the Army Should Do." Rather disingenuously, and especially in view of the fact that its co-author with Ogarev was Nicholas Obruchev, an experienced officer, the article tried to convince soldiers that they could disobey orders without too much risk: "The tsar has signed an order how and when to shoot the people. Why did he get the idea to issue such an order and to have it printed? It is obvious he is frightened of the people. And if a man is frightened then he is weak." One by one the authors take up all possible objections to their appeal. The soldier's oath? —But can an oath bind a man to do something sinful, such as shooting peasants who want land or Poles who want national freedom? If a given regiment were to disobey, wouldn't other troops be brought in against them? —Well, perhaps the first soldier or officer who refused an order might be shot, "but then other soldiers and officers would follow their example, soon all of them." What would the tsar do then? —"Obviously he will have to give the people land and freedom, and that is all that the people want." But isn't it a rebellion when soldiers refuse to obey the law? —"Now, if the people say, 'We shall pay taxes for general needs, give us land so that everybody has enough, abolish all peasant payments and obligations, let us rule ourselves as best we know how, without landlords and officials,' then they are speaking God's truth and this in no sense can be taken as lawbreaking and rebellion!"

As in Chernyshevsky's *To the Landlords' Peasants,* so in this appeal to the soldiers one is struck by the authors' naive Machiavellianism. They seem oblivious to the possibility that uneducated and even illiterate people might be intelligent, that the average peasant and soldier would naturally grow suspicious when addressed by a social superior in exaggeratedly

[19]"Letters Without an Address."

"folksy" language, and that even the stupidest private would find it hard to believe that the overthrow of Russia's social and political system was really a very simple thing: "If the soldiers don't fight the people, the nation will receive land and freedom without any slaughter, without a single drop of blood being shed, in perfect peace."

"What the Army Should Do" was circulated by members of Land and Freedom among some regiments and naval units, but it met with practically no response. How badly its authors misunderstood the mentality of the common soldier can be demonstrated by one of the few examples which the revolutionaries alleged to prove the success of their propaganda. Colonel Andrew Krasovsky, when ordered to put down a peasant disorder in June 1862, appealed to his own regiment "not to be like soldiers who crucified Christ." When he was betrayed to the authorities and was in jail awaiting his death sentence, he received a message of sympathy from a handful of his soldiers: "There are a few of us who . . . really understand you, Your Honor. . . . We shall pray so that the all-merciful God may help you."[20] But not a single one lifted a finger on behalf of their popular commander.

It might appear strange that Herzen, who for all his "breach" with Alexander II and excitement over the student riots preserved a great deal of political common sense, would allow himself to become entangled in conspiratorial affairs. But toward the end of 1861 another force appeared which in addition to Ogarev was pushing him into extremism. Michael Bakunin arrived in London.

It was said of the famous anarchist that while irreplaceable on the first day of a revolution he should be shot on the next. Bakunin's whole career casts doubt on the first part of this statement. In fact he messed up and compromised practically every revolutionary undertaking to which he lent his hand. His arrival in London was viewed by Herzen with some trepidation, but he could not reject or keep at a distance from this old Moscow friend and world-renowned revolutionary.

Born in 1814 to a noble family, Bakunin had belonged to various philosophical circles of Moscow in the 1830s. He then continued his studies in Berlin, where he acquired that lifelong interest in German social thought and detestation of everything else German which seems to have been a common characteristic of practically all Russian radicals. A career as an itinerant revolutionary followed: the barricades in Prague in 1848, the Dresden uprising in 1849, arrest and death sentence—but then he was turned over to the Russian police and in 1851 incarcerated in the Petropavlovsk fortress.

[20]Cited in Vladimir Burtsev, *One Hundred Years,* London 1897 (in Russian), 48.

It was here that Bakunin wrote his famous confession, which fortunately for his revolutionary reputation did not come to light until after the Revolution of 1917. In it Bakunin flattered and eulogized Nicholas I and denounced Western liberals and institutions. Nicholas read the document with interest, but the tsar being unsentimental, its only result was Bakunin's transfer to Schlüsselburg, an even more fearsome place of incarceration. Only in 1857, after another humble petition, this time to Alexander II, was he allowed to exchange this most dreaded prison for lifetime exile in Siberia.

Eastern Siberia was then ruled by Nicholas Muraviev. And as it happened, the Bakunins and Muravievs were related. (Bakunin himself in his middle age when he grew fat and slovenly bore a certain resemblance, ideologically embarassing to both sides, to the "hangman" Muraviev.) Though imperious and imperial-minded—it was he who was instrumental in annexing from China what is now the Soviet Far East Maritime Province and who founded Vladivostok, "the ruler of the East"—Muraviev was in line with the older tradition of his family, tolerant and humane toward political exiles. Bakunin struck up a friendship with his understanding relative, and also with his chief of staff, Boleslaw Kukiel. Kukiel was a Pole, and with Poles Bakunin always got on famously. (He had even, though sexually impotent, married a Polish girl.) It is therefore not surprising that he was not watched very carefully, and in June 1861 he was able to bolt to Japan and from there to the United States.

In his impressions of the transatlantic democracy Bakunin not only advanced a theory about the "convergence" of Russia and America some one hundred years before American political scientists came up with it, but also revealed his rather curious thought processes. "I spent one month in America and learned a great deal," he wrote. "I saw how this country through demagoguery reached as deplorable a situation as we have through despotism. In fact America and Russia have a great deal in common. What is most important for me, I found in America universal and unconditional sympathy toward Russia and faith in the future of the Russian nation. And so despite everything I myself heard and saw, I left America as a resolute partisan of the United States."[21] Most of Bakunin's enterprises were to bear the mark of similar logic.

On December 15 this big revolutionary child was in London and, as he wrote, "welcomed by Herzen and Ogarev like a brother." Years later Herzen was to describe his final accession to Land and Freedom as due to "Bakunin's passion for agitation and Ogarev's fanaticism."

The year when the conspiracy would recruit members and try to absorb various radical circles already in existence in the Russian provinces was

[21]Quoted in Michael Lemke, *Studies in the Liberation Movement of the Sixties,* St. Petersburg 1908, 134–35.

1862. In March Longin Panteleyev, who had been expelled from Petersburg University, was invited by a fellow expellee and inmate of Petropavlovsk fortress to join a secret organization. Upon agreeing, he was brought to a session with Sleptsov who, without identifying himself as one of its leaders, expounded both the purpose and the organizational structure of Land and Freedom. For the time being it was to be composed of cells consisting of not more than five people. Every cell member would eventually recruit four others, etc. Thus each conspirator would be known personally only to eight other people.

To be sure, granted the "broad Russian nature" if nothing else, this somewhat puerile recruiting scheme was bound to break down at once. Members of Panteleyev's cell had been reading all those proclamations, all the articles in *The Bell* and *The Contemporary*. They immediately fell into agitated speculation as to who the other members were. Surely Chernyshevsky . . . ? A chess club had recently opened in St. Petersburg, and while in fact some members of it devoted themselves to this noble game in which Russians have always excelled, nobody (including, as it was to turn out, the Third Department) could miss the fact that it was also attended by various radical luminaries, including Chernyshevsky, who instead of concentrating over the chessboard held conversations in low tones. And then Nicholas Serno-Solovievich—again everybody knew that he had resigned from government service and opened a bookstore and rental library which had also become a gathering point for political malcontents. No doubt the popularity of his undertaking and its frequentation by young officers was also due to the fact that some young and liberated women from the upper classes served as salesladies.

In fact excessive secrecy in the beginning of 1862 seemed unnecessary. The government was concentrating on suppressing open, even quite loyal criticism of its policies. Spokesmen for the nobility of Tver province selflessly and respectfully petitioned the tsar to place the financial burden of the serfs' emancipation on all classes rather than on just the peasants, and expressed the conviction that on this and other reforms the tsar should seek the advice of elected representatives of the whole nation. For this moderate petition thirteen Tver noblemen were arrested and spent five months in prison. In contrast to such vigilance against loyal opposition, the government appeared for the moment to neglect real revolutionaries, as the following story amply illustrates.

Panteleyev went to Moscow to try to recruit two local revolutionaries, Pericles Argiropulo and Peter Zaichnevsky. There was a slight complication, in that they were currently in jail. But it seems to have been a very unusual jail. In it the nineteen-year-old Zaichnevsky had just completed the writing of a blood-curdling proclamation, *Young Russia*, signed by something called Russian Central Revolutionary Committee. In addition to such old chestnuts as the demands for a republican-federative system and for agrarian socialism, the document asked for the abolition of marriage and the family altogether. The whole imperial tribe was to be extirpated to the last man and woman and, if necessary, all those who would try to save them from this fate. An obliging prison guard had conveyed this document to an illegal printing shop, whence it hit the streets. It is therefore not surprising that Panteleyev easily gained access to the young lunatic who proudly presented him with the proclamation and asked what he thought of it: " 'Very powerful,' I answered diplomatically. I did not like the proclamation but thought it necessary to conceal my opinion so as not to spoil our further negotiations."[22] But Zaichnevsky said he would join Land and Freedom only if it would adopt *his* program, and that far Panteleyev was unable to go, especially since Zaichnevsky's entire "party" consisted of some four or five people. (Zaichnevsky's authorship was never discovered by the authorities. He spent the rest of his life in administrative exile in Siberian and provincial places. Wherever he went there were soon small conspiratorial circles, and complaints of local fathers that he was leading their daughters astray, not only politically. He died in 1896, faithful to the last to his Jacobinical creed: "Any revolution afraid to go too far is not really a revolution.")

The revolutionary recruiter then repaired to his native Vologda. But Panteleyev local contact in this dismal provincial hole informed him that the situation was unpromising. There were a few radically minded officials, but their radicalism sprang from the circumstance that they had not received expected promotions. Some Poles were interested, but they told Panteleyev that they would join his organization only if it would set as one of its main aims the restoration of an independent Poland with the frontiers of 1772. He thus returned to Petersburg with empty hands.

Panteleyev's memoirs, written in 1905, by which time he had turned into a liberal, have been severely criticized by historians such as Lemke, as well as most Soviet students of the 1860s. Yet there can be no doubt that the impression he conveys of the amateurishness of the whole conspiratorial effort and of the numerical insignificance of Land and Freedom is in general correct. Still, in the longer run the group's historical importance cannot be questioned: it laid the foundation for the conspiratorial and eventually terrorist mentality of Russian dissent; and it polarized Russian society between those (most of the *intelligentsia* and the young) who, while not participating or even approving of the activities of the handful of conspirators,[23] still considered them as fighters for freedom and the government as

[22]Panteleyev, 300.

[23]The membership of Land and Freedom at its height and in its most optimistic assessments is estimated at 3000. Most likely it was closer to 1000.

the oppressor; and the rest of society, who learned to look on political dissent as subversion and on repression as the only means of dealing with it.

In May 1862 a series of conflagrations erupted in St. Petersburg. They struck for most part the poorer sections of the city. The biggest one, on May 28, destroyed the Apraxin market, a huge conglomeration of shops and warehouses. Fires in Russian cities, with their multitude of wooden structures and inadequate precautions and fire-fighting facilities, were quite frequent. But for many people, and not only among the city proletariat, there was an ominous coincidence between the conflagration and the revolutionary agitation. *Young Russia,* with its attacks on private property and the family, was just being circulated. Was the arson the work of Polish agents? Or perhaps some students were paying back the urban lower classes for their attitude during the university troubles the preceding fall? The special investigating committee could never discover the guilty, if indeed it was arson. But the government now felt strong support among the population, if not among the educated classes, for its taking resolute measures against what the conservatives felt were the main sources of immorality and subversion. All the Sunday schools were ordered closed until new regulations could assure that they would not spread "untrustworthy ideas." And the two main organs of what was now becoming known as "nihilism," *The Contemporary* and *The Russian Word*, were suspended for eight months.

The Third Department was still blissfully unaware of the existence of Land and Freedom, but at the end of June it finally felt that it had the goods on Chernyshevsky. Herzen, as he grew more reckless politically, became rather careless in keeping secret his contacts with the homeland. During a large party in a London restaurant he had talked freely about an acquaintance of his who was going to Russia with letters from himself, Ogarev, and Bakunin. One of the guests was a government agent.

The carrier of the secret correspondence was arrested on arrival on Russian soil, and the Third Department found a lot of interesting material. The addressees had long been in the secret police files as among those suspected of harboring "untrustworthy views" or "a subversive turn of mind." Their arrest in turn revealed much more correspondence, not only "with the London propagandists against the Russian state," as Herzen and company were officially designated, but also with people like Turgenev. But the main catch was Herzen's letter to Nicholas Serno-Solovievich in which, after referring to the recent closing of *The Contemporary,* Herzen expressed his readiness to publish it abroad together with Chernyshevsky.[24]

Chernyshevsky had been under police surveillance since October. (Police surveillance in tsarist Russia was of two kinds: "open" when its object was

[24]Michael Lemke, *Political Trials in Russia of the 1860s,* Moscow 1923, 182.

informed that he was being watched, and "secret" when he was not. One would think that the first variety would tend to defeat its own purpose but then logic was not a strong point of the tsarist government, any more than of most of its enemies.) Chernyshevsky's janitor and cook provided such fascinating and important information as that he seemed to sleep only two or three hours, spending the rest of the night behind the locked door of his study—and that he was visited by army officers, by the Serno-Solovievich brothers, and by suspected Poles. Obviously as early as April the Third Department was itching to get its hands on the writer, for in the same month an aide to Prince Suvorov paid him a visit.[25] But until the hysteria arose over the fires, lack of hard evidence caused the government to hesitate, knowing that the arrest would bring a violent reaction from the *intelligentsia*.

On July 7 Chernyshevsky and Nicholas Serno-Solovievich were arrested. One begins to sympathize with the more extreme of the revolutionaries when one reads that both were imprisoned for two years before the senate even rendered a judgment as to their guilt or innocence. In the case of Nicholas Serno-Solovievich nothing more compromising could be found among his papers than his correspondence with the London exiles and numerous drafts of various petitions to the emperor and of laws to reconstruct the Russian political and social system, by which this indefatigable writer of memoranda planned to persuade the regime to mend its ways. All of them, as well as his petitions from the jail, where he argued that what he was striving for was to have Russia become a constitutional monarchy like England, "where the government joins its interests with those of the nation . . . and leads it to glory and felicity," were characterized in the senate verdict as "insolent attacks upon the government's policies and the state system."[26] And so though his link with the real conspiracy was never uncovered, Nicholas Serno-Solovievich was sentenced to six years at hard labor and thereafter lifetime exile in Siberia. But he died in Irkutsk only four years later under rather mysterious circumstances.

Chernyshevsky's arrest and his subsequent martyrdom was a major psychological error on the part of the government. Given the students' changeable moods, his domination of their radical wing was bound to end before too long, just as Herzen's once much greater sway over public opinion was soon to become a thing of the past. If the government had disposed of hard evidence, and if the trial had been in open court (a practice which began only in 1865, with the new judicial reforms), it is possible that the political consequences would have been different. But under the actual circum-

[25] *The Red Archive*, I (14), Moscow 1926, 119. We know from other sources that on this occasion Suvorov urged Chernyshevsky to go abroad and offered to provide him with a passport.
[26] Lemke, *Studies in the Liberation Movement of the Sixties*, 221.

stances Chernyshevsky's martyrdom helped to crystallize progressive Russia's hostility to the political order, and perhaps even more than his teachings helped to steer the militant minority into the path of conspiracy, thus preparing the psychological ground for the catastrophe of 1866 and for the further terrorist attempts which were to bar the path to a constitutional and liberal Russia.

Chernyshevsky defended himself with skill and persistence. (Also, when the authorities refused visiting rights to his wife he went on a hunger strike —possibly the first use of this technique, which became a frequent tactic of political prisoners—and won his point.) His only contacts with Herzen, he explained, were due to his efforts to warn the editor of *The Bell* not to stir up the young at home to senseless revolutionary enterprises. How could he have close relations with the man who had slandered *The Contemporary* in the Ogarev inheritance business? We cannot chastise him for such prevarications in view of what threatened him; but it is interesting that historians like Lemke who praise Chernyshevsky's behavior show less understanding for a very similar lack of frankness on the part of Ivan Turgenev, who was at the same time being tried *in absentia* for his contacts with Herzen and Bakunin, and who asserted not quite truthfully that he had broken with Herzen over his recent political attitudes and helped Bakunin financially only out of charity. They blame the great writer for cowardice and hypocrisy: what else can you expect from a liberal and resolute enemy of revolution!

To establish Chernyshevsky's guilt the Third Department had recourse to falsification and provocation. Vsevolod Kostomarov, who had fingered Mikhailov in 1861 and who at the time was ignorant as to the authorship of other proclamations in his possession, was now, for the promise of freedom and a few rubles, made to confess that *To the Landlords' Peasants* had been written by Chernyshevsky. To be sure this was a correct guess, but the secret police produced the information by contemptible means, for Kostomarov was made to write letters to fictitious addressees, further implicating Chernyshevsky, and very probably he forged an incriminating letter by his victim. Chernyshevsky was sentenced on several counts: "illegal contacts with the exile Herzen, who through propaganda has attempted to overthrow the existing system of government . . . authorship of a seditious appeal to . . . the peasants . . . his knowledge of other evil-doers who are disturbing the social peace with proclamations."[27] And so the "retired titular councillor" Nicholas Chernyshevsky was sentenced to twelve years at hard labor (reduced by the emperor's grace to six) and thereafter lifetime exile in Siberia. The government was determined that this man who poisoned the minds of a whole generation should never be free.

[27]Lemke, *Political Trials*, 483–85.

When the poet Alexis Tolstoy, an intimate friend of the imperial couple, tried to plead for Chernyshevsky with the emperor, Alexander warned him never to discuss this subject and turned his back on him.

On May 19, 1864 the "civic execution" of Chernyshevsky took place. But this time the public, unlike the audience at Vladimir Obruchev's similar ordeal, was composed largely of the *intelligentsia* and was sympathetic. A few people tried to toss flowers to the scaffold where the senseless and repulsive rite was taking place.

During Chernyshevsky's preliminary imprisonment, the spring of 1863, in which he had so confidently expected a general peasant uprising, came and passed without any significant developments. His sentence, coming after the crushing of the Polish insurrection and Herzen's political bankruptcy, marked in the opinion of the government the final blow to those revolutionary agitators who had disturbed the social peace ever since 1861. But for all the temporary ebb of the actual revolutionary wave, the imperial government, and largely because of its treatment of Chernyshevsky, helped to create a legend from which new generations of revolutionary conspirators would draw their inspiration. In 1902, writing a handbook of political tactics for the party which fifteen years later was to seize power in Russia, Vladimir Lenin chose for its title the one Chernyshevsky had given to his utopia: *What Is To Be Done?*

SIX

NIHILISM

In reading the reports of the investigations on Chernyshevsky and Serno-Solovievich as well as the Third Department's files on them, which became available after 1917, one is puzzled that the secret police did not unravel right away in 1862 the existence of Land and Freedom and its links with the Polish revolutionaries. Its agents' reports clearly established that Chernyshevsky had contacts with Nicholas Obruchev as well as with Josaphat Ohryzko, an official in the finance ministry who was publisher of a Polish newspaper and the Polish nationalists' liaison with the Russian conspirators. Yet Obruchev and Ohryzko were not touched. Nor was Sleptsov, known as a close friend of Nicholas Serno-Solovievich.

One is left with several intriguing hypotheses. One, that they had friends within the secret police and the ministry of the interior who protected them, as some members of Land and Freedom boasted. Another, that some high officials, perhaps the emperor himself, believed that once the sources of revolutionary pollution were suppressed it would be a mistake to cast the net too widely; that once Herzen was exposed as a dangerous contact and Chernyshevsky was under lock and key, the amateurish conspiracies would collapse of themselves. And it cannot be excluded that some members of the Third Department hoped that the conspiracy would be allowed to continue for the moment because they might identify as its members or sympathizers such liberal-minded officials as Prince Suvorov, the minister of war Dmitri Milyutin, and perhaps Grand Duke Constantine himself.[1]

In any case, Land and Freedom continued its clandestine existence. Its directing group, which was rather grandiosely called the Central Committee, was complemented, after the arrest of Nicholas Serno-Solovievich and the flight abroad of his brother Alexander, by Nicholas Utin (the ex-student who initiated Longin Panteleyev into the conspiracy) and Gregory Blagosvetlov. Its other members remained Nicholas Obruchev, Alexander Sleptsov, and Vasili Kurochkin. The treasurer of the organization was Lieutenant-Colonel Alexander Putiata, lecturer in a military school. Putiata's career again was peculiar, or would have been in any other society except Russia of those years. He became an object of suspicion to the government, which was natural enough, but also to the members of the revolutionary movement, where it was widely believed that most of the money he collected went into his own pocket rather than to the cause.[2] Dismissed from the army in 1864, he was caught in the dragnet after Karakozov's attempt on the life of the tsar, but "sat" only four months. After an interval in private employment (and under police surveillance), Putiata became a high civil servant in an establishment for which both sides of his reputation seemed to make him less than suitable—the ministry of education.

Land and Freedom's activity was still concentrated on recruitment. Sometime in the summer of 1862 the conspiracy was joined by Yuri Molosov who brought with him his circle, the so-called Library of Kazan Students, which in 1859 he had secretly organized at Moscow University. But as indicated above, the general effect of its membership drive among the young and the *intelligentsia* was not impressive. Recent Soviet historians, to be sure, tend to discount Panteleyev's testimony on this count, and would include in the conspiracy anybody and everybody involved then (1862–63) and subsequently in revolutionary activity. (This, one suspects, is largely because during the Stalin era the study of Land and Freedom was not a very safe occupation for a historian: treason within the army, encouragement of Polish and Ukrainian secessionism, etc.—too suggestive. Hence beginning in the 1950s one sees a tendency to overcompensate for the previous neglect.) But while it is true that many future revolutionaries had contacts and friends in Land and Freedom, it is still unreasonable to classify them as members of the conspiracy or to consider the organization itself as a disciplined party on the order of the People's Will of the late 1870s, not to mention the Russian Marxists and the Socialist Revolutionaries in the

---

[1] It is interesting to speculate whether Stalin ever studied the secret police files of this period, whether the real though fantastic-sounding ramifications of the conspiracy of the 1860s might have inspired him in weaving the phantasmagoric scenario of alleged plots and treason which served as his rationalization for the great terror of the 1930s.

[2] L.F. Panteleyev, *Memoirs,* Moscow 1958, 322. Some of the funds for Land and Freedom came evidently from Utin's father, a rich Jewish entrepreneur.

twentieth century. What united these various conspiratorial groups was not so much a common program, though Ogarev's *What the People Need* served as a surrogate program, as a hope and a target date.

The hope was that in the spring of 1863 two simultaneous disasters would strike Russia (or as the conspirators would put it, the imperial government). Firstly the peasants would rise once their new freedom was fully exposed as a fraud. In thinking of the dimensions of this uprising, the revolutionaries thought of the vast jacqueries of the past, of Stenka Razin's rebellion in 1670–71, and of Yemelyan Pugachev's uprising in 1773. To be sure both of those folk heroes were essentially bandit chieftains (Pugachev representing himself as Tsar Peter III), but their enterprises gained support and momentum because of the genuine grievances of the peasant and Cossack masses, to whom they appealed to massacre officials and landlords and to whom they promised freedom from serfdom and taxation. The rebellions were localized, but at one time they (especially Pugachev's) engulfed a vast area comprising the lower Volga region and much of the Urals.

Secondly the conspirators believed—and here their prognosis was realistic—that an armed rebellion in Poland was inevitable. Herzen was quite disingenuous in his oft-repeated statements in *The Bell* that if Poland rose, the Volga, Don (Razin was a Don Cossack), and Urals would respond. It would then be up to Land and Freedom to assume the direction of the rebellion, to prevent it from turning into an indiscriminate slaughter-and-looting affair on the Pugachev–Razin model, and to ensure that the imperial government (assuming that it had not collapsed altogether) would grant independence to Poland, and "land" (i.e., full pre-1861 allotments without any payment to the peasants) and "freedom" (i.e., a representative assembly) to the Russian people.

The notion of a peasants' revolt was a vain dream. Herzen and others forgot that Razin's and Pugachev's rebellions took place before the era of railway and telegraph, when a local uprising on the periphery of the state could gather force for weeks and months without the government's being able to choke it off. Besides, nothing indicated that the peasants' disappointment over the terms of their emancipation would take the form of an active uprising. Even at Bezdna, theirs had been but passive resistance. And throughout 1862 the number of peasant disorders declined drastically. The wager on the Polish uprising was on the contrary to prove correct, but its consequences were to be the opposite of what the revolutionaries hoped.

In the Kingdom of Poland by the end of 1861 agitation for independence and conspiratorial activity had reached fever pitch. Radical sentiment had permeated the majority of the gentry and the urban classes, including Jews and the urban proletariat. The imperial government, or at least the emperor himself, had resolved on a number of far-reaching reforms. But just as in Russia Alexander would not grant a constitution, so for Poland he would not accede to what was the minimal demand of the *moderate* patriots: restoration of the Kingdom's legislature and independence, its union with the empire to be maintained merely through the person of the sovereign. This was the "idle dream" which Alexander had decried in 1856. He had hoped that a series of palliatives, such as staffing the administration with Poles and restoring the institutions of higher learning abolished by Nicholas, would stem the rising tide of discontent and violence. But of course such measures had the opposite effect. The local authorities floundered in indecision and the revolutionaries grew bolder. Between 1861 and mid-1862 four successive Russian viceroys tried alternative policies of toughness and concession, each having to acknowledge within weeks that he could not control the situation. The atmosphere can be illustrated by a story which, though confirmed by both Polish and Russian sources, still sounds fantastic. In October 1861, as we have already seen, Russian troops entered some Catholic churches in Poland to clear them of demonstrators. Thereupon all places of worship—Catholic, Protestant, and Jewish—shut down in protest. The then viceroy, Charles Lambert, bitterly quarreled with the commander of the Warsaw region, General Alexander Gerschtenzweig, over what he thought were the latter's needlessly provocative measures. Each viewed this dispute over public policy as a personal affront, and agreed that it was an affair of honor which must be resolved by what was then known as an "American duel," drawing lots, with the loser pledging to commit suicide. Gershtenzweig lost and shot himself. Lambert resigned.[3]

By the beginning of 1862 plans for a Polish insurrection had ripened. The more conservative among the nationalists, known as the "Whites," set up what was in effect an underground government. Collaborating with it to some extent but bent upon a more radical political program was a committee of the "Reds," whose leader was Jaroslav Dombrowski, captain formerly of the general staff but assigned in February 1862 to Warsaw.

We have already met Dombrowski[4] as a member of the Polish revolutionary officers' circle in Petersburg which was headed by Sierakowski and undoubtedly had connections with Nicholas Obruchev and other military members of what became Land and Freedom. And here we come to the serious side of this conspiracy—its infiltration of the officer corps of the Russian troops stationed in Poland. One of the main organizers of this infiltration was Andrew Potebnya, an infantry lieutenant of Ukrainian descent and a former military schoolmate of Dombrowski's. In 1861 Potebnya was already in contact with Herzen, keeping him informed of the existence

[3]V. M. Misko, *The Polish Insurrection of 1863,* Moscow 1962, 73. How this appalling practice came to receive this name is a mystery. The average literate Russian's knowledge of America was then largely based on novels by James Fenimore Cooper and Harriet Beecher Stowe.
[4]The usual Polish spelling is Dąbrowski.

of this revolutionary circle of Russian officers. In April 1862 three Russian officers in Poland were court-martialled for spreading revolutionary propaganda among their soldiers and were sentenced to death. Potebnya's answer was to shoot and wound the acting viceroy, Alexander Liders, on June 15, 1862. He then went underground and in the course of the year visited the London exiles several times, bringing with him lists of fellow members of the officers' revolutionary group.

Their number, at least on paper, was impressive.[5] To be sure most of them were not directly connected with Land and Freedom. A sizeable proportion was, as it might be expected, of Polish origin. And, as events were to show, most were not revolutionaries eager to overthrow the tsarist government (even though in *its* eyes they were traitors subject to hard labor and worse if unmasked), as was Potebnya, but simply progressive young men unwilling to serve as armed oppressors of their own or of any other Slavic nation. But what has been said here about the overall amateurishness of Land and Freedom must now be qualified, for its military branch undoubtedly served as the initiator and catalyst of the secret officers' organization in the Kingdom of Poland. And it is only reasonable to assume that some of its members and sympathizers in the war ministry and the general staff were instrumental in having people like Dombrowski posted for duty in the area, which quite predictably and quickly became a theater of a military insurrection.

Yet from the beginning the cooperation between Russian revolutionaries and Polish nationalists was beset with ominous ambiguities which were eventually to lead to tragedy for Poland, and a grave setback not only for the revolutionary cause in Russia but for Russian liberalism as well. Relations between the two nations had known periods of friendship as well as of conflict. The history of revolutionary movements in both nations bears witness to close cooperation and heroic sacrifices for the common cause. But there is one word which is very difficult to use when characterizing the attitude of either side, even in such joint endeavors: trust.

With tragic premonition, the Poles always suspected even their warmest Russian friends of what Lenin himself was to suspect his fellow Bolsheviks: "Scratch a Russian Communist and you will find a Great Russian chauvinist."[6] And the most Polonophile Russians could never shake off the suspicion that to a Polish nationalist, even a "Red" one, Polish independence meant not only freedom for ethnically Polish areas, but also, as in the days of the old Polish Commonwealth before 1772, Polish lordship over regions

[5] The list, reconstructed largely from Ogarev's private notes, has 449 names on it. V. A. Dyakov, "Herzen, Ogarev, and the Committee of Russian Officers in Poland," in a volume of M. V. Nechkina, ed., *The Revolutionary Situation in Russia, 1859–1861,* Moscow 1963, 3–81.
[6] *Protocols of the Eighth Congress of the Communist Party* (1919), Moscow 1933, 107.

where the gentry and city-dwellers might be Polish but the vast mass of the population was Ukrainian and Byelorussian and hence, in the thinking of an average nineteenth-century inhabitant of the empire, of *essentially* Russian nationality. We have seen how far the progenitors of Land and Freedom, the *Great Russian* committee, were willing to go in meeting such Polish aspirations, and how they admitted that in the case of a successful revolution Ukrainians and Byelorussians could themselves choose with which country they would become associated. But with some "scratching" —i.e., with the moment of insurrection approaching and with the Polish underground government openly proclaiming its intention to liberate not only Poland proper, but those Ukrainian, Byelorussian, and Lithuanian lands that were currently integral parts of the empire—the most fervent Russian revolutionary and friend of the Polish cause was bound to experience a conflict between his nationalist feelings and his revolutionary convictions.

For their own part, the Polish nationalists could not quite shed the apprehension that their Russian friends wished them success mainly so as to have them help overthrow their own hated regime; they were not without that expansionist itch which once in power seemed to the Poles always to afflict their fellow Slavs, whether conservative, liberal, or socialist. Bakunin and, in a more serious sense, Herzen were of course recognized as genuine friends of Polish freedom. But even *they* talked at times of a federation of Slavic nations, membership in which was to be, of course, entirely voluntary, all national partners absolutely equal, but still. . . .

For the more conservative Poles the mere espousal of their cause by the Russian radicals was already an embarrassment and danger. They had no faith whatsoever in the success of a revolutionary movement in Russia or in its ability to render them significant help. They counted on such help from the Great Powers, France mainly and then Britain and Austria. And it did not aid the Polish cause in the eyes of the West European courts and cabinets that it was being espoused by international anarchists and socialists. And for the Russian revolutionary, the albeit tempestuous collaboration between the Polish "Reds" like Dombrowski and the "Whites," with their roots in the gentry, the business world, and the Catholic clergy, made him wonder whether a successful Polish revolution might not perpetuate the Polish landlord's sway over his Ukrainian and Byelorussian, not to mention his Polish, peasants.

To be sure emissaries of the Polish revolutionaries reached a sort of agreement with Herzen's group in September of 1862, and with the Russian center of Land and Freedom in December, which was ambiguous enough to assuage both sides. The Poles, while still proclaiming their goal of recovering the frontiers of 1772, promised that non-Polish areas would enjoy equality and presumably (though this was not spelled out) the right of

secession. They also reassured their Russian associates that the aim of their
revolution was not only national but also social, and that the peasants would
be freed with land (again they did not spell out details). For their own part
Herzen on the London end and Utin in Petersburg assured the Poles that
the Russian revolutionary movement would throw all its resources into the
struggle against the common enemy. But they begged them to postpone
their rising until *the* day: that spring of 1863 when the "Don, Volga, and
Urals" were supposed to respond. The Poles would not promise this. Already they could hardly contain the hotheads in their own camp, and they
pointed out to their Russian interlocutors that the number of peasant
uprisings was catastrophically declining: as against 784 riots in 1861, the
number in 1862 had fallen to about a half and they were now on a much
smaller scale.[7]

Meanwhile the emperor had not abandoned his efforts at conciliation of
his unruly subjects. In the spring of 1862, Grand Duke Constantine, well
known for his liberal views, was appointed viceroy. The actual administration of Polish affairs was entrusted to a native, Marquis Alexander Wielopolski. Few even among the most radical of his countrymen considered
Wielopolski a "collaborator" in the sense rendered odious during World
War II. He was genuinely convinced that any attempt to win independence
through an uprising was foredoomed, that the hopes his excitable fellow
nationals put in Napoleon III or the Russian revolutionaries were chimerical. To him the path toward eventual freedom led through evolution and
through cooperation with Russia, a country which, if liberally minded,
presented less of a danger to the Polish nation than the Germanic powers.
But he was also a man of abrasive and authoritarian character, and his
advice to the Grand Duke turned out to be fatal. On June 21 Constantine
was shot at and wounded by a tailor's apprentice. Wielopolski then declared
that those who wanted to dishonor the Polish nation through such criminal
acts should direct their fire against him, and he had his wish granted: two
unsuccessful assassination attempts against him followed. All three would-
be assassins were publicly hanged.

If some of the Poles understood the mood of the Russian masses better
than Herzen, Wielopolski for his part showed a crass misunderstanding of
his countrymen's psychology. It is just possible that Constantine, who
despite his experience remained bent upon conciliation, would have won
over the "Whites" and avoided catastrophe. But Wielopolski "knew" his
countrymen and "knew" that only exemplary severity would cure them of
their senseless dreams. He now thought of a way to weed out the more
hot-headed among them: a special conscription levy was secretly set for the

[7]Joseph Kowalski, *Russian Revolutionary Democracy and the January Uprising,* Warsaw 1949,
97.

night of January 2–3; those forcibly conscripted would then be sent for army service in the depths of the Russian Empire, and they would include the most turbulent city youths, the rank and file of the revolutionary movement. Warned by its agents within the administration, the underground government ordered an uprising. The would-be recruits fled the cities into the countryside, formed partisan bands, and attacked isolated Russian units.

Without foreign intervention the Polish uprising was doomed to failure. Some twenty or thirty thousand poorly armed partisans (sometimes with nothing but scythes mounted on poles) could not hold out against upward of 100,000 regular Russian troops. Yet as the memoirs of Russian statesmen of the period indicate, the first reaction of the imperial government was one of virtual panic. The regime had more than an inkling of the relations between the Polish insurgents and the Russian revolutionaries. Tsar Alexander II, in his first public reaction to the outbreak of guerrilla war in his Polish kingdom, said, "[It is] the work of the revolutionary party striving everywhere to subvert the legal order. I know that this party counts on traitors within our own ranks."[8] Muraviev the Hangman, before setting out on the mission where he would earn that sobriquet, paid a visit to the empress and found her in a defeatist mood: "Oh, if we could only hold on to Lithuania [i.e., the northwest provinces of the empire]," she is alleged to have said.[9] Poland proper was evidently in some circles considered as good as lost.

This gloom reflected the fear that the Polish insurrection in addition to provoking internal disorders in Russia would bring the intervention of the Western powers. On April 5, Britain, France, and Austria addressed notes to the Russian court reminding it that under the Treaty of Vienna of 1815 Russia undertook to respect Poland's internal autonomy, and that the cause of the present disturbances and the general threat to European peace lay in Nicholas' abrogation of this autonomous status for Poland in 1832. But —and this situation was to repeat itself much more tragically after World War II—the Poles' hopes that the West would save them from Russian oppression were to be exposed as vain. As on the latter occasion, the Western powers' intervention on behalf of the unfortunate country was limited to diplomatic rhetoric. As the imperial government realized this and its initial fears receded, it haughtily informed France and Britain that they had no right to interfere in Russia's internal affairs.

But the Polish insurrection was to have momentous international repercussions. Russia's only diplomatic ally in Europe at the time was Prussia, already guided by Bismarck. And so Alexander's government watched with

---

[8] He was addressing army officers. S. Nevedensky, *Katkov and His Times,* St. Petersburg 1888, 170.

[9] *Ibid.,* 196.

indifference, if not indeed satisfaction, when Prussia trounced Austria in 1866 and France in 1870–71, and established a united Germany, a new nation which was to become the dominant continental power and a much greater threat to Russia during the next seventy years than an autonomous or independent Poland could ever have been. (Another, indirect result of the Polish insurrection was that the American flag now waves over Alaska. The United States government, then in the middle of the Civil War, in view of Britain's and France's rather friendly attitude toward the Confederate States, refused to join in the remonstrations on behalf of Poland. "The federal government," wrote a grateful Prince Gorchakov, Russian foreign minister, "has thus given an example of straightforwardness and honesty which has increased the respect of our August Sovereign toward the American people." And as a token of gratitude the emperor in 1867 sold the then barren waste for $7 million to the U.S.[10])

Relieved of its fears about foreign intervention and spurred on by a nationalistic upsurge in public opinion, the government embarked in the spring and summer upon a policy of ruthless suppression. To the northwest provinces went Muraviev, and we have already recounted his exploits there. In Poland proper, Grand Duke Constantine, who pleaded to the last for a policy of moderation and conciliation, was replaced by another elderly martinet, General Theodor Berg. While not a tyrant quite in Muraviev's manner, Berg's shortcomings in this respect were amply compensated for by the barbarity of his chief assistant, Trepov. When the ladies of Warsaw donned mourning for their country as well as for their sons, brothers, and husbands dead in the fighting, Trepov ordered that any woman wearing black would be fined.[11] By midsummer 1864 the uprising had sputtered to an end. Members of the Polish underground government were apprehended, and on August 5 five of them were publicly hanged. (Strange coincidence: every major revolutionary eruption in nineteenth-century Russia, those of the Decembrists, this uprising in Poland, and the People's Will in 1881, was to end with the gallows claiming five victims.) Poland lay prostrate: some twenty thousand insurgents had been killed in fighting, four hundred executed, and upward of eighteen thousand sent to hard labor and exile in Siberia.[12]

What had happened to the Russian revolutionary movement all this while? Why did not the "Don, Volga, and the Urals" respond to Poland's cry for help in her fight for freedom? What of some five hundred officers of the imperial army who pledged never to lead their troops against fellow Slavs seeking their rights?

[10]Tatishchev, *Emperor Alexander II*, St. Petersburg 1903, I, 487.
[11]*Ibid.,* 476.
[12]Misko, 317.

On the news of the uprising Herzen unhesitatingly threw his support to the Polish cause. But he was soon made to realize that it was one thing to support the Poles when they were demonstrating for independence, and another when they were killing Russian soldiers. In Herzen's entourage there was at the time one Peter Martianov. Born a serf, he could claim with some justification to be the only genuine representative of "the people" among the London exiles. As early as May 1, 1861, when *The Bell* had espoused the cause of Polish freedom, Martianov came to Herzen and said, "Today you have buried *The Bell*."[13] And Martianov would have nothing further to do with men who justified the killing of their countrymen. He went back to Russia, where as a reward for this patriotic gesture he was immediately arrested and given five years at hard labor. (His crimes included not only consorting with "the Russian exiles in London" but also the fact that in writing a letter to Alexander II he had signed it "your humble servant" rather than as a dutiful subject should, your "most loyal servant.")

But the common sense of a peasant could not prevail over the heady influence of Ogarev and Bakunin. Herzen's personal attachments as well as his genuine compassion for the sufferings of the Poles made him throw his last restraints to the wind. In February 1863 Sleptsov, who had witnessed the beginning of the uprising in Warsaw, arrived in London. There he assumed a lordly tone with Herzen, demanding that *The Bell* become formally subordinate to the Central Committee of Land and Freedom (in effect to himself). Herzen's first impulse was to show him the door, and he told the self-proclaimed leader of the Russian revolution that he did not believe that Land and Freedom amounted to much. Yet within days the pleas of his friends made him change his mind. Hence a grotesque agreement was reached between Ogarev and Herzen on one hand and Sleptsov on the other that the former would become official representatives of Land and Freedom abroad and *The Bell* would be its official organ.[14] On February 28 Herzen and Ogarev published a letter in London's *Morning Star* telling the whole world "that all secret societies in Russia have now been united under the leadership of its Central Committee into one *large* organization called Land and Freedom, expressing all the desires of the Russian people: the right of everybody to have land and an elective and federal government."[15] All Russians abroad were invited to join.

This formal affiliation could not bring anything but harm both to the cause of Poland, now in the eyes of the West allied with the international

[13]N.A. Tuchkova-Ogareva, *Memoirs,* Moscow 1895, 183.
[14]Alexander Herzen, *Works,* Michael Lemke, ed., Petersburg 1919, 10, 96.
[15]J. I. Linkov, *The Revolutionary Struggle of A. I. Herzen and N. P. Ogarev and the Secret Society "Land and Freedom" of the Sixties,* Moscow 1964, 344. My italics.

revolutionary movement, and to Land and Freedom, which to many of its former sympathizers, especially within the officer corps, must now appear to have passed the boundary between revolutionary dissent and outright treason. Previously one could believe oneself to be a good Russian and yet wish for the freedom of a fellow Slav nation. Now, with wild stories circulating of Polish partisans butchering Russian soldiers asleep in their barracks, and with the main European powers threatening the empire, many a young radical began to feel that it was not the tsar's government that was being challenged but the Russian nation. Land and Freedom's proclamation to the Russian soldiers in Poland—"Instead of . . . killing Poles, turn your sword against the common enemy: leave Poland with her stolen freedom restored and come here to our fatherland to free it from the cause of all national miseries—the imperial government"—was to fall on deaf ears.

What help the Russian revolutionaries were able to render their Polish comrades centered on two incidents, one to conclude in a tragedy, another in tragicomedy.

The tragedy took place in the province of Kazan. Here an enterprising Pole, Jerome Kieniewicz, decided to stir up a peasant uprising à la Pugachev. A Moscow Land and Freedom member, Julian Benzenger, prepared for him a fake imperial manifesto to give to the peasants, in which the emperor granted land immediately and freely, freed the peasants from all taxes and military duties, and urged them to fight any officials who would try to thwart his will. Kieniewicz had thousands of these phony declarations printed on a secret press in Vilna.[16] Despite some doubts about this technique for inciting peasants—which were based, as Herzen said, not on the inherent immorality of the enterprise, but on the fact that it perpetuated the myth of the emperor's benevolence—Kieniewicz enlisted the assistance of some Polish-born officers and a group of Kazan students. The plans included not only stirring up the countryside but also seizing the city of Kazan. But before the scheme could get very far it was denounced to the authorities by one of the participants. In April–May 1863 most of the plotters were arrested. Kieniewicz and the officers among the conspirators were ordered shot, others sentenced to hard labor. Thus ended the only attempt to raise the ghosts of Razin and Pugachev in the very area in which they had once inflamed the peasant masses.[17]

The irrepressible Bakunin was not going to watch a rebellion and merely cheer on the sidelines. Along with a group of Polish emigrés he procured an English steamer which was to carry the little legion and some munitions through the Baltic to a landing place where they could join with the Polish partisans fighting in northern Lithuania. The English captain's apprehen-

[16]Kowalski, 217.
[17]The story is colorfully related in E. H. Carr, *The Romantic Exiles,* London 1949, 267–84.

sions, anxiety about encountering a Russian man-of-war, and finally the British government's instructions to its diplomats in Scandinavia led to the group's being sequestered in a Swedish port. Some of the expedition members slipped out in a boat, but after several of them had been drowned trying to land near the Russian border, the rest returned in discomfiture to England. Bakunin himself spent several months in Sweden trying to recruit natives for the revolutionary cause, but in October he too skulked back to London. His breach with Herzen now became complete and the two erstwhile friends were to follow different political paths.

As for the revolutionary officers' organization, its help to the Polish cause fell tragically short of what had been expected. The sudden, and from its point of view premature, eruption of the rebellion made it impossible for its members to bring their units over to the partisans' side even if they had planned to. Jaroslaw Dombrowski had already been arrested in 1862[18] and Potebnya was to die while fighting with a Polish guerrilla unit. Sierakowski, who assumed command of the uprising in western Lithuania, planned to occupy the small port where Bakunin's ill-fated expedition was supposed to land. But his outfit, which was better organized and led than most of the partisan bands, was surprised and surrounded by a superior Russian force. Wounded and taken prisoner, Sierakowski was on Muraviev's personal order denied a soldier's death by shooting and, like a criminal, hanged. Thus died a man whose personal qualities and idealism were commemorated by Herzen and Chernyshevsky, and who had been one of the most insistent advocates of the abolition of corporal punishment in the Russian army.

But a mass defection among the officer corps, hoped for by the revolutionaries and feared by the government, did not take place. A recent Soviet study lists only about a hundred officers as having joined the uprising and of them an overwhelming majority were Polish.[19] The imperial authorities, displaying rare intelligence, allowed some commanders of doubtful loyalty to take sick leaves, or transferred them away from the theater.

"We hold Poland for our own self-preservation. . . . We have never reaped any benefit from our rule of the Polish Kingdom. . . . The Russian nation has shown that while it sympathizes with the real Polish people this is something vastly different from a self-betrayal [of its own interest]."[20] The writer of these words now became the voice and inspiration of that Russian nationalism which for the moment had buried the hopes of both the Russian radicals and the Polish insurgents. More than that, Michael Katkov's im-

[18]He would escape from a Moscow jail in 1864 with the help of some future participants in the Karakozov affair. In 1871 Dombrowski would be killed while commanding the forces of the Paris Commune.

[19]V.A. Dyakov and I.S. Miller, *The Revolutionary Movement in the Russian Army and the Uprising of 1863,* Moscow 1964, 163.

[20]M. N. Katkov, *Collection of Editorials for 1863,* Moscow 1897, 245.

passioned rhetoric and demagoguery did something the tsarist government's repression and chicanery could never have achieved alone: it dealt
a final blow to Herzen's mastery over the educated Russian's mind. It is not
too much to credit Katkov with the articulation of that militant nationalism
which has marked modern Russian history—which survived the empire of
the tsars, had its rebirth in the Soviet Union when threatened by foreign
enemies in the 1930s and 1940s, and remains to this day the most dependable
psychological bulwark of the Soviet regime. It is difficult to think of Chernyshevsky living and writing in Soviet Russia, inconceivable in the case of
Herzen, but with a few minor changes and updatings in his fiery editorials
of 1863 and 1864 you can imagine Katkov as a leading publicist for Stalin
or Stalin's successors—thundering against the renegades who, for the profit
of the foreign enemy, slander the democratic traditions of the Russian
nation and try to destroy its greatness by encouraging dissent and disunity
within the Russian state.

On the Polish issue Katkov performed a tour de force reminiscent of
Stalin's argument during World War II that it was the Polish Communists
in Moscow, and not the government in exile in London and its underground
in German-occupied Poland, who represented the majority of the nation;
or Brezhnev's that the Soviet intervention in Prague in 1968 was necessary
to save the Czechoslovak people from the designs of NATO and the "West-
German revanchists." As Katkov expressed it: "The Polish state was the
property of the Polish nobility. . . . The real Polish people were betrayed
by their nobles to the Germans. The inhabitants of Silesia, Western Prussia
are ethnically Polish, but instead of defending their ethnic brothers and
leading them, the nobles pushed eastward, and profiting by the historical
misfortunes of the Russian people enslaved them brutally. . . . Poland torn
away from Russia will inevitably be taken over by Germany."[21] And so in
fighting against the Polish movement for independence Russia was selflessly
struggling to save the Polish people from its exploiting upper classes, as well
as frustrating the designs of the international revolutionary movement.
Change the last two terms to "capitalism," rephrase Katkov's alleged solicitude for the freedom of the Slavs by "the interests of the socialist camp,"
and his editorial might well appear in *Pravda*.

And yet this apostle of Russian chauvinism and imperialism came from
the same intellectual milieu which produced Herzen, Belinsky, and Bakunin, and he had been their close companion in his university days in Moscow. Along with them he had decried the oppression and inanities of the
Nicholas era. A man of wide erudition and learning, this future enemy of
cosmospolitanism had initiated Belinsky (who did not know German) into
the philosophy of Hegel and Schelling. Katkov seemed destined for a bril-

---

[21] *Ibid.*, 241, 245.

liant university career, and it was only the government's decision to suppress the teaching of philosophy as conducive to subversion which turned him to journalism. The Alexander era found him a liberal proponent of an English-type constitution for Russia. Even as late as the 1850s he protested against the oppression of Poland and the civil disabilities endured by Jews. What turned this talented and enlightened man into a reactionary who applauded Muraviev the Hangman and considered the more liberal members of Alexander's government traitors? It was principally what he conceived to be the danger to Russia and the government's initial pusillanimous reaction to it that triggered off this transformation. But there was a personal element as well.

In the early 1860s Katkov was one of those who repeated, perhaps not without a touch of envy, that Herzen was the second, unofficial government of Russia. As his old acquaintance became more radical, Katkov saw an opportunity to challenge him for this high position. In 1862 in his *Russian Messenger* Katkov attacked the London exiles in general and Herzen in particular. The exiles, he said, were allowing themselves to become tools of the international revolutionary conspiracy, which, despairing of success elsewhere, had decided to destroy Russian society. "Our foreign refugees find that Europe has passed its [revolutionary] apogee, that revolution there cannot succeed because of such obstacles to progress as science, civilization, freedom, i.e., the rights of property and person . . . hence the blessed thought to choose Russia for their experiment, where, in their opinion, those obstacles are not strong enough or do not exist. . . . [They believe] she will let be done to her what one wills, will submit to anything that would be insufferable in any other society."[22] It was in its way a perceptive judgment on those revolutionaries who believed that "in our backwardness lies our salvation." As for Herzen himself, Katkov attacked him in terms suggesting an old-standing personal bitterness, but again he did not fall short of the mark: Herzen was intellectually restless and irresponsible, he claimed; incapable of moderation, he either praised the regime with extravagant affectation—"Thou hast conquered, O Galilean"—or attacked it in most inflammatory tones.

To a degree Katkov succeeded in his bid for power: by the mid-1860s he had become a political and intellectual force in Russian life. His *Russian Messenger* enlisted the collaboration of such greats as Turgenev, Leo Tolstoy, and Dostoyevsky and achieved a circulation second only to that of *The Contemporary.* In 1863 Katkov also secured control of the newspaper *Moscow News,* and began his evolution toward an extreme reactionary and chauvinistic position. He was no longer satisfied with a "populistic" ratio-

[22]Quoted in N. A. Lyubimov, *Michael Katkov and His Historical Achievements,* St. Petersburg 1889, 200.

nale for the Russian position on Poland, or with mere verbal attacks upon
the political exiles. All of Russia's internal problems and troubles were now
seen as the result "of a perfidious Jesuit plot." (The Catholic Church and
hence the Jesuits were assumed to be allied with the Poles; this has its
analogy in the "Zionist–Wall Street conspiracy" so favored by Soviet propaganda until the arrival of détente.) It was this plot which had been responsible "for the complete anarchy in our system of education," for liberal
professors teaching "cosmopolitanism and atheism," and for the absurd and
subversive notion that there was such an entity as the Ukrainian nation.[23]
Katkov, whose doctoral dissertation had been in linguistics, now assured
the reader that the Ukrainian, not to mention the Byelorussian, language
did not exist; they were just local dialects; and if an inhabitant of Kiev
province talked a bit differently from a Muscovite, it was only because long
years of foreign rule had polluted his basically Russian speech with a few
Polish words and usages. In the 1870s the imperial government was to ban
books and publications written in the "Little Russian dialect." Not until
1906 was Ukrainian officially acknowledged as a separate language.

Katkov's undoubted popularity did not make him "a second government" in the sense that Herzen had been between 1857 and 1862: he lacked
that moral force and eloquence which made the London exile listened to
and respected by all shades of opinion from conservative to revolutionary.
Yet for a while his hold on the mind of what might be called the middle
Russian—the average landowner, city merchant, lower government official
—was very strong indeed. He appealed to their freshly aroused nationalist
indignation against the "jesuitical Poles," to their fears of "nihilists" who
were corrupting their children and wanted to abolish the family and private
property, and to that craving people frequently experience when confronted
with a perplexing social and political crisis, a craving to blame the whole
thing on some far-reaching plot. Several associations and bodies of nobility
presented Katkov with messages of thanks for his stance, and the Moscow
Old Believers asked him to draft an address to Alexander II expressing their
loyalty and patriotism in this hour of Russia's danger.

This last item must have led to particularly bitter reflections on the part
of Ogarev and the Land and Freedom Committee. One of the most fertile
fields of revolutionary agitation, they had thought, lay among the Old
Believers, subject as they still were to religious persecution and civil disabilities. In fact Herzen and Ogarev put out a few issues of a journal directed
especially at this persecuted religious minority, with Vasili Kelsiev as a sort
of revolutionary minister in charge of propaganda among religious dissenters.

But in fact the whole revolutionary enterprise, both at its London and

---

[23]Katkov, 326.

domestic ends, was by the middle of 1863 in shambles. *The Bell*'s circulation fell from its previous high of 3000 to about 500. Even more important, most of its Russian contacts and correspondents were swept by nationalist hysteria and stopped writing for it. The atmosphere in London became suffocating for Herzen. His companion spoke for him when she wrote, "Certainly among Englishmen there are a lot of fine people, but the exiles had to deal with the acquisitive bourgeoisie, the most unpleasant class everywhere and especially in England."[24] In 1864 he and his entourage resumed their continental wanderings. *The Bell* was transferred in 1865 to Geneva. But its old resonance was gone, and in 1867 the journal that had once been the voice of hope and freedom for all that was best in Russia concluded its brief existence.

By the end of 1863 the same could be said of Land and Freedom. A loose confederation of "circles," the conspiracy depended on the energy and enterprise of a handful of leaders. But its most active organizer, Sleptsov, had been out of Russia since January, and when he became ill that year he abandoned all revolutionary work, returning home in 1864 to resume a decorous civil-service career. The most fiery of the younger leaders, Nicholas Utin, fled Russia in May to avoid arrest, his Polish contacts having been uncovered. But his life continued to be tempestuous. He joined the First International,[25] and in the struggle which ensued for its control between Bakunin and Marx took the latter's side; it was he who proposed on behalf of Marx's followers the resolution which led to Bakunin's expulsion at the meeting of the International in 1872. Incongruously Utin at the same time became a foreign representative of the Russian railway magnates, the Poliakovs, and was undoubtedly in Bakunin's mind when he indulged in his vulgar anti-Semitic outburst against Marx: "Himself a Jew, he attracts whether in London . . . or especially in Germany, a whole heap of Yids, more or less intelligent, intriguers, busybodies, and speculators as Jews are likely to be, commercial and bank agents . . . who stand one foot in the world of finance and the other in socialism."[26] In 1877 Utin's influential employers secured for him a pardon and permission to return to his native land.

Nicholas Obruchev's career, as we have noted, was but briefly interrupted. But in a strange and indirect way he was to contribute to the greatest revolutionary enterprise of all. It was he who in 1892 worked out with his French opposite number the exact procedures which the two general staffs would follow in the case of an outbreak of war with Germany. And to a large extent these plans were put into effect in August 1914. And

[24]Tuchkova-Ogareva, 102.
[25]The initial reason for this union of radical and socialist organizations, founded in 1864, was to render help to Poland.
[26]Y. M. Steklov, *Fighters for Socialism,* Moscow 1923, I, 288.

thus General Obruchev was one of the chief military planners of the great conflagration which destroyed the empire and made possible that revolution which he as a young officer had so fervently believed in and worked for.

There still lingers an air of mystery about Land and Freedom, the first attempt to create a revolutionary party in Russia. Certainly it is striking that while quite a few of its rank-and-file members were apprehended, most of the leaders escaped not only arrest but also, apparently, detection. Even more striking than the case of Obruchev is that of Sleptsov. In 1863 the Polish underground government's delegate for Lithuania, Oskar Aveyde, was arrested in Vilna. Threatened with the gallows, Aveyde made a full and lengthy confession which the imperial authorities thought was so revelatory that they published it in 1866 in book form. There, in black and white, is mentioned "one Sleptsov" as a member of the central committee of Russian revolutionaries who had contacts with the Poles.[27] Granted that this is not an unusual Russian name, still one would think that somebody in the Third Department or the ministry of finance, where Sleptsov then served, would have scratched his head: could this be state counciller Sleptsov who had traveled so much abroad in 1860–63? But Sleptsov went on undisturbed, retiring in 1886 with a generous pension and the order of St. Stanislaus.[28]

The end of Land and Freedom (it was dissolved by its remaining members early in 1864) did not mean the extinction of the revolutionary tradition, however. On the contrary, various ideological and tactical components of the defunct organization—conspiracy, socialism, populism—remained in the soil of Russian radicalism and would re-emerge in different combinations in future revolutionary enterprises.

The revolutionary mood of the 1860s passed into popular parlance both in Russia and abroad under the name of nihilism. Few terms have had as dazzling and long-lasting careers. Nihilism, not without a strong contribution from such writers as Katkov, who should have and did know better, became a stereotype for everything which was deemed revolutionary, anarchist, and antisocial in Russia, especially among the young. The term caught on in the West, and as late as November 1917 some quite respectable British and French journals informed their readers that the party which had just seized power in Russia was that of the "nihilists" headed by Lenin.

Real nihilism in the beginning meant something quite different. Its prototype was of course Eugene Bazarov, the hero of Turgenev's *Fathers and Sons,* which appeared in 1862 and created a veritable storm in the intellectual and radical establishment. Reading Turgenev's masterpiece today one

---

[27] *Confessions and Notes about the January Uprising by Oskar Aveyde,* Moscow 1961, 494, 496.

[28] His premature retirement was due to his incompetence, Panteleyev writes poisonously, 331. He himself, not so lucky as Sleptsov, was denounced in 1864 by an arrested Polish insurgent, and spent several years in Siberian exile.

feels that he treats his nihilist with a sympathy bordering on pity, and that his nihilism is first cousin to what we would call alienation (also an abused and overused term). "Bazarov needs and fears no one, loves nobody, and consequently does not spare anything or anybody."[29] He rejects all faiths, conventions, and ideologies, anything he does not need or cannot control. In brief he stands for the defiant spirit of youth, except that his self-assurance and indifference to others makes defiance almost superfluous. In fact, writes Pisarev approvingly, his hostility to polite conventions comes out of "the same impulse which makes Americans put their feet on the table and spit tobacco juice on the floor of a luxury hotel."[30] The only worthwhile pursuit for Bazarov is natural science, and Turgenev makes him die (with perhaps more symbolism than the critics noticed) from an infection he catches while dissecting a corpse.

Though the book does not lack an occasional light touch it is a serious and compassionate depiction of the perennial conflict of generations. But while the "men of the sixties" were in other respects very un-Victorian they were amply endowed with that moral earnestness so characteristic of the era. So *Fathers and Sons* was received not as the great novel it is but as either a caricature or a defense of the "new men" and their ethos—nihilism. Among the radicals it was widely and incorrectly believed that the character of Bazarov was based upon the recently deceased Dobrolyubov. Michael Antonovich, a poison-pen reviewer for *The Contemporary,* not only attacked Turgenev, with whom the magazine had long accounts to settle, and derided the novel as being of no artistic value, but took Bazarov as a libel on all progressive youth.

But Turgenev found a defender in an unexpected quarter: Dmitri Pisarev, the new star of radical journalism (b. 1840), defended the artistic merits of *Fathers and Sons* and proclaimed Bazarovshchina-nihilism not as a term of opprobrium but as a realistic and positive description of the attitude of young *intelligentsia.* "If Bazarovshchina is a sickness, then it is a sickness of our generation, and it must be gone through. Look at it as you will, that is up to you, but you will not be able to stop it."[31] Bazarov's sort of nihilism represents most of all the enormous strength and self-confidence of the new generation, its ability to look at life soberly and scientifically.

Turgenev was rather appalled by the controversy his novel aroused. One of the few great Russian writers who would not assume the mantle of a prophet or social activist, he was by the same token a man of moderation and humane impulses, and—the usual fate of such a person—became the object of attack and derision from both the reactionary and the revolution-

---

[29]Dmitri J. Pisarev, *Works,* St. Petersburg 1897, II, 386.

[30]*Ibid.* Why is it always our less admirable characteristics which arouse the envy and emulation of Russia's youthful dissenters?

[31]*Ibid.,* 384.

ary camps. Bismarck after a conversation with him expressed the opinion that Turgenev should be Russia's prime minister, a suggestion which at first strikes one as jocular, but on second thought Russia could have done, in fact did, worse.

The conflict in the radical camp between *The Contemporary* on one hand and *The Russian Word,* on the other of which twenty-two-year-old Pisarev was the leading light, went beyond the merits of *Fathers and Sons.* To an outsider both were organs of nihilism and to the conservative their internecine quarrel a source of great amusement. But in fact it was only *The Russian Word* which proudly claimed the banner of nihilism as its own, and to the followers of *The Contemporary* nihilism at first had a far from positive (that is, revolutionary) meaning. Did it not extol individual selfishness and lack of concern for the social question? Why did not Bazarov propagandize the peasants rather than spend all his time dissecting frogs and corpses? And the editor of *The Word,* Blagosvetlov, for all his revolutionary connections had a reputation of personal dishonesty[32] which unlike Nekrasov's could not be excused by poetic genius.

But such subtle distinctions were beyond the Third Department. Following the fires in the spring of 1862 both *The Contemporary* and *The Russian Word* were suspended for eight months. Pisarev, like Chernyshevsky, found himself behind the walls of the Petropavlovsk fortress.

The circumstances of Pisarev's arrest and ordeal throw a grim light on the morals not only of the government but of some revolutionaries as well. In June the police had arrested a former student, Peter Ballod, and found in his possession a hand press and a number of revolutionary proclamations. One which he had not succeeded in distributing was entitled "The Russian Government under the Protection of Schedo-Ferrotti." The latter was a pseudonym for a government propagandist who had been commissioned to write a pamphlet against Herzen, which was publicly circulated in Russia. Though tendentious it did not transcend the bounds of civilized polemic. It chided rather than vilified Herzen for his views and in fact it was attacked by Katkov as an example of the government's softness toward subversion. Ballod had decided to print a violent reply to this provocation by the government.

At this point his acquaintance Pisarev had confided that he was brokenhearted over his beloved's recent marriage to someone else. As the poor standard-bearer of nihilism confessed, in a very un-Bazarov-like fashion, "Before, I thought, I shall get married, I shall have a loving wife, I shall earn four thousand a year in journalism. And now it is all dust."[33] In order to forget his sorrow, he wanted to join a revolutionary circle. Ballod ex-

---

[32] *The Sixties: Memoirs of M.A. Antonovich and G. Z. Yeliseyev,* Moscow 1933, 313.

[33]Quoted in B.V. Gorev and B.N. Kozmin, eds., *The Revolutionary Movement of the Sixties,* Moscow 1932, 133.

plained that the revolutionary circles had dispersed for the university summer vacation and he would have to wait until the fall; but perhaps in the
meantime he could draft a suitable reply to Schedo-Ferrotti's libel of
Herzen? Pisarev obliged, and his personal anguish undoubtedly contributed
to the pamphlet's violence, to passages culminating in such denunciations
as: "The Romanov dynasty and the St. Petersburg bureaucracy ought to
perish."

When this document was found among Ballod's papers, he without much
prompting revealed its authorship to the police. Prudence as well as compassion would have dictated leniency: Pisarev was a popular writer, and he
suffered from intermittent mental illness. And he pleaded for mercy in
heart-rending terms: "I am so young, so prone to be carried away, often I
cannot rationally weigh my words and actions."[34] But he was imprisoned
in the grim fortress for four years. Strangely enough, and mainly through
the intercession of that veritable guardian angel of political prisoners,
Prince Suvorov, the authorities allowed Pisarev to continue his journalistic
career while imprisoned, his pieces appearing in *The Russian Word* on its
revival in February 1863. Released in 1866, Pisarev drowned, possibly a
suicide, two years later.

The puerility of much of Pisarev's writing, his proneness to enthusiasm
over the latest quasi-scientific intellectual trends,[35] should not make us
overlook the fact that he wrote much that was thoughtful and significant.
He became notorious for a scathing attack on Pushkin, calling him, for
example, a "lofty cretin." But when he forgot to try to shock, the young
critic referred to the poet as one of those with "real, vast talent" who, like
Shakespeare, Cervantes, and Byron, would always be read.[36] His most
famous and startling statement is often taken as the essence of nihilism:
". . . here is the slogan of our camp: everything which can be destroyed must
be so; only that which can withstand a blow is worthy of preservation; what
falls into pieces is nothing but rubbish; in any case hit out left and right."[37]
But the actual context of the piece in which this alleged call for universal
anarchy is made makes it clear that Pisarev is making a very sensible plea,
especially for the Russia of his day, that *intellectual* traditions and fads
should not be made into cults, and their representatives (even Chernyshevsky, whom he respected) should not be elevated into prophets. "One
will say, 'but Hegel says. . . .' Another would answer, 'so what?' " This was
not a superfluous warning in a society where intellectual discourse often

[34]Lemke, *Political Trials in Russia of the 1860s,* Moscow 1923, 563.

[35]He took seriously such scientific discoveries of the school of Feuerbach that the subjection
of the Irish to the English had a biological basis: how could a nation which subsisted on
potatoes resist one which grew strong on roast beef?

[36]Pisarev, II, 200.

[37]*Ibid.,* I, 375.

turned on what the infallible authority—be it Chernyshevsky, Tolstoy, or Karl Marx—had to say on the subject, and where even today practically every book on social and political and philosophical problems carries the sacremental "as V. I. Lenin wrote. . . ." And then there is another piece of advice which many might well heed: "What is of least use to the young generation is precisely to praise it inordinately. The more you want to help the young the less you should talk about their virtues, but think rather about their intellectual needs. . . . Make sure that a young man who picks up a journal for amusement . . . will find in it a reasonable spectrum of opinions and a thoroughly civilized approach. . . . Then you will see that the youth will consider you as their friend, even if you do not say a single word in their praise."[38] Pisarev did not always follow his own precept, but how different this is from the doctrinaire and didactic tone of Chernyshevsky, Dobrolyubov, or Lavrov!

And so nihilism *in its original meaning* was quite different from that cult of negation and universal anarchy which the term became known for in the popular mind, an incorrect definition that has spilled into the pages of serious historical works. But in a way this distortion is understandable. Few people can abide by the imperative of nihilism as Pisarev formulated it: to reject all traditional authority and convention and to examine each idea and institution in the cold light of reason and utility. The real-life Bazarovs soon yearn for a dogma, and for a wider field of activity than their laboratory. And if conventional morals and religion were but superstitions, didn't political goals and activism transcend any ethical considerations whatsoever? Thus the nihilist, in the popular stereotype, became a revolutionary who believed that the end justified any means, including terror. And then this stereotype crowded out the original meaning. In the 1860s, those whom society considered nihilists, and who in many cases accepted this description of themselves, came to reject the original popularizer of the term: in their eyes Pisarev was a phrase-monger, prattling about the necessity of self-improvement and of critical examination of every ideology; while they craved commitment and believed they were chosen by history to remake the world.

Those whom society called nihilists were in fact in most cases Chernyshevsky's "new men," and their bible was *What Is To Be Done?* George Plekhanov, the father of Russian Marxism, wrote, "We have all drawn [from the novel] moral strength and faith in a better future. . . . From the moment when the printing press was introduced in Russia until now [the end of the nineteenth century] no printed work has had such success as *What Is To Be Done?*"[39] This was quite a claim in a century which had seen

---

[38] *Ibid.,* III, 266.
[39] George Plekhanov, *Works,* Moscow 1924, V, 115.

Dead Souls, War and Peace, and *The Brothers Karamazov.*

Chernyshevsky wrote his masterpiece in the Petropavlovsk fortress. That this work, full of revolutionary allusions and written by an imprisoned state criminal, was passed by the censor and published legitimately might appear and in fact is strange. Vladimir Nabokov explains it by suggesting that the government thought that the novel was so inept and unconsciously funny that it would cover its author and the revolutionary cause with ridicule. But though this judgment of its artistic merits must be endorsed by today's readers, it is unreasonable to credit the tsarist authorities with such discernment and such touching faith in the literary taste of the younger generation. The real reason was an administrative foul-up, and the fact that the censor who passed on it was a man of progressive ideas.[40]

Subtitled "Tales of The New Men" (with no sexist connotation: on the contrary), the book is a rather preposterous mixture of a mystery story, a sentimental romance, and social utopia. But if the characters drawn by Chernyshevsky seem fantastic it is because they are largely based on real people of those fantastic times, members of his entourage. The heroine, Vera Pavlovna, is mainly drawn from Maria Obruchev, sister of Vladimir. This "new woman" in order to escape her hateful parents contracts one of those "blank marriages," so fashionable at the time, with a medical student, Lopukhov—again taken from a real character, Chernyshevsky's own doctor and friend, Peter Bokov. In the novel the spouses have separate bedrooms and meet only in the neutral zone of the drawing room to drink tea and hold interminable discussions about the philosophy of life. Then another man appears in Vera's life, and to clear the road for his friend Lopukhov blows his brains out. Vera then settles down to real marital bliss with her beloved, also a "new man" and medical student, Kirsanov. Years later a mysterious "North American Beaumont" appears, marries a patient of Kirsanov's (now a famous doctor), and the two couples decide to "live in harmony and friendship, at once quietly and boisterously, gaily and actively."[41] Does the "perspicacious reader," as Chernyshevsky addresses him repeatedly, have to be told that Beaumont is really Lopukhov, who had only simulated suicide?[42]

But it was not this exemplary romance–friendship combination which

[40]Nekrasov, who was to publish it in *The Contemporary,* lost the whole manuscript while returning home at night from a party. Fortunately for the future course of Russian radicalism it was found and returned by a passerby.

[41]N. G. Chernyshevsky, *What Is To Be Done?,* Moscow 1939, 564.

[42]Panteleyev, who knew and hated Bokov, questioned this traditional decoding of the figures of the novel. The Obrucheva-Bokov marriage, he claims, was a real one, and it broke down because Bokov was an incorrigible seducer of his female patients. And it was only in 1875 that Maria linked with "Kirsanov," in real life the well-known physiologist Ivan Sechenov. Bokov's medical and romantic practice flourished allegedly because of his "Lopukhov" fame. Panteleyev, 335.

enraptured readers, for whom both "blank" and "civic" marriages were old stuff, so much as two other elements in the novel. One was Vera's social activism. She organizes seamstresses' cooperatives, where the girls work and live together and share the profits equally—clearly an echo of Chernyshevsky's one-time infatuation with the idea of phalansteries developed by the French utopian socialist Fourier. Also in line with Fourier's ideas are Vera's dreams where she sees society freed from poverty and oppression and where women have become liberated. The whole country had been transformed into one vast flowering garden, with occasional palaces of glass and steel which are centers of mirthful and elevating social activity: "Everybody lives as he wishes."

But of course this utopia will not come of itself or even through the propagation of cooperative communes. Throughout the book there are veiled hints of a coming revolution. And Chernyshevsky offers us the archetypal "new man," who might be called the positive nihilist, Rakhmetov. Though from a noble and rich family, Rakhmetov, like Bazarov, is brusque and scornful of polite convention. He reads only books which are original and written in a scientific spirit; everything else is trash. But unlike Bazarov he cares for the people, and he eats only the kind of food which in any given locality can be afforded by the poor. The only exception to this rule is raw beef, which Rakhmetov consumes in huge quantities to give him strength, presumably for his future revolutionary tasks. Also, as part of his revolutionary training he sleeps on nails. Rakhmetov is evidently derived from Chernyshevsky's notion of himself (the ability to decide in five minutes whether a given book is scientific or trash!), the Polish patriot Sierakowski, and an absolutely unbelievable but real eccentric named Bakhmetev. (Bakhmetev visited Herzen in London, deposited with him a fund for the revolutionary cause, about which later, and then set out to establish a socialist community on some Pacific island near New Guinea. He was never heard of again.)

It is easy to be sarcastic about *What Is To Be Done?* and the radicals' reaction to it: cooperatives of every sort burgeoned all over the Russian social landscape; many young men developed digestive troubles in trying to emulate Rakhmetov's consumption of gigantic portions of raw beef. One must note also that the "great revolutionary democrat" shows himself something of an elitist and a snob. His "new men" are quite sure that they stand above the vulgar multitude and that it is up to them to remake the world. Rakhmetov's noble lineage is dwelt on in great detail.

But then on second thought one begins to feel a certain sympathy with Chernyshevsky and an understanding of the reaction this silly book evoked. As if in a convex glass, the characters of *What Is To Be Done?* represent Chernyshevsky's own aspirations and the pathetic realization of how far short he fell of them. Rakhmetov is a man of great physical strength and self-assurance: Chernyshevsky was frail and awkward in dealing with those of higher social status. Lopukhov easily becomes a "North American": Chernyshevsky, who read voluminously in all major European languages, could not understand or deliver a single intelligible sentence in any of them. (His only trip abroad to see Herzen was almost aborted when he misplaced his only suit in a German hotel, and his efforts to find his way around in London attracted small crowds who, with shouts and in sign language, would try to instruct the gentleman speaking an incomprehensible gibberish which he believed was English.) The almost continuous revelry in his postrevolutionary utopia is again a compensatory dream of a bookworm whose only diversion was his work. And, most poignant of all, the cloudless marital bliss of his two couples reflect the writer's lifelong uncertainty whether his idolized wife reciprocated his affection.

Equally saddening are some of the deeper reasons for the popularity of the book. "How sad is our Russia!" Pushkin is supposed to have said after reading Gogol's *Dead Souls.* How gay is the Russia of Chernyshevsky's fantasy! Here young men and women overcame that peculiar heaviness in Russian life which permeated every social relationship, be it the family or the workshop. They dared to be free and happy and their existence was both individually satisfying and socially constructive.

What, then, stood in the way of this human spontaneity and fulfillment? Of course it was the ubiquitous government, and in a way it was unimportant how liberal the tsar was, or how much land the peasants got. It was still the autocracy, Big Brother was watching you, even if the imperial government did not have the technological accoutrements of Orwell's twentieth-century monster. It is not surprising that we find in the men of the sixties some of the same anxieties and aspirations which our own overpoliticized and overindustrialized world breeds in the young, and that their quest for a new faith and for fellowship led them to revolutionary strivings.

III

THE POSSESSED

"ONLY IN SAVAGE and decadent na-
tions is history made by assassinations," wrote Herzen in 1866 when the
news of Karakozov's shot reached him in Geneva. This condemnation of
terrorism by the father of the Russian liberation movement infuriated many
of the "new men" who considered Karakozov a martyr for liberty. The
tempestuous Alexander Serno-Solovievich, whom we have already met as
one of the founders of Land and Freedom and as the lover-victim of Mme.
Shelgunova, made this remark one of the central points in a scathing
indictment of Herzen which he circulated among the Russian emigrés:
"Your statement about Karakozov: those words you will never be able to
live down."[1] Can one draw a line between revolutionary violence-terrorism
and crime, between fanaticism on behalf of a political cause and madness?
For many Russian radicals those distinctions had by 1865–66 become
blurred, and we shall try to see why.

What is more puzzling is that the problem has received but little attention
from most Soviet historians, and is equally ignored by those Russian and
foreign writers who, while not Communist, are sympathetic to the nineteenth-century revolutionary movement. Yet it is precisely the people who

[1]Michael Lemke, *Studies in the Liberation Movement of the Sixties,* St. Petersburg 1908, 270.
Serno was soon to beg Herzen for forgiveness. Trying to flee the monstrous woman who kept
putting him in an asylum, he sought temporary shelter with the man whom he had denigrated,
and Herzen compassionately granted it. In 1869, convinced that he was really going mad, the
tortured young man committed suicide.

revere the Russian revolutionary tradition who should be most eager to establish the distinction. Whatever one thinks of terrorism as a means of political struggle, one ought to recognize a vast difference between those who advocated and followed that path in the 1860s, and the terrorists of the People's Will of the late 1870s and 1880s. Morally, politically, and psychologically the main figures in the two movements were almost entirely different breeds. Karakozov, Ishutin, Khudyakov, and Nechayev, who are the chief characters in the drama this section unfolds, were all clearly psychopaths. Under investigation and during the trial most of those connected with the Karakozov affair cringed, implicated each other, and begged for mercy. Though their activities had a political background, no one who studies their story can fail to conclude that what mainly prompted them was a sheer passion for violence.

How different in all those respects are the leaders of the People's Will— Tikhomirov, Zhelyabov, Vera Figner, and most of their associates; fanatics or idealists, depending on one's viewpoint, but in any case people whose sanity cannot be questioned. To be sure, there were morally repugnant incidents in the activity of the People's Will, even in terms of revolutionary ethics, yet what motivated most of its members was a sincere belief that terror was a legitimate weapon of struggle against a government that allowed no legal outlet for political dissent. Before the court, with their lives at stake, most of the assassins of Alexander II, and later on, Vera Figner, were proudly unrepentant, and their testimony became an indictment of the regime, which in their view criminally oppressed the people of Russia.

And yet . . . even the heroes of the People's Will would acknowledge Karakozov and Nechayev as their predecessors in the struggle for freedom. The cult of violence among the Russian radicals reminds one of the history of many a religion: conceived first by a fanatic who somehow convinces a small group of followers to accept his pronouncements for reality, it grows with the passage of time into a faith and ritual observed by quite reasonable people. The zealots among them will take literally the preachings of the founder. Others will observe only the external requirements of the cult but view with awe and occasional envy those who give witness to their faith by deeds. Even after 1906, when Russia did have a parliament of sorts, solid lawyers, professors, and doctors, people who themselves would not and could not have perpetrated the slightest act of violence, would still "understand" and even openly approve the assassination of a tsarist official, and sigh over the fate of the culprit if apprehended. Such assassinations in time were taken as facts of life by the population at large in imperial Russia. "It is nothing to you . . ." said a policeman to a questioning passerby, after Pleve, minister of the interior, was blown up by a bomb in 1904. "He whose business it was got killed."

How did this cult of violence get started? The main thrust of revolutionary propaganda and activity prior to 1864 was not (except in Warsaw in 1862) toward acts of *individual* terrorism. The revolutionaries wanted Russia to "lift up the axe," that is, they wanted the peasant masses to rise, but Land and Freedom hoped then to utilize and control this uprising and not allow it to become an indiscriminate slaughter of landlords and officials. To be sure, there was some strong language in those revolutionary proclamations: "we would not hesitate to slit up the throats of 100,000 landowners" in *To the Young Generation,* but still, no call for individual acts of terror. Such distinctions are very important for the history and psychology of the Russian revolutionary movement. *Young Russia* is an exception; it was imbued with a lust for violence, and indeed its author, Zaichnevsky, shared quite a few traits with the terrorists of the Ishutin-Nechayev school.

The revolutionaries of that period did toy with the idea of individual terror. Yeliseyev, whom we shall meet again, was reputed to have contemplated kidnapping the heir to the throne to force the tsar to grant a constitution. Also unverified is a story passed on by Panteleyev: after a young collaborator of *The Contemporary* committed suicide, Chernyshevsky allegedly commented that if one is going to kill oneself anyway, it would be silly not to take someone else with him.[2] But in his serious moments Chernyshevsky, as well as the most radical members of Land and Freedom, would have conceded that killing "someone else," i.e., the emperor, would have been the greatest mistake the revolutionary movement could make. The masses believed in the tsar, especially the peasants, who blamed the shortcomings of the Emancipation on the officials and nobles. A regicide would be pointless; another Romanov would take over. It would most likely also lead to a pogrom of the radical *intelligentsia;* the urban masses had been quite close to this in 1862 when they held the "nihilists" guilty of widespread arson.

But after 1864 such rational considerations and inhibitions were more likely to be brushed aside. Russian radicalism found itself defeated and leaderless, and with the extinction of Land and Freedom the "new men" —or nihilists, to give them the now generally accepted name—lapsed into a multitude of tiny groups. Much more than before 1862, these groups began to resemble little sects, their members no longer united by faith in an imminent revolution, but sustained in their subversive activities by their sense of the real and alleged injustices which society, or as they would put it the regime, had inflicted upon them, and by an almost mystic belief that the day must come when their own and the Russian people's wrongs would be avenged. The nature of their membership had also undergone a change. The army officer or bureaucrat who was also a part-time revolutionary had now become a rarity. He either had been alienated from radicalism during

---

[2]L.F. Panteleyev, *Memoirs,* Moscow 1958, 296.

the nationalist reaction which followed the Polish uprising, or had concluded after the great disillusionment of 1863 that he should steer clear of politics. The literary people and *intelligentsia*, in general mindful of the fate of Chernyshevsky and Pisarev, also grew more prudent. Most of the *intelligentsia* who had been members or fellow travellers of Land and Freedom were still hostile to the regime and faithful to the idea of revolution, but their relations with the activists became more circumspect.

The latter now tended to be recruited very largely amongst students and ex-students drawn from plebeian and poor gentry backgrounds, many of them misfits who could not have found a profession under any circumstance, eking out their livelihood by private tutoring or with charity donated by their more affluent comrades. Hating the regime, feeling themselves betrayed by "society"—i.e., the radical *intelligentsia* who, they believed (not without some foundation), stood ready to applaud others' revolutionary deeds but without exposing their own persons to danger—they wove phantasmagoric dreams of violence directed not only against government officials, but as in Nechayev's case also against those of their fellow radicals who were too fastidious or prudent to resort to terrorism. The erstwhile great names of the movement meant little to them or had become odious: Herzen in his luxurious abode in Switzerland, alternatively sighing over and extolling the new men; even Pisarev, prattling about the need for self-improvement and the guiding light of science. The real nihilists, in contrast, rejected scientific pursuits as well as all professional activity, thus partly rationalizing their personal failures. As one of them said, even higher education was an impermissible luxury when the people were oppressed and ignorant: "The mass of the people is uneducated, and hence we do not have the right to study. . . . One does not need to know much to explain to the people that they are being deceived and robbed."[3] One figure with whom most nihilists identified was the martyred Chernyshevsky. Their main form of nonviolent political activity, and a meeting ground with radicals of a different ilk, was to organize those cooperatives–communes which had been extolled in *What Is To Be Done?* as the most effective way of propagandizing the masses. But it was really the Rakhmetov aspect of the novel which fascinated the young hotheads: he did not content himself with cooperatives and Sunday schools but was in constant training to become a professional revolutionary, obviously (though Chernyshevsky could not spell it out) to perform some deed that would change the course of history.

What the nihilist hated and feared more than anything else was the prospect of Russia's peaceful evolution into a constitutional society—in which case all his preparations for revolution, all his self-denial, would be

---

[3]M.M. Klevensky and K.G. Kotelnikov, eds., *The Karakozov Attempt: A Stenographic Account of the Trial of D. Karakozov, I. Khudyakov, and N. Ishutin,* Moscow 1928, I, 8.

in vain. As Ishutin was to testify, he had told his comrades that if the liberals were to prevail, "The people's condition will become a hundred times worse than now, because they will devise some form of constitution . . . and will make Russian life like that of the West; this constitution would find support in the middle and upper classes because it would *guarantee personal freedom* and prompt the growth of industry and commerce but would not prevent, but rather facilitate the growth of the proletariat and pauperism."[4]

The unhappy possibility that Russia would receive liberties and institutions of the Western variety never appeared stronger than in 1864–65. With a stroke of pen, Alexander II transformed Russia's judicial system from Europe's most backward into one of the most progressive in the world. To conceive of what justice in Russia had been before 1864 it is well to list the essentials of the reforms that were enacted in that year: "The judicial branch was separated from the executive. . . . In civil suits judicial organs were divorced from the administrative ones, in criminal ones from the prosecution. . . . Trials were to be public, both civil and criminal, judges were made irremovable. . . . The institution of the prosecutor was introduced, and so was the Bar, i.e., independent advocacy. . . . Appellate courts were created."[5] Juries, defense lawyers, open trials—this against the background of the Romanov autocracy seemed like a dream come true and must have disturbed the spirit of Nicholas I more than anything else. The reform was greeted with an enthusiasm in which even a man as reactionary as Katkov now was could join.[6]

The other reform, which at the time seemed hardly less momentous, was the 1864 law introducing local self-government in provinces and counties of the Russian parts of the empire. To be sure, the system of election to these assemblies assured their domination by the gentry, but the peasants as well as the middle class were also to be represented, though the emperor angrily rejected the suggestion that this was a step in the direction of a national parliament. Many people, including the representatives of the Moscow nobility who voted in this sense in January 1865 by a majority of 270 to 36,

[4] *Ibid.*, 8. My italics. The Soviet commentator adds, "This is pure Populism"; as we shall see, it is not.
[5] Tatishchev, *Emperor Alexander II,* St. Petersburg 1903, 523.
[6] On many issues this spokesman for Russian jingoism retained vestiges of his previous liberalism. He continued to argue the cause of civil emancipation of the Jews, and perhaps no one in the history of Russian journalism approached him in his admiration for American democracy and the conviction that Russia and America were natural allies. "An alliance with the United States would be for us the only desirable alliance . . . whose consequences would be incalculable for civilization and general progress." M.N. Katkov, *Collection of Editorials for 1866,* Moscow 1897, 374. In both cases, to be sure, there was nationalistic rationale for Katkov's pleadings. Emancipated Jews, he hoped, would become russified and thus an additional element of strength for Russian rule in Poland, the Ukraine, and Lithuania, where they constituted a sizable proportion of the urban population. An alliance with the U.S. would be a warning to Britain, then Russia's rival in Asia, and a barrier to her ambitions in the Balkans.

felt that the edifice of reforms should be crowned "by an assembly of representatives of the Russian land to consider common needs of the country."[7]

As against this panorama of progress and nationwide approval, how insignificant seemed the activities of the revolutionaries, whether quarrelling abroad at the deathbed of *The Bell* in Geneva, or ineffectually weaving their schemes of violence and revenge in small circles of Petersburg and Moscow. "Official" Russian radicalism as represented by *The Contemporary* and *The Russian Word* appeared to be divided by a struggle partly ideological and literary, partly, one suspects, motivated by competition for subscribers, since their circulation had been affected when the educated class became cooler toward radicalism, and by the inroads of Katkov's *Russian Messenger.* Always on the lookout for rising literary talent, Nekrasov secured for his journal the collaboration of Michael Saltykov-Shchedrin. But this great satirist, a man of progressive views, allowed himself in 1864 to indulge in some literary and philosophical criticism of *What Is To Be Done?,* and this brought forth a burst of thunder from *The Russian Word,* where Pisarev (still in the fortress) published a denigrating critique of Saltykov's own literary efforts. (Saltykov was in any case already under a shadow in the radical camp. He had been a civil servant, and in 1861 as vice-governor of Tver he had received and turned over to the police a copy of *The Great Russian.* The handwriting on the envelope was deciphered as that of Vladimir Obruchev.) In brief, when both reaction and constitution were threatening, the remains of the revolutionary movement, those to whom young people had previously looked for guidance, engaged in senseless philosophical and literary squabbles.

The revolutionary activist's sense of isolation and betrayal was increased by a literary campaign against radicalism which began in 1863 with the publication of Alexis Pisemski's *Troubled Seas,* and continued with a whole wave of so-called anti-nihilist novels.[8] Though among the writers were people of great artistic achievement such as Ivan Goncharov and Nicholas Leskov, the literary merit of the typical anti-nihilist novel may not unfairly be compared to that of *What Is To Be Done?* (Turgenev's and Dostoyevsky's literary descriptions of the radical milieu cannot, of course, be put in the same class.) In fact their theme and moral is often that of Chernyshevsky's novel turned upside down. The hero is almost invariably that archetypal nihilist the student, but how dissimilar in his characteristics from Lopukhov or Rakhmetov! Weak morally and physically, he is easily seduced without any real conviction on his part into some ruinous and subversive political enterprise, the villain-seducer being in most cases a Pole. The

[7]Tatishchev, I, 525.
[8]*See* Charles A. Moser, *Anti-Nihilism in the Russian Novel of the 1860s,* The Hague 1964.

sexual mores of the heroes and heroines of the anti-nihilist novels are what might be expected, but bitter indeed are the fruits of those illegal couplings! These sinful people do not as in Chernyshevsky "live in harmony and friendship, at once quietly and boisterously, gaily and actively." They live in fear and shame. Broken lives, miscarriages, and suicide are the final retribution for the immature rejection of religion and patriotism.

SEVEN

HELL

The old saw that life is stranger than fiction is dramatically illustrated by the story of Organization, the group from which came Dmitri Karakozov, the would-be assassin of Tsar Alexander II. No author of an anti-nihilist novel would have dared to project a tale as fantastic as that of the Karakozov attempt. Dostoyevsky's *Possessed* is based very largely on the Nechayev affair, as revealed to the Russian public in the beginning of the 1870s. It still strikes us, as does the story which inspired it, as almost surrealistic in the horror it evokes. But Nechayev's activity was a replay, almost certainly consciously so, of one act of the Karakozov drama: the plan of some members of Organization to create a special subgroup of assassins, appropriately named Hell, who would perpetrate acts of terror not only against government officials, wealthy nobles, merchants, etc., but also against such of their comrades as refused to submit to their rule. Karakozov himself would today doubtless be declared not responsible for his actions by reason of insanity, and he was a tool in the hands of two people who had exhibited signs of serious mental instability and who were to end their lives mad: Nicholas Ishutin and Ivan Khudyakov.

About the latter we have the priceless testimony of an *Autobiography*, written in exile in Siberia before darkness overcame him, and somehow smuggled abroad, where it was published in 1876.[1] Though Khudyakov manages, for obvious reasons, to conceal or distort his various con-

---

[1] Reprinted in 1930 in Moscow under a rather misleading title, *Notes of a Karakozovite.*

spiratorial enterprises, he is quite uninhibited about his personal life and only a bit less so about his political feelings, and they make a pathetic story.

Born in 1842, he came from an old Siberian family of petty officials. At the age of five he had an unpleasant experience which according to his own testimony marked him for the rest of his life: he kept pulling a horse's tail (an unreasonable diversion, one would think, even for a child brought up among domestic animals), and the horse reacted appropriately. The kick in the groin laid the boy low for several months and, the Khudyakov believed, left him with the outward characteristics of a eunuch, a high-pitched voice and sparsity of facial hair.[2] Religious fervor and sexual worries marked his stay in the Tobolsk *gymnasium*. Neither is unusual at that age, but Khudyakov's comment on a common practice deserves to be quoted: in his high school, he tells us, masturbation was developed to a frightening extent. "Some by the age of eighteen have tasted of the tree of knowledge not less than one thousand times and that at a time when blood is much needed for growing and strength."[3] He graduated with a gold medal, but the tensions to which he alludes left him a veritable skeleton.

For a boy from a Siberian backwater, a university town like Kazan might have appeared to offer enough diversions to cure an excessive introspection, especially in those euphoric post-Nicholas days, but Khudyakov was an eternal malcontent and killjoy. Kazan was known in the 1850s as the drunken university, but our young man refused to partake of this traditional ingredient of student life. He read Herzen and became a freethinker and republican. Believing Kazan hopeless, and having participated in some demonstrations against unpopular professors, Khudyakov transferred to Moscow, where he expected to find teachers more interesting and students more civically minded, i.e., radical. On both counts he was disappointed. Professors were either dull or taught their subject from the official point of view or both. Soon Khudyakov was suspended for complaining about an allegedly abusive teacher. Readmitted, he found himself in the tempestuous student autumn of 1861. He went back to Kazan to receive a candidate's (master's) degree, which would enable him to teach in regular schools, and again his aim was frustrated by the intrigue of an unfriendly professor.

By 1862 the young man had developed considerable interest in Russian folklore, in collecting popular songs and folk tales. But though his first two little books were published, the authorities were bound to look with suspicion at an ex-student engaging in this type of activity: after all, a whole body of literature for and about peasants had arisen which under the guise of preserving folk wisdom and educating the masses sought to indoctrinate the latter with "untrustworthy ideas." Khudyakov's proposal to edit a journal

[2] *Ibid.,* 23.
[3] *Ibid.,* 29.

devoted to folklore was vetoed by the ministry of education, his new compilations were stopped by censorship. He sought a job as a university librarian, but the Petersburg curator of higher education, Ivan Delianov—then reputed a liberal, later on a very reactionary minister of education—was unfavorably impressed by the young man's appearance. "Are you engaged in political dreams?" he asked, adding that all such dreamers were, as in poor Khudyakov's case, pale.[4] The interview ended on a "don't-call-us, we'll-call-you" note.

It is not surprising that the young man's sense of being persecuted, already strong in his school days, was nourished and grew stronger through such incidents. He had a high opinion of his own literary and scholarly work —he proudly recalls that some contemporaries thought him a veritable magician for being able to extract such riches from popular tradition. But the same government which in his eyes was somehow responsible for the deplorable self-abuse of Tobolsk high-school students, now through censorship barred his way to literary and scholarly fame. In 1862–63 Khudyakov was undoubtedly on at least the periphery of the revolutionary movement, and attended social-political gatherings of the radical youth.

One such evening was to have a decisive influence on his life. At a musical soiree in the apartment of Vladimir Lebedev (who had been wounded and imprisoned during the student riots of 1861) he met the latter's sister, Leonilla. It was at first the usual story in the style of *What Is To Be Done?*: Leonilla wanted to get away from her hateful mother but needed money to be on her own and join a commune. The unsuspecting Khudyakov (he still cherished the memory of his childhood sweetheart, though she now had a "civic" husband) hired Leonilla as his research assistant at twenty-five rubles a month. But it was not folklore or the commune that the young girl really had her eye on. Soon a research session was interrupted by an embrace, and three evenings later Leonilla fell on his bosom and the "civic" marriage was consummated. Khudyakov's health improved, and he was overjoyed to have a wife who shared his political views. But, alas, Leonilla now pleaded for a legal marriage, on grounds that it would bring her an inheritance of 3000 rubles which they could give to the cause. Khudyakov reluctantly agreed; he tells us touchingly that he believed that since he had lived among many families and under various situations he could cope with marriage and cohabitation. The hateful church ceremony was endured. But then . . . "I was happy, in love, only till the marriage." His wife began to neglect her duties as his research assistant. What was worse, "all her energy now went into the most passionate physical love. Farewell my moderation, farewell my health."[5] Like many a husband Khudyakov discovered that his

[4] *Ibid.*, 68.
[5] *Ibid.*, 92–93.

wife was very much like her mother whom she had hated for her bourgeois ways: Leonilla craved creature comforts, was lazy, capricious, and quarrelsome. She was also, the poor man adds, very unlike himself physically: strong and beautiful. Occasionally Khudyakov would think of suicide, but then would revert to the hope of reforming Leonilla, who was after all a good nihilist basically and whose excesses were undoubtedly caused by her mother who had always made her wear a corset!

Such was the inner tragedy of the youth whom Professor Franco Venturi calls "one of the most typical figures of the Populism of his times and unquestionably one of the men who best expresses the ideology of the entire movement."[6]

By Khudyakov's own testimony it is rather difficult to discover what his ideology was. In prison he was to write a memorandum asking the tsar to grant Russia the "English type" of constitution. But this was a typical gambit of terrorists on trial for their lives. Even Nechayev, whose ideas on parliamentarism were hardly in advance of those of Ivan the Terrible, exclaimed before the court, "Long live the National Assembly!" Unlike the real Populists of the 1870s, Khudyakov had a low opinion of "the people." His researches among the common folk gave him a wider experience of peasant mentality than that possessed by most of his radical contemporaries. Peasants, in his own words, were ignorant, indeed stupid in the indifference with which they endured their exploitation. He put his hand to the kind of literature which in simple language and sometimes through the exploitation of a religious motif sought to stir up the masses, and to catalyze the peasants' allegedly instinctive antiauthority feelings into action, but he never had much confidence in that kind of activity. Like most men of the 1860s, his first preference was for conspiratorial work, and after the failure of 1863–64 his thoughts turned more and more toward a violent coup.

His actual conspiratorial work before 1865 cannot be traced with any precision. After the dissolution of Land and Freedom some of its former cells preserved loose contact with each other, as well as with some of the former leaders of the organization, such as Yeliseyev, collaborator on *The Contemporary,* as well as with Putiata (despite, as we have seen, the almost universal conviction in radical circles that he was a crook). The one revolutionary deed which can be definitely traced to collaboration amongst these fragments of revolutionary organization in Petersburg and Moscow was the arrangement for the flight of Jaroslav Dombrowski. Arrested, as we have seen, in Warsaw in 1862, he was by 1864 in a Moscow jail, in transit to hard labor in Siberia. On December 1 he skipped jail and for some days was hidden by members of Ishutin's circle. In January 1865 he was in Petersburg, sheltered by the Khudyakov group, and from there he fled abroad—

[6]Franco Venturi, *Roots of Revolution,* New York 1960, 338.

to fall fighting in 1871 as a general of the Paris Commune.[7]

But apart from this one success, the scattered and leaderless bands of conspirators could not point to a single tangible achievement between the dissolution of Land and Freedom and April 4, 1866. To be sure there was a lot of scheming, when young men and women met for an evening of revolutionary talk combined with tea and wine drinking. There were some abortive plots. It would be strange if Khudyakov, a native of Siberia, had not been in touch with those of his fellow countrymen and ex-students who in 1864–65 conceived an ambitious plan for a rebellion which would make the vast area an independent republic.[8] The main initiator of that plan, Nicholas Yadrintsev, later on a well-known publicist and ethnographer, was arrested in 1865. The seed of the misbegotten plot might have been planted by Herzen's editorial in 1862 where, writing of Poland's right to independence, he said *en passant* that if tomorrow Siberia declared her independence "we" would be the first to welcome it. Like all famous men he should have heeded the advice succinctly expressed a century later in a schoolboy's essay on John XXIII: "Since the Pope is infallible, he has to be very careful about what he says."

The recurrent motif in these nocturnal discussions and schemings after 1864 was the need to find some way to promote the escape of Nicholas Serno-Solovievich and, especially, Chernyshevsky, and indeed during the next fifteen years several attempts were made to free the spiritual father of the "new men." But for the conspirators even these important plans—not to mention the work on the cooperatives–communes where they encountered "respectable" radicals—was but a surrogate for real revolutionary action. How to overthrow the hated government? There was now a new target date for a peasant uprising: 1870, when, under the Emancipation Edict, the peasants could terminate their obligations toward the landlords whose tenants they were and leave their land, unless in the meantime the proprietors sold it to them. Hence the radicals' hope, weaker than before 1863, that this would be the day. But it was so distant! They would be middle-aged, and the way things were going, Russia might have a constitution by that time!

The assassination of Abraham Lincoln in April 1865 created, many contemporaries testify, great excitement among the Russian radicals. John Wilkes Booth's "Sic semper tyrannis" was being repeated with approval in some student circles.[9] This throws a curious light on the mentality of those

[7]M.M. Klevensky and K.G. Kotelnikov, eds., *The Karakozov Attempt: A Stenographic Account of the Trial of D. Karakozov, I. Khudyakov, and N. Ishutin,* Moscow 1928, I, 305.

[8]Some of them counted on help from the United States! More realistic were the expectations that thousands of Polish exiles in the region would join the uprising.

[9]From the recollections of Zemfir K. Ralli in B. V. Gorev and B. N. Kozmin, eds., *The Revolutionary Movement of the Sixties,* Moscow 1932, 139. Ralli was then a student in Moscow.

young people. To all progressive, not to mention radical, public opinion in Europe, Lincoln was a champion of freedom. The Confederate cause on whose behalf (as he imagined) Booth committed his deed was considered to be that of the blackest reaction. But assassination is a very exciting and often contagious thing. And so the idea of *individual* terror, with which some radicals had toyed, began now to be seriously discussed in revolutionary circles. To the more unbalanced members the deed itself was tempting, and even their more sensible colleagues began to look for a possible rationalization: perhaps killing the emperor would wake up the masses; or, if properly done and if the peasants still retained their idiotic faith in the tsar, they would blame the deed on the landlords and officials.

Though Khudyakov may not strike us as a born leader of men, he was by 1865 the guide of a small group of conspirators based in Petersburg. The reason for his position lay in his literary reputation as much as in his contacts with some former notables of Land and Freedom such as Gregory Yeliseyev, in whose house he once lived,[10] the poet and editor Vasili Kurochkin, and his brother Nicholas, a doctor, all of whom had been members of its central committee. People of that sort were not going to stick their necks out in a dangerous undertaking, but they maintained a discreet liaison with the activists, offering them advice and keeping informed on what the young hotheads were up to.

Two men in Khudyakov's group were especially close to him. One was Alexander Nikolsky, who married Leonilla's sister Barbara, and the other was Nicholas Nozhin.[11] Let us pause for a moment on Nozhin. He was a young man (b. 1841) with scientific interests. Between 1860 and late 1864 he lived abroad, studying at Heidelberg, in contact with revolutionary exiles, among others Bakunin. Returning to Russia, he struck up a friendship and shared an apartment with a contemporary, Nicholas Mikhailovsky, who one day would inherit the sceptre of Chernyshevsky and Lavrov as the intellectual leader of Russian radicalism.[12] Nozhin professed and affected the external appearance of a nihilist. In the summer of 1865 his sister Maria, being one of those damsels who could not bear her parents, by whom she was virtually imprisoned, escaped with his help, and, in view of her being underage, he was put under secret police supervision. But as we shall see, this supervision cannot have been very thorough.

To be sure there were other members of the group whom Khudyakov would not mention for a variety of reasons: obviously his other brother-in-law, Lebedev, who was to rat on him during the investigation; Herman

[10]E. M. Vilenskaya, *The Revolutionary Underground in Russia in the Mid 1860s*, Moscow 1965, 314.

[11]Kievensky and Kotelnikov, *The Karakozov Attempt*, I, 41.

[12]James H. Billington, *Mikhailovsky and Russian Populism*, New York 1958, 23.

Lopatin, who provides a living link between the conspirators of the 1860s and the People's Will, and whom we shall meet engaged in all sorts of revolutionary heroics in the 1870s and 1880s; and *possibly* Dr. Alexander Kobilin, the most enigmatic figure of all in the Karakozov drama. It would be difficult to estimate the exact number in Khudyakov's conspiratorial circle, and it was in the nature of things that there should be no clear dividing line between those who participated in a social evening when talk was rife about freeing Chernyshevsky and ridding Russia of the scoundrels who ruled it, and the people who put their heads together to accomplish these aims.

The other conspiratorial center, Ishutin's group in Moscow, was more organized. Nicholas Ishutin, first cousin[13] of Dmitri Karakozov, was born in 1840 in the Saratov province. Childhood and adolescent ailments, quite possibly of a mental nature, delayed his entrance to the *gymnasium* in Penza until the late age of fifteen, and he left in 1862 without graduating. From then on he was in Moscow, for a time as a free auditor at the university and in 1862–63 on the periphery of Land and Freedom.

In Ishutin we first encounter the revolutionary Svengali type of which the classic embodiment was Nechayev, a man who operated mainly through mystification and who consciously or unconsciously invented nonexistent organizations and plots to impress and gain power over the minds of his fellow conspirators. The political aims of the conspiracy, even of the terrorism, became secondary to his need to dominate others and secure absolute obedience from them. To be sure Ishutin was but a pale preview of Nechayev: he lacked the latter's personal magnetism, enormous energy, and gall, and was something of a coward, which certainly cannot be said of the latter psychopath.[14] But already in his Penza days, Ishutin had gathered a handful of followers, fellow students in the local schools who were impressed by his revolutionary talk and the intimations that he was a member of some secret organization. He renewed these contacts in Moscow and by 1863 headed a little group, the hard core of which were fellow alumni of the two Penza high schools, the *gymnasium* and the nobles' institute. Sometime in 1864 the group adopted the name Organization. Ishutin carried on his game: his fellow members were given to understand that he was in close contact with Land and Freedom, which actually had in the meantime been dissolved. Unlike some of Khudyakov's contacts and associates, members of Organization were with few exceptions very young, in their late teens or early twenties, without a definite profession, most often ex-students and

[13]In Russian, as in most Slavic languages, first cousins were called brother or sister once removed, and addressed each other accordingly.

[14]Ishutin broke down during the investigation and tried to shift responsibility for his own action and words onto others. During the actual trial his testimony was interrupted by fits of sobbing. Klevensky and Kotelnikov, I, 70.

auditors. (An interesting exception is Alexander Malikov [b. 1839], who had served in a provincial prosecutor's office. His role in Organization was secondary, and when eventually he was sentenced it was to "free" exile in European Russia. In the 1870s, abandoning his revolutionary beliefs, he organized a religious sect and was arrested again, this time for propagating heresy. He then lived for a while in a religious commune in the United States, returning to Russia in 1878 to pursue the prosaic occupation of a railway administrator.)

At its height, Organization is said to have had fifty-three members, though again it is difficult to see how one can be so precise.[15] And what a motley crew of characters they were! Some were just immature youths hypnotized by Ishutin, who after serving their sentences for collusion in the Karakozov affair were able to turn to useful professional life. A few remained lifelong revolutionaries but managed to shed that morbid criminal streak which characterized Organization. But there was also one Victor Fedoseyev, who by his own admission planned with the help of some comrades to poison his father in order to use his inheritance for the revolutionary cause. As for the economic situation of most of those young men, it ranged from that of Peter Yermolov, son of a rich landowner, to that of Osip Motkov, born a serf. Yermolov, to whom the trustee of his estate unwisely turned over large sums, practically financed the whole Ishutin enterprise. Motkov's story, as told to the trial court, was heartrending. His education, financed by a sponsor, had to be interrupted at fourteen because his father, formerly a cabman, became an invalid, and Motkov felt he had to earn money for his numerous family. They all lived in one small room in which his mother also worked as a laundress. He tried to give private lessons, but one after another of his employers would fire him because of his shabby clothes. He fell in with a member of the Ishutin group and they gave him help. Yermolov placed Motkov's ailing sister in a seamstress' cooperative; some others offered him rooms in their communes as well as a few rubles from time to time.[16] It is noteworthy that this sole representative of "the people" among the conspirators aroused great personal hostility among some of his fellow accused, and Khudyakov in his autobiography is scathing about Motkov, branding him a "denouncer." To be sure Motkov "sang" during the investigation, but so did the others, including Khudyakov himself. One has a strong impression that Motkov's relative lack of education and polish contributed to the antagonism.

In some ways Organization functioned like many other radical circles of the time: its members set up cooperatives–communes of seamstresses, bookbinders, etc., and carried on propaganda through the Sunday schools. But

[15]Vilenskaya, 418.
[16]Klevensky and Kotelnikov, II, 328–30.

Ishutin would not be content with agitation among the adults, although he had a plan to organize and instill revolutionary ideas in Moscow cabmen. An affluent sympathizer opened a free school for children of poor background with Ishutin as director and his comrades as instructors. "We shall make revolutionaries out of those tiny tots," proudly exclaimed the director.[17] But this school was shut down in June 1865 not by the authorities but by the founder, who found it a veritable bedlam. And the Ishutinists had other, more exciting things on their minds.

They are reputed to have been great admirers of Chernyshevsky, their leader being on record as saying that this great "revolutionary democrat" was one of the three great men of history along with Jesus and St. Paul. But it is clear that in trying to spring Chernyshevsky from Siberia they were motivated by some rather special reasons. "Yermolov said that Chernyshevsky, in return for being liberated, would have to pledge to publish a journal abroad, and that this journal would have the orientation prescribed by us and its whole content would be controlled by Organization."[18] The purpose was evidently not so much to free Chernyshevsky as to capture the writer and to turn him into a tool of Ishutin and Organization.

The link-up between Khudyakov's associates in Petersburg and Organization was in existence at least by the end of 1864. Most Soviet historians make an ideological distinction between the two groups: the Petersburgers were more moderate and political, Organization extreme and completely unconcerned with any political reform. But this is largely an unreal distinction. Both groups thought in terms of violence and, increasingly, individual terror. Khudyakov, being to some extent under the influence of older people such as Yeliseyev and the Kurochkins, was more deliberate and less prone to the wild fantasies spun by Ishutin and his comrades.

Whatever the difference in their approach, Khudyakov and Ishutin were in frequent contact during the first part of 1865. And in July Ishutin gave Khudyakov money (procured from Yermolov) for a trip to contact the Russian revolutionaries in Geneva. Khudyakov had another reason for going abroad: he hoped to shed, at least for a while, his insatiable wife. But Leonilla insisted on tagging along. Occasionally by this time she would drive her usually abstemious husband to the nearest bar. "Now I understood why many husbands become hopeless alcoholics," said Khudyakov.

Despite her enervating presence Khudyakov accomplished quite a bit during his August-November stay in Europe. He wrote and printed in Geneva a pamphlet entitled *For True Christians,* a collection of real and invented maxims from the Bible to be used for propaganda work among the peasants[19] and purporting to show that religion teaches that kings should

[17]*Ibid.,* I, 305.
[18]*Ibid.,* I, 309.
[19]Venturi, 342.

be elected and land held communally. He saw a lot of revolutionaries, but found most of the older emigrés not to his taste. Herzen lived in a lordly manner and would offer only 150 francs for the revolutionary work in Russia. To be sure, Khudyakov found a more kindred spirit in Ogarev, and it is possible that it was the latter who fed him the political fantasies which he was to repeat with such fatal consequences on his return.

Khudyakov could have stayed longer had it not been for his wife. He conceived a strategem: he would go back alone. "I was hoping they would arrest me and send me far away."[20] Leonilla, without any means of her own, would remain abroad and find a lover or, alternatively, would seriously pursue her vocation as a singer.

Khudyakov's revulsion against his own society comes out vividly in his description of the return voyage. Once you entered Russia, he noted, at every station there were masses of soldiers and policemen. On his train, "the first- and second-class carriages [were] full of officials of the Third Department and other bloodsuckers and in the third class a revolting mess of Baltic Germans, Yids, Latvians, etc."[21] And his hopes of a quiet life upon his return were soon shattered. He was not arrested, and, worse, Leonilla reappeared on the scene. At first Khudyakov would not agree to renewed cohabitation, but soon she prevailed upon him to take her back "for one month."

Open as he was about his personal life, Khudyakov was quite rational and even clever about concealing his conspiratorial links and not saying anything that was not already known to the authorities by the time he wrote (1867–68). It is from other sources that we learn what he reported to Ishutin and others about his impressions abroad. According to depositions before Muraviev's investigating committee and before the court, Khudyakov informed several of them of the existence of an international revolutionary association. But here comes the contentious point: was Khudyakov talking about the First International, just organized (1864), as well as about some *past* foreign conspiracies, such as that of the Carbonari in Italy, or was he saying more? As Ishutin transmitted to his group the alleged intelligence received from Khudyakov, it was a fantastic tale. There existed a European revolutionary committee whose aim was the assassination of all monarchs. Soon, in Bukovina (then an Austrian province), this committee would hold a meeting with Mazzini, Ogarev, and Herzen in attendance. They would provide the Russian revolutionaries with 10,000 rubles and special new bombs.[22] Now it is unlikely that Khudyakov could have narrated such a fantastic tale, and in court he stoutly denied the entire story; certainly he

[20] Khudyakov, 98.

[21] *Ibid.*, 100. However, the total personnel of the Third Department was, as we saw, about seventy, and they were concentrated in Petersburg.

[22] This story is discussed by M. Klevensky in "The European Revolutionary Committee and the Karakozov Affair," in Gorev and Kozmin, 145ff. The author considers the *whole history* as Ishutin's invention.

would not have included Herzen as one of the masterminds of this terrorist international. But he and Ishutin did discuss the possibility and desirability of regicide, and Ishutin then embroidered Khudyakov's report with improbable details when he passed it on to his Moscow faithful.

Perhaps "faithful" is not quite the right word, for in January 1866 Ishutin's leadership of the circle was challenged. He had just conceived of an administrative reorganization of his group: within Organization there would be a smaller body named Hell. Members of it would devote themselves exclusively to terror: assassination, armed robbery, blackmail of the rich, etc. The rest would go on with the prosaic work: communes, schools, and libraries with subversive propaganda, agitation in the provinces. But Hell's members would eschew such peaceful pursuits; in fact, in order to conceal their purpose they should adopt the outward characteristics of profligates, drunks, etc. Any member performing an assassination should carry on his person acid, to destroy his facial features after the deed, and poison, to commit suicide after disfiguring himself. To be sure there would be some "minor" tasks for Hell: some of its associates would hire themselves out as servants in rich households to rob and/or blackmail their employers. *After* the revolution Hell would continue, so as to spy on and liquidate unworthy members of the revolutionary regime.

Before the court Ishutin was to say, "Hell did not exist. This was nothing more than foolish talk under the influence of alcohol."[23] And he was *half* truthful. These victims of group psychosis talked in their agitated way about all kinds of terror, about the circumstances under which it could or should be perpetrated. Ought one to begin with the assassination of the tsar or some "petty" terror? Should Organization bide its time until 1870 and the expected peasant uprising? The subject of regicide was a recurrent motif, and Ishutin, after denying it several times, was finally to confess that he was its strongest proponent.

Practically all historians have embraced the thesis that at this point Organization split: its moderate wing, led by Motkov, opposed the proponents of Hell. But this is a misreading of the situation. Here is how one of the "moderates" described how they proposed to deal with the "extremists." "[They] would compel the Ipatovites [Ishutin and his closest partisans, who lived communally in the home of one Ipatov], under the threat of death, to reveal all their secrets. . . . Then they would hang Ishutin and Karakozov. Yermolov would be sent to his estate. . . . Stranden would allegedly be sent after Chernyshevsky . . . and be killed on the way."[24] The

[23]Klevensky and Kotelnikov, I, 28.

[24]*Ibid.*, I, 306. The Soviet commentator blithely notes that maybe this version is a bit exaggerated, but it shows "how sharp was the hostility of the right wing of Organization to the left"!

vocabulary of politics or political analysis is completely inapplicable to this situation. What was going on was a struggle for power between Ishutin on the one hand and Motkov on the other, its deeper cause having nothing to do with the question of assassinating the tsar. There is a taint of perversion about the whole business.[25]

Enter Karakozov, Dmitri Ivanovich, Ishutin's first cousin. A weird story. Born 1840, graduated from the Penza high school, thrown out of Kazan University for participating in student riots, from the Moscow one for not paying tuition. An early member of the circle headed by his first cousin. All his acquaintances report him as unusually taciturn, a bad sign in a young Russian of the period, and once when assassination was being discussed he observed that this was something one did but should not talk about. Partly deaf and with recurrent stomach troubles, Karakozov occasionally confessed that, being hopelessly ill, he was going to take his own life. Most of his fellow conspirators believed him somewhat mad, which considering their own mental state is rather impressive.

All this talk of violence for months on end, and no deeds! Studying the conflicting mass of evidence one must lean to the hypothesis that the initiative for the actual deed of April 4 came from the Petersburg end of the conspiracy. If so, the likely scenario would have Ishutin informing Khudyakov that his cousin, intent on taking his own life, expressed interest in combining his suicide with an assassination, and then insinuating this idea to the mad youth. But Ishutin had a certain element of prudence in his own makeup, so he and his fellow partisans would not furnish Karakozov with a gun or poison, etc. Karakozov himself would get them in Petersburg, and Organization would not necessarily be incriminated if something went wrong. In any event at the beginning of March Karakozov went to Petersburg for what was the first of two trips. His comrades were later on to profess ignorance of his whereabouts and to insist that they learned about them only when Khudyakov came to Moscow around March 20, wherupon they sent some of their members to bring Karakozov back. But they also confessed that they had heard Karakozov talk about killing Alexander.

The trouble is that madmen don't necessarily make dependable assassins. On his first trip to Petersburg Karakozov lodged at first in several rooming houses, but, since he had little money and no identity papers (without which then as now in Russia one cannot procure the necessary residence permit from the police), he was turned out of each. He evidently hesitated about performing the dreadful deed and whiled away his time by propagandizing workers.

In testimony at his trial Karakozov insisted that two people in Petersburg

[25]Motkov originally had supported Hell.

knew he was going to try to kill the tsar: Khudyakov and young Dr. Alexander Kobilin. Even though coming from Karakozov and even though Dr. Kobilin was subsequently acquitted of any complicity, this testimony must be accepted.

Consider the facts: Khudyakov by his own admission saw Karakozov several times and gave him money. Karakozov insisted that he had told Khudyakov what it was needed for: to buy the gun which Karakozov would fire on April 4.

Consider Karakozov's connection with Dr. Kobilin. One does not want to slight posthumously the reputation of the good doctor, and it is just possible that indeed, as the court decided, he was entirely innocent. But what would a modern jury think of the following story? By Dr. Kobilin's own testimony he first met Karakozov when the latter turned up early in March at the Petersburg hospital where Dr. Kobilin was resident and complained of a variety of ailments. His appearance was unusual; obviously an educated man, he was dressed like an artisan. Dr. Kobilin examined him, found no ailment beyond constipation, and dismissed his patient with some pills. Two days later, and Karakozov again appeared in his clinic. The doctor was now convinced that he had a hypochondriac, to say the least, on his hands. Notwithstanding, when his patient explained his trouble in finding lodgings, Kobilin generously offered him a bed in the apartment he shared with his brother. There Karakozov spent three nights, during one of which he and the doctor had a lengthy conversation, mostly about literature. Then his lodger left, assuring the doctor he was returning to Moscow.

Imagine his surprise, continued Dr. Kobilin before the court, when he came to his clinic sometime in the next week and Karakozov was again there. This was too much for even his Christian charity, but he offered to take his visitor to spend a night with a friend, Alexander Putiata. First coincidence: Putiata had been up to his ears in the revolutionary movement. Karakozov, however, refused this offer, saying that Putiata was a crook.[26] The discussion must have been very tiring because both of them fell asleep on the two sofas in the doctor's office and did not wake up until the morning. Then, according to Dr. Kobilin, they parted. The importunate patient would not, however, give up. That same evening, Karakozov appeared at Dr. Kobilin's father's house where the doctor was attending a party. Dr. Kobilin claimed that he now told the pest off stiffly and never saw him again.

But Dr. Kobilin must somehow have had foreknowledge of Karakozov's leaving St. Petersburg and coming back again, for, as he admitted, he had told "the maiden Komarova," as the indictment identifies her, to prepare lodgings for Karakozov sometime late in March. Another coincidence: "the

[26]Klevensky and Kotelnikov, I, 233.

maiden Komarova," belying that classification, was the "civic" wife of Vladimir Lebedev, whom we have already met.[27]

Karakozov represented his relationship with Dr. Kobilin quite differently. It was the doctor, he said, who gave him the strychnine, prussic acid, and morphine which were found on his person after his arrest on April 4. When he informed Dr. Kobilin about his plan to kill the tsar, the latter had not only not discouraged him but had told him that this would be very much in the interest of "Constantine's party." This was a group of high officials who wanted to dispose of Alexander II so that his brother would take over and grant a constitution.

Some Soviet historians have swallowed the story of "Constantine's party" and of Dr. Kobilin's being its agent.[28] But the notion that the Grand Duke connived at the murder of his brother is not only monstrous but preposterous. Tsar Alexander had five surviving sons, two of whom were of age in 1866, so Constantine would not even be regent on the death of the tsar. To be sure, the Grand Duke was known as the head of the liberal faction at the court, but despite their frequent political clashes and differing temperaments the two brothers were united by strong affection, and Constantine continued to hold high state positions as long as Alexander lived. That he or any of his fellow liberals in the government like Golovnin or Milyutin would for a second consider regicide was something that only an extreme reactionary or an extreme radical—people who would believe in anything —could give credence to. But the rumor was being circulated, and it is likely that it was insinuated to Karakozov, who was obviously hesitating about getting on with his dreadful task, that he might not even be punished for the assassination. Perhaps he even thought "Constantine's party" would give the revolutionaries money for performing the deed.

If so, Khudyakov's trip to Moscow was for exactly the opposite reason to that asserted by some members of Ishutin's circle when they testified in court that he came after March 20 to warn them that Karakozov had the mad scheme of killing the tsar. Rather, he came to complain that the man selected for the task was not getting on with the job.[29]

[27]She had been the fiancée of the writer Nicholas Pomyalovsky (1835–1863), who drank himself to death. His novel, entitled for its energetic hero *Molotov*, is now forgotten, but it may well have inspired a young engineering student, Scriabin, in 1910 to adopt it as his revolutionary name, under which he would become world-famous. Alexandra Komarova turned state's evidence (without telling all she knew). Later on she wrote a novel about the nihilists.

[28]E.g., Vilenskaya, 470.

[29]We have seen that the proclamations Karakozov was spreading specified that the deed would be accomplished *by* March 20. The proclamation itself, "To Worker Friends," was written in a "popular" style, e.g., "If the people will make an end of Alexander, their main enemy, their other petty enemies, landlords, potentates, officials, etc., will give up because there are so few of them. Then you will have real freedom . . . everybody will be well off . . . all will be equal . . . no one will be envious." Klevensky and Kotelnikov, I, 294. It is doubtful whether Karakozov, often incoherent in his speech and letters, could have com-

In Moscow Khudyakov must have been shocked to find a conflict within Organization between Ishutin and his fellow partisans of Hell, and Motkov and the others. The latter by now were frightened by the idea of regicide, and Motkov even suggested to Khudyakov that he should inform the police about Karakozov. Instead, two members, Yermolov and Nicholas Stranden, were sent to bring the reluctant assassin back, and Karakozov did return to Moscow on March 24. It is clear that by now most of the Moscow people were frightened of the whole idea, but also it is certain that Ishutin, the only person with whom Khudyakov could be frank on the subject, was still for it. On March 29 Karakozov was back in St. Petersburg.

Here, as they say, the plot thickens. We have mentioned Nicholas Nozhin, the revolutionary who by Khudyakov's own testimony was one of the two people closest to him politically. At the end of March Nozhin, then sharing an apartment in St. Petersburg with Nicholas Kurochkin, became violently ill. Kurochkin, though himself a doctor, had in view of his literary and revolutionary preoccupations not practiced much and felt the need of more professional help for his friend. Another coincidence: the man he summoned to the bedside of Nozhin was none other than Dr. Kobilin. When Kurochkin related the incident to the Muraviev commission he added hurriedly that he was seeing Dr. Kobilin for the first time in his life.[30] Despite Dr. Kobilin's ministrations the patient's condition worsened and on April 2 he was taken to hospital. In the memoirs of two officials, contemporaries of the events, it is asserted that from the hospital Nozhin dispatched a letter (here they differ: one version has it to Prince Suvorov, another to the Petersburg chief of police, Annenkov) saying that in view of his approaching death he felt that he had to divulge an important secret, and begging the addressee to visit him.[31] But on April 3 Nozhin died. His friend and in some ways disciple Mikhailovsky was to refer to Nozhin's death many years later in his recollections: "Through the unfathomable will of fate he died under very strange, and for me still unclear, circumstances. . . ."[32]

One does not have to be Doctor Freud to submit that with one part of his sick mind Karakozov wanted to betray the people who were pushing him to his deed. When arrested, he had on his person, in addition to the objects we have already mentioned, a scrap of paper with some words, the only legible one being "Kobilin," and a letter addressed to Nicholas Andreyevich (i.e., Ishutin). And when his real identity was finally established

posed it, and quite likely its real author was Khudyakov, who had considerable experience at this type of propaganda.
[30]Eugene Kolosov, "N.K. Mikhailovsky and the Karakozov Affair," in *The Past*, No. 23 (Moscow 1924), 67.
[31]*Ibid.*, 73.
[32]Quoted in *ibid.*, 64. Mikhailovsky wrote this, of course, in tsarist times.

by the janitor of his last lodging house, an envelope was found in his room with Ishutin's full name and address in Moscow. And soon after, on April 7, when he gave up the pretense of being someone else, Karakozov "fingered" Khudyakov as the man who had given him money for the gun and knew its purpose, and Dr. Kobilin as the person who provided the poisons and allowed him to sleep in his office in the hospital some time before the attempt.[33]

Karakozov's letter to Ishutin began: "Dear friend: You are a swine, brother Nicholas, you did not know how to set the problem right. . . ."[34] Incoherent gibberish follows but occasionally a meaningful sentence shines through: ". . . my acquaintances about whom I talked with you propose to do the thing soon. . . . It is clear that any single deed would now be extremely useful for the shareholders of both of our firms. . . . Well, goodbye, friends, and let us hope for good results." In trying to explain the letter Karakozov held that "both of our firms" was a code for the real revolutionaries on the one hand and "Constantine's party" on the other.

We already know that the assassination attempt was followed almost immediately by a wave of arrests of radicals of all descriptions. In writing about the atmosphere of those days, Khudyakov made one serious slip: ". . . On April 6 I learned from a friend that Kobilin had been arrested. I had in my pocket only two rubles. I had a lot of debts. And so in view of this news I asked the friend to lend me ten rubles."[35] But in court both gentlemen testified that they had encountered each other only once before, without being introduced, when Khudyakov brought Karakozov some money when the latter was staying with Kobilin.

In studying the work of Muraviev's investigating commission one reaches the melancholy conclusion that General Muraviev was much better at hanging people than at uncovering the roots of treason and plots. And a modern KGB official would hardly believe his eyes studying its results: here the government had under lock and key *all* the spreaders of intellectual poison and instigators of treason, both before and after April 4, all those Kurochkins, Putiatas, Yeliseyevs, etc., and then it let them all go free on the grounds that there was no hard evidence that would stand up in court. Instead the government turned over for prosecution a handful of lunatics and a bunch of deluded adolescents who needed a reform school rather than Siberia and hard labor (which in fact would make real revolutionaries of some of them). But as contrasted with modern totalitarian investigators, Muraviev worked at some disadvantage: he could not use torture. Some Soviet authors assert that indeed it was used, and a few Western historians

[33]Klevensky and Kotelnikov, I, 9.
[34]*Ibid.*, I, 294.
[35]Khudyakov, 117.

have been taken in by such tales. But anyone reading the actual documents as published during the Soviet period will not find the slightest documentation for such a charge. To be sure Khudyakov claims that he was beaten.[36] But neither he nor his defender mentioned it before the court—the latter composed mainly of officials who were well-known enemies of Muraviev and who would have welcomed anything to discredit the Hangman.

But the most fundamental mistake the government made was not to publish the minutes of the investigation as well as the court proceedings, which thus remained unknown to the Russian public until after the Revolution of 1917. No subsequent "affair," not even Dostoyevsky's great novel, could have made the people see terrorism in its real light as this true story would have, compounded as it was of madness, criminality, and youth's immature delusions. The official reason for suppressing it was the fear of giving further currency to the "Constantine's party" legend. But that in itself was so fantastic that no rational person could have believed it.

And so Karakozov and others were permitted, largely through official stupidity, to enter the roll of martyrs for freedom. A myth grew about their heroic behavior, and about the fact that if they confessed, they did so as Khudyakov did because they had been beaten. In fact most of them broke down easily, implicated others, and begged for clemency. The miserable Ishutin professed himself before Muraviev a believer in autocracy: "Your excellency, I could not list all the beneficial results of a trusting attitude of the government toward the young educated elements. One result would make it impossible to be dissatisfied with the Sovereign."[37] And so, he begged, please treat Karakozov's attempt as sheer childishness. He, Ishutin, and his comrades, would help the emperor if they were freed. It was "lack of trust and persecutions which [led] to fanaticism." Well, he had something there. At another session Ishutin said that even under socialism the emperor should be retained: "he has given freedom to millions. . . . God sees my repentance."[38] Khudyakov, in his book, boasted that he braved Muraviev. But in fact, though less abject than most of the others, he implicated several members of the Moscow group and himself begged for mercy.[39] And Khudyakov recounts how he, who despised Herzen as a moderate, wrote a memorandum for Muraviev arguing for an English type of constitution: ". . . such a measure would bring the imperial house the kind of deep affection and loyalty which the English queen enjoys, she who is never afraid of an assassin. The people will then gladly pay millions for the

[36] *Ibid.*, 129.
[37] Selections from the testimony, as edited by Alexis Shilov, in "Karakozov's Attempt," in *The Red Archive*, XVII (4), Moscow 1926, 97.
[38] *Ibid.*, 129.
[39] *Ibid.*, 109.

maintenance of the imperial house which safeguards national freedom."[40]
And this is taken by some authorities as a serious political document.

Having most wretchedly performed his task, Muraviev turned over to the
minister of justice thirty-six of the conspirators to be tried for participation
and collusion in the assassination plot. Haunted by a sense of failure—none
of his enemies such as Suvorov or Constantine were implicated—and by the
obvious disenchantment with him expressed by representatives of the right
like Katkov, the old scoundrel retired to his estate. Tsar Alexander, instead
of rewarding him with a princely title or at least a general-adjutancy as he
had hoped, sent him some diamond trinkets. Even before they reached him
and before he could have the consolation of seeing at least one of the accused
hanged, Count Muraviev of Vilna succumbed to a stroke.

The same consideration which barred publicity made the government
reject the idea of a jury trial, as was supposedly required by the recent
judicial reform. Instead, an imperial decree set up a special Supreme Criminal Court composed of high officials. But this autocratic act had certainly
fortunate consequences for many of the defenders. Given the current public
mood it was most unlikely that twelve ordinary citizens of Petersburg would
have been content with just one hanging. But most of the judges were
septuagenarians (one of them had to be carried into the court in a wheel-
chair), and it would appear that they viewed some of the defendants with
a degree of compassion, as still mere boys, beguiled by Ishutin. Evidently
their elderly minds were not nimble enough to cope with the mass of often
contradictory evidence. In marked contrast to his judicial colleagues insofar
as both compassion and mental alertness was concerned was Prince Peter
of Oldenburg, the emperor's cousin. "How can you defend such scoundrels?" his Imperial Highness asked Ishutin's lawyer.[41] He also caught on
to Khudyakov's principal role in the plot. But Oldenburg's influence was
offset by that of the president of the court, Prince Paul Gagarin. This
illiberal but kindly old man was appalled at the youth and naiveté of most
of the defendants, and at times tried to stop their testimony when in fear
and befuddlement they went beyond the bill of indictment in implicating
themselves in the crime.

The trial itself was an incongruous mixture of the old and the new,
certainly not in accordance with what we know as Anglo-Saxon principles
of judicial procedure. (Yet if we compare the proceedings and verdicts with
those of the military commission which tried the alleged accomplices in
President Lincoln's assassination, the comparison will not be favorable to

---

[40]Khudyakov, 146.

[41]Dmitri Stasov, "The Karakozov Trial" in *The Past,* No. 4 (Moscow 1906), 286. Stasov was
a member of a family very prominent in the professional and artistic life of Petersburg. His
daughter, Helen, an important Bolshevik activist, *de facto* secretary of the Party 1918-19,
managed to survive the Stalin era in obscurity and died in 1966 at the age of ninety-three.

the American court.) However, for the first time in the history of Russian political trials the accused were defended by attorneys, and some of the latter, though inexperienced (the Russian Bar has just been instituted), performed their task with a skill and courage which might have been envied by the most renowned British barrister or American criminal lawyer. Khudyakov's attorney almost convinced the majority of the judges of his client's innocence. As it was, Khudyakov was convicted and sentenced to Siberian exile only for not informing about the existence of the Ishutin circle, something he considered as unjust, "because members of the Moscow circle were sentenced to simple exile"[42]—not true, as we shall see. That most of the Moscow accused were guilty, at least in the sense of having *listened* to the plans for killing Alexander II, there could be no doubt; it was confirmed by their own testimony. Nothing could save Karakozov, for in the light of prevalent medical opinion he was responsible for his acts, and indeed in his court appearance he was more lucid than before and claimed that his attempt had been made in a fit of *temporary* insanity. (During his imprisonment Karakozov underwent a religious conversion. When the rumors of it reached progressive circles it was taken as prima facie evidence that he had been tortured.) He repeated his charges against Kobilin and Khudyakov.

Ishutin interrupted his sobbing denials to admit emphatically that it was he who had initiated the talk about killing the tsar.[43] Both he and Karakozov were sentenced to death by hanging (Gagarin voted against the death sentence for Ishutin), Karakozov's execution taking place on September 3. Ishutin was on the scaffold with the rope around his neck when it was announced that the sentence was commuted to life imprisonment at hard labor. This savage "mercy" must have hastened his illness, for soon he became hopelessly insane, dying in 1879. Khudyakov was dispatched to the furthest regions of Siberia. His wife, who must have loved this strange man and who bore his child, offered to accompany him but he refused. At first he busied himself with collecting the folklore of the Yakut natives, but in 1870 fell mentally ill. He died in an asylum in 1876.

Most of the members of the Hell wing of Organization were sentenced to several years at hard labor, to be followed by exile. A few, judged to have been on the periphery of the conspiracy, got away with a few months of imprisonment or went scot-free. Paul Mayevsky, however, who was not in Organization at all but was its liaison with the Polish rebels, and who almost uniquely among the accused denied every charge against him during the course of the investigation and trial, was sent to life-time exile in Siberia, where in 1905 he shot himself.

[42]Khudyakov, 162.
[43]Klevensky and Kotelnikov, I, 71.

And now Dr. Kobilin: he defended himself stoutly against Karakozov's accusations, though as we have seen he had in the main confirmed them insofar as their meetings in Petersburg were concerned. And "the maiden Komarova" added a seemingly damning corroboration: yes, Dr. Kobilin *had* asked her in late March to find lodgings for Karakozov on the eve of his attempt at regicide.[44] Thanks to minor discrepancies in Karakozov's story, Dr. Kobilin was able to bring witnesses to testify that at the time Karakozov claimed he handed him the poison, Dr. Kobilin was elsewhere, in their company. But those witnesses would not inspire a modern juror with excessive confidence. One was the wife of Putiata, and the other was "the maiden Beliakova," obviously the doctor's girlfriend. The nosy Oldenburg got her to admit on the stand that she visited Dr. Kobilin alone in his apartment, something well-brought-up young ladies did not do with casual acquaintances. But the prosecuting attorney, minister of justice Dmitri Zamyatnin, a typical bumbling bureaucrat, withdrew the charge against Kobilin. This under the procedure did not automatically quash the indictment but pretty much determined the issue.

The court's verdicts, unlike its proceedings, were rendered in public. And when Kobilin's was to be pronounced, his mother ran to the judges' bench, fell on her knees, and cried, "Little fathers, spare him." He was soon in her arms as Prince Gagarin pronounced him a free man and read a fatherly lesson on his imprudence: how could he have sheltered an unbalanced man who, as he knew, had forged identity papers!

Dr. Kobilin clearly had "pull." He had relatives in high court circles. His boss, Dr. Serge Botkin, already the country's most famous diagnostician and the father of Russian clinical medicine, had influential patients. Somebody, perhaps Dr. Kobilin's ultimate superior (he served in a military hospital), Dmitri Milyutin, might have shrugged his shoulders: maybe the young fool[45] was really innocent; in any case he was a promising doctor who would have learned his lesson. Less trusting than the court, the fellow doctors in his clinic refused to serve with him, and Milyutin had him transferred to Warsaw. The Third Department kept Kobilin under its discreet surveillance until 1879,[46] but he fulfilled the expectations of his anonymous protector: a successful and decorous medical practice culminated in 1895–1902 when he was the chief medical consultant to the war office. He died in 1924, and contemporaries and historians alike have paid but scant attention to this most enigmatic figure in a still mysterious affair.

[44] *Ibid.,* 250.
[45] There is a discrepancy about his age: before the court he stated it to be twenty-three. Other sources give his birth date as 1840.
[46] "Activists of the Revolutionary Movement," in A.A. Shilov and M.G. Karnovkhova, eds., *Russia: A Biographical Dictionary,* Moscow 1928, I, 171.

And so ended the great trial, the first in Russian history of which we have a stenographic (though garbled) record. What was the point of this whole plot, which—probably even more than its successful repetition on March 1, 1881—changed the course of Russia history? What did the people who inspired Karakozov really intend to accomplish? To repeat: despite all the legend to the contrary, the would-be assassin's only words when seized and asked by the emperor what he wanted were "Nothing, nothing."

EIGHT

THE PRANKSTER

Was he a bold and enterprising revolutionary with some flaws, perhaps even a criminal streak, in his character? Or was he a cross between a sadist and a charlatan masquerading as a fighter for freedom? Historians have varied in their appraisal of Serge Gennadievich Nechayev. The reader will have to judge for himself. But whatever he was, he will never be forgotten or remain a mere figure in Russia's past. For the crime he committed is the most famous single act of violence in modern history, since it provided the theme for one of the greatest novels of all times.

The period between Karakozov's shot in 1866 and November 25, 1869, when a body was discovered in a pond of Petrovsky Park in Moscow, has passed into history books as the "years of white terror"—an expression first used by the Geneva *Bell*. Even a liberal pre-Revolutionary historian found the ultimate cause of the Nechayev affair to be this white terror, "the wild excesses of the government, the denial of the freedom of the press, and the terror which our government imposed upon society after 1866."[1] We who in this century have seen what real terror is, whether "white" or "red," cannot so quickly endorse the use of this term for what happened following April 4, 1866: perhaps a score of intellectuals were detained for a few weeks and then released, even though some of them, like Putiata and Yeliseyev, had undoubted links with revolutionary activities; two radical journals were shut down, although their editors, Nekrasov and Blagosvetlov, soon ac-

---

[1] A. A. Kornilov, *The Social Movement Under Alexander II*, Moscow 1909, 188, 200.

quired other periodicals, in which they more circumspectly continued to propagate "untrustworthy ideas"; discussion took place within the government whether the new censorship law of 1865 (which enlarged the scope of press freedom and was in comparison with similar laws in force in all other Continental countries quite liberal) should not be revised, but it was not. If this be terror, Indira Gandhi's recent measures in India might be compared to those of Ivan the Terrible! And it can be confidently asserted that even had all those measures of oppression not taken place, Nechayev would have remained Nechayev and would still have found accomplices for his savage deeds.

But while Alexander's government may not have entered on a course of terror, the regime had certainly turned in a reactionary direction. To be more precise, the emperor had lost confidence that further reforms could be reconciled with public order and, dismissing some of his most liberal and innovative officials, he was tending to listen more to the careerists and conservatives in his entourage.

This in turn explains not so much the Nechayev affair itself—for as we have amply demonstrated if there was one thing an extreme radical hated more than autocracy it was the idea of Russia becoming a constitutional state—but the amazingly mild reaction to Nechayev's crime on the part of Russia's educated classes. The court proceedings in the case of Nechayev's murder of Ivan Ivanov were public (unlike the Karakozov trial), and thus the crime and the background to it became known in their full, hideous details. And there could not be in this case (again unlike the 1866 event) even a pretense of a political justification for the deed. One would have thought that in 1871, when the facts became fully known, even the most radical critic of the tsarist regime would be seized by revulsion against the conspiratorial method of pursuing the "struggle for liberation," not to mention the murderers themselves. Yet a liberal Petersburg journal, published legally under the oppressive censorship law, *The European Messenger,* writing of Nechayev's accomplices, said: "They were almost without exception people quite young . . . prone to overexcitement, but diligent, filled with the desire to serve the general public welfare." To be sure the author (a well-known lawyer, Constantine Arseniev), goes on to admit that they had been seduced from this laudable purpose by Nechayev's fantasies, but even Nechayev is not criticized in clear-cut terms, and the article finds some logic in the argument with which he allegedly beguiled these young men to abandon their peaceful pursuits and become murderers and blackmailers: "He showed them that organizing communal workshops and associations is in the eyes of the government practically the same thing as committing a political crime."[2] Presumably it then becomes not too surprising that four

[2] *The European Messenger,* VI (St. Petersburg 1871), 289.

of them agreed to assist in murdering an entirely innocent man, and a comrade of theirs to boot!

This tragic moral obtuseness on the part of the progressive *intelligentsia* shows best in the following passage from the same article: "The system [the government's distrust of society], just as any other policy, should be judged mainly by its results. If this system could stop all disorders at their inception, could quiet minds, if the application of really severe measures could obviate their repetition over the long run, then one could say that the system worked and has proven its beneficence and necessity."[3] The author seems not to perceive that he is in fact arguing for a ruthless police state, such as Russia had under Nicholas I and before long would receive again in more modern and drastic form, and suggesting that in the absence of either complete freedom or complete tyranny, the individual as well as society is absolved from moral responsibility, from the duty to decide what is political dissent and what is crime.

As we have seen, something like this attitude could be observed even before 1866. But Karakozov's attempt at killing Tsar Alexander set up a veritable vicious circle: the government abandoned its zeal to reform Russian life without at the same time being able to reinstitute a thoroughgoing police state. And the educated class, "society" in contemporary parlance, having lost that panicky fear of authority which characterized it under Nicholas I, in turn tended to lose its respect for the government. It now acquired a feeling of critical detachment toward politics which enabled it to look with equanimity even at the most repugnant acts of violence, as long as they were committed allegedly against the existing political order. This in turn strengthened the tendency of some government officials to consider the *intelligentsia* and, especially, the young as a hotbed of potential sedition and thus to alienate them still further.

The evil of the whole system was brilliantly analyzed by Michael Katkov. This spokesman of the right, morbidly unbalanced on anything which touched his nationalist phobias—the Poles, Ukrainians, Baltic Germans, etc.—still remained sane and perceptive about Russia's political problems. Take England, he wrote, commenting on the Nechayev affair: there you have *"habeas corpus,* in virtue of which no one can be arrested or searched without a court warrant. . . . England has a cohesive society, which preserves law and order more diligently and effectively than could any police force by itself."[4] What would happen if the tsar's government should ban preventive arrests and exile by administrative fiat? (He has in mind a law of 1871 which allowed local authorities, without a court sanction, to arrest and temporarily exile people suspected of subversive and criminal inten-

[3] *Ibid.,* 292.
[4] M.N. Katkov, *Collection of Editorials from the* Moscow News *in 1872,* Moscow 1897, 72.

tions.) Katkov was willing to wager that society would then recognize its responsibility to help preserve law and order. Was he right? As it happened no tsarist government was willing to make this wager: by 1906 imperial Russia would have a parliament, but never habeas corpus. It would only appear, a macabre joke, in Stalin's Constitution of 1936, which solemnly proclaimed that "no person may be placed under arrest except by decision of a court" and guaranteed "the inviolability of the homes of the citizens."

The government's inability to lay to rest the ghost of revolution—a ghost that haunted the autocracy until 1881 and, after an interval, until 1917—was, then, due to the absence of an effective principle or ideology which would secure the allegiance of the educated class and instill self-confidence in the rulers themselves.

Of the traditional props of the regime, religion, as represented by the Orthodox Church, had long since ceased to play a meaningful part in the lives of most educated Russians. Religious sentiments retained their hold on the peasantry, witness the continuous attempts by radicals, atheists, or free thinkers to exploit the religious motif in their propaganda among the masses, whether Orthodox or Old Believers. But spiritually and intellectually the Orthodox Church could contribute but little to the solution of the great social and political problems confronting Russia. Most of its hierarchy had been opposed to the great reforms. The Metropolitan Philaret of Moscow had held that the abolition of serfdom and the curtailment of corporal punishment would lead to general lawlessness and anarchy. As for the rank-and-file clergy, that so many radicals came from priests' families and/or were alumni of religious seminaries speaks for itself.

Then as now, there was one great force whose skillful manipulation could secure the government widespread popularity and support—Russian nationalism. Indeed after the experience of 1863–64 the most radical revolutionaries eschewed any plea for self-determination and freedom for any non-Russian nationalities of the empire, and this remained true into the twentieth century. But unlike their Communist successors, the Romanovs could but seldom harness Russian nationalism to their own political interests and find in it a sure bulwark of their power. For all of Russia's continuing expansion in Asia, the traditional goal of her policy—the ejection of Turkey from Europe—remained unconsummated, Nicholas I's efforts in this direction ending in a military debacle in the Crimea, and Alexander's in a diplomatic one in 1877–78.[5] In fact, Russian nationalism instead of being a source of support for the autocratic system, often served to increase society's dissatisfaction with Tsar Alexander's regime. For all his frequently

---

[5]Even Herzen, reputedly the most un-jingoistic of Russians, is on record as saying, "Sometime Constantinople will be Russia's capital. The Turks have no right to be in Europe." Tuchkova-Ogareva, *Memoirs,* Moscow 1859, 234.

voiced disdain of the "rotten West," a patriotic Russian, even if conservative, was bound to feel secret irritation with his country's political and social backwardness. He could not console himself, as a loyal citizen of the USSR can, with the reflection that Britain, France, or Germany, while freer and richer than his own country, were weaker militarily and industrially, doomed by the forces of history as revealed in the pusillanimity of their leaders and total lack of social discipline among their peoples. On the contrary, in the late nineteenth century freedom and power went hand in hand. Britain was the world's leading nation; Bismarck's Germany was soon to have a parliament and universal suffrage. Russia for all her enormous resources remained backward and relatively weak because her people were unfree.

Tsar Alexander once declared to a progressive nobleman that he would sign any kind of a constitution his visitor might desire, if he were not so sure that the country then would fall to pieces. But the point was not that Russia should immediately be transformed into a constitutional monarchy with a responsible government, but simply that the momentum of the great reforms should be preserved. The cessation of this momentum in 1866 made the previous achievements act only as irritants to society, rather than as a solid foundation for public order and loyalty to the throne. Awareness of this paradox penetrated into official circles—hence the other paradox we have observed and will see again in connection with the Nechayev affair: while in no other European country could a man be so readily arrested and exiled for a trivial offence, nowhere else could a serious criminal get off as lightly as in Russia.

In addition to being autocratic, partly perhaps because of it, the political system was inefficient. Apart from the emperor himself there was no unifying force in national policy; no prime minister, no council of ministers in the real sense of the word. The tsar himself lacked a personal secretariat, in fact had no regular secretary. The most trivial issue, as well as state matters of the highest importance, required his personal attention and decision, usually to be communicated in his own handwriting or in a personal interview with the relevant minister.

After 1866 most of the progressive bureaucrats who had contributed so much to the modernization of Russia during the preceding decade disappeared from the scene or were relegated to honorific posts of little importance. The man who for a while had the emperor's ear was Count Peter Shuvalov, the new head of the Third Department. Indeed his generally reactionary influence was reputed to be so great that he was dubbed by Herzen Peter IV. But to render him justice, he was, in contrast with his predecessor and successors, an efficient head of the secret police, and his diplomatic exile (he was made ambassador to London in 1874, a consequence allegedly of his having made some incautious remarks about the tsar's mistress) weakened that vital mainstay of the autocracy. There remained in the imperial administration men who realized that the spirit of the times called for further reforms. One was Grand Duke Constantine, president of the State Council until his brother's death. But for all his liberal ideas, Constantine had a volatile as well as an authoritarian character which alienated other notables, in fact reminded some of them of his mad grandfather Emperor Paul and his scarcely less unbalanced uncle, Grand Duke Constantine Pavlovich. The man who in view of both his ability and ideas was preeminently suited to become prime minister was Dmitri Milyutin. He appreciated the urgency of further political and administrative changes and, uniquely among the high officials, had an understanding of and contact with the *intelligentsia* and the young. But while Alexander retained him as minister of war, Milyutin's previously considerable influence in other spheres of social activity, such as education, was severely circumscribed after 1866. In the eyes of the reactionaries such as Count Shuvalov and the new minister of education, Dmitri Tolstoy, the war minister was a dangerous radical and a protector of people with "untrustworthy ideas," the last charge being, we have seen, not entirely undeserved.[6]

In the last resort the strength and popularity of the autocracy had to reflect the personality and prestige of the Autocrat. By the end of the 1860s Alexander had dissipated much of that capital of enthusiasm and goodwill which was his upon accession to the throne and after February 19, 1861. Quite apart from his disenchantment with reform, his personality and his conduct after 1866 explain this. There was something about the former which made even his most loyal servants unable to feel warm toward the Tsar Liberator. Herzen hit on a sensitive spot when at one stage in his adulation-hatred of Alexander he called him the "German Tsar." This was not the matter of bloodlines, since Alexander III, even more "German,"[7] seemed to be the embodiment of "the broad Russian nature," but of manner and temperament; Alexander II struck his close acquaintances as quite un-Russian in his mixture of sentimentality and a certain grossness, rather than that jovial brutality and awesomeness which many Russians expected in their rulers. Nationalists viewed with apprehension his partiality for Prussia (which, with Russia's benevolent neutrality, was allowed to swallow up Germany and humiliate France), a partiality largely ascribed to Alexander's excessive affection for his uncle, the Emperor William I. And, though excellently brought up (Nicholas, despite all that might have been expected to the contrary, was a loving and enlightened father), the emperor had no

[6]Milyutin did not die until 1912, at the age of ninety-six. As a nonagenarian he wrote an article prophesying the use of armored vehicles in a future war.

[7]All the Romanov emperors but one married German princesses, and, assuming that Catherine the Great's husband was the father of Paul I, the real name of the imperial family should have been Holstein Gottorp, as the revolutionaries never ceased to proclaim in their propaganda.

artistic or scientific interests, and except for his friendship with Alexis Tolstoy, no contact with the world of letters—this at the time when Russian literature was in its most glorious period. (His much less cultured son, the future Alexander III, befriended Dostoyevsky.)

The emperor's prestige was further undermined, especially in conservative circles, by his liaison with Catherine Dolgorukova, the daughter of an impoverished princely family.[8] It was not because fashionable society, in which the affair became known soon after its beginning in 1866, begrudged the monarch an occasional diversion: Nicholas had been notorious for his forays among ladies-in-waiting and dancers of the Imperial Ballet. It was the intensity of Alexander's feeling and the character of the mistress which created a scandal. The forty-eight-year-old emperor fell in love like a schoolboy (anyway, as schoolboys used to fall in love) rather than in the lighthearted and elegant manner befitting a prince. Catherine, as he proclaimed in a letter, was his wife "before God," and he made other tasteless religious references about the adulterous relationship. The object of his passion was a badly educated nineteen-year-old girl. The notion that amorous exertions adversely affect health was evidently widespread among Russians of all political persuasions (witness Khudyakov), for Alexander's ministers increasingly attributed his frequent fatigue and inattention to state business to this "unnatural" relationship with a woman twenty-eight years his junior. Contrariwise, a modern reader might well conclude that if Alexander, a sufferer from severe asthma who was also beset by personal tragedies—the deaths of his eldest daughter and son, the attempted elopement of another son with a dancer, the chronic illness of his wife—and political disappointments, survived in reasonable shape until his assassination at sixty-two, this might well have been due to the happiness provided by his romance. In any event Catherine is alleged to have used her influence both in politics and for financial gain, but it is difficult to evaluate those rumors. Whatever the case the liaison further undermined the emperor's prestige among those who should have been the staunchest supporters of the throne.

Court intrigues and the persistence of the revolutionary virus should not have been allowed, so it seems, to damage the fabric of national life. Russia was going through a great cultural efflorescence such as few societies have experienced. With the abolition of serfdom there began a period of rapid industrialization and a great expansion of railway building; factories sprang up in a hitherto almost entirely agrarian society; new territories were added to the empire in Central Asia and on the Pacific. It would appear that for young Russians this should have been the period of "new frontiers" in science, industry, the arts, that people disenchanted with politics or the claustrophobic atmosphere of old Russia would seek new opportunities in

[8]It is described in great detail in Alexander Tarsaidze, *Katia,* New York 1971.

colonizing Turkestan or the Far East, in commerce with China and Persia, in developing the mineral riches of the Caucasus and Siberia. And many in fact did. But for some of Russia's youth the burden of the recent past was too heavy for them to seek any other avenue of self-expression than politics, and this path almost inevitably led to conspiracy.

Thus Nechayev. One can imagine him in a different society, say post–Civil-War America, employing his enormous energy and talent for deception to become an entrepreneur-swindler or, just barely possible, a respectable captain of industry or finance, thus satisfying his main craving: for power. But in the Russia of his time, another career beckoned men of his type. He was certainly a self-made man. Born the son of a bartender in 1847, he spent his childhood in what used to be the village of Ivanovo-Voznesensk, but already in the 1860s was becoming a textile center which would earn it the sobriquet of the Manchester of Russia. Sympathetic historians have tried to explain what they admit are certain quirks in Nechayev's character by his childhood environment and impressions: here is this poor boy serving as a messenger in a factory who sees all around him the growing wealth and luxury in which new capitalists are living. But this was true of many Russians.

Nechayev managed to finish the local high school and in 1865 left for Moscow. He found a patron, a well-known professor of history and a publicist, Michael Pogodin, in whose house Nechayev lived for a time while performing some secretarial duties. His benefactor's personality could not have left a good impression on the youth, for in a list he composed in 1869 of people who should be liquidated by his conspiracy prior to the revolution, Pogodin, an entirely harmless and then rather apolitical old man, may be found in the company of more distinguished and (from the revolutionary point of view) more logical targets for assassination such as Count Shuvalov and Michael Katkov. Failing to obtain a teacher's diploma, Nechayev transferred in 1866 to Petersburg, where after finally passing the required examination the next year, he obtained a position as a grammar-school teacher with a room to live in on the premises of the school. The subject in which he instructed being religion, the young man's heart could not have been in his pedagogical work—and this is witnessed to among other things by the testimony of the school janitor. This man of the people, on whom evidently Nechayev failed to exercise that magnetism which many of his intellectual associates found irresistible, wrote to the authorities complaining that Nechayev was often absent from his classes, let the children run wildly, entertained, and got drunk with all sorts of suspicious people. But the body which corresponded to the school board had to exonerate Nechayev when the complainant appeared at the hearing completely drunk himself; it is impossible not to see in this the hand of Nechayev himself, who was as prone to pranks as to murder. What renders the janitor's testimony credible was that the few months before his complaint (January, 1869) were for Nechayev a period of feverish activity among the Petersburg students. (He had become in September 1868 an auditor at the university.)

Nechayev appears to have been predestined for a conspiratorial and/or criminal career, but in fact he did have a political mentor. This was Peter Tkachev, a lawyer and a publicist of some renown among the radical *intelligentsia*. Though only three years older than Nechayev, Tkachev in 1868 already had a rich revolutionary past. He had been involved in the student riots of 1861; he was another alumnus of the Petropovlovsk and Kronstadt jails. He had indirect connection with the first "Nechayevist" type of revolutionary, Peter Zaichnevsky, author of the bloodthirsty *Young Russia*. Tkachev had worked on Blagosvetlov's *Russian Word* and, like its editor, experienced some unpleasantness after the 1866 assassination attempt (in his case it was limited to a police search of his apartment and a questioning). After his first stay in jail, Tkachev stated that a regeneration of Russia would require the physical liquidation of everybody over twenty-five.[9] He was just the man to introduce Nechayev into the revolutionary world, and it is undoubtedly from him that the younger man heard tantalizing tales of Land and Freedom and the Karakozov affair.

To be sure, by the time they met Tkachev was already more of a writer and theorist of revolutionary conspiracies than an activist. Unlike Khudyakov, Ishutin, or Nechayev, Tkachev could be described as a political thinker for whom visions of slaughter and assassination did not entirely obscure the revolutionary goal. While writing for various radical journals, he kept in touch with what remained of the Petersburg underground after Khudyakov's arrest and with such figures in it as Herman Lopatin and Zemfir Ralli.[10] Tkachev also had a civic wife, the eighteen-year-old Alexandra Dementieva, who from a revolutionary point of view had assets more important than beauty or brains: a printing press. But to run it she needed money, more specifically three thousand rubles left to her by her mother which would be hers only upon a (legal) marriage. Tkachev, having perhaps heard of Khudyakov's experience with marital bonds, was wary of solemnizing their union, alleging his revolutionary reputation as the obstacle. But

[9]B. Kozmin, *P. N. Tkachev and the Revolutionary Movement of the Sixties,* Moscow 1922, 19. The author adds reassuringly that as he grew older, Tkachev gave up this idea. In *The Possessed* one character has an even more drastic recipe for transforming society: "I would take nine-tenths of mankind and blow them up since they are hopeless; this would leave a small minority of educated people, who would then be able to live in a cultured way." Dostoyevsky, Paris 1960 (in Russian), 429.

[10]Lopatin, who was but briefly retained in connection with the Karakozov attempt and then headed what remained of Khudyakov's circle, wrote subsequently that "Tkachev was morally rotten." G. A. Lopatin, *Autobiography,* Petrograd 1922, 174. Considering the morals of some of the people with whom Lopatin associated in his long revolutionary career, this is an intriguing statement.

this could not have been the real reason, for he tried to persuade various radical associates to contract a church wedding with his beloved and thus get hold of the money. However, eventually some affluent comrade provided funds and the press was in business, printing clandestine revolutionary proclamations along with some innocent literature.[11] One of the proclamations, probably co-authored by Tkachev and Nechayev, appeared on March 20, 1869, under the title *To Society*. Referring to the recent student troubles, it stated among other things, "Our protest is unanimous and firm. We are prepared to die in exile or dungeons rather than to stifle morally in our decadent colleges and universities."[12]

Tkachev's and Nechayev's collaboration resulted also in a program for a new conspiracy to pick up where Land and Freedom left off. Notes entitled *Program of Revolutionary Activities,* composed during the winter of 1868–69, were subsequently found by the police during the arrest of a member of the Nechayev group.[13] The document called for the creation of revolutionary circles in university cities throughout the spring of 1869; action was then supposed to spread to other urban centers and, after October, among the peasants; then—and here a familiar motif is repeated—on the ninth anniversary of the Emancipation Edict, February 19, 1870, the peasants would finally see the fraud and injustice of the land settlement and would start widespread popular uprisings.[14]

But Nechayev was not a man to spend his time writing programs or for long to remain a mere disciple. Throughout 1868 he cut a wide swath among radical circles in St. Petersburg. He was becoming, or rather was creating his own legend: as a peasant boy who could not read or write until the age of sixteen and now, only four years later, could quote Kant! Since only a few of his acquaintances knew that he had in fact attended school, or were able themselves to read the German philosopher, it took some time to establish that the quotations were fictitious and that Nechayev did not know a word of German. In addition to this reputation as self-taught erudite man

---

[11]Dementieva's further career deserves notice. Tried with the Nechayev groups, she shocked the judges when upon being asked to state her name, she burst out laughing and said, "Dementieva or Tkacheva, doesn't matter." When her lover fled abroad from his exile, Dementieva was allowed to go to France to join him. There they were finally wedded, but their "real" marriage turned out to be unhappy and brief. She obtained a doctor's diploma and in 1903 was allowed to return to her native country. In 1904 she volunteered for medical duty at the front during the Russo-Japanese war and was probably the first female doctor to become a war prisoner. Alas, upon her return from captivity, instead of being greeted as a heroine she was clapped in jail for having conducted revolutionary propaganda among Russian prisoners of war.

[12]B. Kozmin, *Nechayev and the Nechayevites,* Moscow 1931, 9.

[13]Kozmin, *Tkachev,* 145.

[14]Kozmin doubts Tkachev's participation in the program on the ground that he was a believer in a *coûp d'état* and rejected the possibility of a national uprising, but that development came later, as we shall see.

of the people, there was something at once menacing and attractive in Nechayev's personality. Many well-born but radically inclined ladies found this combination irresistible. Alexandra Uspenskaya, whose husband as the result of his association with and faith in Nechayev was to die a horrible death, could still describe him decades later as "a simple Russian boy ... smart, very energetic, with his whole soul devoted to the cause."[15] How could Dostoyevsky libel and caricature such a noble character, who in addition to his high moral qualities was so full of fun? "He loved to joke and had such a good-natured laugh." Alexandra's sister, Vera Zasulich, soon to become famous as a revolutionary in her own right, had a teen-age crush on Nechayev. But his main confidante during that winter in Petersburg was a mature woman, Elisabeth Tomilova, a colonel's wife who helped him in his conspiratorial undertakings, and whom he left as a sort of deputy after his first flight abroad. (Where was Colonel Tomilov all this time? History remains silent.) It is almost certain that none of those relations Nechayev had with various women had sexual consequences. He cared for women and money only as means to one end: power.

Among men, reactions to Nechayev varied. Some were impressed by his posture as an indomitable revolutionary who had forsaken everything—a brilliant career as an expert on German philosophy, any family life of his own, pursuit of material gain—for the cause. Quite a few of his acquaintances were to confess later that they were physically frightened of him. And indeed already in 1868 this twenty-one-year-old youth showed that he was not a man to be trifled with.

It was another fall and winter of student unrest. The indirect reason, as in 1861, lay in the government's stupidity. Minister of Education Dmitri Tolstoy had in 1867 published a new set of university regulations which among other things banned mass meetings in the academic precincts, as well as unauthorized associations of student self-help. For a while the reverberations of the Karakozov affair helped keep things quiet, but in 1869 the pot began to boil. An incident at the School of Medicine in St. Petersburg in the fall gave rise to demonstrations that soon spread to other Petersburg academic institutions.

The files of the Third Department attest that the student protest movement was at first aimed entirely at liberalization of the regulations but that from the beginning three people were especially active in the agitation to push it into political channels: Tkachev, Nechayev, and Nechayev's fellow teacher and occasional roommate, Vladimir Orlov. Many students, even politically inclined ones, resented Nechayev's attempts to seize the leadership of the movement, especially since by then his philosophical pretensions had been pretty well unmasked and some now called him a charlatan. He

[15]In her "Recollections of a Woman of the Sixties," *The Post,* No. 18 (Moscow 1922), 33.

was not yet ready for physical violence, but he would send a few of his most uncompromising enemies, whose mail he surmised was being opened by the police, subversive literature, and as a result the foes would find themselves in jail. In January Nechayev himself was invited for a talk with the police. He was not detained, but it may be that several students who were subsequently arrested were caught as the result of Nechayev's interview with the security official.

Nechayev may well have begun to sense that his bid for leadership had failed and that furthermore, in view of the rumors about him, Petersburg was becoming unsafe. He sold his belongings and intimated to acquaintances that he thought of leaving for America. It is rather tantalizing to speculate where he might have gone: Indian territory? the Far West? Harvard? (We shall see another Russian assassin transformed into a placid American college professor.) But as usual Nechayev was just fooling.

In any case, one day he disappeared. The same evening, Vera Zasulich received a letter[16] in which an anonymous writer told that he had met a prisoners' van out of whose window a piece of paper was thrown while a voice inside called, "If you are a student, deliver to the addressee!" An enclosed note revealed a hasty message scribbled by Nechayev: "I am being taken to a fortress. Tell our comrades. I hope to see them. Let them carry on."[17] One would have thought that even an eighteen-year-old girl would have been suspicious of this story, especially when inquiries of the police brought a categorical denial that Nechayev was under arrest. But this served only to resuscitate his legend and increase hostility toward the authorities: what barbarism to arrest a man and to deny the fact. Skeptics pointed out that Nechayev had sold his books some time before and had been studying French, but soon *they* in turn were arrested. Nechayev's martyrdom enhanced the revolutionary mood of the young: their meetings now became secret, and there was no more talk of university reforms; instead they recited new revolutionary poems by Nekrasov, such as the one in which he ironically addresses a nineteen-year-old idealist: "How brazen of you to think to overthrow the government and to beat up an inspector!" Indeed, as Vera Zasulich testified, a police inspector was beaten up by some students and the talk in her circle turned more and more toward "the overthrow."

In the meantime, Nechayev was wending his way south to Moscow. Here there was an obvious meeting point for radicals. Alexander Cherkesov[18] had

[16]Notice the excellence of the Petersburg postal system.
[17]Vera Zasulich, *Memoirs,* Moscow 1931, 25.
[18]Not to be confused with Varlaam Cherkeźov, a Caucasian prince, also mixed up in the Karakozov and Nechayev affairs.

sometime before taken over a bookshop and lending library in Petersburg once run by Serno-Solovievich, using it for the same purposes as the previous owner. He then opened a similar establishment in Moscow. Since Cherkesov led a respectable lawyer's existence in Petersburg, his library-revolutionary center in Moscow was run by twenty-two-year-old Peter Uspensky, married to Vera Zasulich's sister Alexandra. Uspensky put Nechayev in touch with another youth, Nicholas Nikolayev, currently working as a prison guard. Having such respectable employment, it was not difficult for Nikolayev to procure a passport to go abroad. And it was with this passport that Nechayev, on March 4, 1869, sailed west from Odessa.

His destination was Geneva. It is possible to reconstruct what was in his ingenious mind. Here, after the three years of "white terror" and the consequent disheartening quiet in Russia, Russian exiles would see before them a young man who would rouse the masses to revolt, a man whom the government had already thought so dangerous that they had tried to liquidate him in secret, but a man who had frustrated the police by performing the incredible feat of escaping from the Petropavlovsk fortress. This was the phase of his legend which Nechayev propagated in Switzerland. Surely those veterans of the liberation movement Ogarev and Bakunin would take him to their bosom, and with their blessing and prestige thrown behind him, as well as with some of Herzen's fabulous wealth, he would go back to Russia to become the leader of a vast conspiracy that would guide the mass uprising in 1870.

He was *almost* correct in the first part of his calculations. The key to his success was the impression he made on Bakunin, whom he met in Geneva in the beginning of April.[19] The renowned revolutionary was in a deplorable state, physically, morally, and politically. Though in fact only fifty-five, he was old beyond his years, suffering from what today would probably be diagnosed as emphysema. As usual he was broke. All his life a sponger living off the charity of his brothers who lived in Russia and of Herzen, Turgenev, etc. (except that he was childish, a stronger word would be appropriate: when he fled Siberia he took with him 3500 rubles entrusted to him by local merchants), Bakunin now also had to and could not provide for his family, his beloved "Antosia" and the children she bore by another man. Though outwardly cheerful about this situation, it still affected him and, perhaps, contributed to his infatuation with somebody so masculine in every respect as Nechayev appeared to be.

Another internal torment must have troubled Bakunin even more deeply, and helped to kindle that *verbal* violence to which this man, kind and nonviolent in his personal behavior, was so prone, and which acted as a self-intoxicant. This torment, unlike his impotence, was a secret none of his

---

[19]We are now under the Western calendar.

friends and associates knew of: the self-abasing confession he had written for Nicholas I in 1851 when in the Petropavlovsk fortress: "Sire, I do not deserve such indulgence, and I blush when I recall what I insolently spoke and wrote about the relentless severity of Your Majesty. . . . Now I have understood how my schemes and activities were in fact ridiculous, thoughtless, insolent crimes, against You my Sovereign, against Russia my country, against all political, moral, divine, and human laws."[20] Signed a "repentant sinner," this abject declaration must have been on Bakunin's mind whenever Karl Marx, whom he came to hate as much as he had Nicholas, and his "bunch of Yids and Germans" circulated rumors that Bakunin was a secret agent of the Russian government!

Politically his affairs were at a low ebb. The International Alliance, in which he played the leading role and which he hoped would overshadow or take over Marx's First International, was in the process of dissolution and what remained of it would soon become a section of the latter organization. There Bakunin's influence was strong enough to wreck the First International altogether but not to wrest it from the domination of his hated enemy. (Despite his racial and personal prejudice the old anarchist respected Marx as a revolutionary but loathed Marxism—and who can now quarrel with his insight?—for advocating an even more centralized state than the bourgeois one.)

Nechayev's appearance and the tales he brought, not only of his own "escape" but of equally fictitious widespread peasant disorders—everything pointing to a mass rising in 1870—must have seemed to Bakunin a miracle come true. He was not a fool and probably allowed for some exaggeration in the young man's story: no one had previously managed to escape from Petropavlovsk. But as he was to write pathetically to Nechayev after their break: "I said to myself and to Ogarev that we did not have time to wait for another man, we were both old and were not likely to meet another man like you, so devoted [to revolution], so capable; and that if we wanted to take a hand [again] in the work in Russia, we had to come with you and no one else. . . . We knew nothing about your Committee and the whole organization and had to depend on what you told us."[21] Of course there was no "Committee" and no organization. But through Nechayev Bakunin hoped to get a grip on revolutionary activities inside Russia, a goal which had hitherto eluded him.

Ogarev, by now a walking ruin of a man, sustained only by the companionship of the woman he had picked up from London's streets, was almost as impressed by Nechayev as Bakunin was. He hastened to notify Herzen

[20]Bakunin, *Works,* Y. M. Steklov, ed., IV, Moscow 1935, 100, 149.

[21]Arthur Lehning, ed., *Michael Bakunin and His Relations with Serge Nechayev,* London 1971 (in French, with Russian and German texts), 106.

of the arrival of this marvel, "the student who has just escaped from the Petropavlovsk fortress" and who was asking Herzen to print a proclamation to Nechayev's followers in Russia acquainting them with his miraculous escape.[22] Both Bakunin and Ogarev now began to pressure their old friend to deliver to Nechayev the Bakhmetev fund of which he was a co-trustee. This money, as we have seen, was left at Ogarev's and Herzen's disposal by the mysterious eccentric who disappeared in 1858. The capital was £800, or 20,000 francs, to be spent for revolutionary purposes. Herzen, who got to Geneva in May, had a very negative impression of Nechayev, and scolded Ogarev for his new associations and "bloodthirsty inclinations." But once again he felt unable to refuse anything to his life-long friend, for whose personal tragedy he felt partly responsible. It is possible that he was also physically afraid of Nechayev. In any case he hastened to leave Geneva and soon transferred 10,000 francs to Ogarev, who through Bakunin conveyed them to their new associate.

The "Triumvirs," as Herzen called them, were engaged in hectic writing of revolutionary proclamations to be conveyed to Russia. Ogarev's share in this effort, hampered as he was by his alcoholism, was minor. Also, as he explained in a letter to Nechayev which began "from granddaddy to his little grandson,"[23] he could not quite approve the thesis that one of the mainstays of the future Russian revolution would be found in the criminal element of Russia's population. But he dedicated to Nechayev a short and awful poem entitled "The Student": "Pursued by the tsar's vengeance and fears of the great, he chose the life of an exile so as to rouse the people to revolt."

"The little grandson," or "boy," as Bakunin called him (it was one of the few English words he ever learned), basked in this renown, but also kept a wary eye on the Russian revolutionaries in Switzerland who, like Herman Lopatin, knew that he was an impostor and tried to warn the exile colony against him. He hurried to extract from Bakunin as much as possible in the way of collaboration before returning to Russia and assuming the leadership of the revolutionary movement.

The most famous of these revolutionary proclamations has passed into history as the *Revolutionary's Catechism*.[24] It lays down the rules for a conspiracy operation: it should consist (this was reminiscent of Land and Freedom) of cells of five or six people. Other organizational hints follow: the conspiracy should spread subversive rumors via prostitutes, infiltrate

[22]E.L. Rudnitskaya, *N.P. Ogarev in the Russian Revolutionary Movement*, Moscow 1969, 382.

[23]*Ibid.*, 388. It was more symbolic, perhaps, than Ogarev intended.

[24]Subsequent quotations are from the text as presented in the indictment of Nechayev's associates before the St. Petersburg Court on July 1, 1871, and quoted in B. Bazilevsky (pseudonym of Vasili Yakovlev), *State Crimes in Russia*, I; *1825–1876*, Stuttgart 1903 (in Russian).

the police, establish contacts "with the so-called criminal part of the population." The revolutionary must be a consecrated man. "He has no personal interests or activities, no private feelings, attachments, or property, not even a name. He is absorbed by one single aim, thought, passion—revolution." He is to despise public opinion and all learning; he should know only one science, "that of destruction." "Moved by the sober passion for revolution he should stifle in himself all considerations of kinship, love, friendship, and even honor."[25] Then, somewhat repetitiously, the revolutionaries are urged to infiltrate everything: the bureaucracy, the Third Department, "the Winter Palace." The conspiracy was to be hierarchical: there were to be second- and third-class revolutionaries not privy to the secrets of the elite, which was to use them freely for the benefit of the cause.

After this promising beginning the declaration goes on to describe how the revolutionaries are to deal with various elements in this "wretched society": 1) people who are to be liquidated right away; 2) persons allowed to live temporarily, "so that through their beastliness they will provoke the people to irreversible revolt";[26] 3) those influential people who are stupid and can be exploited; 4) various kinds of liberals, whom one can pretend to work with, whose secrets one can learn, whom one can compromise, *so that they foul up the state by their own hand*;[27] 5) doctrinaires and revolutionaries of different ilk, whom one should try to push into extreme actions "so that most of them will be completely destroyed" and a small remainder will be worthy to join the "true" revolutionaries; and 6) "an important category—women," "empty-head ones" treatable in the same way as numbers 3 and 4 of men, while "others, passionate, devoted, able, but not ours" are to be considered as number 5, and finally "our type" of women, who "are to be treasured as our greatest asset, indispensable to our purposes."[28] At least no woman is to be treated like numbers 1 or 2 of men, which supports the thesis of those scholars who attribute the authorship of the *Catechism* primarily to Bakunin, since it is unlikely that Nechayev was capable of such delicacy and restraint.

It would be tedious to go through most of the other fruits of the Bakunin-Nechayev collaboration or to try to determine the extent to which one or the other contributed to this or that proclamation. But we must note two other works. One is signed by "The descendants of Rurik [semi-legendary founder of the Russian state and the highest nobility] and the party of independent nobility" and addressed "to the Russian aristocracy." It is clearly the product of Bakunin's childish mind, since Nechayev's acquaint-

[25] *Ibid.*, 333–34.
[26] *Ibid.*, 471
[27] My italics.
[28] *Ibid.*, 336–37

ance with this social stratum was rather limited. It calls upon the Russian nobility to rise against Alexander II, "that insignificant descendant of a petty German prince," and all the "Germans" around him. It lists the historical merits of the nobility—suppression of revolts, subjugation of Poland, defense of the autocracy, etc.—and asks how Alexander II had rewarded it for all those brilliant achievements? He had taken the nobles' land and given it to the peasants! Bakunin's Soviet biographer, who is eager to credit this "outstanding revolutionary" with the exclusive authorship of as many of those proclamations as possible, concludes sadly that this one "is not so much shameless as stupid"—distinguished in this regard, one assumes, from, say, the *Catechism.*[29]

But skipping most other Bakunin-Nechayev products of those spring-summer months of 1869 we must turn to one that was without doubt authored mainly or solely by Nechayev. This is the broadside entitled *The People's Justice.* (This is a necessarily awkward translation of the Russian word *rasprava,* the meaning of which is somewhere between justice-vindication and punishment-settling of accounts.) It was published on behalf of the committee of the organization called the People's Justice of February 19, 1870, the committee as well as the organization consisting for the time being of Nechayev. "A general uprising of the tormented Russian people is inevitable and at hand," it begins.[30] "The beginning of our sacred task was laid in the morning [actually the afternoon] of April 4, 1866, by Dmitri Karakozov." To prepare for the accomplishment of this task the Committee recommends diligent reading of some recent writings by Bakunin and Nechayev, as well as works whose authors are not specified (in fact also Bakunin-Nechayev). But unlike Karakozov, the Committee does not propose to *begin* assassinations with the tsar's. First and immediately various ministers and courtiers should be killed, as well as "the scum of contemporary Russian learning and literature . . . the mass of publicists, hacks, and pseudo-scientists." A sample of names follows, including the harmless Pogodin who had befriended Nechayev. And Alexander II? *"Him* we shall spare for a painful and solemn execution before the whole people once the entire state lies in ruin."

What use was made of this rather remarkable politico-literary output? The *Catechism,* as the organizational blueprint, was kept secret and was not discovered by the police until after Ivanov's murder in November. But much of the money extorted from Herzen must have been spent on postage. For beginning in the spring post offices in Russia's main cities were deluged with packages containing the Nechayev-Bakunin proclamations. The po-

---

[29]Y. M. Steklov, *Bakunin,* III, Moscow 1927, 456.
[30]Its partial text is in Vladimir Burtsev, *One Hundred Years,* London 1897 (in Russian), 90–96. A somewhat different version of a fragment of it is in Bazilevsky, 322.

lice, as the playful terrorist must have known, had for long been opening packages and letters coming from Switzerland. And indeed in Petersburg alone 500 pieces of such mail addressed to 387 people were intercepted by the authorities.[31] It must have hugely amused Nechayev to think of how his various enemies, casual acquaintances, and people chosen at random as addressees were being questioned and often detained. To make sure of this, in some cases he would sign letters with his real name. One unfortunate victim of these pranks, who had not seen Nechayev since 1864, was arrested and when he refused the Third Department's offer to go to Geneva and spy for it, he lost his job and remained under police surveillance for the rest of his life. It is not surprising that some radicals became convinced that Nechayev was a police *provocateur* and retained this belief until his trial in 1873.

But all this writing and games could not for long satisfy a man of action. Nechayev manufactured a "certificate" dated May 12 proclaiming, "The carrier of this is one of the confidential representatives of the Russian section of the World Revolutionary Alliance, no. 2771." The document bore a seal engraved "The European Revolutionary Alliance—General Committee" and was signed Michael Bakunin. Even though practically all authorities assert that Bakunin willingly participated in this hoax, his much later letter to Nechayev casts some doubt on this point.

With the certificate and the *Catechism* as his treasures, in August Nechayev left Switzerland, and on September 3 was in Moscow. Too many people in St. Petersburg knew or suspected what he was, and he had heard that his friend Tomilova was under police supervision. But in Moscow many radicals were confused as to the fate of this already semilegendary figure. Had Nechayev really escaped and been abroad, as his acknowledged authorship of the recent pamphlets would indicate, or had he died at the hands of the police on the road to Siberia, as the first circular of *The People's Justice* and the conclusion of Ogarev's poem, "He died in the snowy wastes of Siberia," asserted? But Peter Uspensky, into whose two-room apartment Nechayev moved upon his arrival, knew the identity of his guest. To most others whom he recruited into his circle during the next two months, Nechayev was known as Pavlov.[32]

Uspensky, who became Nechayev's main lieutenant, had a somewhat ambiguous reputation in the radical world. He had tried to join the Ishutin circle and had been rejected. Then, when some Moscow radicals were briefly detained in April 1869, Uspensky, though close to them, was unmo-

[31]B. Kozmin, "New Facts About Nechayev" in *The Red Archive,* I (14), Moscow 1926, 149.
[32]Uspenskaya, 32. There are certain discrepancies between her *memoires* and those of her sister Vera. Alexandra hints that Vera had a crush on Nechayev; the latter, whose recollections were also recorded in her old age, admits that she was impressed by him, but rejected his declaration of love.

lested. He thus had an added incentive for demonstrating his devotion to the cause. The police had undoubtedly felt it was more convenient to keep him under surveillance, so as to trap his contacts during any future trouble. But these suspicions were to follow Uspensky in his exile to Siberia and contribute to his terrible end.

As laid down in the *Catechism,* Uspensky and his guest set out to organize a cell of revolutionaries which Pavlov-Nechayev, representative of the World Revolutionary Alliance, announced would be a unit of that alliance's subdivision in "The People's Justice" of February 19, 1870. This cell would be supervised by the clandestine Committee of which he, Pavlov, was also the representative. There is no question that before too long members of the cell saw through the more obvious part of this mystification—the Committee was Nechayev—and, though some of them were to deny this in court, they also learned his real identity. The cell went beyond the prescribed five or six members, but we shall concentrate on four others. One was Nikolayev, whom we have already met as the man who gave Nechayev his identity papers in March; after that he had had to leave his job and hide in the provinces whence on October 20 he was summoned to Moscow by Nechayev. Nikolayev, like Nechayev, had been born in Ivanovo and, though three years younger, had probably known Nechayev as a boy. Another, Ivan Ivanov, born in 1847, was a student in the Petrovsky Agricultural Academy.[33]

Forty-two-year-old Ivan Prizhov was an exception in this group of very young men. The story of Prizhov's life, as he rather incoherently sketched it for his lawyer while awaiting trial, had been pathetic.[34] The son of a retired soldier who was subsequently a hospital clerk, Prizhov from his early years combined an interest in a rather unusual branch of folklore—that dealing with beggars, "holy fools," and drunkards—with an inability to hold a regular job because like the subjects of some of his studies he very early became an alcoholic. In his more sober moments he wrote books on *The Poor People in Old Russia, A History of Russian Taverns,* and similar subjects. His literary efforts did not bring him much money, and he subsisted largely on free drinks and meals offered him in bars—emoluments he received, he assures us, for lecturing barflies about social problems of the day. The opening of his autobiographical sketch, "I have had a dog's life," expresses not only a sense of grievance but also Prizhov's strong affection for, one might almost say identification with, dogs! The only being he refers to warmly is not his wife but his old dog Leporello. Once, having decided

[33]Venturi mistakenly identifies Ivanov as the man who furnished Nechayev with his passport. Franco Venturi, *Roots of the Revolution,* New York 1970, 775.

[34]J.G. Prizhov, *Essays, Articles, Letters,* M. J. Altman, ed., Moscow 1934. His "confession," written obviously in an intoxicated state, in which he sometimes refers to himself in the third person, is on pp. 11–29.

to end his life, he jumped with his companion into a lake. But the dog, not comprehending its master's intention, swam around and Prizhov was pulled out. His arrest in the Nechayev affair interrupted Prizhov as he worked on *The Dog in the History of Human Beliefs.* Both his literary interests and radical views made Prizhov hang around Cherkesov's library. (He believed all major popular uprisings had their inception in alcohol, a statement which a sober historian will not reject out of hand, since both Stenka Razin and Pugachev were far from being teetotalers.) Uspensky recommended him to Nechayev as obviously the ideal man to establish contact between the People's Justice and the "lower depths" of Moscow's population.

And to complete the famous six we have Alexis Kuznetsov. Born in 1846 of a merchant family, Kuznetsov was the only one of the main actors in the drama who lived into and played a part in twentieth-century politics, taking a very active part in the revolution of 1905 in Siberia. He was sentenced to death, pardoned, and survived into the Soviet period.

The conspiracy was now in business. Members of the original circle were given numbers. Thus Ivanov was 2, Kuznetsov 3, according to the *Catechism*'s injunction that "the revolutionary has no name of his own." Each then was to build up a five-or-six-member cell of conspirators, *their* numbers having two digits, beginning with their leader's. (Thus Ivanov's followers would be 21, 22, and so on.) In addition a wider recruitment and a propaganda campaign was to be conducted among various elements of Moscow's population: Ivanov was to work among the students, Kuznetsov had the merchant class, and Prizhov's apostolate was, of course, to criminals, drunkards, and prostitutes. Nechayev, in addition to his duties as the representative of the Committee and the World Revolutionary Alliance, took on the task of recruiting among officers. Nikolayev, when he was brought in, was called variously the representative of the peasants or the special inspector from the Committee. He was slavishly devoted to Nechayev, and usually remained silent, arousing among some fellow members almost as much fear as did his fellow townsman.

Fantastic though it may seem, the circle grew in numbers. Kuznetsov's later statement, that in two weeks the net of circles organized by Nechayev expanded from eight original members to about four hundred,[35] is greatly exaggerated, but when the murder of November 21 put a stop to the whole enterprise there were probably some seventy or eighty people in various degrees of initiation in the Moscow branch of the People's Justice. The Committee kept a vigilant eye on the activities of the organization; Nechayev would express surprise at the speed with which it learned what was going on in his organization, noticed the slightest transgression of the conspiratorial rules, heard about doubts expressed among members con-

[35]Quoted in Zasulich, 125.

cerning the aims of the society, and hastened to issue appropriate warnings (through him). Strangely enough, Nechayev himself was never reprimanded even when, the explicit rules to the contrary, he took a hand in recruiting members for cells other than his own. His proselytizing efforts varied. To some who professed themselves apolitical he explained that they should join for their own safety; they were then sure to be spared in the great slaughter which would take place after February 19, 1870. Sometimes he was more direct: one student later testified that he joined after Nechayev pulled a knife on him.[36] But many were impressed by the tales he told about himself and by his boundless energy. Prizhov, as we know, could not help admiring a peasant lad who was illiterate until sixteen and now would quote freely from Kant's *Critique of Pure Reason.*

What did all the converts do? The cells held biweekly meetings in which the rich harvest of the Bakunin-Nechayev literary collaboration was discussed. But there were more practical concerns: all revolutionary enterprises need money. Nechayev had procured printed membership blanks with the legend "The People's Justice of February 19, 1870," encircling its emblem: the axe. Armed with these credentials emissaries visited people of means believed to be susceptible to such methods of persuasion and demanded money for the cause. Prizhov was sent to Nechayev's hometown to solicit 10,000 rubles from a rich merchant, but having hardly the personality of an "enforcer" his mission met with failure.[37] Some other efforts at fund-raising were more successful. Nechayev still had contacts in St. Petersburg, among them a noble-born young lady, Catherine Likhutin, with whom he had kept in touch while in Switzerland, and her two brothers, Ivan and Vladimir. One day in late September Nechayev, always very circumspect in his visits to the capital, appeared suddenly in the apartment of the Likhutins and persuaded Ivan to accompany him back to Moscow to see with his own eyes how splendidly the revolutionary work was going on. "Here you are asleep. . . . [In Moscow] things are buzzing, people are awake and getting together."[38] Nechayev explained that it would be a great thing to persuade their common acquaintance, one Andrew Kolachevsky, to contribute to the cause, and he suggested a way. Likhutin went back to St. Petersburg and, with his sister's and friend's help, put the scheme into motion. He invited Kolachevsky for tea and handed him some subversive literature as they parted. Once in the street poor Kolachevsky was seized by two "police agents": these were actually Vladimir Likhutin and a friend dressed in appropriate uniforms, with false beards and wigs. Kolachevsky was given alternatives: either the Third Department and all that it meant,

---

[36]Bazilevsky, 318.

[37]*Ibid.,* 304.

[38]*Ibid.,* 384.

or a note for six thousand rubles. Naturally he gave them the latter.[39] Although he helped Nechayev to collect funds, Likhutin, as he explained at his trial, had reservations about his friend's ideological approach: "I sympathized with revolutionary ideas and hoped to achieve them through an insurrection, but not one of the democratic kind Nechayev desired[!] but one with the goal of representative government, with relatively greater freedoms of the individual and of speech."[40]

What other ingenious ideas must have circulated through Nechayev's mind! At his instructions Prizhov acquired a whole wardrobe: priest's robes and various regimental uniforms. Was one of the conspirators planning to appear in the cathedral and call upon the faithful to rise against the tsar? Would false officers lead their regiments and Cossack squadrons in attacks upon government offices? Alas, his enterprise had no recruits apart from a few students: all efforts to enlist peasants and criminals bore little fruit. Some of Prizhov's associates, suspecting that his preaching to the underworld might not be effective, insisted on accompanying him to a saloon known as a thieves' den. But its sights and smells proved too much for their nerves, and they wisely left this line of work to their older colleague. And one may question Venturi's assertion that Nechayev "seems to have had another base among the workmen of the Tula munitions factories."[41] The grounds for this statement can only be another fantasy of that intrepid liar Nechayev: after the murder, and when members of his Moscow organization had already been arrested, Nechayev told Prince Varlaam Cherkežov, from whom he was seeking money and help for his flight abroad, not to worry about the People's Justice: he himself had to leave the country for a while, but in September he had come to Russia not alone but with sixteen other delegates of the World Revolutionary Alliance who now remained undetected and were doing splendid work in various other parts of Russia; thus "Tula, and especially its armament workers, were about to rise."[42]

By November 1869 Nechayev felt that the flourishing state of his enterprise in Russia should be communicated both to his associates and to

[39]The incident is referred to by Venturi as something "between farce and blackmail" (378). To support the "farce" side of the statement he goes on to say, "the victim shortly afterwards married the sister of the fake policeman and [later became] minister of finance in Witte's government between 1900 and 1902." But Venturi has confused Kolachevsky with one Vladimir Kovalevsky. *He* was a very different person: far from being the victim, he helped to plan the robbery; he married Catherine Likhutin and became not minister but deputy minister of finance under Witte. To add insult to injury, the victim Kolachevsky was subsequently arrested as a member of the Nechayev circle and spent a year and a half in jail before being exonerated by the court. Ivan and Catherine Likhutin (Vladimir died in the meantime) and Kovalevsky also faced the court. Ivan was sentenced to sixteen months in prison, and the other two were acquitted.

[40]Bazilevsky, 386.

[41]Venturi, 380.

[42]Bazilevsky, 353.

skeptics among the political exiles in Switzerland. Did she know French and German, he asked his hostess, and upon an affirmative answer said to Uspenskaya, "Would you go to Switzerland to see Bakunin, Ogarev, and Herzen?"[43] Would she! "I would not have dared dream about such luck." There was only one inconvenient detail: she was in advanced pregnancy. Nechayev was not without an understanding of psychology: "Say simply that you do not want to go. I have not expected that from you. Your sister Vera would not have refused." But this did not help. He made the same proposal to several other ladies of his acquaintance, realizing perhaps that none of his male associates would make a suitable impression upon the notables in Switzerland. (And who knows; an enthusiastic woman might even persuade Herzen to change his attitude toward him.)

On November 16 Nechayev announced to his future accomplices his decision to kill the student Ivan Ivanov. Almost all versions of the history maintain that his reason for this was a suspicion that Ivanov was going to inform or already had informed the police about the People's Justice. But nobody who has studied the trial records concerning his four fellow assassins and Nechayev himself[44] can endorse this conclusion. The four accomplices testified repeatedly that the only reason for Nechayev's decision was his personal hostility toward Ivanov. This hostility had arisen, some of them deduced, from a trivial incident. On November 4 Nechayev ordered Ivanov to distribute antigovernment leaflets in the restaurant of the Petrovsky Agricultural Academy. Ivanov objected. The Academy's students were in many ways a privileged group among the youth of Moscow's educational institutions—half of them lived in free quarters on the premises of the school, itself situated in a large pleasant park; their restaurant was subsidized; the administration was liberal, unlike the one at Moscow University; and no one thought of enforcing rules against student meetings and associations—but if subversive literature was found in its precincts, all those privileges might be curtailed. In any case the recruiting effort among students was going well: there was no need for useless bravado which might only draw the authorities' attention. It is doubtful that, as Uspensky and Prizhov testified, Ivanov then became a frequent opponent of Nechayev, questioning the existence of the Committee and threatening to leave the organization and form his own revolutionary group. He certainly took no steps in this direction in the weeks that followed his disagreement with Nechayev, and he would not have unsuspectingly obeyed the latter's summons to meet him in a secluded spot on that fatal evening had he been involved in a violent dispute with him. But, as the sequence of events will show, Nechayev was by instinct a murderer: sadism fought with lust to

[43]Uspenskaya, 34.
[44]They are cited in Bazilevsky, 289–342 and 415–56, respectively.

power for mastery of his mind. He rather easily convinced Uspensky, Prizhov, Nikolayev, and Kuznetsov that Ivanov should be killed. They of course claimed that they objected, and finally assented only from fear of Nechayev. This is credible enough but throws a revealing light on the mentality of those men, three of whom were vigorous and young.[45]

In the early afternoon of November 21 the five assassins gathered in Kuznetsov's apartment. Nikolayev was sent out after the victim. He found him drinking tea and having a boisterous discussion with some fellow students. But Ivanov followed without any hesitation on being told that the cell was to have an emergency meeting: some printing equipment had been discovered hidden on the grounds of the Academy and they were going to pick it up and discuss its possible use. Back in Kuznetsov's apartment the two found only Prizhov; the others had, on the approach of the victim and his companion, jumped into a cab and driven to Petrovsky Park to set the stage for the crime. The printing equipment was supposed to be in a half-ruined artificial grotto some thirty steps from a pond. Uspensky began to tie bricks to a rope, Nechayev tested ice on the pond. Kuznetsov stood on the path to signal when the others appeared. It took some time because Prizhov, who had been forbidden by Nechayev to have any drink that morning, insisted that he, Nikolayev, and Ivanov stop at a bar. It was five o'clock and dark when they finally arrived at the park. Nikolayev, after bringing Ivanov into the grotto, grabbed him but immediately let go for Nechayev had pounced on him, mistaking him in the darkness for the victim. Nikolayev wrested himself from the grip of the maniac shouting, "Not me! I'm Nikolayev!" while Ivanov tried to flee, crying, "What have I done to you?" and was brought down by the others. Nechayev now had the right man, but the others were not helping and he had difficulty strangling his victim. Ivanov sank his teeth in his hand.[46] Impelled by Nechayev's curses, two of the others finally came to his assistance: Kuznetsov sat on the victim's legs, Nechayev sat on his chest, and Nikolayev grabbed the throat. The autopsy established beyond doubt that Ivanov's death was by strangulation, but for some reason, probably to see blood, Nechayev took Nikolayev's gun and shot what was by now the corpse through the head. Nechayev was the only one of the five cold-blooded enough to be able then to go through Ivanov's clothes: he removed his wallet, cigars, etc. But, whether through negligence or from some sudden mad design, he left in Ivanov's jacket the two most incriminating possible items: a watch, which would immediately tell the police that robbery had not been the motive for the crime, and a card to Cherkesov's lending library issued to Kuznetsov.

[45]"The accused, Kuznetsov, Prizhov, and Nikolayev, explained their part in the crime as being motivated by fear that their refusal would have exposed them to Nechayev's vengeance and that they were afraid for their own lives." *Ibid.,* 421.

[46]More than three years later doctors testified that the scars on Nechayev's wrists and fingers dated from that time.

Then the ice on the pond was broken and Ivanov's body, weighed down with the bricks, was thrown in.

The murderers then gathered in Kuznetsov's apartment. Here they burnt Ivanov's belongings and some of their bloodied clothes. Then a peculiar sequence of events took place: Nechayev fired the gun, and the bullet missed Prizhov only by inches. "Well, if you were killed, all this could be blamed on you." Prizhov ran out but then came back, allegedly to pick up his scarf but probably because he realized that one could not run away from this terrible man. Nechayev grabbed him and kissed him on the head.[47] Who, seeing such a scene in a gangster drama, would not exclaim that such things simply don't happen in real life?

The next day Nechayev left for St. Petersburg, taking with him Kuznetsov, whose function for the next few days would be to find out who would give Nechayev shelter and money. On November 25 Ivanov's body was discovered, and the next day the police raided Cherkesov's bookstore and Uspensky's apartment. In both was found much Bakunin-Nechayev literature, including the *Catechism,* in an easily decipherable code, a partial list of members in the Nechayev conspiracy, and other incriminating material. On December 1 Kuznetsov was arrested in Petersburg, and soon others involved or only remotely connected with Nechayev in Petersburg and Moscow were put under lock and key. He himself managed to skip again. With money provided by Prince Cherkezov he went back to Moscow, picked up a female acquaintance, and by the middle of December was out of Russia. The lady in question, one Barbara Alexandrovskaya, the thirty-six-year-old wife of a customs official, found Nechayev a most unsatisfactory traveling companion. She was back in Russia by January 1870. Arrested, she recounted to the police how her presumably romantic expectations were disappointed: "No matter how much I watched after him I could not get his attention; he would not talk, do, or even think about anything except his enterprise. The social question occupies him to the point of physical exhaustion. . . . He drinks but little . . . and [even in his sleep] mumbles incoherent words concerning his business." The scorned woman then offered her services to help lure Nechayev to Dresden where he could be snatched and extradited to Russia.[48]

His accomplices having fully confessed, garbled stories of the murder began to reach Switzerland early in 1870. And if Nechayev even today manages to convince a distinguished modern historian that "he was inspired by a definite picture of the future" and possessed "ruthless, violent dignity,"[49] it is not too surprising that he was still a revolutionary hero to a majority of his radical contemporaries. The one man who would have cried

[47]Bazilevsky, 437.
[48]Kozmin, *Nechayev and Nechayevites,* 140.
[49]Venturi, 379 and 387.

out in outrage was no more. On January 21, 1870, Alexander Herzen died in Paris. To the Russian liberation movement which was his creation he left an ambiguous legacy: both an uncompromising passion for freedom, and that inability to discern clearly and reject those who under its banner would seek new despotism.

Bakunin greeted Nechayev with open arms. Not having money even for the short trip to Geneva where Nechayev was hiding, the old anarchist invited him to Locarno, promising "shelter, bed, room with a table, and the deepest secrecy."[50] The visit took place in February and the encounter was cordial. Nechayev was able to render Bakunin an important service. The latter in his penury had taken on a most uncongenial job: translating Karl Marx's *Capital* I for a Russian publisher. Since Bakunin had never been able really to finish any of his own books, it is not surprising that he was not getting on with the translation, and the publisher's Swiss representative kept demanding either proof of some progress or return of the advance. Nechayev now wrote to the publisher telling him to leave Bakunin in peace or otherwise the People's Justice would take care of him.

Bakunin and Ogarev tried to reconstitute their "Triumvirate" with Nechayev, an effort in which they did not hesitate to exploit their dead friend's name and money. Ogarev secured the second part of the Bakhmatev fund from Herzen's son, and he persuaded Herzen's daughter Natalia (known as Tata, to distinguish her from the two other Natalias in Herzen's life) to come to Geneva and join the trio in their revolutionary propaganda. There was a new flurry of Bakunin-Nechayev proclamations to various classes in Russia, most of them simply a rehash of the 1869 productions. Ogarev and Nechayev set out to revive *The Bell,* but after six issues this sacrilegious enterprise collapsed.

Tata Herzen was then a girl of twenty-five. Having been affected by the sequence of tragedies which befell her family, hurt by her father's denigration of most of the men attracted to her, she now found herself briefly under Nechayev's spell. He played on his old theme with rich women: that those who had lived on the fruits of exploitation had a duty to sacrifice all for the cause, i.e., for himself. But Tuchkova-Ogareva, her stepmother, kept warning Tata against her new acquaintance. She received in return a message from the People's Justice warning her to omit from the publication of Herzen's last writings those passages decrying violence, threatening "decisive measures" if she did not comply.[51] What at first seemed a promising romance, especially financially promising, was to Nechayev's fury turning sour. This sequence of excerpts from his letters to Tata speaks for itself:

May 26: ". . . You have been totally under the influence of your milieu

[50]Y.M. Steklov, *Fighters for Socialism,* Moscow 1923, III, 495.
[51]Tuchkova-Ogareva, 260.

(and it has been a very bad one). . . . This is why Natalia Alexeyevna [Tuchkova]—herself already an effete woman—regards you with pity and believes that without her advice you will perish."

May 27: "I do not think it is necessary to explain my desires, my aspirations to see you a *real woman*. . . . I love you."

May 30: "For the sake of the 'cause,' for the sake of everything you hold sacred . . . come to me as an old comrade, as a dear friend with complete trust. . . ."

And then June: "What intrigues are *you* writing about, you who are a participant in the foulest of intrigues, the exploitation of millions . . . who have done nothing and refuse to work for a cause?"[52]

At the same time another and older associate was also rejecting Nechayev. Bakunin was becoming thoroughly disillusioned with the "boy." February 19, 1870, had come and gone and not a whisper of a peasant revolt. Bakunin realized what in some ways he had always known but tried not to believe: there had never been any Committee or revolutionary movement behind Nechayev in Russia, only at most those seventy to eighty people, now under arrest. And in his old age he, his wife, and her bastards would be left without any means of support, for the Bakhmatev money was gone and Nechayev had scared off his Russian publishers. All these pent-up grievances exploded in a letter he wrote to his erstwhile protégé on June 2.[53] It gives a good picture of how this basically childish man was yet not without cunning, and how his by now almost complete moral obtuseness did not completely extinguish personal kindness.

The theme of the letter is "you have deceived me" and "you have used me." "You used me to build an organization in Russia. Many people really believed that I was head of a secret organization, about which as you know, I myself was completely ignorant."[54] Reading the first part one might conclude that Bakunin had mended his ways, that he had rejected the "criminal-is-the-natural-revolutionary" theme and believed only in, as he says, "spontaneous popular revolutions." But then, alas, "I do not like criminals, but if I am to choose between those who are on the throne and 'people's criminals' I prefer the latter." And so he lapsed back into fantasies. Criminals and the peasant commune were the two principal resources for the revolutionaries; let Nechayev mend his ways, submit all his future plans to Bakunin, and he would agree to collaborate again with Boy. He also hints at his financial needs.

Ivanov's murder, about which Bakunin must have had by now fairly

---

[52]Quotations in Michael Confino, *Daughter of a Revolutionary: Natalie Herzen and the Bakunin-Nechayev Circle,* La Salle, Ill., 1973, 178, 182, 184, 186.
[53]Its Russian text in Lehning, 103–35.
[54]*Ibid.,* 111.

extensive information? Not a word. But "I must confess, dear friend, that your ways of blackmailing and frightening Tata were not to my liking."[55] He compared Nechayev to Savanarola, Machiavelli, and Loyola—a notably frightful example of his utter lack of a sense of proportion and decency.

The net was closing in. Nechayev's associates having made complete confessions, the Russian government now demanded his extradition as a common criminal. The adjective was incorrect, but so was the counterargument in progressive circles that his crime had been politically motivated. In July he had his last interview with Ogarev and Bakunin, and they advised him to leave for America. Instead, having stolen documents from both of them, he repaired to London and tried to enlist as a member of the First International. He was vetoed by Marx, more on account of his previous connection with Bakunin than because of other aspects of his reputation.[56] The socialist press in Belgium, Germany, and Switzerland gave full credence to Nechayev's stories: articles supported the killing of Ivanov as perfectly justified, and described in lurid terms how the Russian police tortured the revolutionaries who had disposed of the despicable *provocateur.* Mme. Uspenskaya, arrested and refused any help in delivery of her child, it was said, "expired after terrible sufferings."[57] (It is perhaps interesting to note the actual report of the Third Department agent on this lady, who of course lived to hale old age: "But what shall we do with Uspenskaya? She is very poor, the baby has not yet been baptized. I have given her twenty-five rubles because with the baby being breast-fed she cannot be moved from the apartment." Prizhov, who was having dt's, was attended by a prison doctor. His comrade Uspensky, who had already fully confessed, advised the police, "Give Prizhov vodka, he will tell the true story."[58])

In the spring of 1872 Nechayev moved to Zurich where he lived under an assumed name, his real identity being known to a handful of Russian and Polish refugees. One of the latter, Adolf Stempkowski, betrayed him to the police. There was a great deal of agitation and indignation among radical and liberal circles when it was announced that the Swiss authorities would return Nechayev to Russia. Even Tuchkova-Ogareva recounts how she pleaded with a Swiss official to let him escape provided he promised to go to America. But despite all such efforts, on October 19 he was in Petersburg and this time found himself really in the Petropavlovsk fortress.

By the time of his arrest the facts about his crime and his general activities were fully known, the trials of his accomplices as well as of a number of people alleged to have been members of the People's Justice having taken

[55] *Ibid.,* 128.
[56] *Ibid., lxv.*
[57] *Ibid.,* 334.
[58] "The Story of the Nechayev Trial," *The Red Archive,* VI (33), Moscow 1930, 127, 157.

place during the summer of 1871. This time the proceedings had been public, but as usual the government did not fail to display its complete assininity when it came to dealing with public opinion. One would have thought that from the legal point of view, not to mention the psychological impact on the public, it was imperative to judge the four partners in the assassination separately. Instead the government joined their case to that of seven others who had political and personal connections with Nechayev—such as Tkachev, his playful "wife," Dementieva, etc. Other trials of "Nechayevites" followed, the total number of accused reaching eighty-seven, some of whom in fact had been Nechayev's victims rather than associates (such as poor Kolachevsky) or people on whom he had planted his revolutionary proclamations. Thus the facts of the vicious murder were largely obscured in the public mind by irrelevant stories about student disorders in 1869, disputed facts as to whether or not some of the accused had circulated manifestos received from Switzerland, etc. Consequently the general mood toward the accused was quite different from that which prevailed toward the main figures in the Karakozov affair of 1866. A Third Department agent dispatched to appraise reactions of the court audience had a depressing tale for his superiors: the prosecutor was inept; the defending lawyers' speeches verged on the seditious; the president of the court, determined to display his liberalism, allowed the accused to read newspapers and wave to the public during the proceedings; the audience, "composed largely of students, young ladies, and artillery officers," was not unsympathetic; there were whispers of "brave boys and girls, they do not lose heart."[59]

It is safe to say that no court in any other country at the time would have failed to dispatch the four partners in this unprovoked, deliberate, and sadistic murder to the gallows. In fact Uspensky, Kuznetsov, Prizhov, and Nikolayev were sentenced to fifteen, ten, twelve, and seven years at hard labor, respectively. (On December 27, 1881, Uspensky was hanged by some of his fellow exiles in Siberia, who were convinced that he was an informer. The comrades' court held afterward decided that the charges had been unfounded.) Twenty-nine others received prison terms (Dementieva, who kept bursting into laughter during the proceedings, got four months); the rest were acquitted, including people who like Tomilova and Catherine Likhutina were clear accessories to Nechayev's crimes other than the murder. On freeing them the presiding judge declared, "Ladies and gentlemen, justice has spoken; from now on your place is not among the accused but with free citizens, with the rest of us." The depressed Third Department agent decided to test the public reaction to this verdict: in the city's bars he discovered that it was held that "the court was too soft with those criminals. They should be hanged as an example to others" or "whipped

[59]Kozmin, *Nechayev and Nechayevites,* 169.

until all that stupidity leaves their heads" and then "settled forever in distant parts of Siberia."[60]

On January 8, 1873, Nechayev himself faced the Moscow court. To give him his due he displayed in court the same gall which characterized his previous activities: he would not defend himself or accept a lawyer, since he did not consider himself a Russian subject and hence the court had no jurisdiction over him. The jury having found him guilty of Ivanov's murder, he was sentenced to twenty years at hard labor, and was dragged out of the courtroom shouting "Long live the National Assembly! Down with despotism!"

When much later it was learned that the criminal, instead of being sent to forced labor in some Siberian mine by personal decision of the emperor had been confined to the Petropavlovsk fortress, a wave of indignation swept progressive circles. The government had compounded its cruelty by this double cross: it had secured Nechayev's extradition on the grounds that he was a common criminal, but as such he had the *right* to be sent to Siberia rather than be locked in solitary confinement. The reasons for both the decision and the indignation are obvious. No one could believe that an enterprising lad like Nechayev could be safely kept in some Siberian locality; soon, possibly having convinced the wife of the local police chief to accompany him, he would turn up in Western Europe.

Instead he was confined in one of the grimmest of tsarist jails: the Alexis Ravelin, within the Petropavlovsk fortress. Even here his ingenuity and gall did not abandon him. In 1876 he addressed a petition to "His Imperial Majesty the Sovereign Emperor" in which he complained that he had not been given the chance to defend himself for his "political crime" and asked the emperor as the "highest guardian of law" to order a retrial.[61] The emperor's answer was to order Nechayev to be deprived of writing materials. Apprised of the result of his petition, Nechayev threw a fit, breaking windows in his cell, and for some time afterward his hands and legs were manacled. By 1880 this incredible man managed to subvert some soldiers in the fortress' garrison. Many of the guards had been stationed there for years, their condition not much different from that of the prisoners. Through them he established links with the current generation of revolutionaries, the People's Will. The latter held some discussions about the feasibility of raiding the fortress and freeing Nechayev, but the story that Nechayev, given the option as to whether the first priority should be to the assassination of Alexander II or to freeing him, decided for the former is

[60]*Ibid.*, 170.
[61]P. Shchegolev, "S.G. Nechayev in the Alexis Ravelin," in *The Red Archive*, IV (Moscow 1923), 256.

a sheer invention,[62] like Karakozov's "I did it for you, brothers" and Khudyakov's being tortured. What *is* credible is the story that following the assassination of Alexander II, Nechayev wrote to those members of the People's Will who were still at large suggesting various new strategems. One was to fake a proclamation from the new tsar ordering peasants to be returned to their former masters and lengthening the term of military service; another was to circularize priests in the name of the Holy Synod, announcing that God had stricken Alexander III with insanity and asking them to offer public prayers for his recovery. But his contacts with the guards were discovered in the course of 1881, and he was put under stricter surveillance. On November 21, 1882, thirteen years to the day after Ivan Ivanov had been strangled, Nechayev died of dropsy.

". . . One cannot but be amazed at his will power and the strength of his character. One must render justice to the selflessness of his behavior. He utterly lacked personal ambition, and his devotion to the revolutionary cause was genuine and boundless," wrote Vera Figner.[63] Did Nechayev in fact do *anything* for the revolutionary cause? The only recorded and reliable record of Nechayev's revolutionary activity among "the people" is the story of his subversion of the prison guards in the Alexis Ravelin. But this was hardly a case of ideological conversion. As the story of the trial of those simple men shows, he first gained their confidence by the usual fantasies—he was an agent of high-placed personages belonging to the party of the heir to the throne, which would come to power once the emperor died—then procured their services by bribing them with money received from outside. Was he "inspired by a very definite vision of the future"? Yes, but his vision did not go beyond an indiscriminate slaughter. Did his personality have about it "something inspiring, compelling submission, acting on simple souls like hypnosis," as Vera Figner also admiringly asserts? Yes, but this power extended only to green youths, guilt-stricken girls from the upper classes, and aging wives of minor officials; and it was as much a case of physical fear as of "inspiration." Vera Figner, of course, never met Nechayev and heard of him in her capacity as a member of the Executive Committee of the People's Will. But hers and other Russian revolutionaries' reluctance to exclude him from the mainstream of the "liberation movement" was due not only to a lack of personal contact with this allegedly charismatic personality, but also to the one characteristic he undoubtedly did possess: boundless energy. And this belief that energy is the revolutionary's highest virtue was to have a fateful effect on the history of the movement. It would be absurd to see Nechayev as a prototype of Lenin, or even Stalin. But both of them ascended to the top partly because of the

[62]See Vera Figner, *Collected Works,* I, Moscow n.d., 232.
[63]*Ibid.,* I, 235.

Party's conviction that their rivals, while perhaps superior to them morally and intellectually, lacked the main prerequisite of revolutionary leadership: ruthless energy. Maxim Gorky, commenting in 1922, not so much on politics as on Russian life in general, wrote: "History offers a clear answer as to gradations of cruelty: he who is most active is most cruel."[64]

In our own century, as much fascinated by violence as were the Russian radicals of the 1860s and 1870s, Nechayev has appeared to some as the prototype of the existentialist hero. For Camus revolution for the first time with him "transcends considerations of love and friendship. . . . [Nechayev's] originality thus lies in the justification of violence to one's brothers." This is elegant nonsense. Nechayev's only claim to originality lies in the fact that his character combined two usually distinct types of criminal: the murderer and the confidence man.

---

[64]Maxim Gorky, *About the Russian Peasant,* Berlin 1922 (in Russian), 19.

IV

THE
REVOLUTIONARY
CRUSADE

NINE

THE QUIET BEAST

One of Nechayev's most intransigent opponents during the student troubles in Petersburg in 1868–69 was an earnest young Jew, Mark Natanson. As against revolutionary adventurism, Natanson preached the gospel according to Pisarev: self-improvement and instruction among the young must precede any political action. In pursuit of this idea he gathered around him a circle of fellow medical students who, eschewing revolutionary heroics, read and discussed books on current social problems. This serious and thoroughly unsubversive occupation was disrupted at its start by two arrests. Shortly before his first flight from Russia, Nechayev denounced Natanson to the authorities, and it took six weeks spent by Natanson in jail before the misunderstanding was cleared up. The prankster did not easily give up: early in 1870 a package of subversive literature addressed to Natanson arrived from Switzerland, and this time Natanson stayed in Petropavlovsk fortress for two weeks.

Despite such interruptions, the work of the circle went on, and it was natural that gradually its young men reached out beyond the student world. Pisarev's fad was giving way among the radical youth to that of a new intellectual light: in 1870 there were published, perfectly legally, the soon-to-be renowned *Historical Letters* by Mirtov, the pseudonym, as everybody knew, of Peter Lavrov, who had just escaped from Russia after a period of political exile. The exact message of the new sage could not, because of its murky prose, be readily digested. But it was easy to get the main drift: self-improvement was not enough, the educated class owed a debt to the people to instruct and improve the condition of their underprivileged brethren. And so the activities of the Natanson circle branched out into occasional contacts with, and the provision of cheap books for, the rapidly growing worker population of the capital. The group also grew, some of the new members being people in or on the periphery of former revolutionary circles, such as Khudyakov's, but who had become disgusted with the conspiratorial methods revealed in the Nechayev affair and were seeking new ways to serve the cause.

At the same time, and quite independently, a group of even more earnest young women was also following the path of self-improvement through serious study. The feminist movement in Russia was about to pass beyond the demand for mere sexual equality, as emblazoned in the manifestos of 1860s radicalism, preached by Chernyshevsky, and epitomized by Liudmila Shelgunova. Women now sought to be men's equals in professional life, as doctors, scientists and . . . revolutionaries. A pioneering venture in this direction was a course of scientific lectures organized by some university professors in 1868 in a high school in Petersburg. And of course since male students had their circles, so would the young ladies who attended this course.

The one of interest to us was formed in 1869 by the Kornilov sisters, three of whom were to play important roles in the revolutionary movement. They were children of a leading Petersburg manufacturer, a man of advanced views, as witnessed by the fact that he allowed his daughters the kind of freedom which even today many a parent would consider excessive for teen-age girls. In the summer of 1869 Alexandra Kornilova, then seventeen years old, decided that it would be a capital idea if she and her friends, who were spending their vacation working in a chemistry lab, moved from their parents' houses and established a female commune in a suburban cottage.[1] One of the participants was a small, intense-looking teen-ager whose name would one day resound throughout the world, Sophia Perovskaya. The only older woman in the group, a general's daughter, Sophia Leshern Von Hertzfeldt (b. 1840), was hardly a suitable chaperon. Soon she herself would plunge into revolutionary work that would conclude with a lifetime sentence at hard labor. The circle did not dissolve when at the summer's end the girls returned to their parental homes. Its twenty or so members continued to meet in the Kornilov mansion, whose owner, so his daughter assured us, being crippled by arthritis, enjoyed having young people around him. But it is unlikely that the circle's sessions produced much girlish laughter or other gaiety. These were very serious young ladies who when they were not studying geometry and chemistry were discussing the latest book on the social question.

[1]"Alexandra Kornilova, Sophia Perovskaya, and the Founding of the Chaykovsky Circle," *Hard Labor and Exile,* XXII (Moscow 1926), 10.

The atmosphere of the Kornilov circle was, one might say, of female chauvinism, no man being allowed to approach. Indeed some of its more extreme members, like Perovskaya, believed that one should avoid contacts with one's male contemporaries altogether, the latter, no matter how high-minded, being always bound to try to dominate and exploit one. Alexandra Kornilova tells us that at the time she would not tolerate even the thought of marriage: how could a woman do any serious work if burdened by children and household tasks? But gradually their prejudices softened when they heard of a group of young men as virtuous and serious in their pursuits as themselves—the Natanson circle. To be sure, there were some tense moments before the full merger of the two could be effected. One of the "Natansonites" turned out to be the proverbial snake in the grass or, less metaphorically, a skirt chaser, who dared to propose to Alexandra that they go abroad together, not to do jointly serious scientific or revolutionary work but as a lark. She indignantly refused, and soon the unsuccessful wooer was dismissed from the now amalgamated circle "for an attitude toward women irreconcilable with the ethical rules of the organization." The new bisexual circle began to function in the second half of 1871. But almost immediately Natanson was arrested and spent the next four years in exile away from the capital. And so this group of serious young men and women who became the pioneers and most famous figures of the Pilgrimage to the People in 1874 passed into history under the name of the Chaykovsky Circle.

Nicholas Chaykovsky, born in 1850 and one of Mark Natanson's earliest collaborators, flashed through the Russian revolutionary scene of the 1870s like a meteor. After his friend's arrest, he managed to enlarge the membership of Natanson's group, drawing into it such future stars of the revolutionary movement as Peter Kropotkin and Lev Tikhomirov. More importantly, under his leadership the circle shed its original character as part club, part monastic order, and became the nucleus of a large propaganda organization. No longer were its members content with living in communes where they subsisted on Spartan meals and discussion of Chernyshevsky or Lavrov (a typical menu was soup and horsemeat). They now embarked on systematic propaganda among the workers of Petersburg as well as missionary activity in the provinces. Unlike the earlier revolutionary conspiracies (and a conspiracy was what the Chaykovsky circle was becoming, at least in the eyes of the law) this one was neither centralized nor hierarchical. "We were in friendly relations with most other [propaganda] groups; we helped them, they helped us, but we did not encroach on their independence."[2]

Chaykovsky must have been an unusually engaging character, since he managed to enroll in his growing organization people who were to follow most divergent paths: future anarchists, terrorists, the first Russian followers of Karl Marx. "I never subsequently met people of such moral purity

[2]Peter Kropotkin, *Notes of a Revolutionary,* Moscow 1966, 273.

and elevation . . . as the ones I encountered at the first meeting of the Chaykovsky circle," Kropotkin was to write many years later. But the same religious fervor which guided Chaykovsky in his propaganda activity soon led to his separation from the mainstream of Russian radicalism. In 1874 he fell under the influence of a "God-in-man" religious sect established by Alexander Malikov, whom we have already met as a secondary figure in the Karakozov affair. Along with some fellow sectarians, Chaykovsky then migrated to establish a religious commune in the United States. In the New World he joined the Shakers for a time, and indeed their creed, which exacts complete sexual abstinence, may have appeared to him as the logical extension of views entertained in the Natanson and Kornilov circles. Chaykovsky returned to Russia only after the Revolution of 1905, and like most of the survivors of the Populism of the 1870s joined the Socialist-Revolutionary party. After 1917 and Lenin's triumph, when the British landed in Archangel the now venerable revolutionary veteran briefly headed the anti-Bolshevik "government" in North Russia, something which helps to explain Soviet historians' lack of interest in the man who pioneered the first mass revolutionary movement in Russia. He died in London in 1926.

Chaykovsky's spiritual wanderings epitomize much of the character of Russian Populism. The term has come to be used as a catchall description of all strains of Russian radicalism, beginning with Herzen and going into the 1890s when Marxism-socialism appears on the scene. To be sure, the belief that the Russian peasant was an instinctive socialist, and the notion that the upper classes had an obligation to their oppressed brothers, does start with Herzen. But the young radical of the early 1870s was disenchanted with his predecessors' attitude toward "the people." For all their revolutionary fervor, their attitude toward the common man was, as we would say today, elitist. Even Chernyshevsky's "new men" were quite sure they stood above the vulgar multitudes that would one day, as *What Is To Be Done?* proclaims, call " 'Save us,' and whatever they say would then be done by all." The older radicals expected the peasant masses to do their work for them: to rise up in 1863 . . . in 1870 . . . and only then would the revolutionary *intelligentsia* take over and lead Russia into the promised land of socialism. But the new breed of revolutionaries, as they emerged from the Chaykovsky group and its offshoots, longed above all to become one with the people, to shed their upper-class and *intelligent* accoutrements, to guide the peasants to socialism and revolution not through conspiracies and manipulation, but by serving them and sharing their lives. And in 1872–73 many of them were ready to obey the summons proclaimed by Herzen way back in 1861, *"To the people, to the people,* there is your place, you exiles from seats of learning. Show . . . that you will become warriors on behalf of the Russian people."

The new bearer of this message, and the most potent intellectual influence in the inception of Russian Populism, was Peter Lavrov. A seemingly unlikely character to stir up the passions of the young, this middle-aged closet philospher and former army colonel! Son of a rich landowner (b. 1823) and thus in Nicholas' Russia almost inevitably slated for military life, Lavrov spent his entire officer's career, twenty-two years, as a lecturer on mathematics in the artillery school and at other military academies. Always a rebel by temperament, Lavrov could express his true feelings only through poems safely committed (as he thought at the time) to a drawer: "Stand, O Tsar [Nicholas], before the Court of history, nation, and God; you rejected the truth, you suppressed freedom, you ruined Russia. . . . Wake up, my country—ravaged by thieves, kept in bondage and chains by the government and its spies."[3] But under Alexander II Lavrov could display his multifarious talents to the public. He published some poems anonymously in *The Bell*, a treatise on philosophy under his own name and in Russia, as well as articles on assorted social and political subjects.

Of all the branches of the armed forces the artillery corps produced the greatest proportion of officers with "untrustworthy ideas" and outright revolutionaries. Lavrov's long pedagogical activity amidst it may not be unconnected. But the first intimation that this erudite and gentle officer had seditious proclivities came in September 1861 when, in his full-dress uniform with decorations, Lavrov addressed the Petersburg University students and, in the words of a Third Department spy who was present, "expressed sympathy for their riotous behavior."[4] Strangely enough, he was allowed to continue to teach. But then, he was a revolutionary *voyeur* rather than an activist, on the periphery of such enterprises as Land and Freedom and Khudyakov's circle but not privy to their conspiracies. He might well have reached decorous retirement except for Karakozov's shot, which changed the course of his life as it did Russia's. In the wake of the assassination attempt, Muraviev's agents searched his apartment and discovered all the subversive poetry, letters from those "state criminals" Chernyshevsky and Utin, and other compromising material. Dismissed from the army and imprisoned for nine months, Lavrov was then exiled to the Vologda region. There, in a succession of bleak provincial towns he whiled away his time by writing essays, published anonymously and quite legally in the radical journal *The Week,* and carried on an amorous intrigue with a fellow exile, the Polishwoman Anna Chaplitska. When his friend fled abroad, he begged the authorities to let him emigrate, but his appeals were unavailing. Lavrov seemed destined to live out his life in the inhospitable north, separated from his beloved and—which he missed almost as much—from a good library. His myopia and clumsiness being as legendary as Chernyshevsky's, it was

[3]Quoted in Ivan Knizhnik, *P.L. Lavrov,* Leningrad 1925, 20.
[4]*Ibid,* 27.

---

out of the question for Lavrov to attempt to escape by himself.

Providentially there appeared on the scene the knight-errant of the revolutionary movement, Herman Lopatin. In 1866 Lopatin had covered up the traces of what remained of the Khudyakov circle while impressing the Muraviev commission that a lad with his "broad Russian nature" could not be a dangerous revolutionary. For the next eighteen years he was involved in a number of daredevil adventures—skipping over prison walls almost at will, commuting between the West (where he hobnobbed with Marx and Bakunin) and Siberia (where he tried to rescue Chernyshevsky), supervising the "execution" of a dangerous secret police official. Only in 1884 did his luck finally run out, and he spent the next twenty years in prison.

In 1870 Lopatin had just fled from jail and was about to go to Switzerland to warn the Russian exiles there about Nechayev, whom he blamed for his arrest, when he heard of Lavrov's plight. Immediately he offered his own (forged) passport and personal help to free this new luminary of radical thought. In the disguise of an officer, Lopatin arrived in Lavrov's place of exile, bundled the sage into a sleigh, and shepherded him to Petersburg, whence Lavrov managed to reach Paris without a mishap. He was already abroad when "Mirtov's" *Historical Letters* appeared in Russia.

The enormous impact of this work came as a surprise to its author. "Several times in the course of writing it I felt I should shorten the work," he confessed later on. And well he might: it is a heavy, repetitious, cliché-ridden treatise of some 250 pages, which would gain in clarity and readability if not originality were it one-tenth the length. Even a worshipful contributor to a symposium celebrating its fiftieth anniversary, who hails the *Historical Letters* "as a major landmark in the development of our social consciousness," was constrained to add that the book was written "drily, boringly, overabstractly; it has hardly any literary quality at all."[5]

But we should not be surprised. We have seen in our own times how abstruse, virtually unreadable philosophical and sociological treatises are proclaimed as revolutionary manifestos and/or revelations of a new social order. One strongly suspects that people who enthuse over these proclamations of past and future shocks, of equality as the basis of justice, etc., seldom read them through. But one does not have to! A hasty perusal of a few pages will persuade the reader that what the author has in mind is what he himself has felt all along but could not express in such elaborate and scientific form.

History calls for sacrifices. They are brought in themselves and around themselves, by those who undertake the great and dangerous task of fighting for their own and others' development. . . . A better historical future has to be conquered: before every individuality that has realized the consciousness of the need for devel-

[5] *Forward! A Collection in the Memory of Peter Lavrovich Lavrov,* Petrograd 1920, II.

opment lies the somber choice: will you be one of those ready for all sacrifices and sufferings, so as to become a conscious and understanding activist for progress; or will you stand on the sidelines, a passive observer of the mass of evil which has been taking place around you, conscious that you have abandoned the path toward development, the need for which you yourself once felt? Take your choice.[6]

Here—and a translation can hardly do justice to the muddled, indeed ungrammatical quality of the original—is the message that inspired droves of young men and women to become "activists for progress" in the Russian countryside and in the workers' quarters of Russian cities.

Lavrov did manage to touch one sensitive spot in the psychology of educated young Russians: the feeling of guilt. Previous generations of Russian radicals had found their mainstay in the "repentant nobleman" and the "enraged plebeian"—famous terms coined by Nicholas Mikhailovsky, Lavrov's successor as the intellectual guide of Populism and a much more lucid thinker and writer. One was repentant about serfdom, the other enraged by humilation in a privilege-ridden society. But now serfdom lay in the past, and though Russia was still a class society, it was probably easier for a talented "plebeian," a peasant's or priest's son, or a Jew to make his way up in the world and become a doctor, professor, or even entrepreneur in Russia than in Britain, say, during the same period. But while following such paths, sensitive young men could not overlook the fact that most people still remained wretchedly poor and, above all, ignorant. In his labored prose, Lavrov gave a severe answer to the youth's unspoken question: "One has to agree that under the present condition of [our] society, personal comforts (*and* privileges) are not only incompatible with justice but its clear contradiction. . . . Our present economic system is incorrect. It *inevitably* leads to inequality and limits freedom for the majority." And if it were not enough to acknowledge one's debts in the present, Lavrov would have Russian youth stand guilt-stricken before past generations: "The individual owes an enormous debt to the preceding generations for their terrible sufferings which have enabled the present one to achieve a modicum of comfort and well-being."

Most religions start with the notion of guilt. And so in a sense Populism was born as the worship of "the people," and the faith that only through serving the people selflessly could one expiate the sins of one's upper-class origin or privileged position. When many of the Populists discovered that their god had failed them, they would not, as did so many of the men of the 1860s, resume their careers to become writers, generals, state councillors, and professors, but sought other gods. Some found them in orthodox or sectarian varieties of Christianity, others in Karl Marx, and quite a few chose the cult of terror. For from the beginning the world of Populism was

[6]Peter Lavrov, *Historical Letters*, St. Petersburg n.d., 386.

stalked by the ghosts of Karakozov and Nechayev. Spirtually the new breed of radicals longed for a creed free of falsehood and violence. Intellectually they rejected terror and the other manipulative and destructive methods used by their predecessors , as Lavrov did in the beginning. And yet, being young, their imagination was stirred by what they believed had been heroic and sacrificial deeds. Vladimir Debogori Mokrievich, a typical Populist, reports how the trial of the Nechayevites in 1871 aroused in him and his friends ambivalent feelings: they could not but deplore the assassins' methods and "jesuitic" mentality, and yet they felt that here were genuine "martyrs of the people's cause."[7]

Most Soviet historians divide the early Populists into Lavrovists, devoted to the idea of serving the peasant masses, and "rebels," followers of Bakunin, who while not eschewing that same task also tried to stir up the people into active resistance against the government. But Bakunin was known to the younger generation mainly as a legend from the past, a man whom one went to visit when in Switzerland as the relic of the Moscow intellectual circle of the 1840s, a comrade of Herzen's, a figure in the *international* revolutionary movement. If his name was invoked within Russia, it was because it had a more respectable sound than Nechayev's. And so we might classify the "rebels" as followers of Lavrov's gospel but who from the beginning had a somewhat guilty hankering for the world of heroics, violence, and mystification which had been embodied in Nechayev's People's Justice. In due time, as we shall see, many of those who began as peaceful propagandists among, and servants of, the people would succumb to the lure of terror.

Populism's incongruous mixture of ideas and sentiments can be seen already in a group which while it preceded the main thrust of the Pilgrimage to the People already epitomized some of its strivings and dilemmas—the Dolgushin circle.

Alexander Dolgushin as a student fell under the spell of Nechayev, but being of an independent turn of mind decided to organize his own circle. Its structure to be sure was to be somewhat different from that of the People's Justice. It envisaged cells of ten, rather than five, members. But when it came to a political platform, so to speak, the source of Dolgushin's ideas is obvious, one of these ideas being "to liquidate highly placed people, including the imperial family."[8] Before his enterprise could gather steam, Dolgushin found himself in jail as a "Nechayevite." He was acquitted in one of the trials of 1871. During his more than a year in jail, his wife gave birth to a son, but Dolgushin's first words to her when they were reunited were: "How are things in

---

[7]Vladimir Debogori Mokrievich, *Memoirs,* Paris 1894 (in Russian), 9.

[8]A. Kunkl, *The Dolgushin Group,* Moscow 1931, 51.

France? Is Napoleon III still alive?"[9] Nechayev's methods being in disrepute, Dolgushin now became a pioneer of the movement "to the people."

This movement was supposed to be almost apolitical during its first phase. The revolutionaries were to lose themselves in the peasant mass, either sharing completely their way of life or serving them as teachers, nurses, midwives, etc. The radical message was to be conveyed by osmosis as it were, and only after the peasants genuinely felt they were not being lectured to or propagandized by a social superior, but were discussing problems of everyday life with someone who was one of their own, albeit perhaps better informed. Or at least this was the formula as one can discern it in Lavrov's murky prose.

But a peasant entering the cottage which Dolgushin bought in a village near Moscow would hardly have felt at home. To be sure a wooden cross hung on the wall, but the inscriptions carved on it were of an unorthodox variety: "in the name of Jesus Christ" and "liberty, equality, fraternity." The walls were covered with suggestive slogans in Latin, English, French, and Italian: "Oh God, oh soul, oh glory of liberty!" "What cannot be cured by medicine can be remedied by steel; what steel cannot cure fire will." "Serve no one but the people, its cause is sacred because it suffers, and everyone who helps the people is sent by God."[10] Yet the religious motif was meant seriously, as had not been the case in the propaganda of the 1860s, and it was not just a bow to peasant "superstitions." Dolgushin was deeply influenced by a contemporary radical writer, William Bervi, who taught that revolution can succeed only by creating a new religion, and not just using religion as a propaganda gimmick.[11]

There was something heroically preposterous about Dolgushin's enterprise. He and his few associates set out in the spring of 1873 to convert the neighboring peasantry to a revolutionary creed couched in a religious idiom. They were all students or former students, except for Ananias Vasiliev, an eighteen-year-old of peasant origin who combined the role of propagandist with that of Dolgushin's domestic. Perhaps not surprisingly it was Vasiliev who, despite his youth and mental instability, proved the most successful propagandist. But in general, the indoctrination brought but

[9] *Ibid.*, 41.

[10] From a police protocol, as quoted in court proceedings, B. Bazilevsky, *State Crimes in Russia*, I: *1825–1876*, Stuttgart 1903 (in Russian), 463.

[11] William Bervi (of English descent) had been an official in the ministry of justice until 1862, when he wrote a letter to Alexander II protesting the imprisonment of thirteen Tver noblemen who had petitioned the tsar for a national assembly. This led to his being confined to a lunatic asylum for six months, at the end of which time, proclaimed sane but subversive, he was dismissed from the civil service. He then became a publicist writing under the pseudonym Flerovsky. His books, *The Condition of the Working Class in Russia* (1869) and the *ABC of the Social Sciences* (1871), enjoyed a vogue among Populists second only to Lavrov's.

meager results. The peasants were intractable—at once too ignorant and too sophisticated to be converted to revolution or socialism; the situation, premonitory of the future failure of the Pilgrimage to the People and the heartrending frustration of the more than a thousand young men and women who set out on their mission with such great hopes. Dolgushin would lecture villagers on how the government oppressed them through taxation. A listener would object: didn't our Lord teach, "Render unto Caesar that which is Caesar's?" and would be unconvinced by the propagandist's lame reply that this injunction was valid only when Christ was on earth! Religion was taken very literally and not just as a set of ethical principles. It would be asked, "How will it be in the next world?" and the confused lecturer could only mumble that this was something they would discuss on another occasion. Already Dolgushin had reasons to suspect that the cardinal tenet of radical belief, that the peasant was an instinctive socialist, was a myth. Equality ordained by nature? "Look at your hand," exclaimed a peasant, "you have five fingers. Are they equal? You talk nonsense."[12]

An associate of Dolgushin's, Dmitri Gamov, after similar disheartening experiences reached a desperate conclusion. "[The peasants] consider the tsar as God's anointed, and thus one cannot move them against him. One has to *invent* a religion that would be against the tsar and the government."[13] Having begun with a genuine conviction that the peasant could be converted to revolution by agitation, by propaganda that stressed the ethical precepts of Christianity, Dolgushin's group was almost immediately driven into the path of propaganda by deceit: phony religious texts, specially edited parts of the Bible, etc. Dolgushin acquired a printing press and composed and circulated proclamations: *To the Intelligentsia* and *To the Russian People*. The language of the second of these is expressive of his frustration: "And when you will demand a better life for yourselves, evil people, scoundrels, will shout that you are rebels, that you want to slaughter everybody, and such stuff. But it is always that way. Remember what Jesus says: 'Be on your guard against those people, because they will drag you into courts and temples and will flog you. And then they will bring you before the great ones and the Tsars to be a witness for Me against them and the Pagans.' "[14] Hatred of the emperor, faith in whom seemed like an unbreachable dam against which beat in vain the waves of all such revolutionary rhetoric, is evident in another "religious" tract published on Dolgushin's press. This one was written especially for him by Bervi, whom the young man, despair-

---

[12]Kunkl, 108.

[13]Quoted in O. V. Aptekman, *The Society of Land and Freedom of the 1870s*, Petrograd 1924, 93. My italics.

[14]*Ibid.*, 96.

ing of his own pamphleteering ability, visited and asked for agitational material. Entitled *About the Martyr Nicholas and How Man Should Live According to the Laws of Truth and Nature,* the pamphlet contains a lurid, though one must admit not *entirely* inaccurate, history of the institution of monarchy in Russia. "The great ones and courtiers, because of the evil in them, [at will] enthrone and then throw out and kill Tsars whenever it is convenient for them."[15] Then they bribe priests to proclaim their creatures as legitimate rulers. Burdened by his sins, the leaflet goes on, Nicholas I committed suicide, and Karakozov was executed only because the nobles could not tolerate a mere student poaching on their prerogative to kill tsars.

With the young men displaying hardly any conspiratorial precautions— Dolgushin would threaten peasants with a gun if they gossiped about the stranger preaching in their midst—Dolgushin's enterprise was doomed from the start. It is a measure of the incompetence of the police that it could be carried on at all for some months in a village not far from Moscow. And it was due to an accident that the whole enterprise was discovered: a hostile relative denounced one of Dolgushin's associates. When the police searched his apartment they found a doctored version of the Gospels, the *Communist Manifesto*, writings by Lavrov and Bervi-Flerovsky, a revolver, and Mrs. Dolgushin's Moscow address. Completely unsophisticated about politics and also not very bright, Agrafena Dolgushin spilled the whole story to the police, and her husband was arrested in the fall of 1873.

The propagandists faced the court in July 1874. At another time their youth—Dolgushin was twenty-five and most of his associates were in their early twenties—and the ineffectiveness and puerility of their enterprise might have argued for a mild sentence, say a couple of years' exile in a provincial town. But now, with the countryside rife with agitation, the authorities were in an ugly mood. Dolgushin and his chief helper, Leon Dmochowski, were sentenced to ten years at hard labor, others to lesser terms. And the emperor unexpectedly refused to reduce their sentences, except in the case of Vasiliev, a mere boy, who suffered a mental collapse during the investigation and crossed himself over and over again while testifying. The cruelty of the verdict was enhanced by the government's not sending the convicts to Siberia right away, but holding them for years in jail. Perhaps this was because the Siberian authorities at the time were notoriously "soft" on political prisoners, clerical work being often substituted for real hard labor, and occasionally a humane local commandant would allow convicts to live as settlers outside the prison camp altogether. Only in 1880 were survivors of the group sent on the long trek; two of them

---

[15]Quoted in Kunkl, 209. Except for the rhetoric, this is not a bad summary of the history of imperial succession between Peter the Great's death in 1725 and Paul I's assassination in 1801.

in the meantime had gone mad and died. In 1883 Dolgushin, as punishment for helping a fellow Siberian prisoner escape, was returned to Russia and placed in Schlüsselburg, along with the Alexis Ravelin the most dreaded of tsarist jails. There in 1885 he died of consumption.

What were he and his associates after? How could they think that a handful of propagandists (twelve, to be exact) and a printing press could change Russia's destiny? Their ideology was a vague blend of anarchism and agrarian socialism. Russia after the revolution, Gamov believed, should be transformed into a loose confederation of twenty-nine ethnic units, and then gradually evolve toward anarchic communism, a free union of communes, in which private property would be abolished. As for the second question, we cannot begrudge members of the Dolgushin group that often abused term: they were idealists.

And idealism was also the impulse that sent so many young men and women into the countryside, beginning in the fall of 1873 and going on to the end of the decade. The movement reached a crescendo with the Pilgrimage to the People in the summer of 1874. Though the Pilgrimage was undoubtedly the first mass revolutionary movement in modern Russian history, we must not exaggerate its extent, as did some government officials at the time and many historians later on, jumping to the conclusion that the entire Russian countryside was seized by tremors and that practically every educated young woman and man in the land was plunging into agitation. The actual number of people apprehended for what the government considered subversive activities was 770 (612 men and 158 women) of whom 265 were considered seriously enough compromised to be detained; many others were kept under surveillance.[16] Even if we assume that in view of the inefficiency of the police, about half the "pilgrims" remained undetected or fled, we arrive at the figure of about 1500, which is an impressive number compared with the Chaykovsky circle but hardly a tidal wave of revolutionary activism such as was to sweep Russia in 1905 and again in 1917.

One of the most engaging participants of the Pilgrimage wrote after it that he had wanted to avoid "getting stuck in the swamp of everyday official or bourgeois existence."[17] Like many others, he was tragically to have his wish: a brief period of peaceful propaganda and agitation among "the people" was followed by arrest, protracted "preliminary" imprisonment, and the famous trial of "the 193." After the age of twenty-two Serge Sinegub was never again to be a free man in the real sense of the word. He was released from imprisonment in 1881, eight years after his arrest, but European Russia was barred to him, and he died in Siberia in his mid-fifties, in 1907. Other stories were more dramatic: some would escape, participate in

[16]Tatishchev, *Emperor Alexander II,* St. Petersburg 1903, II, 590.
[17]Serge Sinegub, *Recollections of a Chaykovite,* Moscow 1929, 24.

real revolutionary ventures, be caught, spend years at hard labor or, worse, within the walls of Petropavlovsk and Schlüsselburg. A few would end up on the gallows. Perhaps those who perished in the struggle would not have envied those of their comrades who lived to see Soviet Russia, especially the octogenarians who survived into the Stalin era: what were the grievances of the peasants under Alexander when compared with the martyrdom of a whole class during the forced collectivization? How feeble and tolerant the autocracy must have seemed as against the horrors perpetrated by the totalitarian state in the great terror of 1936–39.

What prompted so many young Russians to choose this perilous path at precisely this moment? Idealism and a sense of adventure are not precise enough answers. The first could have led to selfless service to the people but without revolutionary undertones or dangerous consequences, and indeed thousands of people, forsaking more worldly pursuits, worked among the peasants in this fashion—teachers, agronomists, midwives. As for the adventure, we have already spoken of the opportunities presented by Russia's expansion and economic growth following the Emancipation. And yet the career that many longed for, including men and women of great abilities, was that of the revolutionary.

If we listen to a representative of this doomed generation, we should be ashamed of seeking sophisticated answers: "It was not so simple as one thinks: that the young people have read a half-dozen tendentious books, have listened to Bakunin and Lavrov and 'have gone to the people.' No! This was [the result of] a shattering spiritual uplift, of painful self-questioning. . . . I myself have seen how young people, going among the peasants, read the Gospels and sobbed. . . . What did they seek in them? . . . I myself went through that then, and therefore I became a Christian, because of my deep spiritual need, because of my love for Christ."[18] Writing some years after the event, this memoirist, both a Jew and a freethinker, still cannot explain the step except as prompted by that religious fervor and faith in the people which seized so many of his contemporaries.

And it was not as simple as Aptekman presents it either. Populism was the first Russian revolutionary movement to have a sizable Jewish component, unlike, say, the first Land and Freedom, which had but few Jews in its ranks, the only one of any prominence, Nicholas Utin, coming from a thoroughly russified family. This development was the paradoxical result of the much more liberal policies toward the Jews initiated under Alexander II. Under Nicholas I, a strong Judophobe, a person of Jewish faith could not, with few exceptions, live anywhere but in the Western provinces of the empire, the so-called Pale of Settlement. But throughout, the basis of discrimination was religious and not racial. A converted Jew, such as Yegor

---

[18]Aptekman, 91.

Abramovich Peretz, who became secretary of the State Council in the 1870s, would not be barred from a high position in the government and society. Under Alexander, then, Jews could enter institutions of higher learning. Laws restraining them from residence in Russia proper were diluted to the point where they had no practical effect. To the bulk of the Jewish population, Alexander II became known as "the good emperor."

Given an opportunity to enter the hitherto forbidden sphere, many a young Jew experienced double rebellion: against his own heritage, associated in his mind with an ethnocentric and ritualistic religion, and against the regime which denied to "the people" as well as to the Jews full civic rights and human dignity. Some Jewish radicals in their revulsion against their own religious and ethnic background used arguments that one day would become the staple of anti-Semitic folklore. When anti-Jewish riots broke out in Odessa in 1871, as yet a feeble preview of future *pogroms,* young Lev Deich and his fellow members of a radical circle, mostly Jewish, discussed "whether Jews are also responsible for the hatred felt against them by Christians. Some, including myself, admitted that our fellow tribesmen have given sufficient reasons for the hostile attitudes toward them, the main one being their preference for nonproductive and profitable occupations."[19]

Similar hostility toward the social sphere from which they came was not absent in non-Jewish members of the movement. Prince Peter Kropotkin relates how even as a child he was impressed by the contrast between the parasitism of his father and his father's fellow landowners, their harshness toward their inferiors, their fawning attitude toward important officials, and what he saw as the natural kindness and dignity, as well as patient endurance, of the family serfs. Her peasant nanny, writes Vera Figner, was "during the first ten years of my life, the only human being with whom we [children] felt free and who would not oppress us."[20]

Noblemen; Jews, both children of rich contractors and merchants and those fresh from the *shtetl;* sons and daughters of high officials—what traits did they have in common to prompt them to go among the people and then into outright revolutionary struggle? A devotee of a psycho-historical approach might encourage the ready answer: an unhappy family background. And indeed, superficially there appears to be plenty of evidence to support this conclusion. Many of the revolutionaries describe their childhood in terms epitomized by Vera Figner's recollections: "We were kept strictly, very strictly in our family; our father was prompt to go into a rage, severe and despotic. Mother was kind, mild, but without a will of her own."[21] Four

---

[19] Lev Deich, *After Half a Century,* I, Berlin 1923 (in Russian), 34.
[20] Vera Figner, *Collected Works,* I, Moscow 1928, 24.
[21] *Ibid.,* I, 24.

Figner sisters became revolutionaries. So did two Kropotkin brothers, Peter, the famous one, recalling bitterly how little attention, not to mention love, they had received from their father and stepmother. Sophia Perovskaya's father, city governor of St. Petersburg, was discharged along with his superior, Prince Suvorov, during the events that occurred in the wake of Karakozov's shot. Lev Perovsky, accustomed to living in high style but now deprived of his official emoluments and pressed by his hitherto indulgent creditors, was forced to sell most of his estates. Always a martinet, he now became a domestic bully, tyrannizing over his wife and making life insufferable for his children. Or at least such is the picture drawn by his son Vassily, who like his sister, but not with the same tragic consequences, followed the revolutionary's path.

As one scans the biographical dictionary of the revolutionaries of the 1870s, one is struck that so many of the leading figures had brothers and sisters who chose the same career. Were tyrannical fathers the root cause of this generation of rebels?

Before we endorse such a facile verdict, it is well to consider some other testimony. Take the case of Eugene Semianovsky. Sentenced to hard labor in Siberia for having conducted propaganda among soldiers, Semianovsky and his fellow political convicts were allowed by the local commander to live as settlers outside the prison camp. But in 1880 categorical orders came from St. Petersburg: such scandalous lenience had to be terminated. Unable to face the prospect of again being locked up, the young man decided to kill himself and wrote his father begging for forgiveness: "Farewell forever, my dearest kindest father. I never thought of you but with gratitude, loved and venerated you as parent and friend."[22] Serge Sinegub, to take another, was the child of his father's old age, and in solitary confinement in the Petropavlovsk fortress he would think about the old man, a landlord and retired army officer, who never understood what "got into" his son, "but no other man I met in my life was so kind and so good."[23] Nicholas Morozov, a leading exponent of terrorism among the Populists, might be thought to be a prime example of a rebel created by parental tyranny. His nobleman father never bothered to legalize a union with his peasant-born mother, and he tried hard to keep Morozov away from revolutionary activities, used "pull" to have him released on bail, and tried to persuade his son to make a clean breast to the authorities of his associations. But Morozov wrote that it was a great solace to him, throughout his later life, to remember that before the gates of Schlüsselburg closed behind him, he and his father embraced and forgave each other. And there are more such tales.

We might go further and assert, paradoxical as it sounds, that the famous

[22]Quoted in Aptekman, 116.
[23]Sinegub, 169.

generation gap is never so wide in a truly revolutionary situation as it is in normal times. In general fathers themselves have to be somewhat unsure of their own, or traditional values, for their sons and daughters to become open rebels. The generation that spawned the revolutionaries of the 1870s had grown up in the oppressive social and political atmosphere of Nicholas' Russia but then experienced what by comparison was exhilarating freedom during the first years of Alexander. Thus it was natural for them to feel that they ought not to rear their children in the way they themselves had been raised by their elders, and to try to view their social and even political nonconformity with understanding, if not sympathy. Vera Figner's father remained indeed a man of the old school: "The era of Nicholas left its imprint on his personality and his views how children should be brought up. . . . You rise and go to sleep at the given hours; always wear the same kind of formal dress; comb your hair in a certain way; don't dare to forget the formulas for greeting your parents and saying goodbye to them, or to cross yourself and thank them after every meal; don't talk behind the table; wait your turn after the grown-ups . . . finish every last bit of food."[24]

Nicholas Figner was a relatively minor official, and people of his class and mentality tend to hew to the old ways. But take this description of parental laxity among the upper classes as given by a scandalized minister of justice in the 1870s, Count Constantine Pahlen: ". . . The rich and no longer young landlord, Sophia Subbotina, not only herself led revolutionary agitation among the peasants, but recruited her niece, and sent her underage daughters to finish their education in Zurich [where young Russian ladies went officially to study medicine, but in many cases to finish their revolutionary indoctrination]. A former province treasurer, Pletnev, being shown a revolutionary book found in his home, announced frankly that he was preparing his teen-age son 'to serve the people.' . . . Daughters of privy councillors, Natalia Armfeldt, Sophia Perovskaya . . . and many others went 'to the people,' engaged in physical labor, slept side by side with peasants, their fellow workers, and not only were not criticized for this scandalous behavior . . . by their relatives and acquaintances, but found among them sympathy and approval."[25]

Thus complex and varied intellectual and psychological motivation drove many Russians to seek communion with "the people" and in the process to try to undermine the edifice of autocracy. A few were men already, so to speak, established in life. Peter Kropotkin, much older than the average "pilgrim" (b. 1842), had not only an ancient title, but quite a reputation as a geographer and explorer when he decided to sacrifice all on the altar of revolution. Serge Kovalik, another "oldster" (b. 1846), had been elected by

---

[24]Figner, 24.
[25]Quoted in Vladimir Burtsev, *One Hundred Years,* London 1897 (in Russian), 120.

his fellow landlords as chairman of justices of peace for his county and seemed on the threshold of a promising career in local self-government. But something, maybe his Cossack blood, would not allow him to settle down to useful but quiet existence. He went abroad in 1873, saw revolutionary exiles such as Lavrov and Bakunin, and then returned to plunge into political agitation.

But most of those who went "to the people" in 1873–74 were very young —in their teens and early twenties. Some tried plying the revolutionary's trade as a part-time job in the evening, after university lectures, and during the summer vacations. Thus Morozov, drawn into a revolutionary circle in Moscow via the drawing room of a charming society lady, had a passion for natural science and tried to combine his first agitational trips with geological explorations. But in general the revolutionary code forbade such compromises. "A resolute revolutionary was expected to sacrifice all for the people. . . . It was even thought contemptible to graduate from educational institutions, as that would give one the possibility to occupy a privileged position! A true revolutionary was expected to burn his bridges behind him and after some preparations set off among the people."[26] Michael Frolenko, whom we shall meet as a participant in some of the most daredevil revolutionary escapades, gives a more disarming version of this injunction: "[We felt] that we already knew so much that if the people were taught one-tenth of it, Russia would become the first country in the world."[27] To be sure, he referred to *theoretical* knowledge: the propagandists had their heads stuffed with Chernyshevsky, Lavrov, Bervi-Flerovsky, occasionally some Marx,[28] and if the peasants would grasp and endorse one-tenth of *that,* Russia indeed would become the first country in the world, according to the revolutionary's scale of values: i.e., she would be plunged into complete anarchy!

Much more troublesome was the injunction for some "preparation" prior to the agitational propaganda work. This meant acquisition of some manual skill which at once would give the young *intelligent* some common ground with "the people," and provide him with a means of subsistence and a pretext for living in a village or in workers' quarters. Thus Deich tried his hand consecutively at carpentry, work in a railway depot, and finally common peasant labor. Morozov went into training to become an itinerant cobbler. The net effect of such endeavors was usually tragicomic. The average middle- or upper-class Russian, brought up in a household full of

[26]Deich, I, 68.

[27]*Hard Labor and Exile,* II (Moscow 1924), 11.

[28]The first volume of *Capital* was translated into Russian in 1872 and Marx was respected by the Populists as a revolutionary, though his stress on the *industrial* worker and condemnation of the "idiocy of rural life" were unacceptable to them.

servants, would have had no need or occasion to develop any manual skills at all. Sports and hobbies were frowned on by serious young men and women as aristocratic diversions. Chernyshevsky's Rakhmetov, as we know, toughened himself up for revolutionary work by sleeping on a bed of nails, but in real life many a young zealot discovered that his ascetic and feverish existence as a member of some student radical circle made him unfit for heavy physical exertion: he would collapse after a day in the fields, or, drinking being almost an invariable accompaniment of serious discussion among peasants (except for some sectarians), our young propagandist could hardly steer the conversation to a discussion of the evils of Russia's social system before a glass or two of the home brew took its effect and he would pass out.

Especially difficult in this respect was the situation of young ladies who joined the movement. Even though Vera Zasulich came from an impoverished family, it was a gentry one, and never throughout her long revolutionary existence did she learn how to make a bed. When her group decided to "go to the people" by opening a tea shop in a village, the enterprise was doomed from the beginning: she refused to cook the traditional Easter pastry and would not even make tea. "Vera Ivanovna did not have the slightest inclination toward household chores," one of her companions confessed.[29] For a while she tried to learn midwifery, but what she liked best was to ride around the countryside with a pistol strapped to her belt. And to tell the truth, despite her social background and her avocation as a terrorist, Vera was not very good at shooting either: in her famous assassination attempt she failed to kill Trepov even though she shot him point-blank.

In view of this general incapacity for artisans' skills or for work on the soil or factory labor, quite a few young rebels chose a more reasonable way to expiate their class origin and gain the peasants' confidence, occupations which to be sure might set them apart from "the people" but which would at least bring them into their midst: teaching, midwivery, being a *feldsher* (a medical practitioner standing halfway between a nurse and a licensed doctor). Prince Kropotkin traveled for a while in the countryside as an itinerant painter of holy pictures. Sophia Perovskaya worked as a nurse at several rural locations, vaccinating villagers against smallpox.

When we come to the political content of the Pilgrimage the picture becomes extraordinarily confused. The first phase of the campaign was to eschew even propaganda in the strict sense of the word, the missionary Populists trying first simply to earn the confidence of peasants and workers by identifying with their life. But this, like many beautiful theories, proved hardly possible in practice. No sooner did Morozov and some other would-be pilgrims enroll as apprentices at a master shoemaker's than they forgot

[29] *Hard Labor and Exile,* II, 244.

their new roles and "instead of working, fell into a dispute about [the form of] the future social system based on equality, fraternity and liberty."[30] Then disenchantment set in: "What use to us to learn to make boots and slippers when the peasants go about barefoot or in bast shoes? . . . What does shoemaking have in common with revolution?"

Members of the Chaykovsky circle, the nucleus of the movement, began with what on the face of it was a sensible compromise: that propaganda should at first be focused on factory workers in large cities. The average worker at the time had been born a peasant and in many cases was just a few years away from his village. If some of them could be converted, then of course *they* could carry the message of Populism into the countryside much more effectively than their *intelligentsia* mentors.

But the purists among the revolutionaries objected. The "city spoiled the peasant" was a frequent saying among them; they believed that after a few years in the money-grubbing urban atmosphere, the peasant ceased to be a noble savage, as the eighteenth-century philosopher would have called him, or an instinctive socialist and enemy of all authority, as Lavrov and Bakunin currently described him. And it is true that to the first generation of industrial workers, shop assistants and the like, even their hard work and low pay often represented an improvement over their previous condition. We have also seen how the city proletariat behaved toward the students in 1861. Individual workers were indeed recruited to the cause of revolution, but until the end of the century the task of propagandizing them remained almost as frustrating as that of destroying the peasant's faith in the tsar. As one of the first serious students of Marx in Russia, Professor Nicholas Ziber, used to say, to be made into a socialist "the peasant must be first thoroughly boiled in the capitalist cauldron."

Propaganda among the workers also had some obvious practical disadvantages: one had to evangelize right under the nose of the authorities in Moscow or Petersburg, as opposed to in some rural wilderness where one could live for months without encountering a constable. For some revolutionaries the mission to the people ended very abruptly, even before the great summer of the Pilgrimage: apprehended by the police for agitation, they spent three or four years in the Petropavlovsk fortress (and then in the prison for preliminary detention), then were sent to Siberia, where a few, like Sinegub, passed the rest of their lives.

When he came to describe what set him on this path, Sinegub, an unusually fair and valuable witness to the atmosphere of those days, paraphrased Lavrov: "For the youth of those days, the main task appeared to be to decide what activity to choose to help the people, to whom they felt they owed an unpayable debt, their privileged position having been purchased

[30]Nicholas Morozov, *Tales of My Life,* Moscow 1917, I, 25.

by the people's immeasurable sufferings."[31] The beginning of his propaganda activity was not only innocent but within the law (rather rare in tsarist Russia): a progressive proprietor of a chemical factory asked him and some other members of his Chaykovsky circle to instruct his workers in grammar, history, and geography. After a while Sinegub and his fellow teachers, who had been instructed in modern socialist thought by an artillery officer, tried to turn their pupils' attention to "social questions." The reaction of the listeners was typical: did not Sinegub teach them himself, asked one worker, that such talk had brought religious dissension and peasant wars in Germany? Did they wish similar misfortunes to befall Russia? All in all, several months of this combined instruction and agitation produced but meagre results: at most, five workers, Sinegub recalled, turned their attention to the "social question." He thus welcomed an opportunity to get away from these rather fruitless endeavors and go on an unusual errand.

One of the female members of his cell-commune had recently been a teacher in a church school for girls in Vyatka. There she had converted to the cause of progress—or corrupted, whatever interpretation you choose— one of her students. And now sixteen-year-old Larissa found the atmosphere of the parental home stifling, and wrote her former schoolmistress to find her a person with whom she could contract a legal but "blank" marriage and thus escape domestic imprisonment. Sinegub volunteered.

The task was easier than might have been imagined. The father, a boisterous Orthodox priest, far from being a domestic ogre, proved to be a loving parent, enchanted that his daughter during her stay in Vyatka had found herself such a respectable swain, a rich nobleman—which Sinegub was by birth. (Having in the meantime become a "nihilist" who lived and dressed accordingly, he had been equipped by his friends, prior to setting on his rescue mission, with suits, shirts, and pocket money appropriate to his role.) The distasteful social preliminaries and the hateful church ceremony were heroically endured by the two conspirators, and back in Petersburg, Sinegub delivered Larissa, free and untouched, to the female contingent of his propaganda circle. "People talked about my fictitious marriage, and I became something of a hero."[32] But there was one difficulty: he had fallen in love with his bride.

To betray this emotion in the slightest "would have been criminal, an assault on her freedom, since I was her legal husband." The unhappy young man sought distraction in intensified propaganda work, but he still ran into Larissa, now a propagandist in her own right. And so Sinegub decided to shift his base of operations: he would become a rural teacher. A position

[31]Sinegub, 15.
[32]*Ibid.*, 83.

opened in the village of Gubin, but one of the prerequisites was that the teacher be married. It was all very simple, he explained to the female members of his circle: one of them could exchange identity papers with his legal wife, and then go with him to live and agitate in Gubin. Somehow no one volunteered, but to his surprise Larissa herself expressed a willingness to foresake the attractions of the capital to return to rural life, which she had once hated so much. "Willy-nilly I had to go with my fictitious wife," wrote Sinegub, who for all his knowledge of Herzen, Lavrov, and the laws governing social development must have been a charmingly obtuse young man. But whatever strain he would have to endure as the result of this proximity, he was glad to acquire such an able assistant for his pedagogical and revolutionary work.

The social scene in the village of Gubin, in the Tver province, was bound to produce a shock in an idealistic young Populist. For a start the local villagers were quite well-to-do. In fact they were in the process of ceasing to be peasants, and beginning to wear urban clothes. Quite a few of them had watches, mirrors, and other accoutrements of a bourgeois life. Furthermore, this progress-corruption was directly traceable to a man who epitomized the type the revolutionaries hated even more than the tsar: the village capitalist. He, one Martynov, a self-made man, employed most of his fellow villagers in making shoes for a large shoe store he owned in Petersburg, where he boasted of acquaintance in high circles, extending to the imperial family. Through his ideological eyes, so to speak, Sinegub saw Martynov as a "ruthless exploiter of the peasants," but he had to admit that he was also a most generous benefactor. Any native of Gubin in need could count on Martynov: he would provide them with free seeds and grain after a bad harvest, replace their sick cattle, pay for their daughters' weddings and dowry out of his own pocket. And he had founded and supported the village's school and old folks' home.

In fact Martynov was sort of a local Peter the Great, and if the imperial government had closely studied his system of rule over Gubin, it might have nipped the revolutionary movement in the bud. To be sure Martynov also shared some vices of his great predecessor: he was quite despotic and often drunk. Scratch many a revolutionary and you will find a prude: Sinegub, who had moved in circles where fictitious and "civic" marriages were taken for granted, was scandalized to learn that the local tsar was an old lecher who kept his wife in the capital while in Gubin he lived with a twenty-four-year-old girl!

Sinegub's revolutionary virtue was exposed to an almost intolerable strain: Martynov liked him and provided him and his wife with free and very comfortable quarters, and with a more than adequate salary. Sinegub undoubtedly would have chucked all those temptations and fled back to Petersburg, poverty, and danger, except that during one of the evenings when he and Larissa "discussed various moral and social themes, the discourse, through an association of ideas, led to the problem of love."[33] Larissa confessed her feelings, and their marriage became a real one. And so perhaps they would have succumbed to the lure of a quiet family life had it not been for an unfortunate incident.

One spring evening the ruler of Gubin paid a sudden visit to his domain. The whole village was aroused that night to celebrate his arrival: men to drink, girls to sing and dance by torchlight. Some time after this bacchanalia Martynov, in his underwear and accompanied by his mistress, suddenly put in an appearance at Sinegub's class and drunkenly began to recite prayers before the stupefied pupils. Sinegub, outraged, sent the children home. There followed a protracted quarrel, with the village elders summoned to arbitrate about who should apologize to whom. Eventually, to the peasants' joy, peace was made, with Martynov (still drunk) ordering the elders to kneel before the teacher to beg him not to leave the village and school. But at the end of the term Sinegub and his wife had had enough and returned to their Petersburg circle and to propaganda among the workers. In November 1873 the police carried out their first raids among the propagandists. Sinegub was arrested. He would not be reunited with Larissa until more than four years later, when she chose to follow him to Siberia after his trial and conviction.

Apart from its comic and romantic aspects, Sinegub's saga illustrates a generality which the Populists were to discover in the next few years: there was no such thing as "the people"—millions of peasants sharing the same economic conditions, endowed with the same craving for equality and communal living. In some places the natives lived indeed under the most primitive conditions, and their mentality, as Chigirin's story will show, was still much the same as that of their medieval ancestors. But Gubin was on the threshold of the industrial age. The Russian peasantry was already going through what the Marxists called class differentiation. Some well-to-do villagers were *kulaks* to their fellows—"tight-fisted ones," men who exploited their poorer neighbors by lending them money and seed at extortionate rates or employing them for pennies. But others were helpful and respected in their community as plucky and hard-working men. Not all employers were "ruthless exploiters." Few European or American employers of the time would have emulated Zhdanov, the proprietor of the chemical plant, who felt that he had an obligation to educate his workers, and invited Sinegub and other people to fill this gap even though he knew they harbored "untrustworthy ideas." Martynov was perhaps harsh on peasants from other villages, but he made Gubin into a miniature welfare state.

Many, many other people—beyond the group of revolutionaries—acknowledged their obligation to participate in the uplifting of the peasant masses. As director of elementary schools in the province of Simbirsk, Lenin's father, Ilya Ulyanov, traveled on horseback ceaselessly over the execrable Russian roads to check on rural instruction and to take the place of sick teachers. Some men abandoned lucrative medical practices or promising government careers to bring medicine to villages, to work as agronomists for the *zemstvos,* etc. Peter Lavrov, now abroad, attacked such constructive endeavor in his inimitable prose: "Those members of the *intelligentsia* who acknowledge the existing regime and are ready to assist in its 'reforms' take their place among the enemies of the people, who have always brought perdition and misery to the people, who cannot bring them anything else even if they would wish to. . . . By the nature of things they cannot really wish the people's welfare because their very existence is based upon the continuous exploitation of the masses."[34] Residence abroad did not improve Lavrov's logic or syntax, but the radical sage, taunted by his fellow exiles like Bakunin and Tkachev for his moderation, forgot his previous theory that the revolutionary appeal should be preceded by a lengthy period of peaceful propaganda, and sternly admonished the *intelligentsia* "to bring the propaganda of socialism and radical revolution to the masses. . . . It is so simple that its meaning, once explained, is immediately translated into the revolutionary movement and the task of a national uprising." But no conspiracies à la Bakunin-Nechayev, please! "The conspirators are quite capable of disregarding the people's aims, the social revolution. They often do not know the people." Such confused messages now flowed into Russia through the pages of *Forward,* which Lavrov had been editing since 1873, and which became a successor of *The Bell* insofar as the radical *intelligentsia* was concerned (though the contrast between Lavrov's prose and Herzen's is on the order of the difference between *What Is To Be Done?* and *Anna Karenina*).

Appropriately enough, this call to action by a former artillery colonel was immediately answered by two young ex-artillery officers, Serge Kravchinsky and Dmitri Rogachev (both b. 1851). In October 1873 the two daredevil youths put on peasant dress and set out for the countryside. Their methods were hardly subtle. As Kravchinsky recounted to Kropotkin, they once met a peasant driving a sled: "We started to tell him that one should not pay taxes, that officials are robbers, and that the Bible preaches the need for a revolution. The peasant urged on his horse, we hastened our step. He put it into a trot, but we kept running, shouting about taxes and revolution . . . until we could not breathe."[35] Not surprisingly, after one month of this "peaceful agitation" they were detained by a village elder, but they fled

[34]Lavrov, *Collected Socio-Political Works,* Moscow 1934, III, 145.
[35]Kropotkin, 284.

before they could be turned over to the police. Upon their return to their friends in Moscow and Petersburg, Kravchinsky and Rogachev painted their experiences in rosy colors: it was all nonsense that one needed a long period of preparation and study to embark on propaganda work as Lavrov once taught: look at the success of their own campaign!

In Moscow the news of Kravchinsky-Rogachev's direct technique of going to the people was greeted with enthusiasm by Michael Frolenko. He and his fellow revolutionaries were, like their corresponding number in Petersburg, trying to convert city workers, and were having about as much success as Sinegub had had. "I was astonished that they [the workers] all looked at the village and peasant with irony and condescension, considering themselves as having a higher status, as smarter. No one would even dream of, having learned something himself, going to the countryside and helping the peasant."[36] And now experience showed that propaganda in the country could be carried out by anybody. "It is enough to don a simple dress, learn some artisan skill, and go forward."

The prospect of going right to "the people" also gladdened the heart of Nicholas Morozov, when he heard the story of Kravchinsky's successful ventures from his own lips, in Olympia Alexeyeva's drawing room in Moscow. Radicalism was as popular among young society ladies in the older capital as in Petersburg. The wife of the governor of Moscow was once abashed upon entering her niece's room to find a strange man undressing there. Timidly she asked her niece for an explanation, only to be silenced by the reply that she would leave her relatives' home if they continued to spy on her. Of course it was nothing so innocent as trysting: Morozov was using a casual acquaintance's house to change to appropriate clothes prior to going to propagandize in the workers' quarters.[37] But as in Frolenko's case, he found this work not much to his liking. To be sure, the workers' living conditions were not as bad as he had thought on the basis of such exposés as Flerovsky's: "I had believed they lived in pigsties like animals," while in fact their apartments were quite clean, with some furniture and even books. But the houses smelled of cabbage and other unpleasant odors. And so the nineteen-year-old nature-lover and revolution-lover in this year of the Pilgrimage set out on foot on long tours of the countryside.

There was now a body of literature suitable, it was thought, for revolutionary propaganda among the peasants. The idea of exploiting the peasants' religious feelings by means of pseudo-religious tracts with radical motifs still persisted, and Morozov carried in his knapsack quite a few of these, stamped fraudulently "with the blessings of the Holy Synod." Some of the youthful revolutionaries tried their own hands at composing readable

[36]Michael Frolenko, *Works,* I, Moscow 1932, 104.
[37]Morozov, I, 190.

folktales with subversive themes. One of the most frequently used was *The Tale of Four Brothers* by the famous future terrorist and then "renegade" Lev Tikhomirov. In it, the four brothers, upon emerging from the forest where they have lived in perfect freedom and equality, are amazed to find the outside world full of oppression and misery; they travel to the four corners of Russia, everywhere encountering the tears and groans of the people. And of course bowdlerized versions were prepared of the stories of Stenka Razin and Yemyelyan Pugachev, in which bandit chieftains were depicted as fighters for freedom.

Morozov was an itinerant propagandist, not one of those who settled in a given locality and tried to saturate it with the Populist gospel. He was discovering real people different from the ones he knew in books. In one county a friendly landlord told him he would never get anywhere with peasants as long as he masqueraded: they would listen to a man of higher status, but otherwise would laugh at anything so young a man might tell them. Elsewhere he was shocked to find that the old folks claimed they had been quite happy under serfdom, while young village lads were contemptuous of landlords because they had given up their seignorial rights without a fight. New ideas were slow to make inroads in the countryside. Could he imagine, exclaimed one peasant to Morozov, the telegraph operator in a nearby town had tried to tell him God did not exist? As for all the tracts disguised so cleverly as religious and folktales, which Morozov was carrying at the risk of his own personal freedom, what did the literate peasants *do* with the pamphlets he distributed? They tore them up to roll cigarettes— paper was so scarce, they explained[38]—and one may assume they used them for less delicate purposes as well. After a walking tour of some three hundred miles (Morozov was, as will become apparent, a man of unusual stamina) "which went like a whirlwind, with a mass of new impressions every day," Morozov returned to Moscow to recount his manifold frustrations and a few apparent successes to his fellow radicals who gathered in Alexeyeva's rooms.

Olympia Alexeyeva would greet him with open arms, literally. The wife of a rich landowner who was confined to a mental institution, his patroness dabbled in revolutionary propaganda while making her home a haven for radical youth. Morozov was disingenuous when recalling his romantic as well as his political activities and emotions, to the point where it is hard to believe that most of the narrative was recorded by a middle-aged man writing in a prison cell and not by a raw teen-ager. He was of an amorous disposition, but for all the hugging and kissing which went on between him and Olympia, Morozov felt he could go no further, since he was destined eventually for lifetime imprisonment or the gallows. The same lack of logic

[38] *Ibid.,* I, 239.

characterized his political views. The fascination with terror, of which he
was to become a strong exponent, can be traced to his early ambition to
become the Russian William Tell and to fell the country's oppressor at one
blow. At other times he and Olympia would dream about starting partisan
warfare in the countryside, and yet another dream was of Russia's becoming
a republic like the United States. (Fortunately for this dream, Morozov who
like most Populists believed in the abolition of private property, was not
acquainted with the political and economic condition of the United States,
then under the administration of Ulysses S. Grant.) But of course the
Russian republic could not have a universal franchise, added the young
Populist: "Illiterates [the then majority of the Russian people] would have
to be excluded . . . otherwise the illiterate citizens would vote to restore the
old order, not understanding the superiority of the new one."[39]

Yet Morozov, so childish and confused about politics and love, was in
intellect and strength of character perhaps the outstanding figure in the
whole Populist movement. He was to endure more than twenty years of
solitary imprisonment in Schlüsselburg, where others after a few years had
died or gone insane. And while a handful who also achieved this feat, such
as Vera Figner or Lopatin, were sustained by the revolutionary's craving
for martyrdom, Nicholas Morozov spent the time in learning advanced
mathematics and physics. He emerged after the amnesty of 1905 to make
distinguished contributions to science and to plunge back into revolutionary
work. In 1932 he became an honorary member of the Soviet Academy of
Science. This incredible man died in 1946, ninety-two years of age. The
Soviets were to honor him in the space age: an asteroid and a crater on the
dark side of the moon (perhaps unwittingly symbolic of the Communist
appraisal of Populism) perpetuate the name of the intrepid revolutionary
and scientist.

His comrades' awareness of both his potential and his limitations brought
the first phase of Morozov's revolutionary activity to an end. After the
arrest of most of the participants in the Pilgrimage to the People, at the end
of 1874, Morozov was sent abroad "to study sciences and to publish a
journal for the [Russian] workers." The prospect of meeting such giants of
revolutionary thought as Lavrov, Bakunin, and Tkachev reconciled Morozov to separation from Olympia. (He was to meet her again, along with most
of his old acquaintances, as a fellow-accused in the monster trial of "the 193"
in 1877–78. His enchantress had been freed on bail while he was a prisoner.
Another incongruity of tsarist justice: she was acquitted, while he received
a mild sentence for having been a member of "Alexeyeva's circle"!) During
his absence, first in Switzerland and then in jail, Olympia's husband had
died and she had remarried. But she would be glad to continue to see him,

she told him in 1877 with a smile, provided he was not "dangerous." The young ass assumed her to refer to politics, and since he was quite determined to continue as a revolutionary, he did not seek her out again. "Thus ended the third platonic love in my life."[40] To tell the truth he had fallen under the spell of Vera Figner in the meantime, a much more suitable object of affection for a future terrorist.

Both Sinegub and Morozov would have been shocked to realize that their attitude toward the peasant was, each in their own way, condescending. And indeed, after the disheartening experiences of the Pilgrimage many an idealist came to suspect that what the French socialist Proudhon had said so ruthlessly was true: the people was a quiet beast interested only in eating, sleeping, and lovemaking! But some, while losing many illusions, stuck to the original tenets of Populist faith. Aptekman was both appalled and strangely attracted by the real peasant as he found him in the course of his pilgrimage. On the one hand he was struck "by the extraordinarily low, almost primitive level, of the people's needs . . . whether cultural, physical or spiritual."[41] This was not the peasant of Nekrasov's poetry, of Lavrov, of Flerovsky. Whether rich or poor, they appeared to him equally dirty and devoid of any intellectual or esthetic interest. And yet he came to envy their inner peace: "By himself man without God is [for the peasant] nothing— chaff blown by the wind. No one has the right to say simply, I want things to be this way or that way." He exaggerated, of course, as to both the villagers' backwardness and the prevalence of religious fatalism. But more than most Populists, this young Jew, his childhood spent in a religious school reading and memorizing pasages from the Old Testament and Talmud, fell under the spell of the Russian peasant, and he took to heart the injunction to learn about and become one of the people. Some of his experiences have a familiar ring. He is asked by some villagers to tell them how peasants fare in other countries: excellently informed on the subject (by Marx's *Capital* I), Aptekman recounts the horrifying story of rural England under capitalism. His listeners are in tears: how could the landlords impoverish the simple folk, make them go out into the world practically naked? "It could not happen here—we have the tsar!" Well, perhaps something closer to home would be more effective; here is an article deploring "class differentiation" in the Russian countryside, recounting how the *kulak* sucks the blood of his less fortunate fellow villagers. This brings an unexpected explosion from his listeners: "Lies, all that is written there is lies. . . . Those fine gentlemen cannot stand the fact that some peasants now are better off."[42] One of the peasants sighs and begins patiently to explain that not

[40]*Ibid.*, III, 241.
[41]Aptekman, 152.
[42]*Ibid.*, 154.

every well-to-do peasant is a *kulak;* and those gentlemen in the city don't understand real peasant life.

And so our propagandist becomes a split personality. His brain still operates on the wavelength set by his student discussion circle in Petersburg, but his eyes and ears make him occasionally suspect that it is perhaps his own skull rather than the peasant's which is thick. Take the peasants' alleged lack of esthetic sense. Superficially this thesis appeared to be confirmed when Aptekman persuaded a female fellow propagandist to read some of the most heartrending of Nekrasov's poems to a village assembly. "The people's poet" left the people cold. So did some short stories by a writer much estimated in radical circles for his knowledge of rural life: "Why do they all write about us?" asked the peasants. "This is not a tale, but something we all know." As a last resort the carriers of culture to the masses tried Pushkin—although how could a "nobleman poet" find acceptance among those who scorned Nekrasov? "A tremendous effect. Rapture! They liked everything: form, rhythm, content." They begged for more. And so "there is some esthetic sense among those uneducated people!" Perhaps, though Aptekman does not say it, the average peasant had better taste in poetry than Chernyshevsky or Pisarev.

A Ukrainian peasant gave Aptekman sound practical advice, which he followed only after some fifteen years marked by imprisonments and a Siberian exile. Seeing him trying vainly to master carpentry and knowing that he had been a medical student, his village host said, "Give it up young man. . . . I will give you good advice: there is no better vocation than that of a doctor,"[43] and he brushed off Aptekman's objection that by becoming a doctor he would be in a privileged position, apart from the people. "This is all nonsense you learned from your books."

Deciding on a compromise between Lavrov and popular wisdom, Aptekman decided to continue as propagandist but combine it with work as a *feldsher* in a rural hospital established by the philantropic and eccentric princess Maria Dondukov-Korsakov. Here new temptation assailed his revolutionary virtue. The princess, herself a convert to an evangelical sect, was after his soul. (She subsequently used her quite high connections to be allowed to visit political prisoners and to try to convert them to her creed of nonviolence. Among others she tried to proselytize Vera Figner and of course failed.) Aptekman, as prone to spiritual seductions as Morozov was to physical ones, resisted her arguments that he should become a religious rather than revolutionary missionary, but became quite close to "this most sincere [woman], purest in her beliefs."

But imperceptibly peasant life grew on him. "Peasant faces, their views and morals, became more and more understandable and dear to me." What wisdom in these people whom *he* was presuming to teach! A peasant wife

[43] *Ibid.,* 145.

with a delicate problem turned to the village assembly for its solution: her husband had contracted syphilis but still claimed conjugal rights. The decision: the woman was to be sent to her parents' house until a doctor certified her husband was healed. This common-sense verdict became for Aptekman "Solomon's judgment! What could be wiser than that?"

Spiritual and physical temptations combined in one Praskovia, a peasant nurse. "I never met such a beauty in the countryside, but even in *intelligentsia* circles such a personality would be very, very rare." A strange courtship of mutual indoctrination ensued, Praskovia trying to gain Aptekman for Orthodox Christianity, he her for socialism. In a way they both succeeded, but with results fatal to their romance. Praskovia went back to her native village to propagate socialism of a strictly peaceful variety; Aptekman, though determined to convert, decided to go back to Petersburg to recharge his faltering revolutionary resolve. He never got to her village, and his letters to her went unanswered, possibly because though now formally a Christian (and spiritually too, he would say), he would not give up his revolutionary activity.

His spiritual and romantic preoccupation kept Aptekman from more flagrant agitation (Praskovia, he confessed, was his only convert to socialism), which by the late fall of 1874 landed hundreds of his fellow pilgrims in jail. And so in the spring of 1875 he renewed his medical-propaganda practice in the province of Penza. He believed naively that now as a Christian he would be more successful in reaching the masses, but again frustration! Like the tsarist government, the average Populist seldom learned from experience. Though he should not have been, Aptekman was ever surprised afresh that criticism of religion or of the tsar usually met with a hostile reaction among the people. The by now conventional literature designed to stir up rebellious feelings among the peasants was worse than useless. Some very old people had heard from their parents firsthand impressions of the Pugachev rebellion (1773), which had spilled over into the Penza province. In the popular tradition Pugachev was quite different from the would-be liberator of the propaganda pamphlet: cruel, feared by the common people, and far from a Robin Hood, who gave to the poor what he took from the rich. The use of the Bible for revolutionary purposes also had its limitations. "I developed this theme [of the difficulty the rich would have in passing through the heavenly gates] as sanctioning active struggle, with the rich as exploiters of the working masses," but one erudite listener objected. Hadn't Job finally reached paradise? Doing some violence to what he had learned both as Jew and as Christian, Aptekman hastily resorted to an improvization on the Biblical text: Job gained this promotion, to be sure, he said, but only *after* he had lost all his riches. He assures us that his audience was appeased, but one remains skeptical.[44]

---

[44]*Ibid.*, 175.

The peasants were more responsive when he told them things they knew to be true: how much of the state domain had been given free to imperial officials and favorites; how heavy the burden of taxation was. But the conclusions they drew from this social criticism were hardly welcome to a Populist. After the national uprising, he taught them, all land, woods, etc., would be the people's, to do with as they would. At this seductive prospect, one of his listeners could not contain himself: "Oh, how wonderful when we shall redistribute land! I shall hire two workers and live like a lord!"[45]

For all his frustrations in political propaganda work, Aptekman was one of the few pilgrims of whom it can honestly be said that they genuinely liked peasants and in return were accepted and respected by them. Other propagandists, such as Sophia Perovskaya, who found themselves isolated in obscure villages, gave vent to near despair in their letters to ideological friends. Living conditions were harsh, the peasants were intractable, and perhaps most of all, they mourned the absence of fellow intellectuals and radicals who would dissipate their doubts and sustain their revolutionary faith. Some who plunged into the darkest of Russia found their already strong, if unconscious, elitism turn to virtual loathing of the peasants. It had been part of the conventional revolutionary wisdom ever since Land and Freedom that one of the most promising areas for propaganda was among the Old Believers, as well as those odd religious sects of which Russia had a greater profusion than any other country in the civilized world, and which in varying degrees were persecuted by the government. (It is difficult to criticize imperial authorities for their negative attitude toward such as the Eunuchs, who castrated themselves and propagandized this road to salvation among the most ignorant of villagers, or Khlysty, whose revival meetings turned into sexual orgies.) Aptekman tried to propagandize among one of the more reasonable sects, the so-called Milk Drinkers, and found them, he writes, "too dogmatic" to be won over to socialism. But another Populist missionary who addressed a sectarian gathering was to his horror only too successful: his listeners fell into a trance, dancing and shouting, "He has come! He is here! He is with us!" He had been taken for Jesus Christ.[46]

It is quite likely that, had the wave of arrests not intervened in the fall of 1874, most of the Populists would have given up their fruitless missionary work, many abandoning politics altogether, some choosing the path of conspiracy and terror right away, and a few continuing to serve "the people" but with no ulterior purpose. The last choice was evidently very tempting to Aptekman. But how could he or any like-minded people abandon their revolutionary goals, when so many friends and associates were now in jail, with the threat of Siberia or a long prison term hanging over

[45] *Ibid.*, 172.
[46] Deich, I, 220.

them? Though he saw clearly that the people did not want his socialism or a revolution—"You may have thousands upon thousands of propagandists; all the same we will not win over the people, will not budge them"[47]—this conclusion did not make him give up his resolve to "save the people" through revolution, but only made him choose a different path toward the same goal.

In February 1876 Aptekman was in Petersburg, his rural phase definitely behind him, eagerly awaiting the man who was supposed to set Populism on a new course: Mark Natanson, just returned from exile. It is one of those historical ironies that Natanson, who in reaction to Nechayev and his methods had founded the circle from which Populism grew, now helped to turn it into a conspiracy with terror and mystification as its ultimate destiny: the second Land and Freedom.

[47]Aptekman, 178.

TEN

SEEDS OF VIOLENCE

The unflattering impression young Lev Deich formed in his youth of the so-called learned profession was confirmed, he wrote in his old age, by a lifetime's experience. "All professors, whether in Russia, Western Europe, or the United States, tend . . . to be devoid of energy, weak, lacking in initiative. . . . The drudgery of teaching, the monotony of repeating the same thing over and over again, leads to apathy, narrowness, and an inability to become excited about anything beyond their professional interests."[1] On the one hand, this is a good example of the enduring Russian propensity to arrive at categorical judgments on the basis of little or no practical experience. Barely had Herzen crossed the Russian frontier when he saw clearly how hopelessly materialistic and corrupt the West was. A few weeks in London persuaded Lenin that *all* English workers lived in slums. And Alexander Solzhenitsyn was quite sure, at least until he met George Meany, that no one in America understood the evil and threat of Communism.

On the other hand, young Deich's judgment reflected the revolutionaries' disenchantment with their own "professors"—Lavrov, Bervi, and, despite appearances to the contrary, Bakunin as well—whose lessons had launched them into the countryside and among the city proletariat. It would be impossible to say that they were disenchanted with the ideology, for *populism never had a precise ideology, only illusions.* Lavrov's was that a well-prepared propagandist would catalyze the instinctive socialism of the

---

[1]Lev Deich, *After Half a Century,* I, Berlin 1923 (in Russian), 132.

234

masses, or (really another version of the same) that the peasants loathed any form of centralized authority and were by nature anarchists. On both counts the experience of 1873–74 was crushing. Aptekman was lucky in that his "instinctive socialists" merely refused to listen to him when he extolled the benefits of communal ownership. In many other cases the preaching led, in the words of a police official, to "fatal results [for the propagandist,] who would be turned over to the authorities by the peasants."[2] As for alleged hatred of all centralized authority, which Bakunin extravagantly believed ran in all true Slavs' blood,[3] on the contrary, the peasant looked upon the tsar as his protector. This was not, as the Populists thought, the result of mere ignorance and superstition—faith in "God's anointed"—but also the effect of a quite rational deduction that what little protection they had had from a grasping landlord and an oppressive or corrupt local official came from the central authorities.

Why then didn't the young revolutionary give up his Populist faith and try to channel his alienation into some other belief—the "God in man" faith, which in a modified version soon found an adherent in Leo Tolstoy; or Marxism, already on the Russian horizon? The answer, unsophisticated though it may seem, is simple: both Tolstoy's Christian anarchism and Marxism preached in their separate ways patience; spiritual regeneration for one, a long-lasting economic transformation for the other must precede the establishment of social justice and harmony. The Populists were, as befitted their age and temperament, an impatient lot. "I cannot wait more than four years for a revolution," said one of Morozov's fellow pilgrims. But a revolution must have a cause. And so of the original device of the Pilgrimage—"everything for the people, everything through the people"—those who kept their revolutionary resolve abandoned only the second part.

The shift in emphasis from propaganda to conspiracy is described by many historians as the triumph of Bakunin's idea of insurrectionary tactics over that of Lavrov—peaceful agitation. But when it comes to nineteenth-century revolutionaries one cannot employ such rigid ideological classifications. The intellectual baggage that an average Populist took with him on his pilgrimage contained, as we have seen in the case of Morozov, a veritable mishmash of ideas and emotions rather than a definite ideology: odds and ends of socialism and anarchism of all sorts, held together only by a sense

<hr>

[2]Ibid., II, 34.

[3]He was in many ways a pioneer of racist thinking in politics. For Bakunin the state was a concept alien to the Slavic and Latin "races"; in Russia's case it was the product of Tartar-Germanic (!) influence. Capitalism, of course, was largely a Jewish invention. Racism, reinforced by misuse of the Darwinism just coming into vogue in Russia, was not a negligible factor in the thinking of many luminaries of the liberation movement. Bartholemew Zaytsev, a collaborator of Pisarev's on *The Russian Word,* and then of Bakunin's in Switzerland, wrote articles "proving" that the structure of the Negro's skull made him intellectually inferior.

of obligation to "the people" and hatred of the tsarist regime. Aptekman
was the classic example of a "peaceful propagandist," but only in the sense
that he preached the necessity of an armed uprising against the "exploiters"
rather than actually trying to organize one. If the revolutionaries themselves
ascribed the shift of Populism to conspiracy as "the triumph of Bakuninism
in Russia" (this was for example the subtitle of the second part of Deich's
memoirs), they did it for obvious psychological reasons: it was difficult to
admit, even to themselves, that in resorting to the adventurous tactics of
conspiracy, mystification, and terror they were following more and more in
the footsteps of Ishutin and Nechayev, rather than being inspired by a
"respectable" revolutionary such as Bakunin.

The course of conspiracy was dictated by another lesson of the great
Pilgrimage: it had lacked central direction and coordination. Some attempts
had been made to gather delegates of various circles to plan joint strategy,
but by and large they had proved fruitless.[4] There were some regional
centers of the movement, such as Alexeyeva's salon in Moscow, and as we
have seen a shoe-making shop in Saratov, where in addition to learning this
useful trade the revolutionary apprentices manufactured false identity papers and maintained a clandestine printing press. The circles, and individual
pilgrims, corresponded freely with each other, observing for the most part
little caution. Once the Saratov circle was "busted" in the summer of 1874,
it was easy for the authorities to unravel what they believed, prematurely,
to be the threads of an organized conspiracy. Of the 770 pilgrims arrested
in the course of the year, 265 were detained in jails.

A "plot" of this size bedeviled the government of Tsar Alexander II. The
imperial authorities saw before them a veritable hydra-headed monster
which, though for the moment decapitated, was already sprouting new
heads and limbs. "The losses within the ranks of the propagandists were
quickly filled by new activists drawn from university youth, thoroughly
indoctrinated by anarchist teachings, and also from those abroad, men and
especially women, who hurried back to join the common effort.[5] The government now regretted the ultimatum it had issued in 1873 to Russian girls
studying in Switzerland to come home. This unwittingly humorous document bewailed the fact that especially in Zurich, "in the midst of Russian
students of both sexes, there have developed all sorts of political parties of
the most extreme tendencies. . . . Political agitation turns inexperienced
heads," and, most horrifying of all, many "succumb to Communist theories
of free love, and under the cover of fictitious marriages lose sight of the most
basic moral principles and feminine chastity"—something His Majesty's
Government could not remain indifferent to, "since those women would

[4]B. L. Itenberg, *The Revolutionary Populist Movement,* Moscow 1965, 291–94.
[5]Tatishchev, *Emperor Alexander II,* St. Petersburg 1903, II, 590.

come back sometime to become wives and mothers."[6] And indeed many of these girls hastened back, either then or after a suitable delay, as Vera Figner did, just to show their contempt for the government rescript, but not to become wives and mothers. In fact, no other radical movement before or after in Russia or anywhere else had such a strong female component, both quantitatively and in terms of leadership, as did revolutionary Populism between 1875 and 1883. This only compounded the government's problems in dealing with what it saw as a tidal wave of subversion: even the staunchest defender of law and order was shocked at this virtually unprecedented phenomenon in Russian and European history: young girls, often from the "best families," facing long imprisonment, hard labor in Siberia, and in one case the gallows.

In its predicament the government thought of the traditional (though by the same token, not invariably wrong) explanation of revolutionary epidemics: "outside agitators." Hence an even more ridiculous summons: in 1874 an official communiqué solemnly called on nineteen Russian political emigrés, "illegally abroad," to come back within six months, or else. It must have been a thoroughly humorless official who thought that people like Michael Bakunin and Nicholas Ogarev would heed this call to spend the evening of their lives in the warm embrace of the secret police, or that others, e.g., Tkachev, shunned even by his fellow exiles for his extremism, would obediently exchange the pure air of Switzerland for a cell in Schlüsselburg. And in fact the two veterans were in no condition to return even if they wished to. Bakunin, though still fulminating with vigor against his old enemies, Marx and the tsarist government, was physically fading and was to die in July 1876, followed within a year by his old friend, long an invalid. The mortal remains of Nicholas Ogarev, buried in Greenwich by his Mary, who took care of him to the last, were reburied on Russian soil only in 1966. One cannot be sure that he would have appreciated this gesture on the part of the Soviet government: when Ogarev left Russia in 1856 he pledged not to return until his country was free.

The old guard was passing just as the new generation of conspirators was to revert to the old device and name, Land and Freedom. But while much of the intellectual inspiration for subversion came, as it had in the 1860s, from abroad, its character and especially its dimension were powerfully affected by domestic factors, among them the government's policies.

It is only fair to acknowledge that the imperial government was faced by a problem which was then unprecedented and which today is found virtually intractable by many governments, democratic as well as authoritarian: how, short of outright terror, to master a revolutionary movement which, though numerically insignificant, finds constant replenishment from the ranks of alienated youth, and sympathy if not actual support from part of the intellectual establishment. What could be done with some three hundred or so youths detained for what undoubtedly had been incitement to subversion, no matter how "peaceful"? In the past, when dealing with much smaller numbers, the choice was simple: imprisonment or Siberia for a few ringleaders, temporary banishment to an out-of-the-way place for the rest. But now the tsarist government was dealing with a movement that had no leaders, and with a type of revolutionary propaganda which could not be undercut by the old and tried method of administrative exile. If the Populists were sent to an obscure town or village, the government believed, they would simply renew their vicious propaganda in a more favorable environment, "whose population, ignorant of the real cause of their exile, would greet them with compassion and sympathy, and thus fall under their influence."[7] One member of the special ministerial commission convoked by Alexander II in 1875 to consider the problem had an innovative idea: to gather all the troublemakers in a single spot. But this was the nineteenth century, and the world was not ready for concentration camps. Send the whole lot of them to Siberia? The government, which had resorted to this measure in regard to thousands of Poles following the 1863 insurrection, felt it could not outrage *Russian* public opinion by doing this to "our children": these were sons and daughters of governors, generals, leading manufacturers. To deal with them thus would have made the breach between the government and society irreparable. And so while committees deliberated and ministers exchanged memoranda, some hundreds of young men and women found themselves incarcerated or on bail, awaiting a trial which would not take place until three or four years from the time of their original detention.

It would have required extraordinary political astuteness for the tsarist government to realize that the best course would be to do almost nothing: perhaps an occasional slap on the wrist, a few weeks' imprisonment for the noisiest of the agitators. By late 1874, revolutionary Populism lay buried under the weight of its collapsed illusion, just as had the first Land and Freedom in 1864. No doubt a few of the hard-core revolutionaries would have persisted in their struggle: a Vera Figner in her search for martyrdom, a Morozov to fulfill his adolescent dream of becoming the Russian William Tell. But most would have desisted, just as did so many radicals of the early 1860s, when with inspired inefficiency the authorities managed to lay their hands only on a handful of military and civilian conspirators. Now the jails and fortresses would become incubators for a ferocious revolutionary mood in the late 1870s. For those Populists who remained free, the imprisonment of their comrades became a psychological barrier to defection from the

[7]Tatishchev, II, 487.

revolutionary ranks and a stimulus to seek more efficacious means of struggle. Most important of all, society at large, outraged by the government's clumsy repression, looked with understanding and even sympathy at revolutionary heroics.

The government was no more successful in evoking fear than in exacting respect. The average revolutionary had come to accept arrest, imprisonment, and exile as (temporary) facts of life, rather than as a definite termination of his or her activity. An inmate of Stalin's *Gulag Archipelago* would consider the life of an average tsarist prisoner as verging on luxury, and by the standard of today's treatment of political dissenters, whether in Soviet Russia or in Chile, those of the 1870s still appear lenient. Food in the Petropavlovsk fortress, Sinegub writes incredibly, was not merely good but excellent, and so plentiful that often he could not finish it.[8] The commandant was humane: he would often drop in on prisoners to chat and bring them new books. Being a nobleman, Sinegub was addressed by the prison guards as "sir." When he was released on bail, Morozov had a hard time persuading his father's friends, members of the highest ranks of St. Petersburg society, that far from having been tortured by the Third Department, he was treated by its officials quite courteously. They sought to extract information through persuasion ("think what this is doing to your father") rather than by threats.[9] And indeed prisoners from the upper crust were often visited by high officials or even, as in the case of Sinegub and Kropotkin, by the emperor's brother who would, of course, fruitlessly try to make them see what harm they were doing to their own lives and to those dear to them. When prior to the actual trial most of "the 193" were concentrated in the preliminary arrest jail, it took on the appearance of a revolutionary club: prisoners communicated freely by shouting into windows while on walks, by the time-honored sending of messages by coded taps on walls, by receiving visits not only from relatives but from fellow revolutionaries who were still at large. There was, until it was to be rudely interrupted, almost a frolicsome spirit among these youngsters: for all their personal worries, they would not let a great revolutionary event pass without special notice. Somehow Morozov procured a quantity of cloth and dyes, and on the hundredth anniversary of the birth of "the great transatlantic republic," to the stupefaction of jailers a homemade Stars and Stripes flew out of many prison windows.

But this leniency served only to underline the irrationality of the system which detained hundreds of people for years, when the least it could do both on humane and political grounds would have been to bring them to a speedy trial. In fact the very laxity of the prison regime often had a destructive

[8]Serge Sinegub, *Recollections of a Chaykovite,* Moscow 1929, 143. He was not being ironical.
[9]Nicholas Morozov, *Tales of My Life,* Moscow 1917, III, 159.

effect on young and exalted natures; for the young, inactivity and uncertainty about the future tend to be more physically and psychologically debilitating than hard labor. From his own experiences and that of the Gulag's other inmates, Solzhenitsyn has drawn the paradoxical conclusion that in prison "a human being confronts his grief face to face. . . . This is the highest form of moral effort, which has always ennobled every human being."[10] But while this may occasionally have been true in Stalin's jails, it was certainly not so in Alexander II's. In the former case the prisoner's grief was for his own and society's utter helplessness in the face of tyranny; in the latter rage against a regime that robbed him of his best years and hope that it could be overthrown were the prisoner's principal emotions, rather than grief and soul-searching. The lax tsarist prison bred the most uncompromising revolutionary and terrorist of them all and he in turn forced the regime to become more brutal, even if not more efficient, in dealing with subversion. Schlüsselburg and Alexis Ravelin were already worthy predecessors of Stalin's jails; the Kara center in Siberia became in the 1880s a miniscule preview of the Soviet forced-labor camps.

We spoke before of those whose temperament would have brought them into the ranks of terrorists no matter what the political circumstances: whether the tsarist government had been wise instead of foolish in the way it dealt with subversion, whether it had followed the path of reform instead of freezing in the posture of reaction after 1866. By the same token, some representative figures in the liberation movement were clearly radicalized by the politics of the day, turning to violence because it was in the atmosphere surrounding them.

Sinegub was a strong opponent of terror even while in jail, he acknowledged, adding that at the time (1878) Sophia Perovskaya shared this attitude. "But afterward I changed my views on terror. . . . I saw it as a fateful, unavoidable phenomenon of Russian political life . . . a response to the corrosive effect of oppression practiced by the cruel, ruthless, and well-organized gang of criminals, murderers, liars, and debauchees who held political power in their hands."[11] Peter Kropotkin passed into history as a veritable revolutionary saint, a propagator of the ideal of a peaceful achievement of anarchism based on voluntary associations. But he was far from being a peaceful propagandist in Russia of the early 1870s: he was the first within the Chaykovsky circle to propose stirring up peasant rebellions, and his year and a half in jail turned him into a ferocious enemy not only of the autocratic system but of the monarch himself. Few memoirs by revolution-

[10] *The Gulag Archipelago Two,* Thomas P. Whitney, trans., New York 1975, 619.

[11] Sinegub, 224. Being then in Siberian exile, Sinegub never had occasion to practice what he preached. But tragically his views must have influenced his son. Lev Sinegub was hanged in 1906 for the attempted assassination of a tsarist minister.

aries exhibit such intemperate personal hatred of Alexander II as do the *Notes* of this scion of one of the most ancient noble families, compared with whom the Romanovs were relative *parvenus.* [12] This hatred is perhaps explained by a family tragedy. When Kropotkin was arrested in 1874, his brother Alexander, though himself politically compromised, hastened from Switzerland to Russia to try to free him. But instead of being able to help him, Alexander was himself arrested for no greater crime then mere correspondence with such political exiles as Lavrov. The emperor, furious that sedition should find recruits in the ranks of the highest aristocracy, confirmed the elder Kropotkin's sentence of twelve years' exile to Siberia. [13] One recalls how in the early 1860s writers such as Turgenev and government officials corresponded with and visited Herzen in London, with the police for the most part looking through their fingers at such goings-on.

"The older I grew the more I became repentant about my part in that affair; how much I would give to undo this wretched business. . . . Even the fact that I was so young at the time does not soften the pangs of remorse I feel when I recall those events." [14] Thus after almost fifty years Lev Deich looked at an "escapade" of his youth as a revolting act of terror directed not against a government official but a comrade who Deich and two others decided on rather flimsy evidence was an informer. But this incident, to which we shall return, was only the most horrifying of a ferocious phase in Deich's revolutionary youth. He planned to deceive peasants into a bloody uprising "which we envisaged not only as leading to the—seizure of all land but also as a slaughter of all oppressors of the people—landlords, police, officials, priests, well-to-do peasants—something, in a word, on the order of the Haydamak or Pugachev affairs." [15] Another time just for fun (he assures us he believed the gun was unloaded) he aimed and shot at one of his revolutionary companions, the bullet barely missing her. In his youth Deich gave the impression of being addicted to violence to the point of insanity, wrote Lev Tikhomirov. But he was no Nechayev. It is impossible to imagine the latter settling down to a peaceful study and propagation of

[12]In his memoirs written in the 1890s and widely read in the West, Kropotkin did not disdain to repeat the most opprobrious gossip about the late emperor, stories which he must have known to be untrue. Thus, allegedly Alexander II personally ordered several people to be locked up for life in the Alexis Ravelin "because they knew some court secrets which had to be kept from outsiders." *Notes of a Revolutionary,* Moscow 1966, 300.

[13]On its expiration in 1886 Alexander expected to rejoin Peter, then an emigré in England, and wrote to him in this sense. He received an incredibly heartless answer: It would be difficult to support him abroad, Peter said, but if Alexander had to come he must do so alone and leave his wife and children in Russia. This cruelty on the part of the younger brother whom he worshipped and for whom he had sacrificed so much led Alexander to kill himself.

[14]Deich, *After Half a Century* II, 134.

[15]*Ibid.,* I, 53. The Haydamak affair was an uprising of the Ukrainian peasants in the eighteenth century when landlords, Jews, and others were massacred indiscriminately.

socialism, whereas Deich became one of the first defectors from Populism to Marxism. As a social democrat and Menshevik he opposed Lenin in 1917; already in 1879 he was against Populism's definite commitment to individual terror. And so Deich was one of those who turned to violence not because they were psychopaths, like Ishutin and Nechayev, but because their youthful fanaticism could not cope with shattered illusions. The intellectual atmosphere of the period—compounded of philosophers' utopian dreams and society's revulsion against a regime both brutal and clumsy—made people of the most divergent backgrounds seek a solution in violence. Thus a Jew and a prince, one a future adherent of "scientific socialism," the other of peaceful anarchism, found common ground in the belief that only a violent revolution could solve their country's ills.

But violence no more than "peaceful propaganda" can be a substitute for a social philosophy. Nor can a conspiracy by itself be an effective tool of political struggle unless it is backed up by a party with a program. From 1875 revolutionary Populism strove to become a party and to acquire a philosophy. But it would never quite succeed in reaching either goal.

By 1875 Lavrov's reign over the revolutionary mind was a thing of the past. For one thing the incoherent prophet was too impressionable: his views took on the coloration of whomever he was working with at the moment. At one time he was flirting with Marxism; then there was a brief period when Tkachev wrote for his *Forward*. Within the international revolutionary community Lavrov became something of a joke. "He has read too much to know anything," was Karl Marx's verdict. An acidulous Russian exile, Nicholas Sokolov, had another witticism: "You can be what you will, a scoundrel, an idiot, or even a spy, but it is impermissible to become a Lavrov."[16] Lev Tikhomirov found Lavrov's whole career epitomized in a tale that the father of Populism himself reported about his boyhood. Whenever he needed a bath, a servant would bring out a tub, set it by the stream running through the family estate, and fill it up so that the young master would not have to step into the running water.[17] Throughout his life Lavrov bathed in radical rhetoric but never stepped into the mainstream of revolution.

The young zealots in Russia were not vouchsafed personal acquaintance

[16]Sokolov, a former artillery officer and a writer for *The Russian Word*, was a "man of the sixties." He was arrested after Karakozov's shot and though soon released found himself in hot water for a book, *The Alienated*. It was confiscated as containing "attacks on Christianity, incitement to subversion, and denunciation of the right of private property." After a period of imprisonment and exile, Sokolov was spirited abroad by some Populists in order to adorn *Forward* with his literary talent. Despite their common professional background, Lavrov and Sokolov soon quarrelled, and the latter, a man of vile temper, beat up one of Lavrov's followers. His last years were spent in France in poverty and, in the words of a Russian government agent, in "a state of dependence on alcoholic spirits."

[17]*Memoirs of Lev Tikhomirov*, Moscow 1927, 297.

with their erstwhile idol, and hence in the mid-1870s he still remained a revered figure but somewhat in the manner of Chernyshevsky: a man of the past whose teaching no longer suited the impatient mood of the moment. *Forward,* the periodical which he published first in Zurich and then in London until 1876, now bored the young with its lengthy articles and discussions. "Learned Lavrov sat on a turtle and shouted 'Forward' " was a witticism that circulated among the students.

What is to be done became again a pressing problem for the revolutionaries. In their quandary more and more of them longed for the conspiratorial-terrorist tactics of the sixties, even though intellectually they still found them repugnant.

This paradox helps explain the failure of Peter Tkachev to become the successor of Herzen, Chernyshevsky, and Lavrov as the spiritual guide of radical youth. Nechayev's erstwhile associate and mentor had high hopes, on reaching the West in December 1873, of providing the revolutionary movement with what it needed most at the moment: a theory and a strategy. Everything seemed to favor Tkachev's assuming the vacant throne of the "second government": his revolutionary past, wide erudition, and (certainly as compared with Chernyshevsky and Lavrov) lucid thinking and writing. But it was precisely this lucidity which proved his undoing. He made it clear without any obfuscation that he had little use for those two idols of Populism: "the people," and anarchy as the model of future society. To him only an organized and highly disciplined minority could achieve a revolution. "This minority, because of its higher mental and moral development, always has and ought to have intellectual and political power over the majority. . . . We acknowledge anarchy . . . but only as the desirable ideal of the far distant future."[18] To most contemporary revolutionaries this was unbearable. They believed that, in the words of *Forward:* "we do not want to exchange the old authoritarian system for a new one, whatever its nature."[19] Deich records with unconscious irony how shocked the contemporary conspirators were to hear Tkachev preach what in fact *they* were practicing. How scandalous of him to advocate "that a few thousand young revolutionaries can disorganize the regime through regicides and other terrorist acts, and thus easily seize power into their own hands."[20] The People's Will will try to do it with at most a few hundred people! And how scandalous Tkachev's denigration of the whole idea of propaganda among the masses. "The revolutionaries ought to realize that propaganda does not make a revolution possible, but on the contrary only after a revolution will agitation become meaningful. . . . Hence you must organize a monolithic, centralized,

[18]P. N. Tkachev, *Collected Works,* Moscow 1933, III, 223.
[19]*Forward,* II (Zurich 1873), 12.
[20]Lev Deich, *Russian Revolutionary Emigration of the Seventies,* St. Petersburg 1920, 83.

and hierarchically controlled secret conspiracy." And Deich, a member of the second Land and Freedom, an organization which except perhaps for elitism followed exactly this recipe, continues: "We the contemporary socialists rejected this new teaching with indignation. Everything in it clashed drastically with our views, aspirations, and emotions."

Tkachev expressed correctly the impatience of the true revolutionary and the fear, which the Russian variety of the species has always felt, that something—a constitution, the rise of a middle class—might snatch away the longed-for moment of struggle and retribution. "To prepare a revolution is not up to the revolutionary. It is being prepared all the time by the exploiters, capitalists, landowners. . . . The revolutionary does not *prepare* but *makes* the revolution. Then make it. Do it right away. It is criminal to be indecisive, to delay." This was the slogan which in effect Lenin was to make his own in 1917. But Tkachev forgot that the revolutionary *leader*— and this was true especially in Russia—must not be too explicit about his ultimate goal. In 1917 how many even among the Bolsheviks would have followed Lenin had he from the beginning advocated a one-party authoritarian state? And did he himself fully realize that that was his goal?

In short the very fact that he understood and expressed the mood of his young radical contemporaries earned Tkachev their opprobrium. He and the handful of his fellow "Russian Jacobins" found themselves isolated among exiles and without any real influence within Russia.[21] *The Tocsin,* which Tkachev published in Geneva between 1876 and 1881,[22] tolled in vain: it had few readers, in the West or in Russia. In a manner to be made notorious by the Communists, Tkachev went on for a while attributing every upsurge in revolutionary activity in Russia to the influence of his ideas. This in turn increased the revulsion felt against him in revolutionary circles. When in 1882 he became mentally ill, his contemporaries like Lev Tikhomirov attributed this to despondency over his political failure. But since Tkachev's death three years later came from progressive paralysis, his insanity in all likelihood had an organic cause.

It is odd that Tkachev, who whatever his political or personal morals never lent his hand to an actual murder, stood in the eyes of his revolutionary contemporaries several degrees lower than Nechayev.[23] His posthumous

---

[21]Jacobinism is the term applied to what historians have considered the purely power-oriented elitist strain in the Russian revolutionary movement extending from Zaichnevsky of Young Russia fame to Tkachev. Though by now conventional, it is hardly appropriate. The Jacobins of the French Revolution never questioned the principle of popular sovereignty or explicitly advocated rule by a minority.

[22]Practically every political refugee from Russia has dreamed of emulating the enormous success of Herzen's *Bell.*

[23]To be sure several of Tkachev's collaborators were considered outright thugs. The most notorious and colorful was a Polish nobleman, Caspar Turski. After an early involvement in the Polish insurrection of 1863 Turski fought in the Paris Commune, was reputed to have

fame has been largely due to the alleged influence his ideas had on young Lenin. But whatever the truth of such allegations and despite Tkachev's political ineffectiveness, one must acknowledge his acute analytical insight: he sensed what was on the mind of his revolutionary contemporaries, and he uncannily predicted under what conditions the tsarist regime might collapse. All it would take would be two or three military defeats, he said, some peasant uprisings, and an open revolt in the capital. And while in general he remained skeptical of individual terrorist heroics, he foresaw and approved without any qualms the use of *mass* terror by the victorious revolutionaries: "The Russian revolution like any other revolution will not be able to dispense with the hanging and shooting of policemen, prosecutors, merchants, and priests."

But for the moment Populism was a religion without prophets. There was no single gospel which the revolutionary would follow as Aptekman did in 1871 when he carried Lavrov's *Historical Letters* "in my vest pocket next to my heart . . . [since] this book was for me what the Bible or the Koran are for the believers." Those of the devotees who were not in jail carried on with propaganda among the workers or peasants, but simply because they could not think of anything else to do, and without that millenary faith which drove them to the people in 1873–74. Some were on the point of leaving the revolutionary stage, at least for a while. In Zurich Vera Figner was preparing for her final medical exams. The most restless activists such as Serge Kravchinsky and Dmitri Klements, future luminaries of Land and Freedom, were drawn to another struggle: in Herzegovina the Serbs were rising against their Turkish rulers, and many young Russians, from radicals to the most loyal subjects of Alexander II, volunteered their services to "brother Slavs" in a war of national liberation.

But precisely at this point, when the movement appeared in danger of dispersal into a multitude of circles carrying on uncoordinated propaganda and terrorist activities, there appeared what Populism needed more than a prophet, an organizer.

Mark Natanson was the veritable *deus ex machina* of Russian radicalism: making his entrance on the stage when the revolutionary movement was in disarray, creating the organizational nucleus of a new conspiracy, and then vanishing (through arrest). The circumstances of his arrest and exile in 1871, after he had created the Chaykovsky circle, endowed Natanson with special moral authority among his radical contemporaries. (His circle had published and circulated a proscribed book by Flerovsky. During the police

---

engaged in several political assassinations, and appropriately enough was Nechayev's roommate prior to the latter's arrest and extradition from Switzerland. After his collaboration with Tkachev he gravitated back to Polish emigré circles. He became a fervent nationalist after the World War and in 1920, when the Red Army entered Poland, the seventy-three-year-old Turski volunteered for the Polish army.

investigation one of the members was delegated to assume direct responsibility for this act. When he refused Natanson himself volunteered to confess that it was his doing and to suffer the consequences.) Now, with the period of his exile over, Natanson was the one man who could and would unite the dispersed forces of Russian Populism and lead them into a new phase of revolutionary struggle. But then, on the very threshold, in July 1877, a new arrest and another exile removed the intrepid revolutionary from circulation. It was seventeen years before he would be back again in Petersburg, and of course start the cycle all over: another clandestine party, arrest, and exile. In 1905 Natanson, like most ex-Populists, joined the Socialist Revolutionaries. He came back to Russia in 1917 and was instrumental in leading the Left S.R.'s to collaborate with the Bolsheviks. His illness then compelled him to go to Switzerland, where he died in July 1918, just as the Socialist Revolutionaries, the last heirs of Populism, were being liquidated by Lenin and his followers.

In 1875–76 Natanson was dubbed by his admirers as the "gatherer of Russian lands," a jocular allusion to the Muscovy rulers of the fifteenth and sixteenth centuries who conquered dispersed principalities to create the territorial nucleus of the future vast empire. He traveled all over to Moscow, Kiev, Odessa to urge a joint organization. He went abroad to Switzerland, and stirred up the revolutionary conscience of Vera Figner. It was difficult for the twenty-two-year-old girl to give up "the goal which had been before me for years . . . it was still so rare for a woman to become a doctor and surgeon." But she recognized such feelings as compounded of "vanity and selfishness" when reminded of some of her former fellow students, girls who had returned to Russia, taken the most menial factory jobs to serve the cause, and were now awaiting trial and the inevitable prison or exile.[24] And after a painful inner struggle, Vera decided to return to Russia and revolution. She would never achieve her dream of a doctor's diploma, though she was to live sixty-six years longer.

Natanson's organization began to solidify in the summer of 1876. Its first successful revolutionary enterprise was engineering the escape of Peter Kropotkin. While being held for trial along with his fellow "pilgrims," the rebellious prince fell ill and was temporarily transferred to a military hospital. During his convalescence the prisoner was allowed to walk in the hospital courtyard, and on June 30 he ran out through the open gate and, as prearranged, jumped into a carriage drawn by a renowned thoroughbred specially purchased for this purpose.[25] The driver of this get-away cabriolet was Mark Natanson himself, while his political friends engaged every cab

---

[24]From her autobiography in *Granat Encyclopedia,* XL, 463.
[25]Two years later Kravchinsky used the same horse, in fleeing the scene of crime after knifing the chief of the Third Department.

in the vicinity to frustrate the would-be-pursuers. Soon Kropotkin was on a ship which flew the Union Jack, "the flag under which so many Russian, Italian, and other exiles found refuge."[26] Radicals no more than the majority of mankind are immune to snobbery, and so the flight of the prince (and not one of the Caucasian ones, who were a dime a dozen, but a descendant of Rurik) was widely celebrated as a blow to the autocracy. "A tasty morsel was snatched away, and in what artistic fashion, from the hands of the Petersburg government!" wrote that perennial enthusiast Aptekman.

By the fall of 1876 Natanson had achieved a more substantial success. He had organized the Northern Revolutionary Populist Group. This group was officially renamed Land and Freedom in 1878, when it began to publish a clandestine organ by the same name, but in fact the appellation was applied to it from the fall of 1876, and we shall follow this tradition. Why the original name? Well, one must surmise that the "Northern" part of it marked Natanson's initial failure to gain concurrence for his program from various southern revolutionary circles, which were at once more militantly inclined than he was and not enchanted by the idea of centralization, i.e., control by the Petersburg group.

Kiev especially was the center of the "rebels," Populists who gave themselves out as followers of Bakunin while in fact their methods bore an uncanny resemblance to those recommended by Nechayev's People's Justice. As one of them put it bluntly, they had concluded by 1875 that propaganda, whether among workers or peasants, was of little use, and "we believed the only path to socialism was through a bloody revolution."[27] But with one spectacular exception their insurrectionist tactics were not meeting with more success than did those of the peaceful propagandists. As Michael Frolenko tells the story: "In 1876 I found myself in the circle of the Kiev rebels. Here the propaganda phase was definitely over and everything was directed toward organizing an armed group so once the peasants would rise we would join them and lead the rebellion."[28] In pursuit of this fantasy, Frolenko set off for Petersburg to collect money to buy guns. All he could raise for this purpose was five hundred rubles, which at current prices would purchase about twenty revolvers. On his return he found the whole enterprise busted, the presumed leaders of the rebellion having been forced to flee the countryside. Hence, as he puts it briskly, "Activity among the peasants becomes impossible. . . . We shall try in the cities. We are all armed. We decide on individual struggle against the government, armed resistance to arrest; we shall liquidate spies, traitors [and] . . . officials." In brief, individual terror.

[26]Kropotkin, 344.
[27]Vladimir Debogori Mokrievich, *Memoirs,* Paris 1894 (in Russian), 139.
[28]*Granat Encyclopedia,* XL, 510.

This was very far from Natanson's original conception. He had not lost faith in propaganda, but wanted to conduct it under the auspices of a centralized conspiracy rather than through the uncoordinated efforts of individuals, as during the Pilgrimage. But it was impossible to slow the momentum of revolutionary Populism and, with it, of Natanson's organization, toward the idea of terror. His closest associates pointed out with a certain logic that if the group devoted itself purely to propaganda it could hardly count on being more successful or more immune from arrest than had been the case with the dispersed activities of more than a thousand "pilgrims." There was the melancholy lesson of the band of activists that had grandiosely called itself "all-Russian social revolutionary organization." It had originated in 1875 from a fusion between some female returnees from Switzerland and a number of students, mostly from the Caucasus. For a few months it had carried on propaganda among workers in Moscow and three or four other industrial centers. By the end of 1875, having achieved but meagre results, all fifty or so of its members were in jail.

The feverish discussions which accompanied the organization of the Northern Revolutionary Populist Group bared the future schizophrenic character of the second Land and Freedom: intellectually it remained committed to education and agitation among the peasants and the growing industrial proletariat of the big cities; emotionally most of its members became obsessed with terror. In recalling those conversations, Vera Figner mentioned how proposals for a program included the traditional staples of Populism such as the demand to turn all land over to communal ownership, propaganda among the peasants (especially in the area of the Lower Volga, rich in the tradition of popular revolts), and so on; but, she added, "in our meetings it was pointed out that no insurrection can be successful unless part of the revolutionary forces were dedicated to a struggle with the government and the preparation to deal the central authority a decisive blow at the moment of a rebellion in the provinces, a blow which would cripple the apparatus and would enable the people's rebellion to grow in strength and dimensions. The possibility of blowing up the Winter Palace with dynamite was then mentioned, so that the whole imperial family would be buried under its ruins."[29] There is no reason to doubt her account, though it was written years after the events she described—she was to retain excellent memory and lucidity into advanced old age. But when she went on to say, "Both amendments were accepted unanimously by all those present," she evidently confused her later recollections of the People's Will in 1879–80 with discussions during the formative period of the second Land and Freedom, 1876–77; it is unlikely that members of the latter were ready at *that* time to go *that* far. Individual terror was discussed but as yet not approved

[29]Vera Figner, *Collected Works,* I, Moscow 1928, III.

in such stark and uncompromising fashion by Natanson and his followers. This interpretation is confirmed by Figner's avowal that she and several like-minded comrades remained during 1876–77 more or less fellow-travelers of Land and Freedom (they called themselves separatists) rather than outright followers of Natanson.[30]

Though still only toying with the idea of terror, Natanson's group was developing some classical techniques of conspiracy. Previous revolutionary endeavors were usually frustrated or betrayed to the police, due to the proverbial "broad Russian nature"—loose talk and carelessness about observing elementary conspiratorial precautions. Everybody in the early 1860s knew that if you wanted to drop in on some revolutionary talk you went to the Chess Club or Nicholas Serno-Solovievich's book shop. The Ishutin people very conveniently tended to live together. Now only a few among the conspirators were to know where Natanson and his closest collaborators gathered to decide what revolutionary enterprises should be mounted. This as yet untypical secretiveness led Dmitri Klements, then a fellow traveler and from 1878 a member of Land and Freedom, to dub its organizers "troglodytes," a name which gained currency and was taken seriously by some historians as having ideological significance.

The actual program of the organization was worked out early in 1877. Aptekman, one of the founders, writes with typical confusion "that this was, above all, a program à la Bakunin, only more fully reflecting historical data and contemporary conditions."[31] But in fact the second Land and Freedom represented an uneasy compromise between Lavrov's ideas and some of the organizational features of Nechayev's People's Justice, dressed in rhetoric inherited from the inspirers of the organization's namesake of the early sixties: Herzen and Ogarev. The Lavrov strain is unmistakable in the programmatic declaration: "Revolution must be carried out by the masses of the people. It is being prepared by history itself. Revolutionaries by themselves cannot achieve anything. They can serve only as the instrument of history expressing the people's aspirations. . . . Our program places first priority on the peasant question [i.e., communal ownership of all land] and considers that of the industrial [worker] as secondary. . . . The revolutionary movement, having burgeoned out of the land problem, it will next

[30]The historic merit of drawing the Populists' attention to dynamite belongs to Joseph Kablitz. One of those "pilgrims" who escaped the police dragnet, Kablitz persuaded two young ladies who had just inherited some money to finance a trip abroad to learn the properties of this just invented (1867) explosive. He returned from England (according to Figner, or the United States, according to Deich) with what he claimed was a sample of the frightful substance. He carried it in his vest pocket, and after a fiery revolutionary speech would produce a great effect by displaying it to his audience or to select individuals, usually good-looking girls. As might have been expected, when real terror began, this proponent of blowing up the Winter Palace left the revolutionaries' ranks and became a journalist and later a civil servant.

[31]O. V. Aptekman, *The Society of Land and Freedom of the 1870s*, Petrograd 1924, 192.

. . . by itself realize the necessity of expropriating industry and eliminating the capitalist system of production."[32]

This was a rather remarkable conclusion for a handful of revolutionaries, practically all of whom had found, on the basis of their personal experience, that, as Aptekman wrote, "the people do not want socialism" and "thousands upon thousands of propagandists" will not budge them on this issue. Yet they went blithely on advocating communal ownership while professing themselves to be but spokesmen of the people's aspirations. Again it was a case of self-deception rather than conscious hypocrisy, but this self-deception bore the seeds of future tragedy for Land and Freedom.

Aptekman gives us further details of the program: the aim of the organization was to unite "the divided forces of the revolutionary youth." Centralization and strict conspiratorial methods of activity were to be the rule. The organization was to be run by the "basic circle" in the capital, members of which would organize affiliated groups.[33] The basic circle was to have the following sections: a) administrative, which among other numerous tasks ran the "heavenly chancery," i.e., the bureau for producing false identity papers; b) propaganda among the *intelligentsia;* c) ditto for the workers; d) rural affairs. This last was supposed to be the most numerous group, devoted to propaganda among the peasants. As it turned out, we shall see that Land and Freedom almost completely neglected this aspect of its proposed activity. Contrariwise, the part which grew was, e) "the disorganization group."

This last, as even Aptekman admitted, was "because of the nature of its work, of the broad powers it received from the organization, placed in a unique position."[34] "Disorganization" in brief was a euphemism for espionage and terror. Members of this unit were supposed to infiltrate the government apparatus, organize escapes of arrested comrades, and "in the case of proved betrayal [of the conspiracy] by individuals . . . to kill them," as well as government officials who displayed cruelty in dealing with imprisoned revolutionaries. "All activities of the disorganization group were to be conducted in strict secrecy. The Administration and Council [of Land and Freedom as a whole] were to be notified only about the general outlines of a 'disorganizing' endeavor; all details were to be withheld."

This, then, was the entering wedge of terror in the program of Land and Freedom. To be sure, the terror was to be limited to self-defense—the elimination of traitors, police informers, and officials notorious for their cruelty—and not applied for "political" purpose, e.g., regicide. But how realistic was it to expect that such fine distinctions could be observed,

[32]Vladimir Burtsev, *One Hundred Years,* London 1897 (in Russian) 138.
[33]Aptekman, 195–96.
[34]*Ibid.,* 197.

especially since the terrorist section of the organization was to be given a virtually free hand? The "disorganization" aspect of Land and Freedom bears a striking resemblance to some points of the *Revolutionary's Catechism* of Nechayev and Bakunin. The very term in all likelihood was suggested by Tkachev's *Tocsin,* when in 1875 it declared: *"To organize for the purpose of disorganization and annihilation of the existing regime as the immediate and most essential goal:* this should be at present the only program for action of all revolutionaries."[35] For Land and Freedom terror was to be but an auxiliary and subordinate part of its activity, its founders hoped, the main goal remaining the traditional one of Populism, steering the masses toward socialism. Again they were deluding themselves.

How many were in this organization, which along with its later offshoot, the People's Will, was to shake the foundations of the vast empire and affect decisively the course of Russian history? The founding group had precisely twenty-five members. In the course of 1877–78 the "basic circle" grew to about fifty. If we count associates and provincial agents, Land and Freedom at its height and just before its split in the summer of 1879 had, according to Aptekman, just above 200 members.[36] Perhaps this estimate is a bit on the conservative side; its offshoot, the People's Will, according to Tikhomirov, and he in turn very likely exaggerates, had about 500 followers, not necessarily all members but also potential followers ready to obey its Executive Committee's summons. And so it is safe to assume that the parent organization had about three to four hundred members and fellow travelers, enough to fill up a medium-sized auditorium.

That such a miniscule group was able to affect the destiny of a nation of ninety million was due primarily to two reasons. First, as Tikhomirov wrote, "Land and Freedom was a strong and cohesive organization such as had not existed before in Russia."[37] The original Land and Freedom was what might be called a passive conspiracy: it waited upon events, specifically a peasant rebellion, to spring into action. The Ishutin, Khudyakov, and Nechayev circles were in the nature of revolutionary "encounter groups." Here for the first time one may speak of a revolutionary *party,* small in numbers but strong in determination and in the ability of its members to leave their imprint on history. By contrast with the People's Will, not to mention the Bolsheviks, Land and Freedom certainly does not seem to have been very cohesive, but with it we are at the threshold of the tradition that leads to Lenin's party: the idea of party discipline, of the individual revolutionary's submission to the collective will of his comrades, makes its first appearance. Land and Freedom never lived up to what we might describe

[35]Quoted in Burtsev, 135.
[36]Aptekman, 200.
[37]Tikhomirov, 124.

as its subconscious ideal of a militant authoritarian party imposing its will on the masses, but the ideal inspired future generations of revolutionaries until it was made explicit in Lenin's Communist Party, "the vanguard of the proletariat."

The principal reason for the historical significance of Land and Freedom, however, lies not so much in what this handful of revolutionaries themselves were able to achieve, but in what they made the imperial government do to itself. And that in the main has been true of all the principal revolutionary events of the nineteenth century: the shock of the Decembrists' revolt led to Russia's social and political system becoming ossified, while the rest of Europe went through a generation of enormous progress; Karakozov's assassination attempt arrested the momentum of reforms which, apart from their inherent merit, had made Alexander II the most popular monarch in Russia's history; arrests and the long detention of hundreds of ineffectual propagandists led to the government's losing the respect of the educated class, including part of its own officialdom. And the great revolutionary achievement of Land and Freedom and its heir, the People's Will, was to make the government lose faith in itself. Persuaded as it was that by now it was viewed with distaste if not outright hostility by the *intelligentsia,* the imperial regime rightly believed until the late 1870s that it still retained the allegiance of the vast majority of the Russian people. But within a few years this confidence was replaced by veritable panic, and by the feeling that the government was like a beleaguered garrison and could be saved only through the relentless repression of hostile forces. And so it was through self-inflicted wounds that the Russian monarchy was eventually to die, bringing down with it the whole social order. At no time is this suicidal tendency as clearly observable as in the period which now unfolds.

The first political action mounted by Land and Freedom was the demonstration on December 6, 1876, in the square before the Cathedral of Our Lady of Kazan in St. Petersburg. To many Soviet historians, this is an epoch-making date, the beginning of a mass revolutionary movement among Russian workers. Yet in itself the event was not only insignificant, but a tragicomic political failure on the part of the revolutionary group, and one which might well have brought its demise at this nascent stage. What rescued it was as usual the incredible stupidity of the authorities.

The story, when stripped of its mythological excrescences, is most instructive. The Populists, beginning with the Chaykovsky circle, had of course for some time carried on agitation among the growing industrial proletariat of Petersburg. By their own testimony the fruits of this agitation were meager. Some historians point—but they do this with obviously bad conscience—to the growing number of factory disputes and strikes during the first part of the 1870s as indicating a rising revolutionary consciousness. But it is clear that practically all the strikes had to do with conditions of work and pay and had no political background. A conscientious Soviet historian testifies that in many cases the authorities intervened on behalf of the workers: "In the first half of the 1870s, in cases of clear oppression of the workers by their employers the police officials often took the side of the exploited."[38] When the first Populist factory propaganda circle was broken up by the police in 1873–74 several workers volunteered evidence *against* the revolutionaries. Despite such discouraging experiences Land and Freedom decided to renew its effort. The head of its "workers" section became the twenty-year-old George Plekhanov, a former military and engineering student.

The winter of 1876–77 was a hard one for the Petersburg industrial proletariat. Many became unemployed. Rumors circulated that the workers were planning a demonstration, either by marching *en masse* to the residence of the heir to the throne to ask him to intercede for them or, in a less traditional form, by holding a public meeting. Plekhanov's "workers' section" decided to seize the initiative somewhat in the manner of the legendary politician of the French Revolution who, seeing multitudes passing under his windows, shouted, "There is the crowd and I am its leader!" and hurried outside. The first attempt was a total flop—practically nobody showed up at the appointed spot. But on December 6 a memorial mass was being celebrated at Our Lady of Kazan for the Russian volunteers fallen in the Balkan uprising, and one could be sure that a lot of people would be present at the end of the service. That Plekhanov and his associates hoped to assemble three thousand workers, as was subsequently claimed, is most doubtful. But in any case, there was likely to be a goodly crowd of worshippers pouring out of the church, and, to make sure, all available members of Land and Freedom and their friends, some two hundred people, were mobilized for the occasion, as well as any workers they could lay hands on. Whatever the number, it was hoped "to throw a challenge to the authorities, to interrupt the atmosphere of [political] calm, and through sheer brazenness to shock the enemy and to give new courage to our followers."[39]

As an eyewitness describes, "Toward the end of the Mass some two hundred students of both sexes entered the church. . . . They behaved most improperly . . . whispered, laughed, and argued."[40] At the end of the service, the crowd debouched on the square, and here the future father of Russian Marxism made his debut as a public speaker. According to the police report, Plekhanov said, "We observe this day in the memory of martyrs Chernyshevsky . . . Nechayev, Dolgushin, and others." Then he said something about the oppression of peasants, concluding, "Death to the tsar! Long live

[38]E. A. Korolchuk, *The First Labor Demonstration in Russia,* Leningrad 1926, 5.
[39]Figner, I, 114.
[40]Korolchuk, 20.

freedom! Hurrah!" At this point, the demonstrators lifted up a sixteen-year-old boy, this time a genuine worker (he had been in the charge of the two Figner sisters, who had taken him to lunch before shepherding him to the demonstration), who unfurled a red banner with the device "Land and Freedom." A constable blew his whistle, and the police fell upon the crowd. The main impressarios of the affair, Plekhanov and the two Figner girls and the rest of the high command of the revolutionary organization, fled, but some of their hot-blooded followers resisted arrest. A few were roughed up by onlookers who viewed the whole affair with distaste. As an observer noted, "The people on whose behalf all that was allegedly done dealt severely with the demonstrators and helped the police catch them." Thirty-two persons were detained (twenty-one men and eleven women), none of them the principal actors and some of them proverbial "innocent bystanders."

How many workers did actually participate in this "first mass workers' demonstration in Russian history"? Plekhanov and after him most historians quote the figure as being between 200 and 250. But there is a more reliable contemporary estimate adduced by the Soviet authority on the subject: "There were at most fifty workers."[41] Apart from being a total fiasco, the whole business left a bad taste even with radical youth: some dwelt ruefully on the fact that the organizers were the first to flee. And indeed Vera Figner records unabashedly how once they noted they were being followed by a policeman she and her sister jumped into a cab, while their charge, the boy hero of the demonstration, was seized. The unfortunate teen-ager, who to put it bluntly had been hired for the occasion, spent the rest of his life in exile.

Imbecility on the part of the authorities served to transform this ludicrous affair into a great propaganda victory for the revolutionary cause which did "shock the enemy and gave new courage to our followers." The government decided to treat the street brawl that ensued at the end of the Kazan demonstration as if it had been high treason. Twenty-one of those arrested were tried in January 1877, not before a justice of the peace but before the special bench of the senate for state crimes. Three of the accused, in their early twenties, received fifteen years at hard labor; two (one of them a nineteen-year-old medical student), ten. Thus for an offence usually punishable by a fine or a few weeks' arrest they were dealt with more harshly than were four of Nechayev's associates in murder. Of the rest, ten (including a sixteen-year-old girl) were sentenced to Siberian exile of indefinite duration. The emperor confirmed the sentences: society was dumbfounded at this display of official stupidity and savagery.

For the next few years political trials became the most effective means

[41] *Ibid.*, 12.

of revolutionary propaganda, dwarfing in this respect all that the hundreds of revolutionary pilgrims had been able to accomplish. The government spared no effort to surround the proceedings with solemnity and the accused with an aura of martyrdom. Under a law of 1871 political trials would at the discretion of the minister of the interior be held not before a regular court and jury but, as we have just seen, before a special session of the highest tribunal, the senate, assisted by four assessors from organs of local self-government. Many a young man or woman who ordinarily would not dream of engaging in strenuous and dangerous propaganda work was now dazzled by the prospect of "starring" in a spectacle which the whole country followed, of issuing a dramatic defiance to the powers that be, conscious that his words would find a vast audience at home and even abroad.

In February-March came the trial of "the 50," the accused who under the name of the All-Russian Social Revolutionary Organization had tried to propagandize workers in Moscow, Tula, Kiev, and Odessa. Again the old story: upper-class youths taking jobs in factories, distributing to their fellow workers *The Tale of Four Brothers, Pugachev,* etc., and in general with the same negligible results. The trial did display some new features, premonitory of the course the revolutionary movement would take within the next two years. The police testified about the trouble they encountered when they came to arrest two of the accused, a Georgian prince, Alexander Tsitsianov, and his companion, also noble-born, Olga Liubatovich. His Grace shot at the policemen who entered their apartment, but to the disgrace of the Caucasian nobility missed twice at close range, while "the young lady," as the police report refers to her respectfully, tried to choke one of the officers.[42] This was probably the first case of armed resistance to an arrest among the Populists, but not by far the last, and the choleric prince received eight years at hard labor (he was to die insane). Compare this with the sentences received by the Kazan demonstrators for *unarmed* resistance.

Another innovation would also catch on: several of the accused refused lawyers and used their defense speeches to expound their political philosophy. Two of them received wide circulation and became revolutionary classics. Sophia Bardina, if we accept the authenticity of the text, offered an exposé of the principles which guided the group: they proposed to work *peacefully,* through propaganda. How could they be accused of trying to destroy religion and the family if one of their postulates was the abolition of property, hence of poverty, which in turn would put an end to prostitution? In any case "revolutions are made by forces of history and not through agitation by a few individuals."[43] The young girl (b. 1853) concluded, "You have physical force behind you, gentlemen, but we represent moral and

[42]Bazilevsky, II, 277.
[43]*Ibid.,* 405.

historical forces, and ideas cannot be suppressed by bayonets."

Even more defiant and dramatic was the speech of one genuine worker among the principal defendants, Peter Alexeyev. "We, millions of working people, are only now beginning to stand on our own feet. . . . The peasant reform of February 19, 1861 . . . does not secure the minimum needs of the peasants. . . . We as before remain dependent on the capitalist."[44] The worker, said Alexeyev, can expect help only "from our *intelligentsia* youth, which alone refuses to look with equanimity at that tortured mass of the working people groaning under despotism." Here the president of the court is alleged to have shouted "Silence," but Alexeyev continued. "And this *intelligentsia* will march together with us until the moment when the millions-strong working people will raise its muscular arm and the edifice of despotism held up by soldiers' bayonets will crumble into dust."[45]

These speeches are not recorded in the official text of the trials, where it is noted simply that Bardina made a speech in her own defense and that Alexeyev during his had to be reprimanded for "insolent expressions." The text, furnished presumably by somebody who attended the trial, was published abroad in *Forward.* Hence one must express some skepticism as to its accuracy, especially in the case of Alexeyev's speech, which sounds both too polished and too much in accordance with what the revolutionaries believed a man of the people *should* say. And we have one unimpeachable testimony that the radicals, both in Russia and abroad, were not above doctoring or even inventing such texts.

During his stay abroad in 1874–75, Morozov worked in one of the emigré journals, *The Worker,* edited by Zemfir Ralli, a former associate of Bakunin and Nechayev. One day they received a letter from a friend in Russia noting that during his trial a worker named Malinovsky delivered a splendid speech, but the letter did not go into any details. In his childish way Morozov was considerably surprised when the next issue of the journal contained a *verbatim* text of "Malinovsky's" speech, containing passages like: "Those who have not been hungry cannot be just. . . . I despise your morals. Judge me according to your laws, but wherever I am sent I shall call upon the hungry to struggle against the tsar, landlords, and capitalists." When Morozov upbraided him for this improvisation Ralli retorted coolly: "What else could he have said? We know his socialist and revolutionary convictions."[46]

Revolutionary Populism never did sink any roots into the now rapidly growing industrial proletariat of the big cities. At times outright bribery was resorted to in order to bring factory workers into revolutionary circles, and

[44]*Ibid.,* 408.
[45]*Ibid.,* 410.
[46]Morozov, II, 229.

it is not surprising that some of these recruits in turn became police inform-ers. The main reason for the lack of success was the same as for the corresponding failure to get a wide peasant following: Populism was too impatient for a revolution, too engrossed in its ultimate vision of anarchic socialism, to pay close attention to the everyday needs and aspirations of the working people, whether in villages or cities. The more advanced work-ers were beginning to hear of trade unions in the West, of the struggle for higher pay and better working conditions. But most of them still thought of the imperial government as their protector against the bosses, and not without reason, as we have seen. Activities of the workers' section of Land and Freedom were almost entirely directed at undermining this faith rather than agitating for such prosaic and, from the revolutionary's point of view, contemptible goals as better wages and shorter working hours. Indeed these were taken as a prima facie proof of Herzen's assertion that "the worker of all countries will grow into the bourgeois." When some Petersburg workers organized a tiny and short-lived Northern Union of Russian Work-ers in 1879, Land and Freedom reprinted its quite radical manifesto (it called among other things for worker ownership of factories) in its organ, but added an editorial comment that it was insufficiently revolutionary in spirit and devoted too much space to demands for the political freedoms of speech, press, etc.[47] This was "politics," a dirty word for revolutionary Populism, since it was held synonymous with making demands on the government, parleying with the state, rather than working to smash it once and for all.

Thus the two contestants—the regime and the revolutionary. The Popul-ists found themselves in a blind alley precisely because they scorned politics as it is usually defined: the pursuit of power through influencing people's minds. And the government tended to use repression as if it were an end in itself rather than an auxiliary and subordinate means for preserving a viable social and political order. Superficially the revolutionaries appeared to act more and more according to the precept of the *Revolutionary's Catechism:* that the end justifies the means. But in fact they were more naive than Machiavellian: revolutionary heroics became an end in themselves. Eventually they dissipated both their own forces and the moral credit with which the government's imbecilities and harshness endowed them.

Yet if they could argue here in self-defense the organizers of Land and Freedom would repeat their traditional plea, that the government had forced them to take the path of violence. From our perspective we can see another and overwhelming reason: their numerical weakness. During its formative period, the founders hoped that its main activity would be a new Pilgrimage to the People but in a more sophisticated form: propagandists

[47]B. Bogucharsky, *Active Populism of the Seventies,* Moscow 1912, 352.

would go among the peasants not individually but in groups, would not disperse their efforts all over the country but would concentrate on the region of the lower Volga. Yet how could a group with a nucleus of fifty members mount an operation of this kind and make even a dent in the peasant's political apathy?

At the same time that a handful of the new-style propagandists were experiencing the same frustrations as their predecessors in 1874–75, the news was reaching them of bold insurrectionist tactics on the part of the southern "rebels." These, as we have seen, initially rejected formal links with Land and Freedom, believing that the whole idea of "peaceful propaganda" had had its day. And by 1877 they were demonstrating that their conspiratorial tactics, borrowed straight from Nechayev's People's Justice, could create more stir than the eclectic ones of their Petersburg-based comrades.

The Chigirin affair, for all its subsequent condemnation by the leading lights of Populism as dishonest, indeed "jesuitical," in its inception, undoubtedly played an important part in pushing the whole movement toward an all-out commitment to terror and mystification as the means of struggle. Three revolutionaries in the Ukraine had *almost* succeeded in triggering a sizable peasant uprising. The lesson seemed to be that scruples of any kind, even partial renunciation of terror, were an impermissible luxury for a movement with so few members which aspired to appear to the government and society as a mysterious and powerful force.

"As we did not have beds in our room, I would lie on the floor with Stefanovich talking to him late into the night, of course about various problems connected with the future revolutions. . . . And on one such occasion . . . I had the brainstorm that our rebels should use the imperial name to arouse the peasants."[48] Thus Deich describes the inception of the idea of forging an imperial manifesto which would call upon peasants in a district in the Ukraine to organize into armed bands and then upon a signal rise and slaughter the landlords and officials.

The idea was hardly an original one: rebellions under or in the name of tsarist impostors had a history going back at least to the seventeenth century. But except for an abortive attempt in 1863 in the Kazan area when the initiative came from some Poles, the Russian revolutionaries had consistently eschewed the use of this technique on grounds both that it was inherently immoral and that in the end it was bound to be self-defeating. But here were two wild young men for whom such compunctions were meaningless.

Deich, the son of a rich contractor who had gone bankrupt during Lev's youth, and Jacob Stefanovich, from a priestly family, were friends from

[48]Deich, *After Half a Century,* II, 11.

their high-school days—perhaps even more than that. Kravchinsky mentioned rather indiscreetly that the two became so close that, when for conspiratorial reasons they had to separate, they exchanged letters every day, and the relationship was the subject of much joking among their fellow Kiev "rebels."[49] The whole Kiev group counted about twenty members, and its existence and occasional propaganda forays into the countryside were hardly a secret from the authorities. The local head of gendarmes, Baron Gustav Heyking, knew that the local radicals gathered regularly in the house of the parents of one of the "rebels," Vladimir Debogori Mokrievich, but he refrained from raiding it, whether out of liberalism or, as Deich claims, fear. This goes far to explain the brazenness of the Kiev group in mounting an operation which in almost any other region of the empire would have been nipped in the bud.

Stefanovich in the course of his wanderings had become acquainted with an interesting situation which had arisen in a number of villages in the Chigirin region. Following the Emancipation, a dispute had split the ranks of the peasants who had previously belonged to the state. One group was ready to accept the same allotments which they had held as state serfs. The other demanded a general redistribution of land, the new allotments to be based on the number of "souls," i.e., heads in the given household. The "redistributors" kept petitioning the authorities, and when their pleas proved fruitless, refused to sign documents confirming their allotments and obligations, or to pay taxes, and engaged in other forms of passive resistance. Finally the government stationed troops in the district, and the most obstreperous "redistributors" were arrested. Among them was a peasant who claimed that on a visit to Petersburg he got to see the tsar, and that His Majesty looked with compassion and understanding on his loyal subjects and their attempts to secure justice!

This was the situation that Stefanovich found on his forays into the region during the winter of 1875–76. He presented himself as a peasant from another area who had successfully intervened with the tsar on behalf of his fellow villagers and who felt that he could successfully perform a similar errand for the suffering "redistributors" of Chigirin. With that, in February 1876, he vanished from the scene, promising to be back in May with a special message from His Majesty.

Back in Kiev he plunged into preparations for the coup. It proved to take longer than he had expected. One of the comrades had to be dispatched abroad to purchase special printing materials to issue facsimiles of imperial rescripts. Along with this stuff the emissary brought back a discouraging

[49]L. M. Stepniak (Kravchinsky), *Underground Russia,* Petrograd 1917, 30. This book appeared originally in Italian in 1882, and then in several other European languages, becoming, along with Kropotkin's memoirs, the main source of information in the West about the revolutionary movement.

message: the alleged spiritual guide of the "rebels," Bakunin, then in the last months of his life, when apprised of the proposed venture expressed strong disapproval. But this did not diminish the enthusiasm of Stefanovich and his two closest collaborators, Deich and a former student, Ivan Bokhanovsky, for the scheme. But before proceeding with it they took time out for a hideous crime.

In June 1876 their conspiratorial headquarters, then in the town of Elizabethgrad, were visited by twenty-year-old Nicholas Gorinovich. Arrested as one of the "pilgrims" in 1874, Gorinovich had been released in 1875 but placed under police surveillance. It is still not clear whether during his arrest Gorinovich denounced some of his Kiev fellow propagandists, but in any case, without any substantial proof or any decision by their group as whole, Deich and Stefanovich decided that he was a police informer. They lured him to Odessa. Here they beat him—to death, they thought—with the Russian version of the blackjack, an iron ball fastened to a chain, and then they poured acid over his face. Gorinovich survived, miraculously, though he was blinded and his face horribly scarred, and upon his recovery gave the police the full story of his tormentors and information about any other revolutionaries he knew.

It is a measure of the moral deterioration of the revolutionary camp that the perpetrators of this deed, one which in sadism and senselessness rivals the murder of Ivan Ivanov, were not even ostracized by their fellow activists; in 1878 both Deich and Stefanovich were accepted into Land and Freedom. In some circles there was open exultation: "Make more such masks for traitors," urged Tkachev's *Tocsin*. But the would-be assassins eventually paid for their crime. Victor Malinka, Gorinovich's "host" in Odessa, was hanged in 1879. Deich in 1884 was extradited from abroad and sentenced to hard labor in Siberia. Stefanovich, arrested in 1882, "sang" to the police himself and was sent into exile.

But that was later. It is a measure of police incompetence that Deich, Stefanovich, and Bokhanovsky were able to return to Kiev and proceed with the plot. In November 1876 the "emissary to the tsar" returned to the Chigirin district. If the "redistributors" had been put off by his tardiness, they were reassured by the handsome documents Stefanovich brought with him, printed in the imperial chancery and signed with His Majesty's own hand. They gave the dissatisfied peasants all they wished for and more. In the Imperial Charter Alexander II let his faithful subjects in on the troubles he had had with his subordinates, landlords, and indeed his own son and heir, who ever since 1861 had managed to obstruct his benevolent laws and plans concerning the peasants. He now appealed to the peasants for help. "Unite into 'secret bands' in order to prepare a rebellion against the nobles, officials, and all the higher estates of the realm." Then there was a Code, with detailed instructions on how those secret bands were to be organized, how to liquidate disloyal members and spies, etc., and the formula of the solemn oath to be taken by all their members.[50] The beauty of the whole scheme from the revolutionaries' point of view was that once Stefanovich, the "Imperial Commissioner," delivered those documents and appointed the over-all chieftain of the "secret bands," the conspiracy would develop a momentum of its own. Stefanovich and his two closest associates would make brief trips of inspection into the area, but otherwise recruitment and organization of the bands would be done by the initiated peasants themselves. And so membership in the bands grew, and by the time the plot was discovered in September 1877 between one and two thousand peasants were ready to pick up their pikes, axes, and the few firearms they had as soon as the emperor, through his Commissioner, gave the signal for wholesale slaughter of officials and nobles.

Writing in his old age, Deich tried to rationalize this preposterous and —from his later viewpoint as a social democrat—disgraceful scheme: "In every great historical moment a kind of mass hypnosis seizes the most enterprising and active people; without it you could not have any progress throughout history." But it was he and his associates who were suffering from that hypnosis rather than the simple people whom they deceived and who themselves would have been slaughtered if the madcap venture ever reached its designed goal. But almost inevitably the secret leaked out, one version has it through the confessional, another due to a drunken initiate forgetting his oath, and after eight months of existence the bands were liquidated. More than a hundred of their members were arrested, but in this case the authorities showed some understanding, and only four peasants were sentenced to forced settlement in Siberia. The three real culprits were also imprisoned in September, but due to the fantastic incompetence of the Kiev police, Stefanovich, Deich, and Bokhanovsky were able to flee the jail in May 1878.

One would have thought that the attack on Gorinovich and the Chigirin affair would have enabled the government to capitalize on the instinctive revulsion that many people, even within the radical camp, still experienced when confronted with outright thuggery and deception. The tsars' Soviet successors would display great mastery in exploiting the real or alleged crimes of their opponents to mount nationwide propaganda campaigns. *They* certainly would not have missed the opportunity to give the widest possible publicity to what happened to Gorinovich, to dispatch some of the deluded and now repentant victims of the Chigirin fraud to the four corners of the empire, to spread the tale of how the peasant's ignorance and his faith in the tsar had been cruelly exploited by "nihilists." But public relations

---

[50]The quotation and some other details of the Chigirin conspiracy are taken from Daniel Field, *Rebels in the Name of the Tsar,* Boston 1976, 77.

were not, to put it mildly, a strong point of the tsarist government. Poor Gorinovich remained a criminal in the eyes of the law, under indictment for his propaganda activities in 1874, and he faced the court in the trial of "the 193." The Chigirin affair was viewed, on the contrary, as possibly contagious, its details to be hushed up as much as possible. The governor of Kiev province had the imbecility to propose that all peasants even remotely concerned with the business, some five thousand strong, be resettled in a different area of the empire.

Like many species destined for extinction, the imperial government had a short attention span (and this in a different sense was also true of revolutionary Populism). In 1877 its main concern was yet another Balkan crisis, which initiated another Russo-Turkish war, which in its turn threatened a fresh conflict with European powers, in this case Britain and Austria. Though this time the imperial army was victorious, the protracted length of the campaign (a year and a half), and the number of casualties incurred in fighting an army which was (not quite justifiably) held in low esteem, brought fresh disappointments to Russian society. The most jarring was the political outcome of the war. Russia's perennial hopes to have the Russian flag fly over Constantinople, to dominate the Balkan Peninsula, were dashed. The Berlin Congress of the Great Powers in 1878 was widely viewed as representing a diplomatic defeat for the empire, which had to back down on its original exactions from Turkey. In fact under the resultant treaties Russia regained Bessarabia and procured valuable real estate in the Caucasus, as well as autonomy for the Bulgarians under the Turks (which in fact amounted to independence). But this was small compensation for the lives and treasure poured into the conflict. There was a general feeling that Russia had been betrayed by her traditional ally, Germany; Bismarck, who presided over the Congress, had allegedly taken a pro-British position. In view of the close dynastic links between the two states (William I was Alexander's uncle) some of the blame rather illogically was attached to the Russian emperor. Austro-Hungary and Britain had to be appeased with part of the loot: Bosnia, Herzegovina, and Cyprus, respectively. Thus the stage was set for Russia's dramatic shift from an alliance with Germany to one with France, eventually for another "Balkan" crisis in the summer of 1914.

Foreign danger and diplomatic humiliation did not prove an incentive to national cohesion and stability at home. If anything they had the opposite effect. And in July 1877 the news from the theaters of war appeared to many educated Russians to be of lesser consequence than the shocking incident that took place in the preliminary arrest jail in St. Petersburg and that, despite only circumspect references to it in the press, soon became public knowledge.

For political prisoners placed in this jail after a stay in the Petropavlovsk fortress, the misnamed institution (some stayed there for three or four years) represented a distinct improvement. Among other things one did not have the infuriating sound of bells every hour on the hour chiming the liturgical "How Glorious Our Lord in Zion," and twice a day "God Save the Tsar." But the main advantage, as we have already seen, was that though the commandant was a martinet, the sheer quantity of "politicals" awaiting the monster trial of "the 193"[51] made it impossible to enforce strict prison regulations. The inmates communicated practically at will—on their walks, through the walls, shouting and sending written messages to each other from the cell windows. Then, in old Russia's manner, this indulgent atmosphere was sharply transformed by an act of wanton brutality.

General Fyodor Trepov, appointed police chief in 1866, was now governor of the city. The man who while in Warsaw in 1863 fined Polish ladies for wearing mourning for their dead loved ones was not likely to tolerate this institution in his jurisdiction being run as if it were a revolutionary fraternity. On July 13 he dropped in for an inspection. What he saw put him in an ugly mood: prisoners were walking in the courtyard in groups and chatting. He turned on some of them: did they know that people awaiting trial were forbidden to communicate? One of the inmates, Bogolyubov (his real name was Alexis Yemelyanov, and he was one of the original members of Land and Freedom), tried to explain that this regulation did not apply to him since he had already been judged and sentenced (for his part in the Kazan demonstration), but Trepov cut him off. When Bogolyubov persisted, Trepov, now beside himself, shouted that the prisoner was being insolent in addressing an official with his cap on, and with a blow he swept it off. He later ordered Bogolyubov birched. The prisoners watching the drama from their windows burst into a din, smashing furniture in their cells, yelling, and banging on their doors. The guards ran into the noisiest cells, beat the inmates and carried them off to the isolator.

Russian society had seen plenty of "police brutality," but until now it was unprecedented that a political prisoner and an *intelligent* should have corporal punishment inflicted upon him. And in fact as we have seen from Sinegub's and Morozov's accounts, a certain etiquette had prevailed in relations between political prisoners from the upper classes and the authorities, which had made it seem inconceivable that a supposed gentleman, and an adjutant-general of His Majesty at that, should openly threaten let alone strike a man who could not defend himself. The government could have quickly repaired the damage and in fact gained face by firing Trepov. The failure to do so was to have truly historic consequences.

The great trial of those charged with "revolutionary propaganda within

---

[51]The actual number judged was, according to varying sources, four below that, one having "disappeared," three dying in the course of the three-month trial.

the empire" which opened in September was bound to take place in a tense atmosphere, and the Trepov episode helped to exacerbate it, as well as to arouse the general sympathy of society for the accused. Indeed many of the accused adopted a stance of open defiance and obstruction of the proceedings. Some refused to testify and declared that they rejected the legitimacy of the court. The most violent among them, Ippolit Mishkin, one-time stenographer of the General Staff, who in 1866 had been personally commended by the emperor for excellence in his then quite new profession, declared: "This is not a court but a comedy; in fact this is worse than a whorehouse. There a woman sells her body to gain a living, but here, you senators, out of vileness and servility, to gain promotions and awards, traffic in human life."[52] The judges were incapable of stopping such outbursts, indeed of controlling the multitude of defiant youth, who in some cases had to be brought in and carried out by force. Since the proceedings were semipublic—insofar as seats were available, relatives of the accused were allowed in the audience—stories of this judicial bedlam made the rounds of the country and were excellent propaganda for the revolutionary cause. Overlooked in the general indignation at this display of the government's clumsy arbitrariness were incidents that in another setting might have led to revulsion against the accused: the appearance of Gorinovich, with his horridly scarred mask of a face, a recital by another defendant of the often underhanded methods with which "peaceful propaganda" among the workers and peasants had been conducted.

What was for the prestige of the regime a catastrophic effect of this misbegotten judicial enterprise was enhanced by the verdict: all but forty of the accused were set free, either as innocent or as having fulfilled their sentences through the time they had spent in jail awaiting trial. Among them were quite a few who soon would be heard of again: Tikhomirov, Perovskaya (she had been out on bail), Morozov, and many others. And the judges petitioned the emperor to lighten the sentences of the forty who were found guilty. But the public took this not as a proof of magnanimity on the part of the government (no one believed that the senators were independent of the executive) but as a belated and cowardly acknowledgment of its arbitrariness: why did the young men and women have to spend their best years behind bars if they were innocent, or guilty of but trivial offences? (Gorinovich was sentenced but freed in view of his "repentance and candid confessions." Mishkin, one of the five who received the severest sentence, ten years at hard labor, would over the next few years repeatedly bait police authorities and attempt to escape. His turbulent spirit was unable to endure captivity: when finally in Schlüsselburg, he deliberately sought the death penalty and received it for assaulting a prison officer.)

[52]Bazilevsky, III, Paris 1905 (in Russian), 310.

The trial, and Vera Zasulich's attempt to kill General Trepov, which came on January 24, the day after the announcement of the verdict, went far to legitimize terror in the minds of the revolutionaries themselves and, what is more important, of many educated Russians. The latter development was decisively to effect Russian politics for the next three years. By themselves the revolutionaries still remained a tiny minority. While political terror was far from being a uniquely Russian phenomenon in Europe of the 1870s and 1880s—the German emperor was shot at twice, an English Cabinet minister was killed by an Irish assassin—the Russian situation was peculiar in that this means of political struggle was viewed with understanding if not outright sympathy by many solid middle- and upper-class citizens who themselves would not have dreamed of violating the most trivial police regulation. It is only under those conditions that individual terror is resorted to by normal people and can become of political significance. We have seen the two classical stereotypes of Russian radicals: "the guilt-stricken nobleman" and "the enraged plebeian." Now what might be called the "sighing moderate" joined them. Within the revolutionary camp he would still plead that the movement should not swerve from its original goal of educating the masses and liberating their instinctive socialism. But he did not oppose his terrorist comrade's tactics too strenuously: how else could the government be persuaded to allow peaceful propaganda for its own overthrow? Respectable lawyers, professors, and journalists shrugged their shoulders over the latest assassination: perhaps it would teach the regime a lesson, that only by granting a constitution could it put a stop to these horrors; and for all the impermissibility of such methods, one could not but admire the idealism of those young people. . . . Buoyed up by this atmosphere, the terrorists pursued their craft heedless of the fact that it would destroy not only their own and their victims' lives, but also the very movement and the ideal they had set out to serve.

V

THE TRIUMPH OF
REVOLUTIONARY
POPULISM

ELEVEN

THE YEAR OF CHOICE

Vera Zasulich spent the night of January 23, 1878, with her friend Maria Kolenkina. She did not sleep well, had nightmares. The two girls had moved to St. Petersburg after Gorinovich, upon his recovery, had told the police all he knew about the Kiev "rebels." They had specific projects in mind, too: Vera was going to shoot General Trepov, her friend Masha the prosecuting attorney in the trial of "the 193." On the morning of January 24, Zasulich was in the city governor's waiting room; it was the day General Trepov received petitioners. When the satrap and his suite entered Vera handed him an application for a teacher's license. He referred her to a subordinate and turned to another visitor. Thereupon she pulled her German 'Bulldog' out from her muff and shot him in the side. (She had considered a Smith-Wesson but rejected it as too long to be concealed in her clothing.)

What little sympathy was felt for Trepov (who survived the shot) was diminished by the obvious lying in his deposition about the matter. There he claimed that his aides had to wrest the gun from Vera's grasp to prevent her from finishing the job. Apart from the obvious implausibility of a wounded man's paying attention to such details, his own men testified that after the first and only shot Zasulich tossed the gun to the floor. She was a terrorist but not a killer.

There followed a rather Russian scene. The official in whose charge she was placed announced that she would have to be searched. Vera bridled at this proposed affront to her modesty: why should she conceal another weapon—she meant just to shoot Trepov; if they did not believe it they could tie her up.[1] She was put under guard, and one of the soldiers wondered where the young lady had learned to shoot. On being told by this captain's daughter that it was a very simple thing, he expressed his professional disapproval. "Well, you did not learn well," he said. "He will survive." Trepov did in fact speedily recover and lived to an old age.

From the juridical point of view Vera Zasulich's case seemed clear: attempted murder. Though she freely admitted she had done this to avenge Bogolyubov, the government, sick for the moment of political trials, decided to treat it as an ordinary crime and have her tried before a regular court and jury.

"Can you, dear Anatole Fyodorovich, guarantee a conviction?" the minister of justice, Count Pahlen, asked the president of the Petersburg district court, thirty-four-year-old Anatole Koni.[2] Koni expressed proper shock at this question. Years later he was to confess that his feelings were far from impartial, but in a direction opposite to what might be supposed: along with most of St. Petersburg high society and officialdom he considered Trepov a swine and a crook, quite apart from his inexcusable behavior toward Bogolyubov. In fact it was difficult to find a prosecutor for the trial. One official pleaded that he could not undertake the task because his brother was a well-known revolutionary; another would prosecute only if he were allowed to say what he thought of General Trepov. Finally the choice narrowed down to one man who was thought, and amply proved to be, most incompetent.

In the meantime, the fearless Vera Zasulich became the toast not only of revolutionary, but of liberal, and even society circles. Poems and radical broadsides celebrated her as another William Tell or Charlotte Corday. The last comparison has always shocked Soviet historians, and rightly so. Charlotte was of course a royalist and Jean-Paul Marat, whom she killed in his therapeutic bath, was what might be called the Tkachev of the French Revolution. But the comparison, used repeatedly by radicals such as Morozov, shows how fascinated revolutionary Populism had become with the idea of individual terror. Her defense was undertaken by Peter Alexandrov, the Clarence Darrow of the Russian Bar of the period.

The very day the trial opened, March 31, Alexandrov showed his masterful hand and, incidentally, the topsy-turvy character of contemporary Russian society. Government officials were eligible for jury duty, which would seem to us a great threat to impartial justice. Yet with unerring psychological insight the defense counsel used his challenges not against them, but against prospective jurors with lower-class background: merchants and artisans. Thus it was that the prosecutor acquiesced without a single chal-

[1]Vera Zasulich, *Memoirs*, Moscow 1931, 68.
[2]A. Koni, *Works*, Moscow 1966, II, 72.

lenge to a jury composed mainly of officials and *intelligentsia*.

Though it was the Western model which had inspired Russia's great judicial reforms of 1864, it has proved impossible to surround court proceedings with the decorum which agelong tradition has imparted to them in the West. Even in ordinary cases, lawyers on both sides allowed themselves liberties unimaginable in England or France. Civic spirit being undeveloped, juries tended to base their verdicts on the general impression the defendant produced rather than on the weight of evidence. It was notoriously difficult to obtain a conviction, even of a common murderer, if he or she touched the heartstrings of the jurors: life in Russia was so hard—how could a good Christian justify to his conscience, or an *intelligent* square with his beliefs, that a fellow human being should spend years at hard labor in Siberia? Despite his obtuseness Count Pahlen was quite right in being apprehensive about the Zasulich trial.

The cream of St. Petersburg society vied for tickets to the spectacle. As was the custom, the most distinguished spectators were given special seats behind the judges' bench. Among them was the highest official of the empire, the octogenarian Chancellor (foreign minister) Prince Gorchakov, who, one would think, should have been quite busy, since Russia was hovering on the brink of war with Great Britain. Ridiculously vain and despite his years still amorously active—he used to say, "My loves are beneficial to the tranquility of Europe"—the prince, as behooved a childhood friend of Pushkin and the Decembrists, was known to be quite contemptuous of Trepov who in addition to his other sins was of low social origin.

Very soon it became obvious that it was General Trepov rather than his would-be assassin who was really being tried. The court agreed to summon several witnesses to *his* crime, including fellow political prisoners of Bogolyubov, something which would have been unthinkable in a similar trial in England or America. One of them, a woman, broke down when she described, possibly accurately, how she saw out of her window prison guards bringing in "a large number of whips . . . it was clear some sort of torture was being prepared."[3] Handkerchiefs came out again among the audience when Vera and her lawyer described her sad life: arrested at nineteen just because she was an acquaintance of Nechayev, held for two years in jail without a trial, and then four years of exile in the provinces. (She skipped over her revolutionary activity during the previous three years.) As against these idealistic and attractive young women and men, the audience watched the officials who gave state evidence with silent reprobation: they were as inarticulate on the witness stand as they had been clumsy in performing their duties. Zasulich described her motives: "I know by my own experience what an ordeal it is to suffer solitary confinement. And the

[3] *Ibid.*, II, 118.

majority of the prisoners had been there for three and more years. Some
went mad or committed suicide. I could then picture to myself the hellish
impression which this torture must have made on all political prisoners.
. . . It is terrible to aim at a man's life, but I had to do it."⁴ Neither the judges
nor the prosecutor saw fit to ask why, if she was acting from an irresistible
impulse, it took her six months from the time she heard of the incident until
she attempted the act of retribution.

The defense counsel's speech, which to us sounds a bit melodramatic and
which contains some internal inconsistencies that an alert prosecutor would
have immediately seized upon, was in the eyes of Alexandrov's contemporaries an oratorical masterpiece which placed him alongside the great advocates of all ages. The hushed chamber was made to relive the tragedy of the
girl, her nerves already overwrought through her own suffering, when she
heard of the punishment to which a fellow human being had been submitted, the horror of it which, because as a midwife "knowledgeable in the
anatomy of the human body," she could visualize more vividly than most.
(In fact, though like many female "pilgrims" Zasulich had trained to become a midwife, she never practiced the profession.) Imagine the effect the
news had on her when it reached her in the rural wilderness, where she had
secreted herself to forget . . . ! (Here the orator forgot that Vera Zasulich
had testified that she learned the *details* of the whipping only when she
reached the capital. The "rural wilderness" was a revolutionary commune,
with Vera riding around with a gun in her belt.) She waited: surely Trepov
would be punished. But nothing! And then a sudden thought like a lightning
bolt strikes her mind "I myself . . . —enough of the silence about Bogolyubov! Someone has to scream. If my strength allows me I shall scream and
everybody will hear." Alexandrov broadened his indictment: not only Trepov but the whole government now figured as the guilty party. And poor
Bogolyubov: had he not been punished sufficiently for his participation in
a mere demonstration—a crime, to be sure, but one "committed not out of
low or selfish reasons . . . but on the contrary from an honest impulse."⁵

We get an incidental and from the feminist point of view tantalizing
picture of Russian criminal justice when Alexandrov intoned, "These
chambers have seen women who killed their violators; women who imbrued
their hands in the blood of lovers who jilted them or that of their successful
rivals, and who left the court acquitted. This was just, a truly divine judgment which takes into account not only the appearance of the crime but also
its internal sense."⁶ By comparison, he argued, Zasulich's act was one of
pure altruism. He concluded more soberly: "Yes, she may leave here convicted but not dishonored."

⁴*Ibid.*, II, 119.
⁵*Ibid.*, II, 127, 150.
⁶*Ibid.*, II, 156.

The speech was interrupted by applause, but never by the presiding judge, even though Alexandrov's rather far-reaching claims on behalf of women who have been unhappy in love should have, one thinks, drawn comment from the bench. The prosecutor's speech could not compete with this Ciceronian eloquence of Alexandrov. And Koni's summing up made clear where his sympathies were and dwelt at large on the extenuating circumstances. He professed later to have been surprised by the subsequent verdict.

To the first question, "Is Zasulich guilty . . . of having deliberately inflicted with a heavy bullet a wound on Adjutant General Trepov?" the jury answered, "Not guilty." The foreman had barely pronounced "not" when the room exploded; some of the audience sobbed hysterically, others cheered and screamed "Bravo! Our little Vera!" Older people crossed themselves, while in the "democratic part" of the courtroom, as Koni puts it, where the students sat, joy was expressed by people embracing each other. "This is the happiest day of my life," said a high official to the presiding judge, who was not so sure it was his.[7] The police who tried to escort Vera Zasulich out of the building were swept aside by the crowd, which was convinced—and with good reason—that verdict or no verdict the authorities might not let her out of their clutches. Thus ended the Zasulich case, the most momentous trial in the history of imperial Russia.

For its heroine the remaining forty years of her life were bound to be an anticlimax. She was kept hidden by her revolutionary friends. One of them advised her not to leave the country: "You will become a retired hero."[8] But others insisted and she was spirited away to Switzerland. Years passed, the one-time "rebel" became a Marxist and a staunch enemy of terror. Once a friend of Nechayev, she fell under the intellectual spell of a man in every respect his opposite, the father of Russian Marxism, George Plekhanov. Along with him and Lenin she edited the famous *Spark,* the fountainhead of Russian Social Democracy. Once she suggested that young Lev Trotsky, fresh from Siberia, should be taken on as an editor. But Plekhanov would not have it and it was enough for "Georges," as he was known as, to fold his arms and give her a withering look for the famous terrorist to become flustered and beat a retreat. After the revolution of 1905 and political amnesty, she tore herself away from "Georges" to return to her other love, Russia. Vera lived in Russia as she had abroad, quietly and messily—her untidiness was legendary even among the revolutionaries. One day an old friend dropped in. A Social Revolutionary, still a believer in terror, he might well have intended to upbraid Zasulich for her apostasy. But all such thoughts vanished from his mind and tears came to his eyes when he saw

---

[7]The government, though infuriated by Koni's conduct, could not fire him since under the law of 1864 judges were irremovable. He was eventually promoted to be chief prosecutor of the civil department of the senate, but he remained convinced that except for the Zasulich episode he would have become a minister.

[8]Zasulich, 75.

the familiar scene: she was sitting with a book "behind an incredibly messy table. On another table and on the windowsills there were plates with uneaten food, dirty glasses and teacups; in the corner soiled laundry of all kinds. Her bed was unmade. Yes, Vera Ivanovna remained herself to the end."[9] The Bolshevik Revolution meant to her as to Plekhanov the betrayal of everything they had worked for. She died in 1919, less than a year after her beloved "Georges," fortunate in not seeing the full consequences of the events to which her shot contributed in no small measure.

For it is difficult to imagine the now decisive turn of Populism to terror without the Zasulich case. Society seemed to say through the court: yes, it is legitimate and necessary to resort to violence to shake up the autocracy. And the autocracy in turn gave up its last attempts to appease the *intelligentsia* and observe its own laws in dealing with sedition. For the believers in law and order there seemed to open, in Katkov's words, "a chasm between our *intelligentsia* and a sense of reality. Wherever in our national life something is up to the people there with God's blessing we accomplish veritable miracles. But once our *intelligentsia* speaks and acts we begin to totter."[10]

But it was not only the *intelligentsia* which lost touch with reality. The virus of terror spread first in the south. Perhaps as the geographic determinists would have it a milder climate tends to make southerners in every major nation more prone to turbulence and violence than their northern countrymen, whose energies are expended in the struggle with nature. But apart from such dubious generalizations there were tangible reasons for Zasulich's shot to reverberate most loudly in the Ukraine. It was, as we have seen, the hotbed of the "rebels." The as yet inarticulate national grievances of the Ukrainian peasantry, not to mention memories of the semianarchic Cossack commonwealth, facilitated enterprises like the Chigirin affair. And polyglot cities like Odessa with strong Jewish and Greek or, as in Kiev, Polish elements in their population provided a more favorable environment for madcap conspiratorial improvisation than one found in purely Russian towns. The authorities tended to be at once more lax and, in the absence of the inhibitory influence of Petersburg and Moscow liberal society, occasionally more brutal.

And thus six days after the incident in Trepov's office shots rang out in Odessa. The police tried to raid a revolutionary commune and printing press, and were met with fire. This was another "first." Russian policemen of the period did not carry guns but only sabres, more as a symbol than a weapon. Armed resistance by political suspects had until now been felt to

[9]Michael Frolenko, "Recollections of Vera Zasulich," in *Hard Labor and Exile,* X (Moscow 1924), 246.
[10]M. N. Katkov, *Collection of Editorials for 1878,* Moscow 1898, 154.

violate the etiquette governing such proceedings (the only notable exception being that of Prince Tsitsianov, who was half crazed). But the leader of the Odessa group, Ivan Kovalsky, was a declared proponent of armed struggle. (A former "pilgrim," he and his comrades printed a couple of revolutionary proclamations. One, entitled *The Voice of Honest People,* declared, "The social democratic party has begun [armed] struggle against this vile government. . . ."[11] The expression "social democratic party" was of course an improvisation. There was no such party and Kovalsky's group was certainly far from anything resembling social democrats. Another broadside referred to a recent execution of one Lukyanov, a particularly brutal murderer who killed two women in the course of a robbery, and asserted that Lukyanov, was much less guilty than government officials, that it was they who deserved the gallows.) Refusing to be searched, Kovalsky tried to shoot the officer who had led the raid and, when his gun jammed, wounded him with a knife. He was overpowered and dragged out of the apartment, but his comrades shot at the gendarmes and the latter beat a retreat. Soldiers had to be brought in to overcome the revolutionaries' resistance. With the experience of the Zasulich trial, the authorities would not put Kovalsky and his comrades before a regular court. On July 24, he was sentenced to death by a military tribunal and on August 2 he was executed.

Two days after the armed clash in Odessa, on February 2, a Rostov-on-the-Don sieve-maker was killed by two noble-born revolutionaries, one of them the son of a police chief. The victim had belonged to a propaganda circle organized by the two among local workers and had been arrested, whereupon he had told the police all he knew. This was, therefore, the first successful execution of a "traitor." "The shot served as a signal for a large number of acts of violence perpetrated in various places in the south. Quite rightly Vera Zasulich is celebrated as the founder of the terrorist struggle in Russia."[12]

The government, dumbfounded by Vera Zasulich's act and infuriated by the verdict in her favor, replied in the way the revolutionaries hoped it would: by escalating its repression. Tsar Alexander rejected the court's recommendation to soften the terms of punishment for those sentenced in the trial of "the 193." And the head of the Third Department, General Nicholas Mezentsev, received authorization to arrest and send into administrative exile several of those the court had set free. Among them was Lev Tikhomirov, who many years later was to write of the emperor for whose assassination he bore a large part of the responsibility: "When I arrived back in Russia I went to Alexander II's tomb . . . and I prayed to him to be my supplicant before God so that He should forgive me, for I had

---

[11]N.A. Vitashevsky in *The Past,* No. 2 (Petersburg 1906), 228.
[12]Lev Deich, "Valerian Osinsky," in *Hard Labor and Exile,* LIV (Moscow 1929), 27.

sinned against the Martyr-Tsar. And yet without any feeling of malice or hostility . . . my conscience constrains me to say that *then* in 1878 the sovereign punished me unjustly, and thus forced me to give up everything else and to turn to the only thing left for me: the desperate revolutionary struggle."[13] He had been jailed, he writes pathetically, for four years, three months, and six days. And now after a few weeks of freedom he was told to turn himself in to begin exile in Siberia. And so, like Perovskaya, Morozov, and other future luminaries of the People's Will, he decided to go "illegal." It is safe to say that most of the others would have continued their revolutionary activities no matter what. But in Tikhomirov's case there was just a chance that he might have turned to repentance and reaction several years before he actually did so in 1886–88. And without him the story of the People's Will, of which he was to be the brains, might well have been quite different.

Going "illegal" was a fairly simple business. One procured false identity papers, preferably those of somebody who had died recently in a distant locality. The art of photography was in its infancy and the liaison between the central authorities and provincial police officials was very inefficient, so one could lead a clandestine existence for years. The authorities did not catch on to Bogolyubov's real name even after he had been incarcerated, tried, and sentenced. On the other hand a revolutionary who would have to move around a great deal needed not only a false passport, but an organization which would back him up, give him addresses of people he could stay with, etc. Thus for very practical reasons if for no other ones, Tikhomirov and about forty others of the trial of "the 193" who found themselves in a similar predicament gravitated toward Land and Freedom, the only organized conspiracy that could shelter them. And indeed in the summer of 1878 some became members of the "basic circle," others fellow travelers of the then major revolutionary group in Russia. The fusion had met with some obstacles: the idea of belonging to a centralized organization in which one had to submit to party discipline ran against the grain of those accustomed to the looser and more democratic atmosphere in Populist circles of the early 1870s. Sophia Perovskaya especially bridled at the idea of taking orders, especially from a man. Though Land and Freedom did not have a formal leader, after Natanson's arrest and that of his wife late in 1878, Alexander Mikhailov, a matchless conspiratorial organizer, came close to filling that function.[14] But the logic of the situation did dictate unity, and the "troglodytes" received an important accession of strength, not so much

[13] *Memoirs of Lev Tikhomirov,* Moscow 1927, 113.

[14] In addition to Alexander two other Mikhailovs played important roles in the revolutionary story of these years: Adrian, who participated in the assassination of Mezentsev; and Timothy, one of the five hanged for the affair of March 1, 1881.

in numbers as in the ability and zeal of the newcomers.

These fresh forces, and the violence in the air, were bound to transform Land and Freedom. Before that fateful winter-spring of 1878 the terrorist part of its program was surrounded by circumlocutions about self-defense and "disorganization," and remained mostly on paper. (Probably the only victim of the "disorganization" section prior to 1878 was a railwayman who betrayed Natanson to the police in the spring of 1877 and was subsequently killed.) The main thrust had been at propaganda among the urban proletariat and, through the "revolutionary settlements" on the lower Volga, among the peasants. But it was notoriously difficult to recruit and especially to keep workers within the conspiracy. As for work in the villages, emissaries to the lower Volga were soon back in the capital with a familiar story. As Vera Figner described it, "Those three months were for me a great ordeal. . . . I did not as much as get a feel of the real peasants and did not even attempt to propagandize them." And after another try she developed a positive loathing of rural society and, though as a good Populist she cannot quite bring herself to say this, of the peasant himself. "In the struggle for survival victory goes to those who best adjust to the rural environment, and so in the mess which is rural life the top dog is the one who is most shameless and whose aspirations and ideals harmonize with the whole manner of life and a social atmosphere redolent of routine and conservatism."[15]

Terror seemed easier than beating one's head against the wall of peasant indifference and inertia or the worker's "narrow" preoccupation with his economic interests. Revolutionary Populism was incapable of adopting the tactics which were to be the key to the future success of Marxism in Russia: a sharp differention between a programmatic minimum, which was agitation for goals which could be realized in the near future, and an ultimate vision of society. Its activity would have had wide response among the peasant masses had it concentrated on lowering or abolishing oppressive taxes, and among the workers had it stressed the wage-and-hour work issue. In the beginning of the twentieth century this proved to be the kind of agitation that was virtually impossible to stop. And of course in the process of struggling for their economic rights both peasants and workers would develop broader social and political horizons. But temperamentally most of the revolutionary Populists were incapable of such self-restraint. They were young and impatient. They were not going to risk a few months' imprisonment or administrative exile in European Russia for merely advocating the abolition of the salt and poll taxes, which heavily encumbered the peasant and which the imperial government itself was to abolish in the 1880s, or for protesting the manufacturer's garnishing the worker's wages for the misera-

[15]Vera Figner, *Collected Works,* I, Moscow 1928, 126, 142.

ble lodgings and food they provided him. Yet they were ready to lay down their lives or spend years at hard labor in Siberia for the unequal struggle against the Moloch of autocracy.

The other horn of the dilemma was the Populists' insistence that they were not interested in politics. In a deep and tragic sense this was true. Their professed goal of an immediate transformation of Russia into an anarcho-socialist society, most of them realized in their sober moments, was chimerical. But they refused to consider any stops on the road to this grandiose future. The idea of a constitution, a government with a parliament, was as unattractive to most members of the second Land and Freedom as to those of the first. Freedom of speech and press? St. Petersburg workers were severely criticized for stressing this demand by one of the most level-headed of the Land and Freedom leaders, Dmitri Klements: "The whole question of the influence of political freedom on the struggle between the exploited and the exploiters is given too much attention and [the need for such freedoms] is affirmed too categorically—while the question of propaganda through facts [i.e. terror] is not even discussed."[16] No one could believe that if tomorrow by some miracle Russians were to receive universal franchise, a party running under the banner of socialism and republicanism would receive more than a miniscule proportion of votes. Morozov, as we have seen, blurted out what every thoughtful revolutionary knew in his heart, that any new regime would have to ban most Russians from voting: "otherwise illiterate citizens would vote to restore the old order, not understanding the superiority of the new."

So what was left except terror and struggle for their own sakes? Existentialism had not as yet been invented, and these were earnest young men who would have scoffed at any such interpretation of their activities. They fought, they believed, for liberty; but how was this ideal to be practically expressed?

A very unusual man stepped forth from the ranks of Land and Freedom with an idea he believed would solve this ideological-tactical impasse. Valerian Osinsky (b. 1853) was the son of a rich landowner from the south. As a teen-ager he displayed that rebellious and passionate nature which was to bring him fame and early doom. Walking one day in the Summer Garden in Petersburg he found himself on a collision course with a middle-aged man in a general's uniform. Young Valerian must have recalled the famous passage from *What Is To Be Done?* when the hero, Lopukhov, in a similar situation sticks to his rule, "I turn aside first for nobody but women. . . ," and he marched straight at the gentleman. The middle-aged man was Alexander II and Osinsky paid for his rudeness by a couple of days in jail.

[16]M. Burtsev, "The Northern Union of Russian Workers," in *The Past,* No. 1 (St. Petersburg, 1906), 188.

He combined the revolutionary's passion with romantic (in every sense of the word) proclivities, characteristics which made his comrades speculate that he must have been of Polish descent. But we have already seen a similar combination in Morozov. The passionate terrorist did not always fit the two stereotypes of psychic abnormality (Karakozov or Nechayev) or the ascetic. What is more surprising is that this hot-tempered and feverishly sensitive young man endured for three years the prosaic job of being secretary of the county self-government in Rostov-on-the-Don, where as a sideline he organized a radical circle.

Within Land and Freedom, one of whose founders he was, Osinsky soon acquired a unique reputation. "Restless like quicksilver . . . always on the run . . . a walking newspaper. . . . Much of what Valerian told us was worthwhile, but mixed up with exaggerations and piquant tales."[17] Elegance was not a frequent characteristic of the revolutionaries, but Osinsky was always spotlessly attired and sported a pince-nez, then considered a fashionable affectation, something like a monocle among Prussian officers. One need hardly add that he was popular with women and amply returned their affection. And while these traits endeared Osinsky to his comrades, they made him less than an ideal fellow conspirator: he did not blend easily into his surroundings, and his passion for danger got others in trouble. Alexander Mikhailov, who as the man in charge of security arrangements for Land and Freedom was known as "the Guardian," finally decided that Osinsky had to be gotten out of St. Petersburg. "What a character! Always complains that his assignment is not dangerous enough! As if we didn't already live in constant peril. I believe we have to send him south."[18] But it was not only his foolhardiness which made his comrades wish him elsewhere. With his passion for terror and danger Osinsky combined a strong conviction that Land and Freedom should go "political," i.e., should formally demand of the government a constitution and civic liberties. His experience in local government, where he had contacts with liberal landowners and *intelligentsia,* convinced him that terror had to have a rationale in concrete political postulates. Paradoxical though this sounds it had psychological sense behind it: much of liberal public opinion would continue its "sighing tolerance" of individual acts of violence by the revolutionaries only if it remained convinced that these acts served the cause of constitutionalism and civic freedoms. Violence for its own sake or in the name of some formless anarchic ideal would soon alienate society at large, and dry up the sources of that moral, legal, and occasionally financial support which the revolutionary cause received.

But when early in 1878 Osinsky presented his proposals to other members

---

[17] O.V. Aptekman, *The Society of Land and Freedom of the 1870s,* Petrograd 1924, 234.
[18] *Ibid.,* 235.

of the basic circle he found himself almost completely isolated. We have already spelled out the reasons for this stubborn opposition within Land and Freedom to anything which smacked of "politics." Also, Mikhailov and some others who were equally fervent proponents of terror believed that it was still premature to try to escalate the debate to the point where it might split the party. Let Osinsky try his tactics in the south, where people were already getting used to random violence. Valerian was not the kind to hold a grudge—that is, not against his own comrades—a characteristic which distinguished him from Nechayev, whom in some other respects he strongly resembled. So while bidding good-bye to Aptekman, who was one of the main opponents of his constitutional ideas, he almost smothered him in an embrace.

In Kiev where he arrived in late January 1878 Osinsky found an atmosphere congenial to his terrorist designs. The leader of the local radical circle, Vladimir Debogori Mokrievich, was an old friend. He had originally been one of the "Americans," one of the radicals who in the early 1870s thought of following Chaykovsky's and Malikov's example and emigrating to the United States to found communistic religious communities. But then Debogori decided instead to join the "rebels," and his parents' house became their official headquarters. Some more militantly inclined members of the group had about this time returned from St. Petersburg, when Zasulich had anticipated their designs to dispose of Trepov. Toward the end of the month Osinsky held a conclave of the activists, and there were immediate consequences of this gathering: the assassination in Rostov to which we have already referred, whose victim had been a member of the radical group in which Osinsky participated during his stay there in 1873–76 but who subsequently had become a police informer.

This killing could still be fitted into the category of "disorganization" as defined by Land and Freedom, i.e., self-defense against spies and traitors; but Osinsky's subsequent actions showed that he could not be satisfied by such a "narrow" prescription for terror. In fact there can hardly be any doubt that the example which he consciously followed was Nechayev's, his chosen methods some of those laid down in the *Revolutionary's Catechism*. It is straight from Nechayev that he must have derived the idea of publicizing the killings he now undertook as being done at the command of a mysterious body called the Executive Committee of the Russian Social Revolutionary Party. The very seal with which proclamations of this body were stamped was an adaptation of Nechayev's People's Justice seal, except that in addition to the axe it also offered a gun and knife as its emblems. Of course for the moment there was no such party, and its Executive Committee, just like that of the People's Justice, had a membership of one: Osinsky.

In choosing its victims the "Committee" appears to have been inspired by the *Catechism*'s admonition that the most cruel officials should not be among the revolutionary's first targets but on the contrary should be allowed to live "so that through their beastliness they would provoke the people to an irreversible revolt." As Lev Deich, who at the time could hardly be accused of being an enemy of terror, testified, "Despite his preoccupation with all sorts of conceivable affairs, Valerian would take a very active part in terroristic acts, for which there was no sound excuse."[19] Deich and his friends, currently in jail for the Chigirin affair, were excellently informed about what was going on outside, and in fact participated in the deliberations of the Kiev revolutionaries: bribed prison guards provided a steady channel of communication with those at liberty.

One act of terror for which Deich felt there was no "sound excuse" was the attempted assassination of the Kiev prosecutor Kotlyarevsky. A prisoner who was known as a habitual liar had informed his comrades outside that this official had had two young girls stripped naked in his presence after their arrest on political charges. One did not have to be very sophisticated to realize that the accusation had to be false: the news of such an outrage by a court official would have been flashed all over Russia. And Deich and Stefanovich, whose case was in Kotlyarevsky's charge, wrote to Osinsky exposing the falsehood and asking him to desist from his plan. His friend Debogori, while not opposing the "Executive Committee's" decision, begged him not to participate personally in the assassination: he was too high-strung for the job. But he persisted, and on February 23, as Kotlyarevsky, his wife, and a friend were strolling back from the theater Osinsky shot him. It was another case of bad luck attending the revolutionaries when they resorted to the gun: the bullet lodged in the prosecutor's thick fur coat. Osinsky and his two companions, who fled the scene, were dumbfounded to learn next day that Kotlyarevsky was not so much as wounded. Next time, perhaps mindful of the maxim of a great Russian military commander of the eighteenth century, "bullet is a fool, naked steel does the real job," they would resort to the dagger. In the meantime some local students were distributing leaflets all over town with proclamations promising that future assassination attempts would be performed more professionally. As this was done fairly openly, the police interfered and arrested a few of the culprits. This in turn led to student protest meetings, at which Osinsky, now in his capacity as a constitutionalist, urged his listeners to demand political freedom, which further shocked Deich and his friends, since as diehard anarchists they believed that the state has to be destroyed rather than bargained with. In the end the authorities after unsuccessfully pleading with the young felt constrained to expel 120 students, fifteen of whom were sent into exile "in distant northern provinces"

---

[19]Deich, in *Hard Labor and Exile,* LIV, 27.

of European Russia. As these fifteen were passing through Moscow on their way north, radical youth gathered at the railroad station to express their solidarity with the Kiev martyrs. But the intended demonstration fizzled. The Moscow students were set upon (probably with some discreet police encouragement) by a mob of Moscow artisans and the like, what the authorities would call plain people and a revolutionary (if he read Marx) *Lumpenproletariat.* With shouts of "Beat those traitors!" they compelled the demonstrators to make a hasty exit.

In Kiev, Osinsky however was able to continue his activities unhampered. There were fresh attempts at assassination. A local citizen had his carriage stopped one night and a stranger with a gun peered inside. On establishing that this was the wrong person, the gunman said politely, "Excuse me," and withdrew. These tactics did not facilitate Osinsky's other aim, that of establishing an alliance between the liberal elements among the southern landowners and *intelligentsia,* and the terrorists. It is clear what his design was. Terror and deception were not for him, as they had been for Nechayev, ends in themselves; to a considerable extent he anticipated the future strategy of the People's Will and the hopes of its leader, Tikhomirov. Both government and society were to be made to believe that the handful of revolutionaries was in fact a mighty party and its Executive Committee an unconquerable force to be propitiated and negotiated with. As his next target for a spectacular assassination, Osinsky chose the local chief of police, Baron Heyking. This from several points of view was a most unfortunate choice, indeed for Osinsky it was a fatal one. As the situation in Kiev amply demonstrated, Heyking was a very inefficient security chief. He had been considerate to the point of being derelict in his duties in dealing with the revolutionaries. There could not be a shadow of justification for including him in the category of officials whom according to the statute of Land and Freedom its members were authorized to kill. Imprisoned revolutionaries strongly protested when they learned of Osinsky's choice. If Heyking were killed it would be a "political" assassination, done for effect and not, as the rules laid down, to remove a particularly cruel or harmful servant of despotism. "In this choice of Valerian's we saw a proof of his inclination, if not conscious then instinctive, toward the struggle for political freedom, to which we as fervent Bakuninists were then very hostile."[20] Following this logic, Deich and his friends in fact sent a message to Osinsky to spare Heyking; if he must kill somebody, then the governor of the province who had had the Chigirin peasants whipped mercilessly would be a very satisfactory substitute.

But Osinsky insisted on Heyking though this time he delegated the task to someone with a steadier hand. In the late evening of May 24 Heyking

[20] *Ibid.,* 30.

was stabbed in the stomach by Gregory Popko, and the wound was fatal. The assassin fled, shooting one of his pursuers to death.

The consequences of this murder were to prove disastrous not only to the Kiev revolutionaries, but eventually to the movement as a whole. For Heyking's successor was George Sudeykin, a veritable master of the craft of police espionage. Sudeykin, during his brief but momentous police career, first in the south then in the capital, as we shall see virtually invented the modern version of the *agent provocateur,* and raised to a veritable art the long-standing but until now not very effective method of fighting subversive organizations by infiltration.

Two nights later Osinsky and his group pulled another coup. On May 26 they spirited Deich, Stefanovich, and Bokhanovsky out of the Kiev jail. This was rather easy to do since security conditions in that institution were extraordinarily lax. One of the comrades, Michael Frolenko, had had no difficulty in first procuring a job there as a janitor, then advancing within a few weeks to prison guard and then to caretaker, who among his other duties was charged with keys to the cells. The night of the break Stefanovich tossed a book out of his window and the guard on duty on his corridor offered obligingly to go out and bring it back for the "gentleman," as "politicals" were respectfully addressed. Frolenko hastened to open the cells and had the trio out, informing the watchman at the gate that these were guards leaving their shift; one of the escapees convincingly sported a policeman's sabre. Soon they were out of the city in safe shelter, embracing Osinsky and reprimanding him for his un-Populist ways. No one had a greater capacity for spotting a mote in a fellow revolutionary's eye than Deich. So now he and Stefanovich, who had participated in the hideous attempt against Gorinovich, upbraided Valerian for killing the harmless Heyking. And how about this fictitious Executive Committee, protested the authors of the "Imperial" proclamations to the Chigirin peasants? Valerian laughed good-naturedly, but they were scandalized. "Such actions only compromise the revolutionaries and do not frighten anybody."[21] They were wrong, for on June 9 the chief of the Third Department of His Majesty's Chancery circulated other authorities about the activity of "the underground organization operating in Kiev, Kharkov, and Odessa called The Executive Committee of the Russian Social Revolutionary Party."

For the rest of 1878 Osinsky operated with some restraint: no more spectacular killings. This was for both political and personal reasons. He did not want to alienate the Petersburg group of Land and Freedom by wanton acts of violence, especially since he must have realized that they were being won over slowly but surely to his ideas on terror. In the second place he established contacts with local liberals, currently embittered

---

[21] *Ibid.,* 31.

by the dismissal of some Kiev University professors for their alleged complicity in student disorders. In the late fall Osinsky and his comrades held meetings with some landowners and other notables active in local self-government. The revolutionaries offered cessation of all acts of terror except those in self-defense, provided the government granted political liberties and established some system of national representation. Here again was a variant of Nechayev's prescription to pretend to work with liberals, to "learn their secrets," and to force them to compromise themselves with the government. It is doubtful that Osinsky was equally cynical, but he certainly succeeded in entangling his liberal interlocutors in what in the government's eyes was subversion. "The liberals of course could not but approve the demands. . . . But since their fulfillment depended not on themselves but on the government they had to start their agitation without any commitment on the part of the revolutionaries [that they would desist from terror]."[22]

Ivan Petrunkevich, one of Osinsky's liberal contacts, who was a councillor in the Chernigov province assembly, moved that an address to the emperor be prepared. As an answer to the government's recent plea to Russian society to help it fight the spreading epidemic of terrorism and subversion, the representatives of the estates of Chernigov declared that, though filled with sentiments of loyalty to the throne, they were unable to help since, "without having legal guarantees, without freedom of public opinion, which would subdue all antisocial aspirations, deprived of the right to criticize freely ideas which arise in its midst, Russian society is but an atomized, inert mass, capable of absorbing anything, but impotent to struggle against social evils."[23] The address was approved by most of his fellow councillors, but the chairman refused to have it read and voted on. Petrunkevich and a few other progressive councillors were arrested and sent into exile in other provinces. Osinsky's design to push liberals into an open clash with the regime and force them to accept terror as the only viable way to effect political change was bearing fruit.

In the midst of these stratagems he was carrying on a romance. Sophia Leshern von Hertzfeldt was, like Osinsky, a nobleman's and general's child. She was also the kind of woman the *Revolutionary's Catechism* specified as "our kind . . . to be treasured as our greatest asset, indispensable to our purposes." A veteran of revolutionary Populism, she had been tried in the case of "the 193" and after an acquittal placed under police supervision. She had planned to follow her lover, one of the fellow accused, into exile, but after his death she moved to Kiev. Here, as she wrote a Petersburg fellow revolutionary, "I found the kind of friends which I would wish to every

---

[22]A. A. Kornilov, *The Social Movement Under Alexander II*, Moscow 1909, 242.
[23]Quoted in Vladimir Burtsev, *One Hundred Years*, London 1897 (in Russian), 146.

honest person."[24] This was Osinsky's circle. Osinsky himself had not long before, and for a revolutionary rather uncharacteristically, contracted a legal church marriage, but his wife had stayed in Petersburg, and Sophia, thirteen years his senior, became his Kiev "civic wife." Both lovers shared a violent revolutionary temper which was to contribute to the tragic conclusion of their romance.

Sudeykin was no Heyking; by January 1879 he had learned through a student informer the identities and whereabouts of the chief Kiev conspirators. On January 24 Osinsky was stopped by a policeman, and trusting his false passport he followed him to the district station. Here he was greeted by Sudeykin himself. Osinsky pulled out his gun, but the police chief overpowered him before he could shoot. The same day Sophia Leshern was arrested in Osinsky's apartment. She also tried to shoot, but her revolver jammed. In February, while the revolutionaries were celebrating Mardi Gras, their conspiratorial quarters were raided by a police party led by Sudeykin. There was shooting, and two of the revolutionaries were mortally wounded. Debogori, sensible enough not to offer armed resistance, after his arrest, was "introduced" by Sudeykin to a prison guard whom he had bribed; Sudeykin also praised him and his friends' bravery: "You can be proud of yourselves," he said.[25]

The authorities never discovered Osinsky's part in the assassination attempts on Heyking and Kotlyarevsky, but since he and Sophia Leshern had offered armed resistance to the police their case was hopeless. After the recent assassinations and a fresh attempt on the tsar's life, all political crimes were tried by military court. Both of them, and two other men, were sentenced to death; several others, including Debogori, to hard labor in Siberia. Osinsky faced his judges defiantly. He declared—and this would become the regular practice for all revolutionaries in his position—that he was just an agent of the all powerful Executive Committee which had many others under its command ready to take his place. The prosecutor having made reference to the revolutionaries' "dissolute ways," the young man declared: "I turn to remarks about my relationship with Sophia Leshern. The prosecutor asserts that we were lovers and says that obviously to cover us with mud. But I say that it is not up to the prosecutor to judge civic marriages. To understand their idea, one must reach a high level of intellectual and moral development just as one must to understand the concept of socialism. If he meant to make us feel ashamed he has failed."[26] Sophia's sentence was commuted to lifelong hard labor; there was no precedent for executing a woman. Osinsky and two others were originally to face a firing

[24]S.N. Valk, ed., *The Archive of Land and Freedom*, Moscow 1932, 96.
[25]Vladimir Debogori Mokrievich, *Memoirs*, Paris 1894 (in Russian), 321.
[26]*The Literature of the People's Will*, Moscow 1930, 12.

squad, but this was changed to hanging. The revolutionaries were subsequently to claim that the emperor personally prescribed this opprobrious manner of execution, but *The People's Will* of November 10, 1879, states that the decision was that of the local authorities.[27]

The night before the execution, which took place on May 14, Osinsky still attended to conspiratorial matters. From his window he shouted to his comrades messages in a code composed from numbers. He then asked Debogori to sing French songs, his favorite being Beranger's "The Old Corporal," about a soldier of Napoleon who before his death implores his comrades not to weep after he is gone. Debogori complied and sang as long as he could. After he stopped, the prison court grew quiet, its silence interrupted only by Sophia from her women's wing and Osinsky calling out each other's names.[28] She was to die twenty years later in Siberia.

The story of the romantic terrorist became a favorite subject for the revolutionaries' biographies. When Kravchinsky in the 1880s published his *Underground Russia* abroad, the foreign reader could also shed a tear for the gallant lad who was like "a Damascene blade," who "loved women and was loved by them," and who met his doom for an offense as trivial as that of trying to pull out his gun when trapped by the minions of despotism.[29]

Sentimentality apart, Osinsky to his radical contemporaries appeared as a kind of "respectable Nechayev," and as such he very strongly influenced the subsequent history of Land and Freedom and the People's Will. He managed to surround terror with an aura of romanticism, just as Zasulich had made it a legitimate expression of protest against official brutality. It would have required considerable maturity and sobriety, qualities not very widespread among Russian radicals of the day, to perceive that Osinsky's cult of terror, for all the political rationale he sought for it, verged on a strange fascination with death. On the eve of his execution he wrote to his comrades, "We [he and his fellow condemned] do not doubt that your efforts will be directed toward one main goal. . . . Our party is not physically capable of spreading its efforts more widely. To employ terror seriously you need the right people, and means. . . . Good luck to you, brethren, this is our deepest wish before we die. And we do not doubt for a minute *that you will follow us perhaps very soon and will die with the same unconcern with which we go to our death.*"[30] This is hardly a charge to continue the struggle; it sounds more like a call to self-immolation.

In sending Osinsky south the leaders of Land and Freedom, notably Alexander Mikhailov, hoped also, and rather cold-bloodedly, to make Kiev

[27] *Ibid.*, p. 13.
[28] Debogori Mokrievich, 316.
[29] L.M. Stepniak (Kravchinsky), *Underground Russia*, Petrograd 1917, 43.
[30] Quoted in Deich, in *Hard Labor and Exile*, LIV, 54. My italics.

a laboratory where both the effectiveness and the limitations of individual terror could be tried out. Throughout the spring of 1878 they had watched this experiment, and the lessons were embodied in a new program and statutes of the organization worked out during these months. Osinsky's design of tying terror to demands for political and civil rights was as yet unacceptable to the majority of members. Hence the program merely repeated the old Populist clichés about all land going to the peasants, the only variation being a recognition based on the bitter experience of the Pilgrimage that the Russian people might be insufficiently developed intellectually and morally to opt at this point for universal communal ownership of land and a completely anarchic system of government. Thus presumably individual peasant proprietors, and some kind of central government would have to be tolerated for a time. But then immediately and incongruously this concession to political realism is withdrawn: "It is clear that our formula can be put into operation only through a *violent overthrow* of the existing regime. And this must be done as soon as possible because the growth of capitalism and the increasing saturation of national life by the plague of bourgeois civilization . . . threaten to destroy the peasant commune and to distort the people's instincts."[31]

To help "the people" achieve what in their own words they desired less and less, Land and Freedom proposed 1) to help all possible revolutionary elements in Russian society, including "revolutionary-religious sects" and "robbers' groups," "since they all express the people's struggle against the existing social order"; and 2) to weaken "and *disorganize* the power of the state without which . . . no insurrection, no matter how widespread and well-planned, can be successful." This represented a definitive repudiation of the "peaceful propaganda" aspect of revolutionary Populism which had been its main tenet until 1876–77, and a decisive turn toward the philosophy it had rejected at its birth: the Nechayev-Bakunin program of 1869–70. The now considerably expanded scope of "disorganization" ran in the same vein. It was no longer to be the means primarily of self-defense against spies and traitors but was to include: "systematic liquidation of the most harmful and prominent people within the government," and—here for the first time Populism embraced the idea of mass terror—"On the day of decision *mass* extermination of the government, and in general of those people who support or *might* support a social order hateful *to us.*"[32]

It is difficult to imagine a party program more uninhibited in language. In some ways it surpasses Tkachev's and Nechayev's efforts in that direction. The former, while equally elitist and a believer in mass terror, had reservations about political assassinations as wasteful of the revolutionaries'

---

[31]Valk, 56.
[32]*Ibid.,* 57. My italics.

human resources. And the People's Justice, while more vivid in its depiction of mass slaughter on the occasion of the insurrection, gives it at least a democratic gloss: the extirpation of the upper classes is to be done by "the people" and not just because they are "hateful to us." In the final red action there was an effort, not very successful, to soften the most jarring provisions: "systematic liquidation" was substituted for "mass extermination." And article 9 now read: "All means are acceptable provided they do not undermine the authority of the organization,"[33] instead of the previous, "the end justifies the means."

In its internal regulations Land and Freedom sought a compromise between strict centralization and a certain autonomy for groups and individuals like Osinsky, who would carry terror to a length which the organization as a whole was as yet unwilling to endorse. Thus there was a category of "separatist associates" who would not be privy to the secrets of the "basic circle" but would keep in touch with it through a member. Likewise any member of the inner groups could mount a revolutionary enterprise on his own and give his comrades just a general idea of its nature "if the action requires absolute secrecy as a condition of success." In that way Land and Freedom could and would sponsor, without accepting formal responsibility for, such acts as an attempt on the tsar's life or a robbery of state funds, which for most of its members went beyond "acceptable" terror.

Tikhomirov has left a description of his formal initiation into the conspiracy sometime in 1878. Alexander Mikhailov and another member met him in an apartment belonging to a third party: "the conspirators' hiding places were to remain unknown to nonmembers."[34] Mikhailov read the program, "the usual Populist nonsense." He was then asked whether he approved each point of the statute. Would he submit to party discipline and did he accept that "the end justifies the means"? "All of which I subscribed to unconditionally and sincerely," wrote Tikhomirov.

Once initiated, Tikhomirov was given the secret code, passwords, and other pertinent information. The organizational structure of Land and Freedom had by now outgrown its original form of a "circle." Unlike its namesake of the early 1860s, based on a network of five-man cells, the new conspiracy was organized along functional lines, with each section specializing in a different form of clandestine activity: "disorganization," the underground press, manufacturing of false documents, etc. Leaders of each group came from the "basic circle" of about twenty or so people, while the rest of its personnel were not privy to the activities of other branches. And even the leaders were not supposed to know locations and auxiliary personnel of conspiratorial branches other than their own. Only the "guardian," as he

[33]*Ibid.*, p. 83.
[34]Tikhomirov, 122.

was called, (*dvornik*) Alexander Mikhailov, knew the complete organizational chart and personnel. This, of course, was designed to minimize the danger of the police, through arrests or informers, unraveling the conspiracy as a whole. By the same token this arrangement would enable Mikhailov, the one man in possession of all its secrets, to steer Land and Freedom much further in the direction of terrorism than most of its members were prepared to go.

One might well ask how in view of their acceptance of the program, any of the members could still harbor reservations about terror. But these were very young and impulsive people, many of whom simply did not realize what a decisive step they had taken beyond their position of only two years before, and how they had now endorsed terrorism not as a means of self-defense but as an instrument of political action. And the "basic circle" which voted the program was composed only of a minority of the membership, those based in St. Petersburg. The other thirty or so were still dispersed in the countryside, and believed, in the words of Vera Figner (still not converted to "political" terror), that "the city members of Land and Freedom became obsessed with fireworks . . . assassinations of generals and police chiefs . . . enchantment with which was pulling the youth away from the real task, that of working with the peasants who needed their help so much."[35] Lest there should be any misunderstanding, she opposed the shooting of generals and police chiefs only because it was in her and other strict Populists' eyes "less productive and necessary than agrarian terror in villages."

But here was the rub. How could Land and Freedom, with fifty members and some hundred fifty or so fellow travelers who could be enlisted as "separatist members," mount an effective terrorist compaign among the vast masses of the rural population? Here and there a local constable might be shot, a landlord's residence set on fire, but as Figner bemoans, "terrorist acts in the countryside passed virtually unnoticed. You could not even judge what impression they created. . . . They did not excite the village revolutionaries . . . [who] did not experience the fears, dangers, and joy of a [real] struggle." As against this humdrum kind of violence the assassinations of notables created great excitement: "Like electric impulses the news of political assassinations ran through the minds of the young and of society and raised their spirits."[36]

"A man by nature uniquely pure and sincere."[37] Thus Tikhomirov, when already a staunch defender of the autocracy, wrote of Alexander Mikhailov. Of all his associates during the revolutionary, and as he later saw it sinful,

[35]Vera Figner, *Collected Works,* I, Moscow 1928, 150.
[36]*Ibid.,* I, 151. Let us repeat, society for radicals meant in this connection the *intelligentsia.*
[37]Tikhomirov, 94.

period of his life, the "renegade" remembered only Mikhailov with affection and praised him without reservation. The master of conspiratorial terrorism, the main advocate of the assassination of Alexander II, remained for Tikhomirov to the last an idealist who, "believing in revolution for the sake of the people and the Fatherland, gave himself to the cause completely without reservation, not in the name of some dry doctrine, not out of meanness or a sense of obligation . . . but with his whole being." Mikhailov was "vibrant with health, strength, and the joy of life." Among his comrades another one recalled that "he was revered by all and loved by those close to him."[38] And George Plekhanov, whose clash with Mikhailov led to a split within Land and Freedom, later rendered this homage to his antagonist: "He never felt fatigue or tension, but marched ahead with a free and confident gait, as does a man who knows where he is going and why."[39]

But there was another side to Mikhailov. "How could those people like Alexander Mikhailov whom we took for honest revolutionaries resort to impermissible Nechayev-like behavior toward their comrades?"[40] From the point of view of those who rejected political terror, Mikhailov systematically deceived his comrades and abused his authority over Land and Freedom, of which he was the leader from October 1878 till its demise a year later. But the comparison with Nechayev is both inaccurate and unfair. It was Land and Freedom as a whole which became mired in Nechayev-like conspiratorial ways. Unlike the criminal psychopath, Mikhailov did not seek power for the sheer pleasure of manipulating people, did not order assassinations because he enjoyed killing. The leadership was thrust upon him by others who were well aware that, with his fanaticism and conspiratorial ability, he could lead the party where they wanted it to go, to complete dedication to terrorism.

If it is possible for a revolutionary to be completely nonideological, then Mikhailov comes close to fitting this description. Throughout his brief life the craving for fellowship, not the passion for revolution or this or that theory, guided his steps. He began a short autobiographical sketch, composed when he was twenty-four, in a way that is bound to throw a psychohistorian into deep despair: there was no unhappy childhood, no tyrannical father or bullying relatives. On the contrary: "From the earliest youth a lucky star shone over my head. My childhood was one of the happiest one can have. . . . My parental home was like a miraculous world in which ruled harmony and mutual love. . . . There were moments where my child's heart could hardly contain all the happiness and joy with which my surroundings

---

[38]Aptekman, 216.
[39]Quoted in the frontispiece of A.P. Pribilyeva-Korba and V.N. Figner, *A.D. Mikhailov*, Leningrad 1925.
[40]Deich in *Hard Labor and Exile*, VII (Moscow 1923), 11.

filled me. And up to this day as a mature man I love warmly my kind and wise parents."[41] Mikhailov concludes the sketch with an acknowledgment of the expectation of an early death in the struggle. "I have never known another man to whom fate has been so generous. . . . My fondest hopes have been fulfilled. . . . I have lived among the most worthwhile kind of people, and I have always earned their love and friendship. This is the greatest happiness a man can find."[42] This is an almost embarrassingly self-centered statement, but he was always ready to lay down his life for his friends, even the very ones he deceived and lied to. Terror was for Mikhailov not a political weapon, but a sort of communion that united his party-congregation by the bond of adventure and danger.

In another era, or had he lived beyond his allotted span, Mikhailov would almost certainly have turned to religion in the usual sense of the term. In jail and awaiting his end—for he was sure that even if his death sentence were commuted, he would not endure solitary confinement for long—he asked for a Bible and concluded a letter to his brother and sisters: "Your brother and friend till the end here and, yes, over there."[43] Spiritual temptation had assailed him even during his revolutionary activity, when he was delegated to propagandize the Old Believers. Unlike most other Populists who loathed this fruitless work among people whose prejudices were as unshakeable as their own, Mikhailov was enchanted, and if he had not been summoned back to the capital, there is but little doubt he would have become a religious sectarian himself. "This was a wonderful and most instructive time for me, unfortunately too brief. The world of sectarians has captivated me by its independence, its deep spiritual basis, and its strong bond of unity. . . . I became very strongly attached to it." His friends in Petersburg were shocked to discover how deeply he had become immersed in what to them was sheer superstition. As Vera Figner notes with embarrassment, "He had some sort of an idea (confusing to others, because he talked but little about it or perhaps confusing to himself too) that the ideals of social revolution should create a new religion which would embrace the whole essence of man just as the old ones did."[44] In brief, he was the kind of revolutionary Alyosha might have made if, as Dostoyevsky once intimated he would, he had written a sequel to *The Brothers Karamazov* on Alyosha as a terrorist.

Mikhailov's intellectual interests and development fell short of his spiritual ones. Rather uniquely among the revolutionaries he does not refer in his autobiographical sketch to a single book by one of the greats of

[41]Quoted in Pribilyeva-Korba and Figner, 39.
[42]*Ibid.,* 53.
[43]*Ibid.,* 184.
[44]*Ibid.,* 49.

Russian radical thought. And indeed the "lucky star" that shone above him during his childhood and revolutionary days seems to have been eclipsed during his school years. He found the atmosphere of his *gymnasium* oppressive. Mikhailov was an indifferent student,[45] and graduated at the age of twenty, which means he must have had to repeat some classes. In none of his subjects did he receive "excellent" or "good" on the final examination, being graded in all "satisfactory." Not having studied classical languages, the road to the university and the only field of study which mildly interested him, Russian literature, was barred, and after three months in the Petersburg Technological Institute Mikhailov gave up the idea of higher education.

His choice of a profession was influenced almost entirely by personal contacts. His first acquaintance with revolutionary circles took place in Kiev in the winter of 1875 and spring of 1876. "Having studied their programs I did not accede to any. I looked for a real force, for specific and vital activity . . . and here they quarrelled about theories. . . . With my gift for administrative matters I felt, though still an inexperienced youth, that the crux of the problem lay not in the search for the most correct theory but in setting up a really professional organization." He met Gregory Goldenberg, "a good boy devoted to the cause . . . but his stupidity both irritated and amused me," Mikhailov wrote, departing for once from his Christian charity. And indeed one day Goldenberg's fanaticism and stupidity would have tragic consequences.

Back in Petersburg later in 1876 Mikhailov became one of the original members of Land and Freedom. The decisive consideration in his accession was an infatuation with Natanson's wife. "In 1876 I met for the first time a woman to whom I became deeply attached. This was the unforgettable Olga Natanson. But she loved her husband passionately, and I for myself liked and respected Mark. . . . Hence my feeling for Olga never passed the bounds of closest friendship."[46] Indeed Olga, though not a beauty, exercised this spell over quite a few of the young revolutionaries. "If Mark was the head of the conspiracy, then Olga was its heart," Aptekman wrote in his usual gushing way.

Not being an intellectual, Mikhailov felt he could make his contribution to the conspiracy, and incidentally gain points with Olga, through his organizational talents. At first his pestering of the comrades to observe conspiratorial rules, to be always on the alert against a policeman or a spy, brought him good-natured ridicule. Indeed his party sobriquet, *dvornik,* was first used in its other Russian meaning, "janitor." But then he became

---

[45]Valk, 354.

[46]Pribilyeva-Korba and Figner, 41. At the time he wrote this Olga was still alive but in prison and hopelessly ill. She died of tuberculosis in March 1881.

the "guardian," recognized master of conspiratorial technique, and by 1878 no one laughed at him any more and quite a few of his colleagues in addition to affection felt a certain fear of this single-minded youth. Mikhailov would brusquely order a nearsighted comrade to wear glasses, or else: the organization could not tolerate a member who because of vanity was unable to spot a police agent. Uninvited he would drop in on his fellow revolutionaries at any hour of day or night to inspect if they observed proper precautions, and was not embarrassed in the slightest if he surprised them in the midst of some very private business.

Unlike Osinsky and, in a different way, Morozov, Mikhailov was not an instinctive terrorist. We have seen how in the beginning of 1878 he was instrumental in sending Osinsky out of Petersburg, feeling that it was premature and harmful to the organization as a whole to license random assassinations. But being a practitioner rather than a theorist of revolution, he changed his mind when Vera Zasulich's act and the jury verdict in her favor demonstrated the electrifying effect that the killing of "oppressors" had on the public mind. Tikhomirov recalled that shortly after January 24 he attended a student ball and saw Mikhailov in a state of exaltation. Forgetting his own rules about conspiratorial prudence Alexander stopped the band and delivered a short speech, something he did infrequently (he stammered), concluding with a toast to the heroic woman. In subsequent months, as Mikhailov recorded it, "being in full sympathy with the struggle against the regime, I began to participate in some terrorist acts and in arranging rescues of political prisoners."[47] And he personally supervised the first spectacular assassination ordered by the central group of Land and Freedom.

In the summer of 1878 the conspiracy passed a death sentence on General Nicholas Mezentsev, chief of the Third Department. The ostensible reason for this decision was Mezentsev's recommendation that several persons freed in the trial of "the 193" be rearrested and sent into exile. One suspects that another incentive was the recent assassination of Heyking in Kiev, and the feeling within the "basic circle" that the central organization which was about to adopt the name of Land and Freedom formally and publish an underground organ with the same name, could not afford to be outshone by a provincial affiliate. As Anna Korba puts it, "The deed of August 4 was the first and brilliant initiative of the new organization."[48]

The execution was entrusted to Serge Kravchinsky. This flamboyant ex-artillery officer and one of the earliest "pilgrims" had returned in May from abroad with some equipment for the clandestine press. He was a man of great daring and physical strength, and his first idea was to challenge

---

[47]Pribilyeva-Korba and Figner, 50.
[48]*Ibid.*, 13.

Mezentsev to a duel. It was with some difficulty that his comrades persuaded him to choose a more practical method of assassination. On the morning of August 4 while the general was taking a stroll, Kravchinsky walked up to him, his dagger hidden in a newspaper, and stabbed him in the back. He and a fellow conspirator then jumped into a carriage with a speedy horse, the same famous Barbarian that had been used in Kropotkin's escape, and were driven away. Watching the whole drama from a distance was Alexander Mikhailov.

Years later Tikhomirov was to deplore the whole enterprise, not so much from the moral as from what might be called the professional point of view. Mezentsev, like his subordinate Heyking, had been a most inefficient pursuer of subversion. "The Third Department was in a very enfeebled and chaotic condition; it would be difficult to imagine a more decrepit political police. In fact, clever conspirators would have tried to preserve such officials, for if you had serious plans for a *coup d'état,* with them around you could perform veritable miracles."[49] But these were not Tikhomirov's feelings at the moment. It was a dazzling advertisement for the conspiracy: one of the empire's highest dignitaries slain in broad daylight on a crowded street. What enhanced the awe was that the assassination was taken to be revenge for the hanging of Kovalsky on August 2, and of course the revolutionaries did not disabuse the authorities and public of this notion. And so people believed that this indeed must be a very powerful and awesome organization, which within two days of the execution of a fellow revolutionary in a provincial city could react so ruthlessly and efficiently and right in the heart of the empire!

Mezentsev died of the wound, and for quite a while the assassins remained unidentified. Not until 1880 did Adrian Mikhailov (no relative of Alexander), the driver of the getaway cab, reveal their identity to the police. Adrian had been arrested on other charges in 1878, and his "candid confession," as the police phrase went, was to earn him a commutation of death sentence to hard labor. An anonymous pamphlet published in the fall of 1878 by Land and Freedom (written by Kravchinsky) still justified the murder as a measure of self-defense by the revolutionary party. *Death for a Death* argued that the revolutionaries' target was the social system as a whole and not individuals—"Killing is a deplorable thing"—but if the government should continue to answer "peaceful propaganda" by hangings and deportations, terror would go on.

The hero of August 4, Kravchinsky, was the same man who had pleaded with Vera Zasulich after her acquittal not to leave Russia and not to allow herself to become a "heroine in retirement." But this was precisely the course he now took. In November he escaped abroad, never to return. Under the name of Stepniak he became in the 1880s and 1890s the leading

[49]Tikhomirov, 118.

interpreter in the West of the Russian revolutionary movement, the first Russian political emigré whose name became widely known in Britain and the United States. According to Tikhomirov's not unbiased testimony—he hated Kravchinsky not only as a vilifier of the Fatherland, but also as a rival and much more successful emigré publicist—Stepniak and his wife (whose Jewishness enhanced Tikhomirov's hostility toward the couple) grew rich on the proceeds of his unpatriotic activity. The erstwhile romantic terrorist who had courted and escaped death so many times met his end in London in 1895 in an accident, falling under the wheels of a subway train.

The government's reaction to the latest outrage showed the extent of its panic. The series of assassinations, proclaimed the emperor's edict to the senate, was the work of a "circle of criminal conspirators" who "reject any social order, private property, the sanctity of marriage vows, and even faith in God," and who disdain no means to achieve their ends. Henceforth all political crimes would be judged by military courts, their verdicts to be executed without delay.[50] Even more expressive of the government's puzzlement as to how to deal with this escalation of revolutionary activity was its appeal to the public: "The Russian nation and its leading representatives should demonstrate, by deeds, that it will not tolerate such criminals in its midst . . . and that every loyal subject of the sovereign will do everything possible to assist the government in extirpating our internal enemies." There followed a fatuous call to the young. "They should soberly consider the degrading and painful consequences to which they expose themselves by falling under the spell of antisocial doctrines." Such infatuation, the decree went on, in its half-pleading and half-threatening way, bound to create an impression opposite to its intention, has already claimed "many victims among those whose abilities would have secured them a more brilliant future and one more useful for the common good."

Russian society's answer was expressed most uninhibitedly in the resolutions of the Kharkov and Chernigov local assemblies, which protested that in the absence of nationwide representative institutions and civic freedoms, His Majesty's loyal subjects could do little to help the government fight subversion. These resolutions were not allowed to be formally presented to the emperor. As to the young they replied by a new wave of uprisings which, beginning with the Kharkov Veterinary Institute, spread to all institutions of higher education in the capital and elsewhere. Some hundred and fifty students of the Petersburg Medical Academy were thrown into a military prison. The whole affair led to the exclusion of several hundred young persons from those institutions and their deportation to various localities where they would be under police surveillance.[51]

What a fantastic success for the revolutionary cause! The government of

[50]Tatishchev, *Emperor Alexander II,* St. Petersburg 1903, II, 600–601.
[51]*Ibid.,* p. 603.

an empire of some ninety million people was thrown on the defensive, constrained to exasperate society still further, and all on account of the activities of a party whose hard-core membership was about fifty! Whereas those thousands of propagandists in 1874 had made only a slight dent in the government's equanimity, now a few stabs with a dagger and a few shots made the whole establishment tremble and pile one psychological error upon another! Truly the "disorganization" section of Land and Freedom justified its name beyond the fondest hopes of its founders.

So much success frightened even the conspirators themselves. With an instinctive feeling where it would lead them both morally and politically, many of them fought the growing conviction that the party should forget about "the people" and concentrate on terror. In September Alexander Mikhailov departed from Petersburg to carry on the Populist apostolate among the Don Cossacks. Some others also went back among the people, and we can be sure that it was not fear of the police, now feverishly active in the wake of Mezentsev's murder, which was the dominant consideration. They were fleeing from the overwhelming urge to go on killing.

But fate again intervened to drive the revolutionary movement in the direction of terrorism. Increased police watchfulness about the middle of October, and perhaps a denunciation, led to the arrest of key members of the Petersburg "basic circle"—headed by Olga Natanson, Adrian Mikhailov, and Alexis Oboleshev, one of the authors of the original program of Land and Freedom. Oboleshev, who would not reveal his real name even at his trial in 1880, was taken by the authorities to be the killer of Mezentsev. Their elimination forced the recall to the capital of Alexander Mikhailov and other "villagers." The latter now assumed the effective guidance of the conspiracy, and was to lead it in a direction quite different from the one intended by the founders of Populism in the beginning of the decade.

TWELVE

THE BIRTH OF THE PEOPLE'S WILL

News from the outside world seldom penetrated the thick walls of Schlüsselburg. Its inmates, all "politicals," many with death sentences commuted to life or twenty years' imprisonment, were as a rule denied visiting privileges and books and journals touching on current events. But in the mid-1890s an exception was made: the prison library acquired Lev Tikhomirov's *Why I Stopped Being a Revolutionary,* the pamphlet which the erstwhile leader of the People's Will had written in 1888, prior to his pardon by Alexander III and his return to Russia, where he was currently a mainstay of conservative journalism. To those men and women who had endured solitary imprisonment, virtually certain that they would not leave the grim fortress alive, who had witnessed death and insanity among their comrades, this was the most shattering blow of all. The main founder and the intellectual guide of the People's Will, the man who they had believed would through his devotion and ingenuity keep the revolutionary struggle going on in their absence, had become a renegade, a vilifier of the cause he had served so faithfully and of the movement that under his leadership had once appeared to have dealt a deathblow to the autocracy. Painful as the news was, and many cried on first hearing it, it was even more astounding: how could a man exchange a place in history alongside Herzen and Chernyshevsky for the opprobrious role of propagandist for reaction?

"He must have gone mad," tapped Vera Figner on the wall which separated her cell from Morozov's. "No, he always had it in him," tapped back Morozov, with that one-upmanship which he never abandoned throughout his long and amazing life. Eternal optimist that he was, he would intermittently amuse and infuriate his fellow prisoners by assuring them every few months that they were about to be freed. One day in October 1905 he and another inmate had their walk interrupted by a guard: they were wanted in the commandant's office. Why were they being deprived of those precious few moments in the fresh air? his comrade wondered irritably. To be told they had been amnestied, asserted Morozov without a trace of doubt. After twenty years, he was finally proved right.

An indirect result of Tikhomirov's apostasy was a serious underestimation of his historical importance. His ex-comrades retained considerable respect, indeed traces of affection, for the man who while negotiating for a pardon by the imperial government, stipulated that he would never turn informer and betray any revolutionary or sympathizer still at large. But by the same token they, and following them Soviet historians, were loath to concede that the leading role in the revolutionary movement during those years had belonged to a man whose views some ten years later evolved so much to the right that they aroused opposition even in the most conservative government circles, and whose religious fanaticism grew to the point where it occasionally embarrassed the hierarchy of the Orthodox Church. In his own recollections, while he acknowledged his share in the responsibility for the terroristic and other activities of Land and Freedom and the People's Will, Tikhomirov could hardly be expected to admit, even to himself, how great that share in fact was. So for the historian as well as for the general reader, the story of the movement which undermined the Russian autocracy and prepared the ground for the revolutionary convulsions of the twentieth century is dominated by such glamorous, and from the radical point of view virtuous, figures as Alexander Mikhailov, Zhelyabov, and Perovskaya, with Tikhomirov very much in the background, an embarrassing intruder in this galaxy of heroes and idealists. Yet to relegate him to a secondary role means inevitably to distort the character of revolutionary Populism during those years when it shook the foundations of the Russian state and when, due largely to Tikhomirov's insights, it stood on the threshold of a success transcending the crowning act of terror, the assassination of the ruling monarch.

In Tikhomirov we encounter a type hitherto missing in the "liberation movement" as we have followed it in these pages: a politician. The role to which Herzen, Chernyshevsky, and Lavrov aspired was to rule over their contemporaries' minds. Their most devoted worshippers would have found preposterous the notion of any of them becoming a prime minister or leader of a party, attending to the prosaic business of governing or political bargaining rather than proclaiming and elucidating profound truths about life and society. The movement had been rich in would-be prophets, high priests, and grand inquisitors; it lacked men with a practical political knack, men who to the question what is to be done would answer not with visions of an instant utopia or retribution for the people's wrongs, but with a strategy attuned to the political reality of the moment.

Had he been born some fifteen or twenty years later than he was (1852), Tikhomirov would very likely have found fulfillment of his revolutionary and religious cravings in Marxism. The orderly gospel of scientific socialism would have answered his spiritual needs immeasurably better than the ruling radical ideology of the day, with its sentimental enthusiasm for "the people" and its dreamlike vision of an instant egalitarian paradise to follow the revolution. In fact the revolutionary in him always had to struggle with, and was finally overcome by, the Christian believer.

It was a life story worthy of the pen of Dostoyevsky, an admirer of this strange man was to write. The descendant of a long line of Orthodox priests (his father was the first to break with the family tradition and become a military doctor), the ambivalence of Tikhomirov's nature is symbolized by an incident which took place right after his birth. His parents planned to name him Mitrofan. But there had been two elder brothers, one who died in infancy baptized Lev. And now the surviving one insisted "we have again Lev," and the baby was christened accordingly. But in his mind it was Saint Mitrofan who remained his patron—incongruously, even when as a revolutionary Tikhomirov considered himself a freethinker. The saint's picture accompanied him to his prison cell. And on September 30, 1888, he noted in his diary that he pulled the ikon from a drawer and hung it in his Paris apartment. "How frail is human nature! It took me an enormous effort to do this, and all on account of false shame before two or three friends who would be stupefied at this sight."[1] Three years later, when his religiosity turned into a veritable mania, the erstwhile atheist and regicide tried to cure a toothache by rubbing his jaw with holy oil from the shrine of St. Mitrofan: "Thank God it helped, the pain disappeared."[2] In view of the state of dentistry in Russia in 1891, this was not perhaps as irrational as it sounds.

"In the upper classes of my high school, I was already a fully convinced republican. And how could it be otherwise? I would not hear a single word in favor of monarchy. . . . I became a revolutionary. Everybody but everybody whom I read, under whom I studied, pictured revolution as inevitable. For us young people, this was a matter of faith. We believed in revolution as one believes that the earth goes around the sun. Like this law of nature or not, it is still a law. And we believed in socialism with the same unshakable faith."[3] But this picture, drawn by him when already a "renegade," and convinced like most of his ilk that revolutionaries are made through the

---

[1] *Memoirs of Lev Tikhomirov*, Moscow 1927, 255.
[2] *Ibid.*, 390.
[3] *Ibid.*, 30–31.

seduction of immature minds by subversive teaching, does not do justice to Tikhomirov the revolutionary. He was not a passive victim of his environment. Ambition as well as a ruling intellectual fad made him a revolutionary. And rather than being a follower, from his youngest days he was a leader. At twenty he wrote two propaganda pamphlets which became the stock-in-trade of the "pilgrims" of 1874–75, *The Tale of Four Brothers* and *Pugachev.* And on his release from jail following the trial of "the 193," he joined Land and Freedom not as a novice but as an acknowledged master of revolutionary propaganda.

At first his standing in the party was inferior to that of Alexander Mikhailov. But in the history of the Russian radical movement it was the theorist and the writer rather than even the most brilliant organizer who would traditionally be called to lead. It was Lenin who, though he was mostly abroad and not concerned with the day-to-day activities of Bolshevism at home, was the principal leader of Bolshevism between 1903 and 1917, and not the Krasins, Stalins, and Shliapnikovs, and eventually Trotskys who kept the movement going on in Russia, and organized the revolution. Vera Figner thought she was being disparaging when she recalled that "even when young, Tikhomirov gave the impression of being an old man and was called so among the comrades because of his oldish appearance and perhaps because of some intuition on their part." But she forgets that Lenin was also "the old man" (a frequent sobriquet among the Bolsheviks) and not merely on account of his premature baldness, but in recognition of his preeminence as thinker and revolutionary strategist.

Tikhomirov's recollections, for all their inherent limitations, give us some tantalizing glimpses into the revolutionary mind and atmosphere of those feverish years. Though when he wrote them he would have liked to erase that part of his past, Tikhomirov unwittingly enables us to reconstruct his goals and ambitions, the stratagems through which he and a handful of conspirators under his guidance aspired to change the course of Russian history.

His comments about his principal lieutenants are even more revealing about himself. Tikhomirov's tribute to Alexander Mikhailov reflects, it is fair to say, not only the writer's genuine liking of this devoted and idealistic comrade, but also a sense of his own superiority. Mikhailov ideally complemented Tikhomirov, first in the radical wing of Land and Freedom and then in the People's Will: an activist rather than a reflecting mind, a man who would attend to assassinations and other strictly conspiratorial matters without bothering about what overall purpose these activities were supposed to serve. One cannot accept Tikhomirov's contention that he himself was always an enemy of terror and accepted it only at the behest of his comrades. On the contrary he was a strong proponent of this method of political struggle, and as late as 1883 authorized a particularly vicious murder.

Tikhomirov is hardly complimentary in his remarks about his principal colleagues, except for Mikhailov and Zhelyabov. Dmitri Klements, he admits, "was very pleasant and talented," but not endowed with real "intellectual force"—as distinguished presumably from Tikhomirov himself who following Klements' arrest and exile in February 1879 succeeded him as the chief theoretical and journalistic spokesman of the revolutionary camp. (Klements, in Siberia, where he spent the rest of his life, became a famous anthropologist and ethnographer.) To George Plekhanov, in whom he sensed considerable intellectual force and hence viewed as a rival, Tikhomirov was willing to grant wide erudition and a theoretical skill, but not a creative mind: "in his premises and general outlook, [he was] the most banal man of his time." And above all, "not a good man, dry, egotistical, irritable, vengeful, incapable of magnanimity."[4] In some ways this characterization is truer of the author himself.

The younger Tikhomirov is at times hard to discern in his writing as a middle-aged "renegade." But some of the prejudices he displays as a monarchist and religious bigot must have been already present in the revolutionary. No question about it, a male chauvinist, if there ever was one. Thus he wrote about such female luminaries of the revolutionary camp as Olga Natanson and Sophia Perovskaya: "Typical women! Not very smart, but what fanaticism, self-assurance and willpower, the latter to be sure in its lowest denominator: *obstinacy*. Something will get into their heads and you will not dig it out even with a scalpel."[5] Tikhomirov and Perovskaya carried on at one time a romance which never reached the stage of a "civic marriage." And there is a suggestive inconsistency in his depiction of their relations: "With her character, she needed a man who would make her his slave, and I was not the type." When history's most famous female terrorist learned that Tikhomirov was married ("Civically," of course!) she felt "insulted and was furious." But from then on, Sophia "looked at me with new eyes. Evidently in the depth of her soul she now respected me for not letting a 'broad' boss me around."[6]

Sour grapes apart, Tikhomirov's appraisal of the role of the "revolutionary broads," as he calls them, is generally negative. Until she found her lover and master in Zhelyabov, Perovskaya with her quarrelsomeness made life difficult for the leadership of the People's Will (i.e., for himself and Alexander Mikhailov). Vera Figner, who took over the direction of the organization after Tikhomirov fled Russia in 1882, was, to be sure, he grants, very attractive and a passionate terrorist, useful to the cause as long as she was taking orders from a man. But on her own, as a leader, she was hopeless; recruited into the party all sorts of unsuitable people; fell prey to

[4] *Ibid.*, 89.
[5] *Ibid.*, 87.
[6] *Ibid.*, 111.

provocateurs; in brief made such a mess that the People's Will never recovered from it, writes our author indignantly, forgetting that now, as a monarchist, he should applaud this outcome. Yet his appraisal of Figner's stewardship of the movement falls, as we shall see, not far from the mark.

If in his slighting opinion of women he was very untypical of the radical sphere from which he came, the same cannot be said of Tikhomirov's anti-Jewish bias. To be sure, as a young revolutionary he could not have been the outright anti-Semite he was in his forties when he wrote, "The Jews are always partisans of socialism, and understandably so, because if this doctrine prevails they will rule the world."[7] But in general the Populists, including Jews in their midst, argued that the Jews as merchants and middlemen, which was their typical function in the western regions of the Russian Empire, were as much exploiters of the peasants as were Gentile landowners and officials. Beyond this economic rationalization of the prejudice, some revolutionaries, and none more than Tikhomirov, felt that the Jew was essentially an alien and undesirable element within Russian society, his values and aspirations sharply at odds with those of "the people." And if the ignorant masses hated the Jew as moneylender, landowner's agent, or even "Christ killer," how could a good Populist oppose such instinctive if primitive emotions of "the people," rather than try to enlist and utilize them in his struggle against the social order as a whole? After all, revolutionaries who came from the gentry also worked and prayed for the day of retribution when the people's aroused wrath would be visited on the heads of their own kind. Some indeed were to find this reasoning not only fallacious but disgraceful, but not before the cult of violence which they had so eagerly embraced produced its bitter fruits.

The way Tikhomirov characterizes his Jewish comrades calls for no comment. About Aron Zundelevich, who was a sort of business manager first of Land and Freedom and then of the People's Will: "Being Jewish he was very talented in practical matters. To get a man across the frontier, to do anything illegal, for that you could not find a more clever person. . . . A good comrade, a man with strong nerves, which is rare among the Jews, not a coward." Aptekman also earned Tikhomirov's sympathy for "un-Jewish" characteristics, "He was the *good Jew* type, an idealist, sentimental, impractical, all nerves, always excited. . . . He was liked, but neither intellectually (being a good Jew he was rather dumb) nor practically did he contribute much to our organization."[8]

What made a man like this a revolutionary and regicide, comrade and leader of those "revolutionary broads," Jews, both "good" and "bad," and fanatical terrorists, rather than from the beginning an apologist for absolut-

[7] *Ibid.,* 324.
[8] *Ibid.,* 89.

ism and reaction? The most revealing passages of the memoir on this count —and about not only Tikhomirov's mental processes but those of many other Russian radicals down to the Bolsheviks of our era—are his impressions of the West. At first his reaction on crossing the frontier in 1882 was one of tremendous relief. For the first time in years he was really free, did not have to walk in the shadow of the gallows. "To look around, to enjoy the sights and with no fear of the policeman—oh, how pleasant it is." But then immediately he was struck by the thought that this vaunted "Europe" was in some ways ridiculous. How tiny all the countries were! Practically each time you looked out of your car window you were in a new country, with people babbling in a different language. "Switzerland has rather amused me. It is so tiny, tidy, and orderly. Rather than being a real country it reminded me of those games I used to play in my childhood with boxes with miniature houses, farms, and cows in them." And how grandiose Russia was in comparison. Whatever you said about her, she was a real and huge state.

And how bitter for his national pride, the realization of the Fatherland's backwardness. All those orderly and fertile German and Swiss farms represented an accumulation of centuries of labor and civilization. As against that, in Russia one saw "veritable savagery—you look around the countryside and you see nothing but rubbish. No one lives in the same house as his grandfather, for an average [peasant] cottage is destroyed by fire two or three times within a lifetime." What can he, an exile, say about his native country to his son who is growing up a foreigner? "What shall I tell him, I who know that Russia is a million times better than France?"

For all the denigrating things Tikhomirov said about Plekhanov, he was constrained to grant his erstwhile rival one supreme virtue: "In his heart he has remained an unflinching patriot. . . . He sees Russia as the giant socialist state of the future and will not concede a foot of her soil." Plekhanov resolutely rejected all national separatisms; he distrusted and disliked the Poles—"hard as it is for a revolutionary exile to be openly against the Poles, who are a force for revolution"; hated the proponents of Ukrainian independence of autonomy even more than Katkov did. Whatever the validity of this characterization of Plekhanov it certainly fitted Tikhomirov. It was an as yet unconscious nationalism which helped propel Tikhomirov into the revolutionary struggle, a yearning that Russia might shed her backwardness and become the "great socialist country of the future." And when he decided that no such revolution would take place in his time, then his now fully ripened chauvinism drove him into the camp of reaction.

For another guiding passion of Tikhomirov's was power. Not in the sense that a demented conspirator like Ishutin or Nechayev understood it: an ability to mesmerize one's followers and to turn them into slaves. His was the politician's goal: to master the course of events, to leave his imprint on the history of Russia. As he wrote frankly in his confession to Alexander III, "My ambition was to organize a large secret society with its aim a *coup d'état* which would lead either to the summoning of a Constituent Assembly or, depending on circumstances, seizure of power by a revolutionary dictatorship."[10] This in itself sharply distinguishes Tikhomirov from practically all of his revolutionary contemporaries. For them there was no "depending on circumstances"—either a full victory, revolution, followed immediately by a socialist and egalitarian Russia, or Siberia and death.

Land and Freedom was hardly a "large society" when Tikhomirov joined it. And the circumstances of Russian political life precluded the possibility of working for a drastic political change except through the means of a conspiracy. But if conspiracy must of necessity be limited in numbers, it does not follow that it has to be impotent against a regime unsure of itself, confronted by hostility (even if for the moment a passive one) of the educated class and incapable of mobilizing support in the rest of society. A handful of conspirators can still gain wide influence, the first surrogate of power, by repeatedly demonstrating the regime's incapacity to govern, by forcing it to grant concessions or, conversely, to escalate repression; in either case impressing the *intelligentsia* and even segments of the bureaucracy itself that the revolutionary movement is a powerful and indestructible force, an inevitable partner in charting a better future for Russia.

Terror was the only practical means of achieving this. But within Land and Freedom Tikhomirov found himself at first in the paradoxical position of being supported but misunderstood by people like Morozov and Alexander Mikhailov, who were passionate believers in terror but did not appreciate the need of combining it with a flexible political program; and of being well understood but opposed by the diehard Populists, such as Plekhanov and Deich. The latter had no compunction against using violence to wipe out government spies and officials who interfered with "peaceful propaganda" among the rural and urban masses, but they were hostile to "political terror" coupled to concrete political demands. For them this was "liberalism with bombs," an attempt to compel the government to grant a constitution, which would enthrone the middle class as rulers, facilitate the growth of capitalism, and thus lead to even more abject economic enslavement of "the people." The miniscule membership of Land and Freedom could be kept together only through the fiction that the organization remained faithful to its Populist principles, while in fact its activity centered more and more on terror. On being accepted as a member, Tikhomirov was asked whether he agreed with these principles: "the usual Populist nonsense about communal ownership of land, free federation of communes, etc. I expressed my agreement though in fact I already began to develop different

[10]*Ibid.*, 242.

conceptions."[11] But for the time being he would not try to convert others. It was better to have Alexander Mikhailov, universally trusted by his comrades, lead Land and Freedom in the direction he himself wanted it to go. While letting Mikhailov carry on as both the boss of the conspiracy as a whole and the chief organizer of terror, Tikhomirov would hold himself apart from such "dirty work"; he would be the "literary" spokesman of the revolutionary camp. At some time in the future, Tikhomirov might well have fancied, he would be called upon to negotiate on behalf of the revolutionaries with the liberals, perhaps with the government itself, and it would be very helpful if the intermediary were not directly identified with the terrorist side of the conspiracy.

It is difficult to estimate to what extent Tikhomirov manipulated his friend. But Mikhailov was a man of little sophistication. "An idea would get hold of him without his grasping what it was all about," another comrade wrote.[12] When Morozov began to publish the *Bulletin of Land and Freedom,* and some comrades objected that it contained unabashed glorification of terror for its own sake, Mikhailov's answer was typical of his political illiteracy: "What matters what is in the paper? The great thing is that it appears clandestinely and that the police are at their wits' end. . . . For me an ideal paper would be one which had no [political] content at all."[13] A man of subtler intellect would not have found it difficult to dominate this sincere, passionate, but naive revolutionary.

Whatever the extent of his indirect guidance of the conspiracy, Tikhomirov established and cultivated ties with the radical *intelligentsia.* With two of its leading figures, Nicholas Shelgunov and Nicholas Mikhailovsky, he was linked by personal friendship. Shelgunov, whom we already encountered in the 1860s as the author of *To The Young Generation* and a model progressive husband, was currently an editor of *Action,* which insofar as the censor allowed continued the tradition of *The Contemporary* and *The Russian Word.* Under an assumed name Tikhomirov contributed frequently to *Action* as well as to *Fatherland Notes,* the guiding spirit of which was Mikhailovsky, the current intellectual leader of "legal Populism." When, in view of his civic wife's pregnancy, Tikhomirov decided to go through a formal marriage ceremony (which of course had no legal or church validity, since both he and his bride lived under false names), Mikhailovsky acted as his best man. After Tikhomirov's apostasy, this occasion (the only one on which he wore tails in his life!) was to be a bitter memory indeed to the acknowledged heir of Chernyshevsky and Lavrov.

Alexander Mikhailov also had wide contacts beyond the conspiratorial

[11]*Ibid.,* 123.
[12]Michael R. Popov, *Notes of a Member of Land and Freedom,* Moscow 1932, 140.
[13]Tikhomirov, 133.

brotherhood, but they were of a quite different nature. He possessed an unusual knack for spotting and enlisting in the cause people of most varied backgrounds: young men who because of their unstable character could not be enlisted as members of Land and Freedom but might be handy in some particular revolutionary enterprise; young ladies whose moral standards also disqualified them for membership but whose charms could be put to good use; what today we would call young executives and minor bureaucrats craving some excitement—they all seemed somehow to cross his path. One such "find" of Mikhailov's was to prove of inestimable value to the conspiracy. Indeed much of the credit for the success of the revolutionary party between 1879 and 1881 must be attributed to Nicholas Kletochnikov.

His is an unusually pathetic story. A typical "little man," a petty provincial bureaucrat, consumptive, Kletochnikov became convinced at the age of thirty that he did not have much longer to live and hence might as well sacrifice his life in a spectacular fashion for a worthy cause. He chucked his job and went to Petersburg, where in the fall of 1878 he encountered Mikhailov. He begged Mikhailov, who in his eyes epitomized all the qualities to which he aspired, for some suicidal assignment. But the "guardian" did not see Kletochnikov as a terrorist. He had another job for him. One Anna Kutuzov rented out rooms to students and appeared unusually inquisitive about her lodgers' extracurricular activities. Kletochnikov moved in and was soon able to report that indeed the widow Kutuzov worked for the Third Department, whose agents would drop by for an occasional game of cards. Through flattering the harridan and losing regularly at the gambling table (the money came from the treasury of Land and Freedom), Kletochnikov soon earned her friendship, and she recommended him to her employers. There was as yet no such thing as a security check, but it took all of Mikhailov's persuasiveness to make the Kletochnikov take on so loathsome a job. He was first used as an informer, but his superiors finding him unsuitable for that but noting his neat handwriting, assigned him to copying secret memoranda. He was considered an exemplary employee by the Third Department, his efficiency being rewarded by frequent promotions and salary raises and, in April 1880, by being decorated with the order of St. Stanislaus, third class.[14]

Thus from January 1879 on, the revolutionaries had an agent within the headquarters of the secret police who regularly fed them information: what the authorities knew about them, who was in danger of arrest, the names of police informers, etc. The identity of "our man in the Third Department" was withheld by Mikhailov from all but a few of his colleagues, and Kletochnikov in turn was not privy to the activities of Land and Freedom and then the People's Will. After the arrest of the "guardian" at the end of 1880, the conspirators grew more careless in their contacts with Kletochnikov,

[14]S. N. Valk, ed., *The Archive of Land and Freedom*, Moscow 1932, 26.

and on January 28, 1881, he fell into a police trap.

During the subsequent investigation his courage failed him, and he blamed his double-agent role on his fear of the revolutionaries, as well as on the need for more money than the job paid him. (The position of a secret agent, entrusted with the most confidential information, was hardly lucrative. Kletochnikov began at thirty rubles per month, an average servant's wages, and only as a senior clerk was raised to seventy-five rubles. This helps to explain the lamentable quality of tsarist security intelligence.) He also told what little he knew about the secrets of the People's Will. It is only when he found himself on the bench of the accused along with his idol, Alexander Mikhailov, in the "trial of the 20" in 1882 that Kletochnikov recovered his fortitude and became what he aspired to be all his life, a hero. He repudiated his confession and in ringing tones declared his devotion to revolution and his execration of the autocracy: "I embraced him warmly, telling him that we shall die as we had lived, as friends," wrote Mikhailov to his family. Though his death sentence was commuted, a chronic consumptive could not be expected to survive for long the rigors of the Alexis Ravelin. Kletochnikov died on July 13, 1883.

As long as they had their spy within the Third Department the revolutionaries enjoyed relative safety. Relative, because police departments in large cities did not always share their information, or at least not immediately, with the headquarters of the secret police. An unusually enterprising pursuer of sedition such as Sudeykin in Kiev or the prosecutor Alexander Dobzhinsky in Odessa would often act on his own, and only afterward notify the central authorities.

In addition to the possibility of anticipating the authorities' moves, Kletochnikov enabled Mikhailov and Co. to gain an insight into the general operations and mentality of the security organs, and find out who (justifiably or not) were classified as having "untrustworthy ideas" or a "subversive turn of mind." Some such characterizations were close to the mark. Thus we meet repeated references to Mikhailovsky's involvement with the revolutionaries although because of the writer's great prestige among the *intelligentsia*, the authorities could never bring themselves to arrest him. But as one might expect, one finds among the secret police files a great amount of unfounded gossip, denunciations inspired by personal vindictiveness, and just sheer nonsense, the product of some dull-witted informer's imagination or an attempt to attract his superiors' attention by a sensational discovery. Thus one overly eager police collaborator named Michael Saltykov-Shchedrin as being a top leader of the revolutionary party! The great satirist, though a man with radical sympathies and a ruthless critic of contemporary Russian life, never engaged in conspiracy, and was a firm opponent of terror.[15] Officials of the Third Department appear from Kletochnikov's

---

[15]Valk, 214.

reports as for the most part not only venal but primitive and stupid in discharging their duties.

Such a picture of the inner operation of the most secret and, from their point of view, most important part of the tsarist bureaucracy could not but buoy the morale of the conspirators. This was then the true state of the Third Department which for years all Russia had lived in dread of? The revolutionaries could now more readily believe that all those plans for instigating vast popular uprisings, stirring up peasants and Old Believers, were not only impractical but unnecessary. Increasingly they fell prey to the illusion that even such a miniscule organization as their own could, by a few well-placed blows, terrorize and disrupt the workings of the entire rotten apparatus. And whatever moral legitimacy and force the system as a whole still enjoyed in the eyes of the people, it was still inextricably bound up with the life of one man. With Alexander II gone, believed the most sanguine proponents of terror, the imperial government would be forced to its knees or thrown into chaos, which would be the revolutionaries' opportunity.

By the same token, the decision to attempt the assassination of the emperor could not be undertaken even by the most fanatical of the revolutionaries easily and without considerable inner struggle. They were not Nechayevs or Karakozovs. Could they who represented the people's aspirations take the life of a man who for all his sins of commission and omission was still the Tsar Liberator? Politically the deed appeared as hazardous as it was morally questionable, especially to those who hated most the idea of monarchy. It meant abandoning Populism's cardinal tenet, that the people, if their eyes are opened, could and should decide their own destiny. The assassination could be justified only in terms of exacting from Alexander's successor what he himself would not grant: a constitution. And the term itself was as hateful to die-hard Populists as autocracy itself: it brought with it the vision of Russia's becoming like the West, ruled by a parliament with the preponderance of political power going to lawyers, bankers, and industrialists, with the village commune and hence the peasant's instinctive socialism being irretrievably destroyed by advancing capitalism. It is probable that at the beginning of 1879 only Tikhomirov among the leading lights of Land and Freedom fully appreciated the consequences of an all-out commitment to this supreme act of political terror. And it required all his guile as well as the lack of political sophistication on the part of such leaders of the conspiracy as Mikhailov and Morozov to sway revolutionary Populism in a direction which negated its basic ideological premise.

Above all, the idea of regicide was advanced by the rising momentum of violence. On February 9, Prince Dmitri Kropotkin, the governor of Kharkov, was shot in his carriage, and a week later he died of the wounds. First cousin of the famous anarchist—who incidentally could not bring himself to condemn this deed, even though his kinsman had interceded on both his and his brother's behalf when they were jailed— Kropotkin was neither better nor worse than the average official of his rank, and his murder could but with difficulty be classified as "disorganization."

The assassination had been planned in Kiev by Osinsky, but its meticulous preparation and execution bore the imprint of that "professionalism" which Alexander Mikhailov was currently imparting to terrorism —that is, except for the person of the chief assassin, Gregory Goldenberg. A high-strung youth (b. 1855), subject to intermittent bouts of exaltation and depression, Goldenberg undoubtedly would not have been chosen for this task by the "guardian." Goldenberg had five years of revolutionary propaganda behind him when in December 1878 he read *Buried Alive,* a pamphlet written by Dolgushin describing his and other political prisoners' sufferings. At the same time he learned that the Executive Committee, i.e., Osinsky, had passed a death sentence on Kropotkin. The ostensible reason was the turbulence at the Kharkov Veterinary Institute, where students, incensed by the introduction of weekly examinations, had responded by a mass demonstration, which was dispersed by Cossacks wielding whips. The prince was also blamed for the severe regimen in the Kharkov prison, introduced following the revelations of the lax treatment of the "politicals," as exemplified in the flight of Deich and his comrades from the Kiev jail the preceding May. The wrought-up Goldenberg demanded that he be entrusted with the assassination, threatening to shoot anybody who would try to anticipate him in disposing of the tyrannous official.[16]

The pattern of preparation for murder was to become typical in future acts of terror. Goldenberg and the back-up assassin, a young Pole named Louis Kobilyanski, were not left to their own devices. Two other conspirators, posing as a married couple, rented an apartment in Kharkov where the plotters could find shelter and take counsel without attracting the attention of a suspicious landlord or hotel porter. Kropotkin's daily routine had been carefully observed before he was struck down at eleven o'clock at night when returning unescorted to his residence. The crime remained unsolved until Goldenberg provided full details in his famous confession to the police one year later when, seized with remorse the unfortunate fanatic tried to explain to himself and others "what made me, a very humane person, take a gun and kill a man."[17]

Before a month was over, Land and Freedom scored again. This time the assassination was planned by the "basic circle," and its victim could be claimed to be a legitimate prey of its "disorganization" section, a police spy

[16]Vladimir Burtsev, ed., *The Trial of the 16,* St. Petersburg 1906, 84.
[17]*The Red Archive,* V (30), Moscow 1928, 145.

who had infiltrated the revolutionary movement.

Nicholas Reinstein had collaborated with the police for a long time, possibly since joining a radical workers' circle in the early 1870s. But the first indubitable proof of his role as a *provocateur* was furnished by Kletochnikov. " 'Nicky' [Reinstein], as he was called, charmed everybody by his attractive personality and his passionate devotion to the cause."[18] In fact he proclaimed Land and Freedom too conservative in its methods and advocated armed robbery and blackmail as a means of securing funds for the conspiracy, something for which its leadership was not yet ready. Such squeamishness irritated the alleged zealot: "These intellectuals always stop at half measures; we workers are free of such silly scruples." In his *provocateur* work, Reinstein was ably assisted by his wife, Tatiana. She became intimate with Victor Obnorski, a founder of the Northern Russian Workers' Union. Obnorski's horizons were much wider than those of the average worker-collaborator of Land and Freedom: he had lived and worked in the West and was acquainted with European socialist and trade-union movements. The Third Department might well have let Obnorski continue at large, hoping that he would lead them to the center of the conspiracy, but inconveniently Mrs. Reinstein grew fond of her lover, and there was danger that she would reveal her role to him. And so at the end of January, Obnorski, despite the pleadings and tears of his mistress, was ordered detained. His arrest and conviction put an end to the Northern Workers' Union, the most ambitious attempt yet made to organize a clandestine revolutionary organization among the industrial proletariat, and the only one headed by people of a working-class background.

Because of Mikhailov's conspiratorial prudence Reinstein had had no contacts with Land and Freedom's inner core. But Kletochnikov's report made it clear that he had wormed his way into the confidence of its Moscow agents, and it was only a question of time before the whole revolutionary organization there would be busted.

Michael Popov, who was selected by the "guardian" to liquidate the traitor, did not find the task easy. "During his last days Reinstein altered his appearance, carried a gun with him, and in general observed special precautions."[19] But the manner in which Reinstein was finally trapped was characteristic of the brazenness with which the revolutionaries operated at the time. Popov and his accomplice hired a suite of rooms in a Moscow hotel and planted a rumor among the radical youth that a representative of Land and Freedom was inviting those interested to a lecture and discus-

---

[18]Lev Tikhomirov, *The Conspirators and the Police,* Moscow 1928, 193. This pamphlet was written by Tikhomirov when he was still a revolutionary living abroad in the 1880s.
[19]Valk, 163.

sion. An intermediary handed Reinstein a ticket to this social occasion.[20] Reinstein's eagerness for a sensational scoop prevailed over his caution. On arrival at the "lecture" he found himself alone with his executioners, and was stabbed to death. The whole enterprise, as Mikhailov meticulously jotted down in his accounts (he was also the treasurer of the conspiracy), including the hotel bill, railway tickets, and living expenses for the assassins, cost 386 rubles.[21] One might well ask how in view of the fact that the alleged lecture was advertised among dozens of people, no one was found to inform the police before or after the assassination and its perpetrators remained undetected. But in the prevailing atmosphere, an average student or a professional would have considered it dishonorable to carry tales to the police, and would hardly regard the killing of an informer as a serious crime, even if he himself were an enemy of violence and revolution. Dostoyevsky, at the time hardly a liberal, once confided to a journalist friend that he would find it impossible to denounce a man, even if he knew he was planning to dynamite the Winter Palace! It is as if, beginning with Vera Zasulich's shot, a spell had been cast on Russian society, a spell which would be only partly lifted after March 1, 1881.

The annals of terrorism cannot be expected to offer much in the way of comic relief. But one comes perhaps closest to it in some circumstances attending Mikhailov's next enterprise, the attempted assassination of General Alexander Drenteln. This gentleman had succeeded Mezentsev as the head of the Third Department, and during his brief tenure in this office had displayed neither cruelty nor efficiency. In brief there seemed no justification for choosing him as the next target of "disorganization." Perhaps for this reason Mikhailov could not find a volunteer for the task among his comrades, and he was forced to entrust the deed to a man who, all Soviet historians agree, lacked entirely the moral and intellectual fiber to be a serious political terrorist.

If Osinsky was thought by his friends to be of Polish ancestry because of his impulsive and romantic nature, then Leon Mirski fits another, this time pejorative, Russian stereotype of the typical Pole: courageous out of recklessness rather than moral conviction, undependable in any serious business, ready to kill for a woman's favor and to betray a comrade for trivial considerations of personal comfort. Even the sober *Biographical Dictionary of Revolutionary Activists*[22] feels constrained to add, after the usual statement of class origin, "from the nobility," redundantly but significantly "son of a Polish nobleman."

Ethnic prejudices apart, Mirski appears a rather incongruous character

---

[20]Popov, 143.

[21]Valk, 145.

[22]A. A. Shilov and M. G. Karnoukhova, eds., Moscow 1931, II, part 3, 934.

for the chief actor in a revolutionary drama. Nicholas Morozov has left us a tantalizing account of the unfortunate youth and the Drenteln affair.[23] Visiting Alexander Mikhailov one day, he encountered "an elegant and handsome youth, with exquisite aristocratic manners." This was Mirski, who announced that he had decided to kill Drenteln, a more harmful man than the late Mezentsev. Mikhailov added the details: Mirski, as behooved a Polish nobleman, was an excellent rider; posing as a sportsman, he would hire a horse from a livery stable, intercept Drenteln in his carriage, and there!

After his guest had left, Mikhailov filled Morozov in on the background of the elegant would-be assassin. He had met him through Mirski's "civic wife," a young girl of nineteen with the exotic non-Russian name of Vivien de Chateaubriant. "She comes from aristocratic circles and can be very valuable to us." He does not say so, but Morozov obviously insisted on meeting this mysterious charmer, and Mikhailov, though this does not seem to have been prudent from the conspiratorial point of view, yielded to his pleadings. As might be expected of a lady of such high social position, she resided in a luxurious apartment. "We were led first through a large gallery filled with mirrors in bronze settings, and pictures with gold frames . . . finally into a blue-walled boudoir where we saw, reposing on a chaise longue, a slim young lady reading a French novel." She languidly extended her hand to the visitors. "We delicately shook her fingertips without kissing them, even though that would have seemed required by the French court customs of the eighteenth century." The servants served coffee "in precious china cups," and Morozov, prompted by his companion, related to the enchantress what a favorable impression her beloved had made on him, and how happy they were that she sympathized with his design to rub out Drenteln. After some further chitchat about doings in high society, Mikhailov managed to drag his impressionable friend away. On the street Morozov expressed his doubts: she seemed a bit too aristocratic and languid for an assassin's accomplice. On the contrary, said Mikhailov, it was she who had planted the idea in Mirski's head by telling him how much she admired such bold fighters for freedom as Kravchinsky, who had disposed of Drenteln's predecessor. "Quite a few heroic acts have been performed for the sake of a pair of beautiful eyes." Morozov promised his help in the enterprise: he would keep tabs on Drenteln's movements.

Alas, Mikhailov had been less than frank with his friend. The alleged aristocratic beauty's real name was quite common—Helen Kestelman— and that flat, dripping with luxury, belonged to the secretary of a Petersburg

[23]Nicholas Morozov, *Tales of My Life,* Moscow 1918, IV, 212–29. Since the story was published originally before the Revolution, Morozov in a silly transparent way changed the names: Mirski appears as Lubomirski, Drenteln as Dritten, etc.

bank, one Gregory Levenson, with whom Helen had lived for a long time in a rather ill-defined capacity. Both Kestelman and Levenson were among Mikhailov's operatives and, as Kletochnikov's notes indicate, not unknown to the secret police. Far from being languid, Helen was quite busy recruiting agents and contacts for Mikhailov's enterprises, for which, as he noted scrupulously in his accounts, she received regular payments.[24] Why Mikhailov chose to play this masquerade with Morozov, usually eager to assist in any terrorist venture, is not clear, but it is a vivid example of the methods he and Tikhomirov employed on occasion to deceive their comrades. What makes the whole business more bizarre is that there was a real-life Sophia Vivien de Chateaubriant, the same age as Helen Kestelman and mistress of another revolutionary.

Mirski's vanity contributed to the failure of this elaborately contrived enterprise. The horse he chose was, like himself, elegant but unstable. On March 13, mounted on this "noble English steed," he caught up with Drenteln's carriage and shot at him through the glass window. The bullet missed, and Mirski did not get a second chance, since the animal reared and bolted, carrying Mirski for some distance. He was finally unhorsed, but with true nobleman's aplomb he ordered a gaping policeman standing nearby to hold the reins and wait so he could repair someplace and tidy up. The policeman was still holding the horse when General Drenteln and his agents arrived in hot pursuit. Yes, he had seen the rider, but His Excellency should not worry, the young gentleman was quite unharmed!

Some hours later Morozov met with Mirski in Mikhailov's apartment. Mirski was still his elegant self but seemed depressed. Mikhailov whispered the reason: "Vivien de Chateaubriant" on hearing what had happened had thrown a hysterical fit and would not see the man who had risked his life for her. Morozov was indignant: how could she fail to offer solace "to this idealistic and heroic man"? Yet he was pleased that his first impression was so correct: "A woman brought up in a life of indolence admires heroism and self-sacrifice as long as she reads about them, but will recoil with horror and tears from real danger."

The Drenteln business was rather expensive: 786 rubles, noted the account book of Land and Freedom, twice as much as the *successful* Reinstein affair. And Mirski turned out to be the kind of person who gave revolutionary terror a bad name.

Spirited out of Petersburg, the unlucky assassin and lover could not endure the boredom of provincial life. He bombarded his relatives with requests for money, boasting to them and anybody else who would listen about his feat. Finally, due to his carelessness, he was arrested in Taganrog on July 6. At first his bravado did not abandon Mirski. "Come and watch

[24]E.g., Valk, 138 and 140.

me swing when they hang me," he told a fellow prisoner. But when this became more than a mere possibility Mirski began to sing a different tune. Sentenced to death in November, he humbly petitioned the emperor for mercy and declared full contrition for his attempt. In view of Mirski's being underage (twenty) and of his "candid confessions," the sentence was commuted to life imprisonment.

If Mirski's petitioning for mercy was incompatible with the current revolutionary etiquette, then his behavior in prison led future historians to brand him a traitor. It was he, they allege unanimously, who as a fellow prisoner of Nechayev's in the Alexis Ravelin in 1881 betrayed the latter's escape plans and his subversion of prison guards. And he did it for no more weighty reason then to secure some petty favors from the prison administration: better food (including oranges for dessert), more expensive tobacco, and fresh reading matter![25] While the circumstantial evidence based on the official files accessible after 1917 is fairly incriminating, it still does not offer conclusive proof that it was the vainglorious Pole who "ratted" on Nechayev. We shall return to this subject.

In 1884 Mirski was sent to penal servitude in Siberia, and though released from confinement in 1890 he was never allowed to return to European Russia. The usually censorious Deich, who met him in exile, had nothing unfavorable to say about him. And as a middle-aged man Mirski was sufficiently involved in the revolutionary activity of 1905–1906 to be sentenced to death. His punishment once more was commuted to imprisonment. Freed by the Revolution of 1917, Mirski was swallowed up by the chaos which was Siberia during the civil war, his turbulent life ending in obscurity sometime around 1920. Levenson was tried in connection with the attempt on Drenteln, but acquitted for lack of proof, which again throws doubt on Mirski's characterization as a villain. As for the enchantress, she must have continued her very special services to the revolutionary cause, for in 1887 she was sentenced to three years of exile.

The attempt on Drenteln's life increased the unhappiness of the opponents of political terror within Land and Freedom, even though they were left in ignorance of the sordid means through which the would-be assassin had been recruited. What enhanced their rage was the veritable apotheosis of political murder contained in No. 2 of *The Bulletin of Land and Freedom,* which appeared on March 22, 1879. *The Bulletin* was created especially for Morozov, whose views were so extreme that often they could not be aired in the party's official organ, *Land and Freedom.* Now referring to the event of March 13 and calling for more and successful attempts of this kind, Morozov exulted: "Political assassination is the very essence of the revolu-

[25]P. Shchegolev, "L. G. Nechayev in the Alexis Ravelin" in *The Red Archive,* V (1924), 172–212. *Also see* E. M. Feoktistov, *Behind the Scenes of Politics and Literature,* Moscow 1929, 392.

tionary movement. . . . The most effective weapon against our enemies, one which cannot be countered by an army or legions of spies." Aptekman was to write: "I can say with all sincerity that that part of the youth and workers which was at the time occupied in creative organizational work . . . was resolutely opposed to such political experiments of our terrorist comrades."[26] And with Osinsky currently in jail, the terrorist faction took over unabashedly his Nechayev-like system of mystification. Announcements and threats of assassination bore the seal of the "Executive Committee of the Social Revolutionary Party." And about the same time Mikhailov, Tikhomirov, and Morozov and some like-minded comrades created a secret nucleus within Land and Freedom, designed either to convert it or, failing that, to create a new secret organization devoted explicitly to political terror and preparation for a *coup d'état.* Its fifteen or so members, wrote one of them, Anna Yakimova, looked with pitying incomprehension at such diehard Populists as Plekhanov and Aptekman, still trying to propagandize workers and peasants. She herself began to study how to make and use dynamite.[27]

From the terrorists' point of view their designs could be promoted only by an uninterrupted series of successful assassinations of high-placed personages. A few failures, and the fickle *intelligentsia* would grow disenchanted, the government more self-assured and what might be called "fundamentalist." Populism would again gain the upper hand within Land and Freedom. But even from the purely tactical point of view, Mikhailov's choice of the next victim was ill-advised: neither his organization nor society at large was as yet prepared for a repetition of Karakozov's attempt.

The terrorists were to claim subsequently that their hand was forced. Alexander Soloviev, a man in his thirties and a veteran of revolutionary Populism, disgruntled by his fruitless propaganda work among the peasants and unhappy in his personal life, approached Mikhailov in February and proposed to kill Alexander II. He allegedly stated that if the "basic circle" would not help him he would still go ahead with his plan. But there is evidence that Soloviev would have desisted if Mikhailov and his friends had categorically opposed the enterprise. In actual fact Soloviev fitted in perfectly with their plans. There were currently two other volunteers for the regicide: Gregory Goldenberg and Louis Kobilyanski. But both, despite their previous experience in assassination, were thought unfit for the task. Mikhailov argued diplomatically that the emperor should not be killed by a Jew or a Pole in view of the probable consequences for the given ethnic group. (Such considerations were to be disregarded in 1881, when the assas-

[26]Valk, 358.
[27]Yakimova, "The Group Freedom or Death," in *Hard Labor and Exile,* XXIV (Moscow 1926), 15.

sins included a Pole and a Jewess.) But the real reason might well have been Goldenberg's mental unbalance and the fact that Kobilyanski was an epileptic.

At Soloviev's urging and to Mikhailov's discomfiture, the plan had to be presented to the membership of Land and Freedom as a whole. And to be sure this proposal of the furthest reaching act of political terror created a storm. Vasili Ignatov, a future co-founder of the first Russian Marxist group, shouted that they should anonymously notify the police if the prospective killer (Soloviev was not present or identified at the meeting) did not abandon his mad idea. Michael Popov, who as the assassin of Reinstein could hardly be accused of being squeamish about terror, uttered another indirect threat, "If there should be Karakozovs amongst us, can you guarantee that there will not appear a Komissarov [Osip] who would frustrate the assassination, no matter what the organization should decide?" Thereupon Alexander Kviatkovsky, beyond himself, shouted, "If you turn out to be a Komissarov, I shall kill you!"[28] Mikhailov and his friends had to abandon their proposal that Land and Freedom should be associated with the attempt. But it was decided that in view of the inevitable consequences, if the unnamed assassin decided to proceed with his plan, all the members who lived under false papers should leave the capital for a while.

Despite the lack of official sanction, Mikhailov, Zundelevich, and Kviatkovsky planned the deed with Soloviev, and Mikhailov furnished him with a gun.[29] On April 2, while Alexander II was taking his morning walk, Soloviev approached him and opened fire. With the Emperor first running and then crawling on the ground, all four shots missed. The unsuccessful assassin was caught; he swallowed poison but was given an emetic and recovered. Soloviev's separated wife and his sisters helped to identify him and filled in the authorities on his revolutionary connections. During the investigation Soloviev justified Mikhailov's confidence: he stoutly maintained that the idea and execution were entirely his own. The night before the attempt, he said, he had spent with a prostitute. Sentenced to death on May 25, he was hanged three days later.

The revolutionaries' reaction to the attempted regicide bared a virtual split within Land and Freedom. Morozov in *The Bulletin* declared on behalf of the "Executive Committee" that Alexander's performance during his twenty-four–year reign fully merited a death sentence. Interestingly

---

[28]N. Morozov, "Echoes of Old Days," in *The Past,* No. 10 (St. Petersburg 1907), 244.

[29]This weapon played a tragic part in the destiny of one Dr. Orest Weymar. A well-known society doctor with connections at the Court, Weymar had rendered a number of services to the conspirators: had assisted in Kropotkin's escape, had helped to hide Vera Zasulich, etc. At one time he had made a present of a gun to Klements. Eventually the weapon found its way to Mikhailov, and after Soloviev's arrest Weymar was identified as its purchaser. The doctor, who heroically held his tongue, was sentenced to ten years for complicity in a crime with which he had nothing to do. In Siberia he became a drug addict, and he died in 1885.

enough, in addition to internal repression the emperor was blamed for his foreign policy: why had Russia failed to cash in on her victory over Turkey, purchased with so much of the people's blood? In 1914 Morozov was to be an enthusiastic supporter of the Russian war effort. Right now he was eager to turn his organization completely in the direction of terror. Unassuaged by connubial bliss, this eternal adolescent still dreamed of the laurels of the Russian William Tell.

(Morozov finally found romantic fulfillment in Olga Liubatovich, who had been tried in 1876 for, among other things, attempting to choke a policeman, and had recently fled from Siberia. This young lady when a student in Zurich was described as follows: "Behind the table was sitting an emigmatic being whose biological character was at first all but clear to me: a roundish boyish face, short-cut hair, parted askew, enormous blue glasses, a quite youthful, tender-colored face, a coarse jacket, a burning cigarette in the mouth. . . . I looked stealthily under the table and discovered a bright-colored, somewhat faded, cotton skirt." It was love at first sight when they met at a conspirator's party in August 1878.[30])

Within the editorial board of the conspiracy's official journal, April 2 led to strong disagreements. Plekhanov prepared to write an editorial on the Old Believers, completely ignoring terror. Instead the fifth and last issue of *Land and Freedom* of April 16 carried a leader by Tikhomirov advocating *agrarian* terror and partisan warfare in the countryside. The revolutionary party had to conquer the peasant, *replace the emperor in "the people's mind as the symbol of power and legitimacy.* But this would never be done by propaganda, only through violent deeds."[31] That revolution must seize not only power but legitimacy, and that "the party" should wield both was an insight that had been hitherto missing in Russian revolutionary thought; one day it would be brilliantly resurrected and refashioned by Lenin. Elsewhere in the journal the conspirators declared that the government's measures in the wake of Soloviev's shots only strengthened their resolve. "The regime declares itself threatened, opens war not only on the revolutionaries but on all Russia. . . . You may shoot tens of hundreds, exile thousands, but you will not save yourselves by such measures." There was a sarcastic description of the emperor's tearful speech to the Petersburg city council in which, among other things, he allegedly urged house owners and janitors to watch for any unusual activities among their tenants. "You should help the police apprehend suspicious characters. Consider all those assassinations. Soon an honest man will be afraid to go out."[32]

Though Katkov in his editorial on "the miraculous preservation by God

---

[30]Quoted from J. M. Meijer, *Knowledge and Revolution: The Russian Colony in Zurich,* Assen, The Netherlands, 1957, 59.
[31]O. V. Aptekman, *The Society of Land and Freedom of the 1870s,* Petrograd 1924, 363–64.
[32]*Ibid.,* 361.

of the life of His Anointed" asserted that "never was the Russian nation as united and resolute as now in its loyalty to the God-given Leader,"[33] the government felt constrained to adopt new emergency measures. On April 5, the appointment was announced of new governor-generals for Petersburg, Odessa, and Kharkov, who along with their opposite numbers in Moscow, Kiev, and Warsaw were endowed with special powers: they could order civilians tried by military courts, order arrests and send suspects into exile at their discretion, forbid the publication of journals, etc. The three new appointees were all generals with high reputations: to Petersburg went Joseph Gurko; Edward Totleben, who as the defender of besieged Sebastopol had emerged as a national hero from the Crimean War, was appointed to Odessa; and Count Michael Loris-Melikov, an Armenian by birth, famous not only for his exploits in the Russo-Turkish war but as a brilliant administrator whose energetic measures helped stem the spread of the plague in the south, became governor of Kharkov. The new measures reflected a sentiment articulated by Katkov: "Fear can only be conquered by repression. The disastrous fear of some dark forces can be subjugated only by the salutary fear of the legitimate power."[34] But as Tikhomirov was to observe many years later, in themselves such measures could bring but little effect. It was not a new governor but a capable police officer (Sudeykin) who put an end to the reign of terror in Kiev. And indeed with one glittering exception, the new officials, for all their military renown and vastly increased power, proved as incapable of dealing with sedition as had their predecessors.

Peter Valuyev, one of the most perspicacious of Alexander's ministers, was charged by the tsar to report "on reasons for the rapid spread of subversive ideas among the young generation and on the means which would put an end to their propagation." His committee found the situation "while not hopeless . . . still dangerous to the state . . . [because] of the apathy of practically all of the more or less educated part of society toward the government's struggle against a relatively small number of evil-intentioned persons, bent on subverting the basic principles of the political, civic, and social order."[35] The more realistic bureaucrats evidently disagreed with Katkov's vision of Russian society as being "united and resolute . . . in its loyalty to the God-given Leader."

But a solution for this lamentable state of affairs eluded the dignitaries. The minister of national education, Count Dmitri Tolstoy, blamed all the troubles—how familiar this sounds!—on general permissiveness, especially on the part of university and school authorities. No, it went much deeper,

[33]M.N. Katkov, *Collection of Editorials for 1879,* Moscow 1898, 161.
[34]*Ibid,* 162.
[35]Tatishchev, *Emperor Alexander II,* St. Petersburg 1903, II, 605, 606.

argued a colleague: due to the liberal system of government scholarships, too many youths from underprivileged classes were enrolling in universities and then upon graduating finding there were no jobs for them; "hence [they] fall easily under the influence of evil-minded agitators . . . who in this element find . . . collaborators and blind instruments of their designs."[36] Only the war minister, Milyutin, and Valuyev himself began to hint again about the need for *political* reforms.

Far from remedying the situation, the new measures of repression served to accentuate the main cause of the social malaise: the *intelligentsia's* benevolent neutrality toward subversion. By December 1879 the military courts had dispatched sixteen persons to the gallows. The governors, especially Totleben, who sullied his reputation through his excessive and unintelligent severity, used their discretionary powers with abandon: from April 1879 to July 1880, 565 alleged political criminals were dispatched by them into exile, 130 of those to Siberia[37]—all that, on account of plots and proclamations engineered by a group whose nucleus never surpassed some twenty-odd people.

Yet at the same time that Land and Freedom was pushing the regime to the verge of panic, its own internal splits and organizational problems were threatening its continuation. Apart from ideological disagreements the revolutionaries were suffering worrisome money problems. Terrorist activity, as we have already seen, does not come cheaply. And part of the conspiracy's ability to wield power quite disproportionate to its membership depended on its hitherto ample financial resources. Most of the members, as full-time revolutionaries, had to be supported by the organization; additional expenses were incurred for arms and the printing shop; payments had to be made to sympathizers (some in its workers' affiliate had their meager wages supplemented from the Land and Freedom treasury); there were occasional bribes to prison guards and policemen. Where did the money come from? Quite a few solid citizens, government officials among them, demonstrated their devotion to "the liberation movement" and experienced the titillation of danger by contributing a few rubles here and there. Just as during Prohibition in the United States "everybody" had his bootlegger, so in the late 1870s, many lawyers, doctors, and occasionally even merchants in major Russian cities knew at least one young man who could act as a discreet intermediary with the fighters for freedom. But such occasional contributions would hardly have been sufficient to finance operations on the scale of those conducted by Mikhailov and his associates.

The main benefactor of Land and Freedom was one of its original members, Dmitri Lizogub, who inherited extensive estates in the Ukraine. In

[36] *Ibid.,* II, 608.
[37] P.Z. Zayonchkovsky, *The Crisis of the Autocracy,* Moscow 1964, 92.

Stepniak-Kravchinsky's listing of representative Populists, Lizogub is characterized as the revolutionary saint. And indeed this young aristocrat (b. 1848) had from his earliest days forsaken the pleasures and comforts appropriate to his station in life and thrown himself wholeheartedly into the radical movement. He had been one of the "pilgrims" in 1874 and after 1877 carried on revolutionary activity in Kiev and Odessa. Having been detained and interrogated by the police several times before, he was arrested in the latter city in August 1878 on account of his close connection with a fellow radical in whose apartment the police had found a quantity of dynamite. Lizogub had been a generous supporter of the revolutionary movement, not only in the south (where he helped to finance Osinsky's pyrotechnics in Kiev) but also to the central group of Land and Freedom. Anticipating a long imprisonment, Lizogub turned the title to most of his property over to an old friend, Vladimir Drigo, with an understanding that it would continue to be at the disposal of the revolutionary party. Drigo, in the accounts of his contemporaries and historians, appears as a despicable coward, and they have been at a loss to explain what he—given his moral failings and completely apolitical nature—could have had in common with Lizogub, an ascetic whose whole life was bound up with revolution. As long as Osinsky, not a person to trifle with, was at large, Drigo loyally followed Lizogub's instructions and kept giving Osinsky money. But when Osinsky was arrested, Drigo began to have other notions as to how his friend's fortune might be spent. Zundelevich, who under an assumed name was designated as the new contact with Drigo, received 3000 rubles from him in April 1879 but after that it was like pulling teeth. Finally Mikhailov himself decided to try his powers of persuasion on the wretch. Mikhailov demanded 10,000 rubles in cash and 60,000 in promissory notes. Drigo ran to the police, who set up a trap for the stranger, and when Mikhailov, with his usual skill, eluded it, Drigo himself was arrested. The treacherous plenipotentiary was brought to Petersburg and grilled in the Third Department. Here, according to Kletochnikov's notes, he promised further collaboration with the police provided he be allowed to retain part of Lizogub's patrimony for his own use.[38] He was then released in August 1879 and placed under police surveillance. But with Mikhailov now forewarned, Drigo was of little further use to the police. He was rearrested in the summer of 1880. That fall he was tried along with fifteen genuine revolutionaries, and sentenced to fifteen years at hard labor for financing terrorist activities.

Scoundrel though he undoubtedly was, Drigo appears innocent of the universally accepted allegation that out of greed he betrayed and exaggerated his patron's and friend's revolutionary role, thus contributing to Lizogub's condemnation to death. (The latter was hanged on August 10, 1879.) We have a pathetic document written by Drigo in November 1880,

[38]Valk, 224.

after his trial, and since it was addressed to the authorities in the hope of softening his sentence, there is no reason to doubt the veracity of the relevant passages: ". . . The Third Department knows that my revelations had no connection with the death of Lizogub. . . . I loved him more than one could conceive the love of one man for another, and this fact is well known to those who were acquainted with us." He himself was not a revolutionary, though had his friend lived, Drigo admitted, "I would have come to share his views." But after Lizogub was lost he felt free to help the police. He was promised immunity by the Third Department. And now "the question for what I have been condemned preys on my mind day and night. . . . I have awaited [mercy] for days, weeks, listened with hope to every step [outside the cell] and yet nothing, nothing. . . ."[39] The wretched man was to die in exile in Siberia.

The real villain in Lizogub's drama was undoubtedly another informer, Fyodor Kuritsin. A student of veterinary medicine, Kuritsin had been connected with the southern "rebels." Arrested in 1877, he proved so cooperative that the Odessa authorities during the next two years kept assigning him as a cell mate to the most prominent political prisoners, who had no reason to suspect that their comrade of years' standing was reporting their every word to the police. And with some embroidery: Lizogub in Kuritsin's version became not only the financial angel of the revolutionary movement but its virtual head. Hence the reason for Lizogub's doom. Yet for all the rumors about him, it was only after 1905 that the revolutionaries somehow procured the official files bearing on Kuritsin's role.[40] The former *provocateur,* by then head of the veterinary service in Turkestan, would have been well advised to pack up and flee Russia at once. Instead he committed the extraordinary folly of writing to a journal protesting his innocence. Out of the ranks of the Socialist Revolutionaries, continuators of the tradition of Populist terrorism, came an avenger: Kuritsin was murdered on September 18, 1906.

With Lizogub disappeared Land and Freedom's hope of realizing over 100,000 rubles from the sale of his estates. Even before, the revolutionaries had thought of a new way of procuring funds: robbery of state banks and post offices. The first major enterprise of this kind was undertaken by Fyodor Yurkovsky, known to his comrades as "Alex the engineer," who on June 3, 1879, tunnelled successfully under the Kherson territorial treasury and carried out more than a million rubles. Unfortunately, due to the carelessness of a lady associate of Yurkovsky's, most of the money was quickly recovered by the police and the revolutionaries retained only a few thousand.

"Alex the Engineer" made quite an impression on Vera Figner when she

[39] *Hard Labor and Exile,* LIII (Moscow 1929), 97.
[40] Their fullest version may be found in *The Past,* No. 7 (St. Petersburg July 1907), 162–68.

met him after this feat. "Never before or after have I encountered such a restless, vivacious, and bold man."[41] He seemed to her to be a "maverick among our comrades—all of them serious, ascetically inclined, and idealistic," while Yurkovsky was always full of fun and games, especially with ladies. Her comrades in fact believed Yurkovsky to be mad, and while using him kept "Alex the Engineer" at arm's length from the inner core of the conspiracy. In Siberia, where he inevitably landed, he helped to murder a fellow political exile—Peter Uspensky, of Nechayevite fame. He ended his days in Schlüsselburg.

To the believers in pure Populism, the Drigos and Yurkovskys were not accidental flotsam and jetsam on the revolutionary wave, but a symptom of the basic degeneration of their party. In its ideological origins the second Land and Freedom went back to Herzen. Organizationally its roots were in the Chaykovsky circle, with its explicit purpose to purify the "liberation movement" of the excrescences of the Karakozov and Nechayev affairs. And yet here they were resorting to methods that bore a startling resemblance to Nechayev's; gravitating toward a blueprint for revolution which, when first enunciated by Tkachev, had been pronounced by all its leading lights as completely incompatible with Populism.

By the same token the Tikhomirov wing of the party was fed up with their colleagues' compunctions about "political" terror and their obvious blindness to the fact that it was the *intelligentsia* rather than "the people" which was of crucial importance at this stage of the revolutionary struggle. And the *intelligentsia*'s sympathetic interest in the revolutionaries' activities could be changed to outright support only if they openly and without circumlocutions declared for political reforms.

In late spring of 1879 Land and Freedom began to prepare for a party congress which would decide its future direction. Traditionally such meetings had been held unrehearsed, with their participants discussing issues spontaneously and at usually great length. But now the terrorists-constitutionalists decided to arrive at the congress as a bloc, bound to secure control of the whole. With the possible exception of Morozov, they wished to avoid a definite split with "pure" Populists; already their ranks were so pitifully small. But Tikhomirov and his group were determined to steer the party toward one immediate goal: regicide.

Since their actual numbers were miniscule, members of the Freedom or Death faction decided at the last moments to co-opt a few individuals who would assure them a majority at the congress. Michael Frolenko mentioned in this connection a southern Populist, Andrew Zhelyabov. The others scoffed at this suggestion: everyone thought the world of Zhelyabov, but he was known as a "pure" Populist who had had nothing to do with Osinsky

[41]Vera Figner, *Collected Works,* I, Moscow 1928, 190.

during the latter's terrorist reign in the south. Mikhailov, currently on his dangerous mission to extract funds from Drigo, was delegated to feel Zhelyabov out on the question of terror and, if satisfied, to invite him to the caucus of the faction. In Odessa Zhelyabov was frank with his visitor: his heart was still in his work with "the people." He would join the terrorists, but only for one purpose: the assassination of the emperor. After that he must be left free to go back among the peasants.

And so the future organizer of the most famous assassination in the nineteenth century found himself one of eleven conspirators who gathered between June 16 and 20 in the resort town of Lipetsk. Theirs was a double conspiracy—against the government, to be sure, but also to seize control of Land and Freedom without their "pure" Populist comrades' realizing what was actually happening. Hence while ostensibly taking walks and picnicking in the picturesque environs of the town, they heatedly discussed proposals for a new program and a new type of revolutionary organization, as well as a slate of candidates for the leading organs. Adopting Osinsky's technique of mystification (and this, as we saw, went back to Nechayev), the conspirators decided that the party should present itself to the outside world as the Executive Committee, which in fact would consist of all its full members. Tikhomirov, Mikhailov, and Frolenko were elected to the directing body, the Administrative Commission. Tikhomirov and Morozov would be in charge of the clandestine press. "[Tikhomirov] could easily be described as the head of the conspiracy," Frolenko wrote subsequently,[42] though he felt constrained to add that Tikhomirov was of no use in practical matters. But one can see immediately how groundless this qualification was, for Frolenko continues that Tikhomirov and Mikhailov always acted in unison, "so that for a person who did not know them, it was impossible to separate their ideas—they agreed on every issue and every practical step, in fact had planned everything in advance [of the meeting]." Tikhomirov's proposals were "always listened to, sometimes disputed, but in the end usually accepted."

He was the type of leader who prefers to pull strings rather than occupy the center of the stage. Hence, though Tikhomirov knew how to speak persuasively and, to quote Frolenko again, "was recognized as a forceful thinker and writer," he delegated the keynote address to Mikhailov. This was an indictment ending with a demand for the death of Alexander II. The speaker acknowledged the good deeds of the emperor's early years: the Emancipation and the judicial reforms. But the emperor had committed such crimes as the introduction of a classical curriculum into the high school, and cruel persecution of those who would peacefully carry enlightenment among the people. Should the two good deeds of the early years

---

[42] *The Past,* No. 12 (St. Petersburg December 1906), 30.

outweigh the black tyranny of the last thirteen? (Preposterous as this sounds to us, the changes introduced in education after 1866 were to the radicals among the most opprobrious of the regime's actions. To the authors of the revisions, such as the minister of education, Dmitri Tolstoy, their rationale was the conviction that predominantly scientific and practical education furthered materialism and freethinking, hence was the source of subversion among the young. It was overlooked that classical studies, with their stories of republican institutions of the ancient world and tyrannicides, can lead as readily to "untrustworthy ideas.") Solemnly the assembled members pronounced the doom of Alexander, and entrusted his execution to the Executive Committee as a whole.

The general meeting of Land and Freedom was planned for Tambov. The "pure" Populists were not entirely naïve, and they arranged to gather there and caucus before the arrival of the others. But their plans were frustrated. Unlike their terrorist friends, they had been dispersed throughout rural Russia, and only Mikhailov and Tikhomirov knew the addresses of all the "villagers," and somehow neglected to notify some of the staunchest enemies of "political" terror about the gathering. The ten or so who got to Tambov in advance of the scheduled date, June 20, had to leave in a hurry. During a boat ride, Eugenia Figner began to sing and her sonorous voice attracted the attention of strangers, including policemen. Hastily the meeting was transferred to Voronezh.[43]

The term "congress" sounds pretentious to describe a gathering which had twenty-one people. But two other momentous congresses in the history of the revolutionary movement were also scantily attended: the first congress of the Russian Social Democratic Party in 1898, which had nine participants, and the second in 1903 at which Bolshevism was born, and where there were some fifty-odd delegates.

The Lipetsk contingent moved to Voronezh in its entirety, except for Gregory Goldenberg, who, it was felt, would only harm their cause. Since of the eleven remaining participants, some, like Perovskaya and Vera Figner, were emotionally if not yet intellectually drawn to political terror, the days of Land and Freedom in its old form were obviously numbered.

Superficially, there was little to attract the suspicions of strangers in this common summer sight of groups of young people picnicking in the Botanical Garden and the woods on the outskirts of the city, boating on the river Voronezh. And the charming setting seemed to restore harmony among the contesting factions. The congress opened on a high emotional note: Morozov read the letter smuggled out by Osinsky prior to his execution, in which he beseeched his comrades to continue on the terrorist path. This dramatic appeal and the news that Lizogub and some others in Odessa were about to share Osinsky's fate dissipated even the "pure" Populists' scruples concerning regicide. A majority voted that the organization as a whole should support the assassination of Alexander II. This bitter pill was sweetened for "pure" Populists by Tikhomirov's insinuation that the emperor's death was a necessary prelude to a campaign of rural terror, dear to their hearts, and the rather meaningless proviso that terrorist activities should not preempt more than one-third of the party's financial resources, the remainder going to work among the peasants. The Lipetsk faction's victory was underlined by the election of its two candidates, Tikhomirov and Morozov, to be editors of the party's organ.

But soon it became quite clear that the compromise was a hollow one, and that a split was inevitable. This was demonstrated at one tempestuous meeting when Plekhanov lashed out against Morozov for his propagation of political terror as the only practical means of revolutionary struggle. What were they working for, what did they expect from continuous killings? And here Alexander Mikhailov, no politician, dropped the other shoe: "We shall get a constitution, we shall compel the regime to grant it."[44] The fateful and, to diehard Populists, dirty word had been pronounced. Tikhomirov tried to smooth over the impression created by his friend's indiscretion. But Zhelyabov, forgetting his original reservations about "politics" —it was not in his nature *not* to throw himself body and soul into anything he joined—spelled out the new, scandalous strategy: they would have to forget for the moment about the social question, about "the people," and concentrate on terrorist struggle for political reforms. Sometime later, Plekhanov walked out of the congress.

The remaining members of the Voronezh Congress parted amicably. But within three months it became necessary to dissolve Land and Freedom formally. The Lipetsk faction constituted itself as a new party, the People's Will; their opponents, led by Plekhanov, adopted the name of Black Partition, signifying that the group's aim remained that of original Populism— redistribution of all land among peasant communes, and categorical opposition to "politics," in line with the old cliché that a constitution would merely substitute a new set of exploiters for the old one. For the next few years Black Partition led but an anemic existence, especially after Plekhanov's escape abroad in January 1880. Its historical significance, however, was great. For through its offshoot, the Group for Liberation of Labor, which adopted a Marxist program, it became a direct ideological ancestor of Bolshevism.

But, and possibly more significantly, Lenin's party also inherited much of the conspiratorial technique and mystique of the People's Will, which was to dominate the revolutionary scene during the period immediately ahead.

[44]Aptekman, 369.

THIRTEEN

THE ELEGANT AND SLENDER BOMBS

"But this is sheer Nechayev," Vera Figner protested when Morozov asked her at Voronezh to join the nucleus of the People's Will. She soon joined anyway, but her original characterization was apt. In its conspiratorial techniques the new party was greatly indebted to the example of Nechayev's People's Justice. True, in some respects this was but a logical development of past practices of Land and Freedom, and on one point at least the People's Will was more forthright than its parent organization: its program frankly advocated terror, with no circumlocutions about "disorganization." Also, unlike the People's Justice, the mystification and "end justifies means" philosophy of the conspiracy were not the contrivance or invention of one man, but resulted from a decision by the aggregate membership. Yet the fact remains that the first effect of the new conspiracy, as it is clearly discernible in its founding statute (which was to be kept in strict secrecy) was to perpetrate a gross deception on Russian society. Not only the government and the general public, but the party's sympathizers and supporters were to be made to believe that the People's Will was a large organization with membership running into the thousands. At times this myth was presented even more extravagantly. As Alexander Mikhailov alleged at his trial in 1882, the People's Will was not strictly speaking a party but the activist segment of a still larger body, the Russian Social Revolutionary Party. A political party, he said, implied shared political beliefs; an organization such as the People's Will required solidarity of deeds.[1] This whole vast movement

[1] V.Y. Bogucharsky, ed., *The Trial of the 20,* Rostov on the Don 1906, 69.

was presided over by the mysterious Executive Committee, completely immune to detection, as proved by the fact that no single member of it was ever apprehended by the police.

This was, of course, a gigantic hoax. There was no such thing as the Russian Social Revolutionary Party. And the People's Will and its Executive Committee were one and the same thing. The fiction was to be maintained through strict conspiratorial discipline: "No one has the right to acknowledge himself as a member of the Executive Committee. . . . In the presence of outsiders he is allowed to describe himself only as its agent,"[2] proclaimed Article 7 of the statute. Even in recruiting new members or dealing with the conspiracy's affiliates, a party leader could call himself but an agent of the third (highest) degree. After Gregory Goldenberg's arrest and his revelations, the more perceptive officials began to see through the hoax. Still, on the general public the myth for long had its desired effect. Witness this reaction to Zhelyabov's declaration at his trial: "When we read Zhelyabov's statement that he was merely a third-degree agent of the People's Will, we decided that in view of such strength of the revolutionary party . . . the autocracy could not last much longer."[3] And indeed, psychologically, it was a brilliant ruse. If men like Zhelyabov and Alexander Mikhailov were but mere agents, what superhuman beings must be the leaders! As Mikhailov told his judges, "What can I say about the Executive Committee, the leading organ of the People's Will, except that you can never identify, still less catch, its members."[4]

This deception still confuses many writers. In fact, as the greatest historian of the movement calculates, the *total* membership of the People's Will Executive Committee, from its inception to its virtual demise in 1884–85, was but forty-four, and in view of arrests, etc., the number at any given time was never over thirty![5]

To be fair, this small membership reflected a deliberate decision of the founders, rather than an inability to recruit more. In organizing the conspiracy, Mikhailov and Tikhomirov must have harked back to the injunction of the *Revolutionary's Catechism* of Bakunin and Nechayev: the revolutionary must be a consecrated man "who has no personal interests . . . feelings . . . attachments." And so Article 1 of the statute proclaimed: "Only those may become members of the Executive Committee who place their life and property irretrievably at its disposal."[6] Once in it, they may never resign, but can, at their colleagues' discretion, be granted temporary leave. Any

[2] N. Morozov, "The Origin of The People's Will," in *The Past*, No. 12 (St. Petersburg December 1906), 12.

[3] Quoted in *Hard Labor and Exile*, III (Moscow 1926), 96.

[4] Bogucharsky, 69.

[5] V.Y. Bogucharsky (Yakovlev), *From the History of the Political Struggle—The People's Will, Its Origin, Development, and Fall*, St. Petersburg 1912, 46.

[6] Morozov, 12.

revelation of the party's secrets is punishable by death. If arrested, a member may not testify except on matters already known to the police. If condemned to death, he must not petition the emperor for mercy. New members were chosen by co-optation. Decisions of the majority were unconditionally binding. Such centralization and discipline ran both against the proverbial "broad Russian nature" and the hitherto rather anarchistic atmosphere of the revolutionary movement. Only few were capable of submitting to such a regimen, and even so, among these few was an obvious misfit—Goldenberg.

The hierarchical principle of the People's Will precluded any notion of autonomous affiliates in the manner of Land and Freedom's "separatist members." Instead the Executive Committee was to have agents: people not privy to its membership and decisions and subordinate in every respect, thus in no sense party *members.* The elaborate provisions about various grades of agents again partook of Nechayev-like mystification. When at Lipetsk Morozov asked skeptically why one needed all the gradations, Tikhomirov replied, "So that nobody will know how many grades he must advance in order to reach the [Executive] Committee."[7] In fact the whole business about agents remained tomfoolery. Morozov recalls only one agent in the formal sense, Kletochnikov. Bogucharsky adds a few other names. Whenever it was necessary, the Executive Committee recruited accomplices for a given enterprise, such as the assassination of Alexander II, when all four bomb throwers were nonmembers whom no one had bothered to initiate as agents whether of the first or second degree.

On the other hand, the People's Will pioneered (though there had been precedents in the case of Land and Freedom) the use of what was to become known as "front organizations" with Communism. Thus revolutionary circles, usually under the supervision of one or two members of the Executive Committee, were created among workers, army and naval officers, etc. These were also provincial affiliates. We have a model statute for such local branches, and it parallels the conspiratorial and hierarchical features of the organization of the Executive Committee.[8] Each provincial affiliate was to be run by the "central local group" whose membership was not to exceed five. This basic cell was in strict subordination to the Executive Committee, its members placing their life and property at the disposal of that body without, however, having any share in formulating policies of the party as a whole. The "central local group" in its turn was to create special sections for work among the *intelligentsia,* youth, workers, and for terror. Concerning the latter, the group could at its discretion "pass death sentences on private persons, spies in its midst, and government officials all the way up

[7] *Ibid.,* 13.
[8] Reproduced in *The Past,* No. 12 (St. Petersburg December 1906), 34–35.

to the governor, for whose assassination it must have the sanction of the Executive Committee." The local revolutionary directorate was strictly forbidden to initiate any uprising on its own. Like members of the Executive Committee, those of the "central local group" were not allowed to resign. "Not until the overthrow of the regime," added Alexander Mikhailov in an explanatory note.

A veritable conspiratorial pyramid with the apex designed to be invisible and unreachable. In practice, the People's Will could not quite match this blueprint. But the latter never ceased to arouse the admiration of future masters of the revolutionary craft. "Pointing out the necessity of strengthening party discipline and conspiratorial practices, V.I. Lenin urged us to emulate the example of the heroic People's Will."[9]

The high command of the party, especially Tikhomirov, put great emphasis on finding fellow travelers among intellectual and artistic notables of the day, another preview of Communist tactics. The most signal "catch" in this connection was the reigning radical thinker of the day, Nicholas Mikhailovsky.[10] Along with his profuse open publicistic and literary activity, Mikhailovsky wrote under a pseudonym for the party's organ, *The People's Will,* and was a trusted counsellor though never a member or even an "agent." There were also less intimate ties with some of the surviving literary celebrities of the revolutionary movement of the 1860s such as Shelgunov and Nicholas Kurochkin. The revolutionaries aimed even higher: an intermediary arranged a meeting for one of them with Leo Tolstoy, but the great writer was a firm opponent of violence of any kind. "Even if you could kill your enemies just by pushing a button, this would still be completely senseless and useless, and would not advance the cause of freedom or the people's happiness a single bit," he told his interlocutor, who could ponder these words during his twenty years in Schlüsselburg.[11]

To a casual student of history, the People's Will appears as synonymous with terrorism and anarchism. Yet in fact terror in its scheme of things was but an instrument, and not the most important one, to enable the *party* to seize power. This sharply distinguishes the People's Will from previous revolutionary movements which at least in theory sought power for "the people." Moreover the dominant political concept was that of a *centralized* state. To spell out these objectives with full clarity would have meant alienating many radicals who, though reluctantly reconciled to "politics," were still not ready to abandon the hallowed Populist idea that the Russian

[9]Quoted in S.I. Volk, *The People's Will,* Moscow 1966, 450.

[10]"His influence in the 1870s was enormous and together with Lavrov's, practically all-powerful among the young generation of radicals." D.S. Mirsky, *A History of Russian Literature,* New York 1960, 217. By the *late* 1870s this was no longer true of Lavrov.

[11]Bogucharsky, *Political Struggle,* 182.

state should dissolve into a free federation of communes. Hence the public program of the Executive Committee, published in number three of *The People's Will* of January 1, 1880, written mainly by Tikhomirov, was quite circumspect. "By our convictions, we are socialists and Populists," it began. The goal of the party was "to remove the present regime and to have power vested in a sovereign constituent assembly." While professing full readiness to submit to the people's will as embodied in the assembly's decisions, the party proclaimed as its goals: a parliament based on universal (by implication, male) suffrage; preservation and self-government of the peasant communes, in whom *all* land should be vested; ownership of factories by the workers; full freedom of conscience, speech, the press, etc.

As to the means the party proposed to employ these are, first, agitation and propaganda, and then comes "terrorist activity designed to annihilate the most harmful officials. . . ." The rationale here, it is rather frankly stated, is "to undermine [the people's] conviction in the strength of the regime, to demonstrate repeatedly the possibility of fighting the government, and thus to enhance the revolutionary spirit of the people and faith in the ultimate success of the cause." Equally candidly, the People's Will proposed to infiltrate "the higher ranks of administration and the army."

The closest the conspirators came to revealing their *coup d'état* mentality is in a passage stating, "The party should take upon itself the task of overthrowing the regime, rather than waiting for the moment when the people could undertake it by themselves." And the promise of unconditional submission to the will of the constituent assembly must be read in the light of another statement that during the prospective elections to this assembly "the party must fight resolutely against the candidacy of well-to-do peasants and use every means to assure elections of proponents of communal ownership of land."

As against these professions of democracy and "pure" Populism, to be sure not very convincing, one must counterpose the much more elitist and manipulative tone of another document: the guide to party work.[12] The guide discussed various eventualities. For example, the regime may out of weakness grant a "fairly free constitution"; it would then "be more convenient for the party to *postpone* an insurrection in order that, profiting by freedom, it might strengthen its forces and organization."[13] The best moment for an insurrection would be a national catastrophe of some kind: defeat in war, fiscal bancruptcy, a popular uprising. But even without such favorable circumstances one must carry on: "A skillful system of terror that would simultaneously liquidate ten to fifteen main figures of the regime should plunge it into panic . . . and at the same time awaken the masses,

---

[12]Reproduced in B. Bazilevsky, ed., *The Literature of The People's Will,* Paris 1905 (in Russian), 867–78.
[13]My italics.

thus making it convenient to attack." The important thing would be to seize St. Petersburg, though the ground should be prepared in the provinces so that at the news of the *coup d'état* they would at least remain neutral. While mentioning the need to secure the support of city workers in an insurrection, the guide is entirely silent about the peasants. In contrast, "the main resource in preparatory work [for a coup] . . . must be the securing of the sympathy and help of the *intelligentsia*. The local affiliates of the party have, as one of their principal tasks, "maintenance of contacts with local liberals and constitutionalists," persuading them that "under the current conditions our interests coincide and we should act jointly against the government."

The army—here is the key to success! "One might say that having the army behind us, one could overthrow the regime even without any help from the people, but if you have the army against you, you will not get anywhere even with the people's support." Yet it is useless to try to propagandize the soldiers. "It is much more feasible to gain influence among the *officer corps:* its members are more developed, freer, more susceptible to propaganda." Officer associates of the party should endeavor to advance to important commands and to gain popularity among their men.

One should not neglect *foreign* public opinion: "Our party should acquaint Europe with the threat that Russian absolutism poses to European civilization . . . with the significance of our revolutionary movement as expressing the protest of the *whole nation.* "[14] All that, after acknowledging that it is useless to try to convert the mass of peasants and common soldiers to the revolutionary cause!

Notable by its absence in the program and guide is any reference to the non-Russian nationalities of the Empire. This omission is not accidental. The conspirators remembered how the first Land and Freedom collapsed very largely as the result of the nationalist reaction against all radicalism in the wake of the Polish insurrection of 1863. Yet at the same time, the People's Will wanted to exploit the ethnic problem for revolutionary purposes. Typical in this connection was the correspondence between Zhelyabov and one of the fathers of the Ukrainian national renascence, Michael Dragomanov. The former wanted to enlist Dragomanov's pen and prestige for the cause. The latter, then in migration, balked at this suggestion, pointing out that the People's Will had nothing to say about the oppressed nationalities. Zhelyabov answered soothingly: though one could not say it openly, for this would only make enemies, the revolutionaries thought of the future constituent assembly as presiding over the dissolution of the Empire into its national components.[15] For the moment, he implied, not very diplomatically, there was but little support for Ukrainian separatism.

---

[14] My italics.
[15] *The Past,* No. 3, (Petersburg March 1906), 73.

Where are the Ukrainian Parnells and Fenians, he asked rhetorically, referring to the current troubles in Ireland. But Dragomanov should come along,
for the People's Will was the wave of the future: "One more push and the
regime will fall."[16] The Ukrainian writer remained skeptical.

As is often the case in politics, the People's Will tried to get around the
difficulty by saying different things to different audiences. The average
Russian *intelligent* and peasant were fiercely nationalist, it was believed
quite realistically, and their reaction to raising the national question would
very likely be, "again those damned Poles are behind the whole thing." But
the more advanced industrial worker was supposed to be rather cosmopolitan in feeling, in line with the *Communist Manifesto's* phrase[17] "the workers
have no country." Hence the People's Will propaganda broadside to workers[18] contains a brief statement as to the resolution of the national question
after the revolution: "Those nations which have forcibly been annexed to
the empire are free [to decide] to separate or to remain within the all-
Russian union."

All in all, the above demonstrates the considerable political skill of
the leaders of the People's Will. The party was to send its tentacles
throughout society, concentrating on the most influential and malleable
sectors. Strategy was to be flexible, propaganda attuned to the different
aspirations of different groups. If the conspiracy was veiled in Nechayev-like mystification, then its plan of action blended some traditional points of Populism with a *coup d'état* technique à la Tkachev,
and with a clever bid to transform the *intelligentsia's* benevolent neutrality into active support for the revolutionaries by having the latter
pose as constitutionalists and democrats. Were the contrivers of the
scheme power-hungry manipulators? No, with the exception of Tikhomirov, it is unlikely that any of the members of the Executive Committee ever thought of themselves as future ministers or dictators.

How then can one square the Machiavellianism of the document with the
undoubted idealism of its authors? To begin with they were young. At the
time of its inception in 1879, no member of the Executive Committee was
over thirty. While intellectually they could picture themselves as politicians
pulling the strings of a growing conspiracy, emotionally they proved incapable of such restraint. They rushed into the struggle themselves, disregarding
their own carefully laid schemes for awaiting the right moment, and they
perished. All their stratagems were gradually forgotten while they sought
the death of one man, and by killing him they also inflicted a mortal wound
on the People's Will.

[16]*Ibid.,* 72. This was written May 12, 1880.
[17]Intellectually inclined members of the Executive Committee had read in Marx.
[18]The "Program of the Worker Members of The People's Will," in Bogucharsky, *Literature
of The People's Will,* 878–86.

The psychological ambivalence of the movement is epitomized in Andrew Zhelyabov. Here is a heroic figure which dominates the revolutionary stage between 1879 and 1881, even if, contrary to what is usually believed, he was not *the* leader of the People's Will. Of all the members of the Executive Committee, only Zhelyabov and Tikhomirov could be said to have had truly political minds. But unlike his friend[19] Zhelyabov had a passion for revolutionary *action* and for courting danger—admirable characteristics in a soldier of revolution, less so in a leader.

Of the party elite—as a matter of fact, of the whole galaxy of revolutionary notables encountered in these pages—only Zhelyabov can truly be said to have sprung from "the people." Born a serf in 1850, he owed his social advancement to an enlightened landlord, who sent the bright boy to a boarding school, and then to a government scholarship which enabled him to attend the university in Odessa. Married in 1873 to a daughter of a prosperous citizen of that city, Zhelyabov could well have embarked upon an orderly and successful career. But ambition was coupled in his nature with rebelliousness. From his earliest student days he was drawn to radical and illegal activities, threw himself wholeheartedly into the Populist propaganda of the mid-1870s, was arrested, was tried and acquitted in the trial of "the 193." Childhood memories of serfdom rankled in the mature man, whose alienation from his wife was deepened by her participation in the musical evenings of Odessa society: "They play for aristocrats and plutocrats," Zhelyabov is quoted as saying, and the same source attributes Zhelyabov's refusal to participate in the Kiev terrorist circle in 1878 to his dislike of Osinsky as an aristocrat.[20]

But this antipathy was also due to Osinsky's casual attitude toward terror. Paradoxical as it sounds, Zhelyabov, one of history's most famous terrorists, appears to have had a strong inner revulsion against terror. Here was the man who organized the ruthless pursuit of Alexander II and planned in detail its successful conclusion. Yet the one assassination attempt in which Zhelyabov personally participated failed due to his negligence, another one fizzled as a consequence of his refusing to authorize the use of an adequate quantity of dynamite, and on the eve of the final one, in which he delegated to himself the most dangerous, in fact suicidal role, Zhelyabov walked into a police trap. His behavior after his arrest almost suggests relief; his conduct during the investigation and trial was that of a man eager to pay in full for taking another man's life. Perhaps for one born a serf there was an added burden in striking at the man who had set him and his kind free.

[19]Personal intimacy between the martyr-hero and the future renegade has been usually glossed over by memoirists and historians. But there is no question that Zhelyabov and Tikhomirov were very close. The former stood as godfather to Tikhomirov's daughter.

[20]P. Semyenyuta, "Zhelyabov, Recollections," in *The Past*, No. 4 (St. Petersburg April 1906), 221.

Yet Zhelyabov was far from being a squeamish humanitarian, nor was he lost in gloomy introspection. He was ruthless in using people, his own background helped make him utterly unsentimental in his view of the peasant, and most of his acquaintances stressed the attractiveness of his "broad Russian nature" and vitality. Olga Liubatovich, who was very far from being a worshipper—Zhelyabov annoyed her by getting impatient with her lover, Morozov—recalls him as "radiating gaiety, light, and hopefulness."[21] Strong and handsome, vain about his appearance, Zhelyabov seemed the very antithesis of the stereotype of gloomy, furtive, suspicious conspirator. If Tikhomirov born at another time might have become a Soviet dignitary, then Zhelyabov fits another side of Russian Communism: an incomparable agitator and activist, he would have been in his element in October 1917 and as a leader in the Civil War—but not afterward.

The first issue of the party's organ, *The People's Will,* appeared on October 1, 1879. The circulation of this clandestine journal was between 2500 and 3000. On its masthead was a rather humorous notice: "Permanent subscribers not accepted." "And so after several months of silence, free word can be heard again in Petersburg," began the editorial board's announcement explaining the split in and demise of Land and Freedom, and offering an olive branch to those comrades who had followed Plekhanov into Black Partition. But in a lead article purporting to state the new party's position, Tikhomirov made clear how different it was going to be from that of "pure" Populism. Work among "the people" was proclaimed to be virtually futile: ". . . the peasant believes that if he could only reach 'the little father tsar' all would be well." What were the political facts? The days of the regime were numbered. "It is an iron colossus with feet of clay, with no support in the country." When its inevitable overthrow took place the party must be in on it; otherwise it would condemn itself to centuries of impotence. Hence, "It must attack [the autocracy] with all its forces . . . systematically, insistently, and uninterruptedly . . . and we will be supported by every thinking Russian." It was time to give up "the superstition" that by demanding a constitution the "revolutionaries are pulling out chestnuts from the fire for others [the liberals]." On the contrary, the fall of autocracy would make it possible to work for "the people," for socialism. The article began and ended with Cato's famous words, *Delenda est Carthago,* "Carthage must be destroyed."

This was a clever bid for support from the *intelligentsia:* "In the history of Russian thought, you can hardly find a single man who really served his country without being proclaimed a political criminal"—a soothing reassurance that really the People's Will aimed to continue under the Populist and Socialist banner, and yet a barely disguised avowal that the aim of the

[21] *The Past,* No. 6 (St. Petersburg June 1906), 113.

conspirators was to *seize* power. And not a word about terror. To be sure, this omission was in line with the conspirators' hope of preserving for the general public the fiction that the party (and the organ which bore its name) was somewhat distinct from the Executive Committee, which would be granted the hospitality of its pages to announce "executions" and issue warnings about police spies and *provocateurs.* But, also, once the People's Will was born, Tikhomirov began to lose his enthusiasm for terror as such. He could not have brought off the whole business without the exciting idea of the "execution" of Alexander II. But now that that was in principle agreed upon he hoped to turn the attention of his comrades mainly to more productive labor: securing support among the *intelligentsia* and officer corps for a far more exciting goal: a *coup d'état.* But if he was the party's leader, he was far from being its dictator; that, under current conditions of Russian revolutionary life, was unimaginable. As it was he was under constant fire from Morozov and his girlfriend for his "Nechayev-like" and "Jacobin" tendencies. The lovers, for all their political naiveté, discerned what today we would call Tikhomirov's totalitarian proclivities and protested in the Executive Committee that he was trying to replace one authoritarianism with another.[22]

But apart from such clashes, it proved impossible to slow down the momentum of the People's Will or divert it from its initial goal. On August 26 the Executive Committee confirmed its "sentence" on Alexander II. Preparations for the killing of this one man were to absorb more and more of the attention and energies of the Executive Committee, with the result that all other projected activity suffered correspondingly. In fact the whole ambitious scheme of recruiting "agents," erecting a network of cells among workers and students, etc., became subordinated to the search for accomplices for the assassination. The promising beginning made in infiltrating the officer corps was to be completely wasted.

In trying to pose as respectable allies of the *intelligentsia,* as fighters for constitutionalism, the People's Will was handicapped by many of its members' indiscriminate penchant for violence. A liberal lawyer or doctor might secretly sympathize with the goal of regicide: it would wake up Russian society. He was much harder put to rationalize the occasional approval of crime as a form of social protest. The very first issue of *The People's Will* carried the text of a speech delivered before the Kiev court by Alexander Ovchinnikov. The explanatory note stated that "in his childhood and youth Ovchinnikov was tried several times for various crimes and finally arrested on charges of murder." While in jail, it went on, this promising youth became acquainted with some revolutionaries and under their influence became a new man: the next time he found himself in jail it was as a *political*

[22]Olga Liubatovich in *The Past,* No. 6 (St. Petersburg 1906), 122–24.

criminal. The facts were actually a bit different than this laudatory preface would make us believe. The young man did not entirely give up his old profession but merely combined it with membership in a terrorist circle. Judging by his speech, he also acquired the gift of eloquence. He knew very well, said Ovchinnikov, that the prosecutor, "by pointing out my past, intends to humiliate both me and the party to which I belong. . . . He reminds me of those Biblical Pharisees who blamed Christ for not thrusting away from Himself harlots and publicans." Let the judges realize that they are seeing a new Ovchinnikov: "I was a victim of the social system. . . . What led to my spiritual rebirth? The ideas of the social revolutionary party." Being underage, this eloquent murderer and thief was spared the gallows, but his future career did not justify the high hopes placed in him by the People's Will. Sent to Siberia, he became a police informer and on the side continued his original profession.

To be fair, the People's Will never sought out professional criminals in the manner advocated by Bakunin and Nechayev. But robbery of state funds was held to be within the revolutionary etiquette. We have already mentioned "Alex the Engineer" Yurkovsky and his exploit in Kherson. In December 1880 Zhelyabov sent Frolenko and some others to Kishinev to try their luck there. The police, however, became curious about these strangers who were renting rooms in a house across from the local branch of the state bank, and the plan to tunnel into the depository was abandoned in a hurry.

Over and above all other forms and means of violence, the revolutionaries became fascinated with a relatively novel one: dynamite. "What a long road it has been," exclaims Vera Figner, "from our primitive notions on this subject, the road which took us through many adaptations, tests, and improvements to these elegant and slender bombs constructed for [the assassination] of March 1, 1881, by members of the People's Will."[23] *Seven* times did the conspirators plan to or actually use dynamite before the eighth attempt finally succeeded in killing the Autocrat of All Russia. No such systematic hunt after one man had ever taken place before, and even our own times, so advanced in matters of terror, can show nothing comparable to it.

Chronologically the first attempt was planned to take place in Odessa, through which the emperor was to pass in November 1879 on the way back from his Crimean vacation. But with that meticulousness which characterized the entire history of their enterprise, the conspirators in the eventuality of failure in Odessa were preparing simultaneously two other points of assault: near the little town of Alexandrovsk in the south, and near Moscow.

She could not bear the thought, writes Vera Figner, that as a member of the Executive Committee she would bear moral responsibility for terror

[23]Vera Figner, *Collected Works,* I, Moscow 1928, 122.

without participating in it personally and thus sharing her comrades' dangers. "I was reprimanded for seeking to indulge myself, rather than leaving it up to the organization how best to use me. But then [the comrades] yielded to my entreaties and sent me to Odessa with dynamite."[24] There she took some quite unnecessary risks. But for the moment her craving for martyrdom remained unappeased—the emperor changed his plans and did not go through Odessa.

Alexandrovsk: here in October, "merchant Cheremisov" and his wife, having received a license to build a tannery, settled on the outskirts of the town. This was Zhelyabov and another member of the Executive Committee, Anna Yakimova. As collaborators, Zhelyabov enlisted three workers, all of whom had long-time connections with the conspirators. One of them, Ivan Okladsky, was a fairly typical proletarian fellow traveler of the People's Will. Born in 1859, he had been apprenticed to a factory at the age of ten, and at thirteen was a full-fledged member of the Petersburg workers' "educational" group run by the Chaykovsky circle. After both were busted by the police, Okladsky in 1874 found employment in various places in the south, seeking connection with and being on the periphery of the local radical groups everywhere he went.

In September 1879 Okladsky was working in Kharkov and planning along with some comrades to "expropriate" a state treasury. Here he was visited by Zhelyabov, who proposed to him participation in a much more important enterprise. Okladsky agreed. "He then told me that from this moment I must stop all local revolutionary work. . . . As to the expropriation . . . he said that right now the party had enough money. If the local revolutionaries believed that the enterprise was feasible, let them go ahead, but without me."[25]

In Alexandrovsk Okladsky discovered that his and the other helpers' task was to watch out for guards and strangers while Zhelyabov, who insisted on it, performed all the manual and technical labor needed for preparing to blow up the imperial train when it passed by the town. This was far from child's play: crawling through a gully to dig holes in the railway embankment for two cylinders with dynamite, stretching and concealing wires between them and from the battery to the hiding place where they would be detonated; all this in continuous freezing rain. With that equanimity which often comes from an awareness that one was born to a life of hard luck and deprivation, and which was not to abandon him either before the tsarist or the Soviet courts,[26] Okladsky later related the harrowing experiences of the handful of terrorists. There were several close calls; Zhelyabov

---

[24] *Ibid.,* 184.

[25] From Okladsky's confession in *The Case of the Provocateur Okladsky,* Leningrad 1925, 112.

[26] In 1925 he was tried, convicted, and sentenced for the legally rather questionable crime of having served as a police agent under the imperial government.

suffered from night blindness, his nerves were on edge, and he would scream in his sleep.

Finally on November 18, notified in advance about the time of the passage, Zhelyabov and Okladsky were at their post. As the train passed over the mine Okladsky pulled out the ends of the conduit wires, and Zhelyabov closed the circuit. No explosion. The train sped northward. Vera Figner attributes the failure to Zhelyabov's negligence. Some were to claim that Okladsky was already a traitor and sabotaged the undertaking.[27] But this is silly; he was a fervent revolutionary, and, as the Soviet court established, his later betrayal and service to the police can be dated only from 1881.

After the failure, Okladsky asked his leader a very natural question. Why had he chosen him as a collaborator, an ignorant worker, rather than a man with some technical knowledge in such matters? Zhelyabov, according to him, answered, "In the interests of the revolutionary cause and of the party one must demonstrate to the regime and society that from now on workers and peasants will join in the ruthless struggle to topple the autocracy."[28] Illogical as it sounds (were they supposed to be caught?), in view of Zhelyabov's future choice of terrorists this has a true ring.

If throughout November 18 Tsar Alexander remained blissfully unaware of his close call, then the next night brought a shock. The Moscow enterprise had been prepared more methodically: for more than a month it had engaged the efforts of nine people, all but one members of the Executive Committee. Preliminaries were similar to those at Alexandrovsk: a respectable married couple (in fact Perovskaya and a comrade, Lev Hartman) purchased a little house along the railway tracks. Placing the mine was even more hazardous and laborious than it had been in the south; an underground gallery had to be dug from the house to the railway embankment.

At eleven o'clock on the evening of November 19, the charge was detonated and this time it worked: eight carriages were derailed; the one supposedly carrying the tsar was overturned and wrecked. But it was the wrong train! It was carrying his aides and baggage; the emperor's had gone ahead. There were no casualties.

Still, news of the explosion swept an astounded country. The Executive Committee proudly acknowledged its responsibility for the deed and promised a successful repetition unless the emperor handed over his powers to a constituent assembly. The January 1, 1880, number of *The People's Will*, carrying on the fiction that its editors were not privy to the secrets of the dread Executive Committee, contained some reflections on the daring attempt. It would appear, they concluded, that this mysterious body could not be prevented from carrying out its sentence on the tsar: "The only question

---

[27]Thus in a popular Soviet biography by Vadim Prokofief, *Zhelyabov*, Moscow 1960, 166.
[28]*Case of the Provocateur Okladsky*, 121.

is the time and the means—in brief, the details." But, they added, the details were not without interest. Previous attempts to get rid of the tyrant were primitive: one man with a gun. How different the enterprise of November 19! "It was masterfully thought through and prepared . . . [required] considerable amounts of money and manpower as well as technical proficiency." And so the journal would *guess* that the failure resulted from some chance factor, rather than from the fault of the conspirators. (This was true; the sequence of the imperial trains was changed a few stations before Moscow.) "How encouraging and progressive this application of modern techniques to the [revolutionary] struggle."

It hardly needs adding that the Alexandrovsk story remained unknown to the authorities, and the conspirators, with Kletochnikov briefing them, knew that the police were unable to identify the perpetrators of the Moscow explosion—with one exception. This exception was Lev Hartman. He fled to France, where in January 1880 he was arrested. But in view of the outcry raised by French liberals, led by the aged Victor Hugo, the government instead of extraditing Hartman to Russia, expelled him from France. He died in New York in 1908.

There was to be sure one arrest which had fateful consequences for the People's Will. On November 14 at a southern railway station, a policeman had noticed a young man with a heavy trunk acting suspiciously. Upon examination the trunk was found to contain fifty pounds of dynamite, and the young man was within a few days identified as Gregory Goldenberg, who, acknowledging himself a revolutionary, refused to tell the police anything more. Odessa authorities placed him in the same cell with their agent Kuritsin, and he, treated by Goldenberg as a fellow revolutionary, was able to extract some scraps of information from him and give the secret police some clues as to the young man's state of mind.

The conspirators' intelligence service, i.e. Kletochnikov, could not protect them from the consequences of their own imprudence. It was foolish to co-opt into the Executive Committee a man who was all nerves like Goldenberg. And during November and December of 1879 obvious carelessness—passing revolutionary literature to unreliable persons and carrying it on themselves—brought about the arrest of such key figures of the conspiracy as its chief liaison with Russians abroad, Aaron Zundelevich; its expert on dynamite, Stephen Shiryayev; and Alexander Kviatkovsky, a member along with Tikhomirov and Mikhailov of the Administrative Commission of the People's Will. During the search of Kviatkovsky's apartment, the police found along with the dynamite a plan of the Winter Palace with a big "X" pinpointing the emperor's dining room. It was thought advisable to communicate this to the commandant of the imperial residence. The latter, obviously a moron, was soon able to report that the security arrangements at the palace were in perfect shape: he had the room in question and all other premises above ground thoroughly searched, and nothing was out of order!

The police were unable to extract any information from the men they had arrested. Thus the comrades of the latter could proceed with the plan for the most ambitious enterprise to date: to blow up Alexander II in his own residence.

There was, incomprehensible as it seems, no security check of workmen employed at the palace. Stephen Khalturin, a joiner, long sought by the police as one of the organizers of the Northern Union of Russian Workers, found no difficulty in applying for and getting a job there under a false name. Conditions at the palace, judging from his reports to revolutionary friends, epitomized those of Russia itself: the outward splendor of the emperor's residence concealed utter chaos in its management: people wandered in and out, and imperial servants resplendent in livery were paid as little as fifteen rubles a month and hence were compelled to resort to pilfering. The working crew was allowed to sleep in a cellar apartment directly under the dining suite. An obvious idea came to Khalturin's mind. He communicated it to Plekhanov, whom he had known through his work among the Petersburg workers. Plekhanov would have nothing to do with killing the tsar but obligingly put Khalturin in touch with the People's Will. Shortly afterward this inconsistent enemy of "political" terror left Russia, not to return until 1917.[29]

After Kviatkovsky's arrest, Zhelyabov kept in touch with Khalturin and provided him with dynamite, which he kept bringing in small quantities to his cellar dormitory, where first he hid it under his pillow (!) and then put it in his trunk.

He could not kill the emperor with his own hands, Khalturin confessed to Zhelyabov: Alexander appeared kind and considerate in his few encounters with workmen. At the same time, he protested that to do a good job he would need much more dynamite than his leader was willing to give him. But Zhelyabov would not hear of it: the cellar was separated from the dining room by the ground-floor quarters of the palace guard, and there was no sense in increasing the number of innocent victims.

About dinnertime on February 5, 1880, Khalturin lit a fuse, then walked out of the palace. The explosion wrecked the guardroom, causing eleven deaths and injury to fifty-six others. Delayed by a guest, Alexander was not

---

[29]Aptekman, who was one of those who insisted on his departure, was to write decades later, "Forty-three years have passed since, and when I remember it, I keep telling myself, Joseph, you did well to make him leave. . . . Maybe it is the best thing you have done in your life." O.V. Aptekman, *The Society of Land and Freedom of the 1870s,* Petrograd 1924, 226. Certainly it was the most *important* thing, since it is almost inconceivable that young Lenin would have turned to Marxism without Plekhanov's influence. And Plekhanov, a consumptive, would never have survived Schlüsselburg or Siberia.

at the dining table at the time. But even if he had been he would not have been seriously harmed; due to the insufficient quantity of dynamite only the dining room floor was slightly damaged and a few windows broken.

"In pursuance of a decision of the Executive Committee there took place on the fifth of the month a new attempt on the life of Alexander the Hangman, by means of an explosion in the Winter Palace."[30] The failure was blamed, not quite truthfully, on the emperor's regrettable lack of punctuality. "We view with deep distress the deaths among the soldiers who were forced to guard this crowned scoundrel. But as long as the army supports tyranny, and does not realize that its sacred duty is to be with the people against the tsar, such tragedies will remain inevitable." In this proclamation of February 7 the Executive Committee once more promised to persist in its attempts until and unless the emperor turned over his powers to a constituent assembly. "What is most depressing is that so-called political crime has become a veritable national tradition," Katkov wrote.[31] The usually eloquent defender of absolutism could at first find no other words about this latest in the series of outrages.

In its alarm, the regime resorted to a drastic measure: the creation of a Supreme Commission endowed with virtually unlimited power for fighting subversion. As its head, and thus in effect prime minister if not quite the dictator he has sometimes been described as, Alexander designated Count Michael Loris-Melikov. There were many things that distinguished the count from the run-of-the-mill tsarist bureaucrat. The son of an Armenian merchant, he was a self-made man who had earned a brilliant reputation in border warfare in the Caucasus[32] and, more recently, in the Turkish war. Of all the governors-general Loris was the only one to be pronounced an unqualified success: firm in supressing political disorders, yet capable of earning the trust of the local Kharkov *intelligentsia.* His background and his impecunious student days, during which he counted the poet Nekrasov among his friends, provided Loris-Melikov with a different perspective on Russia's problems than that of most high officials. And he was abundantly endowed with that practicality and wiliness often believed characteristic of his countrymen. He was fairly unique among Russian statesmen of the nineteenth century in realizing the importance of what we would call today public relations. His appointment was greeted with hope among liberals and with considerable nervousness by the revolutionaries. It was largely to appease the former that Loris persuaded Alexander to dismiss that most hated reactionary official, the minister of education, Dmitri Tolstoy. He also took another step that was long overdue.

---

[30]Bogucharsky, *Literature of The People's Will,* 893.
[31]M.N. Katkov, *Collection of Editorials for 1880,* Moscow 1898, 88.
[32]He appears briefly in Tolstoy's *Hadji Murad.*

What's in a name? In politics a great deal. Much of the animosity among educated Russians toward the emperor sprang from the very name of the secret police: the Third Department of His Majesty's Chancery. Loris now proposed to erase the unfortunate association by abolishing the unsavory institution and transferring political police functions to the ministry of the interior. The man he appointed to carry out this reorganization had, though the count was undoubtedly ignorant of it, rather unusual qualifications for the job: he had been a political conspirator himself. Ivan Shamshin was in the early 1860s a prominent clandestine member of the first Land and Freedom, and it is very likely that in his investigation of the doomed institution he examined with special attention its records of those years. In any case, as he confided to a fellow bureaucrat, the Third Department was in a disgraceful mess. Of 1500 people currently in exile for "politically untrustworthy ideas," many were found to have been completely innocent when their cases were re-examined,[33] victims of personal malice or the stupidity of some secret agent or the most common type of amateur informer, a janitor. Affairs of the Third Department were in chaos. "Very often important documents could not be found. . . . When he demanded them, the usual answer was that they had been lost. When he threatened that he would complain to Count Loris-Melikov a search for them would start . . . sometimes they would be found in a clerk's home. . . . Names of the paid informers were withheld from the chief of the police under the pretext they might become compromised." On the other hand, the head of the secret police kept tabs on high-ranking dignitaries and knew all about personal lives of officials, whom they visited, their mistresses, etc. "All that, including gossip concerning ministers and other high personages, was regularly transmitted to the emperor." In view of such titillating occupations, it is no wonder that the secret police were lax in catching the terrorists.

Loris-Melikov panicked officialdom by sending out investigators to check up on provincial administrators and their finances. One such audit had unpleasant consequences for his chief rival within the bureaucracy, Minister of State Domains Valuyev. Sometimes Loris' methods were more direct. When bread and flour prices in Petersburg rose inordinately, the count invited local merchants in for a consultation. How could they interfere with the law of supply and demand? they pleaded. "Loris told them he had been speaking to them in his capacity as a minister. . . . He would now say something as the supreme head of the police. . . . If they did not lower the prices within twenty-four hours, they would be exiled from the capital. This speech did not please the merchants . . . but next day there was an announcement that in order to help the needy, several traders were lowering

[33] Peretz, *The Diary of Yegor Peretz*, Moscow 1927, 3.

their prices."[34] There was to be no Loris within the tsarist government in 1917, when bread shortages in the capital led to the riots which ushered in the Revolution.

On February 20, 1880, Ippolit Mlodetsky shot at and missed Count Loris-Melikov. Loris himself overpowered the would-be assassin, who was tried, sentenced, and hanged within forty-eight hours. The Executive Committee hastened to dissociate itself from this attempt. It was true that Mlodetsky had sought its sanction and help, but he had gone ahead without receiving any decision. "Those circumstances were reflected in the technical side of the attempt. Had Loris been sentenced to death, the Executive Committee would have found more efficient means of putting the sentence into effect."[35] The terrorists were very jealous of their reputation; for all the setbacks, as in the Winter Palace affair and the discovery by the police of the press of *The People's Will* on January 17, 1880, the sheer audacity of the Executive Committee's activities tantalized many among the young and in foreign public opinion, where "nihilist" became a household word. "To attract the attention of the whole world: isn't it already a victory?" wrote Plekhanov to his old comrades from abroad.

There was on the other hand the melancholy fact that Loris-Melikov, with his "dictatorship of the heart," as it became known, was making inroads among the fickle *intelligentsia*. There was the dreadful possibility that he might persuade the emperor to proclaim a constitution of sorts. "There was great rejoicing among our [liberal] journalistic friends when the count was appointed vice-emperor," wrote Mikhailovsky ill-humoredly in *The Bulletin of The People's Will* of August 15, 1880. This representative of moderation within the revolutionary camp was not above denigrating Loris on account of his racial origins: "A typical Asian, cunning and cruel." What irritated Mikhailovsky and his friends most was Loris-Melikov's reputation for liberalism. In fact the Armenian was a loathsome creature, "half wolf and half fox."

Hence the urge became frantic to hasten the "execution" of Alexander II before he should have another opportunity to display his "liberator" side. The terrorists did not want their friends among the *intelligentsia* to fall on their knees before Loris, as Mikhailovsky put it in accordance with the saying, "you should pat the janitor's dog so it would not bite." But for a variety of reasons, three projected dynamite enterprises, one in the spring of 1880 in Odessa, two during the summer in Petersburg, had to be given up.

But on March 10, 1880, an event took place that eventually would spell disaster to the whole terrorist campaign. On that day in the Odessa jail

[34] *Ibid.,* 9.
[35] Quoted in Bogucharsky, *The Literature of the People's Will,* 895.

Gregory Goldenberg began to unravel for the authorities the whole mystery of the Executive Committee. This brilliant achievement from the police point of view was largely the work of the assistant prosecutor of the local court, Dobzhinsky. Even before, he had induced Goldenberg to confess his part in the assassination of General Kropotkin, and then the mother of the unfortunate youth was brought down to Odessa to plead with him to tell all. Dobzhinsky knew how to play on his sense of guilt: has not enough blood been spilled already? He drew Goldenberg's attention to some of the most gruesome consequences of conspiratorial terror such as the (true) story of a father who killed his son after learning that he sheltered revolutionaries, and then committed suicide.[36] The youth was made to believe that there was now a new spirit in the government, which planned thoroughgoing reforms. It is usually alleged that Goldenberg was "bought" by the promise of immunity for his fellow terrorists if he would reveal their names. This is not quite true. In Petersburg, where the prisoner was transferred in April, he was visited by Loris-Melikov himself, who in answer to Goldenberg's question whether there would continue to be death sentences for political crimes answered forthrightly, "I don't know; I don't want to deceive you."[37]

What emerges from Goldenberg's last message to his comrades, written after he had already decided to take his own life, is the impression of not only an unbalanced personality but fantastic political naiveté. The source of all Russia's troubles are seen in classical education: "Russia should thank Loris-Melikov for abolition of the classical *gymnasium,* the source of all revolutionary sentiments and terror."[38] And Goldenberg wrote a letter to Loris imploring him that if there should be fresh executions they be by shooting instead of hanging.

In any case, Goldenberg spilled practically all he knew: the conspirators' identities, methods employed in the assassination attempts of 1879, the whole mode of operations of the People's Will. There was thus no reason for the government to grope in the dark or to remain awed by the mysterious Executive Committee. Though thanks to Kletochnikov's inside information the revolutionaries could take some measures to offset the results of Goldenberg's revelations, the whole saga of the People's Will would have ended right then if the tsarist police had been more efficient.

In the Petropavlovsk fortress, Goldenberg met Zundelevich, who made him aware of the enormity of what he had done. Goldenberg then composed his last letter confession "to friends, comrades, acquaintances, strangers,

[36]"Confession of Gregory Goldenberg," *The Red Archive,* V, Moscow, 1928, 162.
[37]*Ibid.,* 169.
[38]*Ibid.,* 171. Actually Loris only fired the minister of education responsible for the classical curriculum.

honest people of the whole world." He implored them to give up terror; assassinations could not solve anything, he wrote. "No, it is better to take one's own life than another's." On July 15, he hanged himself in his cell. After Kviatkovsky had been condemned to death as a result of Goldenberg's revelations, he wrote to his comrades that they should not consider the latter a traitor, he was clearly unhinged. Most historians have been less charitable.

Though the noose was tightening around their necks, the terrorists persisted in their hunt. The idea of regicide appears to have become more of an obsession than a political goal. Here was a man who had hitherto defied all the stratagems and technical sophistication of the Executive Committee. If nothing should happen to Alexander the masses would indeed believe that God was protecting His Anointed. And for all the past experiences, the emperor still continued to behave as if he had a charmed life. Michael Frolenko watched in impotent fury when, during a stop in Kiev, Alexander stepped out of the imperial train to chat and joke with peasant women who had arrived at the station *en masse* to catch a glimpse of him and his wife.[39] There was an unhealthy excitement. "When will they try it next?" was a question very much in the air, as Russia entered the 1880s. A government official in Odessa gave Frolenko a thousand rubles for his organization but specified how it must be used: "to get *him* and for nothing else."[40]

The more level-headed among the conspirators sensed the danger posed by this fascination with terror, and how it harmed their overall revolutionary activity. Early in 1880 "moderates" on the Executive Committee persuaded the most enthusiastic proponent of assassinations, Morozov, to leave Russia. It was represented to him tactfully that he was in imminent danger of arrest, and that in view of his Olga's expecting a child, they should both go abroad for a while. But fatherhood did not alter Morozov's views. In Geneva he wrote a veritable paean in praise of political assassination. Not only in Russia but everywhere else, he wrote, the state is powerless to cope with terror. All one needs to bring down tyrants and reactionaries is a few determined men and a lot of money.[41] He pooh-poohed the notion that a handful of revolutionaries needed allies. To be sure, they would accept a parliament, but if this parliament proved but a tool in the hands of the upper classes, as was currently the case in Germany, they would start killing again.[42] Who needed liberals, with their mealy-mouthed professions of sympathy for the cause of freedom?

All this was deeply embarassing to the Executive Committee, solicitous

---

[39] *Hard Labor and Exile,* XXIV (Moscow 1926), 21.

[40] *Ibid.,* 22.

[41] N. Morozov, *Terrorist War,* London 1880, 7.

[42] *Ibid.,* 11.

of preserving the fiction that it stood at the head of a large clandestine party and was still courting the liberal camp. Zhelyabov denounced Morozov's pamphlet as quite unrepresentative of the People's Will.

Preoccupation with individual terror was bound to interfere with what was in fact the central point of the People's Will's program: preparations to seize power. Of what good could it be to dispose of the emperor, if after this cataclysmic event the party stood at its original strength, some forty members and a few hundred dispersed and loosely connected sympathizers? The program stipulated the need to organize a strong conspiratorial nucleus within the officer corps. Yet not until the fall of 1880 did the Executive Committee undertake serious steps in that direction, and only in the winter of 1882, when the game was up, did the People's Will come out with a program for a Revolutionary Military Organization. Under conditions at that time, the key provision of the document was to sound almost fatuous: "Members of the organization agree to a military uprising whose aims would be to seize power in order to institute a system of national representation."[43]

The initial effort to organize the armed forces was undertaken by Zhelyabov, whose personality and very Russian temperament fitted him ideally for the task. And yet how could the terrorist-in-chief find adequate time and energy for what should have been the key enterprise of the revolutionary party? The main proselytizer among the officers was a naval lieutenant, Nicholas Sukhanov. Though for obvious reasons the party's rules prohibited its officer-sympathizers on active service from participating in terrorist activities, not only was Sukhanov co-opted into the Executive Committee, but his expertise in mining was enlisted for the assassination of March 1, 1881. One of the officer-sympathizers was to recall an evening at Sukhanov's when Zhelyabov made an eloquent appeal for the support of the Russian army in the struggle for freedom. His audience of twenty or so was deeply impressed both by the man and what he had to say. "The points about the constituent assembly and the need to nationalize land were set out clearly and convincingly. *Had the* [revolutionaries'] *program not emphasized terror they would have subscribed to it right then.*"[44]

It fell also to Zhelyabov to organize the workers' affiliate of the People's Will and to edit the first issues of the clandestine *Workers' Gazette.* But brilliant speaker and oral agitator that he was, as a writer he fell short of the mark. He wrote in an artificially folksy style, intended to read as if it came from the pen of a real worker, but awkward and unconvincing. Here is a sample from the December 15, 1880, issue of the journal: "Push some

[43] *Literature of The People's Will,* 887.
[44] Nicholas Asheshev, *Andrei Zhelyabov, Materials for a Biography,* Petrograd 1919, 67. My italics.

uncensored writing under the tsar's nose, and he will writhe like a devil sprinkled with holy water. But the Russian people love to see free writing, and they will read it eagerly, not only those learned persons the *intelligentsia*, but also a lot of literate working folks." The Petersburg workers' affiliate of the People's Will reached a not very impressive membership of nineteen,[45] and intellectually they were hardly among the elite of their class. One of them, when subsequently on trial and asked by a judge how he understood the term "Populist," replied, "It means that when I cannot find employment I should participate in terror."[46] And indeed, instead of nurturing its industrial workers' section carefully and keeping it in reserve for *the* day, the Executive Committee enlisted its members as helpers in the terrorist campaign.

Steady, patient recruitment, marshalling resources for an opportune moment, were simply not in the style of these people, who aimed to give history a push, as Zhelyabov once put it; that as much as their fascination with terror made them neglect their own longer-range stratagems and goals. By the same token, their youthful exuberance made them oblivious to danger, which especially since Goldenberg's breakdown dogged their steps. There were parties at which the conspirators assembled to sing and dance, forgetting that an aroused neighbor, janitor, or passing policeman might cause the "bust" of the whole Executive Committee. Spiritualism was then in fashion and on one social occasion the assembled convoked the spirit of Nicholas I to question him by what means his son would meet his end. There was some not entirely mock discomfiture when the august spirit informed them that Alexander would die by poison. This was not the way they proposed to dispatch him.

The high point of the revolutionaries' social life was undoubtedly the luncheon party held sometime in 1880 to celebrate Tikhomirov's marriage to Catherine Sergeyeva. It was held in a private room in an elegant Petersburg restaurant, which, wrote Vera Figner, self-consciously if rather nostalgically, she visited for the first and last time in her life.[47] She joined in the celebration though she did not think much of the bride. Sergeyeva, Tikhomirov's "civic wife" for more than a year, was blamed by some comrades for much of his "Jacobin" proclivities and his turn from "pure" Populism toward the idea of revolutionary dictatorship. A native of Orel, she had come there under the spell of Peter Zaichnevsky, author of *Young Russia* and the original Russian "Jacobin." (Zaichnevsky, a revolutionary Sven-

---

[45]*Ibid.*, 69.

[46]Bogucharsky, *The Trial of the 20*, 92. One must take with at least a grain of salt the allegation of another, subsequently a police agent, that as an inducement to join the workers were provided with food, vodka, and women (81). Yet without doubt some did receive money.

[47]In her epilogue to Dmitri Kuzmin, *The People's Will and Journalism*, Moscow 1930, 262.

gali, would gather around him in each of his successive places of exile a harem of young maidens, as Tikhomirov calls it, whom he would indoctrinate with his "Jacobinism" and contempt for Populism. Among the revolutionary alumnae of his Orel circle were also three Olovennikov sisters, one of whom, Maria, was an important member of the People's Will.) Still, Sergeyeva was a member in good standing of the Executive Committee and one of the team keeping track of the emperor's comings and goings.

The wedding lunch was sumptuous, and after it Mikhailovsky, who along with some other luminaries of contemporary journalism was gracing the occasion, ordered curaçao with his coffee. "I asked him naively what it was; then tasted the liqueur and liked it," Figner wrote. Dancing followed, and to general applause the bride, though eight months pregnant, joined in. There was a tense moment at the end. The bill amounted to fifty rubles, a respectable monthly wage. Mikhailovsky, who as Russia's Walter Lippmann could well afford it, pulled out his wallet. It would have been a social disgrace, felt Vera, for an outsider to pay for the revolutionaries' feast, even if he *was* a sympathizer and secret collaborator. But to everybody's amazement Tikhomirov announced that there could be no question of anyone but himself paying the bill for his wedding party. The honor of the People's Will was saved! "I was tremendously relieved," recalled Figner fifty years after the event. For all the mean things Tikhomirov had said about her, the "revolutionary broad" kept a warm spot in her heart for her erstwhile leader. Or, perhaps living in Stalin's Russia she had changed her perspective on the renegade.

While the leader of revolutionary Russia and his bride exchanged vows openly, if under false names, about the same time another potentate was forced to marry in secret. "It has pleased His Majesty Lord Emperor of All Russia, Alexander Nicolayevich, on this day, 6 July 1880, to enter into a second, lawful marriage with Princess Catherine Mikhailovna Dolgorukova," read this solemn but a bit awkwardly phrased document deposited in the imperial chapel. (Catherine was created, also in secret, Princess Yurievskaya.) The morganatic union, though lawful, was scandalous in the eyes of many to whom the secret inevitably became known. The Empress Maria had died on May 22, and on the first day allowed by ecclesiastical rules, forty days after her burial, the emperor hastened to marry his mistress, though both church and court conventions would have required at least a year's delay. This unseemly haste, not to mention Alexander's neglect of the empress during her last illness, was bound to have a depressing effect on the traditional-minded, and on enemies of the favorite. When within a few months the emperor met his doom, the more bigoted were to see in it God's judgment on the notorious adulterer.

The emperor's liaison, if not his immediate remarriage, was well-known also to the revolutionaries. A scabrous parody of Alexander's imaginary diary published in the September 20, 1880, *Bulletin of The People's Will* contains in addition to racial slurs about Loris-Melikov the following item: "Could not sleep all night. What if Dolgorukova is a nihilist?" Her Serene Highness, no doubt out of concern for her spouse's life, was known to favor a more liberal course. She was friendly with Loris-Melikov who, the Armenian's enemies gossiped, flattered her in order to strengthen his hold on the emperor.

Though the Supreme Commission was dissolved in August 1880, Loris, now minister of the interior, became more powerful than before. On his agenda were far-reaching reforms designed, along with the continuing war on subversion, to restore domestic tranquility; the peasant's economic situation was to be improved by abolition of the salt and poll taxes, for example. He clearly saw that some system of national representation was required to conciliate "society," i.e., the *intelligentsia,* but "constitution" was a dirty word to many in the administration and to the emperor himself, as to many a revolutionary. Yet, Loris-Melikov believed, one could slip in some form of countrywide assembly, elected by local government units, by making it advisory, rather than legislative in the Western meaning of the term.

The race between reform and terror was on. In the next six months, partisans of terror were dealt repeated blows. In October sixteen of them, or rather fifteen besides Drigo, faced a military tribunal in Petersburg.[48] Thanks to Goldenberg's revelations, the prosecution was in possession of detailed knowledge about the activities of the accused, the gist of what had gone on at Lipetsk and Voronezh, etc. Most of them behaved bravely, Ivan Okladsky among them. Who could have thought that he would soon turn traitor, he who, when asked for his religious affiliation, replied, "Socialist revolutionary." Said Shiryayev: "Our red terror was but an answer to white terror practiced by the government." Still, a few, not to mention Drigo, showed less than exemplary fortitude. Zundelevich, the "brave Jew" of Tikhomirov's description, behaved impeccably from the revolutionary point of view, but was fed up with his fellow accused who ran on and contradicted each other in testimony. He wrote from jail, "Were a single reasonable man among my co-defendants, this trial, in view of the judges' tolerance, could achieve historical importance. But they are all clumsy. . . . The way I feel [now], you could not imagine a man less dangerous to the government than myself. [If acquitted] I would not spend another day in Russia. In prison I fell in love with America the way I used to be with Germany."[49] Zundelevich fully expected to end up on the gallows and found his actual sentence, lifetime at hard labor, incredible. "It is so lenient I am simply dumbfounded."[50] By conviction and temperament he was a social democrat of the German school, and only a sense of duty toward his

[48]Report of the proceedings in Vladimir Burtsev, ed., *The Trial of the 16,* St. Petersburg 1906.
[49]Quoted from *Hard Labor and Exile* (Moscow 1930), III, 99.
[50]*Ibid.,* 100.

comrades kept him in the People's Will. He went abroad as he planned, but only after twenty-five years in Siberia.

Five others were sentenced to death, and while three lives were spared, Kviatkovsky, the original planner of the Winter Palace explosion, and Andrew Presnyakov, who in November 1879 secured the timetable of the imperial train, had their sentences confirmed and were hanged on November 4. The fact that only two hangings followed the trial of the sixteen had already been a surprise. In a letter smuggled to the accused, Mikhailov rather prematurely had written: "Brothers, I am writing you about the last act of your public activity. . . . Yours is the first crown of thorns, and at the same time laurel wreath, to adorn our party."[51] But these two deaths led directly to the most grievous blow yet to the Executive Committee, the loss of Alexander Mikhailov himself.

The "guardian" of conspiratorial discipline fell prey to his own fantastic imprudence. He was eager to have several copies of his martyred friends' photographs, and went to have a professional make them. Such pictures were often distributed for propaganda purposes, or even sold to replenish the party's coffers. On his first visit to the photography shop, the shop manager tried to detain him and Mikhailov left hurriedly. But incredibly he went back to the same place on November 28, and this time police agents were waiting for him. As was the case with practically every member of the Executive Committee, whether in police hands or still at large, Mikhailov's personal characteristics and his role within the conspiracy were well-known to the police from Goldenberg's depositions. There could be no reasonable doubt about his eventual fate.

Mikhailov's loss had as its almost inevitable sequel the arrest within two months of Kletochnikov. With the "guardian" gone, the conspirators grew careless in dealing with their man in the secret police. And so on the eve of its climactic enterprise, the Executive Committee lost its shield.

Preparations for the final act of the drama gathered momentum after the New Year. Sometime before Zhelyabov had new doubts and forebodings. Shouldn't the Executive Committee postpone the "execution" of Alexander? It has been a bad harvest year and famine was sweeping the southern provinces. If his comrades agreed, he would go to the lower Volga region and try to stir up a peasant uprising. This relapse into pure Populism was viewed by his comrades with incomprehension and disapproval: it was now or never as far as the emperor was concerned. Possibly the more intelligent terrorists realized that a few more months and Loris-Melikov might beat them to the punch; some phony reforms, and the already wavering *intelligentsia* would fall to its knees before the Tsar Liberator and make the assassination morally impossible. But some by now could think of nothing

[51]*March 1, 1881: Recollections,* Moscow 1931, 29.

but killing. Maria Olovennikova (usually known by her first married name, Oshanina), who headed the Moscow branch of the People's Will, describes one such type: "I was unpleasantly struck by [Gregory] Isayev. He was far from stupid, and much had been expected from him. Now it turned out he could talk of nothing except dynamite and bombs."[52] She went back to Moscow with a heavy heart: Zhelyabov had confided to her that he expected the whole Petersburg organization to be broken up before or after the attempt. "Remember, if you in Moscow do not take over, it will go hard on us."

Their nerves strained to the utmost, the terrorists were grasping at straws. Shiryayev, incarcerated in the Alexis Ravelin, managed to smuggle out the news that Nechayev, long assumed dead, was not only alive but up to his old tricks. There ensued some correspondence between the Executive Committee and the man whose "methods" they had so often condemned. They communicated their plans concerning Alexander to the prisoners—a fantastic imprudence, since a bribed prison guard could easily win not only his pardon but money and honors by telling his superiors the whole business. For some incomprehensible reason the conspirators, especially Zhelyabov and Vera Figner, became greatly excited by the prospect of springing Nechayev. But it would have to wait. . . .

On December 3, 1880, the couple Kobozev rented the basement premises in No. 4 Little Garden Street, where they established a cheese shop. The street lay in the path the emperor usually took from the Winter Palace to the Hippodrome, where every Sunday various guards' units held exercises and a parade. Less frequently he would vary his route, as the observation team reported, by taking the Catherine Canal Road.

The proprietors of the cheese shop were in fact Anna Yakimova and another member of the Executive Committee, Yuri Bogdanovich. Beginning in January, the "Kobozevs" lived on the premises, and every night a number of conspirators would assemble in the basement for the arduous task of digging a tunnel under Little Garden Street. This was to be the most thoroughgoing terrorist venture yet. If the mine failed to go off or the emperor's carriage followed a different route, the terrorists would have in reserve four bomb throwers. If they too somehow failed, Zhelyabov, who was to direct the whole operation, would attack the tsar with a knife. Thus, for all the taunts about imperial cowardice, the assassins counted on Alexander's fearlessness, counted on his not leaving immediately, as he had not after Karakozov's shot, the scene of an abortive assassination.

In choosing members of the assassination team, Zhelyabov displayed considerable lack of scruples. In his last message to his comrades, Alexander Mikhailov undoubtedly had his dead friend in mind when among his

[52] *The Past*, No. 6 (St. Petersburg June 1907), 7.

requests to them he begged and charged them, "Brothers, do not send mere youngsters to their deaths. Allow them to grow spiritually and to develop their character."[53] But the collaborators Zhelyabov chose from outside the Executive Committee were questionable not only on account of their immaturity and lack of comprehension of what they were getting into. Vasili Merkulov, who posed as the "Kobozevs' " shop assistant, was nineteen years old. His life story is strikingly similar to Okladsky's: an industrial worker, orphaned at nine, he was brought up by revolutionaries and ended up as a traitor and police agent. Timothy Mikhailov was designated to throw the first bomb, so that it could be claimed that the tsar had perished by the hand of one born a peasant. Judging by his testimony at the trial he was a man of subnormal intelligence. He was hardly able to put together a sentence, and, asked what the purpose of terror was, he answered: "To kill spies and bad bosses." A dispassionate observer noted at his trial that he was close to being a moron.[54] Nicholas Rysakov, nineteen, who did throw the first bomb and who then told all he knew to the police, was a typical example of what Alexander Mikhailov meant: psychologically and politically immature, he simply did not understand the consequences of joining what appeared to him as an exciting and glamorous venture. He was a bright but raw youth, mesmerized by Zhelyabov, and his very exaltation at being permitted to participate in the historic deed presaged his ultimate breakdown. Ivan Yemelyanov, twenty-one, was also recruited because of his peasant origin, and Zhelyabov overlooked the fact that because of his unusually great height he was bound to be conspicuous. Yemelyanov was eminently sane, but by the same token his behavior before the court and later on in exile fell short of the standard expected of a revolutionary. He denied his participation in the assassination, petitioned for pardon, and, eventually freed, became a substantial Siberian entrepreneur. The man who actually killed Alexander was Ignat Hrynievicki. And in choosing him Zhelyabov disregarded a revolutionary convention of some years' standing: that because of the possible consequences for the whole ethnic group, a Pole should not be directly involved in an attack on the tsar. A similar injunction was violated by choosing a Jewess, Gesia Helfman, as hostess for a conspiratorial hideaway for the assassins. And, indeed as we shall see, her participation in the affair of March 1 did help bring about a wave of anti-Jewish progroms which swept the Ukraine in the spring and summer of 1881.

It is unlikely that a man as intelligent and thoughtful as Zhelyabov failed to consider these consequences or remained blind to the moral and intellectual defects of some of his chosen. But the fact is that the revolutionaries were shorthanded. In January, three more members of the Executive Com-

[53]The Testament of A. Mikhailov," in *The Past,* No. 2 (Moscow February 1906), 173–74.
[54]*Trial of the Accused of March 1, 1881,* St. Petersburg 1906, 60, and Peretz, 54.

mittee were arrested, including Morozov, caught on his return to Russia while crossing the frontier. With only about twenty of the Executive Committee left at large, they could not afford to be choosy in selecting accomplices. Yet it was not only unscrupulous but foolish to engage people like Timothy Mikhailov and Rysakov.

The strain on Zhelyabov was increased by the circumstances of his private life. For some time now he and Perovskaya had been living as man and wife. Sophia was a much more uncompromising believer in terror than her lover was. Rysakov was to tell the police that he heard her argue "that after disposing of the father [Alexander II] one should go after the son. . . . [She believed] deeply in the possibility of revolution when the supreme power has at least temporarily been annihilated and government had passed into the hands of officials who have no authority among 'the people'. . . . The peasantry, oppressed by hard life, suffering from hunger, and *expecting an improvement in its situation only from the tsar,* upon hearing that the old one had been killed and the new one had been too or was about to be, and that all power has passed into the hands of the 'lords,' would rise."[55] The impassioned woman forgot that in addition to the future Alexander III the emperor had four other sons.

Zhelyabov's inner turmoil and nervous exhaustion may help to explain his behavior on the eve of the fateful date. On February 12 the police had received information from an agent abroad, it was subsequently claimed, that a revolutionary with the nickname Milord had been summoned from Odessa and was currently living in St. Petersburg. It was quite likely that Okladsky, who had by now begun to "sing," was able to inform the police that Milord, called so by his comrades because of his elegant appearance, was Michael Trigoni. But whatever the case, it would have been prudent for Zhelyabov to avoid contacts with Trigoni. Of all the members of the Executive Committee Trigoni alone continued to live under his legal name, and, as the authorities knew, he had been a friend of Zhelyabov's since their school days. It was clearly suicidal for Zhelyabov on February 27 to repair to the boarding house where Trigoni was living.

Trigoni had been under observation for some time, and Zhelyabov, entering his room at seven in the evening, told him unconcernedly that the place smelled of police agents. His friend went out to order tea and was immediately seized. Zhelyabov might have tried to brazen it out: he was just a casual acquaintance, etc. Instead he ran, without even pulling out the gun which he carried on him, and thus ensured his arrest. At first he refused to give his name, but when brought to the police headquarters, he was confronted by Dobzhinsky, the Odessa prosecutor who in view of his brilliant work with Goldenberg had been brought to the capital. He had known

[55]Rysakov's Confessions," in *The Red Archive,* VI, Moscow 1926, 188. My italics.

both prisoners in connection with their Populist agitation in the mid-1870s. "I remember you from 1874," he said to "the man with a remarkably handsome face and long black beard."[56] "Your humble servant," acknowledged Zhelyabov with a laugh. With Trigoni Dobzhinsky was almost reproachful: didn't he know better than to use his real name, when the police for long had had their eye on him? The very same evening Zhelyabov ensured that whatever else happened in two days he would not escape the gallows: quite voluntarily he confessed he had been the organizer and chief executor of the attempt to blow up the imperial train at Alexandrovsk. Some accounts have him saying, as he acknowledged his identity, "This won't help you." But this is an even more absurd invention than Karakozov's "I did it for you, brothers." Zhelyabov was hardly the man to tip off the authorities that something else was coming.

The news of his arrest, though it threw Perovskaya into despair, only fortified her resolve to go through with the attempt against Tsar Alexander planned for Sunday, March 1. There was another reason for not postponing the venture. For some time now, the police officer within whose precinct it was situated had been warning his superiors that there was something suspicious about the cheese shop at No. 4 Little Garden Street: young men and women coming and going at all hours of the night. The engineering expert who in the guise of a sanitary inspector was sent to investigate the premises on the morning of February 28 proved himself a worthy colleague of that commandant of the Winter Palace who was so reassuring about its security. There were numerous barrels in the storeroom (filled with earth from the excavation), but it did not occur to the investigator to look inside one, or to reflect that cheese does not usually come in huge barrels. He did notice that the floor was damp (water had been dripping from the wet soil inside the barrels). Yes, they had spilled some milk, the proprietor explained. The official pronounced himself satisfied and left.

At three in the afternoon, members of the Executive Committee assembled in Vera Figner's flat. It was decided to go through with the assassination. There was still a lot of work to be done. Isayev was dispatched to arm the mine in the underground tunnel. Others spent the evening and night preparing the explosives and fashioning bombs out of kerosene cans. The technical side of the preparations had for long been under the supervision of Nicholas Kibalchich, even though this taciturn and withdrawn former engineering and medical student had never been formally inducted into the Executive Committee. After fifteen hours of incessant labor, at eight o'clock in the morning of March 1, the task was finished and the bombs were carried to another conspiratorial hideout where they would be issued to the four who would carry out the "execution."

[56] *The Past,* No. 3 (Moscow, March 1906), 9.

News of the arrest of Zhelyabov, known from Goldenberg's and Okladsky's depositions to be a key figure in the conspiracy, was brought to Alexander on February 28. But during these last hours of his life the emperor had another and more serious reason to feel relieved. He had finally approved the project to summon elected representatives to advise on legislation, and to allow some of them to join the State Council, whose members had hitherto been nominated. For long he had hesitated—he was afraid, he said once, that it would be a step toward a constitution, and that he should leave it to his son to inaugurate *his* reign with reforms. Finally on the morning of March 1, he told Loris-Melikov his mind was made up, and that the ministerial council to be held on March 4 should work out the details of the project and of his manifesto. With the decision behind him and the terrorist chieftain under lock and key, the emperor's mood, as the courtiers were to recall, became very relaxed. His widow was to relate to the imperial family's physician, Dr. Serge Botkin, a very intimate episode that took place that morning,[57] news which so shocked the distinguished doctor that he would never see Princess Yurievskaya again. After lunching with his morganatic wife and their small children, the emperor set out for the guards' review at the Hippodrome.

The route he took avoided Little Garden Street. He thus arrived unharmed at his destination about 1 o'clock. Had he, upon leaving the review, which took only about forty minutes, driven directly back to his residence the same way he came, it is likely he would have survived, since three of the bombthrowers were still lurking along Little Garden Street. (Timothy Mikhailov had arrived at the designated spot, decided that he had no stomach for the business, gone back to Gesia Helfman's apartment, and turned in his bomb.) But instead he decided to pay a brief visit to a cousin residing at the Michael Palace, from which almost inevitably he would have to drive by the Catherine Canal Road. There was time therefore for Perovskaya to signal the bomb throwers to shift to positions along the canal. Shortly before three o'clock the emperor's carriage, accompanied by six mounted Cossacks, passed Rysakov's station. That morning, his landlady was to testify, he had been in an uncharacteristically gay and talkative mood.[58] Now, he tossed his bomb under the carriage. The explosion hurled one of the Cossacks and a bystander to the pavement, but Alexander was completely unharmed. He ordered the driver to stop and got out. Rysakov was being held by soldiers and policemen, and the emperor, following his fatal habit, walked up to him. At the same moment a military man asked the emperor if he was hurt. "No, thank God," he replied, "but—" and he pointed out the wounded. Here, all the witnesses insist, Rysakov said ironi-

[57] *The Diary of A. S. Suvorin,* Moscow 1923, 66.
[58] *Trial of the Accused of March 1, 1881,* 93.

cally, "Still thanking God?"[59] Rysakov denied this allegation[60] but it stuck and, most likely, cost him his life: except for the fatal effect this levity created, he would very likely have received only a life sentence; he was, after all, a minor. Alexander turned away and began to walk back toward his carriage, coming within a few feet of Hrynievicki, who was leaning against a railing with his bomb wrapped in a newspaper. A few days before the young Pole had written, "Alexander II must die. . . . And we, his assassins, will die with him. . . . Our dear and unhappy country will require many more victims to become free. . . . I shall not be there for the final struggle. . . . But through my death I am doing all I can . . . so that our cause shall triumph."[61] And now he accomplished his dreadful errand.

Both Hrynievicki and Alexander lay mangled and bleeding. His lower extremities torn to shreds, the emperor whispered that he wanted to be taken to the Winter Palace "to die."[62] Placed on a sleigh and conveyed there, Alexander, according to the officers who accompanied him, was still able to talk and enquired whether any of them were wounded.[63] But it is most unlikely that he could have remained conscious so long. It is not only revolutionaries who are prone to fantasies about such occasions. All efforts of Dr. Botkin and his colleagues proving unavailing, the emperor expired at 3:35 P.M., some fifty minutes after the second explosion.

"I cried as did the others. The heavy nightmare which for a decade tortured young Russia was gone. This moment when we took the tsar's life paid us for all: for the horrors of prison and exile, for the brutal repression of hundreds and thousands who thought as we did, for the blood of our martyrs. A heavy burden has been lifted from our shoulders; reaction was about to end and give way to a new Russia."[64]

---

[59]Not, as the remark is usually rendered, "Too early to thank God."

[60]*Trial of the Accused of March 1, 1881,* p. 59.

[61]*First of March 1881 Recollections of Participants and Contemporaries,* Moscow 1931, 22. It is not clear which our "dear and unhappy country" was, Poland or Russia.

[62]*Trial of the Accused of March 1, 1881,* 90.

[63]*Ibid.,* 80.

[64]Figner, I, 248.

VI

THE FALL

FOURTEEN

AFTER THE GALLOWS

People more perspicacious than Vera Figner were ready to believe, when news of the tsar's assassination was officially confirmed, that a new Russia was about to be born. Mikhailovsky thought that a revolution was inevitable. Excitement bordering on exhilaration reigned among the *intelligentsia* sympathetic to the revolutionaries. "They finally got him" is a not unfair description of the mood of "liberation movement" veterans.

But almost immediately excitement began to give way to apprehension. Perhaps the more sober-minded opponents of the autocracy recalled Herzen's words after Karakozov's shot: "Only among savage and decadent nations is history made by assassinations." A friend reported Turgenev's reaction: "I saw him sobbing bitterly and disconsolately." The great writer who in *Virgin Soil* had portrayed the revolutionaries with considerable sympathy, attended a memorial mass for Alexander II.[1] For Lenin's father, "The reign of Alexander II, especially its beginning, [had been] a period of light."[2]

The terrorists themselves were not psychologically prepared, paradoxical as this sounds, for the event for which they had worked so long and arduously. How can one otherwise explain their failure to come up with any program of action, any rousing manifesto, on the day of their triumph? The announcement by the Executive Committee "of the execution of Alexander

[1] *The First of March, 1881,* Moscow 1933, 165.
[2] Anna Ulyanova-Yelizarova, *Recollections of Alexander Ulyanov,* Moscow 1930, 67.

359

in pursuance of the sentence passed on him on 26 August 1879" was grotesque in its disingenuousness, "We remind Alexander III that anyone who oppresses the nation is an enemy of the people." How often would the last term resound during the darkest period of Russia's oppression under Stalin! The Executive Committee now appealed to all brave and patriotic citizens for help "should Alexander III force [!] the revolutionaries to fight against him."[3] Two other documents, prepared in advance for the occasion, are also so embarrassing in content and style that they are usually passed over in silence by historians partial to the People's Will. They exhibit an unconscious mixture of lingering awe of the throne, uncertainty about how "the people" will react to the murder, and hatred of the deceased. One purporting to have been issued by "worker members of the People's Will" affects the popular language:

> On this first of March, Alexander II, torturer of his people, was killed by us socialists. He defended only the rich and himself, feasted and lived in luxury, while the people starved. . . . The tsar ought to be a good shepherd ready to die for his flock. Alexander was a wolf. Now we have Alexander III on the throne. Don't let him follow in the footsteps of his father; let him call to the senate as his advisers those whom the people will elect. Then the tsar will give land to the peasants and will lower taxes. Send petitions to him, you in the towns and villages. If he doesn't listen to the people and gets to be like his daddy, he too will have to be *replaced*. Brothers, remember it is a sin to obey an oppressor.[4]

The "workers" evoke the example of such famous revolutionaries as Ivan Okladsky, who was at the time quite busy helping the government round up the assassins. The Executive Committee appeared here in the guise of "Committee of People's Will," which also signed another "announcement" of the emperor's death addressed to "honest members of rural communes, Orthodox peasants, all Russian folk." The obvious and condescending assumption was that many peasants would take the term "people's will" literally and anyway would not understand expressions like "party" and "executive." The gist of this second announcement, couched in an even more phony-sounding, folksy language, repeated the gist of the "workers' " message, with one significant variation: it was not stated *who* killed Alexander. Having listed the tsar's sins, which somehow brought about his "terrible death," the committee went on to command "the Orthodox Christian folk" in a rather imperious way:

> And this here announcement to be read to everybody at the village meetings, and no man can dare to stop it. And what the meeting will resolve to be dispatched with a dependable spokesman directly to His Majesty the Emperor in St. Petersburg.

[3] *Literature of The People's Will,* 898.
[4] *Ibid.,* 899. My italics.

. . . Open the eyes of Our Sovereign Lord to how the peasant suffers in this Russian land worse than he did under the Tartar yoke."[5]

Only on March 8 did the conspirators meet to consider a more honest statement of their case. What emerged from this consultation was the celebrated *Letter of the Executive Committee* to Alexander III. Composed by Tikhomirov, it was then shown to Mikhailovsky, who made some insignificant changes. Though in a way also disingenuous, the *Letter* has a certain dignity and eloquence entirely missing in the "announcements."

"Your Majesty! With full understanding of the heavy feelings You must be experiencing, the Executive Committee still has no right to yield to the natural sense of delicacy. . . . There is something higher than the most sacred feelings of a [private] person. This is the duty to one's country."[6] The letter went on to point out the futility of all governmental measures hitherto directed against the revolutionaries. If the regime continued the policy of repression, "confidence in the government will continue to decrease, the idea of revolution, of its possibility and inevitability, will continue to grow in Russia. . . . A terrible explosion will climax the process and destroy irretrievably the old order." The Committee wanted to avoid such a gruesome eventuality, but if things went on in the same way, it would have no alternative. "Sire, don't be deceived by your flatterers and servants," for the regicide has been greeted by a "vast proportion" of the population with joy and approval.

Still, further bloodshed could be avoided. "We turn to You as a citizen and an honest man." Let the tsar summon representatives from the whole nation; release all political prisoners. Let elections take place under conditions of full freedom. "We declare before our country and the whole world that our party would submit unconditionally to the decisions of the Constituent Assembly . . . and will desist from any acts of violence against the government sanctioned by the Assembly. Yours is the choice, Sire. We can only pray that Your wisdom and conscience will dictate the path consistent with Your dignity and obligations, and with Russia's happiness."

Ten thousand copies were printed and distributed on March 12. One done on vellum paper was mailed to the Winter Palace. The conspirators were much impressed with their "moderation and tact," as Vera Figner noted. Probably only Tikhomirov realized that the real addressee was not the thirty-five-year-old prince who on March 1 had become Alexander III, but those among the liberal *intelligentsia* who after their initial intoxication with the deed now stood numbed and fearful.

Instead of acknowledging the Executive Committee's offer, the regime continued the ruthless pursuit of its members. As Figner put it, "White

[5] *Ibid.*, 901.
[6] *Ibid.*, 903.

terror has begun." Already on March 2 Rysakov, his bravado gone, had begun to spill to the police all he knew. The same night they raided Gesia Helfman's conspiratorial hideout. She was arrested, her companion shot himself. Next morning a burly man walked into the flat and into the arms of the police. It was Timothy Mikhailov, who compounded his stupidity by trying to shoot his way out. Her friends begged Sophia Perovskaya to leave the capital, but, obsessed with the idea of rescuing her lover, she would not. On March 10 she was stopped in the street, and the agent, refusing a bribe, arrested her. Then it was the turn of Kibalchich.

The news of the tsar's assassination redoubled Zhelyabov's determination that he should not escape the gallows. Unmindful of the woman who loved him, of his friends, and seemingly even of the cause he served, he spared no efforts to make certain that he should be considered the chief figure behind the events of March 1. On March 2, before he learned that Rysakov had turned informer, and fearful that the unfortunate boy would be the only one tried in connection with the murder, Zhelyabov wrote to the prosecutor, "It would be a startling injustice to spare my life. . . . I have several times attempted to assassinate Alexander II and did not physically partici- pate in his actual murder only because of a stupid accident. . . . I am afraid the regime might want to follow the letter of the law rather than justice, and in view of the absence of any formal proofs against me will adorn the new reign with only one corpse, that of the young hero. . . . I protest . . . and demand justice for myself. It would be sheer cowardice on its part if the government were to hang only one man rather than two."[7] In his passion for heroic martyrdom Zhelyabov overlooked both conspiratorial discipline—he could not have been absolutely sure that the Executive Com- mittee would assume the responsibility for the assassination—and any com- passionate consideration—he might have said, "hang me *instead* of Rysa- kov," and even before he knew about Rysakov's betrayal he volunteered the information that Rysakov had begged to be in on the killing.[8] There was nothing subconscious about his own death wish. But does not his behavior suggest that something in him sought to bring down the whole terrorist enterprise? To be sure his party would disintegrate. But in years to come the example of the man who feared nothing unless it was his own conscience inspired many others to follow the path of terror.

The government was in a hurry to get on with the trial and, as it confi- dently expected, the hangings. Formal proceedings before a special panel of the senate opened on March 26—after some hesitation the government had decided on an open trial rather than a court-martial. In addition to Zhelyabov and Rysakov, Timothy Mikhailov, Kibalchich, Helfman, and

[7]Nicholas Asheshov, *Andrei Zhelyabov, Materials for a Biography,* Petrograd 1919, 74.
[8]*Ibid.,* 83.

Perovskaya were the accused. Hryniewicki had died without recovering consciousness and was not identified until April; the reserve bomb thrower, Yemelyanov, and the "Kobozevs" were not apprehended and tried until later.

None of those facing the court—even Zhelyabov—had been so responsible for the terror campaign as Alexander Mikhailov, in prison since November. But for some reason he also was not tried until one year later.

For three days the world's attention was riveted on the courtroom drama in St. Petersburg. Foreign public opinion could not but be impressed by Zhelyabov's impassioned statement of the revolutionaries' case against the government, by the quiet courage and dignified demeanor of the youthful Perovskaya—she looked no more than a teen-ager—and by Kibalchich's bitter avowal of what led him to devote his scientific talents to destruction rather than, as he had dreamed, to helping his own people. If there was one event which caused the West to look at the "nihilists" in a new light, no longer merely as sinister conspirators and senseless killers, it was certainly the Trial of the six.

But within Russia the impression produced was quite different from, in fact almost opposite to, the one created by Vera Zasulich's trial. Zhelyabov, who alone of the accused refused counsel and defended (more properly, helped to convict) himself, clearly overdid his heroics. He chortled at the prosecutor's rather florid description of the tragedy and thus enabled the latter to score a telling point: "I am interrupted by Zhelyabov's ironic laughter, this laughter he indulged in during the investigation. . . . While people weep the Zhelyabovs gloat."[9] Zhelyabov tried valiantly to preserve the mystique of the Executive Committee as a dread and invulnerable force —he and the others but its agents—but again he spoiled the effect through exaggeration: when, he said, he had asked his group who would help him to fulfill the mandate of the Committee, forty-seven people had volunteered their services. Nonsense, retorted the prosecutor, Nicholas Muraviev, one had here "just a few Zhelyabovs . . . intelligent, systematic killers."[10]

No listener at the proceedings or reader of the transcript could fail to be depressed by the appearance of Rysakov. He was frightened and bewildered, and occasionally babbled nonsense; he was an enemy of violence, he said, who joined in the assassination because he believed it would put an end to terror.[11] Timothy Mikhailov stood as living testimony to the unscrupulousness of the conspirators in selecting their accomplices: twentyone, he had learned to read only two years before. He said, "I belong to a party that defends the workers and not the one that seeks an overthrow [of

[9] *Trial of the Accused of March 1, 1881*, St. Petersburg, 1906, 146.
[10] *Ibid.,* 189.
[11] *Ibid.,* 35.

the government] because not being developed or educated enough I do not know about such things."[12] Almost equally appalling was Gesia Helfman's story. She had fled from her Orthodox Jewish parents at the age of sixteen because they wanted to force her into a marriage, and eventually she found shelter with the revolutionaries, where, mainly through inertia, she had moved from one conspiratorial circle to another. It was undoubtedly naiveté rather than an awkward attempt to ingratiate herself with the court that made her explain that she had joined the revolutionary movement "out of love for the people, the love my generation learned from the great Tsar Liberator."[13]

Muraviev's conduct of the case for the prosecution was pronounced by contemporary connoisseurs of such things as a classic masterpiece, worthy of comparison with Alexandrov's defense in Vera Zasulich's trial. As in the latter, Muraviev's summation was long (five hours) and tearful. Describing how the emperor got out of his carriage after the first explosion, the prosecutor drew attention to his solicitude about the wounded: "The saddened Master of the Russian land leaned tenderly over the suffering son of the people." They had heard from the soldiers who picked up the stricken tsar, "like children soothing their dying father," that even then he had asked if others were hurt. Nor did Muraviev—then still a young lawyer, whose performance would bring him promotions, culminating in an ambassadorship—neglect the ideological aspect of the case, launching into a spirited defense of the autocratic principle: "[Under it] we have been spared class hatreds, dominations by the bourgeoisie, and alienation of society from the government. . . . Subversion is impotent, and will remain so, to undermine the Russians' age-old loyalty to the throne."[14] This was not a very good prophecy, but in the trauma of the moment most of his fellow citizens would have agreed.

The verdict was inevitable: six deaths. Yet even if one believes in capital punishment it is hard to justify the death sentence for Rysakov, a minor who cooperated with the police, and for Timothy Mikhailov, who in addition to his limited intelligence had turned back from his lethal errand. Both petitioned for mercy. Kibalchich's last words to the court were not about his own fate, to which he was completely resigned, but about a scientific paper which he had worked on even in jail and which contained a very vague plan for a system of rocket propulsion.

The sentences were confirmed, except that for Gesia Helfman, who was discovered to be pregnant. She died in jail a year later. Tolstoy wrote to Alexander III imploring him, as a Christian, to pardon his father's murder-

[12]*Ibid.*, 225.
[13]*Ibid.*, 204.
[14]*Ibid.*, 187, 191.

ers, and Vladimir Soloviev, then a young professor of philosophy and later a famous writer and mystic, pleaded in the same vein in a public lecture on March 28: "Let the Tsar and Autocrat of Russia show by deed that above all He is a Christian and the leader of a Christian nation."[15] Tolstoy's letter remained unanswered, and the only consequence of Soloviev's appeal was that he was prohibited from lecturing in public (but not, as it is sometimes asserted, dismissed from his chair).

On the morning of April 3, the condemned were placed in carts and, to the roll of drums, paraded to the square where the scaffold with gallows had been erected. Each of the five bore a placard with the inscription "Regicide." A huge throng, estimated by the correspondent of the London *Times* at 100,000, crowded the streets along the way. A last embrace by Sophia Perovskaya for all her companions except Rysakov, and the hangman started on his task. The technical side of the execution, an English journalist reported, was handled very unprofessionally. "The Russian manner of hanging people is but simple strangulation. The whole business was most painful to the viewers as well as to all the participants."[16] At 9:58 the gruesome ceremony was over, there were five dead bodies, and a legend was born.

The legend inspired future generations of revolutionaries, and its echoes were still strong enough in 1934 to worry Stalin. "Look," he said to a lieutenant, "if we bring up our children on stories of the People's Will, we shall make terrorists out of them." Terror like practically everything else, Stalin believed, should be a state monopoly.

But in the immediate context, March 1 and its consequences dealt a more crushing blow to the Executive Committee than to the edifice of autocracy. "[The events] raised the Committee in the eyes of its partisans to unsurpassed heights . . . created an atmosphere that would gladden the heart of the most passionate revolutionary," Vera Figner wrote. But then, with what Tikhomirov would have called feminine logic, she was constrained to add sadly, "In fact the Executive Committee was nearing the end of its existence, and the nucleus of the People's Will could no longer function as before."[17] In April, after further arrests, the conspirators still at large were forced to flee St. Petersburg and relocate in Moscow, whence they would try to reconstruct their shattered organization. But who could lead now? Tikhomirov, "our acknowledged ideological spokesman, theoretician, and best writer," was, as Vera recalled, acting very strangely. He wore mourning for Alexander II and compulsively kept attending masses for the repose of the tsar's soul. His comrades attributed this to excessive prudence, but more

[15] *First of March, 1881,* 148.
[16] *Ibid.,* 251.
[17] Vera Figner, *Collected Works,* I, Moscow 1928, 287.

likely he was beginning to experience that psychological crisis which would lead to his apostasy. Maria Olovennikova was experiencing one of her chronic mental disturbances. The leadership devolved of necessity upon Figner, but though utterly fearless herself, she was unable to impose conspiratorial discipline upon her comrades, and one by one they fell into the hands of the police. And, as events were to show, in choosing new people to replace their dwindling ranks, she and her comrades displayed very bad judgment.

It was not only the emperor and the revolutionary conspiracy that had been mortally wounded by Hrynievicki's bomb. Dead for a whole generation was the cause of reform, and gone forever were both the possibility of tsarist Russia evolving peacefully toward constitutionalism, and the reconciliation of its government with Russian society. "Within a short time Your Excellency has been able to justify the trust placed upon you by the Sovereign and many of society's expectations. You have brought honesty and understanding into the government's attitude toward the people. You have sensed correctly what society desires and needs,"[18] ran the address of the Tver provincial assembly to Loris-Melikov shortly before the catastrophe. But terror had won the race against reform.

The emperor's death left Loris in an unenviable situation. He had failed to protect Alexander's life, and was known to have been excessively deferential to Princess Yurievskaya, which would not endear him to the new tsar who deeply resented his father's liaison and morganatic marriage. But above all—and historians seldom attribute adequate weight to this factor —any reform would now appear to many as a partial capitulation to the terrorists. Though widely known to be in the works, "the Loris-Melikov constitution," as this very modest proposal has extravagantly been dubbed, would undoubtedly have been interpreted by revolutionaries and conservatives alike as prompted by fear. And indeed the regime's immediate reaction to the assassination was one of panic. Trenches were dug around the Winter Palace, and the emperor, to his deep humiliation, was persuaded to remove himself temporarily from St. Petersburg and take up residence in suburban Gatchina. Under the circumstances to appease the *intelligentsia*—who Katkov and others of his ilk, had proclaimed were *morally* responsible for the murder (one day Tikhomirov would echo the charge)—would have taken a man either unusually fainthearted or unusually and intelligently courageous.

Alexander III was neither. We have a testimony, unimpeachable since it comes from a revolutionary, that as heir to the throne he had been popular with the masses, especially among the workers.[19] Since he was also known to be quite conservative, this in all likelihood strengthened his conviction

---

[18]A. A. Kornilov, *The Social Movement Under Alexander II*, Moscow 1909, 257.
[19]Michael R. Popov, *Notes of a Member of Land and Freedom*, Moscow 1932, 96.

that the real Russian people did not desire any Western-style innovations. He had a coarse, rather peasantlike appearance, very simple manners. An exemplary family man, his one major weakness was not uncommon among his subjects—he drank heavily.

Still with all these qualifications for being father of his people, with no parliament coming between them, the emperor hesitated to repudiate what his father had in fact approved. The proposal was after all not for a real parliament, just two commissions elected by the provincial assemblies and city councils of the major municipalities to *advise* the State Council on legislation. And the latter body would remain composed mainly of his appointees, with just a few elected representatives invited, also in an advisory capacity. Alexander III might well have yielded to Loris' and other high officials' arguments—except for one man.

Constantine Pobyedonostsev (b. 1827) had been appointed in 1880, ironically enough on Loris' recommendation, Procurator General of the Holy Synod, i.e., the lay head of the Russian Orthodox Church. Alexander II had taken some persuading: Pobyedonostsev was known to have been critical of his private life. But Loris must have thought that Pobydonostsev's wide erudition, impeccable scholarship, and great personal integrity was precisely what the Church needed in its supervisor. In addition Loris would thereby indebt to himself a man who, as the heir's former tutor and still his confidential adviser, could become an important ally. But Pobyedonostsev was one of those for whom that much abused term "reactionary" has been coined. He had not remained immune to the fashion for reform in the post-Nicholas days, in fact contributed to the reorganization of the judiciary in the 1860s,[20] and as a university teacher he had been popular with the young. But the course of events since 1866 had reinforced his deep pessimism about human, and especially Russian, nature: only unwavering adherence to autocracy and Orthodoxy, he believed, could save Russian society from the moral and political decadence one was witnessing in the West. Explaining to Tolstoy why he could not support the great writer's appeal for mercy for the assassins, the Procurator General wrote, "My Christ stands for strength and truth; He heals the weak; yours is a weakling who himself needs healing."

On March 8 the emperor presided over a meeting of high dignitaries summoned to consider the Loris-Melikov proposals. Most of those present, including Grand Duke Constantine and Milyutin, favored the reform, Milyutin believing it was both "timely and necessary." Then came the turn of the procurator general to speak. "Pale like a sheet" and barely controlling his emotion, he began: "I feel not only depressed but close to despair—this proposal is a fraud."[21] Russia, he went on, drew her strength from "the

---

[20]Robert F. Byrnes, *Pobyedonostsev,* Bloomington, Ind., 1968, 43–74.

[21]Peretz, *The Diary of Yegor Peretz,* Moscow 1927, 37.

unlimited confidence which has prevailed between the tsar and his people.
. . . Some want to impose a constitution on the country, if not now, then
as the next step. What is a constitution? Western Europe gives us an answer
—there, constitutions have served to promote falsehood and intrigue."
They were now reaping the fruit of the unwise reforms in the late reign, he
went on, which made the courts the protectors of lawlessness and licensed
the press to preach sedition. This was too much for some of the others: he
was defaming Alexander II, exclaimed a minister. The emperor deferred his
decision.

For the next few weeks Loris deluded himself that his counsel would
prevail, and he and his ministerial colleagues ostracized Pobyedonostsev.
But Pobyedonostsev kept working on his former pupil. On April 29, to the
complete and anguished surprise of the reform party, an imperial manifesto
drafted by the procurator general proclaimed to the world Alexander III's
unshakable faith "in the strength and justice of autocratic power which We
have been called upon to preserve and reinforce for the weal of the nation."
Loris and Milyutin, as well as some others, tendered their resignations,
which were accepted. And on his own the emperor dismissed another friend
of reform, Grand Duke Constantine, from the presidency of the State
Council. Alexander had long disliked his uncle, not only on account of his
liberal reputation, but also because Constantine had never concealed his low
estimate of his nephew's intellectual powers. Russia would enter the twentieth century an autocracy.

One might interject that Russia has not dealt gently with those of her
rulers who sought, however imperfectly, to expand their subjects' freedoms.
Contrast the fate of Alexander III, who died peacefully, with that of his
father, or, closer to our days, Stalin's fate with Khrushchev's. But just as
one cannot accept strict economic determinism, so one should not succumb
to the national-character fallacy. It certainly would have made a difference
to Russian history had a man as enlightened and resourceful as Loris-
Melikov remained in power. Instead the dominant voice in the counsels of
the empire would be that of a bigot and reactionary. And in 1882, as if
Pobyedonostsev was not enough, the emperor appointed Dmitri Tolstoy to
be minister of the interior. He was the most unpopular man in the country,
remonstrated Tolstoy himself. That did not make any difference, said Alexander III, he had his trust.

The wave of reaction that engulfed the country should, by the same
token, have opened new opportunities for the revolutionaries, and at least
until 1883 the regime, even while it contemptuously dismissed the aspirations of the liberals, could not overcome its fear of them. Arrests continued,
and in the fall of 1881 the government struck the Moscow center of the
People's Will so hard that the chief conspirators, notably Tikhomirov and
Vera Figner, had to flee south. But insofar as the government was concerned, it could not be sure that the back of sedition was broken. That

mysterious beast the Executive Committee was obviously still alive and plotting new outrages. Its underground journals continued to appear, promising fresh attacks. The new tsar having refused the revolutionaries' generous offer, "the violent overthrow of the regime has become even more unavoidable," Tikhomirov wrote in the October 23, 1881, issue of *People's Will.* The same issue spelled out eloquently the revolutionaries' argument that they would gladly repudiate terror as an instrument in the struggle for freedom if Russia's conditions offered an alternative. The president of the United States had just (September 20) succumbed to the wounds inflicted by an assassin, and the Executive Committee hastened with its expressions "of deep sympathy to the American people on the death of James Abraham Garfield." There was no excuse for political terror in a country like America, where freedoms of all sorts flourished and "where the free will of the nation determines not only its laws but who should rule." The assassination was an execrable act. "We are against despotism, whether exercised by a person or a party, and [hold that] violence may be used only to answer violence."

And yet at the very same time the revolutionaries were far from censuring, in fact came close to gloating over, the violence that was being visited upon thousands of defenseless people.

Anti-Jewish pogroms had erupted in the Ukraine as early as April 1881 and continued throughout that spring, returning with new force in the fall and in 1882. They swept not only through cities and towns of the Pale of Jewish Settlement, but through the countryside as well. The pogrom had not been unknown in Russia's southern provinces, but for the first time in a long while it took the more vicious form of being directed not only against the unfortunate victims' property but also against their lives. *The People's Will* of October 23 lists casualties for just one town: "In Elisabethgrad, where the pogroms began, one hundred houses were destroyed, twenty people killed, one hundred wounded. . . ." The author of the report quotes at length from other papers' descriptions of the holocaust—arson, murder, widespread looting of Jews' shops and homes by rampaging mobs. The author then poses an obvious question:

> Concerning the Jewish pogroms, many have been curious about the attitude we socialist revolutionaries adopt toward such cases of popular *retribution.* . . . We do not have the right to condemn or even to remain neutral toward such manifestations of the people's anger. We are duty bound to espouse the aspirations of all those *justly* enraged who enter upon an active struggle, and we must consciously seize *leadership of those forces* and endorse their point of view.[22]

The author's troubled conscience may have been responsible for the awkward language in which he expressed not only approval of the beastly

---

.[22]My italics.

excesses but a hope that the revolutionaries might utilize them for a much more ambitious undertaking: "If the bombs again will not help . . . then we will prevail with the aid of a nationwide wave of terror. . . . Come the day of retribution and the people will be merciless."

The attitude of the People's Will toward the pogroms has been a source of deep embarrassment to many historians of the liberation movement. Some break off the narrative in 1881, largely, one suspects, to avoid dealing with this episode in the history of the party. Others argue, with an obviously bad conscience, that the pogroms had been instigated by the government, and they remain silent concerning the revolutionaries. But while there is no question that in years to come, notably at the beginning of the twentieth century, many tsarist officials looked through their fingers at, and some others even inspired, anti-Jewish violence, this was simply not true in 1881–82. The riots erupted spontaneously, and their timing suggests the fact that there was a Jewess among the "tsar killers" must have had something to do with it. Alexander III could indeed write to a minister that "in the depths of his soul" he sympathized with those who beat the Jews, but, he added immediately, of course such outbreaks must not be tolerated. It was not humanitarian feeling that motivated most of the imperial officials, but the realization that if the government failed to curb such hideous crimes a threat was posed to general law and order. Reactionary though he was, Dmitri Tolstoy on his appointment in 1882 promised to deal resolutely with "those scoundrels," and more than five thousand of them were arrested and turned over to the courts.

By the same token the revolutionaries, even if not anti-Semitic (though some of them undoubtedly were), could not find the fortitude to censure or even dissociate themselves from "the people" who attacked the "exploiters." This might after all be a prelude to even more general mayhem: attacks on the landlords and officials, a great uprising on the order of Pugachev's. One of those co-opted to replenish the Executive Committee after March 1 was a veteran Populist, Vladimir Zhebunyev. In May he hastened to a rural district in the Ukraine to see for himself "the people's" avenging mood.

The local situation, as he wrote in the *Bulletin of the People's Will* of July 22, seemed quite promising: in contrast to what he had seen during the Pilgrimage of 1874–75, the peasants this time were really stirring. There were about 400 Jews as against 5,000 Ukrainian peasants in the area, the first quite fearful, the latter expectant, all aroused by the news of the Elisabethgrad pogroms. "Excitement grew before my eyes. . . . The Jews behaved quite tactlessly toward the peasants. They tried to learn what the crowds thought, spied on them, ran to the police with rumors, and helped the authorities arrest those who were plotting. . . . The well-to-do peasants sided more with the Jews than with their own people." Rumors circulated among the peasants that it was the revolutionaries who had stirred up violence against the Jews, which our reporter took as a high compliment indeed to his party. Before, the peasants believed just in the tsar; "now the people have begun to realize that there exist ordinary mortals who strive manfully for their welfare. This is a great achievement of which every revolutionary ought to be proud."

Then news came of a pogrom quite close by, and tension grew unbearable. "Personally, of course I had no animosity against the Jews, but my thoughts and feelings have become one with those of the people, and I was counting hours, minutes till the pogrom started." It was a market day too, especially appropriate for such fun and games, but the peasants were agonizingly slow to begin action. "This was the second night that I could not sleep waiting for the business to begin." And then the next morning was a cruel disappointment: a detachment of soldiers entered the village to prevent riots. "Though the peasants grumbled sarcastically about the soldiers and their officers they quieted down. . . . The sight of bayonets and soldiers in full array had a most depressing effect." Even when the soldiers departed "the depressing effect" lingered on; the would-be murderers and looters were cowed. Zhebunyev was bitterly disappointed. "There was now nothing to wait for and with a heavy heart and regrets I left the village."

The frustrated *voyeur* was not alone in his feelings, for which it is difficult to find an appropriate description. His comrades, with the revolutionary tide receding, saw in the pogroms a possible means to recoup their fortunes. While there is no evidence that individual members of the People's Will stirred up any of those horrors, the attitude of the party was officially expressed in a manifesto of the Executive Committee, written in Ukrainian and addressed to the "good people and all honest folk in the Ukraine," dated August 30, 1881. It starts, "It is from the Jews that the Ukrainian folk suffer most of all. Who has gobbled up all the lands and forests? Who runs every tavern? Jews! . . . Whatever you do, wherever you turn, you run into the Jew. It is he who bosses and cheats you, he who drinks the peasant's blood."[23]

It was long believed that this remarkable document was written by the then only Jewish member of the Executive Committee, Saveli Zlatopolsky, but it seems that it came from the pen of another recent recuit to the Executive Committee, Gerasim Romanenko. Vera Figner took several copies of it to Odessa, but upon discovering that it aroused scant enthusiasm among the mostly Jewish radical circles there, destroyed them.

In any case, the great hopes which the revolutionaries placed on the anti-Jewish movement as a prelude to a general uprising foundered. And

[23]Quoted in V. Y. Bogucharsky, *From the History of the Political Struggle—The People's Will, Its Origin, Development, and Fall,* St. Petersburg 1912, 221.

the attitude which the People's Will adopted could not but damage still further its reputation among the more enlightened elements of society. This in turn infuriated the revolutionaries against the very people from whom they expected so much. An editorial of *The People's Will* of February 5, 1882, was expressive of such feelings: "Take those lovers of the people, the reformers; . . . they have been sitting quietly numbed by the fear . . . that they would have to pay for the revolutionaries' deeds. . . . Here are your Russian liberals . . . frightful cowards . . . begging slavishly for a constitution." Still, there were some hopeful signs: "One third of Russia has been seized by the anti-Jewish disorders, and the number of people tried on charges of defaming the tsar has grown encouragingly." (It was a tradition inherited from old Muscovy that the police would seek out—naturally mostly in taverns—those who used insulting words about the Sacred Person of His Majesty.) The revolutionaries' organ was also very attentive to gossip: Mme. Pobyedonostseva's father turned out to be a crook who stole state funds, and that paragon of all virtues, his son-in-law, was trying to hush up the business (this was quite true). At the same time the Procurator General was working to have Alexander II canonized, and it was he who was spreading rumors that the late emperor's ghost was frequently seen at night in the Cathedral of Our Lady of Kazan (this was quite untrue: Pobyedonostsev loathed the memory of Alexander II). The present empress was revealed as an enemy of women's liberation. "Women's role," said Her Majesty, "should be that of wife, mother, and housekeeper" (this was quite likely).

Almost obscured by this tittle-tattle was the notice of the recent trial of the 20, the latest and perhaps most cruel blow suffered by the People's Will. The trial had taken place February 9–16, and the issue, dated February 5, actually appeared on February 26. Among those sentenced were such luminaries of its old guard as Alexander Mikhailov, Nicholas Morozov, Anna Yakimova, the "Mrs. Kobozev" of the cheese shop, Nicholas Sukhanov, the soul of the revolutionaries' organization within the officer corps. Incongruously, the authorities placed amidst these Vasili Merkulov, already working for the police. Except for him the accused bore themselves with dignity. Sukhanov,[24] of whom it was expected prior to his arrest that he might become another Zhelyabov, declared that he did not feel that his officer's oath bound him to serve the tsar, but only the nation.

The court's verdict was what might be expected: ten deaths, the rest hard labor. Of the ten, nine had their sentences commuted to what was for most of them a slower and more painful manner of dying, prison terms in Schlüsselburg or the Alexis Ravelin, where Mikhailov would expire on March 18,

---

[24]Perovskaya's last message to her comrades had been, "Take special care of Verochka [Figner] and Sukhanov."

1884. Only a few, such as the future nonagenarians Morozov and Frolenko, emerged alive from the dreaded fortresses in 1905, and Yemelyanov, lucky enough to have been sent to Siberia, ended his days there as a prosperous merchant. Sukhanov received mercy of a different kind—instead of the gallows he was executed by the firing squad. Merkulov, though sentenced, was immediately released to continue his good work for the police.

With the net tightening around him, Tikhomirov applied to the Executive Committee, i.e., in effect to its only other member at large, Vera Figner, for permission to leave Russia. She, naturally, did not understand how anyone could wish to leave the battlefield and pass up the virtual certainty of the gallows or Schlüsselburg. But perhaps the Russian colony abroad needed a new Herzen; for the moment there was nobody of stature there except the old bore Lavrov; and Plekhanov was already flirting with Marxism. And so Tikhomirov was granted an "official" leave of absence. Once on the train Tikhomirov's spirits rose. An Austrian Jew in his compartment praised the rule of the Hapsburgs: in their dominions you could say anything provided you did not violate the law, he said. Quite the opposite in Russia, replied the fleeing chieftain of conspirators: there a man can do anything provided he keeps his mouth shut.

With Tikhomirov's departure in mid-1882 begins the final stage of the disintegration of the People's Will. Of course he was no Herzen, and the hope of creating the kind of intellectual government in exile which the great writer ran between 1857 and 1862 was bound to prove ephemeral. Nor was he a Lenin who in years to come would have a sizable body of supporters in Russia and the backing of an international organization, the Second International, abroad. Except for a few veterans of recent Populism, and some old-timers from the 1860s with whom he would intermittently collaborate and quarrel, Tikhomirov lived in virtual isolation. His *Messenger of the People's Will*, which began to appear in 1883, was but a pale copy of *The Bell* and a faint preview of the Lenin-Plekhanov *Spark*.

And yet before he settled down to his thankless task there appeared before this-revolutionary general with no troops a mirage of what he had sought for the last three years: power. With its organization shattered, with most of its leaders dead or imprisoned, the regime was seeking negotiations with the People's Will!

Following March 1, 1881, some loyal supporters of the autocracy had concluded that it was hopeless to expect the bureacracy, shot through as they believed it was by secret sympathizers with sedition and with namby-pamby liberals, to uproot the evil that had spread in Russian society. Fire had to be fought with fire, and a revolutionary conspiracy by a loyalist one. Hence the genesis of an organization dubbed at first Voluntary Protection, but subsequently known to history as the Sacred Band. As its original name indicates, the primary aim was to save the new emperor from meeting the same end as his father. One of the initiators of the scheme was Serge Witte, then a young engineer, later on a long-time finance minister, negotiator of the peace treaty following the Russo-Japanese War, and prime minister after the revolution of 1905. The Band had highly placed sponsors, including at first Pobyedonostsev and Count Nicholas Ignatiev, minister of the interior.[25] (Ignatiev whose aggressive and inept diplomacy as ambassador to Constantinople helped precipitate the Russo-Turkish War, was known even among his conservative colleagues as a pathological liar and intriguer. Appointed in May 1881 on Pobyedonostsev's recommendation, he was fired also on his advice one year later.) And the head of the Brotherhood, as it was also called, was none other than the minister of the Imperial Court, Count Ilarion Vorontsov-Dashkov.

In the best conspiratorial tradition dating to the first Land and Freedom, the Band was organized into cells of five, each "brother" to be referred to by a number. Thus Count Vorontsov was number six (on some occasions he was referred to as the "Supreme"). The brothers were expected to engage in vigorous spying on the revolutionaries, as well as in tracking down those officials and other high-placed personages who in fact were "double-faced traitors," to use a term coined in Stalin's Russia. As might be expected, this volunteer spying brought in the immediate months after the assassination a rich harvest of nonsensical gossip: it could be expected that some within the Band would come to believe that Grand Duke Constantine had connections with the revolutionaries, but others in cahoots with them were also supposed to be people like Dr. Serge Botkin and the late emperor's widow. Such gossipy "information" when communicated to officials, e.g., Pobyedonostsev, would not be acted upon (as it was, for example, in Stalin's time). The Band mobilized its membership to be present and watch out for trouble during the emperor's very infrequent public appearances, but there were also schemes of a more resolute activity on behalf of law and order. Some brothers felt that one should give the revolutionaries a taste of their own medicine and wipe out a few of them. Peter Kropotkin, then in Switzerland, was supposed to be on the list, and being apprised of the rumor he promptly communicated it to the London *Times.*

But it is one thing to collect gossip and carry on masquerades with "brothers," "fives," etc., and another to set up a workmanlike conspiracy. Nothing came out of this idea of amateur counterterror. Officials like Pobyedonostsev, having recovered from their post-March 1 panic, realized that the government simply could not tolerate activities of this kind. But before disappearing from the scene and being relegated to a footnote in history, the Sacred Band played an important role in an episode which throws a vivid light on the People's Will during the last phase of its existence.

[25]Peter Valuyev, *Diary,* Petrograd 1919, 176.

A year had passed since the ascent to the throne of Alexander III. And yet, unlike what inviolable tradition dictated, no announcement was made about the coronation. The reason was obvious: the ceremonial, staged from time immemorial in Moscow, would require the tsar to appear on several occasions in close proximity to the masses and would bring to the ancient capital a vast influx of people from all over the country. Surely this would be a unique opportunity for the terrorists to repeat their feat of regicide. And one could not curtail or change the ritual without damaging the prestige of the throne and its occupant. That the People's Will, for all the recent blows dealt it, was rendered entirely impotent was something no one dared believe. Political terror was not a mere thing of the past, for on March 18, 1882, General Fyodor Strelnikov, military prosecutor in Odessa, was assassinated by two revolutionaries. And in June a laboratory where bombs were being manufactured was uncovered by the police in St. Petersburg. (Strelnikov had been the prosecutor in the Osinsky trial; one of his assassins, subsequently hanged, was Stephen Khalturin of the Winter Palace explosion fame.)

It is no wonder therefore, that both some government officials and the Sacred Band itself had hit upon the idea of entering on negotiations with the revolutionaries, to learn whether and under what conditions they might agree to give up terror or at least to hold it in abeyance until after the coronation.

The story of these negotiations is very murky on both sides. Did the authorities and the Sacred Band enter upon the dialogue with the serious intention of making concessions if they could thereby safeguard the emperor's life? Or did the authorities intend to enmesh the revolutionaries in a net of provocation so to smash them the more effectively? Did the revolutionaries, who as their recollections clearly show had neither the intention nor the resources to create serious trouble during the coronation, sincerely believe in the possibility of an accommodation with the regime, or did they think merely of gaining a breathing spell, then to launch a new campaign?

The first efforts to establish contacts with the Executive Committee were undertaken by two men who had already gained an enviable reputation in unraveling conspiracies: prosecutor Dobzhinsky and Major Sudeykin. Olga Liubatovich, who had hastened to Russia following her lover's arrest, was herself seized in the fall of 1881. Both officials began immediately to work on her. "Tell me," said Dobzhinsky, "under what conditions would your party give up terror, be it only through the coronation?"[26] This direct approach was not successful, but as Olga recalls a bit guiltily, it was the celebrated Sudeykin who softened her resolve not to negotiate with the

[26]From Liubatovich's recollections in *The Past,* No. 6 (Petersburg June 1906), 149.

oppressors.[27] Even though she was an experienced revolutionary and even though Morozov, the man she loved, was in jail, Olga succumbed to the charm of this unusual policeman: "tall, elegant, still young and full of self-confidence . . . gallant and straightforward. One would forget that he was a policeman." He would visit her cell and hold wide-ranging discussions. Cleverly at times he would let Olga get the better of him in an argument: "He was well acquainted with revolutionary literature . . . obviously a very smart man but theoretically not highly sophisticated." Who knows how far he would have gotten with Olga except for the impatience of his superiors? The police director, Pleve, proposed to Olga that *she* approach her comrades; if she so desired they would release her and let her go abroad for that purpose. She demurred and showed herself not quite liberated: this was a job for a man, she said, but promised to confer about it with Romanenko, also currently in jail. Romanenko, the author of the infamous proclamation to the Ukrainian people about the pogroms, then wrote on his own a letter to the emperor in which he assured him that should the government adopt socialism, the revolutionaries would gladly collaborate with the regime in the joint struggle against the bourgeoisie! Sudeykin tried his seductive methods on another prisoner, Jacob Stefanovich. But while this man, who once tried to kill a comrade suspected of being a spy, now himself told the police much more than he should have, he refused to purchase his freedom by becoming an informer within the Executive Committee. One suspects that he felt that Siberia was safer.

In any case, both official and unofficial protectors of the autocracy realized that anybody released from jail would arouse the suspicions of revolutionary comrades in hiding or abroad. The Sacred Band then hit upon a more elaborate scheme: an agent was dispatched to France to contact Lavrov. The agent posed as the representative of a liberal organization of landowners and officials, the (wholly fictitious) Land League. The league would exact from the government various concessions, he was instructed to say, provided the People's Will undertook to suspend terror. But the negotiations fizzled, since the emissary did not arouse much trust among the conspiratorial representatives with whom Lavrov put him in touch.

And now the Band had recourse to a more suitable go-between. He was Nicholas Nikoladze. A veteran of the revolutionary movement of the 1860s, he had since then followed a path not unusual for people with his past: earning his livelihood in journalism and business, yet keeping in touch with radical circles, which occasionally got him in trouble with the police. Here was a typical *intelligent* of the period—a man bound to know somebody

---

[27]He had been transferred to the capital after March 1 and immediately showed his mettle by bagging a number of revolutionaries. The explosives' laboratory, which he busted in 1882, was in fact making bombs intended for Sudeykin's assassination.

who in turn would know someone else who could get in touch directly with the head of the conspiracy. An agent of the Band, a rather shady journalist named Cornelius Borozdin, drew the attention of his leaders to this Georgian, an old-time acquaintance. Nikoladze was invited for a talk with the "Supreme," Count Vorontsov-Dashkov. Brevity was never a virtue of the Russian *intelligent* and Nikoladze began the meeting with an exhaustive two-hour exposition of the country's social problems, their roots in the past going back to the French Revolution. . . . The speaker noticed that his listener was restless, but attributed this to his aristocratic weariness with life, proper to "a high nobleman, bored and blasé, for whom there was nothing more to aspire to or to work for."[28] But when he could get a word in, Count Vorontsov sounded quite liberal. Thus he quoted Bismarck's saying—little did he or his interlocutor realize how prophetic this was—"If the Russian government should embark on the socialist path . . . then Russia would become the most powerful state in Europe."[29]

There were some further and more businesslike conferences between the two men. The count empowered Nikoladze to seek out the revolutionaries' leaders, if need be abroad, convey to them certain proposals, and then report to him on their reactions. He implied that if the latter were sensible the government, though of course he could not speak for it *quite* officially, would prove amenable on its part. According to Borozdin's version[30] of the whole involved business, the voluble intermediary's motives in undertaking this mission were not entirely selfless: he hoped to be rewarded with money as well as by social peace in Russia. Nikoladze of course indignantly repudiated these insinuations when years later they appeared in print.

Nikoladze went with his story to his friend Mikhailovsky, the latter in turn to his friend Nicholas Shelgunov. The result of those consultations of three Nicholases was that on October 15, 1882, Mikhailovsky appeared at Vera Figner's latest hideout in Kharkov. The regime, he told the only remaining member of the Executive Committee in Russia, wanted an accommodation with the People's Will. It was ready for the following concessions: 1) amnesty for political crimes; 2) freedom of the press; 3) freedom for socialist propaganda. Of course, they could not put them into effect right away, and certainly not if terror continued. But as a token of good will they were ready to release a member of the Executive Committee currently in jail. How about Isayev?

Vera smelled a rat: it reminded her of the Goldenberg story. Well, said Mikhailovsky, since currently you have neither men nor resources for carrying out a terrorist campaign, what do you have to lose? Vera hesitated. In

---

[28]Nikoladze's recollections in *The Past,* No. 9 (Petrograd September 1906), 256.

[29]*Ibid.,* 263.

[30]In *The Past,* No. 9 (September 1907), 123–62.

any case Isayev would not do. The government should release Nechayev. Except that she reported this herself,[31] one might not believe it: suffering the agony of imprisonment in the fortress were currently such heroes of the People's Will as Alexander Mikhailov, her close friend Morozov, and many others. And yet she would have *Nechayev* freed rather than any of them! Finally she announced that she could not herself assume the responsibility of speaking for the Executive Committee. Let Nikoladze go abroad to see Tikhomirov; she would send a courier to let him know in advance.

Figner was a woman of strong personal loyalties. And so her plea on behalf of Nechayev can be explained only by the desperate condition of the People's Will and her conviction that this legendary figure could somehow work a miracle. Nechayev's contacts with the revolutionaries had stopped, as we saw, in 1881. When arrested, both Zhelyabov and Perovskaya were found to possess coded messages concerning Nechayev's subversion of soldiers in the fortress—another reason to doubt that the plot to free him had been betrayed by Mirski. In August 1883 Tikhomirov announced Nechayev's death in the *Messenger of the People's Will,* though he was wrong both as to the date, December 8 (in fact it was November 21, 1882), and the cause, suicide (in fact it was dropsy).

And so Nikoladze, chaperoned on behalf of the Sacred Band by Borozdin, set out in the end of 1882 for Geneva to meet with the leader of the People's Will. One can imagine what went through Tikhomirov's mind at the news that the emissary was on his way to negotiate with him on behalf of, if not the government itself, then of influential circles within the regime. Here he was, almost resigned to an exile's bitter existence, reduced to begging peopled he loathed, like Lavrov and Plekhanov, to help him with his journalistic venture. And suddenly a ray of hope: the *government* sought his help! The mere news of such negotiations taking place would be bound to revivify the People's Will in Russia, bring new adherents into the party, enable him to influence the course of politics. And if the government did make some real concessions, the future might bring even more dazzling opportunities.

After listening to Nikoladze's of course lengthy exposition of the reasons why the revolutionaries should not refuse the regime's proferred hand, of how the country had already suffered from terror, etc., Tikhomirov announced that he could not give him an answer right away. He had to go to Paris, summon a party congress, and see what they decided.

In Paris Tikhomirov held his "congress," i.e., he met with Maria Olovennikova and told her what he proposed to say to Nikoladze, who had followed him to France. "About the middle of December . . . Mr. Tikhomirov brought me the resolution of the Congress of the Russian Socialist Revolu-

[31] *Collected Works,* V, Moscow 1929, 342.

tionary Party that if the government should allow . . . peaceful propaganda of social ideas . . . if it would proclaim an amnesty and permit more free activity for the *intelligentsia* (through the press, in local self-government, etc.), then the party promised to stop its terrorist campaign."[32] Furthermore, if the government adopted real social reforms—improved the conditions of the peasants and so on—then "the party will loyally support the government and with all the means at its disposal and all its members' participation will assist the regime to put into effect such reforms." Conceivably Tikhomirov, a regicide, could already see himself as a minister of Alexander III!

For the immediate future his demands were quite modest: they would refrain from spoiling the coronation by killing the emperor on two conditions: 1) Chernyshevsky had to be allowed to return home from exile; 2) the government had to investigate and correct abuses in the treatment of political convicts in Siberia. The point about Chernyshevsky, apart from humanitarian reasons, which one suspects never greatly influenced Tikhomirov, was a clever one: while the radical sage had been almost forgotten by the terrorists, his was still a name to conjure with among the *intelligentsia*. Highly pleased with the result of his mission, and no doubt foreseeing brilliant prospects for himself as well, Nikoladze set out for Russia.

A cruel blow awaited him. "I barely greeted Count Vorontsov-Dashkov when he announced that all his hopes and calculations had been dashed to the ground. The situation in Petersburg had changed so that he would be incapable of carrying out any of the proposals we had talked about." With a true nobleman's sense of fair play the count told Nikoladze that he should write to his revolutionary acquaintances, telling them that any deal was off, and that they should feel free to do what they would.

What happened was that the indefatigable Sudeykin, having placed an agent of his own within the high command of what remained of the People's Will, was able to inform the authorities that the revolutionary party was in a shambles and that what remained of it he could grab and put away at their convenience. It was absurd, therefore, to negotiate with these people, not to mention offer concessions to them. Many in high positions, notably Pobyedonostsev and Dmitri Tolstoy, had become sick of the Sacred Band. It interfered with the official security organs, and it was suspected, not without reason, that some of its members harbored the subversive design of using the terrorist bogey to sneak in parliamentary institutions for Russia. Thus one such "left-winger," Count Paul Shuvalov (not to be confused with his kinsman Peter, former head of the Third Department), confided to Nikoladze "that he was disappointed with the revolutionary party. They missed a rare chance to [force] the introduction of parliamen-

---

[32]Nikoladze, 270.

tary government in Russia."[33] In any case Count Vorontsov was instructed by the emperor to dissolve the organization, and at the end of 1882 the fantastic enterprise passed out of existence.

Alexander III's coronation took place in May 1883 and passed without any untoward incidents.

The only positive result of the negotiations was a much belated act of compassion. Count Shuvalov, an aide-de-camp to the tsar, used his influence to procure a political pardon for Chernyshevsky. Aged beyond his years by prison and Siberia, the erstwhile intellectual idol of Russia's youth broke down and cried when he was told he would be able to rejoin his family in European Russia.

It is difficult to judge whether anything else might have come out of the whole business. Shuvalov indeed thought all was not lost. He kept dropping in on Nikoladze and expounding to him how the present insufferable political situation could be changed. The count was quite cynical: people cared only about their own hides, he thought. And so he had a capital idea—he would arrange an audience with Alexander III for Nikoladze so he could tell the emperor that "the revolutionaries will without fail and very soon kill him as they killed his father, unless he grants a constitution."[34] Nikoladze, his taste for long conversations with the great of this world definitely gone, begged off this honor. But he could not refuse an invitation from the chief of police, who informed him that as a person who had contacts with revolutionaries he was being placed under "strict police surveillance." This was the only reward Nikoladze received for his patriotic endeavors to bring social peace to Russia. And, he ruefully adds, he was never refunded the money he had spent on his trip.

The Sacred Band would have been dissolved in any case. Yet the fact that the government became so emboldened in December 1882 as to decide it had nothing to fear from the revolutionaries can be traced directly to one person. For the first twenty-eight years of his life he bore the name of Serge Degayev, but it was as Alexander Pell, a respectable retired professor of mathematics, that he died in the environs of Philadelphia in 1921.

When in the late 1870s he first sought to join revolutionary circles, Degayev's credentials were impeccable. Radicalism, it appeared, ran in his blood. His widowed mother was a daughter of a well-known writer of the early nineteenth century who, having suffered at the hands of Nicholas' censors, became something of a hero to the *intelligentsia.* Natalia Degayeva brought up her four children in the modern, i.e., radical, spirit, and all of them, as well as herself, upon moving to Petersburg in 1879 became close acquaintances of several members of the People's Will. The old lady occa-

[33] *Ibid.,* 272.
[34] *Ibid.,* 279.

sionally lent her apartment for conspiratorial purposes and also sheltered revolutionaries.

Serge was an artilleryman, thus in that branch of the army which traditionally produced the highest quota of officers with "untrustworthy ideas." And indeed for harboring those he had been dismissed from the artillery academy and was currently on regimental duty. His appearance was unprepossessing: tiny, almost a dwarf, with a huge head—and a furtive look in his eyes as behooved one of the most famous double agents in history. It is doubtful, however, that the impression he created matched his looks, as some of his victims were to claim. Degayev knew how to charm. Michael Aschenbrenner, whose acquaintance with Degayev earned him twenty years in Schlüsselburg, cannot be accused of partiality when he testifies that he was very popular among his fellow officers.[35] In 1881 Degayev, then a captain, resigned from the army and joined the conspiratorial officers' circle headed by Sukhanov. He kept imploring his friends on the Executive Committee to let him participate in some important enterprise, and was one of those who assisted in digging the tunnel under Little Garden Street. He was briefly arrested in the commotion following March 1, but with no evidence against him was released and continued his new profession as engineer. He felt it prudent to leave the capital for a few months and went to Archangel, where he fell in love and got married. Back in St. Petersburg in the fall he resumed his contacts with the conspirators. As yet he was considered and in fact was entirely devoted to the cause. Sent south to Tiflis, he carried on revolutionary propaganda among officers of regiments stationed in the Caucasus. With Sukhanov gone, Degayev, though now out of the army, appeared to be the ideal man to head the military affiliate of the People's Will, the only branch of the conspiracy left relatively undamaged by the arrests of 1881 and the first half of 1882. It was thus logical for Vera Figner to co-opt this enterprising and knowledgeable man into the Executive Committee and make him privy to all the secrets of the revolutionary party.

Sudeykin had had his eye on the whole Degayev tribe for some time, and no wonder, since with the exception of Serge they were what might be called revolutionary exhibitionists. When Gesia Helfman gave birth in a prison hospital to a daughter, old Mrs. Degayev offered to bring up the child. (The infant was sent to an orphanage, where it soon died.) One Degayev girl boasted to anyone who would listen that during her stay in Paris she had been courted by Peter Lavrov himself, the elderly philosopher still retaining his amorous disposition. And the youngest of the family, Vladimir, though only seventeen, was arrested in 1881 on suspicion of participation in illegal activities. In jail he was visited by Sudeykin with a proposition the young-

---

[35]Michael Aschenbrenner, "The Military Organization of The People's Will," in *The Past*, No. 7 (Petrograd July 1906), 13.

ster found hard to refuse. He would not insult him, said this devilishly clever police chief, by proposing that Degayev become an informer, but he would release him without any conditions: *then* if Vladimir decided so of his own will he would be delighted to employ him. Not, God forbid, to bring Sudeykin any names or other conspiratorial secrets, but simply to keep him abreast of what the revolutionaries thought, and whether there was any chance that the conspirators would give up terror if the government adopted timely reforms. Volodya (his nickname) ran with this story to his brother and other revolutionaries still at large, and filled them in on his own idea: he would become another Kletochnikov and would keep passing to them all the secrets of the police. The idea that a child could fool a man like Sudeykin was of course preposterous, but the revolutionaries were grasping at straws, and perhaps brother Serge already had some special notions of his own. They told the young fool to go ahead.

No one could accuse Sudeykin of not keeping his word: he held long conversations with the youngster, bared his own liberal convictions, and only in the most general way kept inquiring whether there was anything new in the revolutionary world, sighing when informed there was not. But it is more than possible that Sudeykin's subordinates were less honorable than their chief, for some of the revolutionaries whom Volodya visited, in order to report on his brilliant infiltration of the secret police, were after a suitable interval arrested. And so when Volodya went abroad in 1882 to boast to political emigrés how he had this supposedly cunning policeman wrapped around his little finger, the emigrés kept their distance from him. Sudeykin told the boy when he returned to Russia that unfortunately he had no further use for his services, and that he should enlist in the army to stay out of trouble. Vladimir enlisted in an artillery battalion, and no doubt a letter followed to its commander.

And now the trap was baited, and like any master conspirator Sudeykin knew how to wait.

Brother Serge was in the meantime making a tour of all the conspiratorial military organizations of the People's Will. After he had finished it, Vera Figner, who was much taken with him, suggested that he should take over the clandestine press of the People's Will which was being set up in Odessa, and she furnished him with all the conspiratorial addresses in that city. Years later, after she had spent twenty years in prison because of him, and barely escaped the gallows, she wrote rather humorously that Degayev was an "invaluable man for getting around and having connections with all sorts of people."

On December 18, 1882, the press was raided, Degayev and his wife arrested. Whatever his true intentions before, Degayev's current prospects—ranging from the gallows to twenty years in a fortress—made him think of a recent friend of his family's. Sudeykin hurried down to Odessa. Mrs.

Degayev was invited from her prison cell to police headquarters, and there, sitting at a table covered with bottles and hors d'oeuvres, was her husband, chatting amicably with Sudeykin.[36] A few days later Degayev escaped while on the way to the railway station. It was all quite simple, he told Vera Figner at the beginning of February when she greeted him, overjoyed, in her Kharkov hideout: he was being conveyed in a carriage by two policemen when suddenly he threw tobacco in their eyes and jumped out! Vera did not reflect that prisoners on such occasions were usually manacled, but she was a bit surprised: Serge did not smoke. Yes, but he had requested tobacco especially for that purpose. Degayev seemed somewhat nervous, but she attributed this to his concern for his wife, still in prison. Then Degayev become solicitous about his hostess—was she quite safe in Kharkov? Absolutely, she assured him, the only man who could give her away was Merkulov, but he was in Petersburg. Did her apartment have a rear entrance, and what time did she usually go out in the morning? Vera was touched by Degayev's concern and explained in detail all her precautions.

Two days later, February 10, as she left her apartment at the appointed hour who should be walking in the street but Merkulov! A few minutes later she was seized by policemen. At headquarters she confronted the man responsible, she believed, for her arrest. "What a big surprise!" said Merkulov with "his usual boorish insolence." Figner forgot she was a lady and was about to strike him "when, coward that he was, he hastily retreated."[37]

Vera Figner was promptly dispatched to jail in Petersburg, where news of her arrest caused great jubilation in official circles. His Majesty himself deigned to jot down in his diary, "Thank God, they finally got this horrid woman." High officials would visit her cell, and she amiably discussed politics with such as Dmitri Tolstoy, who on leaving said he was sorry he could not spend more time with her. So was she, said Vera; after a few more hours she was sure she could have converted him to her philosophy. People were curious to see this young and attractive woman, the high priestess of terror, who stuck indomitably to her post while her comrades were being seized or fled abroad. Everything considered, Figner was in good spirits. The prison library was excellent. "Only here, where I had nothing else to do, could I devote myself to subjects which especially interested me, history, economics, sociology; I read all of Herbert Spencer." She was under no illusions about her probable fate but confident that she had left her party's affairs in competent hands.

And then one day prosecutor Dobzhinsky showed her a document. "It told the authorities about everything the author knew about our party. Not only its leaders, but rank-and-file members and sympathizers . . . military

---

[36] *Ibid.*
[37] Figner, I, 345.

affiliates in the south and north . . . were named from first to last."[38] It was signed Serge Degayev. "I wanted to die."

As of February 10, 1883, then, the real head of the People's Will in Russia was Colonel Sudeykin. Degayev, his prestige among the conspirators enhanced by news of his heroic escape, systematically turned them over to the police. As in Vera Figner's case the arrests were carried out in a way which would not compromise the ingenious little man. This was rather easy, since during her "reign" Figner had been quite careless, and the people she enlisted as sympathizers told all they knew to the police. A veteran of the period recalled the following dialogue between his two cell-mates in the Odessa jail: "Pesis, I am a scoundrel. I turned you in." "Fradis, I am no better, I denounced you even before then."[39] The last hope of the conspiracy, its branch within the fighting services, was totally destroyed. Its highest ranking member, Colonel Michael Aschenbrenner, was arrested in March. He was to recall that at the time he knew of about four hundred officers who were actual or potential members of the organization, but this figure was undoubtedly inflated; it included those who like practically any educated young Russian of the period occasionally talked revolution without necessarily doing anything about it. In any case, some two hundred naval and army officers were detained, and of them sixty-seven were turned over to the courts. (These numbers are for the whole period 1880–83, but the great majority was after Degayev's betrayal.) Most of these, having expressed "sincere repentance," were let off easily, but eight ringleaders were to face a military court along with Vera Figner in 1884.

By the late spring of 1883 there were only a few interesting revolutionaries left at large in Russia. This was deeply troublesome to both Degayev and Sudeykin: to the first in his capacity as the leader of the conspiracy, to the latter as master policeman whose professional advancement depended on the continuous flow of fresh culprits. To remedy this depressing situation, Degayev proposed to repair where the grass was greener: i.e., among Russian political exiles abroad. Perhaps he might entice some of them back home; in any case he would learn what they were up to. And now it was the turn of Colonel Sudeykin to fall victim to that fatal illusion that there are people you can trust. He agreed.

It is now necessary to try to reconstruct Degayev's motives—not an easy task. There is no doubt that he began as a bona fide revolutionary and quite possible that he still thought of himself as such. Very likely he had not foreseen that he would have to hand over all those officers, but once in Sudeykin's grip he had realized one could not trifle with this man. Now his

---

[38] *Ibid.*, 354.

[39] Victor Sukhomlin, "The Fall of The People's Will," in *Hard Labor and Exile*, XXIV (Moscow 1926), 85.

prospects were far from rosy; if not Sudeykin, then his superiors might decide to discard him—witness Drigo's fate. And when his true role became known, then no other Russian would have as short a life expectancy as Serge Degayev. Why did he not flee to America right then in May? His subsequent behavior suggests that by now Degayev's hatred of Sudeykin was almost as great as fear for his own life. The policeman had tricked him, turned a revolutionary leader into a slave, and the very fact he let him go abroad showed contempt.

To resolve his dilemma Degayev hit upon a seemingly suicidal scheme, but in fact one that demonstrates his profound understanding of the revolutionaries' psychology. After suitable preliminaries he made a clean breast to Tikhomirov, whom he saw in Switzerland—well, not quite clean. As Tikhomirov was later on to recount Degayev's version of his fall: "in a state of spiritual depression and moral collapse, cut off from honest and morally strong comrades who might have saved him, he conceived a scheme of ingratiating himself with the government by betraying into its hands some of its worst enemies, so that having gained the regime's trust he then would deal it a decisive blow." But then to his horror Degayev discovered that Sudeykin would not be satisfied with "a relatively small number of victims." "Realizing his self-deception . . . tormented by his conscience . . . aware that he no longer could expect a brilliant career ahead of him," the contrite sinner stood before Tikhomirov, ready for any punishment the Executive Committee would see fit to impose.[40]

If Tikhomirov were to reveal this story, quite a few people around him would have considered it an honor to strangle the little man, although the murder would close every European country to Russian exiles. Even more important, the story would not only damage irreparably what remained of the People's Will in Russia and abroad, but destroy its prestige and chances of revival among the young and the *intelligentsia*. For the time at least, it had to be hushed up.

What Degayev obviously expected was: 1) he would be told to disappear; 2) the exiles would bend all their efforts to have Sudeykin assassinated. And, just conceivably, Degayev had not given up the dream of "a brilliant career." After his seducer was wiped out, he might be allowed to resume his life as a revolutionary leader.

He was *nearly* correct in his assumptions, but he overlooked one fact—he had done his work as *provocateur* so well that there was no one left in Russia who could be counted upon to arrange the assassination of a man so clever and cautious as Sudeykin. After conferring with Olovennikova, Tikhomirov announced the Executive Committee's verdict: Degayev himself had to do the job, "so that this tireless propagator of political corruption

[40]Quoted in B. Bazilevsky, ed., *The Literature of The People's Will*, Paris 1905, 654.

should be hoist by his own petard, his fate an eloquent lesson that nothing positive can be achieved through the use of *agents-provocateurs.* "[41]

But Tikhomirov's explanation as to why he did not there and then unmask Degayev is largely phony. Quite likely he promised him that if he went back and took care of his seducer, his secret would never be revealed, and if the government should allude to Degayev's double role, the Executive Committee would protect him and brand it as slander.

Degayev had little choice, but his feelings on getting back to Russia may well be imagined. It was one thing to agree in Geneva to assassinate Sudeykin, but once home the mere sight of the huge and immensely strong police chief frightened him greatly. In September he was summoned abroad to explain his dilatoriness. What he heard there increased his agitation, if that was possible: Herman Lopatin, hero of innumerable revolutionary escapades, had joined the People's Will and was going home to rebuild the party.

To explain why he had not done his job, Degayev told a fantastic story: there was no reason to hurry since Sudeykin, unwittingly, was to going to render the revolutionaries important service. After the whole Degayev-Sudeykin mess was out, Tikhomirov repeated the alleged story in a lengthy article in the *Messenger of the People's Will* of April 24, 1884, under the heading "In the World of Villainy and Desolation." Since the source of the tale was a consummate liar and the man who reported it did not always, to put it mildly, tell the whole truth and nothing but the truth, we face a difficult problem of textual criticism: is this a complete fantasy, and who lied more, Degayev or Tikhomirov? Probably the former.

The police chief confided in him, related Degayev, that he was deeply distressed because his great services to his sovereign and the country were not being properly appreciated. He, Sudeykin, single-handedly had smashed the conspiracy, something which had eluded all those generals and ministers. And what have been his rewards? He was still a lieutenant colonel, and the only honor bestowed on him had been the order of St. Vladimir, fourth class, a decoration usually bestowed on deserving high-school directors. And thus he conceived a little scheme to make the government realize how valuable he was. He would resign from the secret police but not as head (through Degayev) of the People's Will. In the latter capacity he would organize a terrorist campaign which could make a bona fide revolutionary green with envy. They would begin modestly by killing a few police spies, but then to real business: under his supervision Degayev and other lads would dispose of Count Dmitri Tolstoy, who as minister of the interior was so unappreciative of his services, and of a grand duke or two—more if the situation demanded. That should make the regime see how irreplaceable

[41] *Ibid.,* 656.

Colonel Sudeykin was. The tsar would summon him to his side, make him a minister, possibly dictator. Amidst this splendor, Sudeykin would not forget his pal Degayev: how would he like to become a deputy minister?

Incredibly, all contemporaries as well as historians of the People's Will accepted this cock-and-bull story as truth. Yet they should have reflected that years later, as a "renegade," Tikhomirov paid tribute to Sudeykin as an efficient and loyal servant of the autocracy.[42] And quite apart from it, Degayev's true role was by now well-known to some of Sudeykin's superiors. Admitting that the colonel did not always tell them everything and that he was undoubtedly hurt by his niggardly treatment, Sudeykin was too smart, if not too scrupulous, to embark on such harebrained schemes.

Whether he himself believed the story or not, Tikhomirov let Degayev go back to Russia. In October Degayev presided over a conclave of what remained of the People's Will, and dutifully reported about it to Sudeykin. But now he had to deal also with a man as fearsome as the police chief. Lopatin years before was capable of frightening Nechayev, and one can imagine what effect his proximity had on a man like our hero. Did Lopatin know? One day over teacups Degayev again went through his contrite confession act. Lopatin was astounded. Tikhomirov had told him nothing about the fact that the man with whom he would be working to rebuild the conspiracy in Russia was a police agent. (When he subsequently upbraided Tikhomirov for this duplicity, which could cost him his life, the latter explained soothingly that he had such a high opinion of Lopatin's moral standards that he was afraid he would never have joined the People's Will had he known about all that filth.) But now Degayev had to go through with the job or else. Realizing that he was squeamish about violence, Lopatin said he would find him assistants. In November Degayev, now resigned, dispatched his wife abroad—to spy on the revolutionaries, he told Sudeykin. Even before he was presented to the helpers Lopatin had procured two hefty thugs commandeered from Kiev, Nicholas Starodvorsky and Vasili Konashevich. When he knew that his police friend was about to visit him, Degayev was supposed to send out his servant (also employed by Sudeykin) and notify his assistants, who would hide inside the apartment and wait. After they had finished off Sudeykin they might start on their host, Lopatin laughingly told them. Twice the trap was all set and twice Degayev panicked and would not let Sudeykin in. Finally on December 16 from his observation post in the bathroom overlooking the staircase, he signaled his partners that the colonel was coming up. On entering his trusted collaborator's antichamber Sudeykin divested himself of his coat, with a gun

---

[42]In his letter to a tsarist official in 1888, Tikhomirov wrote concerning some details of his 1884 characterization of Sudeykin, "Then I believed. . . . Now I know this was a pretentious lie." *Memoirs of Lev Tikhomirov,* Moscow 1927, 235.

in its pocket, and his cane, which had a dagger hidden in the handle. Degayev beckoned him inside and then shot him in the back. Understandably he did not wait for the end of the business but bolted out of the apartment, forgetting, as one of the killers was to testify reproachfully, to shut the door behind him. Though severely wounded, Sudeykin fought desperately, and the two thugs had to belabor him with crowbars for quite a while before he lay dead.

The murder became known the same night, and Degayev's complicity established soon thereafter. The tsarist police printed and circulated a "criminal-wanted" poster, possibly a "first" in Russian history, with the photograph of "retired staff-captain Serge Degayev," promising 5000 rubles for any information about his whereabouts and 10,000 for his actual apprehension. The People's Will in turn, displaying what might be described as excessive solicitude for the fugitive, issued a proclamation assuring those who might seek such rewards that they would not live to enjoy them. Degayev was smuggled abroad, and in Paris Tikhomirov told him to get lost and never dare set foot on Russian soil again.

As a man who craved recognition, Sudeykin would have been pleased by his funeral: several ministers attended it and among the floral offerings was one of white lilies from the empress, inscribed "to the man who carried out his duties honestly till the very end." Less gracious was his send-off by the revolutionaries. In the article to which we have already referred Tikhomirov repeated (and quite likely added to) Degayev's fantasies, but in addition there were some clearly personal touches. "Sudeykin was a plebeian, he came from a gentry, but ruined, family"; he "was thoroughly selfish" and rather cowardly. (In fact several revolutionaries had testified to his physical courage.) This version cannot be entirely explained by Tikhomirov's efforts to obscure his own role in the sordid affair. He felt, and with justification, that it was largely due to Sudeykin that his negotiations with the Sacred Band, and the dreams he had based on them, had fallen through.

Konashevich and Starodvorsky, whom nobody thought of spiriting abroad (what could they tell?), were arrested in the early months of 1884. In Schlüsselburg, where they eventually landed, Konashevich went mad. He imagined himself to be his namesake, a famous Cossack chieftain in the seventeenth century. As such he appointed Morozov, his companion on walks in the prison courtyard, as his diplomatic adviser and would threaten him whenever the latter pleaded his inability to go on a mission to the sultan of Turkey or king of Poland. Starodvorsky, rather ironically in view of what got him there, became an informer, reporting to the authorities on his fellow prisoners. Released in 1905, he continued working for the police until the Revolution.

Far from such harrowing scenes, Degayev, now Alexander Pell, was carving out a new life for himself in the New World. In the robber baron era a man with his endowments might well have gone quite far in business and finance. But instead he sought the more unotrusive rewards of academic life. After receiving a Ph.D. from Johns Hopkins, he eschewed the more prestigious institutions on the Eastern seaboard, where immigrants from Russia were now arriving after the pogroms of the 1880s, and became a professor of mathematics in South Dakota. He was, we are assured, a very popular teacher and became, as behooved an enemy of autocracy, a registered Republican. After some years he shifted—perhaps South Dakota reminded him too much of Siberia—to the Armour Institute of Technology. In 1909 his brother Vladimir, who under an assumed name was the American correspondent of a reactionary Russian journal, informed its readers that it was reliably learned that the notorious Degayev had died in 1908 in New Zealand. In fact Serge was still very much alive, and after retiring from teaching spent his declining years near Philadelphia, where his second (American) wife was a lecturer at Bryn Mawr. Lev Deich, then in New York, learned of his whereabouts before World War I, but remembering the crime of his own youth refrained humanely from publicizing the fact. After the Bolshevik Revolution Degayev-Pell is on record as saying: "Accursed Russia, even after the revolution one cannot live there like a human being."[43] And with this comment the man who dealt the final blow to the once awesome conspiracy fades from the pages of history.

[43] I. Genkin, "The *Provocateur* Degayev in America," in *Hard Labor and Exile,* IX (Moscow 1933), 133.

FIFTEEN

EPILOGUE

The People's Will was dead. Its actual demise was hastened by an outside provocation-virus that entered its bloodstream, but in fact it was already doomed by its congenital disease, terrorism. For long after December 16, 1883, any group that tried to start a revolutionary conspiracy was almost immediately struck by these two ailments which had crippled and destroyed its predecessor and model. On those who venerated the memory of Zhelyabovs and Perovskayas, the news that their party had become entangled in something as sordid as the Degayev-Sudeykin business had a shattering effect. The reaction of a leading representative of the younger generation of revolutionaries, the poet Peter Yakubovich, was typical: "Those political exiles have been discredited by allowing the Degayev affair to develop; they should have the elementary decency to separate themselves from any activities in Russia and to seek oblivion."[1]

Yakubovich and some like-minded radicals then proposed to set up a new party, the Young People's Will. The Young Turks proposed to eschew political terror of the kind practiced by their predecessors, but in its place they planned to introduce large-scale "economic" terror, directed against factory owners, foremen, landlords, and the like. For all their disenchantment with the oldsters, the young revolutionaries felt the need to bring into their enterprise a tried veteran of the People's Will, and their choice fell upon Michael Ovchinnikov,[2] and he, an old associate of Degayev's, was

[1]A. N. Bach, *Memoirs of a Member of The People's Will,* Moscow 1931, 95.
[2]Not to be confused with his namesake, the bandit-revolutionary Alexander, mentioned above.

almost without doubt a police agent himself![3] It had been another of the late lamented Sudeykin's ideas: to try to split the revolutionary movement into hostile factions that would expend their energies in fighting each other.

Abroad Tikhomirov still had not given up hope of breathing new life into the corpse of the People's Will. It is hard to believe but early in 1884 he managed to persuade Herman Lopatin, who had fled Russia after Sudeykin's murder, to go back and try to rebuild the conspiracy. This time there would be no surprises à la Degayev, and he would have plenipotentiary powers. He should attempt to bring the deluded youngsters back into the fold, and persuade them that for all the past unpleasantness, the party was strong, vital, and ready to resume its triumphant march toward the revolution.

The reputed miracle maker was back home in March and summoned the (doubly) rebellious youngsters for a conference. Lopatin explained his plan for revivifying the party. They needed a few spectacular assassinations to build up morale and membership. No one would pay much attention if they killed some obscure industrialists; the logical victims would be prosecutor Muraviev of the March 1 trial fame, Pobyedonostsev, and Katkov. The last two names aroused opposition: "how could a party fighting for freedom remain true to itself if it sentenced to death a clergyman and a journalist, i.e., representatives of ideas, even if the ones they preached were harmful?"[4] Having yielded to their objections, Lopatin secured at least a formal agreement from the dissidents to return to the bosom of the People's Will. They promised to furnish him with those two essentials of revolutionary work: dynamite and a printing press. He was overjoyed: "Gentlemen, you have provided us[5] with a horse and helped us get into the saddle. Now we have to earn our spurs."[6] Yet the reunion was mostly on the surface, both sides trying to recruit partisans for their factions even while cooperating to resurrect the party as a whole. In their membership drive Lopatin and Yakubovich were being discreetly chaperoned by police informers. The latter frustrated some extremely amateurish attempts at new assassinations.

The only tangible product of the revival attempt was the appearance after a two-and-a-half year hiatus of the clandestine party organ. Number 10 of *The People's Will,* dated September 1884, contained what in fact was the obituary of the party, a lengthy, labored, and pompously phrased statement

---

[3]Victor Sukhomlin, about the betrayal of M. Ovchinnikov, in *Hard Labor and Exile,* XXIV (Moscow 1926), 144–51.

[4]Bach, 108. While undoubtedly praiseworthy, this objection shows also the young men's abysmal ignorance of Russian politics and history. Pobyedonostsev was, of course, a layman as had been all the procurators of the Holy Synod, the office designed by Peter the Great to have the Orthodox Church under the firm control of the government.

[5]Presumably the Executive Committee.

[6]Bach, 108. As behooved a Don Quixote, Lopatin was fond of the language of chivalry. His joining of the People's Will he described as offering his sword to the Executive Committee.

of the (Paris) Executive Committee on the Sudeykin-Degayev affair, from which we have already quoted. In addition, Tikhomirov tried to put a brave face on the virtual cessation of revolutionary activities: the Executive Committee had generously refrained from any attacks on the regime until the coronation manifesto, "so as to demonstrate to Russian society that the government, even when not occupied in fighting off the revolutionaries, is incapable of adopting any beneficial reforms." But now (more than a year after the coronation), "The Executive Committee, despite its being engaged in work of the highest importance, will still find the time and means to cleanse resolutely the political atmosphere of the demoralizing legacy of Sudeykin." The colonel's ghost must have laughed at those brave words, for even before the appearance of the journal a wave of arrests had struck the remaining activists of the People's Will, both the old one and the young one, and in October that artful dodger Herman Lopatin himself was seized in Petersburg. He had not succeeded in destroying his address book, which contained names of activists and sympathizers in the eighteen urban centers he had visited since his return to Russia. This time the hero of innumerable escapes was confined in Schlüsselburg, until the amnesty of 1905 opened the prison doors for him and for a handful of other survivors of the passionate band which had dealt the imperial regime a blow from which it never fully recovered.

The ghost of the People's Will stalked both the autocracy and the liberation movement until their respective deaths in February and October 1917. The former would never forget what it took to be the lesson of 1861–81, that in Russia reform is bound to spawn sedition. The latter would never lose its fear of moderation; the memories of Zasulich, Zhelyabov, and Perovskaya shamed and rendered ineffective those who argued for other paths to freedom than that of conspiracy and violence. Even more fateful was the conviction, going back to the beginning of the period we have dealt with, that a small minority has the right to speak and act for the people because *history* had ordered so. Said another would-be assassin of tsars on April 18, 1887, before an imperial court:

> Terror, this form of struggle devised by the nineteenth century, is the only means of defense to which a spiritually strong minority, convinced of its righteousness, can resort against the physical power of the majority. . . . I have often thought about the argument that Russian society does not sympathize with terror, in fact is largely hostile to it. But this is a misunderstanding. . . . Society may not sympathize with terror, but as long as the demand [for freedom] remains the basic aspiration of all educated people, our struggle will remain the struggle of the whole *intelligentsia.*

The speaker was Alexander Ulyanov, one of the organizers of the student group which called itself the Terrorists' Faction of the People's Will.[7] He

[7] *March 1, 1887,* Moscow 1927, 292.

and several companions planned to attack Alexander III with bombs on March 1, 1887, as the latter was repairing to a memorial mass for his father. Ulyanov was the main author of the student group's program which, though represented by Soviet historians as being closer to the ideas of Marxism, was in its main points indistinguishable from the postulates of the People's Will, except that it was even stronger in its emphasis on terror. The conspiracy, unlike its model, was very amateurishly prepared. Rumors about it circulated in student circles in Petersburg and as far away as Vilna for weeks before the target date. Though there is no hard evidence to this effect, there must be a strong presumption that the police had known about it for some time through an informer, but to enhance the dramatic effect chose to seize the six would-be assassins stationed along the route from the palace to the cathedral only shortly before Alexander was to take it. The bombs, when analyzed, were found to be defective and would not have gone off.[8]

Ulyanov's behavior during the investigation and trial was worthy of Zhelyabov, though compared with the latter this promising twenty-one-year-old student of natural science was but a tyro in conspiracy. Along with four other plotters he was hanged on May 8, 1887.

His brother Vladimir, at the time seventeen, and later better known as Lenin, did not often refer to Alexander. But quite likely his futile sacrifice was a powerful factor in Lenin's choosing a different path as a revolutionary. Occasionally he betrayed his impatience with terrorism and the movement that had spawned it. When a newspaper collaborator proposed in 1906 a special commemorative tribute on the twenty-fifth anniversary of Zhelyabov's and Perovskaya's deaths, Lenin replied, "They died, so what? Glory and honor to them, but why should we talk about it?" It was the People's Will's mastery of the conspiratorial craft, its members' dedication as *professional* revolutionaries, which inspired Lenin when he was building his own party, not the romance of their lives and deaths.

For Lenin's successor the whole famous Russian revolutionary tradition offered but a negative lesson. It demonstrated the fatal consequences of any softness in dealing with dissent, whether actual or potential, in society. Intellectuals had to be watched and regimented, the young indoctrinated, the individual of any station or age so frightened for his own and his family's lives that he would hardly have any mental energy left for formulating "untrustworthy ideas," let alone trying to put them into execution. The tsar's prisoners in their court appearances often indicted the autocracy and protested its evils before the country and the world; Stalin's indicted *themselves* and explained the regime's failings by their *own* treason and "wrecking." An assiduous student of history, Stalin must have found ample grounds for reflections in materials bearing on *silent* treason: all those

[8]New data about March 1, 1887, in *Hard Labor and Exile*, X (Moscow 1930), 144.

ministers, generals, court doctors, people close to the throne, who yet had contacts with and protected the revolutionaries, occasionally tried to sneak in reforms which would limit the power of their master.

As long as he had to dispose of his rivals within the party, and then of his allies, the despot had little time or cause to pay much attention to the veterans of the 1870s and 1880s. Though few of them joined the Communist Party, these aged men and women were left in relative peace, often on pensions, allowed to retell their stories in historical journals and memoirs. One can imagine with what feelings those who had joined the revolutionary movement because of the plight of the peasant must have watched the horrors of forced collectivization in the early 1930s, and the new, much more cruel form of serfdom Communism imposed on the majority of their countrymen.

With the assassination of the Leningrad party chief Serge Kirov in December 1934, Stalin's attitude toward the relics of the revolutionary past changed.[9] So they were not harmless, the tales told by those old dodderers and braggarts! The Society of Former Political Prisoners and Exiles was dissolved and its funds confiscated; its journal, *Hard Labor and Exile,* an invaluable historical source, was banned. Another irreplaceable tool of research, *The Biographical Dictionary of the Revolutionary Movement in the Nineteenth Century,* also stopped appearing. It seems incredible, even for Stalin, to persecute people the youngest of whom were in their seventies, but biographical data for a number of fairly prominent Populist veterans end suspiciously with "died after 1930." How except by fear can one explain Michael Frolenko's joining the Communist Party in 1936 at the age of eighty-eight? Historical research on the earlier periods of the revolutionary activity was severely curtailed, and that on the People's Will virtually banned. Only in the last twenty years have Soviet historians become free to write and do research on the movement without which Communism as we know it would not have come into existence.

Apart from its legacy to Communism, the main significance of the revolutionary epic of the 1860s and 1870s as crystallized in the People's Will lies in what effect it had on the imperial regime: it destroyed its power to reform itself. Unable to inspire fear as before 1855, incapable in turn to enlist the support and then to preserve respect among the majority of educated Russians, the autocracy dug its own grave.

The tale of the Russian revolutionary of those years is instructive not only in relation to his country. His story illuminates human aspirations, needs, and anxieties which transcend the era and the society he lived in.

---

[9]Many, both in the Soviet Union and in the West, have seen Stalin's hand behind the assassination. In my *Stalin* (New York 1973) I present what is currently a minority opinion: there is no logical reason, not to speak of hard evidence, to tie Stalin to the murder.

"There were no regrets, only suffering," Vera Figner was to write of her twenty years' solitary confinement. Tried in 1884 along with a number of officers, also betrayed by Degayev, Figner endeavored to make sure that she would be sentenced to death. She filled the court in on details of her revolutionary activity, even those unknown to the prosecution, and expressed regret that she had not participated more directly in several attempts on the life of the emperor. When a fellow accused, under the same sentence, asked her advice as to whether he should petition for mercy, she replied that she could never advise others to do something she herself would never do. Her sentence was commuted to life imprisonment in a fortress, and she exacted a promise from her mother at their parting meeting that she would never petition on her behalf. She was, she wrote, "humiliated and outraged" when informed in 1903 that her mother had broken her pledge and that on her application to the emperor Vera's sentence was going to be commuted to twenty years, i.e., she would be released in 1904. "My first impulse was to break off all relations with my mother. . . . I did not want mercy, I wanted to suffer along with my comrades till the end. . . . Mother has ruined my life."[10] She was only partly mollified when she learned that her mother who had already lost one daughter was in the terminal phase of her own illness.

The craving for martyrdom appears to be particularly unbecoming in a revolutionary. But perhaps Figner and some of her companions sought not to change the world but something else. Before her eyes in later years, when she pondered her own fate and that of others such as Perovskaya, was often, Vera tells us, the famous painting by Surikov, representing the lady Morozova. A member of one of the most ancient Muscovite families, Morozova was among the few aristocrats who in the seventeenth century joined the Old Believers, those among the faithful who rejecting the state-approved church reforms stuck to the old ritual, often giving witness to their faith by enduring martyrdom, including mass self-immolation. Such fanaticism appears incomprehensible to the modern mind, since the differences between the old and new rituals did not pertain to doctrine, but hinged on such details as to whether one was to cross oneself with two or three fingers, the proper spelling of Jesus, and the like. The picture portrays Morozova chained; the carriage conveying her to the prison is surrounded by a part-jeering, part-awed mob; yet she herself is serene, "an expression of firmness on her face, of the determination to endure until the end . . . defiantly thrusting up her hand to cross herself with two fingers."[11]

A spiritual dilemma also preoccupied Lev Tikhomirov. After 1884 the revolutionary and the schemer in him began to give way to the Christian

[10]Vera Figner, *Collected Works*, II, Moscow 1928, 238.
[11]*Ibid.*, I, 252.

believer. No one who reads his diary of those years can conclude that the final conversion and repentance came from cold calculation alone. To be sure the travails of the exile's existence pressed in on all sides: shattered political dreams, gnawing poverty, nostalgia for his native land. No Russian *intelligent* abroad would think of taking a job or earning his livelihood by any other means than writing. And so Tikhomirov with a wife and sick son to support was forced to sponge off friends and even casual acquaintances. "The struggle for daily bread is so hard for me, and I have such high aspirations, that I am continually experiencing nervous crises." The phantom of political greatness was still before his eyes: "I need the kind of political party that would be a real force, a party that could govern,"[12] he wrote as late as September 1887. Yet at the same time his thoughts turned increasingly toward the church of his fathers, toward the spiritual haven where he might expiate his sins and find peace. The decisive turn in this spiritual crisis came with the illness of his little son Alexander. The child fell sick with meningitis and even after his miraculous (as Tikhomirov believed) recovery, the father for years noted with anguish the slightest headache and indisposition of his beloved Sasha. "[Alexander] had taught me so much . . . through the feeling which he inspired in me, through his sufferings, through the love which welled up in me, by his childish questions. He brought me back to God."[13]

At first he did not dare to attend the Russian Orthodox chapel attached to the imperial embassy in Paris, but he became a churchgoer. First Tikhomirov tried a Protestant chapel, and he found it "part barn, part school. I could not feel the presence of God." It was different with Catholic services: "something here touched my heart. . . . I did not quite pray, but still felt moved." And finally he overcame his block and with his son stole into the Orthodox church, fearful to the last that someone might recognize him and say, "What are you doing here? You do not belong among us!" Once the service began Tikhomirov was seized by an indescribable feeling: "I felt the urge to prostrate myself both from despair and happiness, from the shame for my sins and because of the rapture of being finally in my church."[14] And the choice was final when he heard his little son say on leaving the services, "Daddy, let us not go anymore to the Catholic church. Ours is better. . . ." (Alexander became a monk when he grew up. He was consecrated a bishop after the October Revolution and then disappeared, very likely a victim of the Communist persecution of the Church.)

On September 12, 1888 Tikhomirov wrote his petition to Alexander III. "Allow me, merciful Sire, to return to a normal and honest life so that as

[12]*Memoirs of Lev Tikhomirov,* Moscow 1927, 200.
[13]*Ibid.,* 280.
[14]*Ibid.,* 336.

a loyal subject and honest father and son I may erase, if not from my heart then from the memory of those close to me, the nightmare of my foolish past." He had come to understand that the autocratic principle "is a precious blessing for the people, an irreplaceable instrument of its well-being and progress."

There were obvious political advantages to the imperial government in allowing Tikhomirov to return and become an apologist for the autocracy. Still, it was a magnanimous gesture the likes of which no other government could have afforded: the man who bore the political and moral responsibility for a series of murders, including that of the head of state, was not even required to stand trial and after five years was restored to his full civic rights.

But if Tikhomirov hoped to become the ideological guide of the autocracy as he had been of the revolutionary party, then the rest of his life was for him as much of an expiation for his past as Schlüsselburg or foreign exile would have been. Though moderately successful as a journalist and eventually as successor to Katkov as editor of the *Moscow News,* he was a source of embarrassment rather than strength to the conservative camp. The two institutions, autocracy and the Orthodox Church, in which he fervently believed and on behalf of which he wrote as passionately as he had once about revolution decayed before his very eyes. The nationalist in him felt deeply Russia's defeat by Japan in 1905. The fall of old Russia in 1917 could not have surprised the man who had long argued that any concession to liberalism, any effort to combine autocracy with parliamentary institutions, as the imperial government tried between 1905 and 1917, was bound to produce anarchy and bring about revolution. And perhaps Tikhomirov felt a grim satisfaction when the Bolsheviks proceeded to destroy the class in which as a revolutionary he had reposed all his hopes, and on which as a reactionary he blamed all of Russia's ills, the *intelligentsia.* It was Lenin who created the party of which he had dreamed, "one that was a real force and that could govern." In the post-October day when the Communist secret police, the Cheka, and marauding bands of Red sailors killed so many notables of the left and right, Tikhomirov was left alone, a hermit living on a monastery's grounds, and he died there in 1923.

The quest for faith does not fully explain why so many young Russians sought fulfillment in revolutionary work. Is it too frivolous or perverse to suggest that some of them joined conspiracies as much out of a feeling of adventure and youthful ebullience as out of a sense of duty to the oppressed people?

It was not religion or the enjoyment of martyrdom that saved Nicholas Morozov, immured first in the Alexis Ravelin, where all around him his comrades were succumbing to disease or insanity, and then in Schlüsselburg. His legs swelled horribly, a symptom of the almost invariably fatal prison ailment of dropsy. He persuaded the prison chaplain to allow him to receive religious books. Yet there was to be no joy in heaven at the return to the fold of yet another sinner. His reading and conversations with the divine served Morozov to prepare for writing a massive exposé of the sacred texts from the rationalist and scientific point of view. Gradually his range of interests broadened; he read gluttonously in higher mathematics, chemistry, astronomy, and physics, wrote a series of scientific papers of such quantity that in the 1920s, describing his prison education, he confesses that some he had not as yet been able to publish. "It is amazing how quickly time flies when you are in jail," he complained to his fellow inmates.

Released in 1905, Morozov married a young girl who, as he wrote with a touch of male chauvinism, "took care of all the petty details of daily existence so that I could devote myself completely to my researches." To be sure there were still political troubles ahead. For writing some subversive poetry Morozov was locked up for a mere year, an imprisonment not entirely unwelcome, since in the fortress he was able to complete his memoirs and to learn Hebrew. Free again, the sexagenarian youngster took up flying.

Most of the veterans of Populism supported Russia's war effort after 1914, in glaring contrast to Lenin and his party. But Morozov again outdid the others, visiting the front lines and lecturing the troops on patriotic subjects. After the February Revolution, the once extreme exponent of terror, now a liberal, was a strong partisan of the Provisional Government and Kerensky. The Bolshevik coup and especially the dispersal of the Constituent Assembly were mournful events to revolutionaries of Morozov's generation. (He was a member of the Assembly's anti-Bolshevik majority.) That was what they had worked and suffered for, and now after one day's session rowdy sailors at Lenin's command threw out the first freely elected representatives of the Russian people. Even when writing under Soviet rule in 1926, Vera Figner could not contain herself as she described this act of arbitrariness. "The dissolution of the Constituent Assembly was a slap in the face to the generations that left the dream of it as their legacy and to the simple masses who venerated it."[15] More fortunate than most, Morozov could find refuge and consolation in his scientific work, which he carried on until the end of his days. He died, probably the last survivor of the People's Will, in 1946. And if a search for faith inspired many of its members, does not his amazing life epitomize the qualities of another strain in the revolutionary character, as well as something in the Russian national temper: heroism, indomitable vitality, resourcefulness, utter lack of common sense when it comes to politics?

[15] *Granat Encyclopedia, Supplement,* XL, 479.

INDEX

INDEX